66255

P
37
.3
.P8

Psycholinguistic research :

PSYCHOLINGUISTIC RESEARCH:
Implications and Applications

Edited by

DORIS AARONSON
New York University

ROBERT W. RIEBER
John Jay College, CUNY
and
Columbia University,
College of Physicians and Surgeons

 LAWRENCE ERLBAUM ASSOCIATES, PUBLISHERS
1979   Hillsdale, New Jersey

DISTRIBUTED BY THE HALSTED PRESS DIVISION OF
JOHN WILEY & SONS
New York   Toronto   London   Sydney

Lawrence Erlbaum Associates, Inc., Publishers
365 Broadway
Hillsdale, New Jersey 07642

Distributed solely by Halsted Press Division
John Wiley & Sons, Inc., New York

Library of Congress Cataloging in Publication Data

Main entry under title:
Psycholinguistic research.

  Includes indexes.
  1. Psycholinguistics—Research. I. Aaronson,
Doris. II. Rieber, Robert W.
P37.3.P8   301.2'1   79-21529
ISBN 0-470-26878-6

Contents

PART V:
LANGUAGE DEVELOPMENT

PART VI:
PARALINGUISTIC ASPECTS OF COMMUNICATION

Foreword

Precisely where some line of research stops being psycholinguistic and starts being something else is a matter that few workers in this field could agree on. Fortunately, however, there are a few core issues that everyone would accept as the important, constitutive problems of psycholinguistics.

Moreover, these core issues were formulated even before the field acquired the name "psycholinguistics." To an outsider it might seem that they have changed almost as rapidly as women's fashions. Forty years ago the central concerns were lexical, phonological, perceptual. Twenty years ago an infatuation with Chomsky's theories of syntax focused everybody's attention on the grammatical properties of sentences. Today the fad is semantics and pragmatics.

Although these fluctuations have been real enough, it is nonetheless true that certain persisting preoccupations have set psycholinguistics off from general psychology, on the one hand, and from general linguistics, on the other. Everyone would agree, for example, that the development of language in children is, and has always been, a central topic in psycholinguistics. In spite of occasional flirtations with structuralism, everyone would agree that psycholinguistics is, and has always been, concerned with language as a human activity, not as a collection of symbolic objects. And everyone would agree that the essential activities are, and have always been, those activities involved in producing and understanding utterances. It would be difficult for any serious discussion of psycholinguistics to ignore these topics, and, not surprisingly, all of them are well represented in the following pages.

Different authors, however, will be seen to attack these topics from different directions, with different weapons. It is a strength of this book that it makes no attempt to conceal basic disagreements among those who have contributed to it. On the contrary. In these pages, behaviorists have it out with cognitive psychologists, psychologists criticize linguists and vice versa, while the basic and applied contingents exhibit their age-old mutual disdain. Naive readers could easily conclude they had stumbled into a Hobbesian war of every man against every man.

A little contention can add fun to any discussion, but controversy should not be seen as an end in itself. I have sometimes wished that feuding theorists could be locked together in a room (out of my hearing) until they reached agreement. Fortunately, I lack the power to impose such conditions. Next best, however, is to lock their theories together in a book where readers must reach their own resolutions. Something like that has been accomplished in this volume.

Readers may not find satisfactory resolutions easy to reach, however. Decades of disputation are distilled in these chapters. I will not attempt to characterize the dimensions of disagreement that the 19 distinguished contributors to this eclectic volume have explored—Aaronson and Rieber give a good catalogue in Chapter 1.

Differences in preconceptions, in methods of research, and in styles of theory construction have been so great between linguists and psychologists, and between different schools of psychologists, that only a firm sense that all are studying the same phenomena, and that together they *must* converge on a truth that can satisfy any reasonable test, could hold them together in a recognizable scientific discipline. This recognition of shared and persisting problems is an indispensable precondition for the existence of psycholinguistics as an independent field of study.

That reader will profit most, I believe, who fixes his or her attention most firmly on these shared problems, and who is least distracted by the splendid variety of approaches and points of view illustrated in these chapters. Such a reader will be forced to focus on *the growth and function of those human activities involved in speaking and comprehending speech.* Listen for this focus as you would listen for a voice against a background of static, for once that foundation is firmly in place it will be easy for you to decide where you stand with respect to the many heated quarrels that might otherwise seem so disturbing and discouraging.

The Rockefeller University   GEORGE A. MILLER
New York
June 1979

I PAST AND PRESENT ISSUES IN PSYCHOLINGUISTICS

1 Controversial Issues in Psycholinguistics

Doris Aaronson
New York University

R. W. Rieber
John Jay College, CUNY

The word "psycholinguistics" denotes a composite of the two disciplines, psychology and linguistics. The rebirth of this interdisciplinary area after a rocky history (see Rieber & Vetter, Chapter 2, this volume) was stimulated about 20 years ago by the interaction of psychologist George A. Miller with linguist Noam Chomsky. Although this area of investigation has grown markedly in size and strength during the past two decades, the number of occasions on which psychologists and linguists actually combine efforts in a truly interdisciplinary fashion is painfully small. This book represents such an effort, and the chapter authors hope it will provide a stimulus for the readers to continue the active development of an interdisciplinary communication and a merger of ideas between psychology and linguistics.

This book is "interdisciplinary" in a second direction. It combines authors who are concerned with basic research and those whose goal is applied research and research applications to social problems in health and education. Basic researchers frequently add a "social relevance" section at the end of their grant proposals as a political move to increase their chances of funding by government and private sources. Also, people in applied linguistics and psychology occasionally attend basic research conferences. Hopefully, the present combination of authors with basic and applied orientations will lead to a strengthening of communication among others with these two orientations.

This book provides a meeting ground in a third direction: It represents a broad variety of theoretical approaches to psycholinguistics. For example, some authors focus on the surface structure of linguistic strings as the

3

primary correlate of human verbal behavior. Other authors are more concerned with an abstract linguistic analysis of underlying representations and with the cognitive processes that occur when the mind must deal with logical reasoning and information coding associated with communication. The reader may often find more in common theoretically among some chapter authors of different disciplines than among those within the "same" area.

This book covers a broad range of topics in psycholinguistics, but it is not meant to be a comprehensive survey. For example, a thorough treatment of such topics as phonetics, pragmatics, neurolinguistics, and animal communication is missing, although some aspects of these topics are considered when relevant to material in chapters aimed in other directions. The book has four goals: (1) to discuss many of the important contemporary issues in psycholinguistics; (2) to explore the different views on major theoretical controversies; (3) to provide an analysis of background literature as a framework in which to evaluate the issues and controversies; and (4) to describe interesting high-quality research currently being done by the authors and some of their colleagues. Hence, this book is aimed at advanced students who already have a strong background in psychology or linguistics and more particularly at active workers in these fields who desire a critical interdisciplinary examination of contemporary and controversial ideas.

In this chapter, we point out some of the important issues in contemporary psycholinguistics. In particular, we briefly compare and contrast the approaches to these issues taken by authors of the various chapters. Sometimes these approaches are complementary, providing alternative views of the same problem, much as one might describe a painting in terms of its color, its form, or its thematic content. At other times, these approaches are in such sharp conflict that you would not be convinced the authors are even discussing the "same" painting. Points raised by the authors within each section are considered, followed by some general comments.

I. RESEARCH ORIENTATIONS

The chapter authors for the section on methodological orientations are psychologists and hence agree that an understanding of linguistic performance is the primary focus of their research. Linguistic competence is of secondary interest in that it places restrictions on the range of language behaviors that can be emitted by the human being. However, on many methodological and theoretical details, Kurt Salzinger and Doris Aaronson take seemingly opposing, but perhaps complementary, points of view.

Salzinger calls his approach "radical behaviorism," and Aaronson might be classified as a "liberal cognitivist." Let us examine here three issues on which these authors take different stands. Each author's approach is typical of a strong "research camp," but many researchers would also position themselves somewhere between these approaches.

A. The Naturalness of Language Situations in Language Research

Salzinger strongly maintains that the research situation must provide a representative sample of situations in which the language behavior being studied occurs naturally. Otherwise, the results obtained and the theoretical conclusions drawn may be quite misleading. He speaks out against the use of "contrived verbal materials" and unusual environmental contexts that are frequently devised in laboratory research settings. To emphasize these points, Salzinger calls his research approach "Ecolinguistics."

In sharp contrast, Aaronson demonstrates that it is often necessary to distort the situational parameters in order to understand the underlying nature of human language processors, in order to get a picture of the qualitatively different types of language performance possible and of its variability and flexibility from one situation to the next and from one individual to another. If a stimulus overload is created by presenting perhaps two or more verbal messages simultaneously, or at super-fast rates or with degraded intelligibility, the ways in which the human "language processors" break down (as reflected in the number and nature of errors and in the patterns of response latencies) can provide information on how those processors are structured and the range of cognitive functions they can perform.

B. The Role of Environmental Stimuli in Determining Behavior

Salzinger views the stimulus environment as a critical determinant in the control of language behavior. He applies the "classical" and "operant" conditioning models, developed by Pavlov and Skinner in the animal lab, to human language situations. He maintains that verbal and nonverbal discriminative and conditional stimuli for communication, in contingency with appropriate reinforcements and unconditional stimuli, determine the person's linguistic response to that situation. In this view, stimulus generalization is an important theoretical concept. The same types of language behavior learned in one stimulus context will be emitted, in new stimulus situations that share stimulus properties with the initial setting. For example, when the child learns to name objects in the environment, and when adults use similar syntactic structures in related speech contexts, generalization of stimulus control is involved.

Aaronson's contradictory view is that the particular stimulus or stimulus class may have little direct control over human language behavior. She reviews research where language coding behavior and overt language performance learned in one stimulus situation persists even when the stimulus parameters are changed, so that it is no longer optimal to use the originally learned linguistic coding strategies. In other studies, she shows that the exact same stimulus sentences result in drastically different linguistic performance, depending on the cognitive task demands. When people must comprehend sentences, their patterns of word-by-word reading times reflect the semantic organization of the sentence: Prolonged pauses occur at key content words such as the subject and object, and reading times decrease with contextual redundancy. But when people must memorize those exact same stimulus sentences, the above patterns are absent. Instead, reading times reflect the syntactic structure; prolonged pauses occur at phrase boundaries, and reading times increase with accumulating linguistic information from one phrase break to the next.

One must ask whether these differences between a cognitive and a behavioral approach are as great as they appear on the surface. In particular, to what extent might there be a mapping between the concepts of "cognitive task demands" and "stimulus determinants?" Researchers have been debating this question for many decades, and the arguments are still quite lively.

C. The Effect of Reinforcement on Linguistic Performance

For Salzinger, positive and negative reinforcements within a communication context are critical factors for establishing language and for guiding future language behavior. The reinforcement strengthens the relationships between the environmental stimulus context and the linguistic response. He shows that this is a powerful concept when the child learns particular lexical responses and then functionally equivalent semantic response classes. Appropriate reinforcements and patterns or schedules of delivering reinforcement in behavior therapy programs can be used to train autistic children first to utter individual words and eventually to carry on meaningful communication when other verbal and nonverbal therapy programs fail miserably.

Alternatively, Aaronson maintains that the effects of reinforcement are often nonexistent or at best indirect and that they are not a critical link in supporting language behavior. Rather, she emphasizes the importance of subject-controlled cognitive or mental strategies for language perception and production. In this view, reinforcement has its major effect by providing "information feedback" to the human being. The informational components of reinforcement permit the subject to try out a wide range of cognitive-linguistic strategies and to develop flexibility in performance strategies that he can later call upon. In some cases, "reinforcement" for a correct response serves to alter the very stimulus–response contingency to which it was applied.

Again, we must ask whether the cognitive and behavioral approaches can be related theoretically. Such relations will depend on the qualitative nature and the generality of one's definitions for "cognitive strategy" and "reinforcement contingency" and the theoretical overlap between these terms.

II. PHONOLOGY

The two chapter authors on phonology are in agreement that a phonological analysis is needed in addition to a phonetic representation and that a major purpose of phonological theory is to account for the more readily observable surface structure of phonetic strings. But beyond these fundamental points, William Diver and Sandford Schane show little agreement on detail. Diver represents a rather empirical and behavioristic orientation, and Schane's approach is close to traditional generative phonology as developed by Chomsky and Halle. Both men sketch for us a picture of a broad range of views centered about their own positions, and they also question the fruitfulness of ideas within the opposing framework. Let us briefly consider three important issues or dimensions on which Schane and Diver sharply differ, and which are quite controversial in many corners of contemporary phonological investigation.

A. The Abstractness of Phonological Theories

In developing theoretical concepts and hypotheses, Diver presents a strong argument for sticking quite close to observable data. He shows us some intriguing data on "phonotactic skewing" (i.e., on nonuniform distributions of consonant clusters and of consonant–vowel patterns in English words). From these data, he uses an inductive approach to arrive at theoretical dimensions upon which to characterize the sound patterns. His goal is to account for particular phonetic patterns (i.e., very specific sets of linguistic problems) with the minimal amount of theoretical baggage in terms of number of unobservable entities and levels of derivation. He developed an interesting analogy between his approach and the approach taken by physicists to determine planetary orbits. Both observe the regularities in large quantities of empirical data and bring in theoretical hypotheses only as needed to account for the patterns, particularly the departures from uniformity. Physicists accounted for planetary orbits and predicted the existence of new planets based only on observed data, the (empirical) laws of motion, and the theoretical hypothesis of a gravitational force. Diver has accounted for important co-occurrence relations in phonetics in terms of a very few hypotheses that are in accord with other existing knowledge about human physiology and behavior.

In contrast, Schane views phonology as one part of the generative-transformational framework for linguistic analysis — namely, the component to account for sound patterns. He argues that it is important to account for a broad range of phonetic problems and patterns within the same general theoretical structure. A more abstract theory with a greater complexity of derivational rules can be motivated if one wants to account for phonetic patterns that are broad, for example across whole classes of consonants or vowels, perhaps across all phonemes (e.g., pluralization), and even across many languages. Schane takes a deductive approach, starting with a broad theoretical framework. He then considers what constraints might be considered for the nature of derivational rules (e.g., alternation and neutralization conditions) and for the ordering of derivational rules (e.g., bleeding and feeding relations) that could reduce theoretical complexity but still permit the theory to achieve an accurate and useful conceptualization of the surface structure.

B. Higher-Level Linguistic Organization in Phonological Analysis

In line with Diver's research philosophy to develop theory on a level close to the empirical phenomena, he excludes linguistic units of analysis beyond the morpheme. Phonotactic analysis should not transend word boundaries, because "at word boundaries there is almost nothing that could be thought of as phonological that controls the juxtaposition of phonemes" (Diver, this volume, p. 168). Analogously, he maintains that morphological sequences within words are controlled only partially by phonological considerations, that interesting patterns occur within the morpheme that do not occur across morpheme boundaries, and finally, that introducing higher-level theoretical structure would add more fog than light to understanding phonological problems.

On the other hand, Schane argues that not only morphological but also syntactic and semantic information are necessary for a complete and comprehensive generative phonology. For example, he shows (1) that changes in phonemic patterns that occur in suffix pluralization do not occur when the exact same segments are located within a word stem, and (2) that different patterns occur for words of Latinate than of Greek origin.

Further, he argues that some words having a unique phonetic representation must have two different representations at a more abstract phonological level because there are really two different morphemes involved, for example, in homographs.

C. Psychological Motivation for Phonological Rules

Diver's phonological theory is firmly grounded within the context of human physiology and psychology. For example, he shows that classes of consonant sounds can be characterized as being either "stable" (e.g., $/1/$) or "mobile" (e.g., $/r/$) depending on whether or not the articulatory organ used to produce the sound is relatively stationary or violently active during the excitation of the resonant cavity. This classification predicts well the different trends in distributions involving these two types of sounds. He goes further to show that co-occurrence patterns of sounds with like value on the stable–mobile dimension have a higher frequency than patterns with unlike values. Diver argues that this is quite reasonable within a psychologically motivated phonology. It is easier to learn to control a sequential pair of articulatory gestures that both involve rapid movement changes or that both involve a steady, stable pattern than to handle a combination requiring quite different motor patterns for the two components.

Again, in contrast, Schane maintains that psychological and physiological principles have provided little or no help in formulating phonological principles. For example, he suggests that the underlying phonological representation may involve relatively unpronounceable forms that violate the surface structure of a language. He states that much of the research on developmental psycholinguistics concerns the relations between the child's and the adult's surface forms and thus is probably irrelevant to goals in generative phonology of showing relations between the surface form and the underlying abstract representation. Although Schane sees little fruitful interaction between linguists and psychologists to date, he does not close the door on future possibilities. Despite Schane's views on the role of psychology in phonological theory, Aaronson asked him to participate in this collection because his own linguistic research (particularly on interactions between morphology and phonology) was quite relevant to her psychological theories!

III. LANGUAGE AND COGNITION

This section of the book has three authors with quite different backgrounds. Osgood might be classified as a neobehavioral psychologist, McNeill as a cognitive psychologist, and Langendoen as a linguist siding closely with the generative-transformational approach. The three men take rather different methodological and theoretical approaches to the study of language and cognition. However, they appear in general agreement on the important areas of focus and on some of the main points. We consider here two issues that are important to all three chapters.

A. The Relations Between Competence and Performance

Langendoen defines the study of linguistic competence as dealing with the structures of expressions in human languages, and the study of performance as dealing with the appropriate use of those expressions. He suggests two extreme approaches to the relations between competence and performance. One view is that for each language there is exactly one performance grammar which has a one-to-one relation with the competence grammar. An opposing view is that representations of linguistic expressions in performance grammar(s) are constructed with no recourse to the principles of the competence grammar. Langendoen rejects the first alternative on several grounds (including the fact that the set of "grammatical" expressions of a language is not equivalent to the set of "acceptable" expressions), and he casts strong doubts about the second approach. Rather, he takes a middle ground of constructing performance grammars that are separate from competence grammars but nevertheless have performance principles that are in large part a function of competence principles.

McNeill, in his present chapter and elsewhere, is in strong agreement with Langendoen's second (rejected) view on the relation between competence and performance. In a recent volume (1975), McNeill wrote: "My point will be that grammar and performance must be sharply distinguished. Indeed, they are so distinct that it is useless to seek relationships between them. They reflect distinct levels of analysis, each associated with a different range of questions about language [p. 171]." In the present book, McNeill goes one step further. He presents empirical data on pauses and hand gestures during natural conversations that are quite out of phase with any of the usual types of grammatical analyses put forth by linguists or psychologists. For example, with high frequency, pauses occur between a preposition and its noun phrase, between an article and its noun, and between a subordinate conjunction and its clause. The gesture patterns are systematically related to the various types of pauses (e.g., filled, unfilled), and over half the gestures start or end during a pause. McNeill develops a theory of sensory-motor programming with functional (rather than structural) units called *syntagma* that represent a direct connection of meaning with articulation.

Osgood's conceptualization of language structure and use has a rather different organizational framework than we traditionally encounter in psychology or linguistics. He lays out defining characteristics of any language (including animal and insect communication) and additional structural and functional characteristics of human languages. We might categorize some of the characteristics within each of his sets as competence and others as performance criteria. However, Osgood's characteristics don't quite fit into a competence–performance framework. Defining characteristics that appear to be more on the "competence" side are: Use of the (linguistic) forms should follow nonrandom rules of combination and should include potentially infinite numbers of novel combinations. But note that Osgood talks about these as properties of the language user rather than of an abstract corpus. Characteristics that are more performance-oriented are: The forms should be producible and receivable by the same organisms, should follow nonrandom rules of reference to events in "other channels," and should result in nonrandom dependencies between the forms and the behaviors of the users. Many of the *structural* characteristics (competence?) of specifically human languages deal with the auditory–vocal form, and the *functional* characteristics (performance?) outline a hierarchical organization of discrete, noniconic symbols that are transfered to others by experience (learning) rather than inheritance (maturation). In reality, for each of Osgood's characteristics, one can see some aspects of both competence and performance.

B. The Relations Between Structure and Content

Most competence grammars deal with an entire (well-formed) sentence as the unit and have strong ordering constraints in requiring all surface-structure parsing to be completed on the sentence prior to underlying grammatical transformations, which in turn precede the final semantic analyses. Each stage accomplishes a different linguistic task and applies a different logical and nonredundant set of ordered rewriting rules. Langendoen describes performance grammars that function differently but that interact loosely with competence grammars. The performance grammars have several stages that can operate in parallel on different parts of the sentence and that have built-in redundancy with the same functions being performed at different stages. The first stage parses the surface structure into "chunks" that are large enough to be linguistically useful, small enough to fit into the available computational space, and independent enough to keep small the number and kinds of relations that subsequent stages must establish across units. Such chunks correspond roughly to major surface-structure constituents, but the first processing stage may assign subject–predicate relations to an entire sentence if it is short and simple. For long complex sentences, the first stage may section off constituents in left-to-right fashion and send them on to stage two to compute linguistic relations across chunks. Then stage one continues to parse the rest of the sentence while stage two is operating on earlier chunks. Langendoen's linguistic processor appears to have two-way interactions between syntactic structure and semantic content. At the first stage of grammatical parsing, the chunk size is determined in part by the number and complexity of lexical–semantic units. But then at a later stage, the semantic relations among the various constituents are determined by the syntactic relations established during the surface parsing. According to Langendoen, performance grammars must recognize strings as legitimate outputs from a competence grammar, and thus the performance processing complexity must be related to the number of transformations required by a competence grammar.

McNeill's theory of sensory-motor programming is a performance system with two types of interacting units. A "phonemic clause" is defined as a sequence of segmental phonemes containing one primary stress, having one of a small set of intonation contours and bounded by silence or terminal contours. A "sensory-motor idea" comprises one concept from the following set: event, action, state, location, property, entity, and person. Raters can score tape-recorded utterances for either of these two types of units with an interrater reliability of over 80%. We might roughly equate the pattern of phonemic clauses with a kind of surface-structure organization and the relations among semantic ideas with an analysis of semantic content. But we must remember, as noted above, that the parsing resulting from these behaviorally and cognitively defined units does not coincide with the parsing resulting from any standard phrase structure or deep-structure grammar. Although McNeill's "structural" and "content" units are independently defined, they coincide with each other in more than 85% of the cases. When one examines speech dysfluencies, breakdowns in the content stream (e.g., repeats of words, incomplete linguistic units) are associated with increased and irregular pauses. Iconic gesture patterns, which appear to relate phonemic and semantic units, also reflect speech dysfluencies. McNeill hypothesizes that action involved in the structural organization of speech is an essential source of meaningful content in utterances. Both the action and meaning aspects of communication are programmed together by closely coordinated and interacting speech-production systems.

As noted earlier, Osgood's theory does not mesh with more traditional approaches. However, the notions of structure and content are dealt with throughout the various parts of his framework. For example, the defining characteristics of "human" languages include the following criteria: Form-meaning relations that associate linguistic structures to meaningful events in other channels must typically be arbitrary rather than iconic, and the organization of both linguistic structure and content must be hierarchical at all levels. However, it is within the section on "nondefining characteristics of human languages" that we see some of the most interesting interactions between structure and content. The structural organization must permit the creation of propositions that are testable for validity, and, in particular, the structure must permit the creation of prevarication for use in politics, fiction, and sarcasm. Linguistic structure must handle reflexive content (i.e., messages can refer to other messages), and language structures must permit the translation of content from any other human language. Finally, Osgood puts forth two criteria that are quite out of kilter with traditional linguistic theories but quite reasonable for a psychologically based performance grammar. For both structural and content units, the selection and combination rules are statistical rather than absolute, and the combinations (in terms of statistical averages) are according to a least-effort principle: Structures of higher frequency of use are shorter, have fewer subunits, and have a larger number of different meanings.

IV. LANGUAGE DEVELOPMENT

The authors of the two chapters that comprise this section agree that environment plays an important role in children's language acquisition. Jerome Bruner and Michael Maratsos maintain different perspectives, however, in their approaches to the study of the language-acquisition process. Bruner, a cognitive psychologist whose interest lies largely in the area of human development, stresses the early cognitive interaction between mother and child, but he allows for a Language Acquisition Devise (LAD) as an inherited capacity. Maratsos, who is a psycholinguist working in child language development, deals more with the language-acquisition process in terms of linguistic mechanisms rather than cognitive interactions between mother and child. Two of the main issues that these authors address are: the role of environmental factors in language acquisition, and the nature of language-acquisition mechanisms.

A. The Role of Environmental Factors in Language Acquisition

Bruner emphasizes the dependence of language acquisition on the interaction that occurs between mother and child. From this relationship, the child learns to use language in a manner that satisfies the requirements of social living; he learns to speak not only with proper respect to sentence formation and word selection but also with appropriate regard for those with whom he is involved in dialogue. Bruner's view of language acquisition differs from that of most of his predecessors, because he assumes that the child communicates before he acquires language. The progession from primitive procedures for communication to more sophisticated ones in the child is then largely dependent on the mother, who teaches the child to speak. As transactional procedures develop between mother and child, the child also learns about the world, and this simultaneous acquisition of language and world knowledge is a necessary step in the construction of a "linguistic hypothesis."

Maratsos analyzes selected recent developments in the study of how children form generalizations from semantic categories to object-concept categories in the environment. He points out that a set of utterances may be described by numerous analytic devices — purely semantic analyses at fine or general levels, or distributional descriptions of varying specificity. Maratsos describes two possible means of explaining how children can proceed from the storage of individual lexical structural-meaning patterns to the powerful and general transfers of syntactic privilege that eventually yield fluent speech. He touches briefly on the Explicit Statement Model, in which linguistic transfer functions are stated separately as abstract rules, apart from individual lexical storages from which they arise. He then examines in more detail the Implicit Statement Model, in which various structural-meaning correspondences are retained individually in lexical storages.

B. The Nature of Language-Acquisition Mechanisms

Bruner's view is that a child's knowledge of how to communicate in a world where he has already conceptualized in some depth provides a basis for generating and testing hypotheses about the meaning and structure of the linguistic discourse into which he enters. As LAD implies, the child does have a substantial capacity to infer and generate rules, even to overgeneralize them. Bruner asserts that the course of action and the structure of speech are not arbitrarily related but rather are neatly matched and that a fair amount of learning is necessary to master the intricacies of interpersonal interaction, even with language proper. Additionally, he believes that case grammar does not emanate naturally from the mastery of interaction in and of itself, although a knowledge of joint action between people provides useful information to the learner about the linguistic code.

Bruner holds that the child is initially learning as much about rules of dialogue as he is about lexical labels. At an age of about 18 months, however, once the dialogue routine is established, it becomes a framework upon which a new routine is established. Bruner re-emphasizes the importance of interaction by stating that language does not grow solely from its own roots but is dependent on interaction and particularly on the interaction of intentions held by two consenting parties, one of them initially willing and capable of giving the other the benefit of the doubt.

Maratsos, viewing human language as an expression of a tendency toward structure building, finds that people are in part, at least, systematic and clear. Language systems themselves, however, are not models of clarity and order; nevertheless, children are capable of learning them as they are. He sees the individual differences among children as they acquire language as a reflection of the structural variants actually observed in mature language. The study of children's acquisitional processes shows in high relief the processes of the human mind that reflect themselves in language.

V. PARALINGUISTIC ASPECTS OF COMMUNICATION

The authors of the two chapters in this section are in general agreement about the important phenomena, but they differ with respect to which levels of analysis are most fruitful. Starkey Duncan, Jr. is a behavioral scientist whose interest is in face-to-face interaction. Of the authors of the second chapter, Joseph Jaffe is a psychiatrist who works in the area of interpersonal communication, Daniel N. Stern is also a psychiatrist specializing in mother–child interactions, and Samuel W. Anderson is a psychologist interested in the neuropsychology of language. In both chapters, there is general agreement that verbal and nonverbal communication tend to interact and synchronize. Three particular issues that the authors confront in their respective chapters illustrate their different viewpoints: What is the nature of the conceptual framework for communication; what is special about the nature of interactive dialogue; and what are appropriate methods to study communication?

A. What Is the Nature of
the Conceptual Framework for Communication?

In Duncan's discussion of a conceptual framework for face-to-face interaction, there are some primary organizing concepts. The first is convention, which refers to the broad, socially accepted rules, meaningful elements, and other phenomena within which interaction takes place. The second is interaction strategy, which is the set of individual variations on convention. The temporal organization for the phenomena of speaking turns includes the following elements: signals, moves, situational requirements, sanctions, and rules.

The human ethnology approach to the study of communication, according to Duncan, has not sufficiently recognized the importance of analyzing sequences of communicative events. Duncan's structural approach aims at a formal description of these sequences in terms of certain regularities of the interpersonal interaction. A wide range of interactions are analyzed systematically and in terms of their possible co-occurrence.

Whereas Duncan's approach is molar, involving the integrated behaviors that comprise communicative acts, the approach of Jaffe, Anderson, and Stern is basically molecular and analytic. Jaffe et al. state that the search for the various manifestations of rhythmicity helps us to better understand the details of interpersonal dialogue. They consider a class of stochastic models to account for rhythmicity at several levels in a hierarchically structured communication system. They maintain that much of what is meant by "personality" and "cultural pattern" involves the nature of variation and stability in behavioral rates and control of temporal sequencing.

B. What Is Special About the Nature of Interactive Dialogue?

From the viewpoint of his conceptual framework, Duncan focuses upon the interplay of two interaction strategies in a (two-person) face-to-face communication. Each participant must assess the social situation, choose conventions, cooperate in conventions chosen by the partner, adhere to or violate these conventions, to some degree, and exercise options for which the conventions provide. These special aspects of social interaction influence the nature of communications. It is possible, according to Duncan, to describe both conventions and strategies strictly in terms of regularities in observed actions. Once a participant's interaction strategy has been described, it is possible to infer certain specific intentions from that strategy. This approach is concerned mostly with what is going on between the speakers to make a communicative event happen. The quality and quantity of the speakers' behavioral cues are systematically looked at from various semantic and pragmatic perspectives.

For Jaffe et al., stable time constancies such as rhythmic expression help us to recognize other people, and more subtle constancies appear to be an important aspect of individual identity. This approach, suggested by Jaffe et al., is referred to as a "systems approach to conversational rhythms." Here, a rather wide range of communication rhythms is examined. The lowest level — which Jaffe calls level 4 — is called the stress rhythm, and it is defined by alternations of stressed vowels and intervening unstressed segments. A run of alternations between these two states constitutes a phonological phrase, which in turn, when alternated with pauses, comprises the phrase rhythm — level 3 of the system. Level 2 is an alternation of monologues: speaking, preceded and followed by listening. This is the closest phenomenon to Duncan's turn-taking. The two approaches are not identical, because according to Jaffe's definition, when speakers change, one stopping an utterance and the other starting, taking the "floor" is also changed, whereas in Duncan's framework, a brief interruption might not cause a speaker to relinquish his turn. In level 1 of Jaffe's system, dialogue is preceded and followed by breaks, which are really decisions as to whether or not one should initiate further dialogue. Jaffe et al. feel that there is much to be gained from looking at this simple interactive process.

C. What Are Appropriate Methods to Study Communication?

Duncan views the most common methodological weaknesses in structural studies to date as being: (1) the failure to include realistic interaction in the methodology (e.g., studies where one person responds to an inanimate stimulus environment or to an unnaturally behaving "experimental stooge"); and (2) a tendency to take observations on a rather limited number of dependent variables when studying rich multidimensional phenomena. He sees both of these weaknesses as being corrected as research of this sort develops. He explains the development of his own framework, devised with Fiske, as having arisen in the course of considering both the results of studies of speaking turns and related phenomena, and the comments of other investigators.

Jaffe et al. find that Markov models are useful in the study of the communication process and are not incompatible with Chomsky's views on phonology. They further assert that they are good descriptive tools for biological clocks. They state that the question of whether phonology has non-Markovian properties actually depends on one other crucial question: "Does there exist a finite upper limit on the amount of contiguous contextual information that need ever be scanned to determine the sound pattern of any phone in any phonological phrase" (Jaffe et al., this volume, p. 398)? They answer this question, on the bases of intuition and examples, in the affirmative. The authors attempt to show that the theory of Markov models does have an important place in the description and explanation of the communicative process. They believe that the special appropriateness of Markov models for problems of phonology is a strong indication that phonological rhythms belong to a class of biological periodicities that lie at the center of a general theory of behavioral timing in organisms.

VI.   APPLICATIONS OF PSYCHOLINGUISTICS

This section of the book includes three chapters by authors with quite different backgrounds in psychology. Davis Howes is an experimental psychologist, who has done a great deal of work in the area of aphasia.

Donald Spence is a clinically oriented researcher, most of whose work has been in evaluating psychotherapeutic interviews. The research of Carton and Castiglione focuses on educational psychology. All of the authors have different methodological and theoretical approaches to the study of language and thought. Nevertheless, the chapters in this section cover two issues in particular that are of some importance to them all: what information from language disabilities has implications for a model of normal language performance; and what research strategies are most useful?

A. What Information from Disabilities Has Implications for a Model of Normal Language Performance?

The problem of a language disability is approached differently by each of the authors in this section. Howes is concerned with aphasia, which is commonly regarded as a linguistic/symbolic disorder due to cerebral damage. Spence is concerned with language disabilities as manifestations of emotional problems. Carton and Castiglione deal with the concept of language–cognitive disabilities in terms of learning problems in the school setting. These differences in focus are responsible for the variety of approaches taken by these authors. However, all of these researchers view language not as an isolated entity but rather as an integrated part of a total cognitive system.

Howes makes three points initially: (1) the act of naming is fundamental not only to understanding natural language but to understanding how things are known as well; (2) naming is immensely complex in its ramifications; and (3) 2000 years have added little to current knowledge of the subject of naming. Howes shows that the breakdown of the naming function observed in patients with aphasia has implications for the normal process by which words, objects, and meanings are linked. He points out that two elementary facts about aphasia make that condition particularly valuable in the study of normal language. First, aphasias are produced by focal lesions in the brain that invariably encroach upon a specific area. Second, different lesions within this area give rise to qualitative as well as quantitative differences in the pattern of aphasic disorders. These facts mark language as part of the biological inheritance of the species rather than as an invention such as tools. These facts also differentiate language functionally and structurally from other cognitive processes and modes of communication that in normal experience seem to be inseparable from it.

Spence, studying natural language in the psychotherapeutic interview, discusses some common ways in which clinical dialogue uses well-known linguistic phenomena. He asserts that, if a symmetry between language production and language comprehension exists, then the same "additional meanings" coded into surface phrase structures can also be decoded at the other end. The study of natural language, according to Spence, helps to isolate spontaneous examples of such encoding and decoding operations. He views the problem of therapy in part as a problem of translating episodic memory, which is highly personal and subject to forgetting, into semantic memory, which is more abstract and permanent. Although psychotherapy may be viewed as the translation from episodic to semantic memory, timing is crucial, and too hasty a translation can interfere with the process.

Carton and Castiglione, in their concern for a comprehensive view of educational psycholinguistics, focus on the importance of individual differences, both in the learner and in his environment. A language disability might be viewed as the lower extreme in the range of individual learning abilities, as an impoverished learning environment, or, more appropriately, as a nonoptimal environment in terms of the given individual. Carton and Castiglione are cautious in making inferences regarding language learning across learning environments and across populations of individuals, such as normals and those with language learning problems. In their chapter, they do suggest that analyses and comparisons of first-language learning, of "natural" second-language learning, and of formally instructed second-language learning may shed some understanding about language-learning mechanisms. But, in a different context, they show strong reservations about such a theoretical approach. The reinforcement procedures of behavior modification have proved quite successful in teaching language to autistic children, but "there are those who would advise against using methods that work on abnormal populations with normal ones lest the 'natural' mechanisms that facilitate learning be disrupted by artificial educational manipulations" (Carton & Castiglione, this volume, p. 502).

B. What Research Strategies Are Most Useful?

Howes, limiting his discussion of aphasia to confrontation naming, cites four syndromes. Within this focus, he asserts that one can formulate and quantitatively test propositions with evidence from individual case studies. Observation, in his view, holds promise that a rather rigorous theoretical treatment of confrontation naming in specific aphasic syndromes is possible and will, in the long run, provide a better understanding of the complex process of human naming.

Spence holds that examples of encoding and decoding operations from clinical interviews may lead to a greater understanding of the nature of underlying structures. He focuses upon the concept of conversational implicatures, which deals with the distinctions between what is said in conversation and what is meant, implied, or suggested. He has formalized this distinction by breaking it down into four categories modeled after Kant: quantity, quality, relation, and manner. Evidence for these categories can be obtained from a systematic context analysis of the lexical surface structure of a patient's utterances.

Carton and Castiglione recommend a natural-history (i.e., nonlaboratory) approach to the study of educative psycholinguistics. Linguistic phenomena take on importance in terms of their real-world validity, in terms of their usefulness in social, cultural, and educational applications. For example, they concern themselves with an approach to psycholinguistics in which the psychological component would be concerned with personality considerations (e.g., self-image, identity, interpersonal perception) and how language relates to thinking. For them, educational psycholinguistics depends on both a linguistic analysis and an understanding of the learner's mind. Linguistic analysis gains psychological validity by understanding a child's mind in the most economical and useful manner.

VII.   CONCLUSION

We trust that, in this chapter, we have adequately demonstrated the enormous growth that has characterized the area of psycholinguistic research over the last two decades. This sampling of various viewpoints clearly indicates the multifaceted, interdisciplinary interest that this field has generated both in terms of basic and applied research. We envision that these controversial issues and others will continue to stimulate innovative contributions toward an appreciation of how language provides a mirror to help us understand the workings of the human mind.

ACKNOWLEDGMENT

This chapter was supported in part by USPHS Grant MH-16,496 to New York University.

REFERENCE

McNeill, D. The place of grammar in a theory of performance. In D. Aaronson & R. Rieber (Eds.), *Developmental psycholinguistics and communication disorders.* New York: The New York Academy of Science, 1975.

2 Theoretical and Historical Roots of Psycholinguistic Research

R. W. Rieber
John Jay College CUNY

Harold Vetter
University of South Florida, Tampa

> *Philosophical (grammar), examining the power and nature of words, as they are the footsteps and prints of reason: which kind of analogy between words and reason is handled* sparsim, *brokenly, though not entirely; and therefore I cannot report it deficient, though I think it is very worthy to be reduced into a science by itself.*
>
> —Bacon *(Adv. of Learning)*

I. INTRODUCTION

Psycholinguistics can be said to have originated as far back in the history of philosophy as one cares to trace psychology. The widespread use of the term *psycholinguistics* and the development of a distinct discipline with that title, however, go back only to the early 1950s, when George Miller, Charles Osgood, and other psychologists introduced a knowledge of linguistics into the psychological study of language.[1] Prior to that time, psychological studies of "verbal learning" dated from the concern of Ebbinghaus (1885) with memory and are tied to a strand of theory that can be followed back to the associationism of Locke (1632–1704). To the extent that verbal learning theorists in psychology were almost totally lacking in linguistic sophistication, it might be said that their research interests represented precisely what psycholinguistics was *not*.

---

[1] To the best of our knowledge, the first modern usage of the term *psycholinguistics* appeared in Kantor (1936) as an adjective and in Pronko (1946) as a noun.

In the summer of 1951, the Social Science Research Council (SSRC) sponsored an interdisciplinary seminar on language behavior at Cornell University that brought together three psychologists and three linguists.[2] Unlike many well-intentioned mutual efforts of this kind, the Cornell conference produced a number of noteworthy results. In addition to their discovery of methodological kinship, the conferees found themselves in possession of a solid foundation of shared interests in language phenomena and their systematic exploration. Two of the more influential consequences of the conference were not immediately apparent. The first of these was the establishment of the following autumn of a Committee on Linguistics and Psychology by the SSRC, which included psychologists John Carroll, James Jenkins, George Miller, and Charles Osgood, and linguists Joseph Greenberg, Floyd Lounsbury, and Thomas Sebeok. The second important consequence of the Cornell summer seminar was the grassfire rapidity with which the term psycholinguistics entered the lexicon of psychologists and linguists alike.[3]

At least part of the reason for the almost instant popularity of psycholinguistics as a term was the lack of a suitable tag or label for the variety of issues and problems encompassed by the research interests and efforts of linguists and psychologists. Roger Brown (1958) objected to the "absurd but intrusive false etymology" of the term, which tends to support the implication that a "psycho-linguist" is a mentally deranged polyglot. But his more serious concern that the term might limit the field to the traditional objectives of linguistics has fortunately been allayed by subsequent developments in psycholinguistic research. In fact, a broad range of inquiry is presently conducted under the rubric *psycholinguistic*, which fits under the more generous umbrella of the "psychology of language" (see Chapter 1, this volume).

Professional interest in psycholinguistics was further stimulated by the publication in 1954 of a monograph entitled *Psycholinguistics: A Survey of Theory and Research Problems*, which resulted from an SSRC-sponsored conference at Indiana University. As Diebold (1965) pointed out in his editorial postscript to the reissue, this monograph provided a "charter for psycholinguistics" and quickly became a collector's item. Further SSRC conferences were held during the next several years at a variety of locations on such topics as comparative psycholinguistics, bilingualism, content analysis, associative processes in verbal behavior, dimensions of meaning, style in language, aphasia, and language universals. With the publication in 1961 of Sol Saporta's anthology entitled *Psycholinguistics: A Book of Readings,* it

---

[2]For further discussion of this point, see Blumenthal (1970, p. vii) and A. R. Diebold (1965).
[3]This point is discussed further in A. R. Diebold (1965).

was apparent that psycholinguistics, as both a term and an important area of interdisciplinary effort, was here to stay.

During most of the decade between the first SSRC conference and the appearance of Saporta's reader, language analysis was largely dominated by the structural linguistics viewpoint as it had been developed and elaborated by Bloomfield, Fries, Hockett, Pike, and others. During this "formative period" of psycholinguistics, as Maclay (1973) has called it, the harmonious relations between psychologists and linguists were enhanced by their "common commitment to an operationalist philosophy of science and a division of labor that prevented a number of difficulties from becoming overt [p. 570]." This happy state of affairs was not destined to last.

In 1957 there occurred what must be ranked among the several most important intellectual events of this century—the publication of a book entitled *Syntactic Structures* by Noam Chomsky. What Chomsky did in this single volume was nothing less than raise the flag of revolution within the linguistics camp. Much of the impact of Chomsky's critique of structural linguistics centered upon a distinction between competence and performance in language. More specifically, Chomsky challenged the proposition that it is possible to arrive at a comprehensive statement of the former by starting from a description, however detailed and specific, of the latter.

The objective of linguistic theory, in Chomsky's view, is to provide a formal statement of the coherence and consistency of a language (i.e., its *grammar*). Structural linguists assumed that it was possible, given an adequate corpus of utterances by a native speaker, to *infer* the essential features of coherence and consistency that characterize the grammar of a given language. Such a statement might require a volume approaching the size of an unabridged dictionary. How, then, could we reconcile anything so voluminous and elaborate with the effective linguistic performance of the 6-year-old child? Said Carroll (1964): "Either the feat of the child is actually greater than we think it is, or there is something wrong with the assertion that a grammar of a language needs to be voluminous [p. 23]."

Each new reported study tends to deepen our appreciation for the impressiveness of the child's feat in learning his or her native language. But without detracting from the magnitude of such an accomplishment, there is the question of the relationship between linguistic behavior and linguistic theory. Is it really possible to start with the slips, false starts, hesitations, fragmentary sentences, and incomplete utterances of ordinary language behavior and arrive at the coherence and consistency of the language system?

Chomsky (1956, 1957) demonstrated that two of the three models that had been proposed up until that time as devices for generating language utterances were unsuitable for reasons involving inherent limitations on their operations: a *finite-state grammar,* which conceptualizes sentences as sequences of items selected from a large inventory and arranged in such an order that antecedent selections determine the conditional probabilities of subsequent choices (i.e., each selection that is made at some point in the sequence reduces the *potential* number of choices available at later stages); and a *phrase-structure grammar,* which makes provision for the fact that language has hierarchical as well as linear organization of the sentence as a series of constructions *(immediate constituents)* at successive levels.

Chomsky analyzed a number of problems such as constructional homonymity which tax the capacities of either model and proposed that an adequate grammar makes most parsimonious use of a small number of basic elements or *kernel* sentences from which an indefinitely large number of *derived* sentences can be generated by means of rules (called *transformations*) that rearrange the components of a word string. Such transformations involve operations like additions, deletions, permutations, and combinations which convert a sentence with a given constituent structure into a new sentence with a derived constituent structure. It adds considerably to the analytic capabilities of the grammatical model if it makes further provision for distinguishing optional transformational rules from obligatory trans-formational rules.

Chomsky's views quickly attracted a group of disciples who became identified in the aggregate as transformational, or generative, grammarians. In their subsequent interactions with the structural linguists—and with the behaviorists among the ranks of the psychologists—they often seemed to display a frame of mind similar to that of St. Paul after he had experienced his encounter on the road to Damascus. Confrontation escalated into full-scale strife, so that by 1970 Hebb, Lambert, and Tucker were pleading for a DMZ—a demilitarized zone—between the warring camps.

Thomas Kuhn, in the *Structure of Scientific Revolutions* (1970), takes issue with the traditional view of science to which every fledgling scientist is exposed as a student, namely, that scientific progress is linear, that scientific knowledge is cumulative, and that scientific research is directed toward abstract truth. Instead, Kuhn maintains, the history of any given science is revolutionary, not evolutionary. Scientific change comes about, in his view, by a process that bears a closer resemblance to the way in which regimes succeed one another in a banana republic than to the orderly process of transition from one governmental administration to another with which most Americans are familiar. The basic pattern is a clash of paradigms in which one view of nature is overthrown by another.

Much of the dispute that raged during the 1960s and early 1970s over the issue of linguistic competence vs. performance involved a conflict between the paradigms of rationalism and empiricism. This conflict needs to be viewed in historical, as well as in theoretical, perspective. Chomsky (1966), for example, traces his own academic lineaments back to Descartes (1596–1650); and in a recent paper, Sullivan (1977) concludes that if there had been a Cartesian linguistics, it might have borne some resemblance to what Chomsky has proposed. In particular, Descartes's transition from the doctrine of innate ideas to one of innate *powers* is consistent with Chomsky's contention that the generativity or creativity of language presupposes certain innate properties of the mind. If such properties exist, are they species-specific to the human being or are they continuously distributed across the phylogenetic scale? This is a question of considerable contemporary import, given the achievements of a number of investigators who have succeeded in teaching Ameslan (American Sign Language) to chimpanzees. But it was raised as long ago as the middle of the eighteenth century by La Mettrie in *L'Homme Machine* (1746), and it has been posed in various ways and at various times by nearly every person who has seriously pondered the origins of language.

Long before psychology emerged as an autonomous discipline, with roots in both the "descriptive philosophy of experience" and biology, concern for what we would identify today as the psychology of language belonged to the philosopher and the medical practitioner. Language phenomena were often the object of study for the light they might possibly shed on the structure and process of thought or reason, rather than as legitimate objects of inquiry in themselves. When interest was shown in language phenomena per se, the chances were very good that the source of the concern was some type of linguistic aberration or disorder, and that the principal aim of the observer or investigator was to find some method of treatment for the disorder. Clinical preoccupation with the linguistic effects of structural disturbances led, in turn, to an interest in language and the central nervous system. Later, the initial observations of *disturbed language* (as opposed to language disturbance) in schizophrenia led to attempts to relate such phenomena to the kinds of symptoms previously noted in aphasia. Thus, the field of inquiry was broadened to cover the systematic study of communication and its pathology.

We have ordered our review of the historical and theoretical perspectives in psycholinguistics with the above considerations in mind. We believe that these topic headings reflect some of the more significant recurrent themes in the psychology of language:

—Language, Thought, and Behavior
—Language and the Brain
—Communication and Its Pathology
—Comparative Study of Communication

This last section is subtitled (and we ask the reader's pardon) "Hands Across the Phylogenetic Scale." Although this list makes no pretense at being comprehensive, we trust that we have managed to include a representative sample of the historical background of psycholinguistic theory and research.[4]

✕ II. LANGUAGE, THOUGHT, AND BEHAVIOR:
Empiricism Takes a Giant Step and Falls

In language, as in so many other areas of intellectual activity, the Greeks—beginning with the pre-Socratic philosophers in the latter part of the sixth century B.C.—were the initiators of systematic inquiry. They were the first language theorists; they were the first Europeans to concern themselves with the study of written texts; they founded the principles of classical European grammar. They discovered the parts of speech for Greek, and also such syntactic constructions as that of "subject and predicate, and its chief inflectional categories: genders, numbers, cases, persons, tenses, and modes. They defined these not in terms of recognizable linguistic forms, but in abstract terms which were to tell the meaning of the linguistic class" (Bloomfield, 1933, p. 5).

Hellenic interest in language was an outgrowth of philosophic pursuits. It was essentially in response to philosophical questions that Greek scholars speculated on the origin of language, the relationship between words and their meanings, and the application of principles of logic to grammar. Philosophical discussions were often directed toward linguistic problems. One of these discussions, as Ivič (1965) points out, is quite famous—the argument over whether the connection between the meanings of words and their sounds is logical and direct, or arbitrary and capricious. The "analogists" maintained that language is not dependent upon human conventions but is a gift of nature. There was perfect correspondence, in their view, between the sound of a word and its meaning; any imperfections that had arisen in this relationship in the course of time could be explained by etymological research, by systematic studies of words and their origins and derivations. The "anomalists," on the other hand, rejected the notion that there was perfect harmony between the sound and meanings of words. They drew on the existence of synonyms and homonyms, the demonstration of linguistic change over time, and the irregularity of grammar to show the imperfect nature of language.

Aristotle (384–322 B.C.) displayed the same twofold philosophical and scientific interest in language that he exhibited in other phenomena. He believed that language was found exclusively in humans, with the songs of

---

[4]The reader is referred to Robins and Robins (1967), Stam (1976), Blumenthal (1970), and Aarsleff (1967) for more detailed historical background material.

birds the closest approximation among animals. Children, he considered, are not able to speak as adults do only because they have not yet attained control over their tongues; control is perfected through training. Human language differs biologically from the vocalizations of animals, in the Aristotelian view, on the basis of a difference in the locus of sound production and the apparatus of articulation: human language is produced by the action of the tongue and animal sounds by the impact of air on the walls of the trachea. Human language articulation is unlike the expressive sounds produced by children or animals. These can neither be reduced to syllables nor combined to form syllables, as is possible with human speech. He considered language itself as part of the natural order *(physis)* and the meanings of words as man-made *(thesis).*

Aristotle also attempted to establish a means of classifying parts of speech. The basic units of language, he felt, were nouns *(onoma)* and verbs *(rhema)*, because only these words have a distinct meaning of their own; all other words merely serve to relate the logical aspects of the thinking process *(syndesmoi)*.

As in so many other spheres of activity, the Romans borrowed liberally from the Greeks in matters pertaining to language. Thus, when a formal grammar was required by the Romans (100 B.C.–A.D. 200) during the period of their hegemony in order to unify the empire and compose a Latin literature, the model they chose was Greek.

The early Christian leaders considered language as God-given; and differences between languages were solely of pragmatic concern whenever a newly discovered territory needed Christianizing. Although language theorizing was dominated by the theme of divine revelation and concern for biblical exegesis, the natural basis of language was not totally abandoned. Ricobaldo of Ferrara, who believed in the separation of language capacities and languages, was supported in this belief by witnessing a miracle in 1293. When a deaf mute acquired hearing and speech after praying at the tomb of St. Anthony of Padua, he could repeat what was said to him but was unable to understand it. This was said to prove that language capacity was God-given, but that the knowledge of a particular language had to be learned.

Later Renaissance churchmen, such as Pietro Bembo (1470–1547), secretary to Pope Leo X, and Juan Luis Vives (1492–1540), maintained that language has a natural order with which no individual can tamper. Furthermore, these languages undergo changes with time, and the simplest languages are the oldest. Even the skeptic Montaigne (1533–1592) believed in the natural basis of language.

The English philosopher, essayist, and statesman Francis Bacon (1561–1626) approached the study of language as a multilevel process of communication, of which speech is only one of many possible manifestations. Discounting enquiry into the origins of names, Bacon nevertheless allows that names are "the vestiges of reason," and he envisions a philosophical grammar based on a comparison of different idioms—a theory that presupposes the possibility of creating a language entirely on the basis of convention and artifice. ⟩⟨

A. The Cartesians

Marx (1967) noted that the separation between philosophy and science with respect to language began with Descartes (1596–1650). As long as philosophy and natural science were indistinguishable, the philosophic emphasis upon language as the expression of human reason tended to confine to philosophy the consideration of all language elements. However, Descartes drew a further distinction between language and the expression of emotions, which man shares with most animals, and articulation, which he shares with parrots and magpies.

Descartes did not write extensively about language, but his conception of how the mind is related to the body influenced much of the later speculation concerning language. His resolution of the mind–body problem in terms of two substances—"extended" (all objects of the physical world, hence body) and "unextended" (not localized in space, hence mind)—and their interaction at the pineal body, generated the dualistic theory. Thus, mind can be considered as a distinct entity, apart from the body.[5]

Certainly another tenet of Cartesian philosophy that affected conceptualizations of language was the postulation of innate ideas (e.g., God, self, conceptions of time, space, and motion).

Chomsky (1966) paraphrased Descartes to demonstrate Descartes's belief that language is a species-specific capacity, a specific human ability that is independent of intelligence. And, of course, with innate thoughts common to all men, everyone has something to talk about:

> It is a very remarkable fact that there are none so depraved and stupid, without even excepting idiots, that they cannot arrange different words together, forming of them a statement by which they make known their thoughts; while, on the other hand, there is no animal, however perfect and fortunately circumstanced it may be, which can do the same [p. 4].

In Descartes's view, speech is not only the sign of thought, but proof of thought's existence. Descartes's remarks on language aimed to illustrate the distinctness of man as a thinking being and to establish the exemption of *res cogitans* from the mechanical laws regulating the extended world.

---

[5]Margaret Wilson, in a forthcoming book entitled *Body and Mind* (ed. R. W. Rieber, Academic Press, New York, in press), argues that an accurate understanding of Descartes' position leads one to the conclusion that he was not a mind–body dualist in the strict sense of that term.

Despite Descartes's specification of speech as a test for humanity, it fell to Geraud de Cordemoy, in his *Discours physique de la parole* (1668), to offer a Cartesian analysis of human language in depth. Gaining something of the status of Cartesian orthodoxy despite various divergent expositions and conclusions, Cordemoy's works attempted to establish the congruity of the Cartesian system with Christian dogma. In Cordemoy's belief, the surest sign of thought's presence is innovation—a process that displays both voice as it proceeds from the body and idea which emanates from the soul.

B. Locke

Locke (1632–1704) rejected the Cartesian notion of innate ideas, reasserting the Aristotelian conception of mind as a *tabula rasa*. However, he did accept a form of dualism in the mind-body postulation and went on to problems of how the mind comes to perceive the world. Locke found the relationship between ideas and words to be so close that a consideration of language became a necessary preliminary to the contemplation of knowledge (Locke, 1690/1924). The first condition of speech is a natural aptitude of the organism—a condition augmented in man by an ability to "use these words as signs of internal conceptions, and to make them stand as marks for the ideas within his own mind" (Locke, 1690). The use of general terms to mark multitudes of individual experiences refines language and renders it manageable. Language arose out of the need to communicate, through external and sensible signs, ideas that are invisible. For Locke, there is no natural connection between particular articulate sounds and particular ideas—a view that he supports by noting that men do speak different languages, and, even in a common language, particular words possess various significances for different men.

Locke's theory posits that, if the human faculty for articulate expression is natural, the invention of names is conventional and arbitrary. Words originally were particular and were used to indicate individuals, only signifying notions of sensible things. General terms were gradually created to correspond to general ideas, and words which had their origin in sensible ideas were, by analogy and metaphor, transferred to spiritual notions.

Locke's influence on Condillac precipitated certain transformations in Locke's theory. Condillac "radicalized" Locke into a more consistent form of genetic sensationalism, one of the results of which was that the existence of human language as a complete entity awaiting man in the course of his development could not be taken for granted as it had been by Locke. Condillac, projecting Locke's epistomology onto a historical screen, used Locke's explanation of psychological development as a model for the historical progression of the race.

C. Condillac

In his *Essay on the Origin of Human Knowledge* and *Treatise on the Sensation*, Condillac (1715–1780) tries to show that all supposedly independent reflections are derivable as compositions from the data of sense—a view that is at odds with Locke's concession that not all experience is of a sensuous type. Ideas, for Condillac, are formed by a prereflective process or association requiring the use of signs. The reason that our attention focuses first on certain selected perceptions is that those perceptions are associated with our wants, all of which are interdependent and related. Thus, the connection of wants and desires produces association of ideas. But the mechanism of *liaison*—the "real cause of the progress of the imagination, contemplation, and memory"—is the use of signs that reinforce and preserve the association. These signs are the necessary precedent to human language and to the operation of reflection, because it is only at this point that the mind becomes aware of the complexity of its own operations.

Reflection and language reciprocally influence each other, leading to further progression of each and the emergence of more advanced mental faculties. In this schematism Condillac claimed to have given empiricism a more thoroughgoing and consistent rationale than had been accomplished by Locke.

According to Condillac's theory, there is only one method, and that is the method of analysis. All thought consists in analyzing complex knowledge and extracting its simple elements and the relations between those elements. This seemingly paradoxical theory implies that what is unknown must be contained in what is known. Condillac's theory is not altogether paradoxical, however; it rests on his conception of science and of the processes of logic. We find what we do not know in what we do know, for the unknown is the known, because it is the same thing as the known. To proceed from the known to the unknown is therefore to go from the same to the same. Thought is merely a progress of expression.

For Condillac, a science is nothing more than a well-constructed language. In order for such a language to be useful, it must be simple, its signs must be precisely determined and defined, and the language must be formed in accord with the laws of analogy. "The whole art of reasoning, like the whole art of speaking, may be reduced to analogy"[6] (Condillac, 1746).

The first language must have been a kind of chant, with violent inflections accompanying the action of the body. At first, language consisted only of interjections or cries in various notes according to the feelings being expressed. In the beginning, there were only the names of things; the first

---

[6]Humboldt's (1972) contribution stressed the biological basis of language, but with an emphasis upon universality of behavior rather than individual differences (see Stam, 1977).

verbs expressed passive states of mind only. Like Locke, Condillac asserts that words expressing abstract or spiritual ideas originated in sensible ideas.

For Condillac language is not a purely arbitrary institution. The natural movements of the body provide the elements of the language of action, and the cry of passion provides the rudiments of speech. Man, impelled by need, speaks before he has willed to speak. Convention, therefore, only perfects and extends what nature has begun. Condillac believed that the elements of the language of action (i.e., the organs) were born with man. In this sense he believed that there was an innate language, but he strongly opposed the notion of innate ideas. Condillac (1809) puts the matter thus: "The language which I call innate is a language we have not learned, because it is the natural and immediate effect of our conversation. It says at once all we feel; it is therefore not an analytical method ... it therefore affords no ideas."

D. Leibnitz

Leibnitz (1646–1716) maintains that words, originally, did not refer to individuals. For him, general terms would necessarily have been the first exponents of language, since it is as natural to employ general terms as it is to observe resemblances among things (Leibnitz, 1916). Moreover, Leibnitz accepts the theory of the arbitrary origin of speech only with reservation. He does maintain that some reason exists for words being what they are. He nevertheless admits the possibility that some languages are "artificial, dependent on choice, and entirely arbitrary."

Leibnitz envisioned a *"caracteristique universelle"* that would be a philosophical language analogous to the language of mathematics—a proposition that would call for a succinct determination of all elementary forms and a clear delineation of all the possible combinations of these rudimentary concepts. To these simple concepts and their combinations, absolute values would be applied, thus rendering a language of precise expression.

E. John Horne Tooke

Charles de Brosses and Antoine Court de Gébelin proposed that all vowels are interchangeable in matters of derivation; all labials are likewise similar, and so forth. Both men wrote voluminously on etymology, rendering up ultimately one original and sparsely worded language. De Brosses, the first to theorize that *fetichisme* was an important phase of pagan religion, hypothesized that the original language was formed as it had perforce to be formed under the influence of climate and the nature of speech organs. The differentiations of this *langue primordiale* owed their appearance to the changes in the vocal organs themselves and in the various climates into which speaking peoples wandered. Numerous writers took up the banner of de

Brosses in France and in Germany, expanding particularly on language's accountability to climate. John Horne Tooke, in his *ΕΠΕΑ ΠΤΕΡΟΕΝΤΑ* (*Diversions of Purley*, 1798), put forth a compilation of disquisitions on the importance of etymologies and innumerable derivations of individual words. Tooke believed that all linguistic progress had consisted of a tendency toward increased efficiency and atrophy of unnecessary parts. He also held that all parts of speech could be derived from original nouns and verbs. An extensive discussion of Tooke's theory of language can be found in Aarsleff (1967).

F. Nineteenth-Century Romantic Views

Comparative philology and the physiological theory of natural signs have engendered renewed interest in the study of language and its origins. The progress of these two theories has illustrated the inadequacy of eighteenth-century views.

The science of language delineated by Leibnitz led, by 1787, to the assertion of relationship among Sanskrit, Greek, and Latin by William Jones. In 1808, Frederick Schlegl, applying the comparative method, incorporated the languages of India, Persia, Greece, Italy, and Germany into the single category of Indo-Germanic languages. Francis Bopp, in 1816, published *System of conjugation of the Sanscrit tongue, compared with that of the Greek, Latin, Persian, and German*, a work identified as the first truly scientific comparison established between the grammars of the Indo-European languages. William Humboldt, Jacob Grimm, and Eugene Burnouf *(Studies on the Ancient Language of Persia)* completed the foundation of an experimental science of language, resulting in a genealogical classification of languages. The affiliation of languages being established, attention was turned to derivation—a process that was shown to be subject to definite and recognizable laws. By showing that languages are modified according to inevitable laws, comparative philology established that language is a natural product, subject to the laws of life.

G. Max Müller

Max Müller counts comparative philology among the natural sciences. Language has had a development rather than a history. "Although there is a continuous change in language, it is not in the power of any man either to produce it or to prevent it" (Müller, 1890).

Müller's theory may be substantially represented in two statements. In the first place, language is a product of nature; and secondly, man speaks by an instinct consisting of two steps—the formation of ideas and the creation of words to express them. This second thesis rests on the reduction by philosophical analysis of a language or family of languages to 400 or 500 abstract, general roots. M. Michel Breal has proved that these roots, however, cannot be regarded as constitutive elements of a first language, but are rather the remains of former substantives—originally concrete words—that have taken an abstract meaning while passing through the form of the verb.

Müller objected to evolutionary theory on the somewhat dubious basis that, if man's origins lie with some lower animal, it is futile to maintain man's distinctness from lower animals. He dismissed the matter of evolutionary transition by affirming that language is unique to humans.

William Dwight Whitney (1827–1894) attacked Müller, asserting that the latter absurdly concluded that thought and language are identical. Whitney charged that the alleged correlation between thought and language is useless unless the terms are clearly defined. The type of thought involved must be determined—whether simple mental processes, rational thought, or some less conventional type of thought. Despite his objections to Müller, Whitney did not commit himself to Darwinism or to any theory of the origin of language. While maintaining that linguistic meaning is conventionally established, he did not provide an answer to how the conventions themselves were established. In the end, he felt, the evolutionist has no contribution to make to linguistic theory.

H. Physiological Theory of Natural Signs

Physiology has explained the production and significance of natural signs. A gesture that expresses emotion, a sign, an expression, a facial change—each is the beginning of an action. If the face, for instance, by a particular contraction expresses a particular passion or appetite, it is because that contraction is precisely the mechanical condition necessary to satisfy that passion or appetite. This theory of Bell's was accepted and expanded by many others during the nineteenth century (see Darwin, 1873).

In his *Expression of the Emotions*, Darwin accepts Bell's principle that, because humans possessed no organs intended originally for expression, certain human movements became by long association signs of particular internal states. He goes on to account for the phenomena of expression through three principles: the principle of serviceable associative habits, the principle of antithesis, and the principle of involuntary—and to some extent nonhabitual—nervous actions.

According to the serviceable-habits principle, movements that are useful in satisfying a desire eventually emerge, after long association with the particular urging, as an independent reaction—although in a markedly less dramatic form. The somewhat hypothetical principle of antithesis provides that certain expressive movements have no other reason than an original and universal inclination to accompany a feeling with gestures contrary to those which would express an opposite feeling. The third principle—that of involuntary nervous action—is exemplified in the gestures of a furious man that may be attributed in part to an excess of nervous force and that often represent the action of striking.

I. Darwinian Theory

The main discussion of language in the works of Darwin was in a chapter in *The Descent of Man* (1871), in which he compares the mental powers of man and the lower animals. Here, as elsewhere, he proposed to show the genealogical links between species without obliterating specific differences. Agreeing that "the habitual use of articulate language" is peculiar to humans, Darwin goes on to qualify the statement by noting that not all human language is articulate, as in cases of human fear, surprise, and so forth. Moreover, although certain lower animals are capable of reacting to articulate speech or even of producing it to a limited extent, man is differentiated by his "almost infinitely larger power of associating the most diversified sounds and ideas."

To the extent that language is a *differentia specifica*, it is a difference of degree rather than of kind, and, as is the difficulty with all such gradualistic schemes, Darwin's final problem was to define the prior cause. He concluded that a reciprocal influence must have been in force between the development of a more efficient brain and the development of more articulate speech. Darwin also thought that the voice was first used as a means to entice and to ward off competition, and from this additional link between animal expression and human language, Darwin inferred that articulate language was preceded by music. In supporting this belief, Darwin drew heavily on the works of Herbert Spencer according to whom all nuances of the voice—loudness, quality, timbre, pitch, interval, rate of variation—are "the physiological results of variations and feeling."

Applications of the main outlines of Darwinian theory were soon made to the later and better known history of language. Sir Charles Lyell devoted a chapter of *The Antiquity of Man* to a demonstration of the law of gradual transmutation in the history of languages, and Ernst Haeckel reiterated these ideas. Frederic Bateman, who rejected evolution in *Darwinism Tested by Language* (1877), determined that material causes alone could explain neither linguistic competency nor speech failures, thus arguing the "immateriality of the faculty of speech."

III. LANGUAGE AND THE BRAIN:
The Brain's the Thing to Catch
the Consciousness of the King

A group of eighteenth-century philosopher-psychologists known as *associationists*—named in accordance with their prolific writing about the "association of ideas," a phrase popularized by John Locke, and as a testimonial to their interest in the question of how simple ideas go together to form complex ones—gravitated in their studies toward the problem of how individuals learn. Their theories, with the exception of Locke's, attempted to integrate mind and body into one interrelated system. Such men as David Hartley (1749) and Erasmus Darwin (1796/1974) were extremely interested in speech and language, as well as in the normal and abnormal development of speech and language in the child.

The associationists described mental processes in terms of analysis, in light of the *law of congruity*. By this law, the basis of association was the observation that two objects, when they are perceived or thought of simultaneously or in close succession, become associated or linked together.

Hartley indicated that sensations (internal feelings stimulated by external events) are associated with simple brain states (vibrations), and ideas (internal feelings other than sensations) are also related to simple brain states. It was theorized that these bonds tie with the simple states into complex compounds. In terms of understanding language, Hartley believed that we arrive at an understanding of one another through the power of association, a process whereby simple sounds are associated into a whole (i.e., words, sentences, and so on). Hartley, who wrote about auditory images in relation to the development of speech and language in the child, believed that children learn to speak by repeating the sounds that stimulate the organism to respond. Speech disorders were interpreted in similar fashion as in the case of stuttering which, according to Hartley, develops from fear, eagerness, or a violent passion that prevents the child from using his speech mechanism correctly. The resulting confusion disrupts the vibrations traveling via neural pathways to the peripheral speech mechanism, thereby causing the individual to reiterate until he is successful. Hartley pointed out, however, that this problem would generally not develop until the child is of an age to distinguish right from wrong in the pronunciation of speech sounds. Hartley also felt that stuttering may develop from a "defect of memory from passion" and, in some cases, that it can be learned by imitation. He went on to point out that stuttering tends to spread or generalize to other words or situations. It is of interest to note that this basic phenomenon is still being explored by verbal learning theorists interested in the problem of stuttering. As Brett (1921) points out, Hartley had a strong influence on later scientists who studied language and its disorders.

Erasmus Darwin (1794/1974) was another associationist who was interested in language and its disorders. He believed that motions affecting the body might result from the following: *irritations* excited by external factors; *sensation* aroused by pleasure or pain; *volition* aroused by desire or aversion; or *associations* that could be linked with other movements. He interpreted all disorders in terms of one or another of these processes and based his classification of diseases upon this frame of reference. Darwin's hope was that his classification would present a better understanding of the nature of illness or disease. Greatly influenced by Hartley, Darwin classified the problem of stuttering as a disease of volition, developing his theory around the idea that when the stutterer is very much preoccupied with an idea, the corresponding fear of failure is so great that the associations of the muscular motions of articulation become impaired. The stutterer then attempts in vain to gain voluntary control of these broken associations, resulting in a stuttering block that may then cause "various distortions of countenance."

The latter part of the eighteenth century and the early part of the nineteenth century saw the continuing integration of the findings of abnormal psychology with those of general psychology; in other words, the ancient relationship between physiology and pathology was now being applied to the study of the mind. This set the stage for the new "mental physiology" of the late nineteenth century. In the work of Spurtzheim and Combe, phrenology, too, became the model for the normal as well as the abnormal. These systems amount to what we might call a "divorce of convenience" or methodological monism; they deny neither mind nor body, but are centered on one or the other. Often pursued with lack of perspective, they prepared the way for the more radical monisms of extreme idealism and ultramaterialism.

The eighteenth-century faculty psychologists had placed their emphasis on the *universality* of the faculties operating on the human mind. This theme harmonized well with the drive of that age toward centralization and large-scale social and political structures which sought validity in a scientific notion of the "common man" and his capacities. Toward the end of the century, an increased interest in the individual became characteristic of a new philosophy—romanticism. A similar shift of interest took place in psychology as the study of faculties deemphasized what was common to all men and centered on the characteristics unique to each. An early prominent manifestation of this tendency was the new doctrine of phrenology instituted by Gall.

Gall's system postulated that localized physiological functions of the brain were responsible for the psychological strengths and weaknesses of the individual. These functions affected the growth of the skull and could be determined from a careful inventory of the skull's shape. Contemporary with Gall, Cabanis was doing much anatomical work in France to foster the notion of the brain as the organ of thought, from a materialist standpont. Although not materialistic in a strict sense, phrenology obviously had a similar thrust deriving individual psychology from primarily physiological factors. What had formerly been a metaphysical category (i.e., faculty) was now an area of the brain. Phrenology was carried on after Gall's death by his colleague, Spurtzheim, by the brothers Combe in Edinburgh, and by Charles Caldwell and the Fowlers in the United States. Once Kant had raised psychology to a supreme position among the intellectual activities of man, subsequent psychological theories tended to invade every area of life with results that were often bizarre, but also often fruitful. Phrenology offered results of each variety.

As was bound to happen, phrenologists eventually applied themselves to the study of language and language disturbances, and there occurred almost unnoticed a "paradigm drift" of great importance. No longer was the focus on the static concept of pathology of the peripheral speech organ, as in Morgagni (1769); now we find the more dynamic concept of a process instituted by the brain, depending on a language faculty in the brain, and owing its weaknesses to an inadequate faculty of the brain.

Ironically, the experimental psychophysiology that stood diametrically opposed to Gall's conception of the functions of the brain and that reverted to the psychological tradition that he opposed derived its belief in cerebral localization from phrenology. Ferrier, in formulating his view of cerebral localization derived in part from phrenology, used three sources: Broca, Fritsch and Hitzig, and Hughlings Jackson. The views of Broca and Jackson, while not adhered to strictly by Ferrier, grew historically out of phrenology.

Broca's localization of a center for "the faculty of articulate language" was the first localization of a function in the hemisphere to meet with general acceptance from orthodox scientists. Even though Broca did not originate the modern doctrine of cerebral localization, it should be stressed that Broca was the first to confirm this long-suspected localization and to clarify it with clear-cut pathological evidence—although the quality of his original evidence was dubious. What Broca did contribute was a demonstration of this localization at a time when the scientific community was at last prepared to take the issue seriously.

By way of background to Broca's "discovery" and his first case, it should be noted that observations on diseases affecting speech were made as early as the Hippocratic corpus (ca. 400 B.C.), and descriptions of speech pathology are scattered throughout the history of medicine since that time. Accurate descriptions of motor aphasia were made at least as early as the end of the seventeenth century (see Benton & Joynt, 1960), but no important ideas about localization of the lesion had been advanced prior to 1800. Gall is usually credited with "the first complete description of aphasia due to a wound of the brain"—a claim based on the case of a young man who, as a result of a foil wound, was bereft of his memory of names.

While acknowledging that Gall did provide early descriptions of the symptoms of motor aphasia, it should be realized that his conception of the language faculty was hardly adequate from a contemporary point of view. He segregated apparent ability to understand questions from ability to speak voluntarily; he noted that ability to speak could be impaired while ability to move the tongue and pronounce isolated words remained intact; and he observed that ability to express ideas by gestures and to identify objects could remain intact while various modes of more formal expression are impaired.

Broca discussed in detail whether speech is an intellectual or motor function, and—though he considered the question an open one—he inclined to the former view. He believed that the pathological anatomy of aphemia[7] strongly supported the view that speech is an intellectual function. Two prevailing dogmas prevented Broca from regarding aphasia as a motor disturbance. While supporting cerebral localization, he could not believe that the cerebral convolutions were involved in motion; he considered those organs restricted to intellectual functions.

Broca had no doubt that speech was a separate faculty, the apparent discreteness of which rendered it ideal for testing the question of cerebral localization. In a report to the Societe Anatomique de Paris dealing with the case of a patient, "Tan," Broca's description provided excellent data for consideration of the problems of the clinico-pathological method. The patient's history of aphemia, complicated by numerous progressive conditions, would disqualify him from modern clinico-pathological studies, but Broca was prepared to infer at autopsy that the lesion began at the third left frontal convolution—an inference he made in spite of extensive damage throughout the entire hemisphere. Broca's inference was later considered highly speculative.

The same year, Broca presented a second case, basing his conclusions on a strictly limited lesion without complications. By 1863 Broca and his colleagues had collected 20 cases showing some pathological change in the left half of the brain, 19 of them in the third frontal convolution. No exact location of the cortical center was given.

Broca's major contribution was to establish that pathological data support the belief in some form of localized brain function. Hughlings Jackson recognized the impact of Broca's work and agreed with Broca that "Broca's area" was the part of the brain most often damaged in patients suffering from aphasia. However, he pointed out the danger of the trend of claiming exact localized centers. Jackson's own words described this best: "To locate the damage which destroys speech and to locate speech are two different things."

Working in the tradition of Jackson an early twentieth-century Czechoslovakian, Arnold Pick, believed as did Jackson in the necessity of total cortical integration for the production of language [see Jason Brown's (1973) translation of one of Pick's important works].

Perhaps the single most important contribution to the study of language and brain mechanism was made in the work of Kurt Goldstein (1948). Goldstein, using concepts based upon Gestalt psychology, believed that "to every mental performance, there corresponds a dynamic process which concerns the entire cortex. The function of a specific region is characterized

---

[7]Broca used the term *aphemia* for *aphasia*.

by the influence which the particular structure of that region exerts on the total process."

Current work in the neuropsychology of language continues to explore such problems as lateralization of brain function and related problems—see Rieber, *The Neuropsychology of Language* (1976), and Chapter 14 in this volume. It is important to note that Marshall, writing in 1977, specifies the goal of neurolinguistic research in a way not much different than those authors cited above. This goal is "to understand the form of representation of language in the human brain." Marshall goes on to say that:

> An adequate theory might be expected to pair an information processing amount of psycholinguistic functions with a detailed statement of the physiological realization of those functions in terms of neuronal circuitry (and whatever non-neural principles of electrochemical pattern formation that may be found appropriate to the description of central nervous system states) (Morton & Marshall, 1977, p. 127).

IV. COMMUNICATION AND ITS PATHOLOGY: Can Humpty Dumpty Be Put Back Together Again?

The pathology of speech and language has two important functions. First, it is important to the psycholinguist who is concerned with setting up and validating a fruitful theory of language and thought. Second, it specifies boundary conditions that may impose constraints on the form of both competency and performance and their mode of interaction.[8]

The state of the congenitally deaf is particularly interesting. A congenitally deaf person does not learn to speak by the processes available to normal children. It is necessary to ask what is the nature of the defect that leads to this state of affairs and what, if anything, can be done to remedy it. These questions, significant in the seventeenth and eighteenth centuries, continue to be relevant even today. The answer to the first question seems rather obvious: the congenitally deaf person does not learn to speak because he cannot hear the language being spoken around him. In the period under consideration, however, it is clear from the arguments that were advanced that this answer was not at all obvious to the majority of academicians. The solution that is obvious to us today contradicted explicit statements on the subject by Aristotle, whose influence will be briefly discussed shortly.

---

[8]Bever (1975) argues against the use of pathological data for the purpose of gaining knowledge about the normal process of language development. His polemical argument fails to appreciate that normal and abnormal communication are two sides of the same coin. Only an understanding of both facets facilitates understanding of the whole. This position is supported by Furth (1975), Morton and Marshall (1977), and others.

The answer to the second question is still interesting today because the question itself is still relevant. For the psycholinguist, the implications of any specific answers may be far-reaching with regard to the deaf person's own remedy (i.e., a sign language).

A. The Context of the Period

The two leading figures of this period were Francis Bacon (1561–1626), whose major works *The Advancement of Learning* (1605) and *De Augmentis Scientarium* (1622–1623) had a great influence on all the authors discussed here; and Rene Descartes (1596–1650), who is mentioned with suspicious infrequency but whose *Discours de la Methode* (1637) and *Meditationes de Prima Philosophia* (1640) were surely known in England.

Although there is no explicit reference anywhere, there is evidence for the influence of the Port Royal logic and grammar in England at this time. Wilkins in his *Essay* (1668) establishes a rather unusual system for the parts of speech in which lexical items are divided into "integrals" and "particles." The former category includes only the noun (i.e., substantive and adjective) and the "adverb derived." The latter category includes the verb and everything else (Wilkins, 1668, p. 298). On the verb, Wilkins (1668, p. 303) says that it "is really no other than an adjective, and the copula sum affixed to it or contained in it."

Funke (1965, p. 83) considers that "[this] point of view seems quite unique, and among those authorities whom Wilkins mentions we find it nowhere." While this point may be true, Wilkins may have been influenced by Dalgarno (1661, pp. 63–64), who had presented a similar scheme. The scheme becomes even less unique when we note that it can also be found in the Port Royal Grammar of 1660. Kenelm Digby, who was a follower of Descartes and a founder and member of the Royal Society, provides a link with Cartesian philosophy that needs further investigation.

1. Applied Psycholinguistics at the Royal Society

The rise of the experimental sciences was one of the major events of the period, clearly marking it off from the Middle Ages. The universities, as institutions, opposed any backsliding from the prevailing respect for Aristotle and his commentators. This led indirectly to the formation of the great scientific societies where academicians and amateurs alike could carry out experiments and discuss their results with people of like mind. It is surely no coincidence that two of the many authors to be discussed here, Holder and Wallis, were members of the Royal Society and another, Dalgarno, was closely associated with its founder-members. The interest in experiments extended to the attempt to teach articulation and lipreading to a deaf-mute.

Holder and Wallis both published accounts of their work with the deaf in the early numbers of the *Philosophical Transactions of the Royal Society*, which first appeared in 1665.

Interest in linguistics and languages grew rapidly in the seventeenth century. The abstract study of grammar was taken up again where the medieval philosophers had left off. On the one hand, it produced such works as the Port Royal grammar. On the other hand, it attempted to design a universal philosophical language to replace Latin and to reflect more closely the "true" structure of the world. The information explosion and the need to communicate quickly and precisely on scientific topics were probably an important spur. The skepticism about language in its role as a deceiver can be traced directly to the works of Bacon.

Large polyglot dictionaries began to appear in the sixteenth century, containing usually five or six European languages. At the same time, grammars and tutors were written in English for such foreign languages as Dutch, French, Italian (1550), and Spanish for publication in England. Grammars of the vernacular also appeared that explicitly rejected the Latin model, such as Wallis's grammar (1653) (see Kemp, 1972). The modern science of phonetics can certainly trace its origins directly back to this period, and no doubt some of the trend systematization was a result of the study of new languages.

Moves toward spelling reform (by Bullokar, Gil, Hart, and Smith in England), which should be associated with such diverse events as the invention of printing and the need for a standard language consequent upon the rise of the national states, led to important work on phonetics and pronunciation. *This was continued in the seventeenth century*, when more works on general phonetics—such as those by Wallis (1653), Wilkins (1668), and Lodwick—and works on phonetics in the service of the deaf and dumb— such as those by Bonet, Holder, and Amman[9]—began to appear. Other books are those by Cordemoy (1668) and van Helmont (1667), but these do not really achieve as much as they claim. At this period, a rough test of the quality of a phonetician can be made by examining how he understands the nature of the voicing contrast (insofar as it is understood, even today), the function of the velum, and whether he notices the existence of, and correctly describes, [η], the velar nasal.

An exhaustive study of phonetics for this period is not possible here, but some information can be found in Abercrombie, Dobson, (1946), and Griffith (1953).

There are certainly other factors that should be considered, such as the growing interest in educational reform, and the progress made in medicine

---

[9]See reprint in English translation of this book (Amman, 1965) with an introduction by R. W. Rieber.

typified by Harvey's *Exercitatio anatomica de motu cordis et sanguinis in animalibus* (1628). Harvey was a student of Fabricius, professor of anatomy at Padua. The value of experiment and of the reexamination of old medical dogmas was first grasped in Italy, and from there comes the earliest note on the educability of the deaf. Above all, it is impossible to exaggerate the curiosity of men who were freeing themselves to look at anything whatsoever that the exercise of observation, reason, and interaction might serve to illuminate or render useful. There can be no doubt that this attitude benefited at least a few deaf individuals and led utlimately to the systematic institutional training that gradually developed during the eighteenth and nineteenth centuries.

B. The Teaching of Speech and Language to the Deaf

Why is it that of all the senses hearing is most liable to be defective from birth? Now language, which is a kind of voice, seems to be very easily destroyed and to be very difficult to perfect; this is indicated by the fact that we are dumb for a long time after our birth, for at first we simply do not talk at all and then at length begin only to lisp. And because language is easily destroyed, and language (being a kind of voice) and hearing both have the same source, hearing is, as it were, per accidens, thought not per se, the most easily destroyed of the senses (Aristotle, *Problemata* XI, 1).

This short and ambiguous statement is essential to an understanding of much of the seventeenth-century discussion on the deaf. Even though it may seem superfluous nowadays, it sums up almost universally accepted beliefs at a time when Aristotle's word was law. Nobody questioned Aristotle and, because he said that the deaf could never speak or learn language, nobody tried to teach them. Because it was believed that speech was a manifestation of reason, it followed that the deaf were considered to have no ability to reason and were assigned the status of idiots.

It was not realized that the congenitally deaf person could, in most cases, not speak simply because he could not hear what people around him were saying. The chain of causation had been wrongly apprehended. If any attempts at alleviation were made, Aristotle's point of view prevailed.

The earliest major policy statement that ran counter to Aristotle's opinion and also came from a respected and famous authority is to be found in Cardano's *Paraliopomena de humanis civilibus successionibus,* Lib. III, Cap. VIII, entitled "De surdo et muta literas edocto," where it is stated that the deaf can learn to hear by reading and to speak by writing. In another work, *De utilitate ex adversis capienda*, Lib. II, Cap. VII, "De surditate" (Cardan Tom. II, pp. 73–76), Cardano describes three classes of deaf people and suggests that they should be taught to read and write to alleviate their misery. There is no mention of Aristotle. There is no attempt to validate his position apart from a reference to a story of this having already been done successfully. However, Cardano (1501–1576) was a widely read and influential sixteenth-century authority.

The first moderately well-substantiated report of the actual teaching of deaf-mutes comes from Pedro de Ponce of Spain, who died in 1584, and in a book by Francisco de Valles, which appeared in 1587. Both of these works represent an advance on Cardano's suggestions, for the students are taught to articulate. It is not known whether Ponce wrote anything on his method, but it is most likely that it did lead to the first book on the teaching of the deaf, written by Juan Pablo Bonet and published in Madrid in 1620. It does not appear that this book was known in England. However, Kenelm Digby (1603–1665) seems to have witnessed the results of Bonet's labors, probably when he visited Spain in 1622.

It had become clear that the deaf could be taught to speak. The Spanish were successful in their attempts, and the English, particularly John Bulwer, were having an equal amount of good fortune. Nothing is known of Bulwer, except that he was a physician and the author of several books, two of which were published in 1648: *Chirologia: or the Naturall Language of the Hand* and *Philocophus: or the deafe and Dumbe Man's Friend.* Bulwer should be considered the originator of the art of instructing the deaf and dumb in England. However original his work may have been, he was acquainted with some of the research done by the Spanish Benedictine monks Pedro Ponce and Juan Pablo Bonet. He had certainly heard of the case, reported from Spain by Sir Kenelm Digby, of the young boy who was taught to hear, not by listening, but by watching. The second half of his book consists of an analysis of Digby's story.

Bulwer felt that sign language was an efficient means of communication because the hand has a "discoursing facultie" that gave the deaf and dumb the ability to communicate. They can argue rhetorically by using signs. It was clear to him that signs were a perfectly adequate form of communication.

The first 13 chapters of *Philocophus* deal with articulation, interspersed with some rather weak philosophizing on the connection between voluntary actions and motion. Bulwer's knowledge of phonetics was quite limited. Some of the chapter headings give the direction of his point of view: "Of the convenience and excellent situation of the Mouth for the more visible appearance and manifestation of Speech"; "That Words are nothing else but Motion"; "That the formes of Letters, and so consequently of Words, may be punctually observed and took notice of"; "That the motions of the parts of the mouth in Speech are so remarkable, that some have (not without success) attempted to imitate them by mathematicall motions"; and finally, the conclusion: "That Articulate Speech doth not necessarily require the audible sound of the voyce, but may consist without it, and so consequently be seen as well as heard." These titles outline Bulwer's argument on the feasibility of lipreading.

Voice production is explained by analogy with a pipe and he attempts to explain the distinction between, for instance, [p], [b], and [m] by means of varying degrees of impulsion of the air.

One other statement in the first part of Bulwer's book is of interest:

> Many of the learned are of opinion, and persuaded in thier judgments, that the imitation of the motions of our speech may be effected by insensible creatures; if a Dextrous man would employ his time in contriving and making such an instrument to express those different sounds; _____ not having more than seven substantiall Differences; besides, the Vowells (as some who have carefully noted them doe affirme) it would peradventure be no hard matter to compose such an Engine.

Compare Cordemoy, writing in 1668: "I conceive likewise, as I have already said, that Art may go so far as to frame an Engine, that shall articulate words like those, which I pronounce; but then I conceive at the same, that it would only pronounce those, that were design'd it should pronounce, and that it would always pronounce them in the same order." The idea of a machine was prominent in certain parts of Cartesian philosophy and perhaps this was Bulwer's source.[10] It may also have been taken from Baptista Porta whom he mentioned in this connection.

Having once established in this way that lipreading is a theoretical possibility and having given various anecdotes about people who were able to lipread, Bulwer presents Digby's story and carefully analyzes it.

Bulwer understood that speech represents thought and that writing represents speech. He indicated that a deaf person could not learn to speak because he could never imitate or understand his interlocutors. Substantiation for his case came from the fact that people who became deaf from illness did not as a consequence become mute and those that became mute from illness did not grow deaf.

He further argued against a "natural" theory of language because the congenitally deaf cannot speak at all. It was not conceivable to Bulwer that this alleged natural language was merely being suppressed. Man is made to learn to speak, much as he learns any of the arts and sciences. Wilkins even claimed in 1641 that man is equally disposed to learn any language in which he may be instructed. The manner in which children acquire language was a source of academic fascination for Bulwer. He could only conceive that children learned to speak by imitation yet also noted the weakness of such a theory.

Bulwer's books were, on the whole, discursive, derivative, and not necessarily consistent, yet they must have stimulated interest in England. His

---

[10]See John Bulwer, *Chirologia: or the Natural Language of the Hand* (London, 1644), with an introduction by H. R. Gillis; reprinted in *Language, Man, and Society Series* (ed. R. W. Rieber, A.M.S. Press, 1975).

work is also noteworthy for the fact that he recommended the establishment of academies for the deaf. It contains a clear rejection of Aristotle's views and recommends lipreading as the remedy for the disability of the deaf-mute.

John Wallis was a mathematician and cryptographer; he invented the word "interpolation" in mathematics and the symbol ∞ for infinity. He was also a founder-member of the Royal Society and the author of the first grammar of the English language that consciously departed from Latin models. Prefixed to this grammar there is a *Tractatus prooemialis loquela, sine literarum omnium formatione et genuino sono* (Wallis, 1653, pp. 1–37), which he incorrectly claims is the first general treatise on the formation of spoken sounds. Wallis did not write a book on the teaching of the deaf, but refers back to this treatise in subsequent letters. It is, therefore, worth examining— at least his treatment of consonants—because he was certainly one of the first in England to achieve substantial results.

Wallis identified [η], correctly describes it, and gives a number of minimal contrasts with [n]. He correctly analyzes [ʃ], [tʃ], and [dʒ] as composite sounds, but incorrectly describes them as [sy], [ty], and [dj], respectively. He was corrected by Amman, an important teacher of the deaf, in a letter prefixed to his *Dissertation on Speech*, first printed in 1700 in Amsterdam.

Wallis reported on his efforts at teaching the deaf and dumb to speak in three letters: to Boyle (1670), to Brouncker (1678), and to Beverly (1698). In the first of these letters, actually written in March of 1661, Wallis describes his experiences in teaching Daniel Whaley to speak. Whaley, however, was not congenitally deaf; he had suffered an accident at age 5 that cost him his ability to hear and, consequently, his ability to speak. He lost his speech gradually over a period of 6 months. Wallis was affirmed in his belief that the ability to speak followed the ability to hear. The loss of the latter then led to the loss of the former. Speech was not dissipated because of some inability of the organs of speech to produce sounds (i.e., Whaley's muteness was not physical). Thus, in one sense, Wallis had an ideal subject for experiment, because it was known that he was not congenitally dumb. However, the boy was in no sense a *tabula rasa*: by the age of 5 he spoke quite well. Because it is not impossible that his lack of speech did not indicate that he had "forgotten" his language, Wallis's success with Daniel Whaley was by no means a demonstration that he had succeeded in the second part of his task, namely, that of teaching him to understand a language. Wallis himself understood this; the ability to speak does not necessarily signal the ability to understand. A parrot can imitate but that is no indication that it comprehends.

He first discusses the difficulties of teaching "Understanding" (which appears to include syntax and morphology) and compares the difficulties of first- and second-language learning. His opinions are surprising, because he championed the liberation of the grammar of the vernacular from that of Latin. He felt that languages did not differ very much. Because of that, in second-language learning the teacher could use the mother tongue to explain problems in the target language. But because at some level, languages are relatively the same, the student already knows much of what he needs to learn. Nor will those universal aspects of language need to be taught in first-language learning. Deafness, however, makes this latter task more difficult to achieve. Wallis's discussion clearly reflects contemporary discussions of universal grammar.

There still remained the problem of speaking, i.e., the description of articulation. How could one teach sounds when the only language available was signing? Wallis believed that the organs of speech could be taught the proper places and manners of articulation even though these could not be seen or heard. He erred, however, by not discriminating between the congenitally deaf and those who become deaf at a later age. The latter retain their language and ability to speak. Cardano and Bulwer knew this; Wallis did not.

In *De Loquela* (1653), Wallis puts forth his methodology. By using signs, he sought to make the deaf student understand how to use the speech organs to produce sounds. If the student proceeded correctly, he would be commended; if he went about it incorrectly, he would be shown the right way to do it. Wallis was skeptical about lipreading. He believed it was necessary to master oral language first before this skill could be adequately taught. With this knowledge, linguistic redundancy and the linguistic context would facilitate learning to read lips.

After 2 months, Whaley had progressed so far that Wallis (1653) could claim: "There is hardly any Word, which (with Deliberation) he cannot speak [p. 40]." He was presented before the Royal Society in May of 1662 and performed much to the credit of his tutor.

The second letter (Wallis, 1678) is mainly an attempt to dismiss William Holder's priority claim, which will be discussed later. It also contains some of Wallis's most impressive observations with regard to Wilkins's discussion in his *Essay* (Wilkins, 1668). Wallis disagrees with Wilkins's treatment of the voiced-voiceless opposition, in a passage that foreshadows the clear recognition of suprasegmentals. Wilkins had treated whispering as a different kind of articulation, but Wallis ascribes it to the domain of "the whole Tenor of Speech." Included in that category are tone, time, timbre, and pitch. The difference between normal talking and whispering, then, is one of stridence not articulation. There is no need to use different phonetic symbols to characterize the two modes of speech. "Much less is this (as he makes it) the difference between V, F, or D, T, or B, P, &c. that the one is (in this Sense) Sonorous, the other Mute. For we may whisper the words, Ved, Bed, without saying Fet, Pet (Wallis, 1678, p. 18)." This is a very sound observation, but he still maintained one mistaken idea—that the difference between F and V lies "[not in the Lips, nor in the Larynx, but] in the Nostrils."

Wallis then goes on to describe what is characterized today as a difference between distinctive and nondistinctive features. He claims that Wilkins identified sounds using all the features available, not just the ones essential to the designation. With his background in mathematics, Wallis was accustomed to using only those features which were absolutely necessary to form definitions. It was the late nineteenth century before such an examination was tried again. This was probably a consequence of the fact that the study of language slipped out of the grasp of mathematicians and philosophers and into that of those interested in the history of man.

Wallis's third letter (Wallis, 1698) mentions Alexander Popham, the pupil who had occasioned the dispute with Holder. Popham had been Wallis's student about 35 years before and had learned to speak distinctly and understand a language (Wallis feared that Popham may have lost his new ability to speak, however). He also noted that there were some deaf persons whom he did not teach to speak, only to understand and to write. This decline in ambition is due in part to disillusionment or skepticism. At this point Wallis felt that one needs to hear himself speak in order to fully appreciate the beauty of the language he may produce.

As for writing, Wallis felt that this was just as necessary an ability as speaking. He suggests that the pupil should learn a finger alphabet [these were already known at that time (Wilkins, 1641, p. 59) describes a simple one] and then be taught as any child is taught his first language. He did note one difference, however: children learn sounds by the ear but deaf people learn to sign by the eye. But both of these equally signify the same things or motions and are equally arbitrary. He closes his letter with word lists as an aid to teaching English grammar.

Wallis's importance here is less as a creative phonetician than as a teacher with practical experience. He explained clearly, if in less detail than one would wish for and expect from an experimental scientist, what his aims and methods were. There is little other evidence that is so valuable (Bonet may provide some) because in England only William Holder had any practical experience and he was interested only in explaining the teaching of articulation.

William Holder was an English phonetician, music theorist, composer, mathematician, and divine. Holder was born in Nottinghamshire in 1616. Matriculating as a scholar of Pembroke Hall, Cambridge, on July 4, 1633, Holder was elected a fellow of his college and received the M.A. in 1640. About 1642 he became rector of Bletchington, Oxfordshire, and on March 21, 1643 was incorporated M.A. at Oxford. Collated by Bishop Matthew Wren to the third prebendal stall in Ely Cathedral on June 25, 1652, Holder was not actually installed until September 1660 due to the policies of the Cromwell Protectorate. In that same year of the Restoration, he received the Doctor of Divinity degree from Oxford, and on January 27, 1662 was presented by Bishop Wren to the rectory of Northwold in Norfolk and to that of Tidd St. Giles, Isle of Ely.

On May 20, 1663, Holder was elected Fellow of the Royal Society and in May of 1668 published "An Experiment Concerning Deafness" in the

Philosophical Transactions (*3*, 665–668). Here Holder described the method he had employed in teaching the deaf Alexander Popham to speak. Unfortunately Popham later relapsed into dumbness and was subsequently instructed by Dr. John Wallis whom we have already discussed.

The dates are important, for what was at stake was the honor of having been the first man in England to teach a deaf person to speak. There was no denying that Wallis had been successful with Daniel Whaley in the early 1660s. As noted, Wallis exhibited Whaley before Charles II, Prince Rupert, and the Royal Society. But when Popham afterwards came to him, Wallis belittled Holder's prior claim. Holder defended himself in *A Supplement to the Philosophical Transaction of July 1670, with Some Reflexions on Dr. John Wallis, his Letter there Inserted* (London, 1678), only to be counterattacked by Wallis in *A Defense of the Royal Society and the Philosophical Transactions . . . in Answer to the Cavils of Dr. William Holder* (London, 1678).

The *Elements of Speech* was published when Holder was 53 years old. His work on phonetics had actually begun when he undertook to teach a deaf child to speak. The connection between phonological theory and its application in teaching speech to the deaf, as well as teaching English as a second language, is a very important one, and will be developed later on.

Holder (1669) begins his *Elements* by making it clear that no other form of language but the spoken form is "natural." He states that by studying the "natural alphabet" we may discover the basic inadequacies of all other forms of communication. "Letters," or phonemes, as we would describe them today, were thought to be the most natural elements of communication. Holder was clearing writing in the tradition developed by Wilkins in his *Mercury*, as well as his *Essay towards a Real Character*. It was the belief of Holder and many of his contemporaries that the best and perhaps only way in scientific inquiry was the "natural way." This way of nature, as it were, assumed that there were phonological as well as linguistic universals.

These universals were assumed to be readily discernible through observation and experimentation. Holder began his theory by describing the organs of speech, which he divided into two classes: organs of the natural parts of letters, and organs of the formal part of letters. The former are the lungs, trachea, and larynx (pulmonary and phonotory mechanisms) and the uvula, which directs the air to either the nose or the mouth (resonance). The latter are the tongue, hard palate, lips, etc. (articulatory mechanisms). He clearly distinguished between voiced and voiceless sounds, and his description of the consonants bears close resemblance to that of Wilkins.

As for teaching articulation to the deaf, Holder points out that lipreading is limited in scope, but by analogy with the recognition of the voicing contrast in whispered speech (when it is in fact neutralized), he shows (as Wallis did) that context is a sufficient guide to make success possible. This is almost identical to what Wallis says. It is suggested that a model of the tongue and upper jaw might be made to show the articulation of [k] and [g]. After the pronunciation of the letters has been learned, the alphabet is to be taught, followed by a finger alphabet. The pronunciation of monosyllables with increasingly complex initial and final clusters, including some, such as [dla], [dna], [gna], [sdna], which do not exist in English, is suggested as good practice, to be followed by the practicing of actual words.

Holder is obviously a very important figure in the history of psycholinguistics and communication disorders. In his emphasis on articulation as a primary feature of human symbolic activity, and his attempt to work out possible articulations irrespective of their use in language, he was well ahead of his contemporaries in England.

George Dalgarno, another phonetician, was acquainted with Wallis and Wilkins. More often he was treated as one from whom to borrow ideas but not to be mentioned as their source. His treatise *Didascalocophus or the Deaf and Dumb Man's Tutor* (Dalgarno, 1680) is perhaps the most difficult of the works discussed here, chiefly because of its style, but it is also interesting and systematic.

The introduction gives several definitions. *Interpretation* is defined as an act of cognitive power, expressing the inward motions by outward and sensible signs. He lists three kinds of interpretations: supernatural, natural, and artificial or institutional, to which he gives the names of *Chrematology, Physiology,* and *Sematology.* Sematology was a general name for all interpretation by arbitrary signs. This was further divided into the three senses of hearing, seeing, and touching; he labeled the respective aspects of interpretation *pneumatology, schematology,* and *haptology.* These, too, are subdivided into *glossology,* a branch of pneumatology where the sound source is the tongue; *typology,* or *grammatology,* a branch of schematology involving the "impressing of permanent figures upon solid and consisting matter"; and *cheirology* or *dactylology,* where communication takes place "by the transient motions of the fingers."

Dalgarno's main argument is that the principal senses are exactly equivalent in interpretive ability. He bolsters this by a repeated comparison of the capabilities of the blind and the deaf. He is almost diametrically opposed to a natural language theory or an innate hypothesis. He felt that man entered the world *tabula rasa,* ready to have a myriad of different images stamped on his being. The daily experience of blind people gave him evidence of the individual ability of the ear and tongue to advance man's knowledge. An equal degree of knowledge is attainable by the eye and expressible by signing. All signs, whether written or vocal, are equally arbitrary. There is no reason why sounds should better represent an idea than hand characters. Neither is naturally symbolic of anything.

He felt that it is probably just as simple for the deaf child to connect a sign and its reference as it is for a blind child to connect a sound and its reference. The eye is intimately concerned in language learning for, when discussing whether manual signs could be easily remembered, he pointed out that transient motions can make as much of an impression on memory as immovable objects do. As proof, he offered the fact that hearing children learn a language although the movement of the tongue is transient. Signs, however, are much more readily visible.

In a rather strange conceptual experiment, we must imagine two 7-year-old boys, one deaf, one blind, both of whom can write. Both boys are taught the acquisition of a language, the blind boy, Latin, and the deaf boy, his mother's tongue. Their probable progress is estimated and compared. The deaf should have no language and the blind a mother tongue. This should give the blind boy an advantage. If writing has already been learned, then this is hardly an acceptable assumption, and Dalgarno's argument is fallacious.

Dalgarno felt it was neither impossible nor difficult to teach a blind man to write or a deaf man to speak. Teaching the suprasegmentals of speech would be hard, however. There may be simpler characters for writing to teach the blind man and there may also be easier sounds to pronounce for the deaf. He proposed that a blind man and a mute person might communicate by means of an elementary form of a reading machine.

Skepticism of lipreading was characteristic of Dalgarno, too. If lipreading and hearing were of equal value, then a deaf person and a mute person should be equally capable of understanding. But the deaf cannot learn a language as well as the mute. Therefore, not all distinctions of sound can be made in reading lips. He must conclude that the ear has certain advantages in language acquisition that the eye does not because a blind man learns to speak by listening, but a deaf man cannot learn so well by seeing. At any rate, lipreading must be complemented by context and redundancy.

In order to teach a deaf man to read and write, there are two basic ingredients: diligence and slates. A deaf man's dictionary should be ordered in three different ways: first, alphabetically; second, following the order of double consonants at both the beginning and ends of words; and third, reducing it to several classes of objects.

Dalgarno's finger alphabet is two-handed. Letters are mapped on the left hand and pointed to by the right. In order to abbreviate clusters, one may point to all the isngle letters of the double or triple consonant. This should not be confusing, because there is no English word where the order of double consonants is inverted in the beginning of a syllable or the end of a word. He realizes the necessity of, but makes no proposals for, a one-handed alphabet.

Much more progress was made later on in the field of language pathology. The last several scholars whom we have discussed became liberated from the early Aristotelian dogma. As should be expected, later researchers working within new and different paradigms were able to shed more light on this topic.

Dennis Diderot (1713–1784) was an eminent French philosopher, whose *Letter on the Deaf and Dumb* appeared in 1751. It was no particular interest in the problems of deaf people that prompted Diderot to write this book but rather a desire to better understand how ordinary individuals develop knowledge about things in the real world, through an analysis of language and its natural development, as well as a communication disorder known as deafness.

Diderot's *Letter* begins with the linguistic problem of inversions but ranges widely over such topics as the origin and historical development of language, epistemology, rhetoric, and so on.

Through the example of an imaginary deaf person, Diderot attempts to determine the relationship between thought and language. The deaf person represents a hypothetical prelinguistic society. Here Diderot (1751) seems to anticipate modern Gestalt psychology:

> Mind is a moving scene, which we are perpetually copying. We spend a great deal of time in rendering it faithfully; but the original exists as a complete whole, for the mind does not proceed step by step, like expression. The brush takes time to represent what the artist's eye sees in an instant [p. 56].

This statement is as provocative today as it must have been at the time it was written. Neisser (1967) has suggested that the Gestalt school of psychology is the most direct ancestor of current psycholinguistics. Others who follow the Chomskian point of view suggest Wundt, because of Wundt's emphasis upon the sentence as the basic unit of analysis. Those who think in terms of verbal behavior would probably not agree with Blumenthal (1970) but would name Watson as the most likely candidate. No doubt all of the nominees have played an important part, one way or another, in setting the stage for the currently accepted version of the psychology of language.

Diderot, however, did not compromise any of his convictions regarding the psycholinguistic nature of man. He consistently assumed knowledge to be completely dependent upon the senses, and more specifically, to the number of senses actually operating. As an interacting hypothetical experiment he imagines a society made up of five persons, each having only one of the five senses; and he comes to the conclusion that each person in this society would have a view of the world determined by his own sensory modality and that each individual would relate to the others as being senseless. This new and more innovative psychology was quite different from the older, more absolute way of approaching the problem.

During the latter part of the eighteenth century, scholars continued to struggle with this important issue. Two other men (briefly mentioned earlier) are worth mentioning again before we go on to the next century: Erasmus Darwin (1731–1802) and John Horne Tooke (1736–1812). Darwin's two most important works in the area of language and thought are *Zoönomia* (1794–1796) and the *The Temple of Nature* (1803). The first was Darwin's best-received work; the second, containing among other things his theory of evolution and theory of languages, was not well appreciated in his time. Darwin (1774/1974) points out carefully that "Mr. Tooke observes that the first aim of Language was to communicate thoughts, and the second to do it with dispatch, and hence he divides words into those which were necessary to express our thoughts, and those which are observations of the former." As T. Verhave points out, Darwin's psychology is a variant of eighteenth-century association theory and is, in part, a restatement of views stated by David Hartley in his *Observations on Man* (1749). Rieber and Froeschels (1966) discussed Darwin's theory of stuttering, also deriving from the theory of association. This is very similar to Mendelssohn's (1783) viewpoint, which in turn was apparently influenced by a paper written by Spalding, in the Magazine *Erfahrungsseelenkunde*, an introspective report of a case of transitory sensory motor aphasia.

We now move to the latter part of the nineteenth century. Here we shall be concerned with the work of Wilhelm Preyer (1841–1897), a German professor of physiology at the University of Jena. Preyer, although not well known today, was quite influential during the late nineteenth century. His pioneering work helped to establish the field of developmental psychology, and he also wrote significant works on hypnosis and neurophysiology. His most important work, *Die Seele des Kindes* (1881), has recently been reprinted by Arno Press in English *(The Mind of the Child)*, unfortunately without an introduction.

Originally written in Germany, *Die Seele des Kindes* was translated into many other languages, including English. It had a direct influence upon two of the most influential psychological theorists of our time, Jean Piaget and Sigmund Freud. Freud rarely quoted other writers, but it has been possible to establish the fact that he was familiar with Preyer's works; indeed, Freud was under the influence of Preyer's ideas when he established as part of his theoretical system (1) the notion of *the study of abnormal development,* and (2) *the value of using stages of development as a better means of understanding the psychological growth pattern of the child.*

Freud, of course, stressed the affective, psychosexual aspect of maturation, whereas Preyer gave emphasis to the cognitive and conative. Preyer devotes the second volume of his book almost exclusively to the linguistic and cognitive development of the child. A whole chapter deals with speech and language disturbances in adults, particularly aphasia. He then draws a parallel to speech and language disturbances in childhood.

Interest in the problem of the relationship between language and thought was quite strong in the 1880s and 1890s. Max Müller was the major advocate of the notion that thinking was not possible without language. The polemics on this issue were about as bad as the polemics of the last decade regarding competence and performance. Müller, a professor of linguistics (philology) at

Oxford, engaged in active debate, mainly through the journal *Nature*, with such prominent psychologists as Sir Francis Galton and George Romanes.

Galton vehemently denied Müller's contentions, arguing that a careful study of congenitally deaf individuals would prove him wrong. But Galton never carried out the study himself, and it was not until the twentieth century that experimental cognitive psychologists were able to demonstrate what Galton had anticipated. Galton's warning to Müller is worth quoting, for it is as pertinent now as when he wrote it in 1887: "Before a just knowledge can be attained concerning any faculty of the human race, we must inquire into its distribution among all sorts and conditions of men on a large scale, and not among those persons who belong to a highly specialized literary class."

Romanes used an example of a disorder of communication, namely, aphasia, to challenge Müller's thesis. He pointed out that, once attained, symbolic concept formation afterwards continued to operate without the use of words. He continues: "This is not based on one's own personal introspection which no opponent can verify; it is a matter of objectively demonstratable fact. For when a man is suddenly afflicted with aphasia, he does not forthwith become as thoughtless as a brute. Admittedly he has lost all trace of words, but his reason may remain unimpaired."

We have seen, then, even from this capsulized review, that the question of the relationship between thought and language is of long standing. In the seventeenth and eighteenth centuries, Cordemoy and Diderot were making a clear distinction between the processes of thought and language. Although language was for them a magnificent extension of thought, thought was necessary before language acquisition could even begin, even where there was no possibility of language acquisition.

The homogenized, atomistic concepts of associations such as Erasmus Darwin and Horne Tooke tended to blur distinctions between thought and language, just as they did for psychological and physiological processes.

In the nineteenth century tremendous progress in neurophysiology and the treatment of speech disorders gave a new impetus to investigations of the thought-language problem. The accumulated research, particularly on the comparison between speech development in children and adult communication disorders, points to the conclusion that language is indeed an extension of thought, rather than a prerequisite to it.

V. COMPARATIVE STUDY OF COMMUNICATION
(Or Hands Across the Phylogenetic Scale)

In his excellent critical edition of La Mettrie's *L'Homme Machine*, Vartanian (1960) notes that the eighteenth-century French philosopher rejected the long-cherished notion of man's uniqueness on the grounds that "the behavior of human beings, when traced to its instinctual sources, seems to him to differ merely in degree, not in kind, from that of the higher animals [p. 26]." La Mettrie's belief in the continuity of animal and human intelligence ("Des Animaux a l'Homme, la transition n'est pas violente") led him to propose the experiment of teaching an ape to speak. Said Vartanian (1960):

> Ill-advised as this expectation was, and notwithstanding the mockery with which it was promptly greeted, it indicates an experimental approach to animal psychology which, though historically premature, was not without value for the future. More exactly, it was the structural analogy between the brain of man and that of the ape which led La Mettrie to wonder if their considerable difference of behavior might not be due less to any organic dissimilarity than to the educative merit of the environment in which each of the species had lived and developed. This in turn entails the assumption that natural—i.e., prehistoric—man must have been very much like present-day anthropoids [pp. 26–27].

It was not until the twentieth century that La Mettrie's proposed experiment was actually carried out.

A. Viki

A prolonged attempt to teach a chimpanzee human language was reported by Hayes (1951). Keith and Kathy Hayes actually raised a chimp in their home, from the age of 3 days to about 6½ years. The chimp, named Viki, was treated as nearly as possible like a human child in such matters as feeding, toilet training, discipline, and play. Viki not only learned to imitate much of the behavior of the adult humans with whom she lived; she also learned to respond to spoken commands. Nonetheless, to the end of the experiment, she never managed to mouth more than three (or possibly four) words: "papa," "mama," "cup" (and possibly "up"). The various attempts to teach human language to Viki and to other primate subjects was reviewed by Kellogg (1968), just as the remarkable breakthrough of two Nevada psychologists was beginning to attract attention.

B. Washoe

In June of 1966, R. Allen Gardner and Beatrice T. Gardner of the University of Nevada undertook to teach a young female chimpanzee the gesture language of the deaf. They were not so much concerned with language as such, and were in fact rather naïve about the subject when they began. They were interested in the theory of learning and reasoned that in view of past failures and the natural behavior of chimpanzees, an attempt to establish interspecies communication would be more likely to succeed if it were based on gestures. To this end, they began an essentially operant technique of rewarding the animal's own gestures when these happened to resemble the gestures made in the American Sign Language (Ameslan).

The experiment began when Washoe (named after the county in which the University of Nevada at Reno is located) was between 8 and 14 months old, and after 22 months of training and other interaction with the investigators and their assistants, all of whom used only manual language in the presence of the animal, Washoe had a repertory of more than 30 signs. Most of the signs named objects or pictures of objects. Once Washoe had eight or ten signs in her repertory, she began to combine them:

> Among the signs that Washoe has recently acquired are the pronouns "I-me" and "you." When these occur in combinations the result resembles a short sentence. In terms of the eventual level of communication that a chimpanzee might be able to attain, the most promising results have been spontaneous naming, spontaneous transfer to new referents, and spontaneous combinations and recombinations of signs (Gardner & Gardner, 1969, p. 672).

Combining signs in a patterned way constitutes a primitive grammar, and the observation that a rather small list of signs is typically used in combination with signs from a longer list parallels the development of two- and three-word sentences in the process of language acquisition by human children. Washoe was approximately 3 years of age at this stage, and she was a year or so behind the human schedule for language acquisition, but the experiment is a considerable accomplishment for all parties concerned, human and ape.

A year later Washoe's lexicon had increased to 85 or more signs, and the process of forming combinations had advanced slightly (Gardner & Gardner, 1971). If we think of the grammar in terms of the requirements of English, the subsequent development is rather modest—but this is not an appropriate comparison. The American Sign Language lacks many of the grammatical requirements of English (use of a copula, for example), and if we apply the usual criterion of evaluating a system in its own terms, Washoe's language should be compared with the system represented by Ameslan. (As far as we know, there has never been a rudimentary analysis of Ameslan, but see Schlesinger, 1971, for some of the problems in dealing with the grammar of Israeli Sign Language.)

The next step in the interspecific communications research was taken when Dr. Roger Fouts, who worked with the Gardners as a graduate student, took Washoe to the University of Oklahoma Institute for Primate Studies. At the institute, which is under the direction of Dr. William B. Lemmon, Fouts established that Washoe is not unique in her ability to learn Ameslan. Several other chimps made good progress and began to use signs in communicating with one another.

C. Sarah

A somewhat different approach to the language capacities of the chimpanzee has been taken by Premack and Premack (1972). The Premacks taught their chimp named Sarah to manipulate plastic pieces of various colors, shapes, and sizes; each of these pieces represents a different word. As of their 1972 report, Sarah had acquired a vocabulary of some 130 terms, which she employed with a reliability of 75% to 80%. She had also learned to use and understand the negative article, the interrogative, and *wh*-questions, as well as such concepts as "name of," dimensional classes, prepositions, the conditional, and hierarchically organized sentences.

D. Lana

The most recent of the chimp language experiments seems to be that of the Yerkes Regional Primate Center in Atlanta, Georgia. Psychologist Duane Rumbaugh taught a chimp named Lana to read and write simple sentences by using what is, in effect, a rather grotesque typewriter (*Newsweek,* 1974, pp. 75–76). On each plastic key of her computer console, there is a hieroglyphic-type symbol that represents a word. The work was begun in 1972; essentially the same kind of conditioning techniques have been used as were employed in the other chimp experiments. After a year of mere "rote associations," Lana began to form her own sentences, with appropriate punctuation marks. As of the 1974 report, Lana had a vocabulary of some 50 words, but Rumbaugh predicted that this number would be at least doubled.

E. Gorilla

Next to the chimpanzee, the gorilla is generally considered to be the creature closest to man. Francine Patterson, at Stanford University, has begun to teach a young female gorilla Ameslan. In a 1973 personal communication to Fouts (Fouts, 1973a), she reported that the 19-month-old gorilla was using six signs and was combining the "more" sign with "food," "drink," and "out." And Fouts reports (1973b) that he was able in a brief study to teach an infant orangutan (again, somewhat more remotely related to man) several signs, and the orangutan combined them into two-sign sequences.

F. Conclusions

Although the work with apes has intrinsic interest, it also carries implications as to the origins of human language. Lieberman, Crelin, and Klatt (1972) have argued that language must be a recent development, because forms prior to modern man *(Homo sapiens sapiens)* lacked the necessary vocal apparatus.

Whether or not Lieberman and co-workers succeed in convincing us with their argument about the human vocal apparatus, the demonstration that the great apes have at least a rudimentary language capacity and the existence of a highly developed system of manual communication among the deaf suggest that human language may have begun as a gesture system rather than as a vocal-auditory system. This argument has been suggested most strongly by Hewes (1973) and Stokoe (1972).

Even if language began as a gesture system, and even though the deaf can converse manually equally rapidly and over as wide a range of topics as those with hearing, it is customary to define language in terms of vocal symbols. By taking the vocal system as primary, we distinguish language from derived systems such as scripts. Even the manual system of Ameslan is derived, in the sense that the signs are supplemented by finger spelling, which is the equivalent of a script.

The most useful definition of language may still be that of Edward Sapir (1921): "Language is a purely human and non-instinctive method of communicating ideas, emotions, and deisres by a system of voluntarily produced symbols [p. 8]." Washoe's accomplishments notwithstanding, language is still a distinctively human characteristic. But we may have to drastically alter this definition if Washoe and her companions establish their manual communication as a characteristic of the Oklahoma chimp community over several generations.[11]

VI. RETROSPECT AND PROSPECT

Paradigm, as Kuhn (1970) uses the term, connotes much more than merely pattern or design: it implies a *model of reality* that not only orders the phenomena to be studied by a particular discipline but also specifies the appropriate techniques to be employed in their systematic investigation. In Kuhn's view, a scientific revolution occurs when anomalies or "counter-instances" accumulate that resist explanation in terms of the prevailing paradigm of "normal science." Does this description of paradigm clash fit the recent or current circumstances in psycholinguistics?

---

[11]Two recent articles—one by Premack, "The Human Ape," *Sciences*, 1977, and one by H. T. P. Hayes, "The Pursuit of Reason," *New Yorks Times Magazine*, June 12, 1977—point to how the use of language by apes has blurred the line between species. In the Hayes article, a suggestion is attributed to a Newark attorney that intimates that the ape in question has developed a consciousness of self and a rudimentary form of language and is therefore entitled to human rights. A thorough discussion of this issue is not possible in the context of this article; nevertheless, this instance amply illustrates that the issue of the continuum of ape to man has assumed extreme proportions.

Charles E. Osgood does not believe it does. Although Osgood acknowledges the revolutionary impact of Noam Chomsky's work on the field of linguistics, he questions whether we are witnessing in psycholinguistics a true Kuhnian "crisis" or merely a pendulum swing between viable paradigms. As Osgood (1975) sees it, the contributions of Chomsky and their effect upon psycholinguistic research and theory fail to meet the criteria that distinguish a scientific revolution:

> (1) there has been no attempt to incorporate solutions to problems handled successfully by the old paradigm; (2) the old paradigm has not been shown to be insufficient *in principle*; (3) there has been no new paradigm to shift *to*—in the sense of a well-motivated, internally coherent alternative theory of language performance. There has been a shift *away from* behaviorism in any form, but in the absence of any alternative paradigm, this would be better termed "revulsion" than "revolution" [p. 20].

Our historical review provides support for Osgood's conclusions. Study, research, and speculation on the psychology of language and thought have been carried on simultaneously during a period that spans at least five centuries in accordance with the competing paradigms supplied by rationalism and empiricism; and whether the fires of controversy that blazed so fiercely over competence vs. performance in recent years are burnt out or merely banked, there seem to be few prospects for revolutionary change in the immediately forseeable future.

It is important to note that most of Kuhn's examples of paradigm clash leading to crisis and revolution are taken from the physical sciences (e.g., Newton/Einstein, Priestly/Lavoisier, etc.). There are ample grounds for questioning whether the social and behavioral sciences have ever developed paradigms (or "regimes") with the kind of authority enjoyed by paradigms in the physical sciences. Instead, we would have to identify broad divergences in methodological and theoretical emphasis that may reflect a continuum rather than a dichotomy.

At any rate, having ruled out the probability of an imminent revolution in psycholinguistics, Charles Osgood (1975) concludes his "Dinosaur Caper" by venturing a few predictions concerning the future prospects for psycholinguistic research and theory as we approach the year 2000:

> (1) *There will be a complete shift from emphasis upon Competence to emphasis upon Performance.*...
> (2) As part of this shift, *there will be an increasing avoidance of dealing with sentences-in-isolation* (whether in linguistic or psychological methodologies) *and increasing dependence upon sentences-in-context* (in discourse in ordinary conversation, and so on)....

(3) *Semantics will be moving into the foreground as syntax moves, reciprocally, into the background....*

(4) As I have already hinted, *logical, rationalist models of language will be shown to be inappropriate for ordinary speakers and will be superseded by more gutsy, dynamic psycho-logical models....*

(5) *There will be shift from ethno-linguo-centrism toward what might appropriately be called anthropo-linguo-centrism* [pp. 23–24].

The test of these or any predictions can be provided, of course, only by the future, and Osgood acknowledges some serious doubts concerning the ability of mankind to reach the "billennium." While awaiting confirmation or refutation of Osgood's predictions—*all* of them—we should like to indicate that we find Osgood's analysis of the current state of psycholinguistics good, active, and potent.

REFERENCES

Aarsleff, H. *The study of language in England, 1780–1860.* Princeton, N.J.: Princeton University Press, 1967.

Benton, A. L., & Joynt, R. J. Early description of aphasia. *Arch. Neurol.,* 1960, *3.*

Bever, T. G. Some theoretical and empirical issues that arise if we insist on distinguishing language and thought. In D. Aaronson & R. W. Rieber (Eds.), *Developmental psycholinguistics and communication disorders.* New York: New York Academy of Sciences, 1975.

Bloomfield, L. *Language.* New York: Henry Holt, 1933.

Blumenthal, A. L. *Language and psychology.* New York: Wiley, 1970.

Brett, G. S. *A history of psychology* (Vol. 2). London: George Allen and Unwin, 1921.

Brown, J. W. In A. Pick (Ed.), *Aphasia* (J. W. Brown, trans.). Springfield, Ill.: C. C. Thomas, 1973.

Brown, R. *Words and things.* Glencoe, Ill.: Free Press, 1958.

Carroll, J. B. *Language and thought.* Englewood Cliffs, N.J.: Prentice-Hall, 1964.

Chomsky, N. Three models for the description of language. *Proceedings of the Symposium on Information Theory, IRE-Transactions on Information Theory,* 1956, *2,* 113–124.

Chomsky, N. *Syntactic structures.* The Hague: Moriton, 1957.

Chomsky, N. *Cartesian linguistics.* New York: Harper & Row, 1966.

Condillac, E. B. de. *An essay on the origin of human knowledge.* Introduction by J. H. Stam. Published originally in French 1746; published London 1756. [Reprinted in *Language, man, and society series* (R. W. Rieber, Ed.), A.M.S. Press, 1975.]

Condillac, E. B. de. *The logic of Condillac.* Philadelphia, Pa.: 1809.

Cordemoy, G. de. *A philosophical discourse concerning speech.* Introduction by Karl Uitti, London, 1668. [Reprinted in *Language, man, and society series* (R. W. Rieber, Ed.), A.M.S. Press, 1975.]

Dalgarno, G. *Ars Signorum, vulgo Character Universalis et Lingua Philosophica,* London, 1661.

Dalgarno, G. *Didascalocophus* or *The deaf and dumb man's tutor, to which is added a discourse of the nature and number of double consonants.* Oxford: 1680.

Darwin, C. *The descent of man.* London: John Murray, 1871.

Darwin, C. *The expression of emotions in man and animals.* London: 1873.

Darwin, E. *The temple of nature.* New York: P. and J. Swords, 1804. (Originally published London, 1803.)

Darwin, E. *Zoönomia, or the laws of organic life.* Introduction by T. Verhave, London, 1794–1796. [Reprinted in *Language, man, and society series* (R. W. Rieber, Ed.), A.M.S. Press, 1974.

Diebold, A. R. A survey of psycholinguistic research, 1954–1964. In *Psycholinguistics: A survey of theory and research problems.* Bloomington, Ind.: University of Indiana Press, 1965.

Ebbinghaus, H. *Memory: A contribution to experimental psychology.* Dover: 1964 (English trans.). (Originally published in Germany, 1885.)

Fouts, R. S. Acquisition and testing of gestural signs in four young chimpanzees. *Science,* 1973, *180,* 978–980. (a)

Fouts, R. S. *Capacities for language in great apes.* Paper prepared for the 9th International Congress of Anthropological and Ethnological Sciences, Chicago, September 1973. (b)

Funke, O. *Gesammelte Aufsätze zur Anglistik und zur Sprachtheorie.* Berne: 1965.

Furth, H. G. On the nature of language from the perspective of research with profoundly deaf children. In D. Aaronson & R. W. Rieber (Eds.), *Developmental psycholinguistics and communication disorders.* New York: New York Academy of Sciences, 1975.

Gardner, R. A., & Gardner, B. T. Teaching sign language to a chimpanzee. *Science,* 1969, *165,* 664–672.

Gardner, B. T., & Gardner, R. A. Two-way communication with an infant-chimpanzee. In A. Schrier & F. Strollnitz (Eds.), *Behavior of non-human primates.* New York: Academic Press, 1971.

Goldstein, K. *Language and language disorders.* New York: Grune and Stratton, 1948.

Griffith, F. G. De Italica Pronuntiatione. *Italian Studies,* 1953, *8,* 71–82.

Hartley, D. *Observations on man.* London: S. Richardson, 1749.

Hayes, C. *The ape in our house.* New York: Harper & Row, 1951.

van Helmont, F. M. B. *Alphabeti vere Naturalis Hebraici brevissima delineatio.* Sulzback: 1667.

Hewes, G. Primate communication and the gestural origin of language. *Current Anthropology,* 1973, *14,* 5–24.

Holder, W. *Elements of speech: An essay of inquiry into the natural production of letters: With an appendix concerning persons deaf and dumb.* London: 1669.

von Humboldt, W. *Linguistic variability and intellectual development* (English trans. by G. C. Buck, F. A. Raben). University of Pennsylvania Press, 1972. (Originally published in Germany, 1836.)

Ivič, M. *Trends in linguistics.* The Hague: Moriton, 1965.

Kantor, J. R. *An objective psychology of grammar.* Bloomington, Ind.: Indiana University Publications, 1936.

Kellogg, W. N. Communication and language in the home-raised chimpanzee. *Science,* 1968, *162,* 423–427.

Kemp, J. A. *John Wallis' grammar of the English language.* London: Longman, 1972.

Kuhn, T. *The structure of scientific revolutions.* Chicago: University of Chicago Press, 1970.

Leibnitz, G. W. *New essays concerning human understanding.* Chicago: Open Court Press, 1916.

Lieberman, P., Crelin, E. S., & Klatt, D. H. Phonetic ability and related anatomy of the newborn and adult human, Neanderthal man, and the chimpanzee. *American Anthropologist,* 1972, *74,* 287–307.

Locke, J. *An essay concerning human understanding.* Oxford: Clarendon Press, 1924. (Originally published, 1690.)

Maclay, H. Linguistics and psycholinguistics. In B. Kachru (Ed.), *Issues in linguistics: Papers in honor of Henry and Renee Kahane.* Urbana, Ill.: University of Illinois Press, 1973.

Marx, O. The history of the biological basis of language. In E. H. Lenneberg (Ed.), *Biological foundations of language.* New York: Wiley, 1967.

Mendelssohn, M. Psychologische Betrachtungen auf Veranlassung einer von spalding. *Mag. Erfahrungsseelenkunde,* 1783, *1*(pt. 3). (Berlin)

Morgagni, G. B. *The seat and causes of disease* (Book I). Letter XIV, London: 1769.

Morton, J., & Marshall, J. C. (Eds.). *Psycholinguistics: Developmental and pathological.* Ithaca, N.Y.: Cornell University Press, 1977.

Müller, F. M. *Three lectures on the science of language.* Chicago: 1890.

Müller, F. M. *Three introductory lectures on the science of thought.* Chicago: Open Court Press, 1909.

Neisser, U. *Cognitive psychology.* New York: Appleton-Century-Crofts, 1967.

Osgood, C. A dinosaur caper. In D. Aaronson & R. W. Rieber (Eds.), *Developmental psycholinguistics and communication disorders.* New York: New York Academy of Sciences, 1975.

Premack, A. J., & Premack, D. Teaching language to an ape. *Scientific American,* 1972, *227,* 92–99.

Preyer, W. *The mind of the child.* New York: D. Appleton & Co., 1896. (Originally published in Germany, 1881.)

Pronko, N. H. Language and psycholinguistics: A review. *Psychological Bulletin,* 1946, *43.*

Rieber, R. W. Neuropsychological aspects of stuttering and cluttering. In R. W. Rieber (Ed.), *The neuropsychology of language.* New York: Plenum Press, 1976.

Rieber, R. W., & Froeschels, E. An historical review of the European literature in speech pathology. In R. W. Rieber & R. S. Brubaker (Eds.), *Speech pathology.* Amsterdam: North Holland, 1966.

Robins, F. N., & Robins, R. H. *Short history of linguistics.* London: Longmans, Green, & Co., 1967.

Sapir, E. *Language.* New York: Harcourt, Brace & World, 1921.

Saporta, S. *Psycholinguistics: A book of readings.* New York: Holt, Rinehart & Winston, 1961.

Schlesinger, I. M. The grammar of sign language, and the problems of language universals. In J. Morton (Ed.), *Biological and social factors in psycholinguistics.* London: Logos Press, 1971.

Stam, J. H. *Inquiries into the origin of language.* New York: Harper, 1976.

Stam, J. H. The Sapir–Whorf hypothesis in historical perspective. In R. W. Rieber & K. Salzinger (Eds.), *The roots of American psychology.* New York: New York Academy of Science, 1977.

Stokoe, W. *Motor signs as the first form of language.* Paper presented at the 71st annual meeting of the American Anthropological Association, Toronto, December 1972.

Sullivan, J. On Cartesian linguistics. In R. W. Rieber & K. Salzinger (Eds.), *The roots of American psychology.* New York: New York Academy of Science, 1977.

Vartanian, A. La Mettrie's L'Homme Machine. In *A study in the origins of an idea.* Princeton, N.J.: Princeton University Press, 1960.

Wallis, J. *Grammatica linguae anglicanae cui praefigitur, de loquela sive sonorum formatione, tractatus grammatico-physicus.* Oxford: 1653.

Wallis, J. *A defence of the Royal Society, and the philosophical transactions, particularly those of July, 1670, in answer to the cavils of Dr. William Holder.* London: 1678.

Wallis, J. A letter of Dr. John Wallis...to Mr. Thomas Beverly concerning his methods for instructing persons deaf and dumb. *Philosophical Transactions,* 1698, *20,* N. 245, 353–60. (Page refs. to Lock, 1706.)

Wilkins, J. *Mercury: or, the secret and swift messenger.* 1641. (Page refs. to Wilkins, 1802, 1–87.)

Wilkins, J. *An essay towards a real character and a philosophical language.* London: 1668.

II RESEARCH ORIENTATIONS

3 A Cognitive Approach to the Study of Language

Doris Aaronson
New York University

This chapter deals with the cognitive functions involved in handling linguistic information. We shall be concerned throughout with subject coding strategies for verbal strings: with the processing stages comprising a strategy, with the nature of the encoded representation at each stage, and with the time course and the flexibility of processing. Thus, this chapter complements Chapter 4, which emphasizes the environmental influences on language behavior, rather than the underlying mental processes that generate it.

This chapter focuses on the perceptual coding of linguistic stimuli in immediate comprehension and short-term memory tasks. Because the emphasis is on the input stages, I shall consider primarily paradigms with relatively short verbal strings and short intervals between stimulus and response. Perceptual coding will refer loosely to input analyses up to and including semantic identification. In the terms of Craik and Lockhart (1972), this chapter deals with the depth of initial analyses; repetitions of analyses that have already been carried out will be viewed as retention processes. The chapter is organized in two major parts: lexical coding and contextual coding. This breakdown is conceptually useful, because individual words often function as coding units that are subsequently organized into a larger context. Also, the research literature frequently involves experimental paradigms that are focused either on word or context processing. Throughout, however, we should bear in mind that these aspects of processing are not independent, but are interrelated in complex ways that are dependent on current task demands, on previous practice or special training, and on the individual's cognitive and linguistic abilities.

I. LEXICAL CODING

A. Theoretical Framework

Several researchers have hypothesized that in immediate memory and comprehension tasks, at least two main stages of perceptual processing occur. Figure 3.1 illustrates these stages. First, stimulus input enters a very temporary buffer store. During a low-level stage of processing, which I will call *sensing,* an image of the stimulus input is formed, based largely on physical features and patterns. This stage of processing is relatively passive and possibly parallel (i.e., more than one word might be processed at a time) (Aaronson, 1966; Shiffrin & Grantham, 1974; Wolford, 1975). The resultant image may be a direct representation, "much like that of a sound recording" (Pollack, 1959), or a mental photograph (Dick, 1974), and will decay rapidly while in this form. The sensed word is coded sufficiently to be used in certain monitoring, matching, or comparison tasks, but cannot survive the decay and interference in many recall or paraphrase tasks (Aaronson, 1968). Sensed representations are held in a relatively large capacity buffer store (Neisser's "echoic memory," Crowder and Morton's "precategorical acoustic store," Broadbent's "S-system") while waiting for higher-level linguistic encoding (Massaro, 1970a, 1970b, 1972). The higher-level process, which I will call *identifying,* may code a word based on a meaning or verbal label (Pollack's and Crowder & Morton's "categorized" representations, Broadbent's "P-system"). Some psychologists question the inclusion of identification as a perceptual rather than a mnemonic process (Underwood, 1973). However, data to date do not even justify a clear dichotomy between these two levels. We are concerned here primarily with two stages of processing that increase the permanence and usability of the internal representation, whether they be perceptual or early mnemonic stages. After identification the decay rate of the words and their susceptibility to verbal interference is decreased, even though some of the initial sensory information was sacrificed in the lexical-semantic abstraction of properties that occurred in recoding. The higher-level identification process is "active" and at least partly serial [i.e., one word at a time (Broadbent, 1958; Neisser, 1967)]. A major function of this stage is to provide a structural organization for the string. The words are identified in a

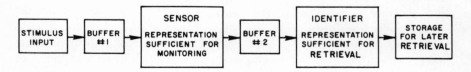

FIG. 3.1. A model of the time-course of perceptual coding for words.

particular order and subjective intonation grouping, which affect the sequential organization during later retrieval (Aaronson, 1967).

Data have been provided on the details of sensing and identifying from studies on perception and short-term memory for characters and words. For example, Sperling (1960) used partial report accuracy of selected rows from a visual display of letters, cued at various postpresentation delays. His accuracy results suggest that we initially (i.e., 0-sec cue delay) sense about nine letters, possibly in parallel, but that their "iconic" or sensory representation decays almost completely in less than a second. In another condition, he observed a linear increase in report accuracy with the delay at which a patterned visual-noise mask followed the display to terminate processing. This linearity provided evidence that we identify verbal items one at a time from the sensory buffer at about 10 msec/item. When subjects must give a *full* rather than a partial verbal report of the letters they have identified, consuming time and creating verbal interference, their short-term memory buffer appears to contain the names of only about 4.5 letters. If the visual display contains letters and digits randomly intermixed, cued partial report of one or the other conceptual category does not yield the nine-item sensory capacity obtained when cueing was based on physical location of the displayed row. Rather, the requirement to identify the character as a member of a (semantic) category yielded the reduced capacity estimate of about four or five items. During the time needed to identify the category meaning of these few items, the remaining contents of the sensory buffer had decayed. Darwin, Turvey, and Crowder (1972) have done analogous work with items spoken over earphones. Their 3 × 3 stereophonic stimulus displays contained three subjective spatial locations in the head (right, middle, and left) for each of three temporally sequenced sets of digits and letters. Their data suggest that the auditory sensing and identifying system has similar trends to the visual one, except that the time course of sensory decay is somewhat over 4 seconds, and the initial capacity may be somewhat less. But the sequential structure of spoken strings (as opposed to the simultaneous structure of visual strings) may permit earlier information to start decaying as subsequent phonemes, syllables, or words are arriving.

B. Temporal Factors in Lexical Coding

The physical quality or linguistic complexity of a word may influence the time needed for sensing or identifying. If the time available is too brief to form an optimal representation of each word in a string, coding backlogs may accumulate over the string and degrade subsequent memory or comprehension performance. When coding the words, the separate temporal parameters — the word durations and the interword pauses — may be differentially important for each stage of processing. Below are three hypotheses regarding the effects of temporal parameters on lexical coding within our theoretical framework.

Hypothesis 1: *Perception is not instantaneous. The encoding time required to make a stimulus representation durable may considerably outlast the stimulus duration.*

When stimulus attributes are varied, keeping the response constant, the corresponding changes in reaction time (RT) have been taken to indicate changes in the time required to perceive the stimulus. For example, Pollack and Rubenstein (1963) measured the time needed to identify single words from message sets of well-known words. Longer RTs for correct responses were obtained for larger stimulus sets, lower S/N ratios, and greater acoustic similarity among words. The RT differences between hard and easy listening conditions often exceeded the stimulus word durations. In Paivio's (1971) experiments, RTs indicated that longer coding times were needed for words in abstract than concrete sentences, and for coding tasks requiring visual imagery than for those simply requiring semantic comprehension. To elicit two levels of linguistic coding, Aaronson (unpublished) varied the subject's task. For short tape-recorded questions, subjects pressed a key as soon as they heard a preassigned target word. The detection RTs were longer when subjects would *later* have to answer the question than when subjects were simply required to detect the target word. At fast presentation rates, RT *differences* between these conditions exceeded the duration of a word and its adjacent pause. Long perceptual delays result when subjects must not only sense the stimulus word, but must also code the semantic meaning of the string.

Alternatively, the time course of perception can be studied by varying the time available for perception, and then observing the resultant response accuracy. Loftus (1974) varied the visual display time for lists of 16 high-frequency nouns from 25 to 500 msec/word. In his Yes-No recognition memory task, subjects were performing close to chance, yielding the signal-detection statistic of $d' = .1$ for display durations of 25 and 50 msec. As displays increased from 75 to 200 msec, recognition accuracy shot up quickly from $d' = .25$ to $d' = 1$. However, for longer durations there was little additional gain, with $d' = 1.5$ at 500 msec. Some of the subjects' scores had already asymptoted by 200 msec. Forster (1970) studied coding time by varying visual presentation time (4 and 16 words per second) and observing the number of errors in the immediate recall of six-word sentences. He found that faster rates markedly decreased coding accuracy and that at each rate accuracy was higher for simple than for complex sentences (i.e., one vs. two deep structure propositions). Forster obtained an interaction suggesting that sentence complexity more strongly affects perception when the available coding time is severely limited. The time required for word processing with the complex sentences in his studies appears to exceed both the word durations and the interword intervals.

Hypothesis 2: *The time intervals during and between words in a string, and immediately following the string are necessary for coding the words.*

The time associated with a stimulus presentation can be divided into three parts: (1) the word durations; (2) the interword pauses; and (3) the time following the last word of a string. Data suggest that these periods play different roles in word processing. The word durations determine the amount of information available for sensing. The interword pauses are used largely for identifying. The poststring time is essential when coding is not completed during the interword pauses. Let us consider the effects on performance of varying these three time periods.

a. The Word Durations. A remarkably short stimulus duration is needed to form the initial sensory image of a word. English is so redundant that only a minimal duration is needed for an iconic or echoic representation, and subsequent identification can proceed from there even after the display is terminated. Studies using speech compression techniques, in which alternate 10–20 msec segments are deleted uniformly from the utterance, suggest that the critical duration for spoken monosyllabic words is about 100 msec (Garvey, 1953a, 1953b; Yntema et al., 1964; Aaronson et al., 1971; Wingfield & Wheale, 1975). Greenberg and co-workers (1968) visually displayed sets of letters or words, such that the second display overprinted and masked the first. For five-letter words, 95–99% correct reports were obtained for onset-to-onset times of only 50–60 msec, supporting Sperling's earlier 10 msec/letter estimate. This high accuracy level was obtained even for on-times as short as 5 or 10 msec, if they were followed by off-times of 50 msec. However, for these intervals more coding time is needed for less redundant strings: accuracy decreased to about 90% for three-letter words, 75% for two random letters, and 50% for six random letters.

Given the minimum "critical" display duration for sensing, further increases in visual or auditory word durations add little to perceptual accuracy. Single spoken words can be compressed by as much as 50–80% of their original duration without intelligibility scores dropping below 95% (Fairbanks et al., 1957; Garvey, 1953a, 1953b). Bergstrom (1907) reported visual memory studies in which the onset-to-onset time was fixed at 768 msec, but word durations varied from 41 to 318 msec. Recall accuracy was unaffected by duration within that range. He concluded that "the process appears to have a period of its own so that the duration of the objective stimulus beyond a certain point is felt to be disagreeable" (p. 224).

b. The Interword Pauses. For auditory presentations, rate is generally increased by a natural speaker speeding up his own vocalizations. As a result, in a confounded manner, the durations of *both* the words and the pauses are decreased, and intonation is also varied. However, two studies used electronically controlled timing to vary rate by varying only the pauses and not the word durations (Aaronson, 1968; Yntema et al., 1964). These studies used rates from 1.5 to 10 words/sec, as fast or faster than normal speech, in an effort to restrict interword coding time. As pause-time decreased, so did recall accuracy. In a stronger test of the coding-time hypothesis, overall rate was held *constant* at 3 words/sec and extra pause time was gained at the *expense* of word duration by "compressing" the speech about 33% (Aaronson et al., 1971). Here again, accuracy improved with the longer pauses, even though one-third of the speech was thrown out. The speech signal actually interferes with coding that can occur during the pauses. The resultant recall improvements were primarily in order information, suggesting that the higher-level identification process was occupying much of the pause time.

The above studies used lists of unrelated verbal items. But similar trends occur for words in sentences. Miron and Brown (1971) increased the speech rate of their sentences in three ways: (1) by speakers speeding up their own vocalizations; (2) by compressing the speech to 30%, 50%, or 70% of the original duration by periodic (uniform) time deletions; (3) by compressing only the pauses by 50% or 100%. For the different methods both subjectively judged rate and errors on a subsequent comprehension test increased with stimulus rate. For all three methods, the critical factor for speech perception may be the decreased pause time. Hutton's (1954) data provide clearer evidence that pauses are important in speech perception. A natural speaker read a message at each of eight rates, and Hutton compressed each of these by five amounts. From his compressed speech one can obtain six sets of three presentations, such that all members of a set have identical rates, but the ratio of speech time to total message time varies within a set. For a fixed speech rate, subject preferences and speech effectiveness were higher for longer pauses, even with the reduced word duration.

Pfafflin (1974) varied off-times from 100 to 325 msec/word for visual displays while keeping the on-time fixed at 50 msec. For her 8- and 16-word grammatical and scrambled sentences, recall accuracy was higher for the longer off-times. Further, linguistic structure and off-time interacted. At short off-times there was relatively little difference between grammatical and scrambled strings. But as off-time increased, recall accuracy increased at a faster *rate* for the grammatical strings. Thus, subjects use the longer pauses between words for higher-level identification processes that make use of the grammatical structure.

c. The Poststring Time Period.   A number of studies have attempted to restrict perceptual coding time by placing interfering events following the last word of a string. According to Conrad (1958, 1960), requiring the subject to interpolate a verbal "naught" just after a digit string decreases recall accuracy because it interferes with immediate postpresentation processing. Brown (1955) held constant the interval between the last stimulus and the recall, but varied the delay between the last stimulus and an interpolated event. Interpolated events occurring within a second after the presentation caused large decrements in recall accuracy, but these decrements decreased and leveled off with further delays of the interpolated item. Hence, the temporal proximity of an interfering item to the relevant words was critical to completing their coding. Mewhort (1972) presented tachistoscopically pseudowords of 0th or 4th-order approximation to English, followed 0 sec or 1 sec later by an interfering digit recall task. Pseudoword recall improved at the 1-sec interference delay for both the 0th- and 4th-order strings. Further, structure and delay interacted. When the interference task was delayed, recall improved by a greater amount for the more richly structured strings. Subjects used the extra time in part for higher-level identification based on sequential relations and pronounceable segments in the 4th-order strings. Crowder and Morton (1969, 1971) have found the effect of poststring interference to be restricted to "suffixes" that are also words, e.g., noise bursts had little detrimental effect. In another study, Crowder's (1973) subjects gave immediate serial recall for strings of short (50 msec) or long (300 msec) spoken vowels presented at 2 vowels/ sec. Again, a verbal suffix, the word "go," had a greater interference effect than a tone, especially on the last few vowels in the string that had not yet been transferred from the "precategorical" (sensed) to the "categorical" (identified) store. Short vowels were interfered with least, either because they tend to be more "categorically perceived" than long vowels, as shown by earlier research, and/or because there was more pause time between short vowels to identify them. Aaronson and Sternberg (1963) hypothesized that the subject's active verbal processing of the interpolated stimulus cue, rather than the stimulus per se, should be the critical determinant of recall decrements. At stimulus delays of 1/6, 3/6, or 5/6 sec after a tape-recorded sequence, their subjects were cued with a left or right light to respond by saying "L" or "R." Subsequent recall accuracy for the sequence differed little with cue delay. But an examination of the response times showed that subjects delayed their interpolated responses longer for early than for late stimulus cues. Further, recall accuracy was lower when subjects responded quickly, within 300 msec of the cue, than when responses were slower, between 300 and 400 msec, as would be predicted by the hypothesis of interference with postpresentation encoding. There was little decrease in recall accuracy from a nonverbal interference task where subjects pressed a right- or left-hand button in response to the cue lights.

Hypothesis 3: *When interword pauses are short, coding delays will accumulate over a string and lead to performance decrements.*

a. The Accumulation of Coding Delays over a String. The needed coding time can exceed the available coding time either when words are presented simultaneously (e.g., dichotically) or serially at high rates. The uncoded or partially coded words accumulate in a buffer while early words are being processed. According to Fig. 3.2, if a string must simply be monitored for a prespecified target word, sensing alone may suffice, but if the string must endure interference and decay while awaiting retrieval, identifying may also be needed. Hence, longer coding times and greater coding accumulations should be reflected in the monitoring RTs for tasks with a requirement for subsequent recall (MR) than for those without (M). In support of these ideas, Aaronson (1968) obtained slower RTs for monitor-plus-recall of seven spoken items than for monitor-only conditions. For fast stimulus rates, the RTs for monitor-plus-recall and the RT differences between monitoring with and without recall increased with the serial position of the target, indicating accumulating coding delays over the string (Fig. 3.2a and b). But, such serial increases did not occur for monitoring-only or for a slow stimulus rate that could provide adequate

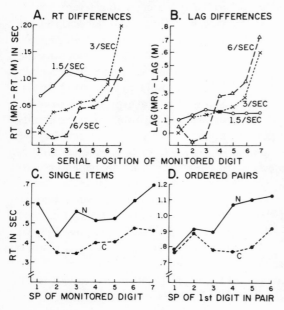

FIG. 3.2. (A) and (B): Differences between monitoring-plus-recall (MR) and monitoring-only (M) for monitoring RTs and for number of items lag between stimulus and response. Parameter is stimulus rate. (C) and (D): RTs to monitor normal (N) and compressed (C) speech for single items and for the order of a pair of items.

identification time. When stimulus rate was held fixed at 3 words/sec but speech-to-pause ratios were varied using identical lists (Aaronson et al., 1971), the monitoring RTs showed greater accumulations for long words (normal speech) with short pauses than for short (compressed) words with long pauses available for identification (Fig. 3.2c). Similar differences between normal and compressed speech occur (Fig. 3.2d) when subjects must monitor for a word pair that will occur in one sequential order (left-key response) or its opposite (right-key response). The similarities in sequential accumulations between monitoring for item (Fig. 3.2c) and order (Fig. 3.2d) information suggest that the words are identified for retrieval in a particular structural order. In Section II we shall see evidence that the coding order reflects the surface structure in recall tasks, but the deep structure and semantic relations in comprehension tasks. Treisman et al. (1974) also obtained evidence for accumulated coding delays when they scored shadowing latencies to one of two dichotic speech channels. At the first two positions the shadowing response followed the stimulus word onset by 540 msec, but these latencies increased over the string and reached 710 msec by the twelfth word. When a synonym of the shadowed word occurred on the nonshadowed channel, shadowing latencies suddenly shot up by about 40 msec, and this added delay from the single synonym persisted for almost the entire string. The increased latency suggests that subjects do identify semantic content from a "nonattended" channel (questioning the selective attention hypothesis), and the persisting delay suggests that linguistic coding is serial in nature.

   b. The Effects of Coding Accumulations on Performance Errors. Coding delays influence the internal representation of both linguistic content (item information) and structure (order information). Delays in identifying verbal items result in their rapid decay and hence in item errors at retrieval. If such identifying delays accumulate over a sequence, item errors should increase with serial position. Accordingly, serial position curves of *item* errors are generally *not* bow-shaped in serial recall tasks. Item errors increase monotonically over the series, except for the last position (Aaronson, 1968; Aaronson & Markowitz, 1971; Ryan, 1969a, 1969b; Glanzer, 1966). Other factors, such as silence after the last item, may increase its recall accuracy. Increasing the presentation rate by decreasing the pause time between items should further increase identification delays, and consequently the frequency of item errors in recall. This was shown with rates of 1.5, 3, and 6 words/sec (Aaronson, 1968). Also, the *slope* of the serial curve of item errors increased with faster presentations, reflecting the increased *rate* of accumulation of unidentified items for later serial positions.

   The order in which sensed words enter the buffer does not strictly determine their recall order (Aaronson, 1966; Aaronson & Markowitz, 1971;

Neisser, 1967). As perceptual delays increase, more words will accumulate in the buffer, and the probability of selecting them in the wrong order for identification will also increase. As the stimulus sequence progresses, for a serial identifier that lags behind the presentation, the buffer accumulation builds up. But, when the stimulus sequence terminates, the buffer size begins decreasing. When items are selected for identification, the chances of selecting them in the wrong order would be higher with larger buffer accumulations, as in the middle of the series, yielding bow-shaped serial position curves of order errors. Accordingly, bow-shaped curves of order errors over a list (Aaronson & Markowitz, 1971) and bow-shaped transitional error probabilities over a sentence (Rosenberg, 1968) reflect the identification of structural information. Further, order errors in recall should increase with decreases in interword intervals that yield larger buffer accumulations. This has been observed when pauses are decreased with word duration held constant (Aaronson, 1968), and even when word durations are increased to fill the decreased pause time, thus maintaining a constant presentation rate (Aaronson et al., 1971).

C. Stimulus Intelligibility and Legibility

Decreasing the signal-to-noise ratio of speech or the clarity of print degrades the intelligibility or the legibility of *individual* words (Miller Heise, & Lichten, 1951; Jerger, 1963; Licklider, 1951; Jeffress, 1970; McCormick, 1957; Corwin & Zamansky, 1976). I will argue in the following pages that such stimulus changes also increase the time a serial processor must spend on individual words, resulting in coding backlogs and delays over the entire string. The interactions of visual or auditory noise with linguistic context suggest that the degraded performance cannot be attributed entirely to masking at a "sensory" level. Noise also disrupts coding and increases the time needed for higher-level identification and structural organization of the lexical items. Although the terms "intelligibility" and "noise" generally refer to speech, I will use them here for both auditory and visual presentations.

a. Word Perception Is Degraded by Noise. When S/N ratio was decreased by 23 dB in a word-identification task, Pollack and Rubenstein's (1963) subjects showed RT *increments* of 300 msec, an amount frequently exceeding the pause durations in natural speech. A control test suggested that this difference was not due to sequentially sensing individual phonemic features. RTs were only 20 msec faster for control words with discriminative features in initial (top vs. pop) than final (top vs. tot) positions. Aaronson (1974) provided additional evidence that the effects of noise cannot simply be attributed to sensory masking. For seven-item strings, on half the trials 54 dB white noise bursts were inserted between the words and *not* simultaneously with them. When subjects monitored the strings for a preassigned item and reported the following item, the noise increased their error rate by only 1.4% over the no-noise trials. However, when subjects had to report the entire string, the noise between words increased the error rate by about 5%. Monitoring RTs suggest that the noise bursts hindered identification during the pauses, resulting in coding backlogs over the string. For target items in serial positions 2, 4, and 6, monitoring RT *difference* scores due to noise were -2, 30, and 84 msec respectively.

For brief simultaneous visual displays, accuracy patterns show strong serial position effects that are considered important indices of information processing in reading. To study these effects, Wolford and Hollingsworth (1974a, 1974b) presented strings of various lengths at various retinal loci, with spaces or with fixed or variable letters placed before or after target letters. In their experimental design, the instructions plus the stimulus patterns separated the direction and the number of letters processed from the direction and number reported. Their data provide evidence that peripheral retinal loci and lateral masking by neighboring letters degrade the quality of sensory representations, but that the direction and number of letters processed affect identification delays. Their RTs to report a preassigned primary target letter increase roughly linearly with the number of other letters that must be covertly processed before the target is encountered in the display. Their RT slope of about 20 msec/letter is close in magnitude to Sperling's estimate of 10 msec/letter. Sperling used visual noise masks of jumbled bits and pieces of letters to terminate letter identification and measured the resultant report accuracy. Wolford and Hollingsworth's data suggest that similar trends are obtained by using RTs to index processing delays.

Sternberg (1967) and Nickerson (1973) both presented clean or "noisy" displays in visual character identification tasks. Sternberg's vector characters were embedded in a black and white checkerboard, while Nickerson's ascii dot characters were embedded in displays of 8, 14, or 20 other random dots. Both series of studies suggest that subjects first "clean up" and identify the name of the displayed character in order to use it for higher-level linguistic processing. Subjects do not use the initial noisy sensory representation in scanning their memory in recognition tasks (Sternberg) or in deciding which of two conceptual categories the character belongs to (Nickerson).

b. Linguistic Context Reduces the Effects of Noise.   When a spoken word must be identified in noise, performance is improved if linguistic context is added (Pollack & Pickett, 1964). Visual transcripts of up to five prior or subsequent words helped the subjects. Providing acoustic context in addition further improved identification. This improvement cannot be attributed either to intersyllabic dependencies, as those do not transcend more than one word boundary, or to repeated samples of the speaker's voice, as repeats of the target word alone did not help. Rather, structural information is gained from the total acoustic contour of changing intonation, stress, pitch, and voice quality. Not only does context reduce the effects of noise, but context and noise interact. For poor listening conditions, contextual information makes little difference, but as the S/N ratio improves, performance improves at a faster *rate* with a richer linguistic context. Miller, Heise and Lichten (1951) obtained this context-by-noise interaction when context was varied by presenting words in isolation or in sentences, or by reducing the size of the text vocabulary. Pickett and Pollack (1963) obtained similar results when the number of words or the amount of speech time following the target word was increased. Miller and Isard (1963) found the interaction when comparing shadowing responses for fully grammatical, semantically anomalous, and ungrammatical word strings. Martin (1968) varied the duration of noisy interword intervals from .5 to 2 sec. His immediate recall scores were lowest for anomalous and ungrammatical strings, and decreases in noise duration improved performance most for the fully grammatical strings. Backward and forward sensory masking effects level off by 100 msec of noise (Hirsch, 1952; Massaro, 1972) and thus cannot even account for the effects on the ungrammatical strings.

When visual stimuli are degraded by noise, linguistic context also improves performance. However, the context-by-noise interaction is in the opposite direction from that obtained with speech. In two studies subjects searched for a preassigned target that occurred either in an expected or an unexpected surrounding context (Fisher, 1975). For some paragraphs, the word and its context were degraded by filling the spaces with characters and/or by alternating upper- and lower-case type in successive letters. Search times were slower for degraded text and for unexpected context. For both experiments, the expected context reduced the RT differences between degraded and normal passages, although these interactions did not quite reach statistical significance. In another study, Stanners et al. (1975) degraded words and pronounceable nonwords by superimposing a random dot pattern. We might view the words, but not the nonwords, as providing a linguistically acceptable context for the component letters. RTs were obtained for subjects to identify the string of letters as either a word or a nonword. RTs were faster for words than for nonwords, and also words significantly reduced the degrading effects of noise on the RTs.

The noise-by-context interactions suggest that for *spoken* stimuli, noise *most* rapidly degrades rich context as it interrupts coding both the items and their relationships. But, for *printed* stimuli noise *least* rapidly degrades contextually rich stimuli as the contextual redundancy aids in coding the degraded words. This inconsistency might be handled in at least three ways.

1. For the most and least degraded stimuli, no words or all words are perceived regardless of context. As noise is reduced, context at first speeds recovery, but this help levels off while the no-context condition catches up. Auditory studies may use a more degraded part of this range than visual studies, yielding the opposite interactions.

2. The temporal structure of speech and the spatial structure of print may cause coding differences between the modalities.

3. "Noisy" auditory and visual stimuli may be qualitatively different. Although modality affects the noise-by-context interactions, their existence implies that noise affects *linguistic* identification. If noise affected only the sensory and not the linguistic coding stages, we would expect additive rather than interactive trends (Sternberg, 1969).

D. Subject Coding Strategies

The two buffer memory stores permit coding flexibility within our theoretical framework (Sec. I,A, Fig. 3.1). Variations can occur (1) in the elapsed time before an item is sensed or identified, (2) in which items are selected for coding from the pool of items in each buffer, and (3) in which processor is activated, and for how many items, before the other is activated. The literature provides evidence that these are aspects of subject-controlled strategies (not necessarily conscious), rather than being strictly stimulus determined, and that they are affected by instructions, current task demands, and prior experience.

a. What Is the Nature of Coding Strategies? For simplicity, let us consider two extremes or "pure" serial coding strategies, although subjects may form mixture strategies. These strategies, illustrated in Fig. 3.3, will be termed an *immediate identification strategy* and a *postponed identification strategy*. With the immediate strategy, subjects sense and then immediately identify one item before going on to another. With the postponed strategy, subjects sense each item as it is presented, but delay identification of early items until later items have been presented and sensed. For short strings, the subject would sense each word during the presentation but identify all words after the stimulus sequence has ended.

Miller (1962) suggests that contextual restrictions play a critical role in determining which strategy subjects use. Based on subjects' speech patterns, Miller hypothesized that they use a "delayed decision" strategy rather than an "immediate decision" strategy more often in shadowing grammatical

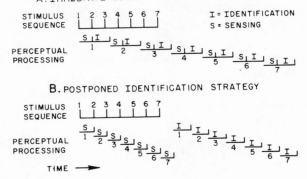

FIG. 3.3.   Two perceptual coding strategies for verbal sequences. (From Aaronson, 1974. Copyright 1974 by Academic Press. *Cognitive Psychology*, 6, p. 143, fig. 4. Reprinted by permission.)

sentences than pseudo (backwards) sentences. "In order to comprehend messages spoken at 150 words/minute, we would presumably have to make about a dozen phonemic decisions every second and perhaps 100 phonetic decisions. . . . A single delayed decision would require far less time than would a series of immediate decisions" [pp. 81, 82]. When Miller inserted a long pause every five words for the pseudo-sentences, subjects switched to a delayed strategy for shadowing, and their accuracy improved.

Moray and Taylor (1958) found that subjects who shadow one of two dichotic messages use an immediate strategy for less redundant stimuli and a postponed strategy for stronger contextual constraints. In addition, such strategies were influenced by individual subject factors. Their subjects could be divided into two distinguishable groups, which used "continuous" and "discontinuous" responses. The former showed "no pauses in speaking longer than the pause between adjacent words, while the latter spoke groups of words with a silent period extending over several words between each output" (p. 107). Belmont and Butterfield (1971) showed that coding strategies for strings of six visual letters are determined by the subject's language skills. For a probe memory task, normal high school students appeared to use an immediate identification strategy and institutionalized retarded teen-agers used a postponed strategy, termed "active" and "passive" strategies by the authors. For subject-paced stimulus displays, normals increased their viewing time as the list progressed and then produced serial position curves of memory errors highly skewed toward the end. In contrast, retarded subjects decreased their viewing time over the string, and produced serial curves with more errors at the beginning positions. These groups did not differ in their total coding time, but differed markedly in the shapes of their serial curves of time and errors.

These studies suggest that subjects may use a postponed strategy in an attempt to reduce perceptual overloads. In Miller's and in Moray and Taylor's work, the richer contextual structure permits subjects to substitute a small number of postponed molar decisions for a large number of immediate molecular decisions. There would be less savings in using a postponed strategy for the less redundant stimuli. Perceptual overloads may occur sooner for Belmont and Butterfield's mentally retarded subjects than for normals. We shall see below that subjects also develop postponed strategies when input overloads are created by presenting stimuli rapidly or mixing them with noise.

b. What Effects Do Strategies Have on Coding Delays? To picture how either strategy would influence coding delays, let us imagine a continuum of diagrams similar to Fig. 3.3, with each representing a different interstimulus interval. For both strategies, delays in both processing stages will increase linearly as the interword intervals decrease. The subjects should select the strategy that will optimize the delays (i.e., minimize the slopes) over the string, as follows. When the stimulus rate is *slower* than the total coding rate, the *immediate strategy* minimizes both sensing and identifying delays. At such slow rates, a postponed strategy would permit wasted pause time while sensed but unidentified items decay. At *fast* rates, when the stimulus rate exceeds the coding rate, the *postponed* strategy minimizes sensing delays, but the immediate strategy minimizes identifying delays. If unsensed items in buffer 1 (acoustic or visual features and patterns not fully analyzed) decay sooner than sensed but unidentified items in buffer 2 (verbal labels and meanings not yet assigned), a postponed strategy would be an advantage at fast rates. Hence, subjects should develop an immediate strategy for slow stimulus rates and a postponed strategy for fast rates. Evidence to test these ideas is provided by studies that vary stimulus rate or that vary coding time (e.g., by degrading the stimuli), as discussed below and in Sec. I,D,3.

After subjects memorized and recalled seven-word strings spoken at 3 or 1.5 words/sec, they assigned scale values to the statements below about listening strategies. Subjects reported postponing their coding more frequently when listening to words spoken at a fast (i.e., statements 1 and 2) than a slow (i.e., statements 3 and 4) rate (Aaronson, 1963).

1. You passively waited for all seven items to be presented and then actively listened to them.
2. You passively waited for the first few items to be presented and then actively listened to those as a group. You passively waited for the rest of the items to be presented and actively listened to them.

3. You actively listened to one item at a time at a slight delay after its presentation.
4. You actively listened to each single item as it was presented.

When two different messages are spoken simultaneously (dichotically) to the two ears (channels), it is assumed that the subject cannot simultaneously code both of them. It is assumed that the free-recall order reflects the perceived word order, and for ordered recall that words coded first will be recalled most accurately. Recall order in free-recall dichotic tasks (Bryden, 1962) indicates that subjects use "temporal alternation" (code one pair at a time) with slow presentation rates, but a "channel" strategy (code words from one ear at a time) with fast rates. At slow rates enough time is available between word pairs to identify both words, but at fast rates subjects can identify at most one word at a time from a single channel (ear) and must postpone the other channel until the presentation has ended. Tolhurst and Peters' (1956) dichotic memory study suggests that speech intensity and intelligibility influence the subject's strategy. As one message was attenuated relative to the other, its response accuracy was decreased, although the combined error rate remained constant. This trend was enhanced when the messages were embedded in white noise. Equal intensities may encourage "temporal alternation," but subjects may postpone coding the less intelligible channel. Corballis and Luthe (1971) required subjects to recall a string of three visual items, each having two attributes, a color and a verbal label. The authors differentially instructed subjects on channel recall (e.g., all colors recalled first) or alternation (e.g., color and label of one item at a time), and they also varied the presentation rate. The error data suggested that the recall requirements did induce the different strategies and that a fast presentation rate interfered more with the alternation than the channel strategy.

c. How Should the Shape of the Serial Position Curve Reflect the Strategy? If coding delays in buffers 1 and 2 cause subsequent retrieval errors, then the strategy used should influence the shape (i.e., skewness) of the serial position curve of errors. A postponed strategy should yield more errors at early positions, whereas an immediate strategy should yield more errors at later positions as observed by comparing Fig. 3.3a and b. For a postponed strategy early positions would suffer from identifying delays, and for an immediate strategy late positions would suffer from sensing delays. Strategy makes relatively little difference in sensing delays for early positions or in identifying delays for late positions. Thus, serial curves should be more negatively skewed for an immediate than for a postponed strategy.

To test these ideas, Aaronson (1968) varied presentation rate during a training session to induce an immediate or a postponed strategy. Then, with *identical* test conditions at an intermediate rate, differences in the error patterns can be attributed to learned strategy differences that persist from the training session. In session 1, subject groups heard 90 strings spoken at 6, 3, or 1.5 words/sec. A week later in session 2, these groups were subdivided: for each training rate, subgroups were tested at each of the three rates. To facilitate the analysis of subject-controlled verbal coding strategies apart from context-determined stimulus effects, random digit strings were used. The *training rate* did influence the error patterns in the later testing session (Fig. 3.4*a*). The serial curve for the intermediate test rate (3 words/sec) is more negatively skewed for subjects previously trained at 1.5 words/sec than it is for those trained at 6 words/sec. These error patterns are consistent with the theory that the slow and fast rates differentially encouraged the immediate and postponed strategies (Sec. I,D,2). Further, for *both* strategies, faster stimulus rates should yield greater backlogs of unsensed and unidentified items over the string. For each training rate, a faster *testing rate* should yield more negatively skewed error curves (Sec. I,D,1), and these data were obtained (Fig. 3.4*b*).

A related study had a slightly different design, less intelligible stimuli (degraded by white noise), and twice the error rate. Group SF heard a *S*low digit rate (1.5/sec) in their first session and a *F*ast rate (3/sec) a week later, while group FS had the reverse order. As expected, group SF shows

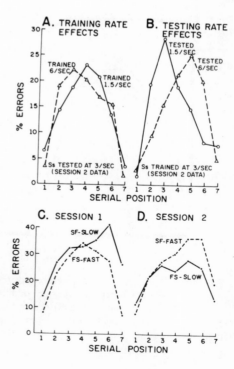

FIG. 3.4.   (A) and (B): Effects of testing and training rates on shape of the serial curve of recall errors during the test session. (C) and (D): Serial curves of recall errors when stimulus rates for two sessions are ordered slow–fast (SF) or fast–slow (FS).

more negatively skewed curves than group FS for both rates, consistent with an immediate strategy for group SF and a postponed strategy for group FS (Fig. 3.4c and d). A final study used the 3/sec and 1.5/sec rates and inserted white noise bursts between the digits, but not during the speech. Group SD had noise first to the *Same* ear and then to a *Different* ear from the digits, and group DS had the reverse order. If noise mixed with the digits on the same "channel" interferes with identification, then a postponed strategy should be developed (group SD); if noise to a different channel can easily be filtered out, then an immediate strategy should be learned (group DS). As expected, (Fig. 3.5) group DS shows more

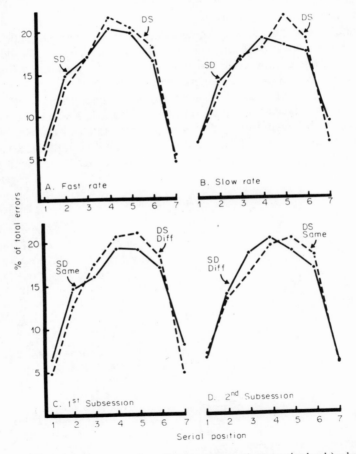

FIG. 3.5. Serial curves of recall errors (averaged over noise levels) when noise and speech are presented to the same or different ears in the order same–different (SD) or different–same (DS). (From Aaronson, 1974. Copyright 1974 by Academic Press. *Cognitive Psychology, 6,* p. 149, fig. 7. Reprinted by permission.)

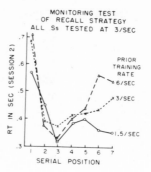

FIG. 3.6. Serial curves of monitoring RTs following training on recall-only with stimulus rates of 6, 3, or 1.5 items/sec. (From Aaronson, 1968. Copyright 1968 by the American Psychological Association. *Journal of Experimental Psychology, 76,* p. 135, fig. 6. Reprinted by permission.)

MONITORING TEST
OF RECALL STRATEGY
ALL Ss TESTED AT 3/SEC

PRIOR
TRAINING
RATE

6/SEC

3/SEC

1.5/SEC

RT IN SEC (SESSION 2)

SERIAL POSITION

negatively skewed curves for both noise conditions and both rate conditions. It is also interesting that group DS, who initially received the more intelligible listening condition, had about half as many item errors in recall as group SD for all experimental conditions.

To test more directly the effects of strategy on coding delays, subjects in the first study above (Fig. 3.3a and b) were given a monitoring RT test after their second session. In addition to recalling the strings, they listened for a preassigned target and pressed a key as soon as they heard it. Their RTs provide an index of coding delays: The greater the delay between presentation and perception of the target, the longer the RT. Figure 3.6 shows the RT data for subjects trained during session 1 at the three stimulus rates, but tested in session 2 for both recall and monitoring at the middle rate. Subjects trained at the faster rates that had insufficient coding time should frequently postpone identification until after the string has ended. Indeed, Fig. 3.6 shows longer RTs and steeper RT slopes over positions 3–7 for the faster training rates. Subjects seem to persist with a postponed strategy when given a slower test rate, even though it may no longer be optimal.

In sum, we see evidence for subject-controlled verbal coding strategies apart from any stimulus effects. Fast speech rates and noisy listening conditions that disrupt higher-level coding induce subjects to postpone lexical identification until after the string has ended. Once subjects have learned such a coding strategy it persists during other stimulus conditions, as much as a week later, and even when it is no longer optimal. Miller (1962) and Moray and Taylor (1958) have shown that a contextually rich phrase structure also encourages subjects to postpone linguistic coding for several words in a shadowing task. In the second part of this chapter we shall see that such a postponed strategy is generally used with natural language in tasks involving verbatim memory. But for comprehension tasks that require little verbatim recall, a coding strategy similar to immediate identification is used.

II. CONTEXTUAL CODING

A. Theoretical Framework

The second part of this chapter concerns the perceptual coding of sentences. It deals with the syntactic and semantic properties of sentences that
influence our mental representation of linguistic information. However, the
"psychological reality" of linguistic components is heavily influenced by the
cognitive demands of the performance task. Thus, a major focus is on the
ways in which the cognitive task affects strategies for linguistic coding.
Green (1975) provides a good example of such effects. Two groups of
subjects listened to the same sentences. One group later gave verbatim
recall and the other created a continuation sentence for each stimulus. The
RTs to probe-nouns that immediately followed the stimulus sentence on
25% of the trials suggest that the "memory" subjects code the words
individually, and perhaps phonemically, but the "continuation" subjects
combine the words into a unified meaningful representation. The evidence
for this was based on a comparison of RTs to probe-nouns that were either
semantically or phonemically related to words in the sentences. For
example, for the sentence, "The large spacious *case* contained the papers,"
the phrase-related semantic probe was "trunk" and the word-related
phonemic probe was "face." The greater the similarity between a probe and
the subjectively coded stimulus words, the longer it should take to reject
the probe as not being in the stimulus. Memory subjects required more
time to reject the phonemic than the semantic probes, and the reverse was
true for the continuation subjects. The linguistic coding for a particular
sentence differed with the nature of the subsequent performance task.

1. The Competence-Performance Distinction

The systematic effects of task demands on linguistic coding have
implications for the controversy about a competence-performance distinction. I will consider two approaches, and Miller (1975) has recently
enumerated seven approaches to this issue. The first approach is analogous
to the "learning-performance" distinction of Tolman and is in line with
traditional psycholinguistics (e.g., as expressed by Chomsky, 1965). Here, a
theory of linguistic competence is the central component of a broader
theory of linguistic performance. The subject is said to possess more
knowledge than the behavioral data reveal. Performance factors such as
memory span, fatigue, distractability, emotional excitement, or drugs
prevent the subject from fully using his linguistic knowledge. Thus, the
experimental criterion for linguistic competence is deterministic and task-

independent: If a subject can respond appropriately to the stimulus sentence at least once in at least one task environment, he has demonstrated competence in processing that linguistic string. Response failures on other occasions are attributed to "nonlinguistic" performance factors.

The second approach is analogous to Gestalt views on figure-ground and reversible-figure perception. Here, the theory of performance *is* the theory of competence; task demands that tap cognitive abilities and capacities modify the linguistic competence at the moment. "Misperceptions" reveal the nature of the processor; they are not taken as measurement artifacts. We are not competent to perceive simultaneously the two aspects of an illusory figure, to proofread for both semantic content and orthographic errors, or to apprehend both meanings of an ambiguous sentence at once. The experimental criteria for linguistic competence are probabilistic and task-dependent. When the task demands activate early processors that filter out or degrade linguistic features, then we are not "competent" to process that information later. Often, we cannot simultaneously engage incompatible processors, particularly in high-information, high-attention tasks. In effect, different task demands result in qualitatively "different" stimuli and "different" subjects. Although both approaches may be useful for the study of psycholinguistics, the following sections are oriented toward the second.

2. A Classification of Performance Tasks

The extent to which the experimental task stresses either verbatim memorization or semantic comprehension appears to influence both the temporal course of coding and the nature of the resultant linguistic code. Indeed, optimal coding for comprehension and for verbatim memory may be incompatible in several ways. For comprehension, the subject may perform transformations on the string to determine deep-structure relationships (Miller & McKeen, 1964); he may abstract key thematic concepts and discard minor details (Bartlett, 1932); he may recode verbal information into visual images that idealize the original or that contain features never presented (Begg & Paivio, 1969) to provide an emphasis or to obtain compatibility with a previously established semantic framework. Such "comprehension" operations may interfere with verbatim memorization. They delete or substitute lexical items resulting in recall errors (Bartlett, 1932). They disturb the linear word ordering found to be most natural in the recall of structured English (Blumenthal, 1966; Coleman, 1963; Deese & Kaufman, 1957). Consequently, they destroy contextual retrieval cues and rearrange structural relations useful in "chunking" adjacent words into more efficient storage units (Miller & Selfridge, 1950; Tulving & Patkau,

1962; Tulving & Pearlstone, 1966). Alternatively, memory tasks may encourage a serially ordered lexical-phonemic code of the surface structure, a code that disrupts semantic integration of nonadjacent constituents (Green, 1975; Aaronson, 1976; Aaronson & Scarborough, 1976). In actuality, most of the laboratory tasks demanding comprehension do not tax mnemonic processes and vice versa. In the following list, performance tasks are roughly ordered from high memory and low comprehension to low memory and high comprehension demands:

1. Serial recall requires retention of all lexical (item) and structural (order) information, but not necessarily its comprehension. For example, a child may recite the Pledge of Allegiance perfectly when many of the words are not in his vocabulary. Many probe-recall tasks also require item and order information, but a less redundant code may suffice, as the probes contain some of the original information.

2. Free recall does not require memory for structure, but subjects often respond with much of the stimulus order intact (Gianutsos, 1972). As stimulus structure is increased, subjects respond with correspondingly more words in their original order (Coleman, 1963; Deese & Kaufman, 1957). Ordered context as well as phonemic and semantic relationships among words provide "retrieval cues" as each word facilitates access to the next word stored in memory (Tulving, 1968).

3. Recognition memory, free-form paraphrasing, and simple transformations (e.g., active–passive) are midway in our ordering. Comprehension aids performance, but subjects also handle anomalous strings and other linguistic nonsense reasonably well (Miller & Isard, 1963; Wang, 1970a). With these tasks, subjects respond correctly with stimulus sentences longer than those used for serial and free recall, suggesting that memory demands are less.

4. Next are tasks that require a meaningful completion of a partial sentence, or a true–false response to a picture as representing a prior sentence or a sentence as representing a picture. To minimize the memory load, these tasks often use short sentences and short stimulus–response time intervals. But also, they often require only partial processing of the stimulus for a highly selective subset of the information (Carpenter & Just, 1975).

5. The last category includes sentence disambiguation and answering questions about the sentence content or about the logical relationships among the words. These tasks generally impose a light memory load; the stimulus is often visually present while the subject is responding. But, these tasks require a rather complete processing of the linguistic information in the sentence.

3. Subject Strategies for Sentence Coding

To handle richly structured strings, the earlier coding model (Fig. 3.1) will be expanded to include an additional buffer storage unit and yet a higher-level processor, which will be called the *context coder* (Fig. 3.7). After individual words are identified, they wait in buffer 3 until they are selected for association, organization and integration with other words in the surrounding linguistic context. As discussed below, the order in which words are selected from buffer 3 for contextual processing depends on the memory and comprehension demands of the performance task. The dashed arrow between processors indicates that context coding interacts with and modifies identification. Some studies considered earlier suggest two ways in which such interactions can occur, affecting the amount and nature of processing, as well as when the processing is done. First, context provides syntactic and semantic redundancy that reduces identification time and errors for the individual words (Pollack & Pickett, 1964; Pickett & Pollack, 1963; Miller, Heise, & Lichten, 1951). Second, context influences the identification strategy, with richer structure leading to a postponed identification strategy, especially in memory tasks (Miller, 1962; Moray & Taylor, 1958). Because of such ongoing interactions between identification of words and contextual organization, subsequent sections will refer loosely to higher-level or linguistic "coding." These sections will describe and provide evidence for two types of interaction patterns, a *memory coding strategy* and a *comprehension coding strategy*. Although extreme forms of these strategies will be emphasized, mixture strategies do occur, in particular for performance tasks in the middle (items 2, 3, and 4) of the task-ordering list just presented.

Below is a brief overview of two aspects of these sentence-coding strategies: the coding procedure, or algorithm, and the resultant coded representation. The coding procedure concerns the subject's methods of

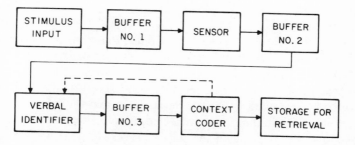

FIG. 3.7. A model of the time-course of perceptual coding of words in context.

linguistic analysis. A coding procedure might be characterized by the temporal course of coding over the sentence and by the organizational units involved. The coded representation concerns the linguistic content and structure that are preserved.

a. The Coding Procedure: The Task Demands Influence the Linguistic Units, the Direction, and the Time Course of Coding. The greater the memory demands, the more likely it is that coding occurs serially through a stimulus sentence, at first word by word, and then phrase by phrase. When memory is required, there is a cumulative integration of linguistic information as successive words are associated and as groups of words are chunked together into larger units for more efficient storage. Hence, coding time will *increase* over the phrase, the clause, or the sentence. Such accumulations will increase with sentence length and with stimulus rate. In contrast, with greater comprehension demands, the word order of higher-level coding is less likely to mirror the stimulus order. Rather, it is more likely that coding units are centered about semantically important anchor points. Coding is focused on the subject noun, the verb, and the object and their interrelationships; auxiliary and modifier information play a secondary role. Coding time will *decrease* over the phrase, the clause, or the sentence, as linguistic predictability increases.

b. The Coded Representation: The Task Demands Influence the Linguistic Level, the Amount, and the Classes of Stimulus Information That Are Preserved. The greater the memory demands the more likely it is that coding will reflect the lexical items and the surface structure useful in subsequent retrieval. The greater the comprehension demands, the more likely it is that a subject will code major content items, quickly eliminating many (but by no means all) lexical and structural details. The resultant code will generally reflect the deep structure and semantic information in the stimulus. For example, synonyms and simplified paraphrases of the original stimulus may be stored.

c. The Coding Procedure and the Coded Representation Are Interrelated. The task demands influence both the coding procedure and the coded representation, yielding correlations between them. Further, the coding procedures in part generate the coded representations. For heavy memory tasks, if coding is done in serial order and the primary organizational process is chunking or concatenating successive items, the coded representation should include the particular lexical items in their (left-to-right) surface structure groupings. For comprehension tasks, if the coding order is determined by key semantic anchor points and the coding rate or the amount coded is determined by linguistic predictability (context

redundancy), the coded representation should reflect the important semantic content, but delete nonessentials and substitute synonyms or paraphrases if they yield a more efficient or effective code. Structural information
may be destroyed by some of those paraphrases, and structural tags (e.g.,
prepositions, conjunctions) may be deleted if they can easily be regener-
ated.

B. Coding for Memory

1. Evidence for a Left-to-Right, Phrase-Unit Coding Procedure

When subjects simultaneously memorize speech and monitor it for a
target phoneme, the monitoring RT data indicate a left-to-right pattern
over the sentence: RTs are longer when the phoneme occurs later in the
sentence (Foss & Lynch, 1969). In addition, the data suggest a phrase-unit
coding pattern: RTs were slower for self-embedded sentences, with long
nested phrases, than for right-branching sentences, with several short
adjacent phrases. Clearer evidence that contextual coding occurs at phrase
breaks was obtained when subjects memorized tape-recorded speech and
judged the pause lengths following preassigned key words (Fillenbaum,
1970a, 1970b). Pauses inserted at major phrase breaks and at sentence
boundaries were judged to be shorter than identical pauses between
modifiers and their nouns within phrases. This would be expected if phrase
breaks were occupied by contextual coding. Miller (1962) hypothesized
that such phrase-unit coding occurs in order to reduce *perceptual* overloads
by substituting a few high-level linguistic decisions for numerous low-level
ones. Alternatively, Wilkes and Kennedy (1969, 1970) theorize that phrase-
unit coding is done to set up pauses as location tags for later *retrieval*. The
first word of each major constituent is stored in a special direct-access
register and serial scanning proceeds from there. Accordingly, they found
high correlations between patterns of word-by-word reading times and
patterns of subsequent recall latencies for those words when they were
probed by the preceding word. Both generally increased over the phrase,
with a prolonged pause at the phrase boundary, where the probe word and
its successor are in separate units.

Recall error data have also been taken to index input coding when the
time between input and output is short and when response interference is
minimized by using short strings. Such data also indicate that words are
coded from left to right and then organized into larger phrase units. When
subjects listen to speech until stopped by a recall cue, bow-shaped accuracy
curves are obtained, with high recall probabilities at clause and sentence
boundaries (Jarvella, 1971; Jarvella & Herman, 1972). The greater bowing

(i.e., higher relative peaking) at sentence than at clause boundaries suggests that clauses were organized into yet larger units. Subjects almost always recalled from left to right, even in free recall tasks, and the syntactic surface structure was almost always correctly maintained. The errors were primarily individual lexical substitutions or omissions and these errors were generally content rather than function words. This suggests that coding was more heavily determined by surface phrase markers than by semantically important content. The similar trends for Rosenberg's (1968) visual displays of all words in a sentence simultaneously and for Jarvella's auditory stimuli indicate that left-to-right phrase-unit coding cannot be attributed solely to Jarvella's sequential presentations having natural acoustic intonation contours. For Rosenberg's sentences, left-to-right transitional error probabilities, TEPs (probability of an error following a correct) were far lower than unconditional error probabilities, again suggesting left-to-right coding. For Rosenberg's low-association sentences, TEPs were lower within than across the phrase boundaries, indicating that words were grouped by phrase structure. For high-association sentences, TEPs showed a mild bow-shaped curve across all sentence positions, suggesting that the two smaller phrase units were organized into one larger unit.

2. Evidence for a Surface-Structure Coded Representation

Data on the time-course of coding provide evidence that the left-to-right, phrase-unit patterns in memory tasks are determined primarily by the surface rather than the deep structure or the semantics. For example, in the above studies, Wilkes and Kennedy (1969, 1970) found no differences between active-passive sentence pairs in mean reading time, in absolute recall latencies, or in latency patterns over the sentences. This occurred even though the surface and deep structures differ radically for passives but are highly correlated for actives. In another study, Kennedy and Wilkes (1971) independently varied the surface and deep structure of sentences in a task requiring recognition memory of word order. For their study, a hierarchical cluster analysis of response latencies showed patterns in accord with the surface structure and *not* with the deep structure. Kolers (1975) examined reading speed for the second reading of a sentence, when the first stimulus had been presented in the same or different typography (upright, inverted), language (English, French), or modality (auditory, visual). If the deep structure and semantics were coded for memory, the second reading should be facilitated when the identical content had been presented in a different typography, language, or modality. But presentation of the same content in a different format showed little facilitation over the first reading, while the identical surface graphemes were read faster the second time. The second reading of an inverted sentence was facilitated far more by a previous inverted one than by a more easily codeable normal presentation of its content.

Recall-accuracy data provide additional evidence that coding in memory tasks heavily reflects the surface structure. When subjects recalled sequences of modifiers terminating with a noun (complete phrase), another adjective (incomplete phrase), or a preposition (impossible phrase), complete phrases were recalled most accurately, but incomplete and impossible phrases did not differ (Dolinsky & Michael, 1969). Whether or not nonphrases were semantically impossible did not matter, suggesting that there was little processing of the semantic information. The critical factor was whether the surface phrase unit was completed. From a hierarchical cluster analysis of conditional word-pair probabilities, clusters of accurately recalled words were in strong accord with the surface phrase structure (Levelt, 1970). Within that structure, strong left-to-right contingencies occurred, but there were no differential patterns of backward contingencies as might be expected for certain deep-structure relationships and transformations. Identical patterns were obtained for sentences of identical surface structure, even though the semantic content differed. Finally, in several recall studies, linguistic depth, as defined by Yngve (1960, 1961) was unrelated to recall accuracy (Perfetti, 1969a, 1969b). Instead, accuracy increased with the ratio of function to content words. Here, as in Jarvella's studies, subjects recalled a greater proportion of structurally important function words than of the semantically important content words. In summary, for high-memory tasks, input coding is determined primarily by the surface structure. It occurs heavily at phrase boundaries, with yet higher-level coding at sentence boundaries. Coding proceeds in a left-to-right direction, and the coding time needed increases with phrase length.

C. Coding for Comprehension

1. Evidence for a Content-Oriented Coding Procedure

For tasks in which comprehension demands predominate over memory demands, the coding procedure should focus on major content words. The context coder should select from buffer 3 (Fig. 3.7) the subject (S), verb (V), and object (O) with high probability, and with an early priority in its coding of the sentence, in contrast to the sequential order of selection apparent for memory tasks. Further, these important semantic components should be integrated *across* phrase boundaries, in contrast to the phrase-unit coding apparent for memory tasks. To study the role of S-V-O relationships in comprehension, Moore (1972) asked subjects to read sentences containing a blank in the S, V, or O position and then to respond yes or no as to whether a test word in the blank position would make the sentence acceptable. Subjects should rapidly reject highly incomprehensible sentences with anomalous connections between major content words. But for more comprehensible sentences subjects should take longer to determine subtle linguistic violations that occur in the final processing stages. Accordingly, for the ungrammatical stimulus sentences, fast, moderate, and slow RTs occurred respectively when all S-V-O connections were violated by the test word, when only one S-V-O connection was violated, and when the S-V-O sequence was intact but modifier relations were violated. Comprehensibility ratings of the completed ungrammatical sentences by other subjects correlated highly with the original RT data, again emphasizing the importance of S-V-O relationships in comprehension.

For comprehension tasks, the context coder should feed information back to the identifier about linguistic relationships in earlier context. This would reduce the information load in subsequent identification, thus *decreasing* the coding time for later words in the clause or the sentence. Again, this is in contrast to the increasing times for memory tasks. Evidence supporting this hypothesis was obtained from eye-fixation data when subjects read five-sentence stories (Mehler, Bever, & Carey, 1967). Fixations occurred more frequently on the first than the second half of each constituent at all levels of structure: two morpheme words, short phrases, subject-predicate clauses, and the entire sentence. Mehler's task ranks near the middle of our ordering, because his subjects had to "retell" or paraphrase the story. Hence, they had to comprehend and remember semantic content but not necessarily the details of structure. A comparison of selected sentence pairs showed that both surface and deep structure influenced coding times. Marks's (1967) RT experiment provided additional evidence that coding time decreases over the sentence for comprehension tasks. First, subjects viewed two standard sentences, one displayed near the left-hand response key and the other near the right. The two standards had identical words, but two different meanings were formed by reversing the subject and object noun-phrases. Then, for test sentences which were intact or distorted by inverting pairs of adjacent words, subjects determined the semantically related standard sentence. Subjects' RTs were faster when the inversion was later in the sentence. All words were displayed simultaneously, and RTs were measured from the sentence onset. Thus, intact context prior to the target words reduced the time needed to determine the meaning of the test sentence. Moore's study above also supported this trend: RTs to detect S-V-O violations decreased from early to middle to late positions in the sentence.

2. Evidence for a Deep-Structure/Semantically Coded Representation

For comprehension tasks, deep structure and semantic factors strongly influence the coded representation, but surface structure continues to play a role. Note that every surface-structure boundary is also a deep-structure boundary, but not vice versa. The three approaches below provide information about the coded representation in comprehension tasks.

   a. Linguistic Correlates.   To predict sentence comprehensibility rankings, Wang (1970a, 1970b) found that only three of eight surface-structure indices yielded significant regression components, and these are also major determinants of deep-structure transformations: linguistic depth, number of self-embeddings, and number of conjoining transformations. These accounted for 45% of the variance, and Wang also attributed the remaining 55% to deep structure and semantic factors. Consistent with Wang's results, surface-structure constituents, deep-structure breaks, and semantic redundancy each predicted a significant proportion of the variance of pause times in oral reading (Brown & Miron, 1971).

Several researchers have constructed stimuli that systematically destroy meaning, structure, or both to examine more directly their relative importance. With this approach, Danks (1969) and Wang (1970a) formed anagrams (that preserved the semantics but scrambled the word order within each sentence) and anomalies (that preserved the grammatical structure but scrambled the words among sentences with identical structure). These were randomized with sentences having both and neither property intact. Danks's subjects either rated sentence comprehensibility (for a factor analysis), pressed a key when they "understood" each five-word sentence, or "corrected the meaning" of anomalous sentences (yielding comprehension times). For these tasks meaningfulness (anomalous or not) was the major determinant of the data, but structure (anagrams or not) also played a role. An interaction indicated that structure simply facilitated arriving at the meaning, if a meaning was there. Lexical attributes, such as word frequency and interword association value had small effects, if any. With 5- to 15-word sentences, Wang found higher comprehensibility ratings for anagrams than anomalies. But for a recognition *memory* task the same subjects produced the opposite results, consistent with Miller and Isard's (1963) shadowing (immediate recall) task that used anagrams and anomalies. Danks, with short visual sentences, and Wang, with long auditory sentences, obtained similar results, suggesting that much of the linguistic coding was independent of modality and length.

b. Propositional Structure.   A number of comprehension studies provide evidence that the coded representation consists of underlying propositions rather than surface structure or lexical properties. To test such a model against data for sentence–picture verification tasks, Carpenter and Just (1975) varied the *number* of propositions that must be comprehended. They maintain that propositions in both the sentence and the picture are coded similarly in an abstract propositional format, and that verification of whether the sentence represents the picture consists of comparing corresponding propositions one pair at a time. In several experiments of their own and of others, the number of propositional comparisons required was varied by changing semantic attributes of the sentence such as its truth value, the number and scope of explicit negatives, of implicit negatives in counterfactuals, and of universal and particular quantifiers. In all cases the sentence–picture verification time increases linearly with the number of propositional comparisons, with a slope of 100–300 msec per comparison. Further, in a self-paced reading task, Kintsch and Kennan (1973) found coding time to increase linearly with the number of propositions in the base structure even when the number of words was controlled. Their subjects recalled the meaning but not necessarily the exact wording, and the number of propositions recalled also increased roughly linearly with the number presented and with the time spent reading the sentence.

In addition to the number of propositions, researchers have varied the *relationships* among them. In the above studies of Kintsch and Keenan, the hierarchical relationships among propositions within a sentence were a strong determinant of recall: The more superordinate propositions were recalled more frequently. In addition, the semantic uniqueness or salience of their modifier propositions influenced recall: Adjectival or adverbial modifiers yielded 30% errors, but only 8% errors occurred for proper names. Using larger textual units, Greeno and Noreen (1974) varied the hierarchical relationships among sentences in seven-sentence paragraphs. The subjects read and recalled the sentences for substance, and then judged them for inference-value and consistency relative to test sentences. Sentences lower in the paragraph hierarchy were read faster when preceded (than when not preceded) by superordinate sentences. But, if the subordinate sentences contradicted expectations set up by prior superordinate ones, they were read more slowly. In sentence–picture and picture–sentence verification tasks, Glucksberg et al. (1973) varied the location of the mismatching proposition (subject, verb, object), as well as the voice (active, passive) and reversability of the subject and object in the sentences. The RTs to detect mismatches for the sentence–picture task increased linearly from verb, to grammatical subject, to grammatical object. This suggests an ordered propositional encoding differing from the surface structure, and a serial self-terminating search in the order V, S, O. A comparison of RT patterns for true–false and active–passive conditions indicates that after comparing the main propositions, subjects process the detailed semantic features (e.g., potency) and the deep-structure relations among propositions (e.g., voice and reversibility).

c. Concreteness and Imagery. Attributes that facilitate semantic coding should increase the speed and durability of coding in comprehension tasks. According to Paivio (1969, 1971), two such attributes are the concreteness and imageability of the stimulus. Paivio proposed a dual-coding theory: that comprehension of concrete sentences depends largely on nonverbal imagery, whereas comprehension of abstract sentences involves intraverbal associations. To test these ideas, Klee and Eysenck's (1973) subjects listened to concrete and abstract sentences that were meaningful or anomalous. The subjects pressed one button if the sentence made sense and another if it did not. On half the trials, extraneous verbal items (digits) or visual items (patterned matrices) were interleaved between words to disrupt verbal or visual coding. In all conditions RTs were faster for concrete than for abstract sentences. But visual interference slowed RTs for concrete sentences, and verbal interference slowed RTs for abstract sentences supporting the dual-coding theory. Further, subjects who were high imagers (according to independent tests) produced faster RTs than low imagers for all conditions, but especially with abstract sentences. Possibly high imagers could use both verbal and visual coding strategies regardless of the semantic attributes of the sentence. Using a true–false RT task, Jorgensen and Kintsch (1973) found high-imagery sentences to be verified faster than low-imagery sentences. Special instructions to use imagery did not further facilitate verification, suggesting that all subjects were already using a semantic coding strategy involving imagery. As both the high- and low-imagery sentences were constructed from concrete words, this is consistent with Klee and Eysenck's results. If sentences had been formed from abstract words, instructions for a visual strategy, in addition to the already used verbal strategy, should facilitate coding.

In summary, when comprehension demands dominate, the perceptual coding procedure is focused on the subject, verb, and object and on their relationships that cut across phrase boundaries. Further, coding time decreases over linguistic units as contextual predictability increases. The resultant coded representation is based largely on meaning rather than structure. The important determinants of meaning include the number and relationships among semantic propositions as well as the concreteness and imageability of those propositions.

D. An Experimental Comparison of Memory and Comprehension Coding

The studies reviewed above provided evidence that different linguistic coding strategies are used in memory and comprehension tasks. The research described below provides clear support for those strategies when two subject groups view the same sentences using identical experimental procedures for input, but have different retrieval requirements that stress memory or comprehension. For both groups word-by-word reading times were obtained to index the temporal course of perceptual coding for sentences that varied in their syntactic and semantic structure. The main trends are described below for research that has been reported more fully elsewhere (Aaronson & Scarborough, 1976, 1977). The data suggest that linguistic strategies differ between the two groups in coding individual words, syntactic structure, and semantic content.

1. Experimental Methods

Forty-eight undergraduates viewed sentences displayed on a computer scope one word at a time, in a self-paced reading task. Each time the subject wanted to read the next word, he pressed a key, and the computer recorded his reading time for the previous word. The words were centered on the scope, and the previous word was extinguished with the appearance of each new word. Two groups of subjects performed different retrieval tasks immediately after viewing a sentence. The *recall* group wrote down the entire sentence in order, and the *comprehension* group answered a yes–no question. The questions were short, three to seven words, and their focus was varied randomly from trial to trial over the various sentence components. There were six practice and 90 test sentences in the 1-hour session.

The same stimulus sentences were used for both groups of subjects. We constructed 45 pairs of sentences such that the later words of the sentences in a pair were identical. Variations in the early words imposed different linguistic structures on the later words (see example in Fig. 3.10). Pairs like these enabled us to attribute differences in reading time to structural factors rather than to particular word properties such as length, frequency, or meaningfulness. Eight sentence frames were determined by varying the type and order of the constituent elements of the sentence. A dependent clause or a complex phrase was added to the main sentence, either before the sentence or between its subject and predicate. The sentences varied with regard to the number of words in these constituents and the serial position of the constituent breaks in the sentence. Sentences were 9–19 words long, with an average of 14.4 words.

We used two methods to decide upon the location and the importance of constituent boundaries for each sentence (Table 3.1). First, we applied standard syntactic definitions (e.g., Chomsky, 1965). We located major constituent breaks just after complex constituents such as clauses and participial phrases. Minor breaks occurred between smaller units, such as noun phrases, infinitives, and prepositional phrases. Second, we asked ten naive subjects to draw lines between "natural divisions" within each sentence. Their judgments were in 98% agreement with our linguistic

TABLE 3.1
Sample Stimulus Sentences[a]

---

1. Because of its lasting construction /// as well as its motor's power /// the boat was of high quality.
   Question: The boat was well made. (Yes)
2. The newly designed outboard motor /// whose large rotary blades / power the boat /// was of high quality.
   Question: The motor was well made. (Yes)
3. In order to make an impression /// Jane wore / an orange and green miniskirt.
   Question: Jane tried to be noticed. (Yes)
4. As a direct result of the dog's help /// the blind teacher was successful.
   Question: The teacher was successful. (Yes)
5. The people // who listened to Bill /// thought carefully // about his words.
   Question: Bill's audience was attentive. (Yes)
6. The obnoxious loud mouthed barber // who had been attending Dave /// talked continuously // about the increased income tax.
   Question: The barber was talkative. (Yes)
7. The politicians // supporting Johnson /// traveled tirelessly // throughout the country.
   Question: Johnson traveled tirelessly. (No)
8. Playing in the woods // when gamesmen are hunting moose /// is dangerous.
   Question: Playing near gamesmen is safe. (No)
9. It was surprising // that only one member of the delegation /// was evicted / from the convention.
   Question: Two delegates were evicted. (No)
10. For his irresponsible reporting /// a member of the press // was censured by the senator.
    Question: A senator was censured. (No)
11. Because of the closeness / of the new manager's control /// the corporation / increased its annual profits.
    Question: The manager encouraged freedom. (No)
12. Because making clothes was a hobby // which the women tried to promote /// sewing novel dresses // became quite popular.
    Question: The women discouraged sewing. (No)

---

[a]Single, double, and triple slashes indicate "natural breaks" marked by 20%–30%, 40%–80%, and 90–100% of the subjects, respectively. The correct responses are indicated after each implied question.

definitions of the *location* of breaks. If frequency of judgment is assumed to index *importance* of the break, there was also high agreement. Each of our major breaks was marked by 80% to 100% of the subjects, but our minor breaks were generally marked by only 40% to 80% of the subjects.

2. Results and Discussion

a. Processing Individual Words. The two groups differed in several ways suggesting that recall (R) subjects form a more durable code and code more information than comprehension (C) subjects. First, the mean reading time was 583 msec per word for recall subjects but only 402 msec per word for comprehension subjects. The 180 msec reading-time difference is enough time for recall subjects to form a durable phonemic identification (Conrad, 1964; Sperling & Speelman, 1970; Landauer, 1962) not needed by the comprehension subjects. Second, as sentence length increased, for group C, mean reading time per word became faster (Fig. 3.8) and response accuracy improved slightly from 91% to 93%. But for group R, reading time remained constant and recall accuracy decreased from 98% to 88%. Comprehension subjects make use of the increased contextual redundancy for the longer sentences, whereas recall subjects continue to fully code each word. Finally, decreases in reading time due to practice were significantly greater for group C than for group R (Fig. 3.9). The comprehension subjects learn well to decrease their linguistic coding time with practice. We shall see later that the decrease selectively affects syntactic information.

b. Processing Phrase Structure. For recall subjects, but not for comprehension subjects, the pattern of reading times over the sentence strongly

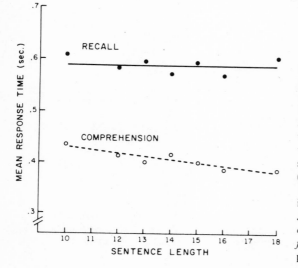

FIG. 3.8. Subject-paced reading time, averaged over all words in the sentence, for sentences of various lengths. (The first and last points are averaged respectively over sentences of 9, 10, 11, and 17, 18, 19 words to roughly equate sample size for all points in the graph.) (From Aaronson & Scarborough, 1976. Copyright 1976 by the American Psychological Association. *Journal of Experimental Psychology: Human Perception and Performance, 2,* fig. 2. Reprinted by permission.)

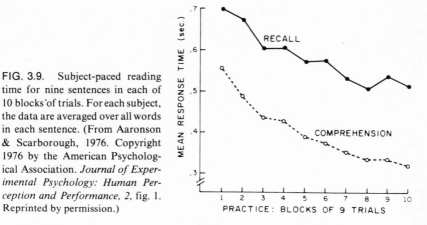

FIG. 3.9. Subject-paced reading time for nine sentences in each of 10 blocks of trials. For each subject, the data are averaged over all words in each sentence. (From Aaronson & Scarborough, 1976. Copyright 1976 by the American Psychological Association. *Journal of Experimental Psychology: Human Perception and Performance, 2,* fig. 1. Reprinted by permission.)

reflected the phrase structure. Figure 3.10 shows the reading time profile for two sentences, averaged over 24 subjects in each group. The y-axis is the mean reading time for each word, and the x-axis is the position of the words in the sentence. For sentence pairs like the one in Fig. 3.10, the response patterns across their identical second halves can be directly compared. The locations of peaks for group R are clearly determined by

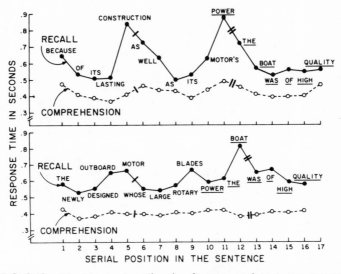

FIG. 3.10. Word-by-word reading time for two sample sentences, averaged for the recall and comprehension groups. (The short line markers on the graphs indicate constituent breaks. Note that response times for the recall group are determined by the phrase structure for the two sentences with identical words in the last seven positions.) (From Aaronson & Scarborough, 1976. Copyright 1976 by the American Psychological Association. *Journal of Experimental Psychology: Human Perception and Performance, 2,* fig. 4. Reprinted by permission.)

the linguistic structure of the sentences, and not by properties of the individual words. For group R, reading-time peaks, or absolute maxima, occurred before or after 90% of the major phrase breaks, with reading times longer than average by 68 and 118 msec respectively. Peaks were 30 to 500 msec higher than the words adjacent to them, with an average of 2.5 peaks per sentence. Group C showed little evidence for phrase-structure coding, with peak increases of 25 msec during the first half-session and 2 msec during the second. Figure 3.11 is a scatter plot for the subjects in each group, showing reading times at phrase breaks (y-axis) versus average word-by-word reading time (x-axis). For group R, the slower subjects are disproportionately slow at phrase breaks. For group C, the subjects hug the diagonal, showing that phrase-break reading times are no longer than average. Figure 3.12 shows that phrase boundary reading times increase over the sentence for group R, but remain constant for group C. The data

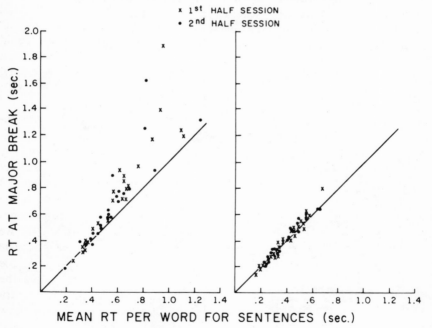

FIG. 3.11. Scatter plots for 24 subjects in each group. (Reading time at the major constituent break for the sentence *versus* mean reading time for all words in the sentence. When these two quantities are equal, points fall on the diagonal line.). (From Aaronson & Scarborough, 1976. Copyright 1976 by the American Psychological Association. *Journal of Experimental Psychology: Human Perception and Performance, 2,* fig. 3. Reprinted by permission.)

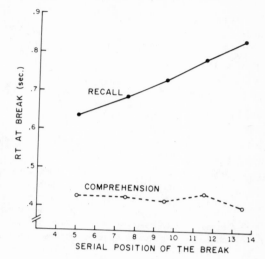

FIG. 3.12. Response time (RT) at major constituent breaks as a function of the serial position of the break in the sentence. (From Aaronson & Scarborough, 1976. Copyright 1976 by the American Psychological Association. *Journal of Experimental Psychology: Human Perception and Performance, 2,* fig. 5. Reprinted by permission.)

in Figs. 3.10–3.12 suggest that recall subjects do much of the perceptual coding selectively at phrase boundaries, and further, that this coding increases over the sentence. Such a phrase-unit coding strategy could facilitate mnemonic processing during perception (Miller, 1962), retention (Miller, 1956; Glanzer & Razel, 1974), and retrieval (Wilkes & Kennedy, 1969, 1970; Tulving & Patterson, 1968).

c. Processing Semantic Content. Whereas recall subjects are predominantly "phrase coders," we find that comprehension subjects are predominantly "content coders." We scored reading times separately for key content words in the subject and predicate of each sentence (e.g., subject and object noun, nominative participle, predicate adjective). Figure 3.13 shows the ratio of these content scores to the mean reading time as the "semantic" ratio, and the ratio of the peak-phrase boundary reading times to the mean reading time as the "syntax" ratio. For "control" ratios we used adjectives and adverbs equal in length to the key content words. The x-axis in all cases represents ten blocks of practice over the session. We see that comprehension subjects spend more time than average coding the important content words. But after only 18 trials, they do not spend extra time coding at phrase breaks. Linguistic ratios for these subjects show strong practice effects over the session. The notion of a subject-determined performance strategy adapted to the task, as opposed to stimulus-bound linguistic processing, implies that the strategy was learned. Although both groups show strong overall practice effects (Fig. 3.9), group C learns to *selectively* code semantic information. In sharp contrast, recall subjects show higher syntactic than semantic ratios and the ratios show *no selective*

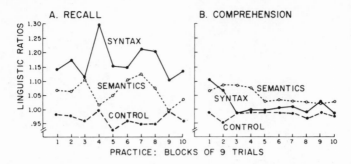

FIG. 3.13. Linguistic ratios for nine sentences in each of 10 blocks of trials. (Syntax ratio: response time at the major constituent break divided by mean response time for all words in the sentence. Semantic ratio: mean response time at major subject and predicate content words divided by mean response time for all words in the sentence. Control ratio: mean response time at minor content words divided by mean response time for all words in the sentence.) (From Aaronson & Scarborough, 1976. Copyright 1976 by the American Psychological Association. *Journal of Experimental Psychology: Human Perception and Performance, 2,* fig. 6. Reprinted by permission.)

practice effects over the session. These content ratios provide a *local* index of semantic coding. A more *global* index was obtained from a subset of 21 matched sentence pairs. One member of each pair was a "causal" sentence and began with the word "Because." The other sentence had a more neutral, descriptive relationship among sentence components (see Fig. 3.10 for an example). Both members of a matched pair have identical words in their second halves, and the causal and neutral sets were equated for number of words and phrases. If comprehension subjects are "semantic coders," they should spend more time integrating semantic information at the ends of causal sentences, with complex logical relationships between major constituents, than at the ends of neutral or descriptive sentences, with relatively unrelated semantic content in the various phrases. We scored two indices of such global semantic integration: mean reading time for the last four words in the sentence, and reading time for the key content word in the final predicate. According to both of these indices, Fig. 3.14 suggests that group C did spend more time integrating semantic content at the end of causal than neutral sentences. This is not the case for group R. For group R the word "Because" may provide a discriminative signal that the sentence is divided into two major phrase units. Hence, for causal sentences, subjects should code the first unit within its display period more frequently, reducing the coding load at later points in the sentence. That is consistent with the trends displayed in Fig. 3.14.

d. Conclusions. This experiment shows that the time course of sentence coding is dependent on both the cognitive task and the linguistic

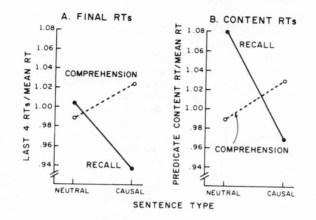

FIG. 3.14. Global indices of semantic processing: ratios of (A) mean of the last four response times in the sentence and (B) response time of the predicate content word in the sentence to the mean response time for all words in the sentence. (Data are for a subset of 21 matched sentence pairs, where one sentence begins with a "causal" and the other with a "neutral descriptive" constituent.) (From Aaronson & Scarborough, 1976. Copyright 1976 by the American Psychological Association. *Journal of Experimental Psychology: Human Perception and Performance, 2,* fig. 7. Reprinted by permission.)

information in the stimulus. The two cognitive tasks induced two perceptual coding strategies, which differentially emphasized the content or the structural aspects of the linguistic stimulus. Recent theories of language processing (Anderson, 1974; Bever et al., 1973; Foss, 1970) maintain that subjects first code the surface structure, then the deep structure, and finally the semantics of a sentence. Our data suggest that subjects are *not* bound to such stages of processing. Rather, their perceptual coding is flexible and learned. It emphasizes the aspects of the linguistic information that are needed for the cognitive task at hand.

ACKNOWLEDGMENTS

Supported in part by USPHS grant MH-16,496 to New York University.

REFERENCES

Aaronson, D. *Effects of presentation rate and recall delay in short term memory.* Unpublished manuscript, University of Pennsylvania, 1963.

Aaronson, D. *Perception and immediate recall of auditory sequences.* Doctoral dissertation, University of Pennsylvania, 1966.

Aaronson, D. Temporal factors in perception and short term memory. *Psychological Bulletin,* 1967, *67,* 130–144.

Aaronson, D. Temporal course of perception in an immediate recall task. *Journal of Experimental Psychology,* 1968, *76,* 129–140.

Aaronson, D. Stimulus factors and listening strategies in auditory memory: An experimental demonstration. *Cognitive Psychology*, 1974, *6*, 133–158.

Aaronson, D. Performance theories for sentence coding: Some qualitative observations. *Journal of Experimental Psychology: Human Perception and Performance*, 1976, *2*, 42–55.

Aaronson, D., Markowitz, N., & Shapiro, H. Perception and immediate recall of normal and "compressed" auditory sequences. *Perception and Psychophysics*, 1971, *9*, 338–344.

Aaronson, D., & Scarborough, H. S. Performance theories for sentence coding: Some quantitative evidence. *Journal of Experimental Psychology: Human Perception and Performance*, 1976, *2*, 56–70.

Aaronson, D., & Scarborough, H. S. Performance theories for sentence coding: Some quantitative models. *Journal of Verbal Learning and Verbal Behavior*, 1977, *16*, 277–303.

Aaronson, D., & Sternberg, S. *Effects of a post-stimulus interference on the immediate recall of auditory sequences.* Unpublished manuscript, University of Pennsylvania, 1963.

Anderson, J. R. Verbatim and propositional representation of sentences in immediate and long-term memory. *Journal of Verbal Learning and Verbal Behavior*, 1974, *13*, 149–162.

Bartlett, F. C. *Remembering: A study in experimental and social psychology.* Cambridge, England: Cambridge University Press, 1932.

Begg, I., & Paivio, A. Concreteness and imagery in sentence meaning. *Journal of Verbal Learning and Verbal Behavior*, 1969, *8*, 821–827.

Belmont, J. M., & Butterfield, E. C. Learning strategies as determinants of memory deficiencies. *Cognitive Psychology*, 1971, *2*, 411–420.

Bergstrom, J. A. Effects of changes in time variables in memorizing together with some discussion of the techniques of memory experimentation. *American Journal of Psychology*, 1907, *18*, 206–238.

Bever, T. G., Garret, M. F., & Hurtig, R. The interaction of perceptual processes and ambiguous sentences. *Memory & Cognition*, 1973, *1*, 277–286.

Blumenthal, A. L. Observations with self-embedded sentences. *Psychonomic Science*, 1966, *6*, 453–454.

Broadbent, D. E. *Perception and communication.* New York: Pergamon Press, 1958.

Brown, E., & Miron, M. S. Lexical and syntactic predictors of the distribution of pause time in reading. *Journal of Verbal Learning and Verbal Behavior*, 1971, *10*, 658–667.

Brown, J. *An experimental study of immediate memory.* Doctoral thesis, University of Cambridge, 1955.

Bryden, M. P. Order of report in dichotic listening. *Canadian Journal of Psychology*, 1962, *16*, 291–299.

Carpenter, P. A., & Just, M. A. Sentence comprehension: A psycholinguistic processing model of verification. *Psychological Review*, 1975, *82*, 45–73.

Chomsky, N. *Aspects of the theory of syntax.* Cambridge, Mass.: MIT Press, 1965.

Coleman, D. B. Approximation to English: Some comments on the method. *American Journal of Psychology*, 1963, *76*, 239–247.

Conrad, R. Accuracy of recall using key set and telephone dial, and the effect of a prefix digit. *Journal of Applied Psychology*, 1958, *42*, 285–288.

Conrad, R. Very brief delay of immediate recall. *Quarterly Journal of Psychology*, 1960, *12*, 45–47.

Conrad, R. Acoustic confusions in immediate memory. *British Journal of Psychology*, 1964, *55*, 75–84.

Corballis, M. C., & Luthe, L. Two-channel visual memory. *Perception and Psychophysics*, 1971, *9*, 361–367.

Corwin, T. R., & Zamansky, H. W. Effects of texture on visual noise masking. *Journal of Experimental Psychology: Human Perception and Performance*, 1976, *2*, 162–166.

Craik, F. I. M., & Lockhart, R. S. Levels of processing: A framework for memory research. *Journal of Verbal Learning and Verbal Behavior*, 1972, *11*, 671–684.

Crowder, R. Waiting for the stimulus suffix: Decay, delay, rhythm, and readout in immediate memory. *Quarterly Journal of Experimental Psychology,* 1971, *23,* 324–340.

Crowder, R. G. Precategorical acoustic storage for vowels of short and long duration. *Perception and Psychophysics,* 1973, *13,* 502–506.

Crowder, R., & Morton, J. Precategorical acoustic store (PAS). *Perception and Psychophysics,* 1969, *5,* 365–373.

Danks, J. H. Grammaticalness and meaningfulness in the comprehension of sentences. *Journal of Verbal Learning and Verbal Behavior,* 1969, *8,* 687–696.

Darwin, C. J., Turvey, M. T., & Crowder, R. G. An auditory analogue of the Sperling partial-report procedure: Evidence for brief auditory storage. *Cognitive Psychology,* 1972, *3,* 255–267.

Deese, J., & Kaufman, R. A. Serial effects in recall of unorganized and sequentially organized verbal material. *Journal of Experimental Psychology,* 1957, *54,* 180–187.

Dick, A. O. Iconic memory and its relation to perceptual processing and other memory mechanisms. *Perception and Psychophysics,* 1974, *16,* 575–596.

Dolinsky, R., & Michael, R. G. Post-integration in the recall of grammatical and ungrammatical word sequences. *Journal of Verbal Learning and Verbal Behavior,* 1969, *8,* 26–29.

Fairbanks, G., Guttman, N., & Miron, M. S. Auditory comprehension in relation to listening rate and selective verbal redundancy. *Journal of Speech and Hearing Disorders,* 1957, *22,* 23–32.

Fillenbaum, S. On the use of memorial techniques to assess syntactic structures. *Psychological Bulletin,* 1970, *73,* 231–237. (a)

Fillenbaum, S. Syntactic locus as a determinant of judged pause duration. *Perception and Psychophysics,* 1970, *9,* 219–221. (b)

Fisher, D. F. Reading and visual search. *Memory and Cognition,* 1975, *3,* 188–196.

Forster, K. Visual perception of rapidly presented word sequences of varying complexity. *Perception and Psychophysics,* 1970, *8,* 215–221.

Foss, D. J. Some effects of ambiguity upon sentence comprehension. *Journal of Verbal Learning and Verbal Behavior,* 1970, *9,* 699–706.

Foss, D. J., & Lynch, R. H., Jr. Decision processes during sentence comprehension: Effects of surface structure on decision times. *Perception and Psychophysics,* 1969, *5,* 145–148.

Garvey, W. D. The intelligibility of speeded speech. *Journal of Experimental Psychology,* 1953, *45,* 102–107. (a)

Garvey, W. D. The intelligibility of abbreviated speech patterns. *Quarterly Journal of Speech,* 1953, *39,* 296–306. (b)

Gianutsos, R. Free recall of grouped words. *Journal of Experimental Psychology,* 1972, *95,* 419–428.

Glanzer, M. Encoding in the perceptual (visual) serial position effect. *Journal of Verbal Learning and Verbal Behavior,* 1966, *5,* 92–97.

Glanzer, M., & Razel, M. The size of the unit in short-term storage. *Journal of Verbal Learning and Verbal Behavior,* 1974, *13,* 114–131.

Glucksberg, S., Trabasso, T., & Wald, J. Linguistic structures and mental operations. *Cognitive Psychology,* 1973, *3,* 338–370.

Green, D. W. The effects of task on the representation of sentences. *Journal of Verbal Learning and Verbal Behavior,* 1975, *14,* 275–283.

Greenberg, M., Helfer, M. S., & Mayzner, M. S. Information processing of letter and word pairs as a function of on and off times. *Perception and Psychophysics,* 1968, *4,* 357–360.

Greeno, J. G., & Noreen, D. Time to read semantically related sentences. *Memory and Cognition,* 1974, *2,* 117–120.

Hirsch, I. *The measurement of hearing.* New York: McGraw-Hill, 1952.

Hutton, C. L. *A psychophysical study of speech rate.* Doctoral thesis, University of Illinois, 1954.

Jarvella, R. J. Syntactic processing of connected speech. *Journal of Verbal Learning and Verbal Behavior*, 1971, *10*, 409–416.

Jarvella, R. J. & Herman, S. J. Clause structure of sentences and speech processing. *Perception and Psychophysics*, 1972, *11*, 381–384.

Jeffress, L. Masking. In J. V. Tobias (Ed.), *Foundations of modern auditory theory*. New York: Academic Press, 1970.

Jerger, J. (Ed.). *Modern developments in audiobiology*. New York: Academic Press, 1963.

Jorgensen, C. C., & Kintsch, W. The role of imagery in the evaluation of sentences. *Cognitive Psychology*, 1973, *1*, 110–116.

Kennedy, R. A., & Wilkes, A. L. Functional structure in sentences: A performance analysis. *Quarterly Journal of Experimental Psychology*, 1971, *23*, 214–224.

Kintsch, W., & Keenan, J. Reading rate and retention as a function of the number of propositions in the base structure of sentences. *Cognitive Psychology*, 1973, *3*, 257–274.

Klee, H., & Eysenck, M. W. Comprehension of abstract and concrete sentences. *Journal of Verbal Learning and Verbal Behavior*, 1973, *12*, 522–529.

Kolers, P. A. Specificity of operations in sentence recognition. *Cognitive Psychology*, 1975, *7*, 289–306.

Landauer, T. K. Rate of implicit speech. *Perception and Motor Skills*, 1962, *15*, 646–648.

Levelt, W. J. M. Hierarchical chunking in sentence processing. *Perception and Psychophysics*, 1970, *8*, 99–103.

Licklider, J. C. R. Basic correlates of the auditory stimulus. In S. S. Stevens (Ed.), *Handbook of experimental psychology*. New York: Wiley, 1951.

Loftus, G. R. Acquisition of information from rapidly presented verbal and non-verbal stimuli. *Memory and Cognition*, 1974, *2*, 545–548.

Marks, L. E. Some structural and sequential factors in the processing of sentences. *Journal of Verbal Learning and Verbal Behavior*, 1967, *6*, 707–713.

Martin, J. G. Temporal word spacing and the perception of ordinary, anomalous and scrambled strings. *Journal of Verbal Learning and Verbal Behavior*, 1968, *7*, 154–157.

Massaro, D. W. Retroactive interference in short-term recognition memory for pitch. *Journal of Experimental Psychology*, 1970, *83*, 32–39. (a)

Massaro, D. W. Consolidation and interference in the perceptual memory system. *Perception and Psychophysics*, 1970, *7*, 153–156. (b)

Massaro, D. W. Perceptual images, processing time, and perceptual units in auditory perception. *Psychological Review*, 1972, *79*, 124–145.

McCormick, D. J. *Human engineering*. New York: McGraw-Hill, 1975.

Mehler, J., Bever, T. G., & Carey, P. What we look at when we read. *Perception and Psychophysics*, 1967, *2*, 213–218.

Mewhort, D. J. K. Scanning, chunking and the familiarity effect in tachistoscopic recognition. *Journal of Experimental Psychology*, 1972, *93*, 69–71.

Miller, G. A. The magic number seven plus or minus two. *Psychological Review*, 1956, *63*, 81–97.

Miller, G. A. Decision units in the perception of speech. *IRE Transactions*, 1962, *IT-8*, 81–83.

Miller, G. A. Some comments on competence and performance. In D. Aaronson & R. Rieber (Eds.), *Developmental psycholinguistics and communication disorders*. New York: The New York Academy of Sciences, 1975.

Miller, G. A., Heise, G. A., & Lichten, W. The intelligibility of speech as a function of the context of test materials. *Journal of Experimental Psychology*, 1951, *41*, 329–335.

Miller, G. A., & Isard, S. Some perceptual consequences of linguistic rules. *Journal of Verbal Learning and Verbal Behavior*, 1963, *2*, 217–228.

Miller, G. A., & McKeen, O. K. A chronometric study of some relations between sentences. *Quarterly Journal of Experimental Psychology*, 1964, *16*, 297–308.

Miller, G. A., & Selfridge, J. A. Verbal context and the recall of meaningful material. *American Journal of Psychology,* 1950, *63,* 176–185.

Miron, M. S., & Brown, E. The comprehension of rate-incremented aural coding. *Journal of Psycholinguistic Research,* 1971, *1,* 65–76.

Moore, T. E. Speeded recognition of ungrammaticality. *Journal of Verbal Learning and Verbal Behavior,* 1972, *11,* 550–560.

Moray, N., & Taylor, A. The effect of redundancy in shadowing one of two dichotic messages. *Language and Speech,* 1958, *1,* 102–109.

Neisser, U. *Cognitive psychology.* New York: Appleton-Century-Crofts, 1967.

Nickerson, R. S. Can characters be classified directly as digits vs. letters or must they be identified first? *Memory and Cognition,* 1973, *1,* 477–484.

Paivio, A. Mental imagery in associative learning and memory. *Psychological Review,* 1969, *76,* 241–263.

Paivio, A. *Imagery and verbal processes.* New York: Holt, Rinehart & Winston, 1971.

Perfetti, C. A. Lexical density and phrase structure depth as variables in sentence retention. *Journal of Verbal Learning and Verbal Behavior,* 1969, *8,* 719–724. (a)

Perfetti, C. A. Sentence retention and the depth hypothesis. *Journal of Verbal Learning and Verbal Behavior,* 1969, *8,* 101–104. (b)

Pfafflin, S. M. The total time hypothesis, recall strategies, and memory for rapidly presented word strings. *Memory and Cognition,* 1974, *2,* 236–240.

Pickett, J. M., & Pollack, I. Intelligibility of excerpts from fluent speech: Effects of rate of utterance and duration of excerpt. *Language and Speech,* 1963, *6,* 151–164.

Pollack, I. Message uncertainty and message reception. *Journal of the Acoustical Society of America,* 1959, *31,* 1500–1508.

Pollack, I., & Pickett, M. Intelligibility of excerpts from fluent speech: Auditory vs. structural context. *Journal of Verbal Learning and Verbal Behavior,* 1964, *3,* 79–84.

Pollack, I., & Rubenstein, H. Response times to known message sets in noise. *Language and Speech,* 1963, *6,* 57–62.

Rosenberg, S. Association and phrase structure in sentence recall. *Journal of Verbal Learning and Verbal Behavior,* 1968, *7,* 1077–1081.

Ryan, J. Grouping and short-term memory: Different means and patterns of grouping. *Quarterly Journal of Experimental Psychology,* 1969, *21,* 137–147. (a)

Ryan, J. Temporal grouping, rehearsal, and short-term memory. *Quarterly Journal of Experimental Psychology,* 1969, *21,* 148–155. (b)

Shiffrin, R. M., & Grantham, D. W. Can attention be allocated to sensory modalities? *Perception and Psychophysics,* 1974, *15,* 460–474.

Sperling, G. The information available in brief visual presentations. *Psychological Monographs,* 1960, *74*(11, Whole No. 498).

Sperling, G., & Speelman, R. Acoustic similarity and auditory short-term memory experiments and a model. In D. A. Norman (Ed.), *Models of human memory.* New York: Academic Press, 1970.

Stanners, R. F., Jastrzembski, J. E., & Westbrook, A. Frequency and visual quality in a word–nonword classification task. *Journal of Verbal Learning and Verbal Behavior,* 1975, *14,* 259–264.

Sternberg, S. Two operations in character recognition: Some evidence from reaction-time measurements. *Perception and Psychophysics,* 1967, *2,* 45–53.

Sternberg, S. The discovery of processing stages: Extensions of Donders' method. *Acta Psychologica,* 1969, *30,* 276–315.

Tolhurst, G. C., & Peters, R. W. Effect of attenuating one channel of a dichotic circuit upon the word reception of dual messages. *Journal of the Acoustical Society of America,* 1956, *28,* 602–605.

Treisman, A., Squire, R., & Green, J. Semantic processes in dichotic listening? A replication. *Memory and Cognition,* 1974, *4,* 641–646.

Tulving, E. Theoretical issues in free recall. In T. R. Dixon & D. L. Horton (Eds.), *Verbal behavior and general behavior theory.* Englewood Cliffs, N.J.: Prentice-Hall, 1968.

Tulving, E., & Patkau, J. E. Concurrent effects of contextual constraint and word frequency on immediate recall and learning of verbal material. *Canadian Journal of Psychology,* 1962, *16,* 83–95.

Tulving, E., & Patterson, R. D. Functional units and retrieval processes in free recall. *Journal of Experimental Psychology,* 1968, *77,* 239–248.

Tulving, E., & Pearlstone, Z. Availability versus accessibility of information in memory for words. *Journal of Verbal Learning and Verbal Behavior,* 1966, *5,* 381–391.

Underwood, G. Concerning the role of perceptual factors in the serial position effect. *Perception and Psychophysics,* 1973, *13,* 344–348.

Wang, M. D. Influence of linguistic structure on comprehensibility and recognition. *Journal of Experimental Psychology,* 1970, *85,* 83–89. (a)

Wang, M. D. The role of syntactic complexity as a determiner of comprehensibility. *Journal of Verbal Learning and Verbal Behavior,* 1970, *9,* 398–404. (b)

Wilkes, A. L., & Kennedy, R. A. Relationship between pausing and retrieval latency in sentences of varying grammatical form. *Journal of Experimental Psychology,* 1969, *79,* 241–245.

Wilkes, A. L., & Kennedy, R. A. Response retrieval in active and passive sentences. *Quarterly Journal of Experimental Psychology,* 1970, *22,* 1–8.

Wingfield, A., & Wheale, J. L. Word rate and intelligibility of alternated speech. *Perception and Psychophysics,* 1975, *18,* 317–320.

Wolford, G. Perturbation model for letter identification. *Psychological Review,* 1975, *82,* 184–199.

Wolford, G., & Hollingsworth, S. Lateral masking in visual information processing. *Perception and Psychophysics,* 1974, *16,* 315–320. (a)

Wolford, G., & Hollingsworth, S. Retinal location and string position as important variables in visual information processing. *Perception and Psychophysics,* 1974, *16,* 437–442. (b)

Yngve, V. H. A model and an hypothesis for language structure. *Proceedings of the American Philosophical Society,* 1960, *104,* 444–466.

Yngve, V. H. The depth hypothesis. In R. Jakobsen (Ed.), *Structure of language and its mathematical aspects: Proceedings, 12th symposium in applied mathematics.* Providence, R.I.: American Mathematical Society, 1961.

Yntema, D. B., Wozencraft, F. T., & Klem, L. *Immediate serial recall of digits presented at very high rates.* Paper presented at the meeting of the Psychonomics Society, Niagara Falls, Ontario, 1964.

4 Ecolinguistics: A Radical Behavior Theory Approach to Language Behavior

Kurt Salzinger[1]
New York State Psychiatric Institute and Polytechnic Institute of New York

The introduction of yet another term to describe what students of language do may appear to be merely one more example of the excesses to which social scientists lend themselves in the delusion that progress in science is produced by the invention of new terms. I submit, however, that the introduction of the new term *ecolinguistics* will aid us in understanding what the proper approach to language should be. Even more important, it serves to include the terms, psycho-, neuro-, and sociolinguistics. Webster's Third New International unabridged dictionary defines the prefix "eco" as "habitat or environment especially as a factor significantly influencing the mode of life or the course of development." In this chapter, I will emphasize the importance of the environment in the study of language, beginning with the assumption that language always occurs in a context and can be understood only in a context. To study language outside of its context or to study it by simulating it—as is done not only with computers but whenever psycholinguists construct some particularly tortuous sentence to test still another wrinkle in transformation theory—is to study a very small, special subset of behavior that is surely unrepresentative of language as it is found among human interlocutors.

I. CONTRASTING ASSUMPTIONS OF DIFFERENT APPROACHES TO LANGUAGE

How do we study the context in which language behavior occurs? By examining the stimuli that constitute it. The stimuli in the presence of which language behavior is emitted must represent a reasonable sample of the kinds of stimuli that are normally present when people engage in this behavior. The

[1]The author is currently on leave of absence at the National Science Foundation. He is grateful to R. S. Feldman for his careful editing of this chapter.

109

population of such stimuli is large; that is, people appear to talk on almost all occasions. However, the occasion on which a psycholinguist or a generativist grammarian constructs a sentence on the basis of some rule(s), changing it until it contains the properties he/she wants it to have to test a theory, is (as already indicated) rather unlikely to produce a good candidate for a representative sample of language behavior.

It is important to point out the assumptions that the generativist psycholinguist makes in contrast to the assumptions that I am trying to make for the field of ecolinguistics. According to the former, the task of the scientist is to study the underlying principles explaining language by manufacturing situations that provide the essential aspects minus the interfering social, psychological, and neural, receptor, and effector factors that serve to obscure those underlying principles. This approach resembles the model employed for the investigation of visual thresholds as a function of wavelength. Blough (1961) trained his pigeons to respond so precisely to the presence or absence of a light that the relative sensitivity curves that he obtained behaviorally, separately for the rods and cones, were almost the same as the ones obtained by the microelectrode and the photochemical absorption method. In this model of the functioning of the eye, it was possible to show that when the behavior was evoked under conditions of sufficient control, it merely mirrored what was happening neurally and biochemically in the retina of the eye of the pigeon.

The question we must ask is whether such a model is appropriate for the study of language, or, put another way, whether the psycholinguist's methods are appropriate for uncovering such information. The generativists assume that some sort of physiological structures correspond to their theory of grammar, that there are templates that are somehow receptive to sentences but not to nonsentences. The basic problem is that the grammatical theory, which corresponds to, say, the photochemical theory of vision in the psychophysics case we just described, does not say what the sentence template is like or how it might function, nor does it even vaguely point in a direction or to a method whereby it might be studied in a physiological way. It is only a metaphor (cf. Salzinger, 1975). Considering what we have been learning about the functioning of the nervous system, the template notion is also of a complexity that seems an unlikely characteristic of the nervous system's functioning. This kind of theory construction is very much like that produced by psychologists at the beginning of this century, although, it should be noted, quite different from the testable behavioral model building that Miller (1962) proposed when he took the generativist theory seriously. Miller did not theorize about the physiological mechanisms involved; he was interested in testing the implications of the transformation model on such behaviors as recall. It is also instructive to note that Miller (Miller & Johnson-Laird, 1976) has turned away from this grammatical approach to the study of the more psychological concept of meaning, which requires that we return once more to considering the environment in which language behavior is emitted.

The ecolinguistic approach is quite different, stemming as it does from behavior theory. It takes the position that we must find a representative sample of behavior obtained under conditions that are representative of the situations in which such behavior occurs. Thus, when the prototype operant conditioning situation for animals was chosen, the idea was to have a simple working space with no distracting stimuli, so that the experimenter could attribute control of the response to a particular class of stimuli, and so that the control would be strong. A single response class was called for, for constant monitoring and measurement. Furthermore, though initially simple, it allowed the experimenter to complicate the situation through the scheduling of reinforcement, thus converting a single-response situation into a multiple-response situation; the method also allowed for the addition of different classes of responses without any difficulty. Further provision was made that the response should be of a form that could be easily emitted (although the amount of energy necessary to emit it was modifiable) and that could be emitted again immediately after it had been reinforced. This arrangement too could be so modified that the reinforcer was not given immediately after the response, and since the manipulandum (e.g., the bar) could be removed, the availability of the response could be controlled as well, although it was commonly assumed that in the typical natural situation the organism can make another response again soon after responding and having received a reinforcer. In any case, the basic arrangement allowed one to determine, in an empirical way, the extent to which any one of these factors was important in controlling the outcome of an experiment. Because it was initially set up in an empirical way, evoking a sample of the kind of behavior we wish to extrapolate to, it allowed for the addition of complicating conditions and other variables.

The generativist method of procedure, which begins with sentences (whatever they are behaviorally) and constructs them on the basis of theory rather than sampling them from actual behavior, cannot add conditions to make the stimulus material more appropriate but must transfer to a different dimension in order to proceed from the contrived sentences to actual language behavior; because there always is a context for every sample of language behavior, whether the behavior is considered either as response or as stimulus, the only way in which the contrived verbal material can be made more like the real thing is to obtain empirical samples and to provide typical stimulus conditions for the language sample being studied. The ecolinguistic approach to be described here will be based on the assumption that language behavior is best studied in representative situations in which we are likely to obtain representative samples of the behavior to which we want to extrapolate.

II. WHY HAS IT TAKEN BEHAVIOR THEORY SO LONG TO BE PRODUCTIVE IN LANGUAGE STUDIES?

First, Skinner's book (1957), which presented a most original conception of language, unfortunately fell between two audiences. The Skinnerians, who should have been most receptive to it, did not quite know where to go after reading it, because unlike Skinner's other books, it presented no data but merely some interesting examples. Some of the research that was stimulated by it rapidly came to be part of the clinical area and gradually turned its focus to behavior therapy, whose emphasis, with some exceptions (Salzinger, 1969a; Staats, 1975), was away from language. The linguists, on the other hand, who might well have been an appropriate audience, were turned off by Chomsky's scathing review (1959), which came to be read more widely than Skinner's book and became a general rallying point of all those who had opposed the behavioral point of view, sometimes on the basis of their own reasons or in areas of research unrelated to language. It is fair to say that most of the newer generation of psycholinguists were brought up thinking that the behavior-theory view is quite irrelevant to the study of language, without their having been given the opportunity to look at what the behavior-theory point of view consists of.

The second reason for behavior theory's early relative obscurity with respect to language is that those psychologists who wrapped themselves in the cloak of behavior theory failed, like the generativists, to take into account the environmental variable. They (e.g., Jenkins & Palermo, 1964) tried valiantly to explain the makings of the sentence (the Holy Grail of psycholinguistics) by various kinds of mediation paradigms, all of which set out to show that a particular verbal response could be called forth exclusively by another verbal response, through a transfer paradigm. But language behavior is never independent of nonverbal context, and consequently they failed to show the viability of their kind of behavior theory for the study of language. Unfortunately, they, and others, generalized these results to all behavior theory.

A third reason for the sluggish development of behavior theory in language was the disappointing result when psychologists tried to train animals to communicate. These experiments, fascinating as they were, might perhaps be best described as a tribute to the concept of resistance to extinction. It was only when psychologists varied their behavior and investigated the act of communicating rather than that of speaking that they succeeded in extinguishing the last claim to uniqueness in the human being; Darwin's theory of evolution referred to *all* functions of human beings, and there was no discontinuity in the emergence of language behavior (Salzinger, 1973a). Thus the Gardners (1969, 1971, 1978), Fouts (1975), and Terrace and Bever (1976) showed that the chimpanzee could learn American Sign Language; Premack (1976) showed that a chimpanzee could learn a language composed of plastic symbols; and Rumbaugh and co-workers (Rumbaugh & Gill, 1976; Rumbaugh, 1977) showed that a chimpanzee could learn to communicate through a computer.

Chomsky's contribution was very important in psychology; almost single-handedly, he revived an interest in the study of language and, with those stalwarts George Miller, Charles Osgood, and J. B. Carroll, showed that there were interesting experiments to be done and that this was an area which was to test the mettle of theories and different approaches to psychology as a whole.

III. WHAT IS THE BEHAVIOR-THEORY APPROACH TO LANGUAGE?

The conception of behavior theory to which we refer is that of radical behavior theory (Skinner, 1974); the notation to be used will come from Salzinger (1969b). We shall explore the two long-accepted types of learning, namely, classical (respondent) and operant (instrumental). We might note here that the clear separation of responses into two obvious classes has been broken down by recent research (Hearst, 1975). Responses arbitrarily placed into one class rather than another were shown to be members of either the other class or members of both (for the example of barking, see Salzinger and Waller, 1962, who showed that barking in dogs was conditionable by regular operant conditioning techniques despite the fact that until then B. F. Skinner and J. B. Scott alike thought the barking response to be a respondent; for autonomic responses, see the work of Miller, 1969, 1973, and Kimmel, 1974). There is also evidence that both types of conditioning occur on all or practically all experimental occasions; the difference apparently inheres in what the experimenter measures for any given experiment. This doesn't wash out the difference between the two types of learning, but it does suggest the importance of examining the stimuli in the situation from the two points of view from the start. As we explore the two types of learning, this point will become more evident. As far as the application of the learning models is concerned, the fact that the same response can be conditioned by both procedures makes the application of the learning models more appropriate, not less so, because it provides still another source for the complicated behavior that we observe.

A. The Classical Conditioning Model

Few models of conditioning are more familiar than the Pavlovian one:

In this diagram US = unconditional stimulus; UR = unconditional response; CS = conditional stimulus; CR = conditional response. The US is conventionally an innately effective stimulus, that is, a stimulus that elicits a response, the UR, from the organism without requiring any previous conditioning; it is a wired-in response. The obvious sample for the UR is the salivation elicited by the placement of food (US) in the mouth of the dog. Other examples of URs are changes in heart rate and galvanic skin resistance due to electric shock. The CS is an initially neutral stimulus, that is, a stimulus that before the necessary conditioning has taken place does not elicit the UR, or the CR for that matter. The CR resembles the UR of salivation and like the UR has other responses accompanying it, such as changes in heart rate and in orientation. The CR typically resembles the UR but is not identical with it, usually differing by having a lesser magnitude but sometimes differing in direction as well, as in the case of the experiments in which shock (the US) increases heart rate while a tone (the CS) decreases the heart rate.

Be that as it may, the conditioning occurs through the pairing of the CS with the US, the CS either preceding or occurring at the same time as the US. (A CS, once an effective stimulus in eliciting a CR, can be used to condition a new CS, thus vastly multiplying the effectiveness of this model.) Despite the increasing evidence, already alluded to, that the same response is capable of being conditioned by two different procedures (operant and classical), it does not now seem likely that the classical conditioning model can be usefully referred to language behavior as response; rather, it is a good candidate for the understanding of language, that is, the behavior of the listener or reader. Classical conditioning then makes available to us one mechanism for what people do when they understand what they hear or read. Language behavior as a stimulus arriving at our sensory gates must have some way of being registered, and the classical conditioning model provides us with one model for that.

Extinction, that is, the loss by the CS of its power to elicit a response, occurs when the CS is repeatedly presented in the absence of the US.

Stimulus generalization stems from the fortunate fact that organisms learn to respond to stimuli as members of classes. Thus, when we have been conditioned to respond to one particular CS, we subsequently generalize to other stimuli with which we had not been confronted in that conditioning context. Dogs conditioned to salivate to a metronome ticking at 60 beats per minute also respond to metronomes ticking at other rates, although the response is diminished; they will also respond to other sounds similar to metronome beats, but again, in diminished magnitude. In this way, we are able to measure the effective, functional distance from stimulus to stimulus by monitoring the magnitude of conditioned responses that the different stimuli elicit.

This has, of course, served as the basis for studies in semantic generalization (see Salzinger, 1978, for examples) showing such interesting findings as the following: Children tend to generalize to words related in sound to the CS, while adults tend to generalize to words related in meaning. This kind of model building relates to Osgood, Suci, and Tannenbaum's (1957) theory of connotative meaning. When the subject views a word in order to rate it, say, on a scale of good to bad, that word first elicits a response from the subject in the classical conditioning sense; probably a response that is generalized because it was not specifically conditioned (paired with any US or with any CS acting as a conditioning stimulus). This elicited response, typically an autonomic response such as heart rate, change of blood pressure, or GSR (Galvanic Skin Response) acts as a discriminative stimulus that controls the operant, the rating which the subject applies to the word on Osgood's semantic differential. It is stimulus generalization that we appeal to for much of what we mean when we say that we understand something that another individual says. This example shows us how the two types of conditioning interact with one another. We hasten to add, however, that we are by no means placing all of our explanatory eggs of understanding into the respondent conditioning basket, for the operant responses to which we are about to turn are very much involved in our understanding of the speech of another.

Work on the respondent conditioning paradigm is not quite as active as it first was in the area of verbal behavior. Nevertheless, investigators such as Staats (1967, 1975), and Mowrer (1954, 1960) have taken the classical conditioning paradigm quite seriously. Mowrer did so mostly theoretically and some years ago; Staats continues to work on that paradigm, although insisting that one must take both it and the operant conditioning paradigm into account at the same time and in their complicated interrelationships with each other. Mowrer (1954), interestingly enough, viewed the sentence as a conditioning device, where the meaning (emotional reaction) of one part of the sentence was conditioned to another part of the sentence, as, for example, in his sentence, "Tom is a thief." Here the meaning of the word "thief" was transferred to the word "Tom." Although Mowrer, like Osgood and Staats, insists on mediating stimuli in language behavior, all of these investigators have made extensive use of the classical conditioning paradigm. Staats, who has done most empirical work in this area, has repeatedly shown that attitudes [expressed through the semantic differential of Osgood (Osgood, Suci, & Tannenbaum, 1957)] can be changed toward nonsense syllables, people's names, and even nations. Clearly, some such conditioning process goes on when we acquire different attitudes toward groups we never meet but have contact with only through the language medium.

Before leaving the phenomenon of respondent conditioning, we must take note of the fact that it can occur with one or both of the critical stimuli inside the organism. Thus it is quite possible that, given the continual flow of internal events, people might well misdiagnose what is happening to them because of such a conditioning procedure. The point is that the effect of such conditioning complicates and obscures the study of "meaning" when we are relating it to private events that in this case are being entirely processed beyond the awareness of the outside observer and often of the person in whom the conditioning is occurring. The other way of viewing interoceptive conditioning is in terms of the multitude of stimuli that eventually become effective in eliciting reactions from individuals and that would then, as newly effective stimuli, also affect both the way a person understands language behavior and the way that person emits it, because those stimuli made effective through a respondent conditioning procedure becomes effective in directing the operant conditioning procedure as well.

B. The Operant Conditioning Model

In operant conditioning, the critical contingency exists between the response and the reinforcer, whereas in respondent conditioning, the critical contingency exists between the stimulus and the reinforcer. Note that it has been the practice in classical conditioning to speak of the US as a reinforcer, that is, the stimulus that strengthens the relationship between the formerly neutral stimulus and the CR. In any case, in operant conditioning, the relationship to be watched is that between the response and its consequence. Interestingly enough, a fortuitous relationship between a response and a reinforcer has the same effect as an arranged consequence on the response occurrence in the future. This means that the relationship can be generalized to a simple temporal one; however, when the response-reinforcer connection is reduced to a temporal relationship, then it resembles respondent conditioning, where the experimenter determines what happens to the subject by manipulating the time periods between the CS and the US.

If, as happens in experiments on superstitious conditioning, the experimenter determines when the reinforcer is delivered (i.e., the delivery of the reinforcer is not contingent on the subject's behavior), then we have a situation very much like that found in temproal classical conditioning, as Hearst (1975) points out. If the two experimental situations are interchangeable, then the question arises whether one can separate operant from respondent conditioning. The answer is that as long as there are different procedures involved in the experiments and in life, then we do have to separate the two kinds of learning, and because it makes sense to separate them in behavior therapy, where human beings are regularly involved, we shall continue to keep these separated for discussions of language behavior as well. This discussion shows that behavior theory is by no means a stable, played-out area of psychology, that on the contrary it is very much in ferment. Although the basic relations still hold very firmly, we ought to keep apprised of newest developments so that we can make use of them, when relevant, in the study of language behavior.

For this discussion, we shall see that the operant conditioning model is most appropriate for gaining an understanding of the speaker and writer, and also of the hearer and reader. The basic concept is the reinforcement contingency. It states that in the presence of a stimulus (the discriminative stimulus, S^D), a response, R, will have a consequence consisting of a reinforcing stimulus, S^R. The formula is:

$$S^D \ldots R \rightarrow S^R$$

Responses occur in the presence of certain stimuli. These stimuli are discriminative in so far as they acquire control over the responses. They are critical in producing the responses at other times. They acquire that control only, however, provided that they are followed by reinforcing stimuli. There are two types of reinforcing stimuli, positive and negative ones. Positive reinforcers are those that strengthen the occurrence of the responses that produce them; negative reinforcers strengthen responses that eliminate or avoid them. Note that aversive stimuli that are contingent on the occurrence of responses, unlike the relationship just outlined for negative reinforcers that gain their strength from affording the subject the opportunity to avoid or escape from them, are called punishing stimuli, not negative reinforcers. Punishing stimuli, as used in their usual way (not in traumatic magnitude), merely suppress the responses they follow; after the passage of a modicum of time, the responses reappear. Sometimes, punishing stimuli appear to be effective because of simultaneous positive reinforcement for responses that are incompatible with the responses being punished.

We must add to this the fact that in social processes, and particularly in language behavior, the most important reinforcers are the conditioned ones, that is, those that are acquired in much the same way as in respondent conditioning by being paired in some way with primary (wired-in) reinforcers. The mechanism believed to underlie the acquisition of conditioned reinforcers is the respondent conditioning paradigm. The stimulus preceding the operant response, the S^D, becomes a conditioned reinforcer, as does any other neutral stimulus that immediately precedes the primary reinforcer, including the emission of the operant response itself. In addition, of course, again as in the case of the respondent conditioning model, conditioned reinforcers themselves become able, by the same paradigm, to produce conditioned reinforcers. Also, positive reinforcers produce new positive reinforcers when they are associated with their occurrence; they make negative reinforcers of those stimuli that are associated with the absence of the positive reinforcers; the reverse holds for the negative reinforcers. Finally, we must add, in this very abbreviated description of operant conditioning, that some reinforcers, such as money, are generalized positive reinforcers for most of us in this society because that kind of reinforcer is regularly paired with a wide variety of other reinforcers—some cynics among us say with all other positive reinforcers.

Reinforcers are not received all of the time, nor for all of one's responses. The explication of this fact is one of Skinner's most important contributions to our understanding of the acquisition of behavior and, perhaps even more significantly, to our understanding of the maintenance of behavior. Whereas most learning theories are concerned with explaining how an individual *acquires* a response, Skinner realized that we must learn to explain how responses are *maintained*. The elimination of responses comes about through the process of extinction, which in operant conditioning consists of the omission of the reinforcer after it has been contingent on the responses.

A question related to maintenance of behavior is how an organism continues to perform a response in the face of intermittent reinforcement when the complete elimination of reinforcement causes a reduction in response rate. The interesting answer that Skinner obtained was that intermittent reinforcement produces behavior that is more resistant to extinction than behavior resulting from continuous reinforcement (reinforcement for each and every response emitted). This finding corresponds to our intuition about how we are reinforced in "real" life. Given the large number of different scheduling effects producing an exquisite variety of response patterns even in the lowly rat and pigeon, the radical behavior-theory model seems a prime candidate for explaining language. Even more important is the finding that more complicated chains of behavior, allowing for choices at various points in the chain, become more, not less, stable when they are intermittently reinforced than when they are continuously reinforced, again supporting the relevance of behavior theory to language. The more the conditions of behavior-theory experiments are modified to approximate natural conditions, the more we find stable behavior.

Two additional important concepts need to be described: response unit and response class. The concept of response unit (Salzinger, 1973b) points up the critical problem of determining what to count. The manner in which this problem is usually solved, particularly in experiments, is through the simplifying assumption of a single standard unit. The word is a frequent candidate for this unit, but others have become the vogue at various times, such as the syllable, the column inch when the language behavior being examined was printed material, the sentence, the idea unit. Skinner's (1957) approach to the problem of unit size is functional. Use of mere topographical description is bound to get one into difficulty, because different size units (in terms of topography) often turn out to be independent of the functional unit size. To take but one simple example, the shouted word "Fire" and the shouted sentence "Help, there's a fire here!" will equally alert people concerned with the control of fires, or for that matter, even mere bystanders. From the point of view of radical behavior theory, adopting a single topographical unit size seems unwise. The proper way to determine unit size is to ascertain how much verbal behavior is necessary for a given effect, how much is produced by the same discriminative stimulus, or whatever other functional relationship can be shown to hold for particular response sizes.

The second concept, that of response class (Salzinger, 1967), is often misunderstood. Critics of behavior theory, having so long said that behavior theory is atomistic, have come to believe that each response is considered separately from every other; assuming such an approach, the critics have asked how behavior theory could possibly deal with the richness and variety that characterize language behavior. The fact of the matter is, however, given the emphasis on functional definitions, that behavior theory must especially take into account classes of response. Verbal responses do not, after all, vary haphazardly and independently of one another. Furthermore, the identification of verbal response classes is an empirical matter to be investigated by appropriate behavioral analyses as in the case of the experimentally defined response class of plural nouns (Salzinger, Portnoy, Zlotogura, & Keisner, 1963) or in the clinically significant case of self-referred affect (Salzinger & Pisoni, 1958, 1960, 1961; Salzinger & Portnoy, 1964).

This concept and the concept of response unit make language behavior and its so-called originality amenable to study by behavioral techniques, as shown for example in Salzinger and Feldman (1973). There, variants of the cloze procedure applied to different types of language samples give rise to surprising regularities in contrast to the surfeit of originality that many psycholinguists repeatedly point to.

Before taking up the various kinds of interactions of the two models of learning and maintenance of language behavior, I would like to comment on an egregious error often committed by critics of behavior theory. The principles of behavior theory as outlined above are often described as being too simplistic (not merely simple, but simplistic) for gaining an understanding of anything so exquisitely complicated as language. I believe that this kind of criticism is based on a misunderstanding of how to deal with the problem of complexity in data. Theories are supposed to deal with complications in data, not by trying to trace or simulate these complications in the theory, but, on the contrary, by beginning with a relatively small number of simple basic premises and by using them so as to generate the complexity of the data. The success of this process is considered a contribution to the understanding of the phenomenon in question. Beginning with the most complicated model makes available to us a description that mimics the complications by a translation into terms equally complicated and therefore is not capable of generating what we normally mean by explanation.

My point is quite simple. When you construct a theory or describe data in abstract terms having some generality, do it in as simple a way as you can. Leave your theory simple and the complexities will take care of themselves.

The complexities inhere in the data; the theory must be employed to explain them by finding basic simple relationships.

C. The Interaction of the Classical and Operant Conditioning Models

Stimuli have a way of ignoring the manner in which you classify them and thus produce the interaction of the two types of learning. This complication that the data of language behavior introduce is no different from the complication introduced by nonverbal behavior. Stimuli have more than one function. A stimulus thus can be a conditional stimulus (CS) in the Pavlovian sense and a discriminative stimulus and positive reinforcer in an operant sense. A negative reinforcer might act as a primary negative reinforcer and a discriminative stimulus for another response in an operant sense and a US in the Pavlovian sense, etc. In language behavior, this taking on of various roles by the same stimuli is even more characteristic than in nonverbal behavior, but it occurs regularly in both types of behavior.

Let us begin somewhere in a temporal sequence of responses and stimuli. We cannot start at the beginning because the stream of behavior and the stimuli that control it are continuous over time. We shall look at a conversation to determine how well this analysis fits.

Two people are having a conversation (you do need at least two people for a conversation). You also need an environment, because conversations take place between people, and people occupy space, no matter where they are; they must be in a particular environment that provides them with stimuli that precede and that follow responses. Let us look at the stimuli that precede the responses of interest. Samantha is seated at her desk, trying to write a letter, when the bell rings. Until that happened, the critical stimuli included the notepaper and pen she was employing in writing her letter. At the sound of the bell, she put down her pen and walked over to the door.

"Hi there, Semmy girl," simpered Sol.

Samantha grimaced predictably. She hated to be called Semmy, and Sol knew she hated it, and what's more, she knew that he knew that she hated it: "And how are you, my puny pen pal?" she finally hissed.

"Pen pal? Aren't you going to invite me in?" Sol began to whine, since Samantha had neither given a sign for him to enter nor made any movement to make such entering possible.

"I don't see why I should, when you begin in that wise-assed manner of yours, do you, sunny Solly?" She finally remembered what he most abhored to hear himself called. "Come on in, Solly, old sock."

"I wish you'd be a little bit more refined sometimes," Sol said once again, but entered meekly anyway.

People's interactions are always complicated, sometimes amusing, some-times repetitious and cliche marked, and always susceptible to at least an attempted reinforcement contingency analysis. Perhaps it would be well to point out at the start that neither interlocutor ever said "yeah," "yes," "mmhm," or even tried to show obvious agreement in this conversation. Literally hundreds of studies (Krasner, 1967; Kanfer, 1968; Salzinger, 1978) have been done using such markers for reinforcers either in experiments or in analyses of actual conversations that had taken place, most usually in the course of therapy when many such interactions are available for analysis. It isn't because of the ubiquity of these reinforcers that they have been employed. It is simply because their effects are so well known and so obvious and because they can be easily inserted in the course of an experiment that they have been used. But none of that suggests that these kinds of remarks are the only or even the most representative or effective reinforcers that maintain conversation under normal circumstances. Everyone has taken part in conversations containing none of these signals and yet has continued those conversations. This does not prove that conversations are continued despite the absence of reinforcers but rather that the class of reinforcers is much larger and more varied than these few words, so often employed in experiments, would indicate.

In a review of much of the behavior theory empirical literature, I (Salzinger, 1978) recently showed how Brown and Hanlon's (1970) analysis of children's and their mothers' interactions shed little light on the role of reinforcement in the acquisition of new structures that children are supposed to be learning at given ages. Brown and Hanlon's definition of what constitutes a reinforcer was altogether too restricted, referring to the formal signals of reinforcers only. The so-called simplicity of the behavior theory lies not in the theory but in the analyses done by those trying so hard to show that it is simplistic. In real life, reinforcers are many and varied. Most of the time, if you ask for salt, sugar, or cream, to be passed to you while you are eating, you are not reinforced by someone saying "mmhmm," no matter how mellifluously that sound is made. Nor does the fact that you repeat your request for the salt, sugar, cream, or whatever only if you have not received it prove that the reinforcer (the particular substance asked for) is not effective. It merely demonstrates, in the great complexity of stimuli in which behavior normally is found, that the appropriate discriminative stimulus marking the occasion for asking for salt, sugar, etc., is the absence of that substance plus an appropriate food such as potatoes or coffee that makes receipt of the salt or sugar reinforcing.

We can now return to our conversation at Samantha's door. A door bell ringing is a very well known and well conditioned discriminative stimulus for most of us, that is, it is typically an occasion for us to get up and "answer the door." Nothing spectacular here, but a good deal of predictability in that event. We must note that first of all Sol did not begin talking until Samantha actually appeared at the door. Samantha was an S^D for his language behavior. Then he uttered a rather universal response, "Hi there, Semmy girl." Certainly the first part of that utterance is quite common, as is the addition of the name of the person and, under some conditions, even of the word "girl," even though currently such usage is definitely viewed with disfavor among feminists. The greeting also includes a deliberate mispronunciation of the woman's name. The emphasis here is not on the speaker's having made a mistake or distorted some truth, but rather that this kind of "mistake" in our society has two possible sources, one of incompetence and the other of making mischief. From the text, we can see that mischief is definitely what was taking place. In fact, apparently what is keeping this conversation going is the alternation of mild insults one after another. We shall talk about the reinforcing quality of these responses shortly.

Also clear in the conversation is the fact that some of the language behavior is occasioned by the time in the visit (the beginning), part by the place (Sol is still at the doorstep and not yet inside). But when Samantha remembers the insult with which she can come back at him and only (or at least most easily) on the occasion of greeting him at the doorstep, she insults him and asks him to enter. Having been insulted once more, Sol is given still another occasion for delivering his insult. This kind of conversation resembles a well-documented kind of conversation sometimes called "playing the dozens" in which it is the task of each interlocutor increasingly to insult the other until one of them can no longer increase the magnitude of the insult. In this entire conversation there were numerous discriminative stimuli, some of the important ones being what had just been uttered by the other speaker, but others, as indicated, referring to time and place of encounter. Samantha's last activity no doubt controlled her utterance of the rather weak epithet, "puny pen pal." Because Sol did not share Samantha's recent discriminative stimuli of writing a letter he appears somewhat puzzled by "pen pal." Still other S^D's are shared by the two speakers through their common reinforcement history, namely, they have engaged in such conversations before and probably a good part has become somewhat stylized, meaning that they are practicing this kind of encounter repeatedly, and, from the point of view of behavior theory, they are reinforcing each other for their language behavior. What is the reinforcer for these interchanges? First of all, the next statement by the other person. Secondly, being let into Samantha's house is reinforcing also; thirdly, their grimaces and gestures, which the author did not tell us about, also must have served as discriminative and as reinforcing stimuli as well.

To this analysis, we must add the response-produced discriminative and reinforcing stimuli. The phrase "puny pen pal" provides us with an example of the action of response-produced discriminative stimuli; in this case, we have the poetic device of alliteration, which in some circles is much reinforced. Here the first subvocal occurrence of "puny" may have suggested "pen pal," or, perhaps more likely, the first subvocal occurrence of "pen pal" gave rise to "puny," so that Samantha then said "puny pen pal." When the sound of an insult came off well, then the feedback of hearing it probably acted as a positive reinforcer just as writing is reinforcing once the writer has expressed an idea that upon rereading is found satisfactory with respect to his/her intent. Note that the word "intent" is not being sneaked in here as a mentalism but is used as a shorthand phrase for a response that resembles other responses that in the past had been reinforced for occurring on such occasions.

The conversation, brief as it was, is very complicated, but our analysis was based on the use of a small number of principles and concepts to explain it. We have said little about positive or negative reinforcers in this conversation. The argument might be made that insults act as negative reinforcers and as escape responses from having been the last person to have sustained an insult. On the other hand, the argument could be made that the conversation was sustained by the positive reinforcement received from having made a "clever" statement. We would need additional examples of conversation between these two interlocutors to determine which kind of reinforcer we are dealing with. In all likelihood, the insults serve both as negative reinforcers for the listener and as positive reinforcers for the speaker.

It is important to point out that the behavior-theory description of this conversation must be placed in the realm of speculation as long as we lack frequency-of-occurrence data. The only way to establish how the various aspects of the conversation are functioning is to analyze repeated samples of conversation, including a description of the nonverbal behavior and of the environment in which the conversation was taking place. The reader will have noticed that the rather simple principles nevertheless gave rise to rather complicated analyses, that we used the concepts of discriminative stimuli, reinforcers, external and response-produced stimuli, verbal and nonverbal discriminative and reinforcing stimuli, and that the history of the interlocutors came into the picture early on, with respect to both recent and remote history.

We must add to this the role of the classical conditioning model. Obviously, the insults have at one time been paired with other CS's of aversive value, or even possibly of appetitive value. It is quite possible that this kind of conversation (CS's) always preceded the interlocutors' getting together to have a marvelous time for hours over dinner, drinks (US's), etc. In any case, the words that were exchanged act not only as S^D's and S^r's but also as CS's and US's in the respondent conditioning paradigm. Therefore, they will be involved in various autonomically controlled responses. Those elicited responses might, if aversive, act as discriminative stimuli for escaping, that is,

Sol's leaving Samantha, whereas, if the elicited responses are appetitive, they might well serve as S^D's for staying, in which case they will be partly responsible for generating further verbal behavior on the part of the visitor so as to be able to stay. In other words part of the function of the language behavior might well have been to enable the two persons to stay together and to be further stimulated by whatever CS's they presented to each other.

IV. DOES LANGUAGE "TEACHING" TAKE PLACE UNDER NATURAL CIRCUMSTANCES?

Part of the behavior theory-generative grammar controversy is colored by the manner in which the latter camp has pictured the learning and conditioning process. Conjuring up the rat or pigeon in a box and constantly reminding us of the precise experimental conditions that are the hallmark of operant and respondent conditioning, the antibehaviorists assure us that no such learning can or does take place in real life. As already indicated, however, this false generalization from experiment to natural conditions and this oversimplification of what conditioning is all about have led to the construction of analyses (Brown & Hanlon, 1970) in which only the most obvious verbal statements of agreement are used in the identification of reinforcers. The error of omitting from these analyses reinforcers such as getting the object, condition, or information asked for, was demonstrated by Salzinger (1978). Here we shall restrict ourselves to examining some studies that have attacked, empirically, the question of what can and does happen in nature.

The generative grammarian's conception of how the child acquires language can, I think, fairly be described as consisting of exposing the child to various sets of sentences at different stages of life, with the limitation that exposure at early stages would simply not be of any use to the child because the basic physiological foundations of rules are not yet available. This view of "learning" (this conception has to be put in quotation marks for any learning theorist) gives the learner only the most minimal role in the process.

Bandura (1977), whose approach to learning differs in some details and in the use of some explanatory concepts from the radical behavior-theory approach espoused here and who places much emphasis on observational learning, nevertheless recognizes, as I do, that observation, imitation, and comprehension all contribute to the process of acquisition of language behavior.

When children observe, it seems reasonable to ask, what are they exposed to? A study by Moerk (1974) supplies us with evidence that mothers change the kinds of things they say to their children depending on what the children say; thus mothers talking with their children varying in age from 2 to 5 steadily increase the length of their statements as their children's statements also increase in length. In addition, Weist and Kruppe (1977) showed that parents, particularly mothers, comprehend their children better than nonparents, suggesting that parents and children learn to comprehend each other. The limitations in memory and ability to pronounce words impose limitations on the children's ability to communicate, and the parents have to learn to pay attention to discriminative stimuli in the children's speech and environment that do not have this function in adult speech. The parents thereby have at least the potential for improving the child's speech, because they understand it better than others.

The experimental literature is replete with examples according to which children without speech at age 4 and later can be trained to speak by means of operant conditioning (Salzinger, Feldman, Cowan, & Salzinger, 1965; Lovaas, 1977); in this procedure, the experimenter reinforces language behavior, at first with edible reinforcers such as M & M's or parts of meals, and later with social reinforcers, such as verbal responses by the experimenter matching the child's length of utterance, agreement, and praise. But even more exciting is the study by Moerk (1976), which analyzed the verbal interactions of 20 mothers with their children who ranged in age from approximately 2 to 5 years. Observing 10 mother–daughter pairs and 10 mother–son pairs, Moerk analyzed hour-long interactions in which the mothers and children followed their normal routines in the presence of a tape recorder. Moerk categorized not only what each interlocutor said to the other but also, and more importantly, the sequences of responses between the two speakers. The investigator found definite evidence of instruction on the part of the mothers: The average number of instructive interactions varied from 1 to 66, with a mean of 37 per hour. The mother as active teacher can no longer be ignored in the scientific literature. The question remains as to how she instructs. She uses the following categories of verbal response: mother corrects or questions the formulation of the response, accepts it as correct answers questions, or responds with a question. For the child, all of these form some type of consequence or reinforcer. The mother also provides discriminative stimuli as shown by these categories: She models from a picture book, describes an object in hand, describes an observed event, utters an incomplete utterance, asks a question, models a phrase from a picture book, prods the child to improve the statement, labels an object, etc. Most important, the author found definite and numerous examples of the mother teaching not only vocabulary and pronunciation but also bound morphemes and syntax. Finally, Moerk was able to show that the amount of this teaching varied inversely with age (–.59) and even more so with child's language level (–.67), showing that the amount of contingent discriminative stimulus and reinforcing stimulus presentation varies with the child's need to be instructed in language behavior. All very "commonsensical" somehow, but this has so long been denied that the empirical demonstration was necessary.

V.   WHAT KIND OF EXPERIMENTS DOES
THE ECOLINGUISTIC APPROACH LEAD TO?

The first rule of the ecolinguistic approach, as suggested above, is generally to make use of language behavior that has been emitted under representative conditions. This should be done, whether the language behavior is used as stimulus or as response. Furthermore, wherever possible, that language behavior should be examined in its environment specified as completely as possible.

An ecolinguist is naturally interested in measuring the relative amount of control that particular parts of the environment exert over the emission of particular classes of language behavior. This can be measured directly by comparing the language behavior typically emitted in different environments. It can be done somewhat more practically, even though indirectly, and with stronger stimulus control, by examining the relationship of the language behavior of the "hearer" (comprehender, recaller, recognizer, etc.) to that of the "speaker" (writer) in the same or different environments. One way of doing that consists of presenting a sample of language to groups of naïve hearers—for some in the presence of the same environment in which the sample was originally emitted, for others in a different but "neutral" environment, and for still others in an environment that evokes verbal responses incompatible with the ones to be remembered. Environment can be controlled systematically by immersing the original speech sample in environments varying in amount of context. The speaker's speech sample can be accompanied by the question that preceded it, or not, or the experimenter can provide the inanimate environment in which the speech was originally emitted as contrasted to a different, possibly incompatible environment.

Various techniques in the psycholinguistic literature can be employed for this manipulation (e.g., Carroll, 1972). Memory tasks constitute one such technique: amount of recall prompted by graded intensity or number of appropriate discriminative stimuli will make clear the amount of control each exerts over language behavior. Various sentence-completion procedures, especially the cloze procedure and its variants (Salzinger & Feldman, 1973), would supply information not only on external stimulus control but also on response-produced stimulus control. In an experiment (Clark, Williams, & Tannenbaum, 1965) that had people make interpretations of abstract paintings and had others fill in the blanks of the mutilated typescripts (every fifth word having been deleted from the interpretations) with and without the availability of the pictures the presence of the pictures was demonstrated to enhance the performance of the "clozers."

An entirely different approach examines the conditions under which new responses are acquired: in artificial language, in the acquisition of a first language (i.e., in young children) and in the acquisition of a second language (i.e., in learning a foreign language), and finally in the reacquisition of language in people who have lost it (i.e., in aphasic patients) or in patients who have become mute in the course of having schizophrenia. Here, we have the opportunity of seeing the contribution made by the various discriminative stimuli as well as the importance of various kinds of reinforcers in the course of acquisition or reacquisition of behavior. Monitoring the process of acquisition and reacquisition also allows us to determine the extent to which response-produced stimuli generated by nonverbal responses as in manipulating objects while learning to describe or label them, act as supporting stimuli to evoke the appropriate language responses.

Still another approach to language behavior is through the study of physical and social stimuli in direct confrontation with each other. This approach allows us to measure the relative effectiveness of the various stimuli, both discriminative and reinforcing, in gaining control over language behavior. The social psychology literature demonstrates the amazing control exerted over people's judgments by the judgments of others in contrast to the physical properties of the objects in the environment supposedly judged. The various parameters controlling these verbal responses are very interesting. They include the age of the child involved, the relationship of the influencing judge over the person's verbal behavior, the number of reinforcements given previously for the correct judgment, etc. (see, e.g., Salzinger & Sanders, 1977).

The study of language behavior is involved in various practical situations, mainly therapeutic ones, such as marital communication situations (Thomas, 1976). Thomas showed how couples can be retrained to improve the way in which they speak to each other by making the reinforcement contingencies systematic and explicit. In the course of accomplishing this, we can learn the conditions that control conversational behavior. In some cases, the only problem is to teach each partner to listen when the other wishes to speak, and to speak when the other wishes to listen. Normal conversation contains discriminative stimuli for change of speaker. By examining these S^D's in therapeutic situations, one can uncover the specific faults in communication—whether they lie in the lack of provision of S^D's by the speaker or in the lack of recognition by the listener.

The use of language behavior in problem solving is a very interesting case that has for too long a time been kept apart from the study of language. Language behavior in the course of problem solving and troubleshooting derives its uniqueness from the fact that so much of it is indirectly reinforced and, even more important, self-reinforced, in that when one solves certain problems, the recognition that one has arrived at the solution is self-evident. In the case of the jigsaw puzzle, for example, there is no doubt when the puzzle has been solved and thereby the problem solver reinforces his/her own language behavior that led to the solution, and all of this without the intervention of another social being. This context of language behavior has been little studied and must be given more attention in order to gain a more complete understanding of the variables that maintain language behavior.

The number of different experiments that lie in store for anyone interested in the ecolinguistic approach is large indeed. What's more, many of the experiments done in psycholinguistics lend themselves to being fit into the ecolinguistic framework of study. The point of this chapter is that, rather than building ever more complicated models of what takes place in the mythical land of the mind, we should embrace that concept only after we have fully exhausted all the other real lands in which our speaking and hearing activities take place, lands that are much more easily charted and that promise much more quickly to pay off in providing us with the treasure of discovery.

REFERENCES

Bandura, A. *Social learning theory.* Englewood Cliffs, N.J.: Prentice-Hall, 1977.

Blough, D. S. Experiments in animal psychophysics. *Scientific American,* 1961, *205,* 113–122.

Brown, R., & Hanlon, C. Derivational complexity and order of acquisition in child speech. In R. J. Hayes (Ed.), *Cognition and the development of language.* New York: Wiley, 1970.

Carroll, J. B. Defining language comprehension: Some speculations. In J. B. Carroll & R. O. Freedle (Eds.), *Language comprehension and the acquisition of knowledge.* Washington, D.C.: V. H. Winston, 1972.

Chomsky, N. Review of Skinner's Verbal Behavior. *Language,* 1959, *35,* 26–58.

Clark, R. A., Williams, F., & Tannenbaum, P. H. Effects of shared referential experience upon encoder–decoder agreement. *Language and Speech,* 1965, *8,* 253–262.

Fouts, R. S. Communication with chimpanzees. In H. Kurth & I. Eibl-Eibesfeldt (Eds.), *Hominisation and behavior.* Stuttgart, Germany: Fischer Verlag, 1975.

Gardner, R. A., & Gardner, B. T. Teaching sign language to a chimpanzee. *Science,* 1969, *165,* 664–672.

Gardner, B. T., & Gardner, R. A. Two-way communication with an infant chimpanzee. In A. M. Schrier & F. Stollnitz (Eds.), *Behavior of nonhuman primates* (Vol. 4). New York: Academic Press, 1971.

Gardner, R. A., & Gardner, B. T. Comparative psychology and language acquisition. In K. Salzinger & F. Denmark (Eds.), *Psychology: The state of the art. Annals of the New York Academy of Sciences,* 1978, *309,* 37–76.

Hearst, E. The classical-instrumental distinction: Reflexes, voluntary behavior, and categories of associative learning. In W. K. Estes (Ed.), *Handbook of learning and cognitive processes* (Vol. 2). Hillsdale, N.J.: Lawrence Erlbaum Associates, 1975.

Jenkins, J. J., & Palermo, D. S. Mediation processes and the acquisition of linguistic structure. In U. Bellugi & R. Brown (Eds.), *The acquisition of language. Monographs of the Society for Research in Child Development,* 1964, *29*(1), 141–169.

Kanfer, F. H. Verbal conditioning: A review of its current status. In T. R. Dixon & D. L. Horton (Eds.), *Verbal behavior and general behavior theory.* Englewood Cliffs, N.J.: Prentice-Hall, 1968.

Kimmel, H. D. Instrumental conditioning of autonomically mediated responses in human beings. *American Psychologist,* 1974, *29,* 325–335.

Krasner, L. Verbal operant conditioning and awareness. In K. Salzinger & S. Salzinger (Eds.), *Research in verbal behavior and some neurophysiological implications.* New York: Academic Press, 1967.

Lovaas, O. I. *The autistic child.* New York: Wiley, 1977.

Miller, G. A. Some psychological studies of grammar. *American Psychologist,* 1962, *17,* 748–762.

Miller, G. A., & Johnson-Laird, P. N. *Language and perception.* Cambridge, Mass.: Harvard University Press, 1976.

Miller, N. E. Learning of visceral and glandular responses. *Science,* 1969, *163,* 434–445.

Miller, N. E. Autonomic learning: Clinical and physiological implications. In M. Hammer, K. Salzinger, & S. Sutton (Eds.), *Psychopathology: Contributions from the social, behavioral and biological sciences.* New York: Wiley, 1973.

Moerk, E. L. Processes of language teaching and training in the interactions of mother–child dyads. *Child Development,* 1976, *47,* 1064–1078.

Moerk, E. L. Changes in verbal child–mother interactions with increasing language skills of the child. *Journal of Psycholinguistic Research,* 1974, *3,* 101–116.

Mowrer, O. H. The psychologist looks at language. *American Psychologist,* 1954, *9,* 660–694.

Mowrer, O. H. *Learning theory and the symbolic processes.* New York: Wiley, 1960.

Osgood, C. E., Suci, G. J., & Tannenbaum, P. H. The measurement of meaning. Urbana: University of Illinois Press, 1957.

Premack, D. *Intelligence in ape and man.* Hillsdale, N.J.: Lawrence Erlbaum Associates, 1976.

Rumbaugh, D. M. (Ed.). *Language learning by a chimpanzee.* New York: Academic Press, 1977.

Rumbaugh, D. M., & Gill, T. V. Language and the acquisition of language-type skills by a chimpanzee (PAN). In K. Salzinger (Ed.), *Psychology in progress. Annals of the New York Academy of Sciences,* 1976, *270,* 90–123.

Salzinger, K. The problem of response class in verbal behavior. In K. Salzinger & S. Salzinger (Eds.), *Research in verbal behavior and some neurophysiological implications.* New York: Academic Press, 1967.

Salzinger, K. The place of operant conditioning of verbal behavior in psychotherapy. In C. Franks (Ed.), *Behavior therapy: Appraisal and status.* New York: McGraw-Hill, 1969. (a)

Salzinger, K. *Psychology, the science of behavior.* New York: Springer, 1969. (b)

Salzinger, K. Animal communication. In D. A. Dewsbury & D. A. Rethlingshafer (Eds.), *Comparative psychology.* New York: McGraw-Hill, 1973. (a)

Salzinger, K. Some problems of response measurement in verbal behavior: The response unit and intraresponse relations. In K. Salzinger & R. S. Feldman (Eds.), *Studies in verbal behavior: An empirical approach.* New York: Pergamon, 1973. (b)

Salzinger, K. Are theories of competence necessary? In D. Aaronson & R. W. Rieber (Eds.), *Developmental psycholinguistics and communication disorders. Annals of the New York Academy of Sciences,* 1975, *263,* 178–196.

Salzinger, K. Language behavior. In A. C. Catania & T. A. Brigham (Eds.), *Handbook of applied behavior analysis: Social and instructional processes.* New York: Halsted, 1978.

Salzinger, K., & Feldman, R. S. (Eds.). *Studies in verbal behavior: An empirical approach.* New York: Pergamon, 1973.

Salzinger, K., Feldman, R. S., Cowan, J. E., & Salzinger, S. Operant conditioning of verbal behavior of two young speech-deficient boys. In L. Krasner & L. P. Ullmann (Eds.), *Research in behavior modification.* New York: Holt, Rinehart & Winston, 1965.

Salzinger, K., & Pisoni, S. Reinforcement of affect responses of schizophrenics during the clinical interview. *Journal of Abnormal and Social Psychology,* 1958, *57,* 84–90.

Salzinger, K., & Pisoni, S. Reinforcement of verbal affect responses of normal subjects during the interview. *Journal of Abnormal and Social Psychology,* 1960, *60,* 127–130.

Salzinger, K., & Pisoni, S. Some parameters of the conditioning of verbal affect responses in schizophrenic subjects. *Journal of Abnormal and Social Psychology,* 1961, *63,* 511–516.

Salzinger, K., & Portnoy, S. Verbal conditioning in interviews: Application to chronic schizophrenics and relationship to prognosis for acute schizophrenics. *Journal of Psychiatric Research,* 1964, *2,* 1–9.

Salzinger, K., Portnoy, S., Zlotogura, P., & Keisner, R. The effect of reinforcement on continuous speech and on plural nouns in grammatical context. *Journal of Verbal Learning and Verbal Behavior,* 1963, *1,* 477–485.

Salzinger, K., & Waller, M. B. The operant control of vocalization in the dog. *Journal of the Experimental Analysis of Behavior,* 1962, *5,* 383–389.

Salzinger, S., & Sanders, R. *The influence of social and physical anchors and type of verbal responses on preschoolers' judgment of weight.* Paper presented at the Eastern Psychological Association meetings, Boston, Mass., March 1977.

Skinner, B. F. *Verbal behavior.* New York: Appleton-Century-Crofts, 1957.

Skinner, B. F. *About behaviorism.* New York: Knopf, 1974.

Staats, A. W. Emotions and images in language: A learning analysis of their acquisition and function. In K. Salzinger & S. Salzinger (Eds.), *Research in verbal behavior.* New York: Academic Press, 1967.

Staats, A. W. *Social behaviorism.* Homewood, Ill.: The Dorsey Press, 1975.

Terrace, H. S., & Bever, T. G. What might be learned from studying language in the chimpanzee? The importance of symbolizing oneself. In S. R. Harnad, H. D. Steklis, & J. Lancaster (Eds.), *Origins and evolution of language and speech. Annals of the New York Academy of Sciences,* 1976, *280,* 579–588.

Thomas, E. J. *Marital communication and decision making.* New York: The Free Press, 1976.

Weist, R. M., & Kruppe, B. Parent and sibling comprehension of children's speech. *Journal of Psycholinguistic Research,* 1977, *6,* 49–58.

III PHONOLOGY

5 A Survey of Generative Phonology

Sanford A. Schane
University of California, San Diego

Generative phonology began, within generative-transformational grammar, as the component for dealing with the sound structure of language.[1] It has, within the last decade, been a dominant force in the shaping of phonological theory and description, particularly in the United States but elsewhere as well. If one can speak—and I believe one can—of an orthodox account of generative phonology, it is to be found in the monumental tome of Noam Chomsky and Morris Halle, *The Sound Pattern of English,* affectionately known as SPE. Here one can find a hearty theoretical discussion of generative phonology and how it differs from other approaches to phonology, an extensive application of the theory to certain aspects of English phonology— notably stress contours and certain vowel alternations, and a brief treatment of the historical evolution of English vowels. To put it mildly, the book has generated ample discussion and dissension.[2] It is still required reading for anyone seriously going into phonology, even though there is no longer a unified doctrine to which all researchers subscribe.

This survey article provides an introduction to the basic assumptions of generative phonology and a discussion of some of the current controversies. We begin by noting that all phonological theories recognize at least two levels of representation—a concrete level encompassing a fairly detailed phonetic

---

[1]Some of the pioneering works in generative phonology are Halle (1959, 1962), Chomsky (1964), and Postal (1968). The grand opus, Chomsky and Halle (1968), provides the codification of the standard theory. An introductory text covering much of the basic material is Schane (1973).

[2]Goyvaerts and Pullum (1976) contains a collection of articles inspired by SPE.

transcription and a more abstract level where phonetic variance is reduced. This two-level system is most easily exemplified by examining the notion of a phoneme and its allophones and by considering the rules for relating one to the other. Phonological theories tend to be in agreement about the nature of the representations at the concrete level. Differences and controversies revolve around the abstract level and the kinds of rules connecting the levels. We then look at the abstract level of representation and the properties of the phonological rules sanctioned within generative phonology. It is these two interrelated aspects of the theory that have led to the two major controversies within phonology: the degree of "abstractness" and the nature of phonological rules. These observations lead to a discussion of some of the proposals for constraining phonological theory.

I. BASIC ASSUMPTIONS
OF GENERATIVE PHONOLOGY

A. Relations Between the Concrete and Abstract Representational Levels

All approaches to phonology have recognized at least two levels of representation: a *concrete* level, where the symbols in the transcription of an utterance depict phonetic detail, and an *abstract* level, where only the essential characteristics of an utterance are indicated. In addition, there is a set of rules relating the two levels.

To give a straightforward example of the two-level approach we can consider the representations of the word *pill*. In English, voiceless stops (*p, t,* and *k*) are phonetically aspirated in certain contexts, such as the beginning of a word; *l* in particular environments is phonetically velarized (the so-called "dark *l*"), one of these contexts being the end of a word. A concrete representation would indicate these phonetic details: $[p^h l l]$.[3] But as the aspiration of voiceless stops and the velarization of *l* are predictable (because one can state the phonetic contexts in which they occur), these traits would not be indicated in the abstract transcription: /pll/. Among the rules linking the two levels of representation are those stating the environments for aspiration and velarization.

Because each language has a mass of phonetic detail and because languages do differ from one another in their phonetics, it is understandable that such

---

[3]Standard notation is generally followed throughout. Concrete or phonetic representations are enclosed in square brackets; the abstract (i.e., phonemic) representations discussed in this section are placed between diagonal bars. In the phonetic notation a superscript *h* represents aspiration and a stroke through *l* indicates velarization.

differences would show up in transcriptions—hence the need for concrete representations. But what about abstract representations? Are they really necessary or are they a mere academic exercise in extracting redundancy? It is precisely such representations that constitute the very foundation of phonology (as opposed to phonetics per se).

Abstract representations capture essential aspects of how sounds are structured in a language. To illustrate this point let us develop further our previous example. As already noted, English voiceless stops are phonetically aspirated in certain environments. One of these contexts, however, is *not* after *s*, so that in this position stops are unaspirated—compare *pill* [pʰIl] with *spill* [spIl]. Precisely because aspiration (or the lack of it) is predictable, we have seen that the abstract representation is not concerned with this detail; therefore, at this level *pill* and *spill* have as their representations /pIl/ and /spIl/ respectively. Now the interesting point is that differing segments in the concrete representations—viz. the initial segment of *pill* [pʰ] and the second segment of *spill* [p]—turn out to be the same in their abstract representations: /p/.

Indeed, phonologists are willing to go a step further and to claim psychological reality for the two levels. Failure, for example, to aspirate in the appropriate contexts may be perceived by speakers of English as a possible source of nonnative pronunciation. Hence, there is an "awareness" of phonetic detail, which is what the concrete representation intends to capture. On the other hand, because [pʰ] and [p] occur in complementary environments (or else in free variation, such as at the end of the word) speakers "conceive" of these segments as manifestations of a single entity; it is this entity alone which in their minds serves to differentiate lexical items—e.g. /pIl/ is opposed to /tIl/ in the same way that /spIl/ is opposed to /stIl/. In fact, the basis of our standard orthography is a representation where predictable phonetic detail is not shown.[4]

The two-level system that we have just outlined represents an approach to phonology that was dominant in American linguistics during the structuralist era of the 1940s and 1950s.[5] The abstract level is known as the *phonemic*, and the concrete as the *phonetic*. The invariant entities of the phonemic representation are called *phonemes*, and there are rules for mapping each

---

[4]Most standard orthographies, due to complicated historical factors, are fairly complex systems; they are not of the simple "phonemic" type (as described in this section), even though spelling reformers have frequently advocated "phonemic" orthography. Note, though, that the spelling reformers do not ask for special symbols for depicting phonetic detail, such as aspiration in English.

[5]Joos (1957) is a collection of articles from this period. A good number of the papers deal specifically with phonemic theory.

phoneme into one or more *allophones*, the predictable phonetic variants of a phoneme.[6]

It is not unfair to characterize the phonemic representations of the structuralists as redundant-free phonetic representations, where the extraction of redundancy depends exclusively on phonological information: The choice of an allophone is due to: (1) its position within the word; (2) the nature of a neighboring segment; or (3) the occurrence of a prosodic feature. Some of the contexts for the presence or absence of aspiration in English illustrate these different phonological environments: (1) aspiration occurs in the word initially (position within the word); (2) it does not occur after *s* (nature of a neighboring segment); and (3) it occurs before a stressed vowel (due to a prosodic feature).

B. Influence of Higher Linguistic Structure on Phonological Representation

Morphological, syntactic, or semantic information was generally not permissible in determining phonemic representations. Within generative phonology, on the other hand, one has recourse to such information. Consequently, the abstract representations of generative phonology will not necessarily be the same as those posited by the phonemicists. To illustrate this difference in abstract representations, let us consider the morphologically related forms *electric* and *electricity*. These words have /əlɛktrIk/ and /əlɛtrIsIti/ as their respective phonemic representations. The final consonant of the stem has the realizations /k/ (/əlɛktrIk/) and /s/ (/əlɛktrIs/); the latter is found before suffixes beginning with /I/. Let us entertain the idea that since /k/ and /s/ are variants here (we are dealing with the same stem), it should be possible to represent them at the abstract level as a unique segment, which we shall assume to be *k*. Then we would have as our abstract representations #ɛlɛktrIk# and #ɛlɛktrIk+Iti#.[7] These representations explicitly show that

---

[6]Within generative phonology, the abstract representations of the structuralists have been variously referred to as taxonomic phonemic (Chomsky, 1964), autonomous phonemic (Postal, 1968) or classical phonemic (Schane, 1971), in contradistinction to systematic phonemic, the abstract representations of generative phonology. Since I shall not be using the latter expression (instead I shall employ *underlying representation*), I shall designate all the former simply as "phonemic." Some of the earlier writings of generative phonologists (Halle, 1959; Chomsky, 1964; Postal, 1968) denied the relevance of phonemic representations for phonological theory. In particular, Chomsky demonstrated that many of the methodological procedures for establishing phonemes, when applied rigorously, would not always yield the desired results. However, Schane (1971) discusses how the notion of phoneme (i.e. surface contrast) might be incorporated into generative phonology.

[7]These abstract representations are not to be equated with phonemic ones. Certain boundary symbols are included in the transcriptions: # denotes the beginning or the end of a word, and + separates affixes from stems or other affixes.

what we consider to be the same stem has the same abstract characterization. Whereas in phonemic theory, we were able, for example, to group [pʰ] and [p] as allophones of a single phoneme /p/, we cannot within that theory state that *k* and *s* are variants of the same phoneme precisely because /k/ and /s/ are already recognized as separate phonemes in English. Furthermore, it is not the case that *k* always becomes *s* when followed by *I*, for most of the time in this context these two segments are in contrast (and hence separate phonemes)—for example, *kit* and *sit*. The change takes place between certain kinds of stems and suffixes. In particular, it occurs in the Latinate part of the vocabulary—e.g., *fanatic, fanaticism*. Words of Greek origin do not undergo this alternation—e.g., *monarch, monarchy*—nor do other non-Latinate forms—e.g., *panic, panicky*. (Note how the spelling deals with the nonalternation.)

Because generative phonology permits access to morphological information, #ɛlɛktrIk# and #ɛlɛktrIk+Iti# are acceptable abstract representations. However, in order to get from the underlying form #ɛlɛktrIk+Iti# to the "surface" form [əlɛktrIsIti] we will need to apply the rule which converts certain occurrences of *k* to *s* when followed by a suffix beginning with *I*.[8]

Another case of this phenomenon is a classic example from German. There are two different words [bunt], one being a noun in the nominative case with the meaning "league" and the other an adjective meaning "colorful." Now when the noun appears in the dative case (where the stem is followed by a vocalic suffix) the stem final consonant is voiced—[bundə]. The adjective too has a special form where a vocalic suffix is added; however the stem final consonant does not vary—[buntə]. Now it is evident that [buntə] and [bundə] contrast so that the difference here is phonemic. Hence *t* and *d* are separate phonemes in German and this distinction would be indicated in a phonemic transcription—/buntə/ and /bundə/. But we would also like to say that [bundə] "league" (dative) and [bunt] "league" (nominative), because they have the same root, should have the same abstract representation for that root. Their forms would be #bund+ə# and #bund#, respectively (as opposed to #bunt+ə# and #bunt# for the two forms of the adjective). But because [bund] is not an acceptable surface form in German, we must apply to underlying #bund# a rule devoicing the word-final consonant.

What is interesting about this German example is that [bunt], a unique representation at the phonetic level, has two different representations at the

---

[8]A "surface" form in generative phonology is the representation resulting from the application of all the phonological rules. Ideally these are concrete representations exhibiting fine phonetic detail. However, because most generative analyses have been concerned with accounting for alternation (such as *electric, electricity*), rules providing phonetic detail (i.e., the allophonic rules of phonemics) are conspicuously lacking. Hence, the derived representations are frequently reminiscent of phonemic transcriptions (Schane, 1971).

abstract level—#bunt# and #bund#—depending on which *morpheme* is involved. (Words are composed of one or more morphemes—i.e., stems, prefixes, suffixes, inflectional endings, etc. Underlying #bund# contains a single morpheme, whereas #bund+ə# is composed of two.) Now, within phonemics, abstract representations such as #bunt# and #bund# would not be sanctioned, precisely because in word-final position [t] and [d] are never in contrast. Furthermore, most phonemicists maintained that from a phonemic representation one should be able to determine uniquely the phonetic representation (up to free variation), and conversely from a phonetic representation one should arrive at a unique phonemic one, a condition known as *bi-uniqueness*. However, if there is no recourse to morphological information (which the phonemicists did not allow), there is no way of knowing whether the abstract representation for phonetic [bunt] should be #bund# or #bunt#. Because of this limitation homophonous forms must have the same representation within phonemic theory: /bunt/ would be the only acceptable abstract representation in that framework.[9]

The English and German examples have dealt with morphemes showing alternation. In generative phonology one tries to give a unique abstract representation to the various alternants of a morpheme. Alternants are separately listed only in cases of *suppletion* (i.e., where there is no systematic basis for the alternation), such as in the case of *go* and *went*. For the alternations presented so far, the underlying form has been equivalent to one of the alternants, but without fine phonetic (i.e., allophonic) detail. In English, where there was alternation between *k* and *s*, the underlying representation contained *k*; and in German, for the alternation between a voiced and voiceless segment, the voiced one was underlying. However, there are cases where no alternant can be considered as basic and where all the alternants have to be derived from an underlying form coinciding with none of them. Yawelmani, a dialect of the Yokuts language of California, presents a situation of this type.[10]

In Yawelmani there are verb forms with a suffix, *it*.

---

[9]Trubetzkoy (1969), one of the founders of the Prague school of phonology, gave priority to neither *t* nor *d* in arriving at the phonemic representation of [bunt]. He claimed that because voicing does not contrast at the end of a word in German, the phonetic value of voicing is predictable and, therefore, should not be indicated in the phonemic representation. Trubetzkoy employed special symbols, called archiphonemes, for such "neutralizations," e.g., /bunT/, where the archiphoneme *T* indicates suspension of the voicing contrast.

[10]The Yawelmani data and discussion are based on Kuroda (1967) and Kisseberth (1969). In the transcriptions for Yawelmani, a colon indicates that the preceding vowel is long, glottal stop (a consonant similar to the break in voicing in the middle of English *uh-uh*) is symbolized by ʔ, and this same symbol joined by a ligature to a preceding consonant (e.g., $\widehat{t^{?}}$) means that that consonant is glottalized; in Yawelmani, a glottalized consonant functions as a unit segment.

xatit	eat
gopit	take care of an infant
giyit	touch
sa:pit	burn
go:b̡it	take in
me:k⁷it	swallow

If the stem vowel is *u* and there is a suffix beginning with *i* (such as *it*), then the suffix vowel "harmonizes" with the stem vowel and it too becomes *u*.

mutut	swear
hudut	recognize

A rule is therefore required that converts *i* to *u*, whenever the preceding stem vowel is *u*. Following are derivations for *go:bit* and *mutut*, where the operation of this rule can be seen.[11]

	#go:b+it#	#mut+it#
harmony	—	#mut+ut#
	[go:bit]	[mutut]

Unexpectedly we find *u* after certain stems containing long *o*.

⁷o:t͡⁷ut	steal
sudo:k͡⁷ut	remove

Compare these forms with a verb like *go:bit* where the *i* suffix vowel occurs. It appears then that in Yawelmani there are two kinds of *o:*—those that "behave" like *u* because they cause a following vowel to become *u*, and those that "behave" normally. But there is a possible explanation for this phenomenon. Long vowels in Yawelmani have a strange distribution. Only *e:*, *a:*, and *o:* occur on the surface; the expected high vowels *i:* and *u:* are missing. Harmony suggests that the underlying long-vowel system is perhaps more symmetrical, that long high vowels occur, and that those *o:* that trigger harmony are to be derived from underlying *u:*. These long high vowels are not found on the surface (i.e., in derived representations) because in the course of

---

[11]The first line of a derivation is the underlying form. Each subsequent line lists a rule and shows the effects of that rule on the immediately preceding representation. A dash indicates that a rule is not applicable. The final derived representation (after application of all rules), with boundary markers removed, appears in square brackets as the last line of a derivation. As we remarked in footnote 8, the derived representation is not necessarily a detailed phonetic one.

the derivation they have merged with the long mid vowels *e:* and *o:*. The underlying forms for the stems "steal" and "remove" must be *ʔu:t̂ʔ-* and *sudu:k̂ʔ-*, respectively. The rule of harmony will then apply correctly; a subsequent rule will lower *u:* to *o:*. Here is the derivation of [ʔo:t̂ʔut].

	#ʔu:t̂ʔ+it#
harmony	#ʔu:t̂ʔ+ut#
lowering	#ʔo:t̂ʔ+ut#
	[ʔo:t̂ʔut]

There is another phonological process in Yawelmani which supports the existence of long high vowels in underlying representations. Certain verb stems of two syllables—what are called "echo verbs"—have identical vowels, except that the first vowel is short whereas the second one is long.

paxa:tit	mourn
yawa:lit	follow
ʔopo:tit	arise from bed

Other forms appear to be exceptions to the occurrence of identical vowels differing only in length.

hibe:yit	bring water
sudo:k̂ʔut	remove

These forms contain a short high vowel in the first syllable and a long mid vowel in the second, instead of an expected short high vowel in the first and a long high one in the second. Once we recognize that long high vowels appear in underlying representations, even though they are not found on the surface, forms such as [hibe:yit] and [sudo:kʔut] are no longer anomalous. The underlying representations of the stems are *hibi:y-* and *sudu:kʔ-*, where both vowels are now identical except for length. The long vowels will be lowered by the rule noted previously.

Because in echo verbs the first vowel is always a shortened version of the second, this vowel becomes predictable and need not necessarily appear in underlying representations. This means that the underlying representations for the stems of [paxa:tit], [ʔopo:tit], [hibe:yit], and [sudo:k̂ʔut] can be: *pxa:t-*, *ʔpo:t-*, *hbi:y-*, and *sdu:k̂ʔ-*, respectively. Because Yawelmani words never begin with two consonants, the actual statement of the echo rule will be such that it inserts a shortened copy of the long vowel between the two consonants of the initial cluster.

The form [sudo:k̂ʔut] is particularly fascinating because the underlying *u:* (which never surfaces as such) accounts for two different phenomena—the appearance of short *u* in the first syllable, where echo verbs have identical vowels, and the occurrence of the suffix *ut*, because of harmony with a preceding *u:*.

	#sdu:k̂ʔ+it#
echo	#sudu:k̂ʔ+it#
harmony	#sudu:k̂ʔ+ut#
lowering	#sudo:k̂ʔ+ut#
	[sudo:k̂ʔut]

We see then that underlying representations may be quite different from derived ones. Yet this difference is not to be had without cost, for whenever an underlying representation "deviates" from the corresponding phonetic one, rules are required to get back to the phonetic form. As the underlying representation increases in "abstractness," the number of rules also increases. Because there is little point in having abstract representations just for the sake of abstractness, one must show that the additional abstractness and the accompanying rules are well motivated. There should be an overall simplification in the grammar. One such simplifying effect is the situation where morphemes show phonological alternation: The lexical representation of a morpheme is simplified if it has a unique underlying form. Yet the rules that produce the various alternants of that morpheme should not just "crank out" the appropriate surface forms but rather should "capture" significant processes operating in the language. In other words, the rules should tell a lot about how the language works. Abstract representations then have an explanatory function: What may appear to be an anomaly on the surface has an explanation at the abstract level. In Yawelmani, it is the underlying long high vowels that explain the peculiar surface manifestations of suffix vowels and of vowels of echo verbs.

C. The Ordering of Phonological Rules

That there may be a high degree of abstractness in underlying representations is one of the principal characteristics of generative phonology. Another important trait has to do with the rules relating abstract representations to their phonetic forms: Many of the phonological rules are *ordered*. What this means is that phonological rules do not apply simultaneously to underlying forms converting them to their surface representations, but rather rules apply sequentially so that the representation resulting from a rule becomes the input to the next rule. Hence, in a derivation there may be several intermediate representations between the underlying one and the final derived one.

An examination of the previously cited derivation of [sudo:k̂ʔut] (from underlying #sdu:k̂ʔ+it#) reveals that some of the rules must be applied in a strict order. In particular, the lowering rule must follow the rules of echo and of harmony. If lowering were to apply first, the underlying *u:* of the stem would be immediately converted to *o:*. Because *u:* would no longer be present, the echoed vowel would show up as *o* (instead of *u*), and harmony could not take place; one would obtain the incorrect form *[sodo:k̂ʔit].[12]

Notice, however, that the echo and harmony rules are not really ordered with respect to each other. Either order of application produces the same result. These two rules do not interact. Rather each rule independently makes reference to the underlying *u:* vowel. Consequently, phonological rules are only partially ordered. Rules are ordered, in the technical sense of the word, if application of the rules in one order results, for some forms, in a different ouput from their application in some other order. Rules are not really ordered if different orders of application produce identical derived forms. Of course, in a derivation, one is compelled to place all rules in some sequence, but this should not be confused with the technical sense of ordered rules. Note that between the underlying and the derived representations, there may be several intermediate representations, one for each of the rules applying to the form in question. These intermediate forms are not of particular theoretical interest. Of the many representatins occurring in a derivation, the important ones are the first and the last—the *underlying* and the *derived*.

Several rules may be ordered with respect to one another. In Yawelmani, long and short vowels normally contrast. However, before two successive consonants, only short vowels appear. We can compare the verb forms cited previously, where the suffix is *it* or *ut*, with a different set of forms, where the suffix is *hin* or *hun*.

xatit	xathin	eat
sa:pit	saphin	burn
gopit	gophin	take care of an infant
go:bit	gobhin	take in
mutut	muthun	swear
ʔo:t̂ʔut	ʔot̂ʔhun	steal

These data illustrate the operation of a rule that shortens long vowels before two consonants. Following is the derivation of [ʔot̂ʔhun].

	#ʔu:t̂ʔ+hin#
harmony	#ʔu:t̂ʔ+hun#
lowering	#ʔo:t̂ʔ+hun#
shortening	#ʔot̂ʔ+hun#
	[ʔot̂ʔhun]

---

[12]An asterisk preceding a form marks it as incorrect. This use of the asterisk should not be confused with its function in historical linguistics, where it indicates an unattested or reconstructed form.

Note that all three rules are crucially ordered. The lowering of long high vowels has to follow harmony for the reasons noted previously. Vowel shortening must follow lowering, for if *u:* were shortened first, it could not be subsequently lowered to *o*, as short vowels are never lowered.

One of the strongest arguments for ordered rules is the case where a rule applies to a structure created through the operation of a previous rule. By allowing the output of one rule to become an input to another rule, one often obviates the necessity of repeating similar environments. As an example, consider the following additional data from Yawelmani.

pa?tit	pa?ithin	fight
?ilkit	?ilikhin	sing
?utyut	?utuyhun	fall

The forms in the first column show that these verb stems terminate in two consonants—*pa?t-*, *?ilk-*, and *?uty-*. Yawelmani does not permit a sequence of more than two consonants word internally. Such a sequence would arise if the stem final consonants were to be followed by a suffix beginning with a consonant, such as *hin* (column 2). To break up this impermissible cluster, there is a rule that inserts the vowel *i* between the two stem consonants when they are followed by a third consonant. For example, this vowel-insertion rule applies to underlying *pa?t+hin* to yield [pa?ithin]. Note however, that the form [?utuyhun] has as its inserted vowel *u*. It is evident that *u* occurs because the stem vowel is also *u*; that is, harmony is at play here. Just as harmony converts the *i* of the suffix *it* to *u*, likewise it affects an inserted *i* also causing it to become *u*.

	#?uty+hin#
insertion	#?utiy+hin#
harmony	#?utuy+hun#
	[?utuyhun]

If there are ordered rules, the output of vowel insertion, which uniquely inserts *i*, can subsequently be harmonized to a preceding *u*. If rules are not ordered it would be necessary to say that *u* (rather than *i*) is inserted whenever the stem vowel is *u*, a statement that partially duplicates the harmony rule.

The preceding example illustrates a rule modifying representations in some way so that a later rule will apply to those changed representations. Whenever two rules are ordered in this fashion, they are said to be in a *feeding* relationship. That is, the first rule "feeds" (i.e., creates additional inputs for) the second rule. There are also instances where the first rule changes the representations so that a later rule will *not* apply. Rules so ordered are in a *bleeding* relationship, for the first rule "bleeds" (i.e., eliminates some of the potential inputs for) the second rule. The Yawelmani vowel-insertion rule interacts in this way with the vowel-shortening rule discussed earlier. There are verb stems whose underlying forms terminate in two consonants preceded by a long vowel: *ʔa:ml-* "help," *ho:tn-* "take the scent." When these stems are combined with the suffix *it*, the stem vowel will become shortened because it is followed by two consonants: [ʔamlit], [hotnit]. However, the vowel is not shortened whenever the stem is followed by a suffix beginning with a consonant, for with three consecutive consonants the vowel *i* must be inserted between the first two. Because of this insertion the vowel of the stem will no longer be followed immediately by two consonants and hence need not undergo shortening.

	#ʔa:ml+hin#	#ʔa:ml+it#
insertion	#ʔa:mil+hin#	—
shortening	—	#ʔaml+it#
	[ʔa:milhin]	[ʔamlit]

Again if the rules were not ordered one would have to complicate the grammar. An additional constraint would be required on the vowel-shortening rule, such that vowels are not shortened if the two consonants are followed by a third one. A constraint of this type seems counterintuitive.

Kiparsky (1968a) has shown that one important way in which dialects of the same language can differ is in their rule ordering. Two dialects may have the same underlying forms and even the same rules, but the rules are applied in a different order. In Finnish, the vowel sequence *ee* diphthongizes to *ie*—for example, *vee* > *vie*. Certain medial voiced continuants have been lost, thus introducing new occurrences of *ee*—for example, *teɣe* > *tee*. It is the preservation of this "historical" order that is found in Standard Finnish where there are surface occurrences of *ee*. This dialect then has the rule ordering:

1. diphthongization
2. loss of medial voiced continuants

However, in other dialects of Finnish, the "new" occurrences of *ee*, which came about after the loss of the medial consonants, in turn became diphthongized—for example, *teɣe* > *tee* > *tie*. In these "innovative" dialects the rule ordering has become:

1. loss of medial voiced continuants
2. diphthongization

Notice that in the innovative dialects the two rules have rearranged themselves into a feeding relationship. The significance of this change will be reconsidered further on.

Fairly abstract underlying representations and ordered rules are perhaps the most conspicuous distinguishing traits of generative phonology. To a certain extent the two go hand in hand. Underlying forms of a high degree of abstraction are far removed from their corresponding surface representations. Many rules are then required to connect the two levels. Because there are complex interrelationships among the various processes and interdependent environments, the actual statement of the processes can be simplified if one can take advantage of such properties of rules as feeding and bleeding relations, which entail of course rule ordering. Contrast this situation with the allophonic rules of phonemics, which are rarely, if ever, ordered, but where the abstract (phonemic) representations are considerably less removed from the phonetic.

D. Distinctive Features and Formal Notation

There are two other characteristics often associated with generative phonology—*distinctive features* and *formal notation*. Segments are not viewed as indivisible entities but are further analyzable into complexes of features. That segments are composed of phonetic properties is by no means novel to generative phonology, for phoneticians have always operated with this assumption. Standard articulatory phonetics, for example, classifies [p] as a voiceless bilabial stop. It is only because sounds are composed of features that we are able to make generalized statements and to refer to entire classes of sounds, such as statements to the effect that in English it is the voiceless stops that are aspirated in certain contexts, or in Yawelmani it is the long high vowels that do not occur on the surface. However, there are some special characteristics about the distinctive features of generative phonology. At the underlying level the values of all features are claimed to be binary—a segment is either [+voiced] or [-voiced] (i.e., voiceless), [+nasal] or [-nasal] (i.e., oral), etc. [13] It is further maintained that the features are universal—that is, they are adequate for characterizing the abstract and surface representations of any language and are capable of describing the natural classes of segments to which phonological rules make reference (i.e., the generalized statements). Finally, the features are part and parcel of the formal notation.

---

[13] Jakobson first made the claim that all features are binary at the classificatory level (see Jakobson, Fant, and Halle, 1963, and for further discussion, Halle, 1957). Ladefoged (1975) has criticized the strict binarity of all features, particularly features representing points along a scale, such as vowel height. It should be evident that a binary system is inadequate for capturing any degree of phonetic detail. Within such a system we can indicate whether or not an attribute is present, but we cannot show *how much* of it is there. Generative phonology recognizes this limitation and at the phonetic level it allows a feature to take on more than two values; these are usually represented by integers. The various values would be supplied by the (allophonic) rules for depicting fine phonetic detail.

The formal notation is basically a system for writing phonological rules. It is intended to reflect "significant" generalizations operating in languages. Distinctive features enable one to refer to whole classes of segments and to state concisely changes affecting those segments. There are also special symbols for indicating boundary phenomena. Other notational devices, such as parentheses and braces, allow what would otherwise be separate rules to be grouped as subparts of a single rule. The following rule for English states that voiceless stops are aspirated in two contexts—word initially and before a stressed vowel.

$$
\begin{bmatrix} -\text{sonorant} \\ -\text{continuant} \\ -\text{voiced} \end{bmatrix} \rightarrow [\text{+aspirated}]/ \begin{Bmatrix} \#\underline{\qquad} \\ \underline{\qquad} \begin{bmatrix} +\text{syllabic} \\ +stress \end{bmatrix} \end{Bmatrix}
$$

The complex of features to the left of the arrow defines a *natural class*, the class of voiceless stops.[14] The feature to the right of the arrow shows how this class of segments is changed—its members become aspirated. The context where this change occurs is found to the right of the diagonal slash. The braces indicate that there are two environments for the change—whenever there is a word boundary to the left or a stressed vowel to the right. (The latter environment should be modified so as not to apply to stops preceded by *s*.)

The notation is supposed to reflect directly the complexity of the phonological change: A more "general" statement should require fewer symbols than a less "general" one. For example, it is a more general (i.e., more inclusive) process for all voiceless stops to become aspirated than for *p* alone to do so. This difference in generality is reflected in the notation as it would require additional features (additional, that is, to those listed above to the left of the arrow) to specify *p*. By the same token, it is "simpler" for voiceless stops to become aspirated in two different contexts than it is for them to become aspirated in only one context and for something else entirely different to happen to them in a second context. Use of the brace notation requires fewer symbols to state the former situation.

This *evaluation metric*—that the complexity of the notation should reflect the complexity of the description—has played an important role in the development of generative phonology. Given two descriptions of the same set of data the analysis that utilizes the fewest formal symbols ideally should be preferred. Yet it is easy enough to construct cases where a correlation in complexity between notation and process does not hold. For example, a rule that causes all consonants to become voiceless word finally would require

---

[14]The sonorant consonants include nasals, liquids (*l* and *r*), and semivowels (*y* and *w*); nonsonorants (obstruents) comprise stops, continuants (such as *s*), and afficates (such as *j*). In the distinctive-feature framework, a stop is defined as a consonant that is nonsonorant and noncontinuant. Vowels are classified as syllabic segments.

fewer symbols (and hence ought to be more "general," for it includes more segments) than the rules affecting only obstruents. Yet such a rule, if possible, would be an extremely rare one among the languages of the world; it would certainly be less "natural" than the rule for the devoicing of obstruents. Because the notation alone is not sufficient for distinguishing between the "naturalness" of different types of segments and of phonological processes, the evaluation metric has been supplemented by other devices, such as *markedness conditions.* The notion of markedness dates back to the Prague school phonologists. It has been reintroduced by Chomsky and Halle (1968).

Markedness is intended to reflect differences in the internal complexity of segments. Two segments can be differentiated by considering one of them to be *unmarked* for a particular feature and the other one to be *marked* for that feature. Important to the notion of markedness is the assumption that the unmarked value represents the less complex, the normal, or the expected state, whereas the marked value of a feature contributes additional complexity to a segment. For example, it is claimed that for obstruent consonants, voicelessness is the unmarked state. To be sure, voiced obstruents readily occur, but they are judged to be more complex (i.e., marked). On the other hand, it is extemely rare for sonorant consonants to be voiceless; for them, the unmarked situation is the voiced one. Neutralization rules tend to make segments less marked. Such a rule is the one in German for devoicing word-final obstruents. Thus, when one of these voiced segments becomes voiceless, it goes from marked to unmarked status. A rule that would devoice all final consonants would be, according to markedness theory, less favored than the German rule, even though superficially it appears to be more general. Such a rule would devoice sonorant consonants as well, causing them to become more marked.

II. CURRENT CONTROVERSIES IN PHONOLOGY

We have mentioned several properties frequently associated with generative phonology: abstract underlying representations, ordered phonological rules, distinctive features, and formal notation. Phonologists today, regardless of their particular persuasion, are pretty much in agreement that it is desirable to have available a universal set of distinctive features for referring to classes of segments and to have at hand a rigorous notation for stating phonological rules. Whether or not there should be an evaluation metric intimately tied with the formal notation is a separate debatable matter. Consequently, distinctive features and a formal notation are no longer necessarily the exclusive domain of generative phonology. The really essential characteristics are the abstract underlying representations and the ordered phonological rules, aspects of which have been under serious question.

A. The Abstractness of Phonological Representation

We have noted that there can be considerable "distance" between underlying and surface representations. The more "removed" the former is from the latter, the more phonological rules are required to connect the two levels. There is little point, however, in setting up complex underlying representations if they cannot be properly motivated. Many phonologists feel that it is important to constrain underlying representations so as to eliminate "clever" analyses whose linguistic justification may be highly dubious. Kiparsky (1968b) was one of the first to propose a constraint on underlying representations—what he called the *strong alternation condition*. He suggested that underlying distinctions should not be set up unless they are realized somewhere as surface distinctions. Such a constraint would severely restrict the types of segments appearing in underlying representations. The advantage would be that underlying distinctions could not be arbitrarily posited, only to be "neutralized" at the surface level; underlying contrasts would also have to be manifested, at least in some of their occurrences, as the same contrasts on the surface. Now the strong alternation condition would effectively rule out the analysis proposed for Yawelmani, where the long high vowels *i:* and *u:*, posited in underlying representations, are subsequently lowered everywhere to *e:* and *o:*, respectively. The reason why the strong alternation condition would exclude *i:* and *u:* as possible underlying vowels is that there are no *surface* alternations between i: and *e:* or between *u:* and *o:*, precisely because on the surface only *e:* and *o:* occur.

Let us see how the strong alternation condition would affect the forms [hibe:yit] and [sudo:k͡ʔut], cited previously, whose stems were set up underlyingly as *hbi:y-* and *sdu:k͡ʔ-*. Recall that for an echo verb the first vowel does not appear in the underlying representation, so that the stem begins with two consonants. The echo rule breaks up this consonant cluster by inserting a shortened version of the following vowel. But in surface representations one finds only *hibe:y-* and *sudo:k͡ʔ-* (or else *hibey-* and *sudok͡ʔ-* if vowel shortening occurs). Because there is never any surface alternation between *i:* and *e:* or between *u:* and *o:*, the underlying representations could not contain the high vowels and instead would have the vowels occurring in surface representations, thus *hbe:y-* and *sdo:k͡ʔ-*. If the latter are the underlying representations, then there is of course no need for the rule of vowel lowering, as there would be no *i:* or *u:* to be lowered. Such rules, which convert a segment to some other segment everywhere—that is, in every possible context—are known as *rules of absolute neutralization*. Thus, the strong alternation condition also has the effect of disallowing rules of absolute neutralization.

Let us compare the Yawelmani case with the German neutralization, where word-final voiced obstruents merged with the corresponding voiceless ones. There underlying #bund# "league" and #bunt# "colorful" both surfaced as

[bunt]. Yet the former is a perfectly acceptable underlying representation and even though the final *d* merges with *t* this merger does not violate the strong alternation condition. The reason is that *d* and *t* both occur on the surface: [bundə] "league"; [buntə] "colorful." In fact, the same root has both of them occurring as variant surface forms: [bundə] "league" (dative); [bunt] "league" (nominative). Furthermore the rule that devoices the *d* of underlying #bund# is not a rule of absolute neutralization. The change does not take place everywhere, but only in one specific context—in word-final position. Another example should help clarify this point. In Yawelmani [mutut] had #mut+it# as its underlying representation. The harmony rule than converted the vowel of the suffix from *i* to *u*. This again is not a case of absolute neutralization, for the change does not occur unconditionally but only when the preceding stem vowel is *u*. Hence the vowel of the suffix will alternate, and indeed both *it* and *ut* are found on the surface.

Given the strong alternation condition, which requires that a form such as [sudo:k̂ʔut] have as its underlying representation #sdo:k̂ʔ+it#, how are we to account for the final shape of the suffix as well as the quality of what will be the first vowel of the stem? How does this form differ from [ʔopo:tit], where the underlying representation appears to be similar (that is, the long vowel of the stem is also *o:*)—#ʔpo:t+it#? One solution is to say that there are two types of *o:*—(1) a normal *o:* such as is found in #ʔpo:t+it#, which in echo verbs has as the first vowel a shortened version of itself and is compatible with suffixes containing the vowel *i*; and (2) a "special" *o:*, as in #sdo:k̂ʔ+it#, which governs *u* in the first syllable of echo verbs and causes a following *i* to become *u*. This solution can be formally implemented by marking all *o:* with an arbitrary diacritic—let us call it [X]. Furthermore, we shall say that all the normal *o:* are marked as [−X], whereas the "special" *o:* will bear the value [+X]. We can then say that in echo verbs the first vowel is normally a shortened version of the second, but if the second vowel bears the diacritic mark [+X] then the first vowel must be high. Because

$$
\begin{array}{l}
\text{+X} \\
\text{#sdo:}\widehat{\text{k}ʔ}\text{+it#}
\end{array}
$$

contains the "special" *o:*—marked with the diacritic [+X]—this would account for the ultimate occurrence of *u* in the first syllable. On the other hand,

$$
\begin{array}{l}
\text{−X} \\
\text{#}ʔ\text{po:t+it#}
\end{array}
$$

has the "normal" *o:*—marked with the diacritic [−X]; hence there will be the expected duplicate short vowel in the first syllable. In addition, the vowel-harmony rule will need to be modified. It must now state that *i* becomes *u* either when the preceding stem vowel is *u* (this part of the rule is required for occurrences of short *u*, such as #mut+it# → [mutut]) or when there is a long rounded vowel marked [+X]. The second condition will account for the *u* suffix vowel of [sudo:k͡ʔut].

Diacritic features are standard fare within generative phonology. They are needed whenever a phonological process applies to certain forms but is inapplicable to other grammatically similar forms where the environmental conditions appear to be met. Earlier we observed that the rule in English that converts *k* to *s* applies only to a particular class of words; hence the forms that undergo this rule would need to be marked by a diacritic, and the rule would apply only to those forms specified for the appropriate value of the diacritic. The use of diacritic features is the formal means for sorting lexical items into various arbitrary classes for the operation of certain phonological rules. Frequently there is a historical explanation for the particular lexical classes. Thus, the rule changing *k* to *s* applies to Latinate forms. One consequence of the strong alternation condition is an increase in the use of diacritics in phonological rules.

A "concrete" analysis of Yawelmani—use of diacritics and concomitantly less abstract underlying forms—has been advocated by Vennemann (1974) in the context of his "natural generative phonology." Proponents of "natural" phonology claim that many of the underlying representations of "standard" generative phonology are much too abstract. They accept then the basic assumptions of the strong alternation condition as one type of constraint for rendering underlying representations more concrete. We have noted that because there are no long high vowels underlyingly in this analysis, there would not be the need for a lowering rule, a rule of absolute neutralization. However, the absence of absolute neutralization renders more complex the statement for echo verbs and for the harmony rule, because one needs to flag with a diacritic those *e:* and *o:* that "behave" as though they were high vowels. This diacritical information needs to be built into the statement of both processes in addition to whatever purely phonological environments are required in the "abstract" solution. Hence the "concrete" analysis entails additional complication in the rules.

To justify the concrete analysis, Vennemann argues that the abstract solution makes incorrect predictions about possible future sound change in Yawelmani. It is recognized by historical linguists that in the course of time phonological rules may be modified or even lost entirely. Given the abstract solution with the high vowels *i:* and *u:* and with a rule of absolute neutralization (the lowering rule), we might suppose that this rule could eventually drop out of the language. If this were to happen then Yawelmani would actually have long high vowels on the surface as there would no longer be a lowering rule to merge them with *e:* and *o:*. Vennemann is correct in noting that this particular change woud be a highly unlikely state of affairs. He then states that rule loss in the concrete solution predicts a more plausible evolution. Because the additional environments with diacritics add complexity to the statement of echo verbs and the harmony process, it is to be expected that there would be a loss of this excess baggage. As a result, both processes would become conditioned by the actually occurring surface vowels. To support this possibility Vennemann cites data (Newman, 1944) from Chukchansi, a dialect closely related to Yawelmani, where echo, but not harmony, is based on the "new" long lowered root vowels.

| Yawelmani: | hibe:yit | sudo:k²ut |
| Chukchansi: | hebe:yit | sodo:k²ut |

The differences between Yawelmani and Chukchansi can be accommodated within the abstract solution by assuming that there is a difference in rule ordering. We already noted that dialects may differ on the basis of the order in which the rules are applied. In Yawelmani both echo and harmony precede the rule of lowering. In Chukchansi harmony still precedes lowering but echo would have to take place after lowering.

Kiparsky (1971) has claimed that when rule reordering occurs, the new order leads to more "transparent" surface forms. Forms are *transparent* (as opposed to *opaque*) whenever the effects of the rule are readily observable on the surface. In Chukchansi, the echoed vowel is an exact (shortened) duplicate of the second vowel; in Yawelmani, the echoed vowel starts out that way but the similarity is subsequently obscured by the lowering rule. In Chukchansi, then, the effects of the echo rule are transparent, whereas in Yawelmani they are opaque.

We observed previously that it would be extremely unlikely for the lowering rule to be lost and for long high vowels to occur suddenly on the surface. This is not to say that rules of absolute neutralization are never lost, but if they are, there would be at the same time restructuring in the underlying forms. The underlying forms would become closer to their surface realizations. "Historical" explanations then, based on projection of future change, are equally plausible in both analyses—standard generative phonology or natural phonology. Such arguments by themselves are not always compelling for choosing between two alternative analyses.

In the quest for constraining excessive abstractness, Vennemann (1974) has made an additional proposal: For morphemes exhibiting alternation, the underlying representation must be equivalent to one of the occurring alternants. There are many situations where this requirement is already met. In Yawelmani the verbal suffix, with alternants *it* and *ut*, has *it* as the underlying representation; in German the morpheme "league" has the alternants *bund* and *bunt*, the former being equivalent to the underlying representation. Standard generative phonology permits also abstract representations coinciding with none of the alternants. Vennemann's proposal, of course, would eliminate these types of representations. However, if this condition were imposed there would be no correct underlying representations for certain undeniable instances of phonological alternation. The following data are from Palauan, spoken in the South Pacific (Flora, 1974):

Present Middle Verb	Future Participle	Future Participle	
	(conservative)	(innovative)	
mə-dáŋəb	dəŋób-l	dəŋəb-áll	"cover opening"
mə-té?əb	tə?ib-l	tə?əb-áll	"pull out"

In Palauan, stress falls on the final vowel if there is a suffix (both future participle forms), but on the penultimate vowel if there is no suffix (the present middle forms). Furthermore, unstressed vowels reduce to schwa. To account for these data the underlying representations of the stems must be:

daŋob   te?ib

The stem is combined with a prefix (present middle) or a suffix (the future participles). Stress is then assigned to the appropriate vowel. Unstressed vowels reduce to schwa: In the present middle the second vowel of the stem becomes schwa, in the conservative future participle it is the first vowel, whereas in the innovative form both vowels reduce. What is significant about these Palauan forms is that the underlying representation of a stem cannot coincide with one of the actually occurring alternants. Rather it is an amalgam of two of them—the first vowel of the present middle and the second vowel of the conservative future participle.

This example demonstrates the untenability of Vennemann's proposal. Notice that Kiparsky's original strong alternation condition does not insist that one of the alternants constitute the underlying representation. The strong alternation condition prohibits postulating underlying segments which never surface anywhere. In the Palauan example, the "full" vowels that are posited in the underlying representations of stems always occur in surface forms although not necessarily in any one form. The strong alternation condition then would permit the segmental composition of an underlying form to be constructed from the segments of its various alternants.

There is a most interesting consequence following from these various proposals for constraining the abstractness of underlying representations: The inventory of underlying segments is a subset of the inventory of occurring surface segments. This is because one cannot posit abstract segments for which there are no actual phonetic correlates.[15]

B. Constraints on Ordering Phonological Rules

We noted previously that highly abstract underlying representations entail ordered rules. It is natural then for one who advocates concrete underlying forms to question the necessity for rule ordering. Vennemann, for example, takes the position that phonological rules are unordered and that they apply any time the relevant conditions are met. A truly interesting proposal has been offered by Koutsoudas, Sanders, and Noll (1971). Although they accept the abstract underlying representations of generative phonology, they claim that phonological rules do not need to be *extrinsically* ordered. Rules are extrinsically ordered if (1) applying the rules in different orders leads to different outputs for some forms, and (2) no matter what order is tried every rule applies to some form or other. If rules can logically apply in only one particular order, then they are *intrinsically* ordered. For example, assume that in a language the main word stress is always introduced by rule (that is, stress does not occur in underlying representations). Assume further that certain stressed vowels become diphthongized. These two rules are ordered intrinsically because the diphthongization rule will never apply anywhere unless the stress rule has previously assigned stress.

Now, the no-ordering hypothesis by Koutsoudas, Sanders, and Noll concerns extrinsic ordering. They argue that the proper ordering can be determined from a few general principles. In essence, for a given form, rules apply whenever they can: They apply simultaneously if possible; otherwise they apply sequentially. These principles favor *nonbleeding* and *feeding* relations. Rules that apply simultaneously are either noninteracting or if they interact they are in a nonbleeding relation. Rules apply sequentially whenever they are in a feeding relation. Let us see how these principles handle some of the ordering constraints established for Yawelmani. Repeated here is the derivation of [ʔotʔhun] from underlying #ʔuːtʔhin#.

	#ʔuːtʔ+hin#
harmony	#ʔuːtʔ+hun#
lowering	#ʔoːtʔ+hun#
shortening	#ʔotʔ+hun#
	[ʔotʔhun]

---

[15]There is a venerable tradition to the claim that the set of underlying segments is drawn from the set of surface segments. McCawley (1967) has attributed this view of underlying structure to the notable Americanist Edward Sapir, considered by some as the "granddaddy" of generative phonology.

Recall that the application of all three rules is critically ordered. Long high vowel lowering has to follow harmony. If *u:* were lowered first, it would become *o:*, and the suffix vowel could not then become *u*. That is, application of long high vowel lowering first would bleed harmony. The rule of vowel shortening has to follow high vowel lowering for a similar reason. If *u:* were shortened first, it could not subsequently be lowered to *o*, since short vowels are never lowered. Again the incorrect order involves a bleeding relationship. The ordering actually exemplified here then is the converse—namely, *nonbleeding*. But observe that if one permits simultaneous rule application, then all three rules can apply instantaneously to the underlying representation #ʔuːtʔ+hin#. Harmony allows the vowel of the suffix to agree with the original stem vowel; at the same time the rules of long high vowel lowering and of vowel shortening will lower and shorten the underlying stem vowel. We see then how nonbleeding order can be translated into simultaneous application. In Yawelmani there are also situations where the no-ordering proposal would require rules to apply sequentially. Earlier we noted the derivation of [ʔutuyhun] from underlying #ʔuty+hin#.

	#ʔuty+hin#
insertion	#ʔutiy+hin#
harmony	#ʔutuy+hun#
	[ʔutuyhun]

The rule of vowel insertion uniquely inserts *i* between the stem consonants whenever they are followed by a third consonant. The harmony rule then changes the inserted *i* to *u*. Because the insertion rule creates a new set of inputs for the harmony rule, these rules are in a *feeding* relationship. Notice that these rules cannot possibly apply simultaneously, for obviously, the *i* has to be created before it can be modified to *u*. The equivalence then between feeding order and sequential application becomes apparent. Note that the harmony rule applies in two different places—to the inserted *i* and to the vowel of the suffix *hin*. Feeding order has relevance only for the former occurrence.

Kiparsky (1968a) had already noted that where dialects differ in the order of their rules, the innovating dialects reorder the rules such that feeding and nonbleeding relations are established. What both of these types have in common is that rule application tends to be maximized—that is, rules apply to as many forms as possible. Kiparsky referred to feeding and nonbleeding as the "unmarked" orders. However, there are cases of reordering not covered by the principle of maximal applicability. To handle these situations Kiparsky has proposed the notions of rule transparency and opacity (as discussed previously). Kiparsky's original observations about feeding and nonbleeding orders pertained to historical change. Koutsoudas, Sanders, and

Noll claim that these concepts also determine how rules are to be ordered in a synchronic description.

To be sure there are situations where rules must enter into either *bleeding* or *nonfeeding* relations, orders that are not accommodated by the proposal. How would one deal with such cases?

An example of bleeding order is the relationship between the rules of vowel shortening and of vowel insertion in Yawelmani. The interaction of these two rules is seen in the derivations of [ʔa:milhin] and [ʔamlit], where the underlying representation of the stem is *ʔa:ml*.

	#ʔa:ml+hin#	#ʔa:ml+it#
insertion	#ʔa:mil+hin#	—
shortening	—	#ʔaml+it#
	[ʔa:milhin]	[ʔamlit]

Recall that vowels are shortened before two consonants. However, the prior application of vowel insertion in the case of [ʔa:milhin] destroys the environment for vowel shortening and hence prevents the rule from applying. In other words, vowel insertion bleeds vowel shortening. Now according to the no-ordering hypothesis, rules should apply simultaneously if possible. Accordingly, the stem vowel would be shortened at the same time that a vowel is inserted to break up the consonant cluster. The result of simultaneous application would be the incorrect *[ʔamilhin].

Perry (1972), working within the same framework, handles this problem by claiming that whenever a bleeding situation arises, one (or more) of the rules must have been improperly formulated. He notes that whenever vowel shortening takes place in Yawelmani, on the surface the shortened vowel is always followed by exactly two consonants—[ʔam*l*it], but [ʔa:*m*ilhin]. From this observation he concludes that vowel shortening must be restricted to take place only when the two consonants are immediately followed by a vowel. If we examine the underlying representation of [ʔa:milhin]—i.e., #ʔa:ml+hin#— we see that the two consonants are followed by a third one. Hence, the rule as restated could not apply, and only vowel insertion will occur. The reformulation of vowel shortening has made the domains of application of the two rules mutually exclusive—that is, vowel shortening and vowel insertion become noninteracting.

Perry argues that the additional constraint imposed on the rule of vowel shortening—that the two consonants be followed by a vowel—is not a trick device to make the proposal work. He insists that the reformulation directly reflects an important constraint operating in Yawelmani—namely, that shortened vowels in a nonfinal syllable are always followed by two consonants and a vowel.

Unfortunately, not all instances of what would be a bleeding order can be eliminated through a simple modification in the statement of the rules.

Portuguese offers an interesting example where the no-ordering proposal fails. In this language certain occurrences of word final *e* are dropped. Also there are forms where *l* is deleted between vowels.

	Singular	Plural
	#murale#	#murale+s#
e-deletion	#mural#	—
l-deletion	—	#murae+s#
	[mural]	[muraes]

Because the final *e* has been deleted in the singular, the *l* is no longer situated intervocalically, and so it cannot undergo deletion. In the plural the final *s* protects the *e* from deletion, because the latter is no longer found finally. Instead the *l*, due to its intervocalic position, becomes deleted. Note that if rules are permitted to apply simultaneously, both rules are potentially applicable in the singular, because in the underlying representation *l* is between vowels and *e* is word final. Simultaneous application, however, would result in the incorrect *[mura]. To circumvent this wrong derivation, one would need to change the environment of *l* deletion, so that it would never apply in the singular. However, there is no obvious way to rewrite this rule such that the restatement of it would be in any way motivated. One is forced to the unavoidable conclusion that these two rules of Portuguese are extrinsically ordered in a bleeding relationship. Of course, there is always the possibility that a thorough reanalysis of the Portuguese data could lead to a description compatible with the proposal.

The no-ordering proposal, as formulated here, may not be sufficient to account for all instances of extrinsic ordering. Yet it does accommodate a substantial number of cases, and for this reason the proposal counts as a significant achievement. Whether the principles, refined further or supplemented by others, will be adequate for explaining all instances of extrinsic ordering remains to be seen. If it indeed turns out that there are principles for predicting the order of application of rules, this discovery does not in any way mean that generative phonology was wrong in assuming the necessity for ordered rules. What will have been demonstrated is that the required ordering is determinable uniquely 'from general principles. Generative phonology has always been in favor of uncovering universal principles for explaining language particular facts.

C. Historical and Psychological Evidence on Generative Phonology

We have seen that the same data may occasion radically different analyses. Yet many linguists would like to believe that there is a unique description and that a theory, if appropriately constrained, would somehow suggest the "correct" analysis. Thus far though, attempts to come up with principles internal to linguistics proper have not been overwhelmingly successful. Some would hope to seek validation of a theory in external evidence, in particular, historical change and psycholinguistic data.[16]

Kiparsky (1968a, 1968b, 1971) has been a strong advocate for language change as a corroborating vehicle for various theoretical assumptions. He has utilized such data to argue for notational devices, notably the use of braces; his claim that feeding and nonbleeding are "unmarked" rule orders is based on cases of historical rule reordering; he has argued that neutralization rules do not apply to nonalternating forms—for example, German *weg* [vek] "away" would terminate underlyingly in a voiceless stop, although historically, as the orthography still shows, it was voiced; and he has presented arguments of a diachronic nature against rules of absolute neutralization, but because of the explanatory power of such rules within synchronic description he has since softened his original strong claim.[17] Earlier we noted an example (the Chukchansi data) where it appeared that competing theories were equally capable of accommodating projected linguistic change. In sum, it seems to me that, for the moment, in the arena of synchronic theoretical disputes, much of the evidence drawn from diachronic change is inconclusive.

Can we expect psycholinguistics to be a savior? Unfortunately, there have been few experimental studies dealing with the two burning controversies within phonology—abstract underlying representations and intricate rule ordering.[18] It is difficult to see how one might tap into highly abstract

---

[16]Schane (1976) is of the view that most arguments utilized in phonology in justification of certain analyses are not convincing, although they frequently have strong aesthetic appeal. Botha (1971, 1973) questions the "internal" and "external" argumentation utilized by generative phonologists, and he claims that, under careful scrutiny, most of the arguments in justification of the theory can be shown to be invalid. Derwing (1973) finds "standard" generative phonology to be dubious as a psychological model.

[17]Kiparsky (1971) consents to allow abstract underlying segments that subsequently undergo absolute neutralization, on the condition that more than one rule makes reference to the abstract segment. This weaker position was in response to data from various languages in support of "abstract" phonology—Arabic (Brame, 1972); Nupe (Hyman, 1970); Yawelmani (Kisseberth, 1969); French (Schane, 1974; Selkirk & Vergnaud, 1973); and Hungarian (Vago, 1973). These researchers try to show for their languages that the strong alternation condition of Kiparsky (1968b) leads in many cases to unenlightening and downright counterintuitive analyses.

[18]M. Ohala (1974) attempts to show that some Hindi speakers may have underlying schwa vowels that do not necessarily occur on the surface; these posited underlying representations are still relatively "shallow" compared to the really "abstract" ones of generative phonology. Several experiments (Ladefoged & Fromkin, 1968; J. Ohala, 1973; and Nessly, 1976) utilize nonsense words to "tease out" speaker awareness of stress patterns and vowel quality in English. Schane, Tranel, and Lane (1976) also use nonsense words to show that English-speaking subjects find it easier to learn a rule deleting consonants if the resulting forms lead to sequences of consonant-vowel alternations rather than to clusters of either consonants or vowels.

underlying forms, because often they are unpronounceable—that is, they may violate the surface structures of a language. One has yet to demonstrate which forms speakers recognize as morphologically related, let alone whether such forms, if related, have a unique representation. Unlike syntax, where novel sentences are created anew, in the domain of the lexicon new words are not being constantly invented. Because the vocabulary, at any given moment, is finite, a good deal of rote learning could be tolerated.

The research on primary language acquisition also has little bearing on the controversies over abstractness and rule ordering. Most developmental studies have dealt with the child's acquisition of adult surface forms. The rules cited are frequently complex and may even involve some depth in ordering, but their intent is to convert adult surface forms into the child's pronunciations.[19] Rule ordering, in relating abstract structures to surface forms, has not been a topic of the acquisitional studies. Nor, of course, has there been a quest for abstract phonological forms.

Are linguists naive in believing that their descriptions ultimately should be psychologically real models of what is going on within the depths of speakers' heads? After all, children do learn languages and speakers do manipulate linguistic data, and it would be undeniably lovely if our theoretical models mirrored whatever it is that learners and speakers do. If we are to ascribe psychological reality to our theories, we shall need confirmatory evidence, and it is natural to expect it to come from psycholinguists. At present, there is little confirmation; whether any will be forthcoming remains part of the future.

REFERENCES

Botha, R. P. *Methodological aspects of transformational generative phonology.* The Hague: Mouton, 1971.

Botha, R. P. *The justification of linguistic hypotheses.* The Hague: Mouton, 1973.

Brame, M. K. On the abstractness of phonology: Maltese ʕ. In M. K. Brame (Ed.), *Contributions to generative phonology.* Austin, Texas: University of Texas Press, 1972.

Chomsky, N. *Current issues in linguistic theory.* The Hague: Mouton, 1964.

Chomsky, N., & Halle, M. *The sound pattern of English.* New York: Harper & Row, 1968.

Derwing, B. L. *Transformational grammar as a theory of language acquisition: A study in the empirical, conceptual, and methodological foundations of contemporary linguistic theory.* Cambridge: Cambridge University Press, 1973.

Flora, M. J. *Palauan phonology and morphology.* Doctoral thesis, University of California, San Diego, 1974.

Goyvaerts, D. L., & Pullum, G. K. *Essays on the sound pattern of English.* Ghent, Belgium: E. Story-Scientia, 1976.

Halle, M. In defense of the number two. In E. Pulgram (Ed.), *Studies presented to Joshua Whatmough on his 60th birthday.* The Hague: Mouton, 1957.

Halle, M. *The sound pattern of Russian.* The Hague: Mouton, 1959.

---

[19]For English the most detailed account of this type of acquisitional study is Smith (1973).

Halle, M. Phonology in a generative grammar. *Word,* 1962, *18,* 54–72.

Hyman, L. How concrete is phonology? *Language,* 1970, *46,* 58–76.

Jakobson, R., Fant, C. G. M., & Halle, M. *Preliminaries to speech analysis.* Cambridge, Mass.: MIT Press, 1963.

Joos, M. *Readings in linguistics I: The development of descriptive linguistics in America 1925–56.* Chicago: University of Chicago Press, 1957.

Kiparsky, P. Linguistic universals and linguistic change. In E. Bach & R. T. Harms (Eds.), *Universals in linguistic theory.* New York: Holt, Rinehart & Winston, 1968. (a)

Kiparsky, P. *How abstract is phonology?* Bloomington, Ind.: Indiana University Linguistics Club, 1968. (b)

Kiparsky, P. Historical linguistics. In W. O. Dingwall (Ed.), *A survey of linguistic science.* College Park, Md.: University of Maryland Press, 1971.

Kisseberth, C. On the abstractness of phonology: The evidence from Yawelmani. *Papers in Linguistics,* 1969, *1,* 248–282.

Kuroda, S.-Y. *Yawelmani phonology.* Cambridge, Mass.: MIT Press, 1967.

Koutsoudas, A., Sanders, G., & Noll, C. *On the application of phonological rules.* Bloomington, Ind.: Indiana University Linguistics Club, 1971.

Ladefoged, P. *A course in phonetics.* New York: Harcourt Brace Janovich, 1975.

Ladefoged, P., & Fromkin, V. A. Experiments on competence and performance. *IEEE Transactions on Audio and Electroacoustics,* 1968, *AU-16*(1), 130–136.

McCawley, J. D. Sapir's phonologic representation. *International Journal of American Linguistics,* 1967, *33,* 106–111.

Nessly, L. *Experimental phonology and English stress.* Bloomington, Ind.: Indiana University Linguistics Club, 1976.

Newman, S. S. *Yokuts language of California* (Viking Fund Publications in Anthropology 2). New York: Viking Press, 1944.

Ohala, J. J. *On phonological experiments I.* Unpublished manuscript, University of California, Berkeley, 1973.

Ohala, M. The abstractness controversy: Experimental input from Hindi. *Language,* 1974, *50,* 225–235.

Perry, T. A. *On two theories of rule application.* Bloomington, Ind.: Indiana University Linguistics Club, 1972.

Postal, P. *Aspects of phonological theory.* New York: Harper & Row, 1968.

Schane, S. A. The phoneme revisited. *Language,* 1971, *47,* 503–521.

Schane, S. A. *Generative phonology.* Englewood Cliffs, N.J.: Prentice-Hall, 1973.

Schane, S. A. Some diachronic deletion processes and their synchronic consequences in French. In M. Saltarelli & D. Wanner (Eds.), *Diachronic studies in Romance linguistics.* The Hague: Mouton, 1974.

Schane, S. A. The best argument is in the mind of the beholder. In J. R. Wirth (Ed.), *Assessing linguistic arguments.* Washington, D.C.: Hemisphere Publishing Co., 1976.

Schane, S. A., Tranel, B., & Lane, H. On the psychological reality of a natural rule of syllable structure. *Cognition,* 1976, *3,* 351–358.

Selkirk, E. O., & Vergnaud, J. R. How abstract is French phonology? *Foundations of Language,* 1973, *10,* 249–254.

Smith, N. V. *The acquisition of phonology.* Cambridge: Cambridge University Press, 1973.

Trubetzkoy, N. S. [*Principles of phonology*] (C. A. M. Baltaxe, trans.). Berkeley, Calif.: University of California Press, 1969. (Originally published, 1939.)

Vago, R. Abstract vowel harmony systems in Uralic and Altaic languages. *Language,* 1973, *49,* 579–605.

Vennemann, T. Phonological concreteness in natural generative grammar. In C.-J. Bailey & R. Shuy (Eds.), *Towards tomorrow's linguistics.* Washington, D.C.: Georgetown University Press, 1974.

6 Phonology as Human Behavior[1]

William Diver
Columbia University

I. PHONETICS AND PHONOLOGY

Do we, in linguistics, need both a phonetics and a phonology? And if we do, what is the relationship between them? The question of the extent to which phonetics is relevant to phonology has long been debated, and the extreme position, that phonetics is entirely irrelevant, has been taken by such otherwise diametrically opposed scholars as Troubetskoy (1949) and Bloomfield (1933). But the opposite view may also be taken: If phonetic research provides us with an accurate acoustic and physiological description of speech sounds, what do we need phonology for?

As between the two extreme positions, there is no doubt that phonetics has the stronger prima facie case. It is all very well to say that physics is not a science of meter reading, but it is equally true that without its meter readings the science of physics would not exist; it would be, not physics, but metaphysics. As for phonetics and phonology, it is phonetics that has the meter readings, and the great weakness in the case for phonology is the curious uncertainty of its relation to the meter readings of phonetics. No linguist, to be sure, would agree that we can dispense with phonology, and phoneticians implicitly agree, in that it is the awareness of phonological problems that generally motivates the exact course of phonetic research.

But what motivates phonology?

The case of Bloomfield and Troubetskoy is instructive, three points in particular being worthy of note. First, neither of them, of course, in spite of

---

[1]Read before the New York Academy of Sciences, March 1975.

his protestations, managed to free himself from phonetics. In Troubetskoy, this is transparently the case. His paradigmatic structure of sounds is clearly based on phonetics, for his categories share or differ in such phonetic features as lateral, nasal, and sonant. Bloomfield's reliance on phonetics is somewhat more subtle His syntagmatic structure has to do with the function of units in the syllable, the main categorical differentiation being that between consonant and vowel. He rejects as irrelevant such phonetic factors as lateral, nasal, and sonant, but that consonant and vowel, as well as syllable, are themselves phonetically based notions is a fact that can hardly be denied.

Second, in turning their backs on phonetics, both Troubetskoy and Bloomfield held concepts of abstract structure that for them provided the motivation for phonological research. They disagreed with each other, of course, in their conceptions of what phonological structure was, and others since have disagreed with both, so it is hardly surprising that we find some difficulty in justifying anew, for ourselves, the choice of these particular motivations. But at any rate, the effect of these strongly held views on structure was to reject phonetics, and responsibility to phonetics, as a control on their procedures. The phonetics, of course, was there and did serve as a control, but for a control to be implicit and unacknowledged, rather than explicit, is undoubtedly always an unhappy state of affairs.

The third point, and here Troubetskoy and Bloomfield are more specifically in agreement, was the identity of the fundamental unit in terms of which the abstract structure was developed; that is, of course, the phoneme. For each, the existence, the reality, the inevitability of the phoneme as the building block for phonological structure was accepted without question. And given their attitude on the irrelevancy of phonetics, it followed quite naturally that neither should have any explicit position on the relation of the phoneme to any kind of phonetic base.

This brings us to the heart of the great paradox of phonemic analysis. There has never been any great difficulty, either for modern phonemicists or ancient alphabet makers, in establishing the existence and identity of phonemes. The area of disagreement in phonemic analysis is small, and the task of reducing languages to writing does not produce wildly disparate results. And yet it is by no means clear exactly what it is that is being done when a phonemic analysis is carried out. Most phonemicists have been avowedly descriptive linguists; their task, they say, is to state the facts. But is that what they are doing? Are phonemes facts, in the sense of observations that can be recorded without recourse to abstraction or explanation. Surely not. That hope was forever exploded with the development of the spectrograph, when it became clear that there was no one-to-one relation between the discrete phonemes and the acoustic reality. Is it the *phonetic* facts they are describing? Obviously not. The trouble with the spectrogram is just that; it presents us with phonetic facts, it describes them for us, and does nothing more. Indeed, much of the point of modern phonemics has been to escape, in the words of Martin Joos (1957, p. 115), the gooey continuity of the phenomena—that is, the phonetics. The meter readings of the phonetician have never been of direct interest to the phonemicist, either in the laboratory or in the field. Even the narrowest of phonetic transcriptions, so-called, is implicitly phonemic; this is indeed as it should be, a first approximation to a phonemic transcription.

The paradox, then, is that the phonemicist can neither get along with phonetics, nor get along without it. And a corollary paradox is that the descriptive linguist is not a descriptive linguist—the reason being that the units, or categories, that he is presumably describing are in fact not directly observable.

The descriptive linguist, among linguists, is the one who has most determinedly refused to entertain a priori assumptions about language in the conduct of his analysis and has most rigorously persisted in a methodology that begins with the raw data; if even he is, in fact, depending on something other than observation. It would appear to be a good idea to take a careful look at the identity of what are regarded as the fundamental units of language and of linguistic analysis.

It is, of course, not only the phoneme that is unobservable in language; all linguistic units are unobservable, regardless of what our intuitions as native speakers may tell us. In this respect, in fact, language appears to be strikingly different from other fields of study, and in particular from the exact sciences, a point generally overlooked by those who would use the exact sciences as models of procedure for linguistics. Indeed, it may be worth our while to spend a few minutes with one of the exact sciences to see what we can learn in terms of a comparison between observable and unobservable units.

II.   DESCRIPTION, EXPLANATION, AND OBSERVABILITY

In the classic area of study, the planetary system, there has never been any doubt as to what was under observation. Certain of the stars, instead of remaining in a fixed position relative to the others, wandered around erratically and were hence dubbed planets. This was entirely on the basis of direct observation, and when the ancients undertook to describe these motions—more accurately, to generate these observations—with the aid of the mathematical model known as the epicycle, the collections of observations they made use of were just that, collections of observations. (Meter readings, if you will.) This epicyclic model, now in the capable hands of the computer, is once again in use today, describing—and predicting within an accuracy of 1 second of time and 1 / 10 minute of arc—the apparent positions of the navigational bodies, all this so that navigators, when they observe these bodies in their turn, can locate their position at sea. We have, then, observable units and the description of observable units, the description being in terms of the various positions (declination and hour angle) the bodies will appear to occupy at various times.

But there is a very interesting and unexpected twist to this problem. When Newton introduced what was called gravitational astronomy, his arguments were at first met with disbelief. Many were reluctant to accept the notion that the effect of gravity, which had been well studied on earth since the time of Galileo, should be extended through vast distances of space to other members of the celestial system. With the acceptance of this idea, however, interest became divided between the practical problem of the apparent motions (useful to navigators) and the scientific problem of the actual motions. For this latter, the mathematical model of the epicycle, already under fire out of considerations of simplicity, now had to yield altogether for a more important reason: Newton's laws of motion now served as an external constraint on the characteristics of any hypothesized orbit; every irregularity in the orbit had to be justified by the gravitational attraction of another body—as much as though this were a problem in ballistics on earth—and the epicycles were a constant source of unmotivated irregularities.

With this development, the stage was now set for reckoning with unobservable, rather than observable, units, and this is what we see happening next. The orbit of the planet Uranus, in order to fit with the observations, would have had to have ascribed to it characteristics that violated the laws of motion. It was, therefore, suggested that this perturbation must be due to the gravitational attraction of some previously unobserved body. The orbit and position of this body was calculated, on the basis of its disturbing influence, a telescope was pointed in the appropriate place, and there it was, the planet that came to be called Neptune.

This discovery is of interest to us because, in a field where all units had been observable, it became possible to describe an unobservable, or at least previously unobserved, unit. Because, in linguistics, all units are unobservable, it is worth spending a little more time to see just how, in principle, this was done.

Let us suppose for the moment that gravitational astronomy, with its external constraints, had not been introduced, and that research had continued with the task of generating the apparent positions of the observed planets, making use of the epicycle as the mathematical model. With the discovery of Uranus, its observed positions, too, would have been submitted to epicyclic analysis. However, there would have been nothing corresponding to the difficulties that actually arose, for there would have been no gravitational theory to act as an external constraint on what combinations of epicycle could be made use of and what ones could not. The epicycle itself doesn't care what positions it generates; it just generates positions. That is, there would have been no norm from which the observations of Uranus would have been departing. Hence, in turn, there would have been no motivation for searching for a previously unobserved body, and no basis on which to conduct such a search. With epicycles, then, there could have been description of observed bodies only, not of unobserved bodies.

In order to describe Neptune, the unobserved unit, it is not sufficient to have a mathematical model that will generate observations; we must also have an understanding of why the motions are what they are, and not otherwise. Without this understanding, we can describe the observable units, but not those that are unobservable.

To put it the other way round: Observable units can be described before they are understood. Description can precede explanation. Unobservable units cannot be described until they have been understood. Description cannot precede explanation.

III.   THE IDENTIFICATION OF UNOBSERVABLE UNITS

Let us now return to the problem of the phoneme as unit. The phoneme being unobservable, as we see on the spectrogram, we cannot reasonably expect to describe it without doing anything else, such as to understand it, to explain it, to come to some comprehension of its characteristics, similar to that provided for the characteristics of the planetary orbit by the laws of motion. And furthermore, because those concerned with the problem, including again the ancient alphabet maker, have always had considerable success in establishing the identity of phonemes, it follows that they must indeed have been doing something more than describing.

Now, as you all know, phonemic practice has never followed the pure principles of phonemic methodology as advocated by the extreme wing of descriptive linguists. Trager and Smith (1952), for example, assure us that the fundamental methodology of descriptive linguistics is the study of distributions, and Zelig Harris (1946), in remarking that "substitution is basic in linguistic analysis," is referring to a particular procedure for the study of distribution. The difficulty with this procedure, of course, is that one cannot establish the existence of units by studying the distribution of those selfsame units, one can only do it on the basis of other units; but when we get down to the bottom of the pyramid, we have no units, we have only the gooey continuity of the phenomena.

In practice, of course, what is described by the methodologists as a shortcut is always used; that is, an appeal to meaning—specifically, to a difference in meaning. This puts the shoe on an entirely different foot. In fact, what I want to suggest to you is that it is this reluctant, this grudging, introduction of meaning that corresponds to the equally reluctant and grudging introduction of Newton's gravitational astronomy into the planetary problem. With it, we can acquire understanding of what is going on and thereby gain the possibility of identifying the unobservable units.

The ancient alphabet maker, apparently, was aware that there was a skewing in the distribution of speech sounds, an irregularity in the phonetics, and that this skewing correlated with certain characteristics of messages that were communicated thereby. He was apparently able to establish that certain gross phonetic characteristics of the sounds were used distinctively in that particular language, and that others were not. This ability is clearly attested to by the changes alphabets undergo as they move from one language to another in the ancient world. There is no suggestion that the alphabet maker, or the alphabet user, was a skilled phonetician or was interested in nice phonetic details, but we can tell from his alphabetical behavior that the early writer of Latin, for example, could hear the difference between [k] and [g], even though the distinction was not made in the alphabet he had borrowed, and that he could ignore the differences among [ci], [ka], and [qu], even though these alphabetical distinctions were available to him.

The ability of the user of a language to establish the existence of unobservable units in this way is very suggestive, particularly in regard to what it is that he is correlating with the phonetic skewing. The ideal terrain for the phonemicist is the minimal pair: two "words" or "morphemes" that are minimally distinct in sound and are also different in meaning. We are thus confronted by, and dependent on, a signal-meaning-pair, the same kind of thing, in principle, that we see in forms of communication outside human language, as in the familiar case of the language of the bees; that is, we are confronted by an ingredient in an act of communication. It has been a considerably moot point for a long time now as to whether communication is a controlling factor in the structure of language. Many have argued that it is not. But this unobservable unit, the phoneme, comes to light only when approached by way of distinctiveness—that is, communication— and it regularly comes to light when it is approached in that way. This has by now happened so often that it is difficult to escape the inference that it is not just coincidence, and that, at least so far as phonology is concerned, communication lies at the heart of linguistic structure, and that what motivates phonemics is the need to establish a relationship between communication and phonetics.

IV. THE CHARACTERIZATION OF UNOBSERVABLE UNITS

With this much clear, let us review our position. Just as the skewing in the motions of the observable unit, Uranus, leads us, when viewed from the orientation of the gravitational astronomy, to the positing of an unobserved unit, Neptune, that produced the skewing in the orbit of Uranus, so also the skewing in the phonetics leads us, when viewed from the point of view of communication, to the positing of a number of unobservable distinctive units (represented by the letters of a phonemic alphabet) whose deployment for the purposes of communication produces the phonetic skewing.

But, and here is where the problem moves into its next stage, although in the case of Neptune we can thus assure ourselves not only of its existence as a unit, but also of its significant characteristics—that is, the nature of its orbit and its position in that orbit at any moment—in the case of the phoneme we are assured only of the fact of its existence: in a particular language, there is a particular number of distinct units. From phonemic analysis alone, we do not know the characteristics of those units, nor even what it means to be a significant characteristic; we only know that they are distinct from each other.

This being the case, it is not surprising that there should be a great uncertainty as to the relation of the phoneme to its phonetic base. (For example, should the phoneme be identified in terms of articulatory or acoustic features? Should *l* be called a liquid or a lateral? Should *p* be called fortis or voiceless? Should we, with the ancients, continue to call *s* a sibilant because it sounds like the hissing of a snake?) Nor is it surprising that for the pure phonemicist there should be a temptation to assert that there is no relationship at all between the phoneme and its phonetic base: as far as distinctiveness alone is concerned, it may be enough to be an abstract unit.

V. STATEMENT OF THE PROBLEM

In moving into the next stage of the problem—that of establishing the characteristics in addition to the identity of the distinctive units—it seems reasonable to follow the same procedure as the one we have been examining; that is, observe a skewing or irregularity, establish an appropriate orientation to act as an external constraint, and devise hypothetical characteristics that, like the orbits, will provide us with an understanding of the skewed observations against the background of the orientation. Specifically then, what is the skewing that poses the problem? What is the orientation? And what are the characteristics that provide a solution to the problem?

First, the skewing. We saw earlier that a skewing in the phonetics posed a problem that, against the background of the communicative factor, has led to the hypothesizing of phonemes, the phoneme thus being the solution to the problem posed by the phonetic skewing. But the phonemes themselves, once hypothesized, are found to have a skewing of their own; namely, that asymmetry in distribution and combination that we study under the name of phonotactics. Let me rephrase the phonotactic problem, however, in terms appropriate to the present research. Given a stock of distinctive units and a large corpus of phonemic transcription, it might be expected that, other things being equal, the phonemes would be distributed symmetrically within the larger linguistic units that they serve to differentiate: the morphemes, words, phrases of the language. We know, of course, that they are not distributed symmetrically, and it is the motivation for the particular skewing we find that constitutes the phonological problem.

Many of you are acquainted with the distinction in Sanskrit between external and internal sandhi. External sandhi describes the phonological interactions that take place at word boundaries; internal sandhi describes those within the word, at morpheme boundaries. In modern phonotactics, the description of skewing covers only that within the word, external sandhi is excluded from consideration. In the present research, I would go one step further and exclude internal sandhi from consideration as well. The motivation for these two exclusions is identical: at word boundaries there is almost nothing that could be thought of as phonological that controls the juxtaposition of phonemes. That juxtaposition is a consequence of the juxtaposition of words, presumably for communicative purposes, and there we may find any word initial occurring together with any word final, in combinations that have nothing to do with those internal to the word. At morpheme boundaries we have a milder form of the same problem: Particularly with a productive morphology, we may find morphologically motivated juxtapositions that are only partially controlled by phonological considerations, and again patterns may occur across morpheme boundaries that do not occur within the morpheme. The classic example is the past tense of *grab: grabbed;* the cluster *bd* occurs in final position only across a morphological boundary. Because the object of our study is to establish the nature of the purely phonological constraints on symmetry of distribution, the introduction of others—morphological considerations, for example— would only muddy the waters. Therefore, they are excluded. The skewings that make up our observations, then, will be those that take place between morphological boundaries, not across them.

As to orientation, we have seen that communication as an orientation is crucial for providing us with a basis for establishing the list of distinctive units, but that the phonemic procedure does not do more than that. To go beyond this point, it has been found necessary, and here we depart considerably from the planetary analogue, to introduce additional orientations. (This will mean, in part, a consideration of phonetics much more explicit than the rough awareness that was sufficient for the alphabet maker, and it is in this way that we shall be led back to a motivated relationship to the phonetic base.) The additional orientations are three in number; they behave in the same way as a single one but with the added complication that they interact with and to some extent contradict each other, adding considerably to the complexity of the problem. The four orientations are: (1) the communicative (which we have already seen); (2) the physiology of the vocal tract; (3) the acoustic medium that is used for transmission; and (4) the orientation that graces the title of this paper—what I shall refer to as the human factor. These provide, you will recall, constraints on the theoretical characteristics to be posited. If the orientations were different, there would, of course, be different constraints. If a part of the human anatomy other than the vocal tract were used—let us say the hands, as in sign language—it is apparent that there would be different constraints; with a different medium—say visual rather than acoustic, as in lipreading, there would again be different constraints; and if the human factor were removed, if we were dealing with a speech synthesizer, even one that could produce only the sounds of the vocal tract, still other constraints would be removed, because the machine is not bothered by such human weaknesses as laziness and its attendant consequences.

Let me pause here to make an important point. Some might tend to identify the orientations I have been mentioning with the notion of an assumption, an initial assumption that can be chosen at will, arbitrarily, as a starting point for research, an assumption whose justification need only be the hoped-for success of the research that follows from it. That is not the nature of our problem here. What I am searching for is understanding, and understanding of the skewings cannot be obtained by relating them to previously untested assumptions. It will come only by placing them against the background of a larger body of information that is known independently of the study, as in the case of the terrestrial background to the celestial motions. For understanding, it is not enough to begin with an assumption that manages to stay out of jail only because nothing is known against it.

Further, the relation we here envision between skewing and orientation also controls the amount of knowledge we require from the orientation. We need not know everything about the physiology of the vocal tract, nor everything about the human mind in order to solve the problem. We need to know only as much as is required for an understanding of the skewing. Our procedure, then, is not to learn everything there is to know about the orientations and then proceed to the problem; quite the contrary, the scope of the problem is determined entirely by the extent of the skewing.

VI.   ANALYSIS

As a final preliminary to settling down with the problem itself, let me sketch briefly the fundamental analytical position:

1. Users of a language behave as though they have learned certain distinctive units, the phonemes, which they deploy for communicative purposes.

2. We cannot observe directly what it is that they behave as though they have learned.
3. We can however observe the phonotactic skewing, a skewing that has been built up over the centuries and millennia in the very mouths of the speakers.
4. We can infer that these long-range skewings represent favorings and disfavorings on the part of the users of the language. (It is to be observed that the skewings are not idiosyncratic to particular languages; their general characteristics recur from language to language.)
5. We then examine the favorings and disfavorings against the background of the orientation—which means with independent knowledge of what kinds of favorings and disfavorings humans are prone to in areas other than the use of language.
6. We can infer that a disfavoring, for example, represents a difficulty in a learning process, and by a close examination of what it is that constitutes a difficulty in the way of a particular learning process, we can infer what it is that is being learned.
7. What it is that is being learned we may identify as a characteristic of the distinctive units.

In sum, then, we pose a hypothesis of the unobservable characteristics of the units, on the basis of the disturbing influence that those characteristics bring to bear on the distribution of the units, in the same way that we hypothesize the characteristics of Neptune on the basis of its disturbing influence on the orbit of Uranus.

We come now to a consideration of the skewings themselves. Let us begin by plunging into the midst of a problem. One of the classic examples of phonotactic skewing is the absence of the cluster *tl-* in English and in many other languages. This absence is best seen against the background of other clusters, containing *r* as well as *l*, as seen in Table 6.1.

TABLE 6.1
Frequency Distributions for Occurrence of *l* and *r* in Initial Clusters

	p	*b*	*t*	*d*	*k*	*g*	*f*	*s*	*š*	*θ*	*Totals*	*Cross Totals*
l	38	42	0	0	54	24					158	
r	42	62	54	40	61	51					310	
l							55	54			109	190
r							32	0			32	419
l									0	0		
r									17	19		

The numbers in the table give the number of monosyllabic words in English beginning with the clusters indicated; for example, there are no words beginning with *tl*-, but 54 beginning with *tr*-. The numbers are drawn from a count, made by me, of all the monosyllables of English (of which there are about 2,500), so arranged that the number of phonemes can be recovered, in any position, either alone or in combination with any other phoneme. Looking first at the zeros, we see that they occur not only at *tl* and *dl* but also at *sr*. (The combinations with *š* and *θ* include variables other than those under immediate consideration, and they will be discussed separately.) But further, if we look at the other figures we are tempted to infer that the zeros are but extreme instances of a skewing that is present throughout: in the first two rows of Table 6.1, the row containing the zeros has smaller numbers in every instance, the totals of the two rows coming to 158 and 310. And in the next two rows of Table 6.1, where 55 to 32 goes along with 54 to 0, we see the same consistency, the totals being 109 to 32. And if we add the totals in crisscross fashion, to group the disfavored rows and favored rows respectively, we have a skewing, 190 to 419, that shows less than half as many disfavored as favored. The nonoccurrence of *tl*-, therefore, appears to be an extreme case rather than an isolated instance.

Now of course what kind of a skewing we get depends on what it is that we count, and the rationale of organization here is transparent. What are traditionally called stops prefer to cluster with *r*, the nonstops prefer *l*. The units involved have been characterized in various ways—stop, occlusive, obstruent, consonant, fricative, spirant, sibilant, liquid, lateral, resonant, etc.—but none of these characterizations illuminates the source of the skewing. Our task here is to provide a characterization that does lead to understanding of the skewing.

A phonetically accurate characteristic of these sounds that is not included in the usual repertoire of phonetic features is that they differ among themselves in being either *stable* or *mobile*. *Stable* indicates that the articulatory organ employed in the production of the sound is relatively stationary during excitation of the resonant cavity. Thus the lip and apex, respectively, are stationary during the production of *fff, sss,* and *lll*. Mobile indicates the opposite: the articulator is necessarily in motion during sound production. For the stops there is explosion of the pent-up air, and the lip, apex, and dorsum respectively are violently displaced. A trilled *r* is vigrorously vibrated, and we shall see in a moment that it is a trilled *r*, characteristic of an earlier stage of the language, that we are here concerned with.

Returning now to the skewings, in terms of stable vs. mobile, we can make the single statement that combinations of sames are favored and combinations of differents are disfavored. That is, the rows containing zero and the lower numbers are mobile plus stable and stable plus mobile; those with the higher numbers are mobile plus mobile and stable plus stable:

	Stable (*l*)	Mobile (*r*)
Mobile (*p, t, k, b, d, g*)	–	+
Stable (*f, s*)	+	–

With this in mind, we can now take a closer look at the instances with *š* and *θ*:

	l	*r*		
š	0	17	**šl-* < OE *skl-*	*šr-* < OE *skr-* (*shrine* < *scrin*)
θ	0	19	*θr-* < *tr-* (*three = tres*)	**θl-* < *tl-* (*θ* disfavored)

In the case of *š*, we see that a sound change within the recorded history of the language has produced a realignment of the stable-mobile relations. As *sk* > *š*, a stable rather than a mobile becomes juxtaposed to the following *l* or *r*, and the modern frequencies, 0 *šl* < *skl* and 17 *šr* < *skr*, still reflect the older distribution and the preference for combinations of sames: stops favor *r* and disfavor *l*. At the same time it is an interesting point that the recouping of clusters since the sound change also follows the formula: already in Middle English we have, coming in from various sources, vocabulary items beginning with the favored combination *skr-*, as in *scribble*, but not with the disfavored combination *skl-*.

The case of *θr* and *θl* represents in part a variant on the same theme, although there are additional complications. *θr-*, which occurs, has as its major etymological source a favored combination by way of Grimm's law, *tr-*, as we see in comparison of *three* with Latin *tres*. We may assume that the presently disfavored *θr-* has lost a considerable amount of ground in the interim—compare its 19 with the 54 of the presently favored *tr*—but it is still hanging on. In contrast, the presently favored *θl-* comes by way of Grimm's law from *tl-*, obviously disfavored, and it would have had to do a great deal of recouping to overcome this initial disadvantage. That has been prevented, however, by the general disfavoring of *θ* itself, which has a low frequency status in the language as a whole (for reasons not being discussed here, but compare its total instances of 99 with the 315 of *f*) and in some dialects has been eliminated outright by phonological change.

Returning now to the formula, we see that the zeros associated with *š* and *θ*, which seem to be turning up in the wrong column, are reflections of additional factors playing a role in these particular instances, and we can with some security restate the position that, in respect to stable and mobile, sames are favored and differents are disfavored.

Some might be tempted to stop here; this is, after all, an impressive generalization. What one could do is impute to a theory the mobile-stable distinction, then make a statement that that theory constrains the combinations of units in terms of the distinction that the theory now contains. To me, however, this would be an extremely uninteresting thing to do; it would be merely a generalized restatement of the facts, made possible by a happy choice of terms. In spite of the façade of theory, it would not provide us with an understanding of why the theory is what it is, and not, for example, the reverse. The reverse, let it be noted, could be stated as a constraint just as easily: differents are favored and sames are disfavored.

We require, then, an external source for an understanding of the particular nature of the skewing, and once we have addressed ourselves directly to the problem, the source is not difficult to find. In this instance we are concerned with an interaction between the physiological orientation and the human factor orientation. A certain musculature, the physiological factor, is being controlled—that is where the human factor comes in—to produce a sequence of articulatory gestures that will in turn produce sounds. We would naturally suppose, in terms of the human factor, that combinations of gestures that are easier to learn to control will be preferred over combinations that are more difficult to learn to control. In the present case, the skewings seem to support this supposition. With *tl-*, for example, we have a violent motion, the explosion, that must immediately be quelled and brought under control so that a gesture of a very different kind can be made. With *tr-*, on the other hand, the violence of the motion can continue unchecked; it is merely transmuted—"steered" perhaps is the term—into another gesture equally violent, and the control problem is greatly lessened. Where we begin with a stable gesture, *s* or *f*, we have the same problem of control in reverse. Further, that it is a problem of control of the musculature that is involved is supported by the subskewings within the skewings. The strongest disfavorings, the zeros, occur where it is exactly the same musculature that has to be brought under control, the apex in both elements of *tl, dl,* and *sr*. Where there is only a change in kind of motion, such as violent to nonviolent, but with different musculatures, the skewing is milder, as in the labial plus apical combinations, *pr* and *br*, or dorsal plus apical in *kr* and *gr*. Here the switch to a somewhat different musculature relieves the problem of control, although the change in degree of violence of motion is still playing a role.

Outside the sphere of language, physical behavior of the type represented by the disfavored combinations—abrupt, jerky transitions from one movement to another—is generally characterized as being awkward and uncoordinated, and it is readily observable that a person who moves in that way has difficulty with problems of control. The golfer or tennis player who is cursed with a jerky swing has a great deal of difficulty in controlling the flight of the ball. He, of course, may not be able to escape his fate, if he insists on playing golf or tennis, but the speaker of a language has options. Confronted by the alternatives of controlling a jerky swing, as it were, and a smooth one, he can abandon the former entirely and concentrate on the latter. For just as in speaking we may avoid the use of a word of whose meaning we are not quite sure, so also may we avoid a word whose pronunciation presents some slight difficulty. In the more difficult cases, and over the long run, such avoidance can reasonably be expected to produce skewings of the kind under examination.

It is by now apparent that explicit introduction of the human factor leads to a consideration of the problem in terms of precision of control over gestures, gestures that in turn produce sounds. For our understanding of skewings we therefore naturally begin to look at well-known variables—outside language—that have an effect on precision of control. For example, a person is called right-handed because his right hand is more adroit than his left; confronted by any task requiring precision of control, wielding a tennis racquet or a pencil, the right-handed person uses his right hand. Similarly, as among lip, apex of the tongue and dorsum, it is apparent that the apex is the most adroit of the three. It is not surprising then that, as has often been remarked, the apical sounds are generally more frequent than the others.

Note that attributing to these sounds a characteristic of dental or alveolar rather than apical does not provide us with an understanding of a greater degree of exploitation based on adroitness; the teeth and alveolae cannot be said to be adroit. The problem with phonetics, of course, is that it gives us a great deal more information about speech sounds than is required by a phonology (hence the controversy about how phonemes are to be labeled), and it is just the task of the phonology to demonstrate that, of all those phonetic characteristics that are undeniably there, only certain ones are of significance for the understanding of the skewing. As seen in the present example, given the importance of precision of control it is evident that the part of the physiology that is subject to control—the articulator rather than the place of articulation—will in general be the provider of the significant characteristic.

Another example of physical control outside language is to be seen in the childhood trick of trying to pat your stomach and rub your head at the same time; that is, trying to perform two different actions at once. This difficulty, too, is reflected in the skewings. In the case of what is called a voiceless stop— t, for example—a single articulator both shapes and excites the resonant cavity; for d on the other hand, an addition articulator—the glottis—is invoked to provide additional excitation, thus changing the character of the acoustic product and adding another distinctive unit to the inventory. But coordination of the glottis with the apex, doing two things at once, requires more control, and the voiced stops suffer in frequency accordingly, another well-known observation.

This matter of "voicing" in terms of the control of two simultaneous movements is closely associated with the phonetic research that has been done on voice-onset time, variation in onset time being obviously related to simultaneity. When we compare different languages, we see that the extent to which "voicing" consists of doing two things at once is a matter of degree, varying from language to language, rather than an absolute. A schematic version of this may be seen in the following where _____ represents the gesture of one articulator, closure and release, and . . . . . represents the other, vibration of the glottis.

Romance	*b*		*p*		
	————	. . . . .	————	. . . . .	———— . . . . .
English			*b*		*p*

In each language category the sound that is written with the letter *p* and that shows greater frequency in frequency counts has a later voice onset, which in turn means that the gesture produced by the glottis is to a lesser extent simultaneous with the gesture of the other articulator. Conversely, the *b* in each category has an earlier voice onset; that means "doing two things at once" to a greater degree, and *b* is accordingly disfavored. The middle member of the trio above is therefore either favored or disfavored depending on the option available in the particular language.

If now we turn to the controversy on whether voice-voiceless or fortis-lenis is the more appropriate characterization of such pairs of sounds—both, again, being phonetically accurate statements—we see from the above that it is the phonetic factor of voice onset that is also a factor in the phonology. By contributing directly to the variable of one articulator vs. two in the makeup of the phonological gesture, it motivates skewings. The fortis-lenis difference, on the other hand, appears to be a consequence of phonological factors rather than a motivator. With only one articulator both shaping and exciting the cavity, as with *p*, crispness of articulation is desirable for optimum excitation; but when a second articulator, the glottis, is assisting with the excitation we can relax, literally, and (here comes the human factor) a lenis articulation results. Lenis, in other words, is merely a failure to do something, when we can get away with it, that would be required under other circumstances.

We may use the figures in Table 6.1 for a first look at the actual skewings involved as we move from one articulator per gesture (both shaping and exciting) to two articulators per gesture. Comparison of the favored and disfavored combinations, the sames and the differents, in terms of voiced vs.

voiceless, reveals that the voiced member of the pair drops much further in frequency than does the voiceless:

	r	*l*	
p	42	38	– 4
b	62	42	–20
t	54	0	
d	40	0	
k	61	54	– 7
g	51	24	–27

For *p*, there is a drop of 4, from 42 to 38, in going from the favored to the disfavored combination; for *b*, there is a drop of 20, from 62 to 42. *t* and *d*, of course, are not usable, since both drop as far as they can, to 0. *k* drops 7, from 61 to 54, but *g*, combining two articulators, drops 27, from 51 to 24.

These figures indicate not only the effect of the combination of two articulators in one gesture as a disfavoring, they also show that we must take into account how many disfavorings are present in a given instance: here, two disfavorings have greater consequences than one. A third disfavoring (already mentioned) is to be seen in the drop of *tl* and *dl* to zero, one that arises when the same musculature is involved in the transition from mobile to stable. Direct comparison of the three disfavorings shows how the drop in frequency accelerates as the difficulties pile up:

			Average Amount of Drop	*Percent of Average Drop*
One disfavoring (mobile + stable)	*pl*	*kl*	5.5	10.7
Two (+ two articulators)	*bl*	*gl*	23.5	41.6
Two or three, one strong (+ same musculature)	*tl*	*dl*	47.0	100.0

In the case of *dl* all three disfavorings are at work, but it is to be noted that *tl* drops to zero with only two disfavorings, not being voiced. This, of course, suggests that the third disfavoring is stronger than the second, since *bl* and *gl*, also with two, do not drop nearly as far. In fact, reuse of the same articulator—i.e., the same musculature—seems itself to be disfavored, even in instances where the reuse is delayed sufficiently so that considerations of abrupt transition cannot be involved. Examples follow, and it will be seen that here, too, the amount of disfavoring is correlated with the degree of additional disfavoring and the consequent piling up of difficulties.

The first two examples, containing a relatively strong additional disfavoring, show an articulator being reused in word-final after appearing in an initial cluster (as will be seen in a moment, it is the cluster that constitutes the extra disfavoring).

ClVC	189 *slip*	CNVC	60 *snip*
CCVl	40 *spill*	CCVN	98 *spin*
ClVl	1 *flail*	CNVN	0 *smin*

First, with *l*, there are 189 words of the type *slip*, with *l* in the initial cluster, and 40 words of the type *spill*, with *l* in final position, in the presence of an initial cluster. But there is only one world, *flail* with *l* in both the initial cluster and final position.

So also with nasals—i.e., with reuse of the musculature that opens and closes the nasal passage. There are 60 words of the type *snip*, with *any* nasal in the initial cluster, and 98 of the type *spin*, with any nasal in final position, but no words of the type *smin*, with any nasal in the initial cluster and any nasal in final position.

We may now reduce the extra disfavoring by moving from examples of the type CCVC to examples in CVC. (For the purposes of the present chapter we shall merely infer the disfavoring of CC- in comparison with C- from the well-known difference in frequency, without going into the question of motivation; the actual numbers of CC- are a much smaller percentage of their mathematical potential than is the case with C-). We are now down to the single disfavoring of reuse of the same articulator at the beginning and end of the word, and we may expect that, as proves to be the case, the drop in frequency will be less marked.

For this example, the labial, apical, and dorsal articulators will be examined as they appear in *p t k* and *b d g*, the type *pit*.

1. Observed initial: labial 86 + apical 72 + dorsal 71 = 229
2. Observed final: labial 59 + apical 108 + dorsal 62 = 229

Of the 229 words both beginning and ending with any one of the six sounds indicated, 86 begin with labials (*p, b*), 72 with apicals (*t, d*), and 71 with dorsals (*k, g*). Of the same 229 words, 59 end with labials, 108 with apicals, and 62 with dorsals. If on this basis we calculate a symmetrical distribution in the combination of initials and finals, assuming that there is no influence from one end of the word to the other, we get the figures in 3.

3. Calculated co-occurrence of initial and final stops:

L+A	L+D	A+L	A+D	D+L	D+A	:	L+L	A+A	D+D	Total
41	23	19	20	18	33	:	22	34	19	229

The calculated values are of course obtained by taking, for example, the proportion of initial labials (86/229) and multiplying that by the proportion of final apicals (108/229), giving the proportion of labial plus apical that could be expected to occur if all initials and finals combined freely with each other:

$$86/229 \ (.376) \times 108/229 \ (.472) = .177$$
$$.177 \times 229 \ = 41$$

The left part of item 3 shows combinations of different articulators at the beginning and end of the word, of the types *bat* (L + A), *pick* (L + D), *tap* (A + L), *dock* (A + D), *cab* (D + L), and *get* (D + A); on the right are combinations of same articulators, of the types *pep* (L + L), *debt* (A + A), and *cog* (D + D).

Comparison of the calculated co-occurrences with the acutal numbers is given in item 4:

4. Calculated vs. observed co-occurrence:

	L+A	L+D	A+L	A+D	D+L	D+A	:	L+L	A+A	D+D	Total
Calc	41	23	19	20	18	33	:	22	34	19	= 229
Obs	43	26	21	23	21	37	:	17	28	13	= 229
Diff	+2	+3	+2	+3	+3	+4	:	−5	−6	−6	

The actual figures for the 229 words show slight departures from the calculation based on symmetry. With different articulators—the left part of item 4—43 rather than 41 for an increase of 2; 26, for an increase of 3; and continuing with increases in each category of 2, 3, 3, and 4. But with same articulators the direction of departure reverses, and we have drops of 5, 6, and 6. That is, all those with different articulators increase a little, and all those with the same articulators drop. Now if our hypothesis were in fact entirely ungrounded, we would expect that in each category there would be a 50-50 chance of departing from the calculated amount either in the direction predicted by the hypothesis or in the opposite direction, just as, in a single toss of a coin we have a 50-50 chance for heads and for tails. But with every individual category departing in the same direction—that is, in the direction predicted by the hypothesis—we have the equivalent of throwing heads nine times in a row. It would appear then that even in the absence of other disfavorings there is a significant avoidance of reuse of the same musculature from one end of the word to the other.

(In this connection is is interesting to observe that in the Semitic languages, in the consonantal structure of the root, there is a widespread avoidance of the same item occurring both at the beginning and at the end of the root, another instance of an extreme case where elsewhere we see only a trend.)

Now what is there about human behavior in general that would provoke skewings reflecting the avoidance of doing the same thing over again? Once more, once the question is posed explicitly, the answer is not far to seek. A direct physiological parallel, having to do with control over the musculature, is to be seen in the fact that in boxing, a skilled boxer is one who can stand off and use his left again and again and again, saving his right for an appropriate moment, whereas the unskilled boxer is one who rushes in in roundhouse style, alternating lefts and rights and relying on brute strength to land something somewhere. The "educated left jab" of the skilled boxer is just that; it takes practice, control, and precision, and not many acquire it. In less directly physical analogues, the same kind of factor seems to be at work; we speak of attention span, boredom, and monotony. If we set a child to picking blueberries at a blueberry farm, he flits about from one bush to another, picking a few here and a few there, instead of working away steadily at one bush, repeating the same operation until the bush is stripped. And we have all felt that irrational impulse, in the middle of some task, to stop for awhile and do something else "for a change."

The general question that confronts us is, how far will such well-known traits of human behavior penetrate into the structure of language? Our only answer lies in the skewed distributions, and the skewings we have been looking at suggest that, in the case of phonology at least, they penetrate very deeply indeed.

Before entering into my concluding remarks, I should like to pick up one more point, because it is already available in the statistics we have been looking at. In the statement of observed initials and finals for type CVC, above, we see that the differentiation in frequency according to articulators is not very great—86, 72, 71—with the labials being somewhat more frequent. In final position however, we see that the apicals far outstrip the labials and dorsals: 108, as against 59 and 62. The greater adroitness of the apex has already been mentioned, but why should this factor be realized so much more strongly in final than in initial position? (To cite an extreme case again, in ancient Greek *only* apical consonants appear in final position.) To understand this we must come back to the communicative orientation. As we proceed through an individual communication, the accumulation of information makes it progressively easier to anticipate what will come next; in fact, we all know people who, as hearers, come in in sympathetic chorus on the final words of sentences. In words too, in any particular context, the early part of the word is likely to give us as much information as we really need to identify that word. Even with a minimal pair differentiated in final position— say, *cat* and *cap*—both words of the pair are not likely to make equally good sense in the particular message: "I have a dog and a c-." The beginnings of words, then, contain a much greater burden of distinctiveness than do the ends. It is entirely understandable that if different gestures present different degrees of difficulty, the more difficult gestures will be disfavored where the motivation for maintaining distinctness is lessened, as in final position. In the present case the greater ease of control inherent in the more adroit articulator accounts for its considerably higher frequency in a position of low communicative load.

So also in final position for another variable we have already examined: one articulator vs. a combination of two articulators; that is, voiceless vs. voiced.

	One Articulator (p t k)	Two Articulators (b d g)
Initial	417	412
Final	616	357

In initial position (high communicative load) there is practical equality between the voiceless stops, 417, and the voiced, 412. But as the need for distinctiveness drops in final position the more difficult task of coordinating two articulators asserts itself, as it were, and leads to a drop in frequency, 616 to 357. Here again we can note an extreme case, the classic examples of German and Russian, where the voiced stops go down to zero frequency in final position.

Earlier, apropos of the methodology of phonemics, reference was made to the question of whether communication is a significant ingredient in determining the structure of language. Here, as there, the answer seems to be a clear affirmative. Not only is communication an essential motivator for the existence of distinctive units in language; it is also a controlling factor in the phonotactic structure of those same units.

I have been able, here, to provide only an excerpt from the research that has been underway at Columbia, but it is probably sufficient for you to see in what direction it is going. Let me review the major points in the line of argument:

1. We begin with phonetic observation, articulatory and acoustic, within which there are no observable units.
2. By means of the communicative orientation we can establish the *number* of distinctive units in a particular language. This is the standard procedure of the phonemicist.
3. Consideration of the acoustic and physiological characteristics associated with these units suggests a variety of possible characterizations; that is, a nonunique terminology for describing the units.
4. In choosing among these possibilities, it is apparent that the characteristics of the units must be of such a kind that the human user of the language can learn them.
5. This means that either
   a. the human learner has an innate capacity for learning these particular characteristics that is entirely independent of his usual ways of learning, or that

b. the human factor, in the ordinary acceptance of the term, is relevant to this learning process, too.

6. The innateness hypothesis is essentially untestable; it is of use only as a residual hypothesis after all others have failed.

7. Proceeding with the human-factor hypothesis, because it can be tested, we do not know in advance, deductively, in exactly what way the human factor will interact with the other orientations.

8. Therefore, we must have some inductive source of information by means of which to assess the degree of penetration of the human factor.

9. That inductive source is the phonotactic skewing, the result of the accumulated learning of many generations.

10. The skewing, viewed in ways that are consistent with the human factor, against the background of communication, acoustics, and physiology, informs us of the kinds of characteristics we are confronted by.

What then are these characteristics? The data given earlier, and the larger area of research that supports it, strongly indicate that the phonological problem has to do in the main with the control of gestures. The key is least effort in terms of precision of control.

There have been three main sources of competition for the description of sounds: articulation, place of articulation, and the acoustic product. The gesture as we have been examining it here corresponds to the articulation; it is the articulation that we learn to control, and we have seen how the skewings respond to the problems of controlling it. The place of articulation is not something that presents us with a learning problem in the same way; it is not a gesture that we need to learn to control, although learning problems associated with a gesture may lead us to prefer one place of articulation over another, as appears in skewings we have not discussed here. In recent decades, acoustics has been a strong rival to physiology as a basis for a classificatory terminology. However, in the investigations that have been conducted so far there appear to be no skewings that would get to be better understood through the establishment of an acoustic categorization. Two roles seem to be played by the acoustic orientation. First, and obviously, the articulatory gesture must help produce a sound, either by shaping or by exciting the cavity. Second, the various distinctive units must produce sounds that are distinct from each other. However, the *particular kind* of acoustic distinctness (what would be a basis for an acoustic classification) has not yet emerged as a motivator of skewings; the mere fact of distinctness, any distinctness, seems to be enough.

The overall interrelationship among phonology, physiological phonetics, and acoustic phonetics can be sketched as follows: the speaker learns the signals of the language (the morphemes) as made up of a limited number of distinct articulatory gestures; these are the phonological units. In the particular circumstance of the individual act of speech, the attempt at the articulatory gesture produces certain vocal movements. These can be recorded and observed on, for instance, X-ray film. The vocal movements in turn shape and excite resonant cavities, and the resulting sounds can be recorded and analyzed with the spectrograph. The movements and sounds, then, are consequences of the articulatory gestures.

Dominating the articulatory gesture as the phonological unit is the problem of precision of control and the human factor, and this brings us sharply back to the question of the unobservability of characteristics. The analytical problem in phonology has always been one of what to select from among the multiplicity of observables offered by the phonetics: as phonemicists, for example, we may select the backing of a vowel as its distinctive characteristic, ignoring the liprounding as redundant, or say that an *f* is phonetically labio-dental but phonemically labial. So also with a universal phonetic alphabet, where distinctiveness within a particular language is not of primary concern, the problem is to decide what is to be recognized and what is to be ignored among the phonetic facts. The unobservability of units has thus manifested itself indirectly in the need for a selection from among observables; if the units themselves were observable, the problem of selection would not arise.

With the introduction of the human factor however, it becomes apparent that phonological characteristics are not confined within the domain of what is phonetically observable. We shift, then, from an area in which there can be arbitrary phonetic description of what is potentially phonological, in advance of the solution of the phonological problem, to an area in which there is nothing to describe until the phonological problem—the understanding of the skewings—has been solved. In the two areas, however, we actually have somewhat different variations on the same theme. In both instances, characteristics must await the solution of the phonological problem. *Description cannot precede understanding.*

VII. CONCLUSION

Do we, now, need a phonology as well as a phonetics? In this chapter, we have been trying to come to an understanding of the skewings in the phonetics. In all areas of scientific investigation, it seems that research is provoked by skewings, by lack of symmetry, in the observations. It is the attempt to come to an understanding of these skewings that leads to the formulation of theories; that is, to the postulating of unobservable—or as yet unobserved—

entities whose characteristics dominate the observable data and thus motivate the skewings. The orbits of Uranus and Neptune are thus theories; we postulate for them those characteristics—consistent with the orientation, the laws of motion—that will provide us with an understanding of why each planet is observed when and where it is. *A theory, therefore, is a solution to a problem, and a phonology is a particular instance of a theory.*

This being the case, we need a phonology if we wish to understand the skewings in the phonetics, and it is of course the nature of such a phonology that it cannot reject phonetics as something outside the interest of phonology. It is also the nature of such a phonology that if it is to provide us with the understanding that is necessary for the characterizing of unobservable units, the theory must operate against the background of orientations comparable to the laws of motion. A significant innovation in this chapter is the point that such a background must include not only acoustics and physiology—the traditional domain of phonetics—but also communication and the human factor. All of this means a distinct step away from any kind of "pure" linguistics; that is, any linguistics that eschews in advance bodies of knowledge that might be associated with the linguistic problem. The principle that determines the scope of the theory and its related orientations must rather be that what is included is exactly what is required for the solution of the problem—no more and no less.

Further, this principle leads in turn to a clear possibility of a delineation of the discipline, both internally and externally. Within the discipline, we have first the phonetic skewings of speech—as opposed to those of music or the waves on a beach. These, the observations or phenomena, are observable, and they pose the problem that confronts the discipline and that motivates its existence. Second is the theory, the postulation of unobservables such as the phonemes and their characteristics that provide understanding of the skewings and thereby solve the problem that has been posed. And third is the orientation—in this case there are four of them—the background information that makes the solution possible. The distinction between the first two factors is, of course, that the one is observable and the other is not; the one is the problem and the other is its solution. The difference between the second and the third is that the theory is a specific response to the skewings whereas the orientations are known independently of any phonetic skewing or phonological theory, just as the laws of motion are known independently of the observations of a particular planet or its orbit.

The external delineation lies in the relation between theory and orientation, for the requirements of the theory control the extent to which the orientation is to be introduced. How much phonetics do we have to know, how much do we have to know about human behavior in order to solve the problem? Strictly speaking, only that much. It is of course inevitable that we should have a larger body of knowledge concerning the orientations, but our knowledge need not be exhaustive, firstly, and the mere fact that we know something, secondly, does not earn it a place in the theory—that is, in the phonology. The phonetic fact that *l* is a lateral does not of itself earn laterality a place in the phonology. For that to be the case, "lateral," like "stable," would have to help provide an understanding of the skewings; until it can be demonstrated that it does so, *l* remains a lateral phonetically, as a matter of observation, but not phonologically, as a solution to a problem.

Another kind of external delineation has to do with what may be referred to as "quasi-orientations." A number of terms that are commonly used in phonetics (and phonology) do not in fact derive from the phonetic orientations at all; that is, from physiology and acoustics. The term "liquid" is commonly applied to *l* and *r*. This term actually derives from the "fluid" status of these consonants in respect to "making position" in the metrics of the classical languages: a syllable consisting of a short vowel followed by a cluster containing a liquid can be "scanned" as either long or short, at the option of the poet, although other clusters of two consonants always make the syllable long. Now I do not suppose that anyone would deliberately suggest that the metrical conventions of a particular culture at a particular time should be regarded as contributing to an understanding of the phonetic skewings of human speech in general, in the way, for example, that the physiology of the human vocal tract does. Yet that is what the use of the term "liquid" in phonetics and phonology implies. And it cannot be ignored that the same is true of the other terms just used: "vowel," "consonant," and "syllable." These, too, are derived from classical metrics, and the long-standing difficulty of providing definitions for them is undoubtedly related to their extraphonetic origin.

The term "quasi-orientation" may thus be applied to a body of knowledge that is influencing attempted solutions of a problem without having any demonstrable relation to the skewings that are under study. Of course, if a relation can be demonstrated, then that body of knowledge becomes an orientation, but there is a distinct burden of proof that must be satisfied; traditional use of a term is not enough. In the planetary analogy there were of course a number of quasi-orientations during the pre-Newtonian period: the harmony of the spheres, the magic number ten, and, most prominently, the sanctity of the circle as the perfect geometric form. In hindsight, we can see very clearly how these quasi-orientations stood as obstacles to the solution of that problem, and there seems no reason to suppose that the same would not be true in another field as well.

As narrow a conception of the term theory as that offered above—a specific solution to a specific problem—is of course quite alien to what is usual in the field of linguistics, but it is not clear that other notions of theory are such as to arouse any great enthusiasm when viewed from the present perspective. In recent years, for example, linguistic theory has taken the form of a universal phonology that is in fact an arbitrary selection from phonetics and a universal grammar that is in effect an attempt to portray the human mind. Because neither phonetics nor the human mind offer us observable units, makeshift units have been borrowed, on the one hand, from the heterogeneous background of phonetic research—part of which has been indicated above—and, on the other hand, from the familiar categories of traditional grammar: sentence, phrase, part of speech, construction, and the like. [It should perhaps be pointed out in passing that the traditional grammar, although an attempt at a theory in the sense in which the term is being used here, has never proved itself empirically adequate. That is, the traditional grammar has never provided an understanding of the skewings in the distribution of the morphology for any language, very probably because its unobservable units, its familiar categories, are based on a quasi-orientation—namely, the notion that the structure of language (e.g., the "deep structure" of a sentence) is a particular instance of the structure of rational thought, and that the units of a theory of language are therefore in some way related to units of logic.]

Further, these makeshifts have been treated as though they were observable units in a successful theory, and as a result what is called linguistic theory has concentrated on the task of linguistic *description,* with the most highly prized theory being that which promises the maximally efficient apparatus for bringing the enormous task of such a description down to a manageable size. Needless to say, this attempt to put description before understanding has not fared particularly well.

One final word. The field of lingustics is notoriously fragmented. This widespread and continuing disagreement may well be the direct consequence of problems of categorization and classification of the kind discussed above. On the one hand, inductively, there are too many factual statements that can be made about various things associated with language. In the absence of a nonarbitrary control—appropriate orientations—attempts at description have led to nonuniqueness in one school and an appeal to a simplicity metric in another. On the other hand, deductively, the study of language has always been a dumping ground for various kinds of philosophical speculation, with the quasi-orientations of each. The consistent failure of these speculative approaches has had the consequence of casting language into the role of something unknowable, mysterious, and remotely abstract and has effectively forestalled any attempt to deal with language as a straightforward analytical problem. I suggest to you that language is knowable and that much of the mystery will disappear if we keep clearly in mind that this most characteristic of man's activities is just that, a manifestation of well-known traits of human behavior.

REFERENCES

Bloomfield, L. *Language* (chap. 8). New York: Holt, Rinehart & Winston, 1933.

Harris, Z. S. From morpheme to utterance. *Language,* 1946, *22,* 161–183.

Joos, M. (Ed.). *Readings in linguistics.* Washington, D.C.: American Council of Learned Societies, 1957.

Trager, G. L., & Smith, H. L., Jr. *An outline of English structure.* Washington, D.C.: American Council of Learned Societies, 1962.

Troubetskoy, N. S. *Principes de phonologie.* Paris: Libraire C. Klincksiek, 1949.

IV LANGUAGE AND COGNITION

7 What Is a Language?

Charles E. Osgood
University of Illinois

What is a language? You may well be wondering why I ask this question when everyone *knows* what a language is—it's what you're expressing and I'm comprehending, you say. Let's change the question's form a bit: How would one identify something as *a language* if he encountered what *might* be one in an obviously nonhuman species—for example, flowing kaleidoscopic color patterns on the bulbous bodies of octopus-like creatures who land in a spaceship right in one's own backyard? And, for that matter, is the natural signing of deaf-mutes a language? The game of chess? And what about the "language" of music or art? Or suppose that pale, eyeless midgets were discovered in extended caverns far below the present floors of the Mammoth Cave—emitting very high-frequency pipings from their rounded mouths and apparently listening with their enormous, rotatable ears. How might one decide whether or not these cave midgets have an identifiably *humanoid language*? Only if one can say what defines a language in general and defines a human language in particular can he go on to offer possible answers to some other very important, questions: Do certain nonhuman animals "have" a language? What is common to prelinguistic cognizing and linguistic sentencing? When does a developing child "have" a language? How may languages have developed in the human species? Answers to all these questions, of course, would have relevance to the basic issue of universals and uniquenesses in human communication.

I. DEFINING CHARACTERISTICS OF LANGUAGE GENERALLY

If anything is to be called "a language," it must satisfy the following criteria: It must (1) involve identifiably different and nonrandomly recurrent physical forms in some communication channel, (2) these forms being producible by the same organisms that receive them, their use (3) resulting in nonrandom dependencies between the forms and the behaviors of the organisms that employ them, (4) following nonrandom rules of reference to events in other channels and (5) nonrandom rules of combination with other forms in the same channel, with (6) the users capable of producing indefinitely long and potentially infinite numbers of novel combinations that satisfy the first five criteria.[1] Now, with our Octopian visitors (from the planetary system of the nearest star, Arcturus, as was later discovered) particularly in mind, I will elaborate a bit on these criteria for something being "a language" in general.

1. The Nonrandom Recurrency Criterion: *Production of identifiably different and nonrandomly recurrent physical forms in some communication channel.* A few years ago there was quite a flurry of excitement over apparently nonrandom, recurrent signals being received over interstellar radio receivers—was it something unusual in sunspot activity or, possibly, communication attempts from some distant form of intelligent life? (As I recall, the decision was in favor of sunspots!) As far as ordinary communication is concerned, humans have opted for the vocal-auditory channel (for reasons that will be considered a bit later), but there are many other possible channels that we *are* aware of, because we have also these sensory modalities (light-visual, pressure, tactile and chemical-odor, at which dogs seem particularly adept), and many others that we are *not* aware of (e.g., radiant wavelengths above or below the visible-to-humans range)—and what about ESP? The only critical thing is that such signals be combined in nonrandom ways to produce energy *forms* that are identifiably different (using special equipment if necessary) and are themselves nonrandom in distribution in time and/or space. Note that there is no requirement that the forms be discretely digital (as is generally the case for human languages); they could be continuously analogic in nature.

Back in our own backyard, having recovered from the shock, and being convinced that our octopus-like visitors intend us no harm, we note that as one Octopian pirouettes slowly, with its whole bulbous body flowing with

---

[1]In formulating my own notions about "what is a language" here and in the sections on human languages that follow, I am indebted to the participants in a conference I attended on *Universals of Language,* sponsored by the Social Science Research Council in 1961 and later published in a volume under the same title edited by Joseph H. Greenberg (1963)—particularly papers by Greenberg, Charles S. Hockett, and Uriel Weinreich.

multicolored visual forms, the other stands "silently" neutral gray—only to begin displaying and turning when the first has become "silent." We begin to think that this *may* be some form of communication—not merely displays of emotional states as in the "blushing" of the chameleon.

2. The Reciprocality Criterion: *These forms being producible by the same organisms that receive them.* It is difficult to imagine a human society in which, say, women were the only ones who could produce language (but not comprehend it, even from other women) and men could only comprehend language (but not produce it). For one thing, knowing what we do about the intimate interactions between comprehending and expressing in the development of language in children, one would be hard put to account for the development of such a system. But what about communication between species? Yucca plants and Yucca moths certainly interact for their common survival, but one would hardly call this communication; the "language of flowers" is only a euphemism—we humans can't smell back! But what about mule drivers and their mules? There is no question but that there is communication here, even though the mule can only "kick" back when ornery, but obviously the same organisms are not both producing and receiving the same forms—indicating clearly that communication is not the same as language. Noting that some of the flowing visual forms produced by Octopian A are reproduced in apparent "response" by Octopian B, always along with some uninterpretable contextual variations—and observing this systematically later with color movie films—we became convince that this may, indeed, be some kind of language.

3. The Pragmatic Criterion: *Use of these forms resulting in nonrandom dependencies between the forms and the behaviors of the organisms that employ them.* This criterion applies most testably to the recipients of messages (behaving in appropriately differential fashion to signals received), but also to the initiators of messages (displaying a nonrandom tendency to communicate about entities and events that are proximal in other channels— see criterion 4 below). This is really the criterion that there *is* communication going on. Except for obviously representational art and music—and for purely affective reactions—this criterion would seem to rule out anything other than euphemistic use of phrases like "the language of art" or "the language of music." There is no doubt that bright dogs (like my poodle, Pierre!) develop a large repertoire of appropriate behaviors dependent upon the verbal commands of their masters (e.g., fetching his bone rather than his ball when requested "go getcha *bone*").

Note, however that there is no implication here that pragmatic dependencies must be acquired through experience (learning), although this is clearly the case for human languages. In the language of the bees, when the observing bees in the hive fly the distance and direction signaled by the returned dancing bees, this satisfies the pragmatic criterion—albeit on an innate, "wired-in" basis. What, then, about communication between a human master and a completely "wired-in" *computer* servant? I would argue that this meets the pragmatic criterion (see Winograd, 1972, for a nice example)—but obviously not others (particularly criterion 6, combinatorial productivity). And what about our Octopian friends? Satisfaction of this criterion would be indicated by, for example, a certain color pattern in Octopian A being conditionally dependent upon the presence in front of their spaceship of some complicated scanning device and, when accompanied by various contextual color patterns, by behaviors with respect to this device (shifting its orientation, taking it back into the ship) on the part of Octopian B.

4. The Semantic Criterion: *Use of these forms following nonrandom rules of reference to events in other channels.* This criterion implies that for anything to be a language it must function so as to *symbolize* (represent for the organism) the not-necessarily-*here* and not-necessarily-*now*. Again, although such representing relations are clearly acquired via learning by humans, the language of the bees again tells us that this is not necessarily the case—their dance, upon returning to the hive, does symbolize the not-here (source of nectar) and the not-now (to be found at some indicated flying time in the near future) on a purely innate basis. This criterion is clearly *not* met by the game of chess (where the pieces, despite their names and their moves, bear no symbolizing relation to anything other than themselves) *or* by the "game" of mathematics (where the symbols are deliberately abstract and bear no necessary relations to anything in the real world, but by virtue of this property are *potentially* relatable to any set of real-word entities). Even in humans, semantic relations are not necessarily arbitrary: there is *onomatopoeia* (the name of a thing or event being based on its characteristic sound, e.g., *cuckoo, cough, hiss, slap* and *wheeze* in English) and there is *phonetic symbolism* (in my classes I like to ask the male students which blind date they would prefer, Miss *Pim*, Miss *Boloav*, or Miss *Lavelle*, and then to describe her probable appearance).

Forms in a language can also be *iconic*—witness much of the natural signing of the deaf as well as the gestural accompaniments by ordinary speakers (e.g., in describing my "blind dates" above)—and *this*, we come to infer, might well be the case, at least in part, for our Octopians: we noted that, on the first appearance of Pierre the poodle in our yard, there was a silvery blob followed by a rising line on Octopian A (possibly a question?—"what on earth [sic!] is that?") answered by a nondescript wobbly fuzz figuring near the bottom of Octopian B's bulbous body (possibly meaning, "I haven't the foggiest idea!"). Later, after we demonstrated feeding doggie biscuits to Pierre, taken from a box (for which one Octopian extended a multiple "fingered" tentacle in request—which needless to say we honored), the appearance of Pierre would produce exchanges of silvery blobs, plus some angular pattern, and one Octopian would slip into the ship and reappear with the box of doggie biscuits. And still later they would "call for" an absent Pierre with his "blob" (and that rising line pattern)—and Pierre in turn quickly learned to come to beg the Octopians for biscuits!

5. The Syntactic Criterion: *Use of these forms following nonrandom rules of combination with other forms in the same channel.* As will be seen, all human languages may be characterized as being *hierarchical* in structure (analyzable in terms of units-within-units); they are also organized *temporally on a "left-to-right" basis*—that is, from prior to subsequent forms at all levels—as a necessary consequence of their utilization of the vocal-auditory channel. But these by no means must be defining characteristics of language in general, and one wonders to what extent space could be substituted for time in the organization of messages by organisms using other channels. Presumably there would be some limit—for example, we might discover (although the "how" of this is not as obvious as with the preceding criteria) that the Octopians "flash" the equivalents of whole paragraphs on their N "panels" as they rotate in the process of communicating, the within-paragraph information being spatially represented—"sentences" thus being an unessential carving up of the information flow (I might note that whole paragraphs, consisting of a single sentence, multiply conjoined and embedded, are not exactly a rarity in, particularly, scholarly writing!). The diverse recursive devices (e.g., as in center-embedded sentencings like *the man the girl the teacher likes married plays poker*) might be entirely unnecessary in a spatially organized language like Octopian.

And yet *some* structuring, representing what is "natural" in sentencing based on prelinguistic cognizing experience—for Octopian "squidsters" just as for human youngsters—might be expected for all organismic languages. For humans, the two basic types of simple cognition appear to be Action and Stative Relations (and both in SVO order), the former highlighting the typically +Animate Actor as subject as against the typically ‾Animate (or at least relatively passive) Recipient as object and the latter highlighting the +Salient Figure as subject against the ‾Salient Ground as object—thus *Pierre chased the ball* and *the ball was on the grass* as simple Action and Stative cognitions respectively.[2]

After having mastered some of the pragmatics and semantics of Octopian, we might study our video-tapes with such Naturalness Principles in mind. For examples: are the visual patterns centered on a "panel" (e.g., the silvery "Pierre" blob) characteristically representations of the more animate and/or

---

[2]See Osgood (1979) for detailing of these Naturalness Principles—including, of course, the fact that human languages also utilize adverbial substitutes for simple junction *(and)* and disjunction *(but)* which permit clausal permutations (which might well be unnecessary in Octopian).

figural entities, and the other blobs with which they are diversely linked radially by angular lines (verb phrases?) characteristically the less animate and/or figural? Is there some spatial ordering discernible for several sets of "conjoined" radial patterns involving same or different centered "topics," and does this ordering typically fit our human notions of naturalness in ordering?

6. **The Combinatorial Productivity Criterion:** *The users of the forms being capable of producing indefinitely long and potentially infinite numbers of novel combinations that satisfy the first five criteria.* At any particular time, synchronically, this novelty in human language lies in the combining and not in what is combined; thus, my statements about the Octopians' linguistic behaviors, although entirely novel as wholes (I presume), utilized thoroughly familiar lexemes (criterion 4) and constructions (criterion 5) in contemporary American English. However, it must be admitted that anyone who has done an analysis of the semantics and syntactics of telephone conversations comes away rather unimpressed with the combinatorial productivity of ordinary speakers using ordinary language. Of course over time, diachronically, human languages do display adaptive changes by both expanding the lexicon (criterion 4) and by changing the rules (criterion 5). Presumably, any organismic language would display such adaptivity—either via evolution over very long periods (for languages with innately based semantics and syntax, like that of the bees) or via learning over relatively short periods, dependent upon changing environmental conditions (for languages with individually acquired semantics and syntax, as happens with human cultures and languages in contact).

Testing for the presence of this combinatorial productivity (criterion 6) in another language—particularly a very strange one like Octopian—would undoubtedly be most difficult. Although nearly all of the communicative exchanges among the Octopians, and between them and ourselves, would seem novel in whole or in part *to us*, that would be no proof that they were not elaborately stereotyped patterns, analogous to most human telephone conversations. Only after we had mastered *their* language to the point where *we* could compose Octopian statements of indubitable novelty for them (and see if they comprehended them) and ask questions requiring indubitably novel answers (and see if they could produce them), could we determine if they had this crucial capability. And—horror of horrors!—we might discover that they did *not*, that they were entirely "programmed" like computers, and in fact were *robots* sent out by the real Arcturians, whatever they might be like. However, one thing this litte experiment by Arcturians would have demonstrated is this: if two species each have a language by these criteria, then either directly (or mediately, via appropriate equipment) they should be able to communicate to some extent with each other; the extent and direction would depend on the amount and balance of intelligence, that organism with the lower channel capacity determining the limit on communication (the dog in effect setting limits for the master).

A. Do Any Other, Nonhuman, Animals Have a Language?

One can trace a continuum of levels of interorganismic communication: from *proximal interactions* (contacting, mating, mothering, fighting and ... consuming!), through *distal SIGNAL sending and receiving* (unintentional odors such as the bitch in heat, mating calls, baboon warning and food-supply noises), through *distal SIGN sending and receiving* (intentional expression of affect, like growls, tail waggings, postural and facial expressions designed to influence the behavior of the receiver), to *SYMBOL creating and interpreting* (the food-supply dance of the bees, "play" in dogs and other higher animals, referential gesturings by chimps and humans). For any given species, we can ask, *does its intraspecies communication satisfy the six criteria for something to be a language?* Take the *clam*—which, if anything, seems to have specialized *away* from communication in its evolution: because, as far as I know, there is no evidence for clam-to-clam nonrandom recurrency of signals in any channel (criterion 1)—and, given the limited motility and reactive capacity ("neck" retracting, shell clamping, and ... ?), it seems likely that communication would be limited to chemical broadcasts at most (unless the clam has been fooling us and specializes in the development of ESP!). If criterion 1 is not satisfied, of course, then none of the others (reciprocality, pragmatics, semantics, syntax, or combinatorial productivity) can be met. The answer to whether this species has a language is, in a clam shell, no! So let's move along up the evolutionary tree.

a. The Bee. Briefly (necessarily),[3] the bee communicates three species-significant things: *showing its pass-badge* (a scent pouch that is opened on entering the hive and, if the scent is wrong—execution); *location of a nectar supply* (the well-known "dance," whose angle with respect to the sun indicates direction, whose number of turns per unit time indicates distance, and whose number of abdomen wags indicates quality of the supply); *location of a new "home"* (a kind of "election" in which, when local supplies have dwindled, that returning bee which gets the crowd at home to follow his dance—usually the one that has found the richest load, has had to fly the shortest distance back, and hence is the most energetic—ends up with the whole hive flying off to his new location). Because the dance forms are obviously nonrandom, because any worker bee functions equivalently as sender or receiver, because

---

[3]See K. von Frisch (1974) and James L. Gould (1975) for updating references on communication in the bee.

behaviors of both are nonrandomly dependent upon the messages, and because the forms have nonrandom rules of reference (to the not-here and not-now nectar locations), criteria 1–4 appear to be clearly met. As far as syntactic criterion 5 is concerned, because the messages involve three types of forms (direction, distance, and quality indicating) that must be combined in certain nonrandom ways, this would seem to be met. But what about criterion 6, the combinatorial-productivity criterion? For any given bee "speaker" or bee "listener," a given combination of direction, distance, and quality indicators must often be novel, yet communication is successful. So we conclude that, within very narrow limits of what can be communicated, "the language of the bee" is not a euphemism—and, most remarkably, it is entirely innate ("wired in").

b. The Bird. The varied calls of the many subspecies of birds (which must be acquired, particularly during an early "imprinting" stage) are sufficient evidence for satisfying criterion 1 (nonrandom recurrency of forms), and the back-and-forth callings that awaken us so pleasantly in the early mornings of spring are evidence for satisfaction of criterion 2 (reciprocality). In the bird-to-bird communication of crows, for example, their "alarm" and "assemble" calls are evidence for at least rudimentary pragmatics and semantics (criteria 3 and 4)—and there are even crow "dialects" (taped *alarm* calls of American crows have been shown to produce *assembling* on the part of French crows!)—but these are essentially absent in bird-to-man communication. Given criteria 1 and 2, plus use of the vocal-auditory channel, one can teach some birds (e.g., parrots, parakeets, myna birds) to talk "human" in limited ways, but these appear to be purely imitative, sensory and motor integrations—meaningless, without expressing representational significances and intentions. I well remember in the early 1950s a research assistant of O. Hobart Mowrer spending many months and thousands of trials trying to get a talkative myna bird to say something like "wanna-eat" and "wanna-drink" (both in its imitative vocabulary) *differentially* for seeds vs. water, when made hungry vs. thirsty and shown the appropriate reinforcers—with never a significant shift from pure chance performance. So the bird appears to be strong on criteria 1 and 2 and weak on 3 and 4, with both 5 (syntax) and 6 (combinatorial productivity) totally lacking—talking birds repeat phrases as wholes, never piecing together parts of different phrases to make new combinations.

c. The Dog. This species might almost be said to have developed "writing" before "talking," because it seems to depend more on persistent (odor) than evanescent (visual or auditory) *denotative* signs—everytime I return to the house, my Pierre has to lift up and sniff my hand, just to make *sure* it's me! However, in dog-to-dog (as well as dog-to-human) communication, connotative meanings (primitive affective Evaluation, Potency and Activity, also found to be universal in human languages—see Osgood, May, and Miron, 1975) are richly displayed and reacted to in gestural-visual and vocal-auditory channels, the dog's tail being a particularly expressive organ: up vs. down signaling the Pleasantness, rigid vs. limp, the Forcefulness, and moving vs. stationary, the Liveliness of the animal's affective states. Dogs can acquire extensive repertoires of differential significances for human-produced signs through training, either formal (for hunting or circus performance) or informal (as pets), and this definitely satisfied both pragmatic (3) and semantic (4) criteria. Thus, in contrast with the bird, the dog is weak on criteria 1 and 2 (dependent on what I call the Integrational Level of behavior) but strong on 3 and 4 (dependent on the representational level). But, like the bird, the dog does not satisfy 5 (syntax) and at best only minimally meets 6 (combinatorial productivity)—and that only in comprehending (e.g., behaving appropriately to the pivot phrase "pick up" plus a new object name like "your leash").

d. The Ape. I use this term to refer to nonhuman, but close-to-human primates—rather than the *chimp*—because others have been shown to have similar capabilities (e.g., recently the gorilla). I will also concentrate on the Gardners' Washoe (R. A. Gardner & B. T. Gardner, 1969; B. T. Gardner & R. A. Gardner, 1975) rather than the Premacks' Sarah (D. Premack, 1971; A. J. Premack & D. Premack, 1972). The laboratory research with Sarah (comprehending sentence-like vertical sequences of plastic symbols and behaving appropriately; producing plastic sentence-like sequences of her own and being differentially reinforced) demonstrates the astonishingly complex cognitive capacity of a chimpanzee: ability to signal the "sameness" or "difference" of object pairs, that symbol X is or is not "the name of" various presented real objects (bananas, apples, etc.), responding appropriately to "clause" pairs conjoined by an "if-then" symbol (e.g., SARAH TAKE APPLE ("if-then") MARY GIVE CHOCOLATE SARAH / MARY NO GIVE CHOCOLATE SARAH), and so forth. However, whether this represents comprehension and production of *sentences* or "simply" complex, differentially reinforced reactions remains obscure (usually only a single set of alternative responses was required on any given problem). And although there is ample evidence for semantics and pragmatics, there is little for syntax or combinatorial productivity.[4] In any case, Sarah's would be a highly

---

[4]With regard to semantics, particularly impressive to me was the fact that Sarah would make the same "semantic-feature" choices for the plastic *sign* of, say, an APPLE (Round rather than Square, Stemmed rather than Nonstemmed) as for the apple object itself—when the sign itself happens to be a flat purple triangle!

arbitrary *written* "language" rather than the gestural–vocal one natural for the chimpanzee.

Prior to the Gardners' work with Washoe, several psychologists (e. g. the Kelloggs' Gua and the Hayes' Viki) had also brought up an infant chimpanzee in their home as they would a child of their own, but the only attempts at "language" seemed to be to teach the ape to talk human—and they failed miserably (Viki ended up with about four imperfectly produced simple words like "papa" and "cup"). Given the lack of hemispheric dominance in nonhuman primates, which is critical for voluntary control over the medially located speech apparatus, this failure was not at all surprising. The decision to bring a chimp up in a human environment, *but with constant exposure to the natural sign language of the deaf-mute,* was long overdue, and one of the most exciting developments in decades resulted.[5] Facial, manual and postural gesturings, along with strong tendencies to imitate, are characteristic of chimps in their natural state, and Washoe took readily to signing, imitating her human companions in the context of meaningful everyday events (with their motivating and reinforcing properties) and babbling away manually on her own (with her companions "shaping" her signs into the human-proper forms). And I understand that Washoe is now in a colony of chimps at Norman, Oklahoma, busily communicating with others just acquiring . . . the language?

So now let's check Washoe's communicative performance (as reported in R. A. Gardner & B. T. Gardner, 1969) against our criteria of something being "a language." Criterion 1 (nonrandom recurrency of forms) is obviously met by the differential use (by age 4) of some 80 gestural signs. Criterion 2 (reciprocality, both sending and receiving) is obviously met—first with humans "at the other end" but more recently with other chimps. Criterion 3 (pragmatics) is satisfied by such evidence as her making the "toothbrush" sign "in a peremptory fashion when its appearance at the end of a meal was delayed," by her signing "open" at the door of a room she was leaving, and so forth *ad infinitum*. There is also no question about satisfying criterion 4 (semantics): her spontaneous "naming" of toothbrushes, with "no obvious motive other than communication"; her learning to sign "dog," mainly to those in picture books, but then signing it spontaneously to the sound of an unseen dog barking outside; her signing "key" not only to keys being presently used to open locks but also to "not-here" keys needed to unlock locks! And there is also no question but that criterion 6 (combinatorial productivity) is satisfied: the Gardners report that as soon as Washoe had a vocabulary of a dozen or so signs (including verbs like "open" and "go," nouns like "key" and

---

[5]I can't resist noting (with no little remorse) that during my tenure on the University of Illinois Research Board in the early 1960s a request for support of precisely this type of study was voted on favorably, but the young couple who were to raise the baby chimp backed out—otherwise this breakthrough might have occurred at the University of Illinois!

"flower," the pronouns "you" and "me," and adverbials (?) like "please," "more," and "hurry") she spontaneously began combining them in sequences like "open flower" (open gate to flower garden), "go sweet" (to be taken to raspberry bush), and "you me out" (you take me outdoors); she also displays the "pivot/open-class" productivity familiar in child language development (e.g., "please sweet drink," "please key," "hurry out," and "please hurry sweet drink").

But what about criterion 5 (syntax)? This has been the focus of most questioning of Washoe's "having a language," and in early critiques both Bronowski and Bellugi (1970, p. 672) and McNeill (1970, p. 55) stress the fact that Washoe's "utterances" display no constraints on "word" order, her signings seemingly having free ordering (e.g., "up please" or "please up," "open key" or "key open"). However, in an equally early commentary, Roger Brown (1970, pp. 224–230) makes several very significant points:

1. that Washoe's linguistic performances should be compared with those of a 3- or 4-year-old *deaf-mute child* rather than with normal children of this age;

2. that just as normal children already control several prosodic patterns when they begin to produce combinations (e.g., the falling pitch of declaratives, the rising pitch of interrogatives), so do the deaf—*and quite spontaneously* (according to the Gardners) *Washoe*—hold for a perceptibly longer period the last sign of a sequence to indicate a question; and

3. that just as in human language development, Washoe displayed a gradual increase over time in the sign length of her "utterances"—two common before three and three common before four—and Brown asks reasonably, "why should this be so if the sign combinations are not constructions [p. 225]?"

Perhaps most significantly, Brown (1970) observes that "there is little or no communication pressure on either children or Washoe to use the right word order for the meanings they intend [p. 229]" when language is being used in contexts that are *perceptually unambiguous* to both producer and receiver— which is the case in much of early child language and in just about all of Washoe's signings (and it should be noted that, although Washoe's companions "corrected" the signings of particular lexical items, they apparently did not "correct" for sign orderings, as do most adult companions of young human children).

Relevant here is an actual experiment with Washoe (B. T. Gardner & R. A. Gardner, 1975) designed to get at evidence for recognition of "sentence constituents" in her communications. In English, answers to *wh*-questions require identification of the relevant NP constituent; given the sentence *Roger put the key on the table*, for example, the question *Who did it?* specifies the subject NP (Roger), the question *What was put somewhere?* specifies the object NP (key), and the question *Where was something put?* specifies the NP-head of the locative phrase. The Gardners were able to demonstrate not only that Washoe's replies (including single-sign) to such *wh*-questions were significantly contingent with the correct NP constituents (at the .00001 level) but also that her 84% correct NP inclusion in replies was superior to the performance of normal children of corresponding linguistic age! It is also interesting that David McNeill, in a recent paper (1974), now concludes that the chimpanizee (Washoe data, primarily) *does* meet criterion 5, "...spontaneously adopting an apparently novel form of syntax based on social relationships (such as addressee and nonaddressee)." Generalizing, it appears that, whereas human language is designed for humans to talk *about* people and things, natural chimp "language" is designed for chimps to talk *to* other chimps (or people, in Washoe's case).

II.   DEFINING CHARACTERISTICS OF HUMAN LANGUAGES

Human languages must, of course, satisfy all the criteria for *anything* to be called a language—thus having nonrandom recurrent signals in some channel, producible by the same organisms that receive them, which display nonrandom pragmatic, semantic, and syntactic dependencies that are combinatorially productive—but there are additional delimiting criteria that must be met if something is to be called a natural *human* language. These additional defining characteristics can be categorized (at least superficially) as either *structural* or *functional*.

A. Structural Characteristics of Human Languages

For something that is a language to be called a *human* language, it must have the following structural characteristics: it must (7) involve use of the vocal–auditory channel, and thus (8) nondirectional transmission but directional reception and (9) evanescence in time of the forms in the channel, these characteristics requiring (10) integration over time of the information derived from the physical forms, but also (11) providing prompt feedback to the sender of his own messages. All of these structural characteristics are direct, combined functions of the physical nature of sound and the biological nature of the human organism.

   7. The Vocal–Auditory Channel Criterion: *All natural human languages use vocalization for production and audition for reception.* This, of course, refers to the primary communication system for humans, there being many other derived systems—the most general being writing (a more lasting gestural-visual sort of channel) but also drum signals, smoke signals, and

Morse code. It should be noted that the vocalic response system is both relatively "lightweight" (in terms of energy required, as compared, say, with locomotion) and minimally interfering with other ongoing activities (like toolmaking, hunting, and fighting)—properties we shall find relevant to the question of the origin of human languages.

8. Nondirectional Transmission, Directional Reception: *In human languages, speaking is broadcast and hearing is selective.* Broadcast transmission is simply a function of the manner of propagation of sound waves—in all directions and, conveniently, around corners (an advantage lacking in visual Octopian, by the way); selective reception is simply a function of the fact that we have a head between our ears, this interaural distance yielding phase differences for sound waves originating in all directions except along the medial line, and hence providing cues for direction of the source. This channel characteristic may well have had significant influence upon the social structures of primitive human groups—Mr. "Big-mouth" being heard by all "Little-mouths" at once, but the "Little-mouths" securing one-to-one privacy only by isolating themselves!

9. The Evanescence-in-Time Characteristic: *Signals in the vocal–auditory channel fade rapidly in intensity over time.* The advantage of such evanescence, of course, is that it minimizes "cluttering up" of the channel—as anyone who has tried to understand what another is saying across an echo chamber fully appreciates. The disadvantage is that it puts a heavy load on short-term as well as long-term memory—the latter undoubtedly being the major reason for the development of writing systems of various types, apparently independently in different human societies as they reached certain levels of complexity. (Parenthetically, it is sobering in this nuclear age to realize that humans have had writing systems for only about 5,000 years.)

10. The Integration-over-Time Requirement: *The distribution of message forms over time on a linear "left-to-right" basis requires temporary storage and integration of information.* Although there is simultaneous patterning within sounds (e.g., chords in music), it is minimal in comparison with vision. A familiar example of such temporal integration in human speech is *prosody*—a falling intonation pattern over time signaling a statement, a rising pattern a question. This constraint also leads speakers to shift "leftward" (earlier in time) message elements that are salient to them (e.g., creating a passive, "Pierre was stung by that bee!"). Of course, our Octopian receivers would have to integrate information over *space* within the "panels" of their bulbous senders' bodies, as well as store it temporarily for integration with information in succeeding "panels."

11. Availability of Prompt Feedback: *The speaker of a human language is normally capable of hearing his own messages as he produces them.* This property of the vocal-auditory channel has significance for development of language in the young of the species as well as for production of language in the mature. Because it is a maxim in language development that, at all stages and in all phases, comprehension typically precedes production, it follows that the sounds of understood adult forms (like "ball") and combinations of forms (like "that's Mommy's shoe") can serve as models against which the child can correct his own productions ("bawh," "dah Mommy show"), and even more complexly develop the syntactic niceties. In the ordinary speech of adults, one notes not only filled and unfilled pauses (time for cognizing to catch up with sentencing) but also retracings with corrections (usually of full constituent length, e.g., "Well, my dear, I did it all in one swell foop . . . /ah/ . . . in one fell swoop and was on my way!"). Under abnormal conditions of *delayed* feedback (via the intervention of tape), one finds he cannot speak, or even read, naturally (as I found when the late Grant Fairbanks had me try to read the statement on a pack of cigarettes, ". . . the Amer-eric-c-can To-to-BACCO Comp-comp-COMPNY! . . ."); under abnormal condition of *no* feedback (via masking with noise), patients in psychotherapy have been found to talk more freely (but often rather incoherently) and without as much self-critical backtracking (Mahl, 1972). One wonders how the Octopian "speakers" would monitor their own communicative displays—by seeing them from within?

The signing of deaf-mutes would be ruled out, as far as being a *natural* human language, by criterion 7 (use of the vocal-auditory channel), but of course it would still satisfy the requirements for being *a language*, even in the chimp, as Washoe has demonstrated. And what about our Cave Midgets—in their domain far beneath the floors of the Mammoth Cave? While we were trying to determine if our visitors from Arcturus had something that could be called "a language," other intrepid human explorers (linguists) were doing the same with the pale little Cave Midgets. Tape recordings of their high-frequency pipings left no doubt but that nonrandom recurrent sound forms were being reciprocally produced and received; the nonrandom dependencies of their use of artifacts in mushroom-and-worm cultivating activities upon these distinctive piping forms clearly satisfied the pragmatic and semantic criteria.

Testing for syntactic structuring and combinatorial productivity took a bit of doing, particularly because our linguists were struggling with very sore throats brought on by continuous whisperings—the big-eared Cave Midgets fly into panic at any loud, low-frequency sound. However, after many sleepless days analyzing visual displays of ultrasonic piping patterns, one linguistic genius demonstrated "noun/verb" selection rules, and, a bit later, another had a brainstorm (not surprisingly, after consuming a worm-and-mushroom pizza) and created a computer-based Cave-Midgetese synthesizer, at least for very simple utterances—and combinatorial productivity was firmly established. So there was no question but that these Cave Midgets had a language—and, given the piping sounds that went whistling around the cavern passageways plus the big ears that rotated to receive them, it seemed obvious that this language met the *structural* requirements for being of the human type—but what about the *functional* requirements?

B. Functional Characteristics of Human Languages

For something to be called a human language, it must also have the following functional characteristics: (12) the semantic relations between forms and meanings must, in general, be arbitrary rather than iconic, and (13) the forms in the channel that distinguish meanings must be discretely rather than continuously variable; further, the forms in the channel must (14) be analyzable hierarchically into levels of units-within-units, with (15) large numbers of units at each higher level being exhaustively analyzable into relatively small numbers of components at each lower level; and finally, (16) extension of a language within the species, both generationally and geographically, must be via experience (learning) rather than via inheritance (maturation). The complex, visual-patterning language of the Octopians seems to fit neither the arbitrariness (12) nor the discreteness (13) criteria, and its efficiency must lie elsewhere than in hierarchical (14) and componential (15) organization. Whether the Octopian language extends itself in time and space on the basis of experience (like human language) or of inheritance (like bee language) we do not know at this point. However, because the Cave Midgets are a somewhat humanoid species of this earth, we would be most interested in seeing how *their* language stacks up against these functional criteria.

   12. Arbitrariness of Form-Meaning Relations: *In human languages the rules relating forms in the communication channel to events in other channels* (cf. criterion 4) *are typically arbitrary rather than iconic.* We must say "typically" because (as noted earlier) human languages do display both onomatopoeia and phonetic symbolism; however, for the most part form-meaning relations are arbitrary (witness *Pferd* in German, *cheval* in Fench, and *horse* in English). Noting the prevalence of phonetic symbolism in the communication of affect—in both natural chimp ("oh-oh-oh" for joy vs. "uu-uu-uu" for sorrow, "eeee!" for fear) and natural human ("boy-oh-boy" for pleasure vs. "ugh" for disgust, "eek!" for the "shriek" of fear)—one might speculate that there has been social evolution from iconic affective signs toward arbitrary denotative signs, particularly as languages became more complex and abstract in their references.

   13. Discreteness of Form Shifts Signaling Differences in Meaning: *In human languages, the changes in form that convey changes in meaning are discretely rather than continuously variable.* This characteristic certainly holds at the phonemic level (the abrupt shifts in distinctive features of sound that distinguish, for example, *fail, gale, male, sail* and *tail*), the morphemic level (the productive pluralizing morphemes for nouns in English are always *either* [-s], [z] or [-iz], conditionally dependent on the voicing or sibilance of the preceding sound, as in *cats, dogs,* and *horses* respectively), the lexical level (a graded speeding up of *walk* into say *wok* doesn't yield the meaning of *run*), and the syntactic level (an NP being signaled by *the singing* and a VP by *was singing,* for a simple example). Such discreteness has certainly simplified the descriptive task for linguistic science. Whether such discrete either/or-ness holds at the level of semantic features is highly debatable—but then meaning is not usually overtly signaled in the surface forms of human languages.

14. The Hierarchical Organization Criterion: *In human languages, the stream of forms in the channel is analyzable into levels of units-within-units.* Complex sentences are analyzable into clauses (or "sentoids"), clauses are analyzable into immediate constituents (concatenations of NPs "hanging on" a VP), constituents into word forms (heads, modifiers, and modulators), words into morphemes (stems and affixes), morphemes into phonemes, and phonemes into distinctive phonetic features. To some extent semantic systems also display hierarchical organizations (particularly for nouns) that are describable in the form of "taxonomic tree" structures—thus the meaning of *bird* is entailed in the meanings of all its exemplars (*sparrow, robin, eagle,* etc.), the meaning of *animal* is entailed in those of *bird, fish, mammal,* and so forth. Implicit in this criterion (and in criterion 15) is the constraint that no higher-level unit can be embedded in a lower-level unit—and this raises some interesting questions about what is the proper linguistic analysis of, for example, sentences with relative clauses (*I've met the girl who arrived late at the party,* where the *Wh*-clause is itself a sentential elaboration of an NP), what I call "commentative" sentences (like *I hope that John will be on time for the wedding* or *It is a fact that John has been married before*) or monstrous center-embedded sentences (like *The boy the girl Pierre likes likes likes spaghetti!*).

15. The Componential Organization Criterion: *In human languages, large numbers of units at each higher level in the hierarchy* (of criterion 14) *are exhaustively analyzable as near-simultaneous combinations of relatively small numbers of units at each next lower level.* Potentially infinite numbers of sentences are analyzable into near-infinite numbers of clausal constituents, these in turn analyzable into some hundreds of thousands of word units that are themselves analyzable into some thousands of morphemes, and these being analyzable into some 40 or so phonemes that can be analyzed into an even smaller number of distinctive phonetic features for any given human language. And this componential analysis is exhaustive at all levels—no leftover pieces! Viewed from bottom to top, from combinations of the smallest units (distinctive features) to the uniquely varied patterns of the largest (sentences), this system represents a remarkably efficient way to satisfy the criterion of combinatorial productivity (6)—which anything must meet if it is to be called "a language." But this is obviously not the only *conceivable* way to achieve efficiency. If, for example, a species were able to increase the number and complexity of units at some lowest, unanalyzable, level (e.g., hundreds of thousands of meaningful "morphemes") and simultaneously increase the complexity of the simultaneous patterning of only one higher level (potentially infinite numbers and complexities of "sentences"), then perhaps even greater efficiency could be achieved, but it would take mental capacities far beyond those available to humans—perhaps those available to Arcturians, however.

In introducing this section on the defining characteristics of human languages, and proposing that they could be categorized as "structural" vs. "functional," I added the parenthetical "hedge" *(at least superficially)*. Now, with specific reference to the hierarchical and componential organization criteria (14 and 15), although they are in no obvious way dependent upon the *peripheral sensory or motor structures* of primates, they may well reflect ways in which the *central nervous systems* of higher organisms have evolved—and hence be just as innately determined as those reflecting the constraints imposed by using the vocal–auditory channel. Note that the same hierarchical-componential organization appears in prelinguistic behavior as well: in the comprehension of complex facial expressions of emotion, with their variable component states (upturned vs. downturned mouth, V-shaped vs. Λ-shaped brows, etc.); in the production of complex skilled acts, like that of "door opening," where locomoting, arm extending, object grasping, and pulling constituents are sequenced in terms of perceptual feedbacks, are themselves composed of finer motor units, and participate in many different intentional acts (e.g., object grasping as part of the acts of "apple eating" and "hand shake greeting" as well as "door-opening").

16. The Transferral-via-Learning Criterion: *Human languages are transferred to other members of the species, both generationally over time and geographically over space, via experience* (learning) *rather than via inheritance* (maturation). There is no evidence whatsoever that the offspring of speakers of some particular human language find it easier to acquire *that* language than any other; in other words, children come into the world cognitively equipped to speak any human-type language—a Japanese infant can learn to speak English or Papago just as easily as Japanese. Of course, this Japanese infant couldn't learn Cave-Midgetese very well (without special equipment), and the same would hold for Cave Midget youngsters learning any existing human language, but this could be due simply to the special adaptation of the Cave Midgets to their cavernous environment over the millennia.

How might our intrepid linguists determine whether or not Cave-Midgetese meets the functional criteria for a language being humanoid in type? Form-meaning arbitrariness (12) and discreteness rather than continuousness in signaling meaning shifts (13) would both require pretty thorough familiarization with the language; given that, one might then determine if the *components* of piping "word" units (analogous to our phonemes) have essentially random relations to their meanings (12) and also whether the shifts in pipings are discretely or continuously variable with respect to shifts in meaning (13) (e.g., if a "vowel" frequency shifted continuously from low to high in order to modulate the meaning of an otherwise constant form to convey "doing something very slowly" to "doing it very rapidly").

But both of these "tests" already presuppose satisfaction of both hierarchical (14) and componential (15) organization, and in some ways "tests" of these characteristics would be easier: One would merely need to demonstrate (using the ultrasonic visual displays) that distinguishable piping forms enter arbitrarily into diverse larger forms that have distinctive meanings, and that these larger forms enter similarly into more diverse, still larger piping sequences, probably separated by identifiable "pauses"—the differences in these larger forms, of course, displaying predictable contingencies with behavioral (pragmatic) and referential (semantic) phenomena, as indicated by use of a vastly improved computerized Cave-Midgetese synthesizer. So, given such demonstrations, it would appear that "the language of Cave Midgets" is indeed a human-type language—developed by an early branch of humanoids that, in the search for bigger and juicier mushrooms and worms, happened to end up in caverns deep in the earth.

III. NONDEFINING CHARACTERISTICS OF HUMAN LANGUAGES

All of the defining characteristics considered so far are, ipso facto, universals. There are many other characteristics of human languages—some of them apparently absolute but many of them only statistical universals—which, I would argue, are not *defining* characteristics. That is, if one encountered something that was *a language* by criteria 1–6 and, further, was a human-type language by criteria 7–16, then, if it failed to display any one or more of the characteristics to be discussed in this section, it would *still* be considered a human language—albeit a rather strange one. We can categorize nondefining characteristics fairly reasonably into two types: (1) those that reflect certain *intellectual and cultural traits that are common to the human species* rather than linguistic regularities per se; (2) those which reflect dynamic *interactions among principles of psycholinguistic performance* and typically yield statistical rather than absolute universals of language. Only very small samples of such nondefining characteristics can be offered here by way of illustration.

A. Based on Intellectual and Cultural Characteristics of Humans

1. Propositionalizing

All known human languages can be used to create propositional sentences that, in principle, are testable as to their truth or falsity. All humans seem capable of cognizing certain regularities and relations in their physical and social environments and expressing these in linguistic assertions—*the sun always rises in the east, a robin is a bird, bears hibernate in the winter,* and so on *ad libitum.* Without such capacities, there could be no science, to be sure, but would we wish to claim that the language of a society of humanoids *sans* science was therefore not a human-type language? The language of our Cave Midgets might well be so characterized. Interesting in this connection is the complete absence of propositional sentences (apparently) in Washoe's signings—and, in fact, McNeill (1974) points out that chimpanzee "syntax" seems to be based on sociality more than objectivity, with the addressee-nonaddressee distinction being crucial for word ordering (witness Washoean "utterances" like *you me out, Roger Washoe out, you Naomi peekaboo* and *you tickle me-Washoe*).

2. Prevarication

In all known human languages, messages can be intentionally false, deceptive, or meaningless. This, in a way, is a consequence of being able to propositionalize. All humans seem to be able to produce sentences analogous to *the moon is made of green cheese, I was not involved in planning the Watergate Caper,* and even *colorless green ideas sleep furiously.* If speakers of an otherwise humanoid language—let's say Cave-Midgetese—couldn't prevaricate, then, of course, they could have neither fiction nor poetry, would be unable to "grease" the social grind with convenient "little white lies," would be incapable of sarcasm ("Thanks a lot!") or irony (saying "Isn't that just great!" while looking at a flat tire on one's car) or any of the little clevernesses with language, like saying of a certain woman "she'll make someone a nice husband." But would such lackluster communication rule out a language as humanoid? I doubt it. One might note in passing that "play" in higher animals (e.g., Pierre making a ferocious growling charge at me that ends in kissing my hand) is a kind of prevarication.

3. Reflexiveness

In all known human languages, messages can be used to talk about other messages and/or their components. In all human languages one can say things like "the word *bachelor* can refer to 'an unmarried adult human male'" but also to 'one who has received the lowest college degree' or even to 'a young male fur seal kept off the breeding grounds by the older males.'" In writing, we usually make use of tricks like italicizing, capitalizing, and quoting to signal the fact that such forms *are* words about words, rather than ordinary communications. And witness performative sentences like *I christen thee "the Jimmy Carter"* for some aircraft carrier of the future, or illocutionary speech acts more generally (see Searle, 1969) like *I state that S, I promise that S, I fear* (am amazed, am sorry) *that S,* and *I know* (believe, doubt, etc.) *that S*—what I have called "commentative" sentences where the so-called matrix sentence (*I verb* that . . .) is some kind of comment on the embedded sentence. If our Cave Midget friends lacked this ability to use language to comment on language, then of course they could have no philosophy, no linguistics, no psycholinguistics . . . and no puns. But they could still be said to have a humanoid language, I think.

4. Learnability

Any natural human language can be acquired by any normal human being. If the acquirer is a child, we speak of first-language larning; if it is an adult, already fluent in his native language, then we speak of second-language learning. We might sometime come across a language used by humanoids so primitive or unintelligent that they just simply were not capable of learning the complex structures of any ordinary human language—and this might well apply to the hypothetical Cave Midgets—but I still think we would have to classify it as *a human language* if it met all of the defining criteria. And the same, of course, would apply in reverse: If it were some humanoid species whose spaceship landed in our backyard, and if they used the vocal-auditory channel and obviously displayed all of our defining characteristics—but their language was so complex in lexicon and in both length and embeddings of sentences that no Earthly human could learn it—then I think we would still humbly have to admit it as a human language.

5. Translatability

Any natural human language can be translated into any other human language. Both the preceding nondefining characteristic (learnability) and this one (translatability) assume, of course, that the lexicon of the acquirer or of the destination language of the translation can be expanded as necessary *or* be handled by circumlocutions (e.g., the "iron horse" used by American Indians as a translation of "locomotive"). And the same complexity constraints apply as above—either the ordinary human source language could be beyond the intellectual capabilities of the destination language users (translating English into Cave-Midgetese) or the extraordinary humanoid source language could be too complex for the users of ordinary human destination languages (translating the language of those godlike humanoids from outer space into ordinary English). But, again, I would argue that these limitations would not rule out the essential "humanness" of the languages involved.

B. Based on Language Performance Principles and Their Interactions

1. Selection and Combination Rules

Across all languages and levels of units, rules of selection and combination of alternative forms are statistical rather than absolute universals (cf. criteria 14 and 15, hierarchical and componential organization of human languages, above). At the phonological level, each language selects from those differences in sound which the human vocalic system makes possible a small subset of differences that will make a difference in meaning (i.e., are phonemic); certain differences (voiced vs. nonvoiced) are much more probable statistically than others (lip flattening vs. lip rounding) across languages. At the syntactic level, each language selects as its grammar a limited subset of "rewrite rules" (for expansion in expression and for contraction in comprehension) from an indefinitely large number of possibilities; again, certain types of grammatical rules are statistically more probable than others (e.g., NP $\leftrightarrow$ N + A about twice as likely across languages as NP $\leftrightarrow$ A + N and for good psycholinguistic reasons). At the semantic level, each language selects from a potentially infinite number of features some subset for differentiating among the items in its lexicon; although many semantic features are universal, many are not—and, in any case, the distributions of feature weights in languages are statistically variable. This differential rule selection and combination at all levels is the reason why any particular human language must be learned—yet is learnable.

2. A Progressive Differentiation Principle

Across all languages and levels of units, a principle of progressive differentiation of meaning-signaling forms operates, but the extent of differentiation varies statistically. In phonology, for example, only if a high–low vowel distinction is phonemic will a lips flattened–rounded distinction also be phonemic—never the reverse order of differentiation. In syntax, one example would be the Keenan-Comrie (1975) "Accessibility Hierarchy" for relative clause formation: Only if a language permits relativization of the subject NP will it also have relativization of the object NP, and only if these are both developed in the language will relativization of the indirect object NP occur—and so forth, but never with the reverse order of differentiation. Greenberg (1966) documents evidence for progressive differentiation across languages for units at all levels; at the semantic level, for example, only if a language already makes a distinction between singular and plural will it also have a further distinction of plural into dual vs. indefinitely plural. Berlin and Kay (1969) offer evidence for progressive differentiation of color terms cross-linguistically—from the most primitive bright vs. dark, to differentiation of the bright into red vs. nonred, further in the red region into red vs. yellow, and later in the blue region into blue vs. green. Our own cross-cultural studies of affective meaning (Osgood, May, & Miron, 1975) suggest that generalized affective Positiveness vs. Negativeness differentiates into $^\pm$Evaluation + $^\pm$Dynamism and thence differentiation of Dynamism into $^\pm$Potency + $^\pm$Activity (i.e., from a one- into a three-feature system). Although the principle of progressive differentiation seems to be a universal of human languages, its interaction with other principles results in a statistical distribution of degrees of differentiation.

3. A Least Effort Principle

Across all languages and levels of units, a principle of least effort operates statistically, such that the higher the frequency-of-usage level (1) *the shorter the length of forms,* (2) *the smaller the number of forms,* and (3) *the larger the number of different meanings* (senses) *of the forms used.* This principle comes from G. Kingsley Zipf (1949), and he offers the entirely delightful analogy of a skilled artisan working at a long bench, with his production (sentence composition) space at one end and his various tools (here, lexical forms) spread out along it; obviously, it would be most efficient to have the tools most often used closest at hand along the bench, and these tools themselves lightweight, few in number and multipurpose in function. Using language data from English mainly, but also some from Chinese and Latin, Zipf was able to report functions that very neatly supported these hypotheses, and there seems to be no reason to doubt that the same would appear for languages generally. Does the Least Effort Principle hold for linguistic levels other than the lexicon? Greenberg (1966), noting Zipf's pioneering studies (p. 64), reports relevant data at the phonological level. Although I know of no explicit evidence, one would expect the same to hold for NP and VP constituents—e.g., that unmodified head nouns would be more frequent than elaborated ones (indeed, that diachronically there would be pressures toward simplification, e.g., from *knob of the door* to *door's knob* to *doorknob*) and that unmodulated verbs (simple presents and pasts, *walks* and *walked*) would be more frequent in ordinary language than modulated ones (like *was walking* or *had been walking* or certainly *would have still been walking*).

4. Affective Polarity

Across all languages and levels of units, it is statistically universal that affectively positive forms are distinguished from affectively negative forms (1) *by marking (either overt or covert) of the negative members of pairs and* (2) *by priority of the positive members of pairs in both development (in the language and in the individual) and form sequencing in messages.* Again Greenberg (1966) provides massive evidence at all levels: thus in phonology, marked nasal vowels are never more frequent in a language than unmarked nonnasal vowels, and Jakobson's general theory of phonemic development (Jakobson & Halle, 1956) includes the principle of priority for unmarked poles of features; thus in syntax it appears to be a universal (Greenberg, 1963) that affirmation is unmarked (X *is* Y) and negation is marked (X *is NOT* Y), and the unmarked active construction (X *verbed* Y) is universally the basic, natural form and the marked passive (X *WAS verbed BY* Y) is always viewed as a transformation; thus, in semantics, Animate is unmarked but INanimate is marked overtly, and affectively Positive *tall* is unmarked but Negative *short* is marked covertly (note that we normally say *how tall is John,* not *how short is John,* unless we are already assuming he is to some degree short). As far as priority of Positive members in the development of language in the species is concerned, the mere fact that it is characteristically Positives that are marked to produce Negatives (*happy/UNhappy* but not *sad/unsad,* although this, too, is only statistically universal, as witness *untroubled/troubled*) clearly implies that the Positives already exist *to be marked*; as far as priority in individual language development is concerned, DiVesta (as reported in Boucher & Osgood, 1969) has shown that in qualifier elicitation from children of various ages the Positives of familiar opposites (*good-bad, big-little,* etc.) typically appear earlier and hold higher frequencies than the Negatives. As to sequencing of such pairs in language production, note first that in stating opposites one usually goes from Positive to Negative (*strong-weak* rather than *weak-strong, fast-slow* rather than *slow-fast,* and so on), and then that familiar idiomatic phrases tend to follow the same rule (see Cooper & Ross, 1975)—*no more ands or buts, they hunted fore and aft, are you for or against me, the pros and cons of it,* but definitely not the reverse orders.

5. The Pollyanna Principle

Across all languages and levels of units, it is statistically universal that affectively Positive forms and constructions are more diversified, more frequently used, and more easily processed cognitively than affectively Negative forms and constructions. The greater diversity of Positives shows up nicely in our cross-linguistic semantic differential data on (now) some 30 language-culture communities around the word—in the eight-octant space defined by $^\pm$Evaluation, $^\pm$Potency and $^\pm$Activity factors (which system is itself a human universal), the + + + octant (Good, Strong, and Active) is much more densely populated with concepts than the - - - octant (Bad, Weak, and Passive), and the same holds for the Positive vs. Negative directions of each factor taken separately. Greenberg (1966), Boucher and Osgood (1969), and Hamilton and Deese (1971) all present evidence that the Positive members of pairs of word forms are significantly more frequent in usage than their Negative counterparts. As to the ease of cognitive processing, both H. Clark and his associates (Clark, 1971; Clark & Chase, 1972) and Hoosain (1973) in my own laboratory have shown that simple sentences with overt (*nots*) or with covert negatives (*short, ugly, weak,* etc.) take significantly longer to comprehend, and both also find that the same holds for incongruent complex sentences conjoined with *but* as compared with congruent ones conjoined with *and*—incongruence being itself a form of negativity. Perhaps the most striking evidence for the Pollyanna Principle will be offered in a paper in preparation by Osgood and Hoosain (1979): Measuring the times required for simply saying appropriately "positive" or "negative" to single words from all sorts of pairs presented randomly, there was a highly significant difference of about 50 msec favoring Positives. In other words, it is easier to "simply get the meaning" of affectively Positive words than the meaning of affectively Negative words, and this even when usage frequency was biased in favor of the Negatives.

IV. HOW MAY HUMAN LANGUAGES HAVE ORIGINATED?

This is a question that has intrigued speculative philosophers of all periods—and it is as purely speculative as anyone could hope, because there is little likelihood that any of the hypotheses will ever be tested empirically. There is no question but humans have the *propensity* for vocal–auditory language: All known normal human groups have such a language; all normal children develop competence in a native language of great complexity in what has often been called "a remarkably short time" (although there are many hours in the busy days of childhood); and, as we have seen (criteria 1–16), all human languages are fundamentally of the same type. Yet, given the essential *arbitrariness* of the phonological, syntactic, and semantic rules of each, particular human languages must be learned.

A. Speculations on the Origin of Language

How did some genius man-ape "get the idea" of communicating with others of his kind by means of vocalizations having distinctive referential properties, thereby enabling him to influence their behaviors? All of the speculations I briefly characterize below—except the first, "mystical" theory—will be seen to contain a grain or two of probable truth, but they are all obviously insufficient. Furthermore, they are limited to "wording" (usually emoting or labeling) and have nothing to say about "sentencing"—but, like the holophrastic stage in child language, it seems certain that the expression of ideas (whole cognitions) would be the fundamental communicative unit.

1. The "Ding-Dong" (Mystical) Theory

Assuming it to be given (1) that meanings are somehow inherent in words and (2) that objects have the power to evoke the words that refer to them, the process of language origin is simply that man-ape sees object DING, DING causes him to say "dong," and "dong" contains the meaning *ding*. Nonsensical as this is, it nevertheless has understandable roots in primitive (?) human behavior—the strong tendency toward *reification of words:* The infant in its random babbling happens to produce the noise "ma-ma" and the fond parent exclaims "Why, the little darling knows me!"; Malinowski (1938) has aptly dubbed this the "bucket theory" of meaning—words, like little buckets, are assumed to pick up their loads of meaning in one person's mind, carry them across the intervening space, and dump them into the mind of another—and he notes that in some societies a man never reveals his real name (rather, inscribing it on a piece of wood or stone and burying it in some secret place) lest some ill-wisher practice magic on it. Other obvious criticisms are: (1) why don't all languages have the same names for things? (2) what about names for object-less "things" like function words, verbs, and abstract concepts generally?

2. The "Bow-Wow" (Imitative) Theory

Assuming it to be given (1) that animals and many other things make or have characteristic sounds and (2) that our man-apes had a spontaneous tendency to imitate noises heard, the process of language origin is simply that dog-produced "bow-wow" already has *dog* meaning as a perceptual sign and man-aped imitative "bow-wow" elicits the same meaning via stimulus generalization. Suggestive evidence would be the use of imitative sounds in most tribal ceremonies and the commonness of onomatopoeia across human languages. Critique: (1) most words in languages are not onomatopoeic; (2) because in different languages there are quite different "natural" imitations of the sounds that *dog, cow, cat, rooster,* etc., make, and they all follow their own phonological rules, we would have to assume that our man-apes already had a language. However, this theory has a grain of probable truth *as a "starter"* on the path toward vocal–auditory language.

3. The "Pooh-Pooh" (Interjectional) Theory

Given (1) that, like ape, man-ape has a repertoire of unlearned vocal expressions of affect (grunts, groans, screams), (2) that these are non-randomly occasioned by the situations he is in, and (3) that these situations (as complexes of perceptual signs) have meanings for him, the "idea" of language originates in the transfer of the meaning of a situation to the vocal interjection as a sign of that situation. Thus Man-ape A breaks the thong he is using to tie his stone axe-head to its handle-stick and mutters a disgusted "pooh-pooh"; and later he says "pooh-pooh, pooh-pooh, pooh-pooh" to ridicule Man-ape B for tripping clumsily over a log—and soon the whole tribe is going around "pooh-pooh"-ing each other! Not only does this theory seem quite reasonable as a "starter" for vocal–auditory language, but it has a pretty solid grain of probable truth in it—prelinguistic cognizing (the meanings of perceived situations) is prior to, and necessary for, linguistic cognizing, a speculation on which I will elaborate momentarily. However, by way of critique: (1) how does the man-ape get beyond the ape—in the naming of entities (NPs) and relations (VPs)? and (2) how does he get from emoting into describing, explaining, warning and the like—that is, into sentencing?

4. The "Yum-Yum" (Gestural) Theory

This was what E. L. Thorndike (see below) dubbed the speculations of Sir Richard Paget (most recently, 1944) about the origin of human languages. Given (1) that our man-ape was a fluent and total gesture maker (with noisy mouth gestures accompanying other bodily gesturings and posturings) and (2) that his gesturing behavior followed the same principle of least effort as that proposed by G. K. Zipf (earliest in *The Psychobiology of Language,* 1935—see Section III, B, 3), language originates as the least effortful and least interfering vocal parts of the gesturing are substituted for the total. Thus anticipatory behavior toward a juicy food-object includes tummy rubbing and lip smacking; when the latter is accompanied by voiced exhaling, "yum-yum-yum" is produced. Now imagine two hungry man-apes squatting beside a grubby rotten log: if they keep rubbing their tummies they can't keep on digging for juicy grubs, but they can keep on "yum-yum"-ing (except when swallowing!)—so the vocalizations become the signs. This also seems reasonable as a "starter" on the path to a human language, and it is consistent with evidence for short-circuiting and amplitude reduction in the acquisition of representation mediators in sign learning (cf. Osgood, 1956, 1979). Critique: (1) we are still left with the problem of how the *meaning* of "yummy" is abstracted from the situational context (so that Man-ape A can point in some direction, say "yum-yum" to Man-ape B, and get B to go to the grubby log); and again, (2) how do we get beyond the ape and satisfy functional criteria 12–16?

5. The "Babble-Lucky" (Associational) Theory

This is E. L. Thorndike's "dubbing" of his own theory (1943) of the origins of language. Given (1) that man-apes already had strong tendencies for vocalic play ("babbling," like human infants), (2) that they already existed in social groups and were surrounded with various natural and artifactual objects, and (3) that they had the cognitive capacities for symbolizing the meanings (Thorndike simply called these X's) of such objects, language evolves as a result of chance associations of certain random babbles with certain objects and events, these *happening* to be observed and imitated by the group, and thus becoming socially standardized (hence the "lucky"). Imagine that a bright man-ape spies some clams along the lake shore and happens to babble "uk-uk"; since he already has a meaning for the perceptual sign of CLAM, he associates "uk" with that meaning; gathering up some clams, he brings them back to the cave, calling "uk-uk-uk!" as he comes; the other, less gifted, man-apes imitate him, while observing and feasting on the clams—and "uk" thus comes to refer to CLAM object and all that it signifies. This theory includes the referential properties of others, but it has the advantage of allowing arbitrariness of form-meaning relations while permitting "bow-wow"s, "pooh-pooh"s and "yum-yum"s as starters. It also introduces the critical notion of *social standardization*. Critique: (1) maybe this mechanism is *too* chancy and (2) too susceptible to social confusion (what with some man-apes in the group "uk-uk"ing, others "yum-yum"ing, and still others "whiss-whiss"ing about the same clams); most critically, (3) it remains simply a theory of "wording," with nothing to say about "sentencing."

B. Speculations on the Evolution of Languages

Is it possible that some prehuman simian species like Pithecanthropus had a human-type language? If so, we would expect it to have been more primitive than existing human languages, which presumably have evolved from simpler origins. It seems most unlikely that humanoids suddenly started talking as they dropped from the trees. Many writers have suggested what at least some of the lines of language evolution must have been. For example, in a paper submitted to a volume *To Honor Roman Jakobson,* J. Bronowski (1967) suggests the following: (1) increasing capacity to delay outgoing vocalization to an incoming auditory message; (2) increasing capacity to separate the affective reactions to, and the denotative significances of, messages; (3) the "prolongation of reference," thus increased ability to refer backward and forward in time; (4) increasing internalization of language, from being primarily a means of social communication to becoming a means of reflecting and reasoning; (5) the "structural activity of reconstitution," increasing analysis and synthesis of messages into rearrangeable components. One might also consider my defining *functional* characteristics—(12) arbitrariness of semantics, (13) discreteness of signals, (14) hierarchical organization, (15) componential organization, and (16) transferral via learning—as *variables* that increase in complexity as languages evolve. Unfortunately, unlike skulls and tools, languages leave no traces in or on the earth, and so there is no *direct* evidence available on language evolution. But what about *indirect* evidence?

1. The Question of "Primitive" Human Languages

Among the many thousands of extant human languages, are there some less and some more "evolved"? The Old Look answered "yes": It was suggested that there were stages in development—from isolating languages like Chinese, through agglutinating languages like Turkish, to highly inflecting languages like ... of course! ... Latin; this notion was dropped when it was realized, with some embarrassment, that most modern Indo-European languages, along with English, were *less* inflecting, *more* isolating, than Latin. The New Look answers with a resounding "NO!": Ethnolinguists have found the languages of *culturally* primitive (near Stone Age level) peoples fully as complex as those of highly civilized (??) peoples "like us"; complexity of language-based conceptual systems (for kinship relations, mythology, etc.) appears to vary quite independently of levels of technological development; so the very question of "relative primitiveness" of extant human languages is meaningless.

But perhaps we need to take a Fresh Look—and ask ourselves just what the *criteria* of "primitiveness" might be.

a. Structural Simplicity Vs. Complexity? Just how this would be indexed—numbers of phonemes, of semantic features, of syntactic rules, or maybe ease of descriptive linguistic analysis?—is entirely unclear; if anything, it would appear that there probably was prehistoric increase in overall complexity but decrease during recent historic times.

b. Size of Vocabulary? This clearly covaries with cultural development (but one should use lay speakers in such comparisons), and, in principle (given criterion 6, combinatorial productivity) any language *can* be used to talk about anything.

c. Efficiency in Communication? In the information-theoretic sense, most languages at most levels (e.g., N-features/N-phonemes) run at about a 50% redundancy level in order to maximize the probabilities of messages "getting through"; in my foreign research travels, however, I have noticed rather marked differences in the length of signs used to communicate the same messages in airlines (e.g., *no smoking, fasten seat belts*)—but then, cultures where we might expect language primitiveness usually don't have airlines!

Maclay and Newman (1960) devised an interesting measure here: the number of *morphemes* needed to communicate the same information when Person A tells Person B on the other side of a screen which forms to select from a set to match his own; there were marked effects of both negative feedback and homogeneity of forms upon increasing the N of morphemes, but unfortunately no comparative studies across languages were made—only American English subjects being used.

d. Degrees of Concreteness? Roger Brown (1970, pp. 19–22) reports a comparison of the nouns and verbs used by adults vs. children in terms of their concreteness (vs. abstractness)—a kind of "picturability" (a point-at-able/ non-point-at-able ratio). For nouns, 67% of the childrens' but only 16% of the adults' 1000 most frequent were "picturable"; for verbs, 67% of childrens' but only 33% of adults' were "picturable." Might *this* be used as an index of "primitiveness"? Perhaps—but this, too, would seem to be more cultural than linguistic, when adult speakers are being compared.

e. Ease of Learning? It seems reasonable that more primitive languages should be easier to learn, but the "how" of going about this is obscure. Could one show that isolating, uninflected Chinese is learned more quickly *as a first language* than is, say, highly agglutinative, inflected, and left-branching Turkish—and just what criteria of "learning" would be used? Could it be shown that Chinese can be learned more quickly by Turks *as a second language* than Turkish can be learned by Chinese? As Uriel Weinreich has amply documented in his *Languages in Contact* (1953), the interactions at all levels of units in second-language learning are incredibly complex and bi-language specific. A related index would be the degree of difference (linguistically described) between adult and child language—comparatively across languages, of course—but at just what level do we define the "child" language?

So, having taken a Fresh Look at the question of relative "primitiveness" of extant languages in terms of criteria that might be used, we seem to be about where we started—with a set of possible criteria but little or no available evidence.

2. The Notion of Recapitulation

The notion that ontogeny (development of the individual organism) recapitulates phylogeny (evolution of its species) is a familiar one. Could we get some idea of how language might have evolved in human species from the regularities of language development in its contemporary offspring? In an early tracing of stages in language development, Ervin and Miller (1963) report that in the course of language development there are increases in the number of phonemic distinctions, the number of grammatical classes, and the average length of utterances; holophrastic words (with contextually redundant remainders of full cognitions unexpressed) appear before word combinations (constructions), lexical word forms (distinctively semantic) before function word forms (primarily syntactic), and ordering rules (e.g., Agent-Action-Recipient) before inflections (which permit permutations in ordering).

More recently, Brown (1973), taking a more sentential approach, specifies five stages in development: (1) expression of relations or roles within simple sentences (the case roles of various noun phrases in relation to the verb phrase); (2) modulations of meaning within the simple sentence (modulating the N with number tags, with qualifiers, and the like, and the V with tense indicators and adverbials); (3) diversifying the modalities of simple declarative sentences (into yes–no questions, *wh*-constituent questions, negations, imperatives and the like); (4) embedding of sentences, expressing simple cognitions, within others (relative clauses, object noun-phrase complements, and the like); and (5) coordination of simple sentences and propositional relations (simple *and/but* complexes, adverbial main/subordinate clauses, and so forth). It should be stressed that Brown believes this 1-5 ordering to be that of development in children.

If we have some faith that ontogeny *does* tend to recapitulate phylogeny, then we might speculate as follows about the evolution of human languages:

1. They probably began with holophrastic expressions of complete perception-based cognitions, with purely semantic (often affective) and pragmatic functions.

2. As the sheer numbers of such expressions increased, the number of phonemic distinctions and grammatical classes had to increase, along with socially agreed upon rules of sequencing the expression of such classes.

3. Starting with the simplest sentential expressions of full cognitions (single-word nominals related in action and stative relations by single-word verbs, like *dog took leg-bone* and *woman (is) in cave*), the pressures to express finer semantic distinctions led to modulations into NPs and VPs (*your mangy mutt sneakily stole away with my juicy leg-bone* and *my woman must have been in your warm cave*) and the needs for more pragmatically effective social communication led to diverse modalities of sentencings (like *where is my woman?, she is not in our cave,* and *tell her to come home*).

4. Relatively late in the evolution of languages, complexes of cognitions came to be conjoined in coordinate and embedded sentential forms, with the rather aesthetic need to avoid repetitive orderings within sentoids (clauses) leading to diverse inflections and transformations—all of which eventuated in sentence lengths getting longer and longer (like this one!).

C. A "Naturalness" (Representational) Theory of the Origin of Languages

I've been unable to come up with a catchy, rhyming dubbing for my own speculations—but perhaps some reader will succeed where I've failed and let me have his suggestion. The broadest notion underlying the general theory of cognizing and sentencing I've been working on (Osgood, 1979) is this: *that, both in the evolution of the species and in the development of the individual human, the cognitive structures that interpret sentences received and initiate sentences produced are established in prelinguistic experience, via the acquisition of adaptive behaviors to entities perceived in diverse action and stative relations.* I suppose one might also call this an "article of faith." However, it follows from two assumptions that would rather obviously seem to be true: (1) that humanoids, before they had language, must have had capacities (a) for cognizing the significances of events going on around them, and (b) for learning to behave appropriately in terms of such significances—if the species were to survive; and (2) that children of contemporary humans, before they have language, display exactly the same capacities for acquiring the significances of perceived events and reacting with appropriate intentional behaviors.

This notion implies what I have called a *Naturalness Principle* for sentencing in language behavior—namely, *that the more sentences produced or received correspond in their surface structures to the cognitive structures developed in adaptive prelinguistic perceptuomotor experience, the greater will be the ease of processing them.* This functional principle in turn has potentially testable implications for what should be *universal* (1) in the development of the language by the young of our species, (2) in the processing of language by the adults, and (3) in the evolution of language in the species itself. As to children (1), the greater the correspondence of alternative structures to the prelinguistically established ones, the earlier should be the acquisition of their processing—in imitating, in comprehending (Simply Acting out), and in expressing (Simply Describing)—both within any given language and cross-linguistically for bilingual children (cf. Slobin, 1973); as to adults (2), the greater the correspondence, the greater will be the speed of comprehending and producing sentences and the more frequently will be the use of such sentences in various communication tasks (e.g., in Simply Describing perceived events); as to language evolution (3), the greater the correspondence, the earlier such structures should appear in, and the more universal they should be across, human languages.[6]

---

[6]And, I would add, the greater the correspondence of competence-based grammars to prelinguistically based cognitive structures, the higher should be their evaluation in competition with alternative grammars.

1. A Bit of Behavior Theory

The specification of what is "natural" involves hypotheses deriving both from Representational Neobehaviorism (see Osgood, 1979) and from psychological intuitions about *what should be natural* in the prelinguistic cognizing of young children[7]—in contrast to linguistic intuitions about *what is grammatical* in the sentencing of adults. So a bit of behavior theory is in order. Our concern here will be limited, first, to presenting a basic *sign-learning principle* and its extension to an equally basic *feature-learning principle*—both being part of my own generalization of classical Hullian (Hull, 1943) mediation theory to a representational and componential mediation theory of meaning—and, second, to emphasizing the intimate parallelism between nonlinguistic and linguistic cognizing (or between "Things and Words," reversing appropriately the title of Roger Brown's justly famous book, 1958) by offering *an "emic" principle* and *an "ambiguity" principle of neobehaviorism.*

a. A Sign-Learning Principle.   Just like apes (and even rodents) before them, it seems likely that humanoids developed the capacity for "getting the meanings of" wholistic perceptual signs of things prior to the capacity for analyzing out the distinctive features that make the differences in meanings. This behavioral principle may be stated as follows: *When a percept that elicits no predictable pattern of behavior has repeated, contiguous, and reinforced pairings with another percept that does elicit predictable behavior, the former will become a sign of the latter as its significate, by virtue of becoming associated with a mediation process, this process* (1) *being some distinctive representation of the total behavior produced by the significant and* (2) *serving to mediate overt behaviors to the sign appropriate to ("taking account of") the significate.* Such a principle has been implicit in all of the speculations above (except the "ding-dong" theory) about the origins of language (e.g., the X's in Thorndike's "babble-lucky" theory). Note that, both in evolution of the species and in development of the individual, nonlinguistic percepts of familiar entities in diverse action and stative relations (DADDY SPANKING FIDO; KITTY BEING ON PILLOW) will acquire meanings prior to the linguistic percepts (word forms) that will later represent ("stand for," "refer to") them—and, indeed, the representational processes formed in such prelinguistic experience will typically provide "prefabricated" mediators in later language acquisition. The representational mediation process that comes to be associated with a sign (perceptual or linguistic) as a dependent event in the nervous system is its *significance* (in comprehending); the same

---

[7]In preliminary mimeographed versions of my evolving APG (Abstract Performance Grammar) I have used as a parenthetical subtitle "Picking Oneself Up by One's Booties"!

process as an antecedent event is the *intention* behind the overt behaviors mediated by a sign (in expressing).

b. A Feature-Learning Principle. Just as the overt behaviors made to significates are typically a *set* of overt responses which together constitute and "act," so also in theory are the mediation processes derived from this total behavior, and now elicited by a sign, a *set* of mediator components. To the extent that pairs of signs elicit *reciprocally antagonistic* mediator components, these componential antagonisms will become the "differences that make a difference" in meaning.

A simple, but paradigmatic, demonstration (Lawrence, 1949) will illustrate: In a simple T-maze, with the upper "arms" at the choice point having both BLACK vs. WHITE walls and CHAINS vs. NO-CHAINS (soft curtain) distinguishing right from left sides (but with random right–left locations across trials), members of one of four possible groups of rat subjects will be rewarded with food pellets if they go toward the BLACK and punished by sudden loss of support if they go toward the WHITE, with the CHAINS/NO-CHAINS location being random with respect to differential reinforcement; being reasonably bright little fellows, these rats rapidly learn to get food and avoid falls. The crucial thing here is that, after this experience, *they will learn to go to the WHITE and avoid the BLACK much more rapidly than to go to the CHAINS and avoid the NO-CHAINS;* in other words, they have learned to "pay attention to" the differences that make a difference in meaning—here, anticipated reinforcement ("hope") vs. anticipated punishment ("fear")—in an otherwise constant behavioral situation and to "disregard" differences that do not make a difference.

I call this little experiment "paradigmatic" because it suggests a general model for the development of both phonemic and semantic distinctive features in human languages. In this connection, it is interesting to me that, although many linguists and most psycholinguists assume that phonemic and semantic feature distinctions must be acquired via experience (given the obvious fact that languages differ in *what* features come to "make a difference"), I have searched in vain for any explication of the crucial *how* of this learning. Note that this feature-learning principle is a logical extension of the sign-learning principle, *once a componential conception of the mediation process is substituted for an undifferentiated global conception.* This is the entrée, I think, of Neobehaviorism to a theory of meaning and reference— and, with structuring of the semantic system, ultimately to a theory of sentencing.

The "emic" principle of Neobehaviorism. By virtue of the fact that both things and organisms are mobile with respect to each other, along with the fact that environmental contexts are changeable, it follows that the distal signs of things will be variable through many stimulus dimensions. Thus, for the human infant, MOTHER'S FACE will vary in retinal-image size as she approaches him and in brightness and hue as time-of-day shifts from dawn through midday into twilight; similarly, for man-ape on the hunt, retinal size of ANTELOPE percept must have varied in size and hue as he moved stealthily in on his prey. But because these varying percepts are associated with the same significate and the behavior it produces (cf. the sign-learning principle above)—mother eventually coddles and comforts baby and antelope eventually gets killed and eaten—there will be extension of the common mediator (meaning) across such sets of percepts. Therefore the differences within such sets will be differences that do *not* make a difference in meaning.

This is the "that-ness" or "thing-ness" in perception, and it is the basis for the *constancy phenomenon*—long familiar to psychologists. Note that what we have here is *a class of variable signs having a common significance*: if we substitute *sounds* for *signs*, we have the definition of the "phoneme" (a class of physically different sounds having the same significance in the phonemic code, e.g., the /k/ in *key, cope* and *coo*); similarly, at the lexical level, word forms like "mother" and "linguist" retain their denotative significance regardless of variations in intonation, stress, or voice quality of the speaker. Equivalently on the output side of the equation, classes of nonlinguistic and/or linguistic behaviors come to be associated with the common mediation process and therefore can be said to be *expressions of the same intention*—the child (older now) or the man-ape locomoting toward, reaching for, grasping, and biting the APPLE object ... but *not* for a percept-class having a different significance, e.g., a RED-HOT COAL!

But there is also a "how-ness" or "where-ness" in perception. Neither human child nor man-ape emits the various responses expressing the same intention at random. Neither would emit biting, then grasping, then reaching movement—in thin air—in that order or before approaching the APPLE, anymore than Caesar would have announced "Vici, vidi, veni"! Rather, *the distinctive percepts as stimuli converge with the stimulus effects of the common mediator to modulate the probabilities of alternative movements* (expressions)—thus, the small visual angle of APPLE (ON-TABLE-OVER-THERE) plus its meaning as an edible object converge on locomoting toward, a larger visual angle plus the same meaning converge on reaching for, and so on. This fusion of convergent and divergent hierarchies is what is called *control* and *decision* in representational neobehaviorism. Note that there is thus *a syntax of behaving* just as there is a syntax of talking—and again, the former is clearly prior to the latter and therefore can serve as a cognitive model for the latter.

   c. *The "Ambiguity" Principle of Neobehaviorism.*   When percepts are constant, but the mediators associated with them are variable, we have the conditions for *perceptual ambiguity*—the same sign having more than one meaning. Familiar examples from the psychological laboratory would be the Necker Cube (an outline cube which flips between "from the side" to "from above" perspectives) and the Miles Kinephantoscope (where the shadow of a rotating bar on a rod can be seen as "flapping toward me," "flapping away from me," "shrinking and expanding," "rotating left or right," etc.), and there are many others. The child may be ambiguated by a fuzzy black something on the floor (BALL OF THREAD or SPIDER?)—until it moves; our man-ape may be ambiguated by a sudden movement of some bushes (WOMAN-APE or SABER-TOOTHED TIGER?)—until it growls!

This is strictly analogous to *linguistic ambiguity*—homonomy, and more generally (and finely) polysemy of forms, at lexical *(he went to the BANK)*, syntactic *(the SHOOTING OF THE HUNTERS was terrible)*, and pragmatic *(CAN you open the window?* as an indirect request or an inquiry as to capability). *Disambiguation* via contextual signs can occur *within channels*: perceptual-by-perceptual, as when that pretty, long-haired person says "where's the toilet?" in a DEEP BASS VOICE; linguistic-by-linguistic, as in *he ROWED to the bank*. Or it can be *across channels*: perceptual-by-linguistic, as when the experimenter induces irresistible shifts in the Kinephantoscope perceptions of the subject from "pirouetting to the left" to "flapping behind" just by saying those words; linguistic-by-perceptual, as when one co-ed says to her companion as another co-ed in a *mini*-miniskirt just passes them on a campus path, "she also dyes her hair"! The cross-channel disambiguations have a most significant implication—namely, *that at some deep cognitive level, nonlinguistic (perceptual) and linguistic "wordings" and "sentencings" must share the same representational system*—otherwise, events in the two channels would pass each other like ships in the night.

2. Some Speculations About Naturalness in Sentencing

In discussing the syntactic criterion (5) for anything to be called a language, in connection with Octopian, I introduced this Naturalness notion. It is assumed that the prelinguistic structures of the simple cognitions underlying sentoid (clause) comprehending and expressing are *tripartite* in nature (cf. Greenberg, 1963), and further that these cognitions are "SVO" in their ordering of components (ENTITY$_1$-RELATION-ENTITY$_2$). This makes the very strong prediction that human languages that are SOV in adult type will display evidence of originating from SVO: There is diachronic evidence for many shifts in type from SOV to SVO in historic times, but not a single case of an SVO-to-SOV shift, without external pressures (invasion, cultural dominance, etc.); in the "diachronics" of language in children, one would expect evidence for SVO ordering in the two- to three-word stages of development in SOV languages before the adult language ordering takes over.[8]

It is also assumed that there are two basic types of SVO cognitions: (1) expressing *action relations* (where ACTOR-ACTION-RECIPIENT is the natural ordering in cognizing, because of the characteristically [+]animate— and often [+]human—semantic coding of actors as against the [-]animate—or at least relatively passive—coding of Recipients); and (2) *stative relations* (where FIGURE-STATE-GROUND is the natural ordering, because of the Gestalt-like characteristic [+]Salience of Figures and [-]Salience of Grounds). Thus, both for all human children and for our hypothetical man-apes *en route* to language, one would expect prelinguistic cognizings like MAN KICK DOG (action) and DOG ON FLOOR (stative) to be more natural than DOG KICKED BY MAN or FLOOR UNDER DOG. If the underlying Naturalness Principle is valid, then one would expect the earliest sentencings—by contemporary child and by now-extinct man-ape—to be active (rather than passive) and "figure-ative" (rather than "ground-ative"). The fact that we don't even have any names for the latter suggests that the cognizing of stative relations may well be more basic and primitive than the cognizing of action relations (again, cf. Osgood, 1979, for elaboration).

What about evidence for these naturalness predictions? Only a bit of the most relevant evidence can be given here. Osgood and Bock (1977) present a reanalysis of data on the simply describing of a variety of little demonstrations with balls, blocks, tubes, poker chips, and the like by adult American English speakers (previously reported in a paper by the first author, titled "Where Do Sentences Come From?"). Evidence for naturalness in describing both action and stative relations was overwhelming: For stative relations, despite the grammatical availability of GROUND-STATE-FIGURE sentencings (e.g., *a plate is holding a ball, a spoon and a poker chip* or *a ball is being held by the man*), these rarely occurred (we got equivalents of *a ball, a spoon and a poker chip are on a plate* [20/0/6][9] and of *the man is holding a ball* [24/1/1]); for action relations, despite the availability of ordinary passives (e.g., affirmatives like *the tube was hit by the orange ball* and negatives like *the tube was not hit by the orange ball*), again they practically never occurred (we got equivalents of *the orange ball hit the upright tube* [21/0/5] and of *the orange ball did not hit* [*missed, passed*, etc.] *the tube* [21/5/0—the "flubs" not expressing negation in any way]). Our Center for Comparative Psycholinguistics is right now in the process of

---

[8]During the summer and fall of 1977, two of my students tested this radical hypothesis—S. N. Sridhar and Annette Zehler in Bangalore and Hiroshima, respectively, Kannada and Japanese both being SOV languages, but otherwise rather different (cf. Osgood, 1979).

[9]With an N of 26 subjects, the first value is the number fitting the naturalness prediction, the second the number of "flubs" (e.g., a subject opened his eyes too late!), and the third is the number contrary to the prediction.

collecting such simply describing data from native speakers of some 20 languages around the world, using a color-film containing 70 similar demonstrations designed with "psycholinguistic malice aforethought"; we want to see how diverse languages equivalently take account of various cognitive distinctions (presumably universal) in the surface structures of their sentences.

At this point one might reasonably ask: why do "unnatural," yet grammatical, sentencings ever occur? The title of the Osgood and Bock (1977) paper, "Salience and Sentencing: Some Production Principles," implies the answer: *All languages provide ways for their speakers to move constituents of messages that are salient to them forward (earlier) in time of production;* this, by the way, is consistent with the Hullian motivation principle (Hull, 1943)—performance equaling habit strength times drive. The *Naturalness* Principle itself is based on the notion of the relative salience of Actors over Recipients and Figures over Ground, other things being equal; the principle can be overridden by (1) the *vividness* (inherent salience, affective intensity, of semantic features) and/or (2) the *motivation of speaker* (attributed salience, due to topicality, interest, identification, etc.) with respect to nonactor or nonfigure constituents.

Kay Bock's thesis (summarized in Osgood and Bock, 1977) investigated the effects of vividness, using a variety of optional transformations in English. In the following examples, I capitalize the noun-phrase alternatives that were assumed to be ⁺Vivid in each case: the dative *(the boy tossed the FRISBEE/ball to the dog/ST. BERNARD / the boy tossed the ST. BERNARD/dog the ball/FRISBEE),* the passive *(the BULLDOZER/truck crushed the flowers/DAFFODILS / the DAFFODILS/flowers were crushed by the truck/BULLDOZER),* the genitive *(the powwow was held in the WIGWAM/tent of the chief/SITTING BULL / the powwow was held in SITTING BULL'S/the chief's tent/WIGWAM),* and a number of others. The prediction was that where the ⁺Vivid alternative was already in the temporally *prior* position *(the boy tossed the FRISBEE to the dog* or *the boy tossed the ST. BERNARD the ball)* there would be few shifts in reproduction, but where the ⁺Vivid was given in the temporally *subsequent* position *(the boy tossed the ball to the ST. BERNARD* or *the boy tossed the dog the FRISBEE)* there would be significant transformational shift tendencies. These vividness predictions had to be tempered by the Naturalness Principle, of course: If the given structures were already ⁺Natural, they would tend to be reproduced that way; if they were ⁻Natural, they would tend to be shifted back into the natural form in reproduction, regardless of the Vividness relations. In other words, 50% of the time Vividness and Naturalness Principles would reinforce each other and 50% of the time they would compete with each other. The results were generally consistent with these expectations.

An hypothesis derived from "putting on the booties of childhood" received interesting support from both cross-language linguistic data and from experimental psycholinguistic data, as reported by Osgood and Tanz (1977). The intuition was about the prelinguistic child's cognizing of bitransitive situations (prototypically, Person A transfers inanimate object X to Person B), where the X is perceptually a part of the transfer relation and Person B perceptually the real object (little Suzie perceiving BIG-BROTHER GIVES-BOOK-TO BIG-SISTER)—and this led to the title of our paper, "Will the Real Direct Object in Bitransitive Sentences Please Stand Up?"

For the cross-language data, a number of predictions were verified such as: (1) that the so-called indirect object (D for dative) should be more frequently marked than the so-called direct object (O for objective) and that this should be more often the case when D is closest to the verb (i.e., the unnatural transform); (2) the strong prediction—that in languages where O is marked in unitransitive clauses but not in bitransitive, the same marker will be applied to the D—was upheld in a surprising number of cases; (3) that in languages where nouns are incorporated in verbs, O-incorporation should be greater than D-incorporation (clearly upheld); and (4) that the natural SVOD structure should be less constrained transformationwise than the unnatural SVDO structure. Three psycholinguistic experiments supported the predictions (5) that natural SVOD forms would be more faithfully recalled as given than SVDO forms; (6) that unnatural SVDO forms would be more frequently shifted to SVOD in recall; and (7) that as probes for single-word associations, V should produce O more often than D, and O should produce V more often than D does. So it would appear that, despite what grammarians have been telling us for centuries, the *real* direct object in bitransitive sentences is the so-called indirect object!

Finally, the Naturalness Principle makes certain predictions about the ordering of clauses in complex, conjoined sentences—namely, that where there is a natural order in prelinguistic experience with complex events, this order in sentencing will be either required or at least preferred across languages. In the simple junction mode of conjoining, either order is natural (*Mary sang and John played the guitar* or the reverse). But for the temporal mode there is a natural order in experience (and thus *Mary got dressed and went to the party,* but not *!Mary went to the party and got dressed*);[10] similarly for the causal mode (*it was raining and John got wet,* but definitely not *!John got wet and it was raining*) and the combined causal-temporal mode (*Dan ate some poisonous mushrooms and got sick* but definitely not *!Dan got sick and ate some poisonous mushrooms*).

Opačić (1973) measured processing times (for judging whether a given pair of clauses, then a given conjoiner, was "possible" or "impossible") and then the complex sentence the subject produced *if* he had said "possible"—for these and other modes of conjoining. For all modes in which two orders are

---

[10]I use the ! symbol to emphasize the fact that although such sentences as these may be completely unacceptable (indeed, mind-boggling), they are *not* ungrammatical—which raises some interesting questions about the notion of grammaticality, which we cannot go into here.

possible, one natural (N) and the other unnatural (U), natural-given and natural-retained (NN) had the shortest latencies, UN were next in ease of processing (i.e., where the subject *restores* the natural order), UU came next (literal memorizing), and NU (shifting from the natural *to* the unnatural ordering) was the most time-consuming.

Results of this sort are most encouraging and support the general notion that the cognitive structures developed in prelinguistic perceptual experience do in fact provide the "most natural" cognitive bases for comprehending and producing sentences—both in the evolution of language in the human species and in the development of its contemporary children. But, of course, neither this nor the demonstrably intimate parallelism between nonlinguistic and linguistic cognizing means that such prelinguistic capacity in itself constitutes "a language." It lacks three of the criteria for *anything* being a language— nonrandomly recurrent signals in some channel, reciprocality in sending and receiving such signals, and combinatorial productivity—precisely because such prelinguistic cognizing cannot be *abstracted* from the perceptual and motor chains that bind it to reality.

REFERENCES

Berlin, E., & Kay, P. *Basic color terms: Their universality and evolution.* Berkeley: University of California Press, 1969.

Boucher, J., & Osgood, C. E. The Pollyanna hypothesis. *Journal of Verbal Learning and Verbal Behavior,* 1969, *8,* 1–8.

Bronowski, J. In *To honor Roman Jakobson.* The Hague: Mouton, 1967.

Bronowski, J., & Bellugi, U. Language, name and concept. *Science,* 1970, *168,* 669–673.

Brown, R. *Words and things.* Glencoe, Ill.: Free Press, 1958.

Brown, R. *Psycholinguistics: Selected papers.* New York: Free Press, 1970.

Brown, R. *A first language: The early stages.* Cambridge, Mass.: Harvard University Press, 1973.

Clark, H. H. *The chronometric study of meaning components.* Paper presented at the CRNS Colloque Internationale sur les Problèmes, Actuels de Psycholinguistique, Paris, December 1971.

Clark, H. H., & Chase, W. G. On the process of comparing sentences against pictures. *Cognitive Psychology,* 1972, *3,* 472–517.

Cooper, W. E., & Ross, J. R. World order. In *Papers from the parasession on functionalism.* Chicago: Chicago Linguistics Society, 1975.

Ervin, S. M., & Miller, W. R. Language development. In *Child psychology,* 62nd Yearbook, National Society for the Study of Education. Chicago: University of Chicago Press, 1963.

Gardner, B. T., & Gardner, R. A. Evidence for sentence constituents in the early utterances of child and chimpanzee. *Journal of Experimental Psychology: General,* 1975, *104,* 244–267.

Gardner, R. A., & Gardner, B. T. Teaching sign language to a chimpanzee. *Science,* 1969, *165,* 664–672.

Gould, J. L. Honey bee recruitment: The dance-language controversy. *Science,* 1975, *189,* 685–692.

Greenberg, J. H. Some universals of grammar with particular reference to the order of meaningful elements. In J. H. Greenberg (Ed.), *Universals of language.* Cambridge, Mass.: MIT Press, 1963.

Greenberg, J. H. Language universals. In T. A. Sebeok (Ed.), *Current trends in linguistics: III. Theoretical foundations*. The Hague: Mouton, 1966.

Hamilton, H. W., & Deese, J. Does linguistic marking have a psychological correlate? *Journal of Verbal Learning and Verbal Behavior*, 1971, *10*, 707–714.

Hoosain, R. The processing of negation. *Journal of Verbal Learning and Verbal Behavior*, 1973, *12*, 618–626.

Hull, C. L. *Principles of behavior: An introduction to behavior theory*. New York: Appleton-Century-Crofts, 1943.

Jakobson, R. C., & Halle, M. *Fundamentals of language*. The Hague: Mouton, 1956.

Keenan, E., & Comrie, B. Noun phrase acceptability and universal grammar. *Linguistic Inquiry*, 1977, *8*, 63–100.

Lawrence, D. H. Acquired distinctiveness of cues: I. Transfer between discriminations on the basis of familiarity with the stimulus. *Journal of Experimental Psychology*, 1949, *39*, 770–784.

Maclay, H., & Newman, S. Two variables affecting the message in communication. In D. Wilner (Ed.), *Decisions, values and groups*. New York: Pergamon Press, 1960.

Mahl, G. F. People talking when they can't hear their voices. In A. Siegman & B. Pope (Eds.), *Studies in dyadic communication*. New York: Pergamon Press, 1972.

Malinowski, B. The problem of learning in primitive languages. Supplement in C. K. Ogden & I. A. Richards (Eds.), *The meaning of meaning*. New York: Harcourt Brace, 1938.

McNeill, D. *The acquisition of language*. New York: Harper, 1970.

McNeill, D. Sentence structure in chimpanzee communication. In K. J. Connolly & J. Bruner (Eds.), *The growth of competence*. New York: Academic Press, 1974.

Opacic, G. *Natural order in cognizing and clause order in the sentencing of conjoined expressions*. Doctoral dissertation, University of Illinois, 1973.

Osgood, C. E. Behavior theory and the social sciences. *Behavioral Science*, 1956, *1*, 167–185.

Osgood, C. E. *Lectures on language performance*. Berlin, Heidelberg, New York: Springer, 1979.

Osgood, C. E., & Bock, J. K. Salience and sentencing: Some production principles. In S. Rosenberg (Ed.), *Sentence production: Developments in research and theory*. Hillsdale, N.J.: Lawrence Erlbaum Associates, 1977.

Osgood, C. E., & Hoosain, R. *Pollyanna II: It is easier to 'simply get the meanings' of affectively positive than affectively negative words*. Manuscript in preparation, 1979.

Osgood, C. E., May, W. H., & Miron, M. S. *Cross-cultural universals of affective meaning*. Urbana, Ill.: University of Illinois Press, 1975.

Osgood, C. E., & Tanz, C. Will the real direct object in bitransitive sentences please stand up? In *Linguistic studies presented to Joseph Greenberg*. Saratoga, Calif.: Anma Libri, 1977.

Paget, R. A. The origin of language. *Science*, 1944, *99*, 14–15.

Premack, A. J., & Premack, D. Teaching language to an ape. *Scientific American*, 1972, *227*, 92–99.

Premack, D. Language in chimpanzee? *Science*, 1971, *172*, 808–822.

Searle, J. R. *Speech acts: An essay in the philosophy of language*. London: Cambridge University Press, 1969.

Slobin, D. I. Cognitive prerequisites for the development of grammar. In C. A. Ferguson & D. I. Slobin (Eds.), *Studies in child language development*. New York: Holt, Rinehart & Winston, 1973.

Thorndike, E. L. The origin of language. *Science*, 1943, *98*, 1–6.

von Frisch, K. Decoding the language of the bees. *Science*, 1974, *185*, 663–668.

Weinreich, U. *Languages in contact*. New York: Linguistic Circle, 1953.

Winograd, T. Understanding natural language. *Cognitive Psychology*, 1972, *3*, 1–191.

Zipf, G. K. *The psychobiology of language*. Boston: Houghton Mifflin, 1935.

Zipf, G. K. *Human behavior and the principle of least effort*. Cambridge, Mass.: Addison-Wesley, 1949.

8 The Role of Grammar in the Use of Language

D. Terence Langendoen
CUNY Graduate Center and Brooklyn College

> *We have seen that a model of sentence comprehension is, in effect, a device which associates token wave forms with messages. Very little is known about how such a device might operate, though I would guess that, if we started now and worked very hard, we might be able to build one in five hundred years or so.*
>
> — J. A. Fodor (1975, p. 167)

I. THE TASK OF LINGUISTICS

Ultimately, the task of linguistics is to give an account of the ability of human beings to produce and to comprehend the expressions of a language in a manner that is appropriate to the contexts in which they are used.[1] As with most tasks of this magnitude, the most effective strategy for dealing with it is a "divide-and-conquer" one, in which the task is broken down into a number of subtasks and the accomplishments in each domain are then integrated into an overall account.[2] For example, we may divide the

---

[1]Throughout this paper I use the term "linguistics," rather than "psycholinguistics." No special significance should be attached to this wording. The ability in question is what Chomsky has called "the creative aspect of language use" (1966, pp. 17–18; 1972a, pp. 11–13).

[2]Specific arguments for adopting a divide-and-conquer strategy in dealing with the task of linguistics are given in the "Introduction" to Bever, Katz, and Langendoen (1976). See also Bever (1974).

task of linguistics into the study of the principles (or rules) that determine the structures of the expressions of human languages and of the principles (or rules) that determine the appropriate use of those expressions. The former study may be called the study of linguistic competence; the latter, the study of linguistic performance.[3] The study of linguistic competence and linguistic performance can be further divided into the study of those aspects that all languages of necessity have in common and of those aspects that are peculiar to individual languages. The study of those aspects of linguistic competence that all human languages of necessity have in common is now generally called the study of universal grammar,[4] and while there is no generally agreed upon term for the study of those aspects of linguistic performance that all languages of necessity have in common, the term "universal performance" suggests itself. We may suppose further that the properties of universal grammar and of universal performance are properties of mind, so that the "necessity" with which all languages have certain common properties is "biological necessity."[5] The further divisions of the study of linguistic competence (both universal and language-particular aspects) into the study of syntax, semantics, morphology, phonology, and phonetics is familiar and requires no further discussion here.[6] On the other hand, how the study of linguistic performance may be further articulated is perhaps less familiar, and some discussion of this matter is called for.

---

[3]This use of the term "linguistic competence" follows that of Chomsky (1965). However, our use of the term "linguistic performance" differs from his, in that Chomsky includes in the study of linguistic performance such phenomena as hesitations, false starts, and slips of the tongue, that clearly have nothing to do with "appropriate use." By "linguistic performance" we have in mind a notion like that of "communicative competence."

[4]This term was commonly employed in this sense in seventeenth-century rationalist discussions of the nature of human language. It fell into disuse with the rise of empiricist views of language, and has only been recently revived. For discussion, see Chomsky (1966).

[5]Alternatively, we may suppose that the systems of universal grammar and/or of universal competence (and similarly the grammars and performance systems of individual languages) are abstract systems that happen to be representable in some form by human minds. Viewed in this way, the "necessity" with which all languages have certain common properties is essentially definitional in nature. The difference between these alternative views of the relation between language and mind are of considerable philosophical interest, but for the present at least have no consequences for the way in which linguistic investigations are carried out.

[6]This is not to say that there is total agreement that all these divisions of the study of linguistic competence are necessary. Indeed, the main theoretical issue separating "generative semantics" (Lakoff, 1971; Postal, 1972) from "interpretive semantics" (Chomsky, 1972b; Jackendoff, 1972; Katz, 1972) is whether syntax and semantics can clearly be isolated as separate aspects of grammatical study, while form-content analysis (discussed in this volume by Diver) makes do without syntax entirely.

II. DIVISIONS OF THE STUDY
OF LINGUISTIC PERFORMANCE

As language users, we either produce or we comprehend linguistic expressions; thus we may broadly divide the study of linguistic performance into the study of production (further divided into the study of the production of speech, of manual signs, and of writing) and of comprehension (further divided into the study of the comprehension of speech, of manual signs, and of writing). Each of these processes not only takes place in time, but ordinarily takes place in no more time than is required to process linguistic expressions as physical events (for example, we ordinarily understand speech in no more time than it takes us to hear it). To account for the extraordinary efficiency of the human language processing mechanisms, we must assume that representations of the significance[7] of expressions are built up as those expressions are being received and produced. Furthermore, it would appear necessary to assume that separate, but integrated, processing subsystems operate simultaneously, in parallel, during the reception and production of linguistic expressions. Accordingly, each performance system is best analyzed as a set of interacting subsystems, much as the system of linguistic competence is.

Because the significance of an expression is usually distinct from what that expression literally means (i.e., distinct from its semantic interpretation), the question arises whether semantic interpretations are computed in the course of obtaining representations of significance. Elementary theoretical considerations would lead one to conclude that they are, and though we lack systematic experimental evidence that would bear on this question, what experimental evidence we do have (Clark & Lucy, 1975) supports that contention. If the contention is correct, then we can divide the components of any performance system into those that are involved in the construction of what expressions mean and those that are involved in determining what they signify in context, given what they mean. The former components of a system of language use are like those of the system of linguistic competence in that they are involved in the construction of the representation of the sound-meaning relations of linguistic expressions.[8] We, therefore, refer to the former components of a performance system as a "performance

---

[7]For this term, see Katz and Langendoen (1976, p. 10). The significance of expression is its meaning in the context of its use.

[8]It is clearly not necessary for a performance system, such as that of speech comprehension, to construct the entire grammatical representation of an expression in order for that expression to be appropriately used. However, we must assume that that system is in principle capable of constructing its entire representation.

grammar" and to the system of linguistic competence as the "competence grammar."

III. THE RELATION OF PERFORMANCE GRAMMARS TO COMPETENCE GRAMMAR

We come now to a problem that has greatly exercised linguists and psychologists alike over the past 15 years or so: what is the exact nature of the relation between the competence grammar of a language and the various performance grammars of that language? At one extreme is the possibility that for each language there is exactly one performance grammar and that it is identical to the competence grammar of that language. At the other extreme is the possibility that performance grammars construct representations of linguistic expressions by principles of their own, without recourse to the principles of competence grammar. Of these two extreme possibilities, the first appears more attractive on general simplicity grounds, and it is, therefore, not surprising that it was this possibility that was first seriously entertained by linguists following the advent of the theory of transformational-generative (TG) grammar. However, it is easy to see that the principles of TG grammar, whether those of Chomsky (1955) and (1957), Chomsky (1965), Chomsky (1972b) and (1975), or even those of Bresnan (1978), cannot possibly serve directly as the principles of performance grammars. First, it is manifest that performance grammars construct representations of linguistic expressions essentially from beginning to end (from left to right, assuming Indo-European writing conventions), whereas the principles of any TG grammar do not. Second, performance systems directly construct, as a first step, representations comparable to surface-structure representations given by TG grammars, whereas TG grammars do not directly construct such representations.[9]

Once it became abundantly clear that the principles of TG grammar cannot themselves serve as the principles of performance grammars, linguists who chose to maintain one form or another of TG grammar as a theory of linguistic competence found themselves compelled to move closer and closer to the second of the two extreme positions just described. At the same time, many other linguists chose simply to ignore the relation between competence and performance grammars entirely, to concentrate their attention solely on the development of performance grammars, and perhaps also to claim that the study of TG-based linguistic competence is

---

[9]For further discussion of the inappropriateness of TG grammars as mechanisms for the construction of structural descriptions in performance, see Fodor, Bever, and Garrett (1974, chaps. 5–6).

devoid of interest (Derwing, 1973). Finally, there has developed a movement to replace or to alter TG theory of linguistic competence in favor of a theory of competence grammar whose principles can be directly used by the various performance systems. Given our discussion so far, it is clear that the grammatical principles that such a theory must provide directly construct surface representations essentially from left to right, whatever else they may do (for example, construct semantic representations). The best-developed theory that meets both of these requirements is that of augmented transition networks (ATNs), formulated initially by Thorne, Bratley, and Dewar (1968), construed as a theory of linguistic competence by Woods (1970), and applied to problems of linguistic analysis by a number of researchers, notably Kaplan (1972) and Wanner and Maratsos (1978). As Woods observes, ATN theory is as capable as that of TG grammar of providing for grammars that generate all and only all of the expressions of a human language.[10] Therefore, in order to determine the adequacy of ATN grammatical theory, relative to the theory of TG grammar, as a theory of linguistic competence, one must assess their relative capacities for expressing true linguistic generalizations.

ATN theory is criticized on these grounds by Dresher and Hornstein (1976), who contend that proponents of ATN theory have ignored the basic questions of grammatical-theory evaluation. However, they are able to sustain this contention only by failing to consider those discussions of ATN theory, in particular Woods (1970), in which those questions are raised. Woods claims, in fact, that ATN theory does provide a notation in which true generalizations about linguistic structure are indicated by the brevity of the statement of the principles that express them, just as in TG theory. Whether this claim can be sustained under close scrutiny, of course, remains to be seen, but it certainly cannot be dismissed out of hand. It is ultimately an empirical question, yet to be decided, whether a theory of grammar, such as ATN theory, in which first surface-structure representations are built up left to right, is to be preferred as a theory of linguistic competence, to a theory, such as that of TG grammar, in which linguistic representations are constructed in some other way.

More important, however, than the question of the adequacy of ATN theory of grammar is the correctness of the claim that the grammar of competence also serves as the grammar of the various performance systems. By definition, the expressions constructed by the competence grammar of a given language are the grammatical expressions of that language. On the other hand, the expressions constructed by a performance grammar of a given language are the acceptable expressions of that

---

[10]Like the theories of TG grammar, ATN theory provides for grammars that are capable of generating every recursively enumerable set; hence of generating every human language.

language. To hold that the competence and performance grammars of a language are the same is to hold that the set of grammatical expressions of a language is identical to the set of acceptable expressions of that language. Now we know that under ordinary conditions, those sets appear to have quite distinct membership: there appear to be grammatical expressions that are unacceptable and acceptable expressions that appear to be ungrammatical (Chomsky, 1965, pp. 12–14; Langendoen & Bever, 1973; Bever, Carroll, & Hurtig, 1976). Thus, the question arises whether under ideal conditions, the acceptable and grammatical expressions of a language converge. Unfortunately, the answer to this question is unknown, though there are fairly good grounds for conjecturing that it is negative (for discussion, see Langendoen, 1977). Hence, we may properly be skeptical about the contention that the performance principles by which linguistic expressions are constructed are to be identified with the principles of competence grammar.

But if this is the case, then the second of the two extreme positions concerning the relation of competence to performance grammars remains a viable option. We can continue to maintain some version of a TG theory of linguistic competence and at the same time to feel free to develop theories of performance grammars as we see fit. Such theories would still bear a significant relation to the theory of competence grammar, in that the performance principles would be formulated as a function in large part of the principles of competence grammar. For example, those principles would presumably make systematic and extensive use of the constructs of competence grammar — the various grammatical (phonetic, phonological, morphological, syntactic, and semantic) categories and relations, etc. However, to make this position at all attractive, it is necessary to go into some detail as to how it might work.

IV. TOWARD AUTONOMOUS PERFORMANCE GRAMMARS

In Section II, it was argued that any given performance system constructs representations of linguistic expressions by means of a set of interacting subsystems operating in parallel. It may be maintained further that the function of the first subsystem (or group of subsystems) of the speech comprehension mechanism that is activated by the perception of linguistic input is to construct a surface representation of the perceived input expression (i.e., to "parse" that expression). Following Fodor, Bever, and Garrett (1974), we may assume that once this subsystem completes the job for some portion of the input material, it sends its analysis off to a second subsystem, which continues the linguistic analysis; meanwhile, the computing space available to the first subsystem is cleared, to make room for computations on the next portion of the input material.

On this view, one of the major problems faced by the first subsystem is how to divide up the input material into units that are large enough so that a significantly useful amount of analysis can be carried out, and yet not so large as to exhaust the relatively small amount of computation space available to it. Ideally also, the units should be as independent from one another as possible, to minimize the number and kinds of relations that subsequent processing subsystems would have to establish among them, in order for the entire input to be comprehended. Reasoning of this sort leads us to expect that the first subsystem will attempt to analyze the input material into units, or "chunks," that correspond to major constituents in the surface-structure representation it is trying to construct, and as far as possible into units that do not appear to have elements missing from them that they ordinarily have. The results of experiments carried out by Carroll (1976) suggest that, indeed, chunking is carried out in this fashion.[11]

Exactly how the first subsystem parses each chunking unit must remain, for the moment, a matter of conjecture.[12] We may, however, presume that the subsystem is constructed as a finite-state transducer that assigns surface structures to input strings up to some fixed finite degree of recursion.[13] Accordingly, the inability of performance systems, under ordinary conditions, to parse multiply center-embedded expressions is simply a consequence of the finite-state character of the first subsystem of those systems.[14] Similarly, the inability of performance systems, under ordinary conditions, to parse multiply right- and left-branching structures that have not been "readjusted" as coordinate-like structures follows from the finite-state character of the first subsystem (Langendoen, 1975).

From this picture of the organization of performance grammars, it follows that the same principles (or principles that have the same function) must belong to separate subsystems. For example, the first subsystem of the system of English speech comprehension must be able to assign the subject–predicate relation to the major constituents of expressions like 1, whereas some subsequent subsystem must do so for expressions like 2.

---

[11]We assume, following Toppino (1974) and Kemper, Catlin, and Bowers (1977), that the results of Bever, Lackner, and Kirk (1969) can be reinterpreted in a way that eliminates the role of deep structure in chunking.

[12]Kimball (1974) presents interesting suggestions as to the nature of the universal-performance principles of surface-structure parsing.

[13]In Langendoen (1975) an algorithm for constructing a finite-state transducer that parses the expressions generated by an arbitrary context-free grammar up to some fixed finite degree of recursion is presented. This algorithm generalizes the one originally presented by Chomsky (1959).

[14]As pointed out at the end of Section III, it is unknown whether the other subsystems can overcome the limitations of the first subsystem under ideal conditions.

1. Doris went to Delaware.
2. The only sister of the best friend of my boss's nephew might want to try to get everyone in the office to go to Delaware.

In 1, the subject and predicate expressions are both contained within the same chunking unit (the sentence as a whole), so that the relation between them can be assigned by the principles of the first subsystem. In 2, on the other hand, the subject and predicate expressions each constitute separate chunking units, so that the operation of relating them as subject and predicate cannot be carried out by the first subsystem. But because 2 is fully comprehensible to normal English speakers under ordinary conditions, some other subsystem must be able to relate its subject and predicate appropriately. This observation, that different subsystems of a performance system appear to be able to carry out the same grammatical functions, provides us with another reason for distinguishing sharply between competence and performance grammars. It is a goal of competence-grammar description to achieve a redundancy-free statement of the principles that are needed to generate the structural descriptions of the expressions of a given language, whereas an adequate account of performance grammars will apparently have to be highly redundant.[15]

V.   FROM SURFACE PARSING TO SEMANTIC INTERPRETATION IN PERFORMANCE GRAMMARS

The construction of a surface parsing for a linguistic expression is a major step in the determination of its semantic representation in performance. We may assume that while the surface parsing of an expression is being built up by the first subsystem, other subsystems are operating to determine the semantic representations of the lexical items and constituents that appear in it. The semantic relations that hold among the various constituents of the expression must then be determined as a function of the syntactic relations that hold among them by virtue of the surface parsing. In some cases, the syntactic relations that are relevant to semantic interpretation can be directly read off of the surface parsing, whereas in other cases they must be reconstructed by indirect procedures. Examples 3 and 4 illustrate these two possibilities.

3. Some people who are pretty angry are roaming the corridors.
4. Some people are roaming the corridors who are pretty angry.

---

[15]See Schane's contribution to this volume for further discussion of the goals of the theory of linguistic competence. Besides the redundancy built into the grammars of each performance system, there is presumably considerable duplication of grammatical principles across the various systems also.

In both 3 and 4, the expression *who are pretty angry* is understood as bearing the syntactic relation of "modifier of" to the expression *some people*. This relation can be read directly off of the surface parsing of 3, because the two expressions form a single constituent *some people who are pretty angry,* in which *who are pretty angry* is syntactically subordinate to *some people*. In the surface parsing of 4, on the other hand, the two expressions do not directly bear any syntactic relation at all. That the expression *who are pretty angry* is a modifier of the expression *some people* in 4 must be reconstructed in performance by a procedure that recognizes (1) that *who are pretty angry* is an expression of the type that can only be construed as a modifier, (2) that the expression *some people* is the only available expression that can plausibly serve as the modified constituent, and (3) that the grammar of English permits the relation to hold in cases like 4.[16]

Formally, the way that a TG competence grammar establishes that *some people* and *who are pretty angry* are syntactically related as modified and modifier in 4 is by deriving that expression from an underlying structure in which the relation holds directly (that is, a structure very much like the surface parsing of 3), by application of a syntactic transformation that destroys that structure, and creates a new structure in which the relation no longer holds. Thus, the task of a performance grammar, when presented with the surface parsing of 4, is to recognize that it is a legitimate output of that transformation. How the performance grammar accomplishes this task need not concern us; it suffices to note that a performance grammar, in processing 4, must carry out certain operations that it does not have to carry out in processing 3.

For convenience, let us call a surface parsing, like that of 3, which provides an adequate basis for computing its semantic interpretation, "canonical." All others we may call "noncanonical."[17] From the foregoing discussion, we have seen that performance systems must carry out certain operations in the processing of expressions that have noncanonical parsings that they do not have to carry out in the processing of those that have canonical ones. Thus we may conclude that, ceteris paribus, expressions that have noncanonical parsings are more difficult to process than those

---

[16]Proviso 3 is necessary to distinguish expression 4 from expressions like *The people are roaming the corridors who are pretty angry,* in which the relation does not hold, even though the counterparts to provisos 1 and 2 are satisfied.

[17]The terms "canonical" and "noncanonical" can also be applied to strings, but not without some difficulty. Some strings are canonical in two different ways (have two different canonical parsings associated with them), for example, *I asked for a reason.* Others may be associated with both a canonical and a noncanonical parsing, for example, *What agency has that spy under surveillance?* Finally, others may be noncanonical in two different ways, for example, *For what reason did you ask?*

that have canonical ones.[18] Because an expression that has a noncanonical parsing has a syntactic derivation in which one or more transformations have applied that alter or destroy syntactic relations, it follows that there is a relation between the complexity of a syntactic derivation of an expression, measured in terms of the number of transformations that have applied, and its processing complexity. However, that relation is not a direct (much less a linear) one: not all transformations have an effect on syntactic relations, the degree to which syntactic relations are altered by a transformation may vary, and other factors may intervene to obscure the relation.[19]

The problem of determining the exact nature of the relation between derivational and processing complexity is further complicated by the fact that there is not complete agreement as to which transformations alter syntactic relations (or if so, in what way), and hence which surface parsings are canonical and which are not. Thus, while it is generally agreed that the *wh-* movement transformation that applies in the derivation of certain interrogative expressions in English alters syntactic relations (except when it affects the subject of the main clause), there is no general agreement as to whether passive expressions in English are derived by means of a transformation that alters syntactic relations.[20] Until such disagreements can be resolved, we can give no systematic interpretation to the results of experimental investigations into the processing complexity of expressions of different syntactic types.

VI.   CONCLUSIONS

To the question "What is the role of grammar in the use of language?" we may reply with another question: "What grammar, competence grammar or performance grammar?" The role of performance grammar is a direct one: It is used to construct the semantic interpretations (and, ultimately,

---

[18]The "ceteris paribus" provision is crucial here. Thus, while example 3 is canonical and 4 is noncanonical, 4 may nevertheless turn out to be easier to process than 3 because its degree of center embedding is less than that of 3.

[19]See footnote 18. Jacques Mehler informs me that something very much like this more restricted version of the "derivational theory of complexity" was in fact entertained by certain researchers in the early 1960s. If so, it was nevertheless quickly supplanted in everyone's minds by the more general theory. When the falsity of that theory was dramatically revealed several years later, the whole field of psycholinguistics was thrown into a disarray from which it has not yet fully recovered.

[20]The traditional view, established by Chomsky (1955, 1957) is that they are. An interesting recent restatement of the traditional view is given by Fiengo (1977). For the alternative view, see Bresnan (1978).

significance) of the linguistic expressions that are used. The role of competence grammar is an indirect one: It provides the vocabulary for the construction of performance grammars, and it presumably interacts with performance grammars in ways that we have not considered here. We have also not considered the ways in which universal grammar and universal performance may be related. Surely the principles that children use in the acquisition of a language and of the systems by which they use that language must be intimately related.

ACKNOWLEDGMENTS

An earlier version of this paper was read at the Universities of Paris, Sussex, Liverpool, Edinburgh, and Groningen, and I thank various members of those audiences for helpful comments and criticisms. Special thanks go to Manfred Bierwisch.

REFERENCES

Bever, T. G. The ascent of the specious or, there's a lot we don't know about mirrors. In D. Cohen (Ed.), *Explaining linguistic phenomena.* Washington, D.C.: Hemisphere Press, 1974.

Bever T. G., Carroll, J. M., Jr., & Hurtig, R. Analogy or, Ungrammatical sequences that are utterable and comprehensible are the origins of new grammars in language acquisition and linguistic evolution. In T. G. Bever, J. J. Katz, & D. T. Langendoen (Eds.), *An integrated theory of linguistic ability.* New York: Thomas Y. Crowell, 1976.

Bever, T. G., Katz, J. J., & Langendoen, D. T. (Eds.). *An integrated theory of linguistic ability.* New York: Thomas Y. Crowell, 1976.

Bever, T. G., Lackner, J. R., & Kirk, R. The underlying structures of sentences are the primary units of immediate speech processing. *Perception and Psychophysics,* 1969, *5,* 225-231.

Bresnan, J. A realistic transformational grammar. In M. Halle, J. Bresnan, & G. A. Miller (Eds.), *Linguistic theory and psychological reality.* Cambridge: MIT Press, 1978.

Carroll, J. M., Jr. *The interaction of structural and functional variables in sentence perception: Some preliminary studies.* Doctoral dissertation, Columbia University, 1976.

Chomsky, N. *The logical structure of linguistic theory.* 1955. Mimeo. (Published with an introduction. New York: Plenum, 1975.)

Chomsky, N. *Syntactic structures.* The Hague: Mouton, 1957.

Chomsky, N. On certain formal properties of grammars. *Information and Control,* 1959, *2,* 137-167.

Chomsky, N. *Aspects of the theory of syntax.* Cambridge: MIT Press, 1965.

Chomsky, N. *Cartesian linguistics.* New York: Harper & Row, 1966.

Chomsky, N. *Language and mind* (2nd ed.). New York: Harcourt, Brace and World, 1972. (a)

Chomsky, N. *Studies on semantics in generative grammar.* The Hague: Mouton, 1972. (b)

Clark, H. H., & Lucy, P. Understanding what is meant from what is said: A study in conversationally conveyed requests. *Journal of Verbal Learning and Verbal Behavior,* 1975, *14,* 56–72.

Derwing, B. L. *Transformational grammar as a theory of language acquisition.* London and New York: Cambridge University Press, 1973.

Dresher, B. E., & Hornstein, N. On some supposed contributions of artificial intelligence to the scientific study of language. *Cognition,* 1976, *4,* 321–398.

Fiengo, R. On trace theory. *Linguistic Inquiry,* 1977, *8,* 35–61.

Fodor, J. A. *The language of thought.* New York: Thomas Y. Crowell, 1975.

Fodor, J. A., Bever, T. G., & Garrett, M. *The psychology of language.* New York: McGraw-Hill, 1974.

Jackendoff, R. S.   *Semantic interpretation in generative grammar.* Cambridge: MIT Press, 1972.

Kaplan, R. M. Augmented transition networks as psychological models of sentence comprehension. *Artificial Intelligence,* 1972, *3,* 77–100.

Katz, J. J. *Semantic theory.* New York: Harper & Row, 1972.

Katz, J. J., & Langendoen, D. T. Pragmatics and presupposition. *Language,* 1976, *52,* 1–17.

Kemper, S., Catlin, J., & Bowers, J. On the surface structure of infinitive-complement sentences. *Journal of Psycholinguistic Research,* 1977, *6,* 1–19.

Kimball, J. Seven principles of surface structure parsing in natural language. *Cognition,* 1974, *2,* 15–47.

Lakoff, G. On generative semantics. In D. D. Steinberg & L. A. Jakobovits (Eds.), *Semantics: An interdisciplinary reader.* London and New York: Cambridge University Press, 1971.

Langendoen, D. T. Finite-state parsing of phrase-structure languages and the status of readjustment rules in grammar. *Linguistic Inquiry,* 1975, *6,* 533–554.

Langendoen, D. T. The inadequacy of type-3 and type-2 grammars for human languages. In P. Hopper (Ed.), *Festschrift for Winfred Lehmann.* Amsterdam: Benjamins, 1977.

Langendoen, D. T., & Bever, T. G. Can a not unhappy person be called a not sad one? In S. A. Anderson & P. Kiparsky (Eds.), *A festschrift for Morris Halle.* New York: Holt, Rinehart & Winston, 1973.

Postal, P. The best theory. In S. Peters (Ed.), *Goals of linguistic theory.* Englewood Cliffs, N.J.: Prentice-Hall, 1972.

Thorne, J. P., Bratley, P., & Dewar, H. The syntactic analysis of English by machine. In D. Mitchie (Ed.), *Machine intelligence 3.* New York: Elsevier, 1968.

Toppino, T. C. The underlying structures of sentences are not the primary units of speech processing: A reinterpretation of Bever, Lackner, and Kirk's findings. *Perception and Psychophysics,* 1974, *15,* 517–518.

Wanner, E., & Maratsos, M. An ATN approach to comprehension. In M. Halle, J. Bresnan, & G. A. Miller (Eds.), *Linguistic theory and psychological reality.* Cambridge: MIT Press, 1978.

Woods, W. A. Transition network grammars for natural language analysis. *Communications of the ACM,* 1970, *13,* 591–606.

9 Natural Processing Units of Speech

David McNeill
University of Chicago

The organization of utterances apparently takes the following form. There is a structure of concepts and relations that corresponds to the speaker's meaning. This structure falls into one or another generalized category of ideas, such as the idea of event, action, state, location, property, entity, or person. The speaker organizes and moves from one of these generalized ideas to another, for example, from the idea of an event to the idea of a location, and in so doing is guided in coordinating the articulation of the speech output. The unit of production, according to this statement, is based on the structure of concepts, and within this conceptual structure there are the processes for coordinating speech output. Kozhevnikov and Chistovich (1965) have defined these meaning units as syntagmata, or meaning units pronounced as single outputs. The output of speech shall be said to be coordinated within syntagmata. As new meanings are organized in the speaker's conceptions fresh syntagmata become available. Hence, there is a coordinated articulation of speech output that corresponds with the organization of meaning.

In contrast to linguistic entities such as phrases, sentences, sentoids, etc., the syntagma is a unit of speech functioning. It may or may not correspond to the familiar structural units of linguistic description. And even when the syntagma does coincide with some structural unit, the claim will be made that the functional unit with which the processing of speech is engaged is the syntagma—the direct connection of meaning with articulation—and not the linguistic structural unit with which it fortuitously corresponds.

The concepts of event, action, state, location, property, entity, and person, are examples of what I will call sensory-motor ideas. This choice of terminology cannot be fully motivated in the present paper, and for further discussion I must refer to a recent longer work (McNeill, 1979). My proposal, briefly, is that part of the meaning of any utterance includes information that can be represented at a sensory-motor level. This level of meaning plays a fundamental role in utterance programming. Such information takes the form of one or more of the sensory-motor ideas mentioned above. For example, a causative action sequence is one type of a sensory-motor representation of an event. The mental representation, or scheme, of this sensory-motor sequence, then, is one kind of an idea of an event. Sensory-motor representations have the capacity of existing simultaneously in two realms, that of meaning and that of action. The sensory-motor level is precisely where these realms meet. This line of thought leads to the following hypothesis.

Let us call the neural system for controlling motor action in the world system A, and the neural system for controlling speech articulation system B; then the sensory-motor level of representation arises from system A and speech from system B. Sensory-motor ideas become important for speech production in the following way. For one to have syntagmata, it is necessary for systems A and B to converge so that A provides the plan, or scheme, of the action and B provides the channel of execution of this scheme. In this way the dual character of sensory-motor representations, as simultaneously part of meaning and part of action, is exploited. Such AB fusions appear at an early point in ontogenesis and remain, we suppose, the fundamental mechanism of speech coordination from the semantic level with adult speakers as well (McNeill, 1975). [This role for sensory-motor action schemes can be related to the description of action control given by Bernstein (1967), Greene (1972), or Turvey (1975); according to them the control of action is accomplished through a hierarchy of processes each level of which manages only a few degrees of freedom, and in these hierarchies the highest level can be identified with the scheme of the action.]

Thus, as speech production proceeds, speakers are presumed to be constantly activating sensory-motor content (A), which they do on the basis of meaning relationships, in order to access and control the articulatory system (B). We should, therefore, expect that measures of the coordination of speech output (phonemic clauses, the place and kind of dysfluency, etc.) will coincide with units of sensory-motor meaning.

My purpose in this paper is to present evidence that the natural units of speech processing do coincide with sensory-motor ideas.

I. SEGMENTATION OF SPONTANEOUS SPEECH

Much of the data I report are based on a two-person conversation which was recorded and transcribed by S. Duncan, Jr. (Duncan & Fiske, 1977), and I am grateful to Duncan for providing this transcription for me to study. The conversation, which lasted about 18 minutes, took place between two well-acquainted adult males, both psychotherapists, who were discussing a female patient. The transcription made use of the conventions of Trager and Smith (1951) and included all the segmental phonemes, the primary stresses, and the terminal contours.

A phonemic clause is defined by Trager and Smith as a sequence of segmental phonemes bounded by silence and/or terminal contours which contains exactly one primary stress. In addition, it has one of a restricted set of intonation patterns. Each combination of these features (a particular tune and stress assignment, and choice of terminal contour) can be thought of as the output of a single speech program. The phonemic clause segmentations of the Duncan corpus can therefore be examined for evidence of being the output of syntagmata. Do they tend to coincide with independently determined semantic segments; for example, the ideas of event, action, location, and others? (A phonemic clause, of course, should not be confused with a grammatical clause; the definitions of the two are entirely independent.)

A second approach to locating natural processing units of speech is to make use of the dysfluencies that appear in a speaker's output. For example, when the structure of the utterance breaks down and some new structure is substituted, what elements does the speaker appear to be manipulating? If there are hesitations, can the places at which they occur be interpreted as points where the speaker is shifting speech programs?

A third approach is to look for a correspondence of paralinguistic features with semantic segments in speech. For example, do hand gesticulations begin and end at points in the speech stream which could be interpreted as outputs of single processing units? Gesticulation is treated, in this interpretation, as a second channel of output from the same syntagma that programs the speech itself. Syntagmata have already been said to be based on fused AB control systems. We are only supposing in addition that system A can continue to have something like its original action output, perhaps in vestigial form, while it programs system B for speech. Hence, there should be a correlation through time between speech and gesticulation, and gesticulation should tend to be iconic with respect to the sensory-motor meaning. In this way, gesticulation can be viewed as an external dynamic trace of the internal process of speech programming.

A. Definitions of Sensory-Motor Concepts

In all investigations where the sensory-motor content of speech has been judged, I have relied on the following definitions which are applied rigorously. These definitions cover more than 95% of the utterances in the adult corpora to which they have been applied (excluding utterances associated with turn exchanges). Experienced judges agree on more than 85%

of the classifications made, and this value rises to more than 95% after comparison and discussion.

> Event—a change of state, e.g., The men stopped their cars.
> Action—the performance due to an agent or actor, e.g., stopped their cars (omitting the agent), or stopped (omitting the object as well).
> State—the condition before or after an event, e.g., the moving cars.
> Property—condition on an event or action, e.g., The men *quickly* stopped their cars.
> Entity—the object concept (cf. Piaget, 1954), e.g., the cars.
> Person—animate being, e.g., the men.
> Location—terminus or source of an event (cf. Piaget, 1954) e.g., The men stopped their cars *before the gate*.

B. Phonemic Clauses

Altogether, the two speakers produced 1438 phonemic clauses; 561 from speaker *L* ("lower" on Duncan's transcript) and 877 from speaker *U* ("upper").

Table 9.1 gives a tabulation of the phonemic clauses in this corpus that did not precede dysfluencies, classified according to the way in which they have been judged to correspond to sensory-motor content.

TABLE 9.1
Phonemic Clauses Compared to Sensory-Motor Ideas

		Lower Speaker		*Upper Speaker*	
		Freq.	*%*	*Freq.*	*%*
Case 1					
PC ⊢——⊣		249	78.8	500	76.1
SM ⊢——⊣					
Case 2					
PC ⊢—+—⊣	2 PC	34	10.8	76	11.7
SM ⊢——⊣	3 PC	3	0.9	8	1.2
	4 PC			1	0.2
Case 3					
PC ⊢——⊣	2 SM	5	1.6	6	0.9
SM ⊢—+—⊣	3 SM	1	0.3		
Case 4					
PC ⊢—+—+—⊣		1	0.3		
SM ⊢—+—⊣					
	Sociocentric	22	7.0	62	9.4
	Unclassified	1	0.3	4	0.6
	Total	316	100.0	657	100.0

a. Case 1. The phonemic clause coincides with a single sensory-motor idea. An example is:

I wónder what | yóu | méant by that |

The first segment refers to an event, "I wonder (something)," the second to a person, "you," and the third to an action. The internal structure of a single sensory-motor idea can be complex, in that it contains other sensory-motor ideas, and some of the sensory-motor ideas that coincide with one phonemic clause are complex in this way. In Case 1, the evidence is that the coordinated articulation that produces a phonemic clause coincides with a single sensory-motor meaning. This evidence is lacking in the remaining cases.

b. Case 2. A sensory-motor idea corresponds to more than one phonemic clause. The meanings that coincide with the phonemic clauses show a real connection, and at least one of them would not be expected to stand alone. The table differentiates entries according to the number of phonemic clauses over which the single sensory-motor idea is spread. For example,

Thát was a | beáutiful | thing she did |

(The indefinite article appears in the first phonemic clause rather than in the second with its NP; this is a common phenomenon, discussed below.) The second and third phonemic clauses together form a single idea of an entity, "[a] beautiful thing she did." The conceptual content of "beautiful" cannot stand alone apart from the rest of this entity, yet was programmed separately. We can speculate that the speaker wished to emphasize the property "beautiful," using primary stress, and also wanted to emphasize "thing"; this doubling of primary stress would induce a terminal contour between the two words in accordance with the principle that each phonemic clause can contain only one primary stress.

c. Case 3. A phonemic clause contains two sensory-motor ideas that one would expect to have been programmed separately. Most of these examples involve adverbials of a type that can optionally appear in alternate sentence positions. Therefore, the adverbial would seem to require separate programming, and most such adverbials in the Duncan corpus do, in fact, occupy separate phonemic clauses; but in Case 3 they appear jointly with other material. For example,

hówever it was | she went to school préviously |

The adverbial "previously" could have occurred, but did not, at the position after the "was" (the example is also missing a conjunction). That it occurred at the end of the sentence should have called for separate programming.

d. Case 4. There is no correspondence of sensory-motor ideas with phonemic clauses. The only example is,

Thén *on* | *that thére* | *was a good year* |
    location existence   entity

C. The Degree of Correspondence

The degree of correspondence between the phonemic clause segmentation of speech output and sensory-motor content has to be estimated in two ways. First, we have to find the percentage of sensory-motor ideas that appear in one phonemic clause; this is the fraction: Case 1/(Case 1 + Case 2). Next, we have to find the percentage of phonemic clauses that contain unified (possibly complex) sensory-motor ideas; this is the fraction: Case 1/(Case 1 + Case 3). These fractions are similar for *L* and *U*, as shown in Table 9.2.

From these results, we can conclude that nearly all the phonemic clauses in the Duncan corpus are segregated into their own sensory-motor ideas, and better than 80% of the sensory-motor ideas coincide with single phonemic clauses. Although phonemic clause boundaries could occur in a variety of positions, they in fact are highly constrained, for the speaker's speech output accurately reflects the underlying sensory-motor content.

Syntagmata appear to be remarkably short, to judge from the length of phonemic clauses in *L*'s and *U*'s output. Table 9.3 gives the distribution of length in number of syllables for the first 102 phonemic clauses that *L* and *U* each produced (phonemic clauses preceding dysfluencies and sociocentric phonemic clauses omitted). The average phonemic clause is 3.02 *syllables* for

TABLE 9.2
Overlap of Phonemic Clauses and Sensory-Motor Ideas

	Percentage of Sensory-Motor Ideas in One Phonemic Clause— Case 1/(Case 1 + Case 2)	*Percentage of Phonemic Clauses in One Sensory-Motor Idea— Case 1/(Case 1 + Case 3)*
Speaker *U*	85.5	98.8
Speaker *L*	87.1	97.6

TABLE 9.3
Length of Phonemic Clauses

	Number of Syllables								
	1	2	3	4	5	6	7	8	9
Speaker *U*	9	28	34	15	13	1	1		1
Speaker *L*	13	30	24	20	9	5		1	

L and 3.08 *syllables* for *U*. In *L*'s speech, the modal length is only 2 *syllables*. At these short lengths, the most typical programming unit would seem to be a single simple sensory-motor idea.

D. Hesitations

Hesitations of various kinds are by far the most frequent form of dysfluency in the Duncan corpus. Several types occur, including filled pauses, unfilled pauses, audible inhalations, and audible glottal clicks. The pauses were recognized subjectively by Duncan. The interrater reliabilities of Duncan's transcriptions range between $r = .80$ and $r = 1.00$ (Duncan, 1965).

A problem in working with hesitation data is that some hesitations may be programmed by the speaker as part of the speech output. There is no definite method for recognizing these programmed hesitations. The interest in this paper, however, focuses on the unprogrammed hesitations that arise when speech programs are changed. Hesitations of this kind indicate, in another way, the boundaries of speech programming units. Therefore, we should try to remove possibly programmed hesitations.

It would seem that inhalations are in some sense programmed. There is evidence of smooth control of the breathing process during speech which is different from normal breathing (see Lieberman, 1967). If all the audible inhalations are excluded from the sample of hesitations, what remains would seem to be more nearly a collection of the hesitations that occur as speech programs change.

As a further attempt to isolate unprogrammed hesitations, we can apply a distinction drawn by Goldman-Eisler (1968) between "grammatical" and "nongrammatical" hesitations. Her investigations show that the latter tend to occur mainly during periods of high hesitancy, when apparently a large amount of concurrent cognitive activity is taking place. Hesitations at "grammatical" points, in contrast, are almost alone in occurring during periods of high fluency. Presumably the speaker's wherewithal for programmed hesitations would be greater when speech is generally fluent. Therefore, if we remove all the "grammatical" hesitations, what remains should come still closer to the desired sample of hesitations that occur at the point of changing programs.

Each hesitation in the Duncan corpus has been classified into one of 11 categories. Nine of these correspond to the definitions in Goldman-Eisler (1968) for "grammatical" hesitations (these consist of her six categories plus three more). The "grammatical" hesitations are: sentence ϕ (where ϕ represents the hesitation); ϕ conjunction; conjunction ϕ; ϕ *wh*- term; *wh*-term ϕ; ϕ quotation; quotation ϕ (the quotes may be direct or indirect); ϕ adverbial of manner, time, or place; and ϕ parenthetical clause (or phrase) ϕ (i.e., at either end). This leaves the two following categories, the ones of primary interest.

1. *Concept ϕ concept.* The hesitation occurs between two sensory-motor ideas. For example:

I just want to ϕ talk with somebody

The first segment is a state (a condition before a change of state of the speaker). The second segment is an action. Thus, the speaker shifted programs at the onset of the idea of an action.

2. *Con ϕ cept.* The hesitation occurs in the middle of a sensory-motor idea. For example:

a very real ϕ thing she was doing

Here, "very real thing" corresponds to the idea of an entity, and it seems that it should have been programmed as a single output. The hesitation therefore interrupts a presumed programming unit.

There are necessarily more places where hesitations could occur within concepts (2) than there are between concepts (1), because the number of syllables within concepts is greater than the number of positions between concepts.

Table 9.4 presents the results of classifying the four types of hesitation into the 11 categories mentioned above. We eliminate all the hesitations consisting of inhalations, and all the hesitations deemed to be grammatical. The

TABLE 9.4
Hesitations in the Spontaneous Speech of Two Speakers

Environment	Type of Hesitation				
	Filled Pause	Unfilled Pause	Glottal Click	Inha-lation	Total
concept ϕ concept	40	61	2	48	151
con ϕ cept	6	9		4	19
sentence ϕ	4	24	2	41	71
ϕ conjunction	1			7	8
conjunction ϕ	8	3	3	4	18
ϕ wh- term					
wh- term ϕ	3	3		2	8
ϕ quote	4	3		4	11
quote ϕ	2	1		1	4
ϕ adverb				1	1
ϕ parenthetical ϕ		2			2
Not classified	2	2		5	9
Total	70	108	7	118	303

remaining 118 hesitations consist of filled pauses, unfilled pauses, and glottal clicks, classified as concept ϕ concept or con ϕ cept. Of these, the great majority (87%) are in the category of concept ϕ concept. In spite of the greater opportunity for con ϕ cept hesitations, this class is comparatively rare.

Thus, we can conclude that spontaneous hesitations generally occur at points where one syntagma gives way to another, and where one sensory-motor idea concludes and another begins. The 67 "grammatical" hesitations in Table 9.4, of course, also can be described in this way, increasing the fraction of concept ϕ concept to 91%. One of the advantages of conceiving of the production of speech in terms of syntagmata based on conceptual content is that we can look beyond contrasts such as "grammatical" and nongrammatical" and find an underlying continuity of processes between these categories.

E. Breakdowns

Certain speech dysfluencies give a vivid picture of the dynamic course of speech processing. The speaker seems to pursue a zigzag path. He begins on a certain structural tack, encounters difficulty, and shifts direction. The new direction usually has particular implications for meaning of its own, so the line of the speech takes a turn, leading eventually to a new interruption, another substitution, and so on. The series of breakdowns this generates provides information about the set of structures that the speaker manipulates. For example:

how 'bout the ϕ the ϕ does that how much do how has that affected you

There is a progression through this breakdown in which later candidate structures retain elements from previous structures. Figure 9.1 suggests how

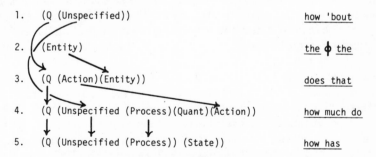

FIG. 9.1. Evolution of structure during a breakdown. (The idea of "unspecified" refers to a conceptual element that seems to be involved in interrogative words such as "how" and in certain constructions with *wh*- words such as relative clauses. For further discussion, see McNeill, 1979.)

the sensory-motor content is built up until the correct combination occurs for the speaker's meaning. This speaker tried out different sensory-motor ideas, such as entity and action, but then abandoned them after second attempts. Only the idea of a state in the ultimate version had not already been tried out in an earlier version during the breakdown. It may have been the linchpin, without which the speaker could not continue speaking. This example shows the speaker searching for a workable combination of sensory-motor ideas. It suggests that dysfluencies can have their own internal organization and that we can speak of a well-formed error. Although the speaker shifts his ground in a way that at first seems random, on closer examination this proves to have a dynamic organization.

F. Grammatical Constituent Structure

Table 9.5 gives a tally of every speech dysfluency in the Duncan corpus that occurred in the context of the following grammatical constructions: prepositional phrases, noun phrases, transitive verb phrases, complements with "that" and "to," subordinate cluases introduced by conjunctions, and intransitive verb phrases with auxiliary verbs.

Table 9.5 is interpreted as follows. A dysfluency after the subject of a transitive verb phrase (she ϕ said something like) would suggest that the subject and verb phrase were programmed as separate units. A dysfluency after the verb (she said ϕ something like) would suggest that the subject and verb were programmed as one unit and the rest of the verb phrase as another unit. Table 9.5 shows that the tendency is much greater to break up the grammatical structure of the verb phrase than to preserve it, 34 to 3. The same is true of other constructions, involving noun phrases. In 11 of 14 prepositional phrases, the preposition was programmed with its antecedent rather than with the rest of the prepositional phrase. In 22 of 23 articles with noun phrases, the article was programmed with its antecedent rather than with the rest of the noun phrase. Complementizers also are programmed with their antecedents rather than with the clauses that they introduce, although this may not be inconsistent with the constituent structure. Finally, auxiliary verbs are programmed with their main verbs, and this is consistent with the constituent structure.

The evidence of the transitive verbs and noun phrases seems to mean that the unit of speech programming is not a grammatical constituent in many utterances. This is not without theoretical interest. The performance device in these utterances cannot be said to have more than a *weak equivalence* with the grammatical description (i.e., they produce the same word strings), and not, as widely assumed (Miller & Chomsky, 1963; Pylyshyn, 1973; Fodor, Bever, & Garrett, 1974; Miller, 1975), a strong equivalence (i.e., produce the same structures).

TABLE 9.5
Dysfluencies in Various Grammatical Contexts

Construction	Lower Speaker	Upper Speaker	Total
Prepositional Phrase			
X^a φ Prep NP	1	2	3
X Prep φ NP	3	8	11
Noun Phrase			
X φ Art N	0	1	1
X Art φ N	14	8	22
Trans. Verb Phrases			
X φ V NP	1	2	3
X V φ NP	15	19	34
That Complement			
X φ that C	1	0	1
X that φ C	8	2	10
To Complement			
X φ to C	1	0	1
X to φ C	3	0	3
Subordinate clause			
X φ Conj S	1	2	3
X Conj φ S	11	5	16
Intrans. Verb phrase			
NP φ Aux V	13	6	19
NP Aux φ V	6	7	13

[a]Indicates antecedent speech.

Now, a subject and transitive verb make an event (she said is an event). The omitted direct object affects the structure of the idea of an action, but not that of the idea of an event. Hence, the subject and transitive verb can form a syntagma. Prepositions, conceptually, belong as much with their prior actions as with their following entities. In an expression such as "move through the door," the preposition relates to a particular kind of movement ("moving *through*") as well as to a particular kind of hole in a partition. Attempts to explain the effects of prepositions only in terms of nouns seem misguided. Thus, a preposition can be programmed with a prior verb as easily as with a following noun, and there seems to be a general tendency to put these words with their antecedents. Articles do not present a clear case, but for whatever reason, they also are programmed into speech before the speaker has programmed the following words. For example, the first article in "the in fact the first interview" was selected and uttered before the rest of the noun phrase was programmed. Auxiliary verbs, in contrast to transitive verbs and prepositions, belong exclusively with their main verbs. The auxiliary is a kind of modulation or temporal specification of the action, and this is programmed with the action.

G. Gesticulations

The rationale for studying gesticulations in relation to speech is that they seem to show directly an involvement of action schemes (system A) in the speech process. The evidence of this is that gesticulations are closely correlated in time with the sensory-motor segments of utterances. The degree of synchronization suggests a common source. The sensory-motor scheme that organizes the output of speech itself, could also activate and entrain gesticulations with the hand.

Kimura (1976) has observed that movements of the right hand are more frequent during speech than during humming or nonverbal problem solving. In the latter cases, the left and right hands move equally often. This difference according to speaking conditions holds for free movements of the hands, but for self touching, the left and right hands are equally involved in both speech and nonspeech. Assuming that speech is organized in the left cerebral hemisphere, these differences suggest an anatomical propinquity of the source of organization of speech and gesticulation.

The examples and data presented below are from a videotaped technical discussion between two professional mathematicians. The advantages of using such abstract technical material are twofold. First, the literal content is highly abstract, a condition that may stimulate gesticulations. Second, the segmentation of speech into conceptual units is much easier with technical material.

The videotape of the discussion was transcribed and the concurrent speech-gesticulation segments carefully correlated in time. The method by which this correlation was made provides an accuracy within one syllable approximately. Not all gesticulations coincide with speech, and the temporal relation of isolated gesticulations to speech is not known; however, less than 1% of gesticulations are isolated. The data reported below are based on the first 500 gesticulations in the transcript that coincided with speech. Nearly all of these were produced by one of the speakers, a fact that reflects the apportionment of speaking time during the discussion.

An example of an utterance accompanied by gesticulation is the following,

[there's a complete] [tensor product in the category]

The brackets indicate the onset and termination of two gesticulations. These are illustrated in Fig. 9.2 (pp. 254–255), drawings of photographs made of stopped video images.

The first of these drawings shows the posture of the hands about 200 msec before the beginning of the utterance. The gesticulation begins abruptly, shown in the second drawing, with the phrase "there's," and consists of the right hand forming a ring with the fingers, then slowly dropping. At the same time, the left hand is rising, the fingers partially extended. The entire

TABLE 9.6
Classification of 500 Gesticulations in Relation to Sensory-
Motor Content

	Consistent	Questionable	Inconsistent
Frequency	432	41	27
Percent	86	8	5

gesticulation is, from the first, formed in all its essentials, which suggests that "there's a complete" was programmed as a single output. Probably the posture of the right hand (the ring) is iconically related to the idea of "complete." The next gesticulation coincides with "tensor product in the category." An abrupt change in the posture of the hands takes place with the word "tensor." This confirms the supposition that "there's a complete" was programmed as a whole. The left hand relaxes and falls to a rest position; the circle that had been formed in the right hand disappears, and the index finger extends outward in its place. Again there are iconic implications of this new gesticulation, possibly referring to the idea of location or to the technical concept of "tensor," or to both. As before, the gesticulation is formed immediately and maintained through the whole phrase, suggesting that "tensor product in the category" was also programmed as a whole.

Table 9.6 shows the result of classifying the 500 gesticulations into three categories: those that are either consistent, questionable, or inconsistent with respect to the sensory-motor segmentation of the co-occurring speech. These terms are defined as follows:

1. *Consistent.* In this category are gesticulations that coincide with sensory-motor ideas. For example:

[ideal]	entity
[same as saying]	state
[it's an inverse limit]	existence of entity
[of Artinian rings]	entity

2. *Questionable.* In this category are gesticulations that coincide with relational terms, the connection of which to sensory-motor content is for one reason or another unclear. These gesticulations do not either correspond to the sensory-motor content or refute it, but occupy some kind of middle ground. For example:

[a] basis
[and uh] have

(A) There's
↑

(B) There's
↑

(C) a complete
↑

(D) a complete
↑

3. *Inconsistent.* In this category, the speech has clear sensory-motor content, but the gesticulation in some way fails to correspond to it. For example:

[group sch]emes
com[plete formalism]

As Table 9.6 shows, very few gesticulations fall into the last category, and only a few more into the questionable category. Most gesticulations are in the consistent category. Table 9.6, therefore, shows that, for a large number of

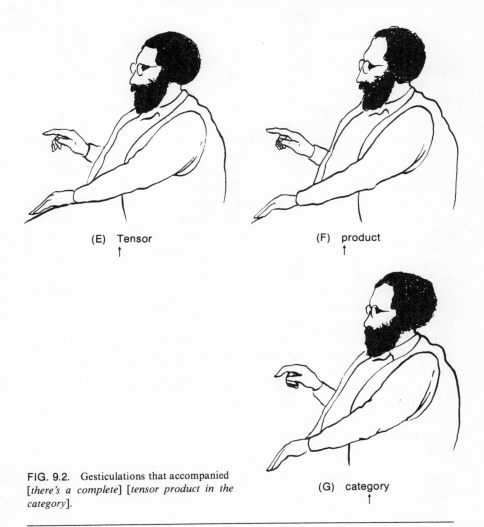

(E) Tensor
      ↑

(F) product
      ↑

(G) category
      ↑

FIG. 9.2.   Gesticulations that accompanied [*there's a complete*] [*tensor product in the category*].

gesticulations, the hand movement begins and ends within one syllable of segments of speech corresonding to sensory-motor ideas. When actual movements co-occurring with speech are taken into account, we find that they are coordinated with the sensory-motor content of speech.

1. Grammatical Constituent Structure from the Point of View of Gesticulation

The co-occurrence of gesticulations with speech provides yet another basis for determining the programming units of speech output that can be

TABLE 9.7
Classification of 500 Gesticulations in Relation to Grammatical Structure

	Single words	Phrases, clauses	Nongrammatical
Frequency	103	219	178
Percentage	21	44	36

compared to grammatical constituent structure. In contrast to Table 9.6, where 86% of 500 gesticulations correspond to the sensory-motor content, Table 9.7 shows that only 44% correspond to grammatical phrases or clauses. Of the gesticulations, 21% correspond to single words, but 36% correspond to nongrammatical segments. Examples of the latter are reminiscent of the segments formed in the Duncan corpus through speech dysfluencies. However, in gesticulation-formed segments, there often was uninterrupted speech. For example, of 92 occurrences of verbs that take objects or complements, the gesticulation organized the verb with its subject and not with the object or complement phrase 62 times. This compares to only 30 occurrences in which the verb was organized with the object or complement phrase and not with the subject. (In addition, gesticulations co-occurred with full clauses 50 times, and with single verbs 12 times.)

These kinds of differences are shown in Table 9.8 for several grammatical constructions. As with dysfluencies, the programming unit of speech appears to require no better than a weak equivalence between grammatical description and linguistic performance in a significant number of cases. Only definite articles reliably appear in units that correspond to a grammatical constituent. The indefinite article is evenly divided between conforming to the constituent structure and disrupting it. This difference obviously corresponds to the difference in meaning between the articles.

In general, however, the degree of correspondence with constituent structure is somewhat better with the mathematician's corpus than with Duncan's corpus. Whether this is due to a difference between the speakers, or

TABLE 9.8
Co-occurrence of Gesticulations with Grammatical
Constructions

Construction	Frequency
X [V Comp. or Obj.]	30
[X V] Comp. or Obj.	62
X [Prep Prep. Phrase]	28
[X Prep] Prep. Phrase	24
X [the NP]	48
[X the] NP	8
X [a(n) NP]	11
[X a(n)] NP	10

a difference between dysfluencies and gesticulations, cannot be said. There is a suggestion that gesticulations may conform more than dysfluencies to constituent structure, in that the dysfluency patterns in the mathematician's corpus were stronger in their deviance than the gesticulation patterns were. With the articles, for example, dysfluencies associated with "the" were as frequent after the article as before (5% and 7% of all occurrences), and dysfluencies associated with "a(n)" were four times more frequent after it than before (19% and 5% of all occurrences).

2. "Fate" of Gesticulations Related to Dysfluencies

Table 9.9 shows the relationship between dysfluencies in the speech sample and gesticulations. The latter are classified as to their "fate" as follows:

1. *Sustained.* This means that the gesticulation started at some point before the dysfluency and the hand posture was held through it without significant further movement or modification.
2. *Continued.* This means that the gesticulation started before the dysfluency and continued to evolve through it. The gesticulation terminates with the end of the dysfluency.
3. *New.* This means that the gesticulation started with the dysfluency (at some point during it) and either continued to evolve or was maintained after the dysfluency ended.
4. *Unique.* This means that the gesticulation started at some point during the dysfluency and ended with it.
5. *Relaxation.* This means that a gesticulation started before the dysfluency, terminated during it, and the hand returned to a rest position.

Several findings are of interest in Table 9.9. Nearly half of all gesticulations associated with unfilled pauses are unique. If unfilled pauses are to some

TABLE 9.9
Gesticulations Related to Dysfluencies

		Gesture Sustained	Gesture Cont'd	New Gesture	Unique Gesture	Relax-ation
Filled	Frequency	7	3	3	1	0
Pause	Percent	50	21	21	7	0
Unfilled	Frequency	5		5	9	1
Pause	Percent	25		25	45	5
Break-	Frequency	5	5	18	3	3
down	Percent	15	15	53	9	9
Build-	Frequency	16	7	14	3	3
up	Percent	7	16	33	7	7

extent associated with word-finding problems, the corresponding gesticulations might be expected to be unique, because they would not relate to any other part of the speech program.

Half of the filled pause gesticulations are sustained. Vocalization continues without articulation, and the gesticulation is also held in place. Continuing a gesticulation in a conversation is a strong cue that suppresses turn-taking attempts (Duncan & Fiske, 1977). Its validity for this function would be explained if it arises from an ongoing intention to program speech.

Half of the breakdown gesticulations are new, compared to only one-seventh that are sustained. A breakdown involves changing speech programs. Accordingly, new gesticulations appear which correspond to the new programs.

A fourth type of dysfluency in Table 9.9 is called a buildup. In this dysfluency, the speaker repeatedly produces the same structure, adding more and more to it on subsequent attempts. As in a breakdown, new material comes into speech during a buildup, and like a filled pause, the intention to speak is maintained. A third of the buildup gesticulations are new, and a third are sustained, corresponding to the programming of this hybrid situation.

Relating the "fate" of gesticulations to the type of dysfluency in speech confirms and extends the conclusions already drawn. We see that the differences between the types of dysfluencies and gesticulations can be understood in terms of the state of the speaker's speech programming. There are different dysfluencies and gesticulations depending on whether an already existing speech program is maintained or a new one is started. In the first situation we find sustained gesticulations, filled pauses, and some buildups; in the second, new gesticulations, breakdowns, and other buildups. It would seem that these correlations between the types of dysfluency and gesticulation cannot be understood without accepting the theory that at some level the speech programs include schemes relating speech to system A of action.

3. Iconic Gesticulations

Iconic gesticulations are defined as hand movements that in configuration and movement refer to some aspect of the semantic content of the corresponding utterance. Such gesticulations show the semantic relevance of sensory-motor ideas most directly. The meaning is expressed simultaneously through two channels, one of them an overt hand movement.

An example of an iconic gesticulation was given earlier. The speaker formed a ring as he said "there's a complete;" then he pointed as he said "tensor product in the category." Three additional examples are shown in Fig. 9.3. In these drawings arrows indicate the direction in which the hand *will move* after the moment shown. In the first example, the hand rolls over just as

FIG. 9.3. *(Opposite page)* Gesticulations that accompanied (A) [*over*] *the ring;* (B) [*consisting*] *of;* and (C) *a*[*n inverse limit*].

over the ring
↑

over the ring
↑

(A)

consisting of
↑

consisting of
↑

(B)

an inverse
↑

inverse limit
↑

(C)

FIG. 9.3

259

the word "over" is said. In the second example, the hand circles in a swirling motion just as the word "consisting" is said. In the third example, a complex rotation of the hand occurs as the speaker said "an inverse limit." This gesticulation was reliably associated with the word "inverse." About 16% of the gesticulations in the mathematicians' corpus appear to me to be iconic, and making an allowance for technical meanings that might have been missed, perhaps 25% of the gesticulations were iconic.

II. SUMMARY AND CONCLUSIONS

The argument of this paper has been that action is an essential source of meaning in utterances. The actions in question are those involved in coordinating speech itself. These actions of speaking are organized into output segments that correspond to sensory-motor ideas. Such ideas have evolved in the first place from external actions toward the world, and they contribute one component of the meaning of utterances—an autochthonous component.

This chapter adds new forms of evidence that utterances are in fact organized in segments that have sensory-motor meanings. Phonemic clauses strongly correlate with sensory-motor content. Dysfluencies form around segments that preserve sensory-motor content. Gesticulations, themselves movements, correlate with sensory-motor content. This latter correlation shows a connection, in utterances conveying even highly abstract meanings, of sensory-motor schemes with both speech and actions of other kinds. And in all these cases, sensory-motor content correlates with the natural processing units of speech more closely than does grammatical constituent structure.

ACKNOWLEDGMENTS

Material in this paper is from *The Conceptual Basis of Language* (by the present author), to be published by Lawrence Erlbaum Associates.

It is a pleasure to thank S. Duncan, Jr., for permission to extract examples and make statistical summaries from his detailed transcription of the conversation between U and L. Duncan's research was supported by PHS grants MH-16210 and MH-17756.

The mathematician's conversation was transcribed by P. Gomperts and N. McNeill, and the drawings were made by D. Novotny. The mathematicians were R. Morris and M. Anderson, who were at the Institute for Advanced Study at the time.

I am grateful to N. McNeill for comments on the manuscript.

The preparation of this paper and the research on which it is based were supported by PHS grant MH-26451 to David McNeill, by National Institute of Education grant NIE C-74-0031 to David McNeill, by a Sloan Foundation grant to the Institute for Advanced Study, and by The University of Chicago.

REFERENCES

Bernstein, N. A. *The co-ordination and regulation of movements.* Oxford: Pergamon, 1967.

Duncan, S. D., Jr. *Paralinguistic behaviors in client-therapist communication in psychotherapy.* Unpublished doctoral dissertation, University of Chicago, 1965.

Duncan, S., & Fiske, D. *Face-to-face interaction: Research, methods, and theory.* Hillsdale, N.J.: Lawrence Erlbaum Associates, 1977.

Fodor, J., Bever, T., & Garrett, M. *The psychology of language.* New York: McGraw-Hill, 1974.

Goldman-Eisler, F. *Psycholinguistics.* New York: Academic Press, 1968.

Greene, P. H. Problems of organization of motor systems. In R. Rosen & F. M. Snell (Eds.), *Progress in theoretical biology* (Vol. 2). New York: Academic Press, 1972.

Kimura, D. The neural basis of language qua gesture. In H. Whitaker & H. A. Whitaker (Eds.), *Studies in neurolinguistics* (Vol. 2). New York: Academic Press, 1976.

Kozhevnikov, V. A., & Chistovich, L. A. *Speech: Articulation and perception.* Washington, D.C.: Joint Publication Research Service, 1965.

Lieberman, P. *Intonation, perception, and language.* Cambridge, Mass.: MIT Press, 1967.

McNeill, D. Semiotic extension. In R. L. Solso (Ed.), *Information processing and cognition: The Loyola Symposium.* Hillsdale, N.J.: Lawrence Erlbaum Associates, 1975.

McNeill, D. *The conceptual basis of language.* Hillsdale, N.J.: Lawrence Erlbaum Associates, 1979.

Miller, G. A. Some comments on competence and performance. In D. Aaronson & R. W. Rieber (Eds.), *Developmental psycholinguistics and communication disorders.* New York: New York Academy of Sciences, 1975.

Miller, G. A., & Chomsky, N. Finitary models of language users. In R. D. Luce, R. R. Bush, & E. Galanter (Eds.), *Handbook of mathematical psychology* (Vol. 2). New York: Wiley, 1963.

Piaget, J. *The construction of reality in the child.* New York: Basic Books, 1954.

Pylyshyn, Z. W. The role of competence theories in cognitive psychology. *Journal of Psycholinguistic Research,* 1973, *2,* 21-50.

Trager, G. L., & Smith, H. L. *Outline of English structure.* Norman, Okla.: Battenburg Press, 1951.

Turvey, M. T. *Preliminaries to a theory of action with reference to vision.* Haskins Laboratories: Status Report on Speech Research SR-41, 1975, 1-49.

V LANGUAGE DEVELOPMENT

10 Learning How To Do Things With Words[1]

Jerome Bruner
Wolfson College, Oxford University

I.

What I shall be discussing is how the human infant learns to use language in a fashion that meets the requirements of social living as a member of a culture-using species. To succeed at such living requires far more than that one speak in well-formed sentences, or that one's words and sentences meet the requirements of reference and meaning and truth-testability. To speak, rather, requires that one's utterances meet criteria of conventional appropriateness or felicity not only with respect to the context in which speech occurs, but also to the acts of those with whom one is involved in dialogue. If I say *Italy is a boot,* the sentence may be well formed, but it is quite unclear whether it is true or false, useful or useless, appropriate or inappropriate unless you know to whom it is addressed and under what circumstances (see, for example, Grice, 1968). To anyone conversant with the debates in linguistics and linguistic philosophy over the last 15 years — ever since John Austin first introduced those matters — this will all have a very commonsensical and familar ring. It is quite plain, of course, that language fulfills various communicative functions — whatever view one wishes to take of such functions (compare Halliday, 1975, and Dore, 1975). But how are communicative functions progressively realized in the life of very young children and how does early nonlinguistic interaction between mother and child provide a matrix for the acquisition of language? Once

[1]This chapter is based upon the Wolfson Lecture, delivered in Oxford in 1976. The work reported was supported by the Social Science Research Council of Great Britain.

one examines the detail of early language acquisition, how the child goes from prelinguistic communication to the early mastery of language, it should come as no surprise that later, the question *How would you feel about a breath of fresh air?* is not interpreted as inquiring into one's naive theory of respiratory physiology but as an invitation to go for a walk.

II.

Before I begin, we require a necrology in order to set the background. It is for LAD, Chomsky's (1962) Language Acquisition Device, a veritable child prodigy that, for its 10 years of sway, helped produce a new way of seeing what is involved in acquiring language — and thereby dug its own grave. LAD, let us recall, was what linguists refer to as a discovery procedure, that is to say, a means of discovering the rules by which acceptable sentences in a language are put together. Its input was a sample of the language, however encountered; its output was the set of syntactical rules that would generate all the well-formed sentences possible in the language and none that were ill-formed. The base of this recognition or discovery program was presumed to be the language-learner's innate grasp of the universals of language. The local language being learned, according to this view, was merely a realization in local form of the syntactic universals of language. The innate grasp of these linguistic universals of language was assumed to be independent of any knowledge of the nonlinguistic world. Nor, indeed, did the recognition program require anything more than that the learner (or discoverer) of the language be a bystander: the spoken corpus of speech flowed round and into him, and the rules came out the other end. It did not require, for example, that he already know what the language referred to — that he have concepts about the real world being referred to — nor that the learner had to enter into particular kinds of dialogue with the speakers of the language. As an enthusiastic David McNeill (1970) put it, "The facts of language acquisition could not be as they are unless the concept of a sentence is available to children at the start of their learning [p. 2]."

A decent necrologist should not carp. There are some features of LAD that are plainly and baldly wrong. The child's knowledge of language is deeply dependent upon a prior mastery of concepts about the world to which language will refer. The work of Brown (1973), Sinclair-de-Zwart (1969), Bloom (1970, 1973), Schlesinger (1974), Greenfield and Smith (1976), and others makes it quite clear that conceptual mastery of the world of referents to which language will relate provides powerful assistance to language acquisition. One can say that much without taking any stand on the question whether the generative base structure of language is semantic either in the manner proposed by Bloom (1970) or implied by Fillmore (1968).

It is also becoming clear how dependent language acquisition is upon the nature of the interaction that takes place between child and mother (e.g., Bates, Volterra, & Camaioni, 1976; Ryan, 1974; Snow, 1976). Being a witness at the feast of language is not enough of an exposure to assure acquisition. There must be contingent interaction. But, for all that, Chomsky has taught us something that is profoundly important. It is that the child is equipped with some means for generating hypotheses about language that could not simply be the result of learning by association and reinforcement what words go with what in the presence of what things. There is indeed something preprogrammed about our language-acquiring capacity. But we need not, as my good friend George Miller once put it, vacillate between an impossible theory that assumes we learn everything by association (the facts deny it and the sheer arithmetic tells us that there would be just too much to learn even in a dozen lifetimes), and, on the other hand, a magical theory that says we already know about sentences before we start. There appears to be some readiness, rather, quickly to grasp certain rules for forming sentences, once we know what the world is about to which the sentences refer. And the rules that govern these sentences are neither imitated — for often one does not find them in the speech of the adults with whom the child is in contact — nor are they to be thought of as simple reflections of the world of concepts that the child has learned for dealing with the extralinguistic environment, though they are plainly related. What Chomsky (1976) has rightly insisted upon is that human language users show a striking sensitivity to structural properties of the kind found in grammar and that there is no way in which these can be learned *just* by learning something about the world or by succeeding in communicating by means other than language. Both of these *help* in language acquisition, but they do not explain how *language itself* is learned — notably the intricate formal structure that mediates between sound and sense (or between sound and speech act, in John Searle's, 1976, rendering). So though we come to bury LAD, we must not be so foolish as to withold all praise.

I should like to propose an alternative way of looking at acquisition, particularly at the role of interaction in the process. I shall take for granted that the child communicates before he has language. He does so in order to carry out certain functions that are general to the species. These primitive communicative acts are effected by gesture, vocalization, and the exploitation of context. There is enough that is universal about such pre-lexico-grammatical communication to suggest that a part of it is innate, and easily triggered. There is a progressive development of these primitive procedures for communicating, and typically they are replaced by less primitive ones until eventually they are replaced by standard linguistic procedures. These progressive changes and procedural leaps are massively dependent upon the interaction of the mother (a word I shall use for "caretaker" generally with a certain statistical licence) and the child. Mothers *teach* their children to speak, however willing the children may be, and I rather take their willingness to be part of the innate preparation for language. Washoe and Sarah and the other talking chimps (Brown, 1973), viewed closely, are *not* eager pupils.

While the child and mother are developing transactional procedures, the child is also learning about the world: about actions, agents, instruments, objects; about possession, location, belongingness; about natural categories, entities and their attributes, etc. These are the universal cognitive structures upon which semantic distinctions in language are going to rest. They might not, *ab initio,* be learned in a fully abstract sense, but *locally,* and then with increasing generality (see de Villiers & de Villiers, 1978). In the same way, there are certain communicative universals that come into evidence early enough to warrant being candidates for the status of innate universals: indicating, demanding, requesting, etc., realized in every language and, indeed, realized prelinguistically as well. Bates, Volterra, and Camaioni refer to the "proto-indicative" and the "proto-imperative" and Halliday (1975) to the pragmatic and mathetic modes operating prelinguistically, most often marked by gesture and intonation (Dore, 1974; Menyuk & Bernholz, 1969).

In my view, the simultaneous development of world knowledge and of communicative competence is a necessary condition for provoking what can properly be called "linguistic hypotheses." These are *not* easily characterized, contrary to Chomsky's (1957, 1965) early hopes. In his initial formulation (presented at three colloquia at the Harvard Center for Cognitive Studies, March 30, April 6, and April 13, 1960, on "Grammatical Factors in the Perception of Sentences"), he likened linguistic hypotheses to perceptual hypotheses, of which some were obviously "primitives" (such as figure-ground and other Gestalt organizing principles), while others were equally compelling and immediate though based as well on some knowledge of the local language. I find myself in sympathy with this view, never fully developed in his writing, although beginning to reappear in his most recent book (1976). What I would propose is that while "structure sensitivity" to language may be an innate capacity of language learners, it cannot express itself without the learner first developing some working knowledge of the world to which it can apply and of the functions which language will subserve.

It is with the communicative side of these issues that the remainder of this chapter is concerned — particularly with the manner in which prelinguistic mastery creates the conditions for linguistic acquisition. Concerned as I shall be with the growth of reference and with the emergence of communication in support of joint action, I shall sketch roughly what I think may be involved in such development.

With respect to reference, it would seem that at the start there is a strong push present in the infant to share features of the sensory world with the mother and an equally strong push for the mother to orient to the features of the world to which the child is attending. At the outset, referential activity on the part of the child is very much captive of his needs. He has intentions and shows them, gesturally and vocally and in appropriate contexts. Mothers invariably interpret signs of desire as intentional communicative acts, and respond appropriately. As Ainsworth and Bell (1974) have shown, the mothers who respond to their children's vocalization during the first half of the first year end up in the last quarter of that year with children who cry less and vocalize and gesture more in a communicative way. In time, the sharing of attention is extended by both parties to matters that are sensorially vivid or surprising or even rare. Indexing procedures, gestural and vocal, emerge and change. They very rarely have the character of being signs for specific events, but, as Harrison (1972) notes, they are procedures for noting which among several candidates for attention has in fact achieved the focus of attention — reaching toward, pointing, etc. Early in life, as the child develops models of what constitutes a steady-state environment, he begins to develop means of indicating objects and events that diverge from his theory or model of that world. It is interesting that a profound change in his signaling occurs at this point. And at the end of the first year, there emerges yet another distinct step: the deep hypothesis that how one vocalizes affects how another's attention can be altered, that sounds and sound patterns have semanticity. At that point, a quite new means of generating hypotheses, strongly influenced by mother's utterances, comes into being. Something more like the philospher's reference and less like ostensive references emerges. We shall see more of this in a moment.

With respect to action and joint action, let me sketch briefly what is at issue. For anybody to understand action, whether he be child or adult, requires being able to categorize a flow of events in a complex, though possibly natural way. Most human action has at least the following minimal set of categorizable components: the act itself, agent, an object, a recipient of the action, an instrument, a locus, and a time marker. Or to say it in common sense, understanding the actions of human beings involves knowing what is done to what, by whom, to whom, where, by what instrument, and in what order. It is also necessary to distinguish its start and its finish. All of that is obvious, and I even suggested that it was "natural," a moot point. In order to communicate in a way that makes possible joint action, there must be, at very least, some way of signaling the intent to act as well as indicating when one's intentions have been fulfilled, but that is scarcely enough for regulation. There must also be a way of indicating what the action is, who is to be the agent and who the recipient, on what object is the action to be performed and with what instrument, where and when. You will immediately recognize my list as being a parallel to the classic case grammar with categories like subject, verb, object, indirect object, locative, instrumentive, plus some form of aspect or tense marker. There must, as well, be some primitive mood-marking procedure to distinguish indicating from commanding or requesting. For full effectiveness, there must be also some way of using these cases in a rule-bound order in an utterance that permits shifting and substitutability. For now I am the agent and you the recipient, and then you become the agent and I the recipient, and sometimes you use the instrument in a particular place, and sometimes I do but in a different place. And to be effective in signaling about the course of an action, I must be able to indicate when something should start and when it should stop — and not just the action as a whole, but those parts of it that are carried by an agent or recipient, are directed to particular objects with particular instruments, etc.

By this recounting of the obvious, I hope I have convinced the reader of three things. The first is that the course of action is nicely matched to the structure of speech: that the two are not arbitrarily related. The second is that it takes a fair amount of early learning to master the intricacies of joint action, even without language proper. And the third is that the conventions and procedures by which we represent the aspects of action — case grammar — do not naturally fall out of our mastery of joint action in and of itself, although a knowledge of the requirements of joint action would surely provide some powerful hints to the learner about the structure of the linguistic code. And perhaps there is a fourth matter that is obvious: that for human beings to share in an action, with or without the aid of regulatory language, there must be a considerable amount of intersubjective sharing between them, a sharing of many presuppositions that buffer the cooperating parties from shocked surprise — the classic problem of "other minds."

III.

We come now to the empirical part of our inquiry. We have been studying children from roughly 3 months of age to about their second birthday, visting them in their homes fortnightly, and video-taping a half-hour of ordinary play interaction between the mother and child, often much enriched by the presence of the experimenter. This has been supplemented by occasional videotapes made by parents of behavior they thought we should see and had not (often very valuable indeed) and by diary records. As a preliminary, we looked at six children in this way; more recently we have concentrated on three, and I shall mostly be telling you about two of them. The object of the exercise was to explore how communication between the pairs was established before language proper came on the scene and how, gradually, the older modes of communication were replaced by more standard language. Our effort, as you may guess from what has already been said, was to explore how language was used, how its forms were made to serve functions. I shall concentrate as noted on two uses of communication: for referring and for carrying out joint action. I choose the two because they may stem from quite different roots, the one relating to the sharing of attention, the other to the management of complementary intentions. In each of them, we shall see the emergence of communicative forms that have language-like properties that, at the opportune moment and with the help of an adult, provide a clue for the child as to how to crack the linguistic code he is encountering. Let me say, before turning to these matters, that I shall not burden you with the dates or milestones at which new forms appear in language, but only with rough indications. It is the order of emergence that matters rather than absolute dates, for some children learn quickly and some less so, with no seeming effect on later performance. Nor is it evident that all children go through precisely the same order, for the literature on the subject and our own data suggest that order is dependent on context in some degree and reflects the individual progress of the mother-infant bond.

So let me turn first to the course of reference. The deep question about reference is how one individual manages to get another to share, attend to, "zero in" upon a topic that is occupying him. At the start, the child can neither reach nor point toward an object that he wants or is interested in. He can of course cry or fret. He can of course look at what interests him, and that, as we shall see, stands him in good stead. As for the mother, her options are almost as limited as the child's: Neither her vocalizations nor her gestures are able to accomplish the end of bringing the child's attention to objects or events she wishes to single out. From the mother's side, her first and most useful basis for sharing the child's "referent" is her power of inference backed by her inevitable theory of what the child is intending. She inevitably interprets the child's actions as related to wants and needs: he cries because he is hungry or wet, stares at something because he wants to take possession of it or, simply, is "fascinated by it." She is not the least disturbed by the difficulty of philosophers in establishing communicative intent, how we know that others are attempting to send a message. She simply assumes it, and indeed, Macfarlane's (1974) study of greeeting rituals of mothers toward their newborns suggests that from the start, the maternal theory is premised on the infant's acts being purposeful and his gestures and vocalizations being attempted communications. It is not surprising, then, that in a recent study by Collis and Schaffer (1975), the mother's line of regard follows the infant's line of regard virtually all the time that the two of them are together in an undistracted situation.

But perhaps more interesting is the infant's behavior. Dr. Michael Scaife (Scaife & Bruner, 1975) working in my laboratory here at Oxford has demonstrated that infants as young as 4 months of age will also follow the mother's line of regard outward to the surrounding environment. To those who have read the literature on infantile egocentrism, this may be a surprise, because the finding indicates that the child can use another axis than his own egocentric one to guide his orientation. Scaife also reports that there are indications that such gaze following may occur even when the child is not interacting directly with the adult involved. If two adults, conversing with each other, now look jointly in a convergent direction, and they are within the infant's range of attention, the infant's line of regard will often converge with theirs, all of this before the infant is much over a year.

Before the child begins his reaching career, his chief focus of attention is his mother's face, eye contact leading to smiles, vocalizations, and a variety of exchange maneuvers — of which more later. Once the child begins reaching for objects, however, *en face* contact between mother and child drops drastically from about 80% of contact time to roughly 15%. Characteristically at this stage, the child either orients to the objects he reaches for, manipulates, and mouths, *or* he orients to the mother. At 5 months, for example, he never looks to the mother when his attempts to reach or to grasp an object fail. He is possessed by the one or the other and does not alternate. At this stage, the chief communicative feature of the child's object-directed activity is his fret vocalization in the event of not being able to reach or get hold of something he wants.

Note the infant's typical reach at this stage. It is an effortful gesture reeking with intention to possess the object: hand and arm fully extended, fist often opening and closing, body bent forward, mouth often working, eyes fixed on the object. This gestural effort, which gives no indication of being communicatively directed toward the mother, is nonetheless treated by her as communicatively intended, and the mother often obtains an object the child cannot reach. The child in time comes to expect this support.

By 8 to 10 months usually, the child's reach metamorphoses. It becomes markedly less exigent, and he begins looking toward the mother while he is in the act of reaching for an object. The gesture is changing from an instrumental reach to something more like an indicator — a semiextended arm, hand held somewhat angled upward, fingers no longer in grasp position, body no longer stretched fully forward. His gaze shifts from object to mother and back. He can now reach for real and reach to signal.

For a few months after the appearance of indicative reaching, there is a transitional phase. Indicative reaching becomes dissociated from the intention to get an object; it may signal only, and the child may not even take an indicated object that is proffered. Indicative reaching increasingly extends outward to objects more remote spatially. And, characteristically, the mother conforms to the change, interpreting reaching as interest rather than as desire, chatting in turn to the child's reach accordingly.

What emerges next suggests that new forms of communication emerge initially to fulfill old functions and then bring in new functions with them. It is the pure point, and in no sense is it gesturally like a reach — forefinger extended, the infant not reaching bodily forward. Initially it is used like an indicating reach. But like most new forms, pointing explodes in usage soon after first appearance. At 13 months, for example, six pure points were observed in Richard in a half hour's play with his mother. At 14 months/3 weeks, in a holiday setting, 29 pure points occurred in the same time, and in a 3-hour observation session the next day, more than 100 were observed. The objects selected as targets were governed by the following rules: (1) objects more than a meter distant and either novel or in an unexpected context; (2) neither novel nor unexpected but a *picture* of a familiar object; and (3) neither novel nor pictured but imaginary or hypothetical, the locus being indicated (as pointing upward to the ceiling, and saying "Bird"). Though Richard had few words, he was working on the hypothesis that his uttered sounds had semanticity. And we should note, finally, that his pointing was typically accompanied by vocalization and by looking back at the interlocutor. Needless to say, his mother interprets his pointing much as she would interpret that of an adult.

I would want to note one thing particularly about the growth of pointing over the next months. It is extended to many things, as in indicating a choice between objects, aiding requests, and so on. But it is also a prime instrument in the children we have studied for exploring the relation between objects and both their loci and possessors. At 15½ months, the turning on of a light evokes in Richard a point toward the ceiling and "li(ght)"; later the sound of an auto in the drive produces a point toward it and "Daddy"; a picture of a wine bottle in a book results in a point to the bare dining table, etc. Such instances are invariably shared by glancing back at the adult. I mention this point here to make clear one matter that tends to be swamped by the implicit notion that referencing or indexing is somehow associative. I would urge that, however associative it may be, such indicating behavior also serves for generating and testing hypotheses, bringing objects, and, indeed, hypothetical ones, into the realm of discourse. This I take to be an aspect of the child's "linguistic hypothesis" at work (Dore, 1976).

Again, the mother goes readily along with the new development and begins incorporating the child's pointing and his interest in semantic or naming sounds into dialogue. Indeed, it was the Russian linguist Shvachkin (1948) who noted that the child's interest in the phonemic system of the language coincided with his interest in naming. The mother's new medium for dialogue in the present case is "book reading," and I have no doubt that cultures without picture books find suitable substitutes.

But by the same token, such changes in the child's interest produce changes in the way in which the mother speaks to the child in order to promote the development (for a review of "Motherese," see de Villiers & de Villiers, 1978).

Looking at picture books together concentrates the joint attention of mother and infant upon highly compressed foci of attention. (For a detailed account of the work on "book-reading," done jointly with Dr. Anat Ninio of The Hebrew University of Jerusalem, see Ninio and Bruner, 1978.) They are foci of attention, moreover, that by virtue of being representations rather than real things, eliminate competition from virtually all other response systems — notably the reaching system. In this sense, the medium is part of the message, and it is not surprising that at the earliest stage, the mother spends hard effort in getting the child into the medium — converting the book from an object to be banged and mauled into a carrier of pictures to be looked at. The end point of that enterprise is the establishment of a dialogue pattern, and that dialogue pattern, we shall see, is crucial to the development of labeling.

There is a period of several months — from 1 year to about 15 months — when the mother's strategy seems to be devoted to getting the child to look, to point, and to vocalize at the right junctures in the dialogue exchanges between them. I fully agree with Catherine Snow (1976) that the establishment of such turn taking, sequenced dialogue is a prerequisite for language acquisition. In Richard's case, the dialogue is controlled by three linguistic devices used by his mother in a highly predictable way. The first is the attentional vocative "Look" or some variant, appropriately accompanied by pointing. The second is a *wh-* question, and it takes the form of some such question as "What's that, Richard?" again often with a supportive point. Interrogatives are not novel: they constitute from one-third to one-half of the mother's utterances during the first year, a matter to which we shall return. The third device is labeling. During this stage and the next, described later, the mother's labels are always nominals — object words or proper names, never attributes or states or actions.

The dialogue exchanges initiated by the mother while she and Richard were looking at pictures together, show the following striking regularity. Where there are two or more rounds in the exchange, in eight cases out of ten, the mother says "Look" before either asking a *wh-* question or proferring a label. If there are only *wh-* questions and labels in the dialogue, the former precede the latter. The almost invariant order was from a vocative through a question to a realization of the label. And each was given in an appropriate context. And so, for example, *wh-* questions follow only upon the child's gesture of pointing, and never upon a vocalization. A wide range of vocalizations are accepted in this first "dialogue establishing" stage as appropriate responses to either an attentional vocative or a *wh-* question, however wide they may be of the standard lexical mark. If Richard responds with a vocalization, mother's response to him in the great majority of cases is a label. Indeed, in mother-initiated dialogues, she responds to Richard's reaction in about 75% of the instances, virtually always giving him full marks for an appropriate communicative intent. A small point adds a sense of the meticulousness of this process. The mother makes a rather sharp distinction between those vocalizations of the child that slot into the dialogue routine of book reading and those that are out of place in the exchange. The latter vocalizations and gestures are treated by the mother as procedural — "You like this book, don't you Richard?" or "Yes, it's very exciting, isn't it?" such remarks always addressed to him directly and without reference to the book.

You are quite right if you infer that the child initially is learning as much about the rules of dialogue as he is about lexical labels. But once the dialogue routine is fully established, at about 18 months or earlier, it becomes the scaffold upon which a new routine is established. For now, the mother comes more sharply to distinguish between vocalizations that are "acceptable" and those that are not. They are now in a "shaping stage." Mother tightens the criterion of acceptablility as soon as there emerges a sign that the child is trying to produce words. I should warn you that my last sentence includes the whole field of developmental phonology, about which I know just enough to know the depth of my ignorance. But it is not the phonologist's theories that interest us here, but the mother's. When Richard slots in a sound that she thinks too wide of the mark, she will now respond not with a label, but with the question, "What's that, Richard?" or with a highly emphasized label.

But to put it that way may seem to give too much of a role to pure imitation. Rather, what is notable is that the child does not learn his labels by directly and immediately imitating his mother's labelings. Compare the likelihood of Richard uttering a label during the second half of his second year of life under two conditions. One is in response to the mother's just previously uttered label. The other is in response to his mother's "What's that?" question. The latter produces four times as many labels as the former. A label for the child is something that slots into a position in a dialogue. Indeed, 65% of the labels uttered by Richard during this second half of the second year were said without the mother having uttered the label in that exchange. And an interesting sidelight: Richard responds to *wh-* questions almost invariably on the first time round. Where he responds with a label in response to a mother's label, it almost invariably requires at least one repetition by his mother to get him to do so. We are not, as a species, copycats.

One regularity during this shaping phase suggests how crucial is the role of the mother in *teaching* language and its use. She is constantly establishing linguistic distinctions between the given and the new, the familiar and unfamiliar. She is, for example, much more likely to use "what" questions with special intonation for pictures the child already knows and can label easily. New or less familiar pictures are labeled forthwith. The result is a presuppositional structure about what one asks about and what one tells.

Perhaps a good way to put the mother's pedagogical role in perspective is to look at it as providing a stablizing scaffold during the two phases of label learning we have been exploring, a stabilizing scaffold with respect to which the child can vary his responses as his mastery permits. And so we find, for example, that the time devoted to dialogue exchange remains constant over these months. The number of turns in an exchange remains roughly the same. The repetition rate for labeling remains the same. The probability of mother's reciprocating the child's response remains unchanged. And once the child is in the shaping stage, mother's rate of confirming correct utterances remains about the same. All of these are controlled by the mother. They are what the child can count on in dialogue with her.

What things change over time, on the other hand, are almost all under the child's control. For one, there is a steady increase in the number of "book reading" exchanges initiated by the child — from 0% to 40%. There is a steady increase in the child's rate of responding to gestural or verbal overtures initiated by the mother. He even learns to respond to repeated rhetorical requests, ones he has just answered, suggesting that he is even learning to conform to the arbitrariness of pedagogical exchanges!

So much then for indexing and referencing. It is a very incomplete story as I have told it, but at least it gives a sense of how related acquistion is to use, to the functions of dialogue and exchange. We turn now to communication in support of joint action.

IV.

I want very briefly to consider three issues. The first has to do with the precursors of modality in grammar. The second follows from this and concerns the differentiation of joint action into its parts, a matter I have already touched on briefly. And the third has to do with starting, regulating, and stopping joint action — a set of procedures related to aspect in grammar.

With respect to mood, let me underline one point made by Catherine Snow (1976):

> One of the most ubiquitous features of . . . mother's speech at even the earliest age . . . [is that] they constantly talked about the child's wishes, needs, and intentions. . . . as if the mother's task was to find out something that the baby already knew . . . Persistent crying was referred to . . . as if it reflected a very well-defined sense of agency; the babies' behavior was never discribed as random and only rarely as a function of physiological variables. It was seen, just as adult behavior was seen, as intended and intentional [pp. 7–8].

And indeed, we know from the work of Ricks (1972) that mothers *can* recognize better than chance what general state produces their baby's cry and act accordingly. Not surprising, then, that the opening months of an infant's life reveal a transformation in the infant's crying from what may be called a demand mode — the standard biological cry, upped when untended to a very wide sound spectrum with a heavy load of high-frequency, fricative noise — to a request mode in which energy is concentrated in a fundamental frequency, with the cry stopped for moments at a time in anticipation of response. Request crying gradually achieves stylization and differentiates to match the context — hunger fretting, wet fretting, and so on. By responding to these cries, as already noted, the mother recruits the child's vocalizations from demand and request into more subtle communicative patterns later in the opening year of life (Ainsworth & Bell, 1974). In mood, then, initial crying is transformed from an exigent demand into anticipatory request, with the infant leaving slots for the mother's response.

What follows is the beginning of exchange and turn-taking, first in vocalization and, then, with the growth of manipulative skill, in the exchange of objects — forerunners of dialogue. Daniel Stern (1975) has shown exquisitely how mother–infant gesturing and vocalizing become synchronized in the opening months, and our own data on the first half year also shows coordinated cycles of eye contact and calling, controlled principally by the mother, of course, but increasingly by the infant. As the months go on he increasingly initiates acts of vocal exchange. The exchanges then are imbedded in anticipatory body games like "Round and Round the Garden" and "This Little Pig" in which vocal exchanges are made contingent on the progress of an interaction and various high-brow technicalities like terminal marking are being mastered in earthy but useful ways.

The next step in interaction appears to be closer to the exchange of objects than to vocalization. Alison Garton, Eileen Caudill, and I were led by this to some rather detailed studies of these exchanges, on the hunch that they might serve as a base for later dialogue. You may by amused by a few details of our expedition into the primitive economics of mother–infant exchange. If a market or economy reliable enough to sustain a steady flow of goods is established, can messages then develop that will flow in the same channels? Obviously, the first step for the mother is to get the infant to enter the game of taking objects, which need not concern us though it is of considerable interest as a chapter in the child's increasing capacity to mobilize not only a motoric response but also his attention upon the task (see Bruner, 1973). We have recorded sessions where more than 50% of the time went into the perfecting of this skill. The mother characteristically assumes that the child *wants* the object; what he must be helped to do is *try*. The next step is getting the child to give the object back. If we define agency as handing off and recipiency as receiving, the child's entry into the exchange economy is steady and striking and surprising to nobody (see Fig. 10.1). Concurrently, another unsurprising but important transition is taking place. Now the child rather than the mother alone begins *initiating* exchange episodes (see Fig. 10.2). As he gets into exchange, he is less

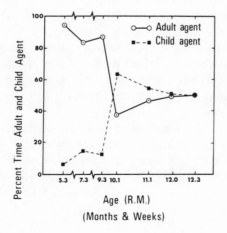

FIG. 10.1.   Shift in role of agent in "give-and-take."

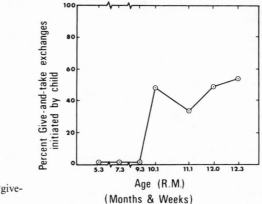

FIG. 10.2.   Initiation of "give-and-take" by child.

reluctant to give up an object: His possession time before handing off drops steadily (see Fig. 10.3). Indeed, by 13 months, the concept of exchange itself, rather than the joy of possession, seems to dominate his play. He is able now to enter a *round* of exchange involving two other persons and to maintain the direction of the exchange flow (see Fig. 10.4).

A stunning number of linguistic prerequisites are being mastered. Role shifting is one. Another is turn-taking. A third is the coordination of signaling and acting, for typical of these exchanges is that the child not only hands off the object in minimal time but looks to the recipient's face as he does so. And should his turn be delayed, he will point, reach, vocalize, or label to get matters righted. Put in the metaphor of case grammar he is differentiating in action between agent and recipient, forming a primitive development of locus with deixis in the sense of

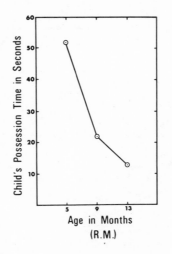

FIG. 10.3.   Child's possession time in "give-and-take."

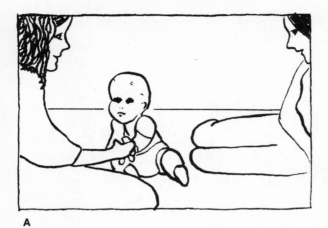

A

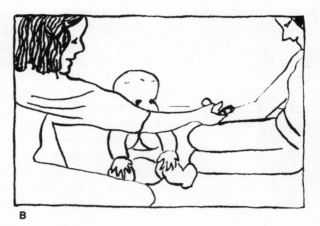

B

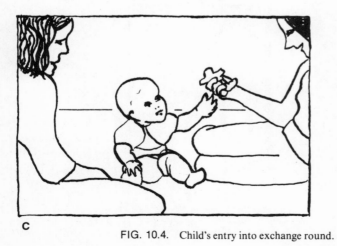

C

FIG. 10.4.   Child's entry into exchange round.

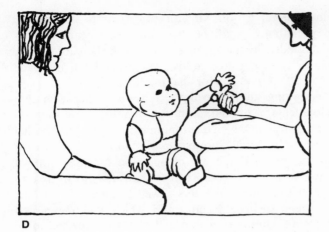

D

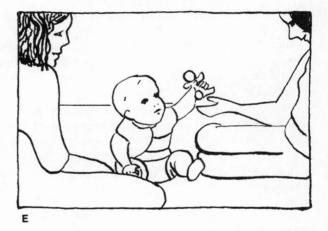

E

FIG. 10.4. *continued*

knowing to whom the object is to be handed in multiple exchange, learning some elements of time marking in the sense of knowing who comes before and who after. And in addition to all this, the child has come not only to participate in exchanges initiated by others, but to initiate them himself.

I wish there were space and that we had the necessary data fully to describe the manner in which the child learns during this period not only how to start but how to stop the action. For it reveals much about the precursory development of negation as a linguistic form. Initially, negation amounts to no more than a resistive gesture directed toward an act directed to the child; the gesture becomes stylized and is used communicatively. In time, such proto-negation is extended to rejection of a specific object, or a specific agent carrying out an action with an object, or to a temporal misplacement (as in peekaboo) — all of these directed toward activity initiated by others. Eventually, by the age of 15 months or thereabouts, the child comes to be able to apply negation to his own acts and will approach a forbidden object saying "No, no" and/or shaking his head.

I cannot resist mentioning an interesting extension of negation that occurs after the developments just noted, around 17 months, for it suggests yet another instance of the way in which a communicative form is extended to new functions. The new functions in question are more referential than pragmatic. A transitional phase is the use of negation for some mix of unexpectedness and inappropriateness, as when Richard fails to be able to put a large object into a thin box and utters a well formed "No." In his record at that time, there are also instances in which the unexpected absence of an object from a container within which it was expected to be provokes a "No." And in the work of Bloom (1973), Greenfield and Smith (1976), and other investigators, one finds instances of negation being used for disappearance of an object, self-produced as in "all-gone" or otherwise produced, or for cessation of an event in the environment. And finally, well into the second year, negation is captured by the rules of dialogue where it can be used for dealing with the linguistic representation of an event contained in a question: "Do you want more milk?" "No."

I hope it has been clear from this very brief account of the development of early communication as a means of regulating joint action that language does not grow solely from its own roots but is dependent upon interaction and particularly the interaction of intentions held by two consenting parties, one of them initially willing and able to give the other the benefit of the doubt.

V.

One last word. I have said very little indeed about the mastery of well-formedness, of grammatical speech per se. I have already said that one cannot learn the rules of grammar from learning either real-world concepts or interaction procedures for managing joint attention and action. I have been tempted in the past by the hypothesis that there is something in the deployment of attention that leads naturally to the child adopting the rule that in sentences agent comes before action and action comes before object, the near universal SVO order, but I think such assumptions about naturalness lull one into intellectual drowsiness. Rather, I would take the view that the child's knowledge of how to communicate in a world he has already conceptualized in some depth provides him with a basis for generating and testing hypotheses about the meaning and structure of the linguistic discourse into which he enters. He does, as LAD would have us believe, have a stunning capacity to infer and to generate rules, indeed to overgeneralize them. His hypotheses are based in part upon his knowledge of the requirements of action and of interacting with another. His mother, the tutor, gives him every hint she can. And her hints are first class, for she is not operating in the dark like a Turing machine. She knows from the start what it will take to speak the native language and treats the child's efforts from the start as if he *were* a native speaker or were soon to be. Her predicitions work out in 99.9% of the cases! There may indeed be something innate about the child's ability so swiftly to crack the linguistic code, once he reaches a given level of conceptual and communicative mastery. But there is almost certainly something innate about the mother's ability to help him to do so.

REFERENCES

Ainsworth, M. D. S., & Bell, S. M. Mother–infant interaction and the development of competence. In K. Connolly & J. S. Bruner (Eds.), *The growth of competence*. London and New York: Academic Press, 1974.

Bates, E., Volterra, V., & Camaioni, L. *La comunicazione nel primo anno di vita*. Turino: Boringhieri, 1976.

Bloom, L. *Language development: Form and function in emerging grammars*. Cambridge, Mass.: MIT Press, 1970.

Bloom, L. *One word at a time: The use of single word utterances before syntax*. The Hague: Mouton, 1973.

Brown, R. *A first language: The early stages*. Cambridge, Mass.: Harvard University Press, 1973.

Bruner, J. S. Organization of early skilled action. *Child Development*, 1973, *44*, 1–11.

Chomsky, N. *Syntactic structures*. The Hague: Mouton, 1957.

Chomsky, N. Explanatory models in linguistics. In E. Nagel, P. Suppes, & A. Tarski (Eds.), *Logic, methodology and the philosophy of science*. Stanford, Calif.: Stanford University Press, 1962.

Chomsky, N. *Aspects of the theory of syntax*. Cambridge, Mass.: MIT Press, 1965.

Chomsky, N. *Reflections on language*. London: Temple Smith, 1976.

Collis, G. M., & Schaffer, H. R. Synchronization of visual attention in mother–infant pairs. *Journal of Child Psychology and Psychiatry*, 1975, *16*(4), 315–320.

de Villiers, J., & de Villiers, P. Semantics and syntax in the first two years: The output of form and function and the form and function of the output. In *Language acquisition*. Cambridge, Mass.: Harvard University Press, 1978.

Dore, J. *Communicative intentions and the pragmatics of language development*. Unpublished manuscript, 1974.

Dore, J. Holophrases, speech acts, and language universals. *Journal of Child Language*, 1975, *2*, 21–40.

Dore, J. Conditions for the acquisition of speech acts. In I. Markova (Ed.), *The social context of language*. London: Wiley, 1976.

Fillmore, C. J. The case for case. In E. Bach & E. T. Harmes (Eds.), *Universals in linguistic theory*. New York: Holt, Rinehart & Winston, 1968.

Greenfield, P. M., & Smith, J. H. *The structure of communication in early language development*. New York: Academic Press, 1976.

Grice, H. P. Utterer's meaning, sentence-meaning, and word-meaning. *Foundations of Language*, 1968, *4*, 1–18.

Halliday, M. A. K. *Learning how to mean*. London: Arnold, 1975.

Harrison, B. *Meaning and structure*. New York and London: Harper & Row, 1972.

MacFarlane, A. If a smile is so important. *New Scientist*, 1974, *62*(895), 173–178.

McNeill, D. *The acquisition of language: The study of developmental psycholinguistics*. New York: Harper & Row, 1970.

Menyuk, P., & Bernholz, N. Prosodic features and children's language productions. *Quart. Prog. Rep. No. 93*. MIT Reasearch Laboratory of Electronics, Cambridge, Mass., 1969, 216–219.

Ninio, A., & Bruner, J. S. The achievement and antecedents of labelling. *J. of Child Language*, 1978, *5*, 1–15.

Ricks, D. M. *The beginnings of vocal communication in infants and autistic children*. Unpublished doctoral thesis, University of London, 1972.

Ryan, J. Early language development: Towards a communicational analysis. In M. P. M. Richards (Ed.), *The integration of the child into a social world*. Cambridge: Cambridge University Press, 1974.

Scaife, M., & Bruner, J. S. The capacity for joint visual attention in the infant. *Nature*, 1975, *253*(5489), 265–266.

Schlesinger, I. M. Relational concepts underlying language. In R. L. Schiefelbusch & L. L. Lloyd (Eds.), *Language perspectives acquistition retardation and intervention*. Baltimore, Md.: University Park Press, 1974.

Searle, J. R. Rules of the language game. *Times Literary Supplement*, September 10, 1976, pp. 1118–1120.

Shvachkin, N. K. The development of phonemic speech perception in early childhood. *Izvestiya Akademii Pedagogcheskikh Nauk RSFSR*, 1948, *13*, 101–132. [In D. I. Slobin & C. A. Ferguson (Eds.) (E. Dernback, trans.), *Studies of child language development*. New York: Holt, Rinehart & Winston, 1973.]

Sinclair-de-Zwart, H. Developmental psycholinguistics. In D. Elkind & J. H. Flavell (Eds.), *Studies in cognitive growth: Essays in honour of Jean Piaget*. New York: Oxford University Press, 1969.

Snow, C. E. The development of conversation between mothers and babies. *Prgamatics Microfiche*, 1976, *A2*, 1.6.

Stern, D., Jaffe, J., Beebe, B., & Bennett, S. *Vocalizing in unison and in alternation: Two modes of communication within the mother-infant dyad*. Paper presented at The Conference on Developmental Psycholinguistics and Communication Disorder, New York Academy of Sciences, New York, January 1975. (To be published in *The Transactions of the New York Academy of Sciences*.)

11 How To Get From Words to Sentences

Michael Maratsos
University of Minnesota

The study of language structure is a study of generalizations, and the study of language acquisition is the study of how children form these generalizations. The essence of language, as Chomsky has emphasized, is its *productivity*: From a finite set of linguistic units such as morphemes, and a finite set of procedures for arranging these units, a speaker of a language can produce, comprehend, and judge an infinite set of utterances. He can do this in novel situations to express and comprehend the expression of novel needs, thoughts, and wishes. He can simultaneously avoid the production of, and judge to be deviant, an even larger infinite set of ungrammatical utterances.

The child begins the task of analysis with only the information afforded by a limited number of instances of language structure in the speech around him, used in a limited number of contexts. Thus the problem for the study of acquisition is the problem of how the child generalizes from this limited number of specific instances to the infinite set that knowledge of a language makes available to him. Though there are some individual differences, speakers of a given language seem to form highly similar generalizations from the diverse data they hear. From this we infer that they are learning a surprisingly general structure instantiated in the diverse speech samples around them, such that the commonalities of the generalizations overwhelm the particular variations in the input data to the various learners.

Determining what the nature of the child is, such that he can form these generalizations, and determining the procedures of data analysis, hypothesis formation, and further analysis that he uses to form these generalizations, is the chief task of studies of grammatical language acquisition. Such a determination depends in a natural way on the nature of the structural generalizations that we describe the child as learning. The field of language acquisition in particular was given its recent great impetus by the formal descriptions of a number of types of generalizations that have come to be called *transformational* relations (Chomsky, 1957; Katz & Postal, 1964; Chomsky, 1965). The important aspect of this description was the abstractness of the structures and rules that it implied the speaker of a language had formulated. The polemical and theoretical analyses of the early 1960s (Chomsky, 1965; McNeill, 1966), with the ensuing continuing debates about the degree to which the child must be attributed with specifically linguistic complex innate ideas, have formed a backdrop for the field ever since.

To a large degree, the nativist position formulated by Chomsky and others has held the role of an antagonist position. Subsequent analysts have spent much effort to show that the structure of language contained considerable roots in nonlinguistic cognition (e.g., Schlesinger, 1971; Sinclair, 1971). The use of cognitively based semantic structures in the description of what children formulate has grown steadily. Analysts have generally continued to attribute to the child considerable powers of general linguistic category formation, however, though these categories may be semantically based categories such as agent and action rather than grammatical ones such as subject and verb. This emphasis on broad semantic categories has recently met, however, with analyses suggesting a more specific, distributionalist bent to the child's early analyses of constructions (Braine, 1976; Clark, 1974). The result is a descriptive flux without apparent satisfactory resolution in favor of one kind of description over another. The question is what can be done about this irresolution.

A primary purpose of the present review will naturally be an attempt to describe this flux. Beyond this, however, a resolution of the issue in favor of one point of view would comprise an unsatisfactory resolution in the sense of its being a false one. For as I shall try to illustrate, human languages consist of structures of varying kinds, and of varying degrees of generality. The beginning directions of children's acquisitional patterns are mirrored in the mature language. In the course of this exposition, I shall also try to illustrate the fruitlessness of seeking any unitary relation between the stratum of general semantic analyses and grammatical analysis. Languages exist for the communication of meanings. But their structures in the end depend on elements and procedures characterized partly by the purely combinatorial properties of linguistic units, properties not completely defined by the meanings they express. The trend in recent research toward emphasizing description of children's early language in terms of direct semantic-structural correspondences (e.g., Schlesinger, 1971) can lead to a lack of recognition of the highly formal nature of the final product of acquisition. In particular I shall try to illustrate how linguistic productivity can be largely formulated as a process of transfer of combinatorial privileges within classes of lexical items and shall seek to show how this kind of process characterizes the various levels of grammatical analysis. In the end we shall see that the implied picture is one of a remarkably flexible organism: one that can make complex analyses in both short-term and long-term memory over whole groups of individual lexical-meaning configurations, an organism in the end able to master both general and specific analyses, along with both sensible and arbitrary formal structures. Simultaneously, a central theme will consist of showing how the child's analyses of patterns in individual lexical configurations, analyses of great specificity, often only slowly proceed to more general formulations of linguistic patterns.

In the past few years many of these issues have been raised most sharply in the study of children's early construction of simple sentences (Bloom, 1970; Bowerman, 1973, 1976; Braine, 1976; Brown, 1973; Schlesinger, 1971). I shall accordingly begin with an examination of the problems of semantic vs. distributional analyses and general vs. specific analyses that have been studied in this area. Research is also available in the study of more advanced syntactic development, which can provide illumination, and relevant work and theorization in the study of the acquisition of morphological and transformational relations will also receive attention. I shall then outline briefly what different kinds of models of the child's processes of formal analysis of rules may be constructed, with particular emphasis on the differences between analyses made in short-term vs. long-term memory. I shall conclude with a description and evaluation of some higher-level generalizations (e.g., Slobin, 1973; Brown, 1973) about the course of acquisition in the child.

I. THE STUDY OF EARLY GRAMMATICAL ACQUISITION

A. The Study of Early Speech Rationalized

The chief stimulus to the greatly accelerated interest in children's acquisition of gramamtical structure lay in the implications of complex transformational grammatical descriptions. Paradoxically, the last years have seen a primary interest in such children's utterances as *mommy push, get ball, daddy chair, no mush, big dog,* and *that car,* for the description of which transformational grammars would never have been formulated. Probably leading to this development was a conviction that such simple combinations form the beginning point of syntactic combination in the child's development. The child's manner of making these initial analyses might give special insight into his primary analytic tendencies.

The particular issue with which investigators have been most concerned is whether the child shows in his initial analyses of language the employment of specifically linguistic innate ideas about the nature of language (McNeill, 1966; Schlesinger, 1971). Supporters of this nativist position have claimed (McNeill, 1966, 1970) that the best analysis of children's early grammatical constructions makes use of purely grammatical relations such as subject, verb, and object. As these have been described for adult grammar, they cannot be tied directly to nonlinguistic bases such as semantic definitions or to surface grammatical analyses of sentences. Children's immediate use of them in analyzing grammatical structure would imply a predisposition that cannot be explained easily without positing their having had an innate propensity to employ specifically linguistic hypotheses immediately.

Other investigators, in opposition, have sought to explain children's earliest acquisitions in terms of cognitively based semantic-structural correspondences or in terms of individual word-structure formulas. It seems to me that at present the best justified analyses have fallen into these latter two categories or mixtures of them and at present dominate the discussion. I shall accordingly begin with an examination of the application of these kinds of descriptions to children's early speech, leaving a discussion of the probable role of grammatical relations until a later section.

B. Semantic Versus Distributional Analyses

Lyons (1968) discusses two major kinds of sentential structural analysis that have recurred in the history of grammatical analysis. The first of these is distributional analysis: an analysis of linguistic units and the procedures for combining them purely in terms of the way in which classes of units combine with each other, largely or completely without reference to meaning. The second of these is semantic-structural analysis, the analysis of major sentence parts in terms of general semantic relations.

The two kinds of analysis can be illustrated briefly (and much too simply) by a consideration of a very small corpus of utterances: *hit ball, get spoon, I hit, you get, find shoe, mommy find, mommy get.* In a distributional analysis, only the combinatorial properties of the utterances are relevant. The terms appear to fall into three classes, which I shall neutrally call X_1, X_2, X_3. Class X_3 consists of those terms which occur only at the ends of utterances: *spoon, dog,* and *shoe.* Class X_1 terms occur only at the beginning: *I, you, mommy.* Class X_2 terms occur either at end or beginning: *hit, get,* and *find.* A final distributional support for this analysis into three classes lies in the fact that X_1 and X_3 terms apparently never occur with each other. There are no utterances such as *mommy ball* or *I dog.* Members of each class co-occur only with members of X_2. The utterances can then be described by a simple pair of rules:

$$\text{Utterance} = \begin{Bmatrix} X_1 + X_2 \\ X_2 + X_3 \end{Bmatrix}$$

Such a rule is more general than the corpus on which it is based. It predicts that the speaker might also utter or accept *mommy hit* or *find ball*. This characteristic of the rules in generating utterances beyond the particular set on which they are based corresponds to their being productive. Later it will be seen how powerful the productivity is that such distributional knowledge can afford a speaker of an adult language.

In a semantic-structural analysis of the above set of utterances, the terms are classified in terms of their general semantic relations to each other. One possible classification scheme is that the utterances consist of three kinds of semantic category: agent, one who initiates an action; action; and patient, the recipient of the force of an action. By this scheme, *mommy, I,* and *you* may all be classified as agents; *hit, get,* and *find* as actions; and *ball, spoon,* and *shoe* as patients. Two rules then account for the corpus above, as well as predicting other possible utterances:

$$\text{Utterance} = \left\{ \begin{array}{l} \text{agent } + \text{ action} \\ \text{action } + \text{ patient} \end{array} \right\}$$

Either description is in formal terms an adequate general description of the corpus of utterances. In psychological terms, of course, they imply very different kinds of understanding. A speaker who in a psychologically real sense used the distributional analysis might or might not be making semantic analyses of the roles of the terms. The point would be, however, that these would be irrelevant to his formulation of the sentential structure. Sentences would be produced by a classification of the terms into different purely positional possibilities. Wishing to say something about finding and a ball, for example, the translation for the concept of finding would be the word *find*, which can appear in either first or second position, while that for ball would be *ball*, which is generally classified as appearing only second, thus dictating the appearance of *find* in first position. The result is the utterance *find ball*. Should the speaker want to say something about some connection between *mommy* and *ball*, he has no means of doing so, for the rules make no provisions for combining these terms.

The semantic analysis claims that just certain aspects of the semantic analysis are relevant to the construction of sentences, namely the relations of agency, patienthood, and action. In talking about hitting and a ball that is hit, because the first of these is an action and the second a patient, the sentence formation rules dictate the placement of *ball* after *hit*. It is only these general semantic analyses that are relevant, furthermore. Though the fact that *hit* requires contact between two objects is relevant to the choice of the word *hit* to describe some activities, it is not relevant for the ordering of the terms.

Other possible rules for sentence formation may easily be found in even this limited corpus, however; these rules vary both in the generality of analysis and in the degree to which combinatorial and semantic formulas are combined. The concepts agent, action, and patient, for example, are very general concepts. To classify hitters, getters, and finders all alike as agents is to abstract from each kind of activity a small part of the conceptual structures of the respective roles. A speaker who produced these utterances, even if using a semantic basis to guide his productions, may have instead learned very specific formulas revolving around the more specific roles involved in finding, getting, and hitting, such as placing the term denoting the finder before the term denoting the action of finding. The speaker's knowledge would thus consist of six binary combinatorial rules: finder + find, find + found, getter + get, get + gotten, hitter + hit, hit + hit object. In the end such a formula would lack generality in the learning of new terms, of course. As new actional words were added, each would have to be learned for its specific semantic structural correspondence.

As a last illustrative example, we could imagine that the speaker's knowledge encompasses a combination of distributional and semantic formulas of the following kind. He knows that each utterance must contain one of the terms that is capable of occurring either first or last, that is, the X_2 class of *get, find,* or *hit.* For each of these terms there is a specific semantic-structural correspondence such as getter + get or get + gotten. As peculiar as this formula seems, it will be seen that it actually comes closest in spirit to much of adult English sentence structure.

The difficulty of making a convincing single choice of an analysis is well illustrated by the plethora of analyses available for the small corpus above. The hypothetical speaker of this hypothetical corpus could be given various learning and judgment tasks to see how he has actually encoded what he has learned. But it is more to the point here to deal with what has been found out about young children. Students of children's language deal with data both richer and more difficult, for the corpora are larger but far less orderly. The ingenuity of investigators in determining as much as they have is considerable.

C. Descriptions of Children's First Combinatorial Sentences

The first description of children's early speech to attract widespread interest comprised a purely distributional one (Braine, 1963). With the cooperation of mothers, Braine collected corpora of the early two-word combinations of three children learning English. The major feature of the data was the frequent use of a few words in mostly fixed position, in combination with a larger set of words that were each used less frequently and not necessarily in fixed position. A typical subset of the utterances from one child's corpus included *want baby, want car, want get, want glasses,* and 11 other combinations of the form *want* + X. Another child produced sentences of the form *X + off: boot off, light off, pants off, shirt off, shoe off, water off.* Braine called the small set of frequently used, fixed-position terms by the name of "pivot words"; the second set came to be called "open words."

Other distributional criteria seemed to converge on the analysis into these two classes. Open words could occasionally occur together, pivot words could not. Open terms could occur alone, while according to Braine's description, pivots tended not to.

Braine's analysis attracted both reinterpretation (McNeill, 1966) and criticism (Bowerman, 1973; Brown, 1973; Bloom, 1970). The criticisms centered around three major points. One of these was that studies of other children seemed to show some for whom the analysis was not profitably applicable at all. More damaging criticisms were also applied to the general adequacy of the description even in the case of corpora to which it might apply. Bowerman (1973) criticized the pivot-open description on purely distributional grounds. In both Braine's original corpus and in corpora of other children, for example, some terms appeared very frequently but in either sentence-initial or sentence-final position.[1] The most damaging criticism, however (Bloom, 1970), arose from the possibility that Braine's analysis underestimated the degree to which children might be encoding semantic-structural correspondences in their speech, rather than simply formulating specific word combinatorial rules. A beginning problem was that Braine's analyses made no reference to the semantic function of expressions, a function that was clear when viewed in the speech context around the child. Bloom (1970), for example, found three children using many pivotlike constructions, such as *no + X* or *more + X*. But it seemed clear that in uttering these sentences they were doing more than combining words; they were encoding particular semantic functions. *No + X* always referred to a disappearance or some other nonexistent state of *X, more + X* to a desired or noted recurrence of *X.* The frequent use of these constructions followed from children's interest in expressing relations such as disappearance, recurrence, naming, and so on.

The more serious difficulty for a pivot-open analysis arose from the possibility that children also encoded more general relations such as agency, possession, location, attribution—relations expressed by the ordering of general semantic categories rather than by single word formulas. A child who says *hit ball, get dog, find shoe* may be analyzed as instantiating the general relation action + patient. In such usages, children seem to have gone beyond single word-positional formulas to the formation of general semantic-class

---

[1]As has been pointed out to me by M. Chalkley, this criticism was partly made on the basis of data from children learning a language with a freer word order, Finnish. Braine's explanation for pivot-open learning, however, presupposed a stable word order in the language, and so the data from freer word-order languages is not particularly relevant. Contrary cases from English were also discussed, however.

combinatorial rules, for the semantic categories are broader than any of the individual terms which instantiate them.

The crucial methodological step in such analyses is that the child's word order seems to match the most common adult word order for what is interpreted as the child's semantic intent, so that some real observance of a structural-semantic rule is involved. A child who wants to refer to an action such as finding and something found may have two words for reference to each, such as *shoe* and *find*. If all he knew, however, was to say the two words together he could produce either *shoe find* or *find shoe* to express the same relation. Children learning English, however, seem generally to choose the word orders an adult would have chosen to refer to the same relation (i.e., *find shoe* in the above). The method of analysis depends on two assumptions: one, that the child's semantic intention can be inferred from conversational context, so it can be compared to his means of expression. Two, the child is compared against the most common order. For example, the most common English order for the relation of possession is possessor-possessed, as in *Harry's chair*. But in fact the other possible order is also used, such as *that chair of Harry's, a chair of Harry's,* and so on. It is the commonness of the possessor-possessed order that makes the analysis a reasonable one.

Bloom made a particularly telling criticism based on combinations found in two of the children she studied. These children produced utterances which would have received a uniform grammatical analysis under a pivot-open description, but which apparently served to express different semantic relations. One child said *mommy sock* in one case referring to herself picking up her mother's sock, and thus seemed to be encoding the related possessor-possessed object. In another context, she used the same combination of words, *mommy sock,* when her mother was putting on the child's sock, leading to Bloom's inference that the child was encoding the relation of agent-patient (one who does something—thing acted on). In numerous cases, the pivot-open analysis would apparently underdescribe what the child knew about the most common ways of arranging general semantic categories in English.

The idea of using semantic-structural correspondences to describe children's early speech, appearing also in a paper by Schlesinger (1971), soon attracted the attention of many analysts. A typical list of commonly proposed two-term relations in children's early speech is adapted here from Brown (1970):

I. *Relations:*   *Examples:*
   Agent-action   (Adam put, Eve read)
   Action-patient   (Put book, Hit ball)
   Agent-patient   (Mommy sock, Mommy lunch)
   Possessor-possessed   (Adam checker, Mommy sock)
   Actional-location   (Walk street, Come here)

Located object-location	(Sweater chair, Book table)[2]
Attribute-modified	(Big train, Red book)
II. *Referential Operations:*	*Examples:*
Nomination:	(That book, it cat)
Notice:	(Hi Mommy, cat, belt, chair)
Recurrence:	(More + milk, cereal, nut, read)
Nonexistence:	(No + rattle, juice, etc.)

Both Brown (1973) and Schlesinger (1974) and others, however, pointed out that a serious problem lies in choosing the appropriate level of generality at which to analyze the child's hypothesized relational rules. The problem is essentially the one pointed out earlier: a corpus that may be analyzed as instantiating more general relational formulas such as agent + action might in fact consist of a set of lower-level rules such as hitter + hit, getter + get, finder + find, or some mixture of these. The question is one of how decisions can be made about the child's actual mode of analysis.

If the presence of a range of combinations is not enough to justify securely the analysis of a general relational rule, what is? No perfectly satisfactory answer can be given. But a number of possible developmental outcomes would support the generality of a categorical analysis in a positive way, though it is not clear that their failure to occur would invalidate the analysis.

Schlesinger (1974) suggested one possible analytic procedure, that of noting what structural-semantic correspondences were exemplified in word-order combinations that emerged nearly simultaneously in a child's speech. If a child suddenly started using many terms that exemplified the relation action-patient, the evidence would support the psychological reality of the action-patient formulation in the child's own analysis of the speech around him. Or conversely, he might only formulate a small subclass of the possible actional-patient combinations, supporting his having analyzed the data in terms of smaller semantic-structural patterns.

Braine (1976) applied this method to the analysis of data from 16 corpora of children's early speech, including 3 he had the most extensive data from. The data supported the psychological reality of one fairly broad structural-semantic correspondence, that of mover-movement. But often the semantic breadth of the categories employed in the word combinations that emerged together was quite narrow. One such acquisition, for example, was the acquisition of the pattern *want + X (want cereal, want shoe, want hat),* emerging without the simultaneous use of other word combinations that denoted an experience or feeling + the thing experienced. Or a child might learn together the use of a few terms instantiating a limited semantic category,

---

[2]These utterances are typically glossed as meaning the same locational relations as the adult sentences, "The sweater's on the chair," and "The book's on the table."

such as the encoding of actions denoting oral consumption *(eat + X, bite + X, drink + X)*, or terms concerning the movements of vehicles *(drive/pull/tow + X)*. Similarly, Braine found little evidence for children's use of a general analysis such as attribute + object.

Bowerman (1976) has similarly reported on two of her own children, making an interesting contrast between the structural acquisition patterns of the two. These children were observed intensively enough so that both multiword combinations and their concurrent single-word combinations were available as data. One of these children, Eva, seemed clearly to be initially learning the combinatorial properties of single words. As Bowerman writes:

> For example, the first week of word combination at about 17½ months was characterized by the sudden production of a large number of constructions involving the word "want," in sentences like "want bottle," "want juice," "want see," and "want change." At the same time that Eva began to combine "want" with other words she was using approximately 25 other verbs of adult English as single-word utterances.... However, none of these verbs began to enter into combination for another month [p. 173].

Bowerman reports that Eva began to learn prenominal determiner and modifier combinations in a similar word-by-word fashion. For example, even as she put the referential term *more* before other words to denote recurrence, she failed to make combinations with the similar terms *again, no more,* or *all gone*.

Thus, even though such a child might later instantiate a wide variety of what we could analyze as action-patient or attribute-entity semantic structural relations, it appears that these broad categories did not guide the initial productivity of the child's speech.

The absence of initial positive evidence, however, does not constitute certain evidence that broader semantic categorical rules are not eventually attained. The child might make a later integration of the related instances, drawing out the generalization only after storage of a number of more specific analyses. Later discussion will uncover instances in children's acquisition of morphological structure in which this is known with some certainty to happen. In the particular case of semantic-structural rules, such a development might be found in a sudden spurt of growth of combinations across a wide range described by broad categories such as agent-action or attribute-entity after the initial period of specific learning.

Bowerman (1976) reporting on Eva, does not say how she evaluated this possibility of later integration, but she reports:

> Nor was there evidence for the operation at a later time of rules at an intermediate semantic level, which would indicate that after a period of experience with the syntax of particular words Eva had reorganized her

information about them according to simpler superordinate semantic categories like "agent" and "action" [p. 173].

In the end, Eva went:

> rather swiftly from an approach based on learning sequentially how to make constructions with particular lexical items to a much more mature system in which words of virtually all semantic subtypes were dealt with fluently.... There is no evidence that she achieved this with the aid of relational concepts at a level of abstraction between the semantics of particular words and syntactic notions that are independent of any particular semantic content, such as "subject" and "direct object" [p. 174].

Braine similarly found little such evidence in a number of analyses.

Another of Bowerman's children, Christy, did display the use of some higher superordinate semantic categories in her acquisitional patterns. Christy refrained, for example, from using possible modifiers with nouns for some period of time. Then within a short period she assembled sentences in a predicate-nominal or predicate-adjective pattern, using sentences like *that wet, daddy hot, bottle all gone,* and *that airplane.* The emergence is somewhat puzzling in purely semantic terms, because *that airplane* does not instantiate a description of a property as directly as the sentences with *wet, hot,* and *all gone.* The pattern could be one of a broader attribution of properties and categories to objects, or one based on the more distributionally based adult pattern NP + *be* + *X.* Christy also simultaneously organized some information with action words according to a fairly broad movement category, including X + *up, down, on, off, back* (object + direction of movement), and a number of agent + action patterns.

Children's early combinations, then, seem to range from organization in terms of specific lexical meaning-distribution formulas to organization employing the use of semantic-structural rules of varying generality. Furthermore, the possibility must always be entertained that even combinations that seem most easily described in broad combinatorial formulas may be instantiations of more particular formulas. Some children that have been studied, for example, appear to express the relation located object + location with a variety of terms, producing sentences such as *sweater chair* (said referring to a sweater that is on a chair) or *book table* (said of a book on a table). In such cases, analysis in terms of a general relation of location seems particularly attractive, for the child makes no mention of more specific locative relations, such as *in* or *on.* Thus, such a case contrasts with the problem of classifying an utterance like *eat cereal,* in which *eat* specifically encodes a range of possible relations ranging from very specific to very general.

Even in cases such as *sweater chair,* however, the child may have learned, and may be encoding, a more specific relation. Most of these early locative utterances of the form located object + locative object can be interpreted as encoding the semantic relations appropriate to the specific prepositions *in* and *on,* which are in fact the first prepositions to emerge in children's speech. Children might be encoding according to the more specific formula $X + Y = $ "X ON Y" or "X IN Y". Without a wider range of developmental data, the problems of proving a more general categorization can be quite severe.

There is a natural inclination, perhaps, to think of such initial learning in terms of small meaning-distribution formulas as an unnatural way into the realm of adult English syntax, which makes productive use of rules combining broad categories of word classes. An approach to the final state through the linkage of structural configurations to large semantic relations, characteristic of many recent analyses in the field, may appear a more natural way for entry into adult grammar. Bowerman (1976), for example, seems to express such a view.

It is not so clear, however, that this is so. In the next section I shall try to point out some relevant characteristics about English constituent structure. The major arguments I shall make are these:

1. The regularities of English syntax are *not* very directly tied to general semantic-structural relations, although there are some generalizations of reasonably wide application. Rather, particularly in verb configurations, many regularities of grammatical structure fail to follow uniform semantic-structural patterns.

2. General semantic relations, at least when considered with respect to adult use, turn out to be difficult to specify and list convincingly, particularly for use in classifying the major roles of noun phrases in sentences.

3. Attention to highly specific lexical patterns remains a constant feature even in adult syntax. Adult English requires much specific semantic-syntactic memorization of the speaker, down to a level of near idiomaticness for many usages. The emphasis on the generality summarized by sentence structure rules, well justified in many respects, has served to obscure this fact.

The outcome will be to show that the various analytic tracks that children seem to take in early speech turn out to be ones that are all variously useful for the acquisition of sentence structure—a fact that is probably no coincidence.

More positively, I shall also try to elucidate some of the nature of grammatical productivity, concentrating on how language structure consists of vast networks of transfers of distributional privileges that apply to large numbers of individual terms. Finally I shall return to the discussion of children's early acquisition, which will be more clearly seen as but a beginning, however reasonable, in the acquisition of a mature linguistic competence.

II. SEMANTIC STRUCTURAL RELATIONS, DISTRIBUTIONAL ANALYSIS, AND CONSTITUENT STRUCTURE

A. Nongovernance of Simple Sentence Structure by Semantic Roles

Even if general semantic relations could be clearly defined, a child who learned language by forming structural correspondences to very general semantic relations and attempting to subordinate all his future learning to this principle would encounter difficulties. For a characteristic of English (and all other languages) is that the same general semantic relations may be read out even into simple sentences in a multiplicity of ways, particularly in relations revolving around verbs and adjectives. This can be illustrated by the use of sentential pairs in which identical or near identical relations are encoded by quite different orders of NPs, and even different constituent types. Consider the following pair:

John likes tables.
Tables please John.

The general semantic relations between *tables* and *John* are quite similar in both sentences, as are the general constituent analyses: NP + V + NP. In both sentences, *John* is experiencer, *tables,* stimulus. But for *like,* the experiencer occupies subject position, and for *please,* object position.

Or consider, similarly, the relation possessor-possessed as exemplified in the following sentences:

John owns this house.
This house belongs to John.

Again the same general relations are read out into different NP orders, and in this case, into different constituent configurations as well. The following sentence groups all illustrate the same point:

The monkey's antics amused John.
John was amused at the monkey's antics. (Not a passive.)
John sold a car to Mary.
Mary bought a car from John.
John gave a comb to Mary.
Mary {received, got} a comb from John.
I think he'll come.
It seems to me he'll come.
He'll probably come.

Sometimes even the same verb arranges its roles differently, depending on the prepositions:

We got the message to Mary.
Mary got the message from us.

It is obvious that the verbs of English show no clear structural-semantic relational match. In a very real way, learning English often requires an item-by-item learning of structural-semantic formulas for verbs.

It is true that some semantic relations show a more general degree of meaning-structural correspondence. Agents, if present, occur overwhelmingly often in initial NP position in simple sentences, though there are exceptions even to this generalization *(John received a blow on the head from Mary)*. Other semantic relations show a mixed structure-position regularity. Locative relations may be encoded a number of ways, either in a verb or by a prepositional phrase or an adverb:

Forty marbles were in this box.
This box contained forty marbles.

If encoded by a prepositional phrase or adverb, locatives in simple sentences generally follow the verb phrase. The case is similar for temporal phrases *(yesterday, at ten o'clock)*; manner phrases *(nastily, in a nasty manner)*; duration phrases *(for 3 hours, a long time)*; and others.

B. Some Difficulties of Semantic Role Classifications of NPs

Even in simple sentences, then, English does not afford a straightforward relation between structure and general meanings. Adult linguistic structures afford problems to another aspect of general semantic role classification, even apart from the use of such roles as possible governors of sentence structure. The difficulty is that it is not certain that there is a small set of unitary, clear, mutually exclusive semantic roles such that every NP of a sentence can be assigned just one such role. It was early recognized in recent linguistic work that an NP might not take just one major semantic role in a sentence. For example, consider the relation theme (Fillmore, 1971; Jackendoff, 1972), the entity whose movement or location is described. In the sentence *John got out of bed, John* is clearly a theme, but also an agent, because the action is intentional. Or, in another mixture, in *John looked at the dog, John* is both an experiencer of sensory input, and an agent, the intentional initiator of the activity of looking.

This problem, however, is not as potentially interesting as several others, though its effects can already be seen in current developmental research (e.g., Bloom, Miller, & Hood, 1975). For the semantic categories themselves do not appear to be unitary and distinct, but rather to share various meaningful dimensions in overlapping ways. Both agent and instruments, for example, involve the notion of causal force. As such, rather than being distinct, they are more similar to each other than to relations like locative. Consider further the following three sentences:

The army destroyed the village.
The cannon destroyed the village.
The earthquake destroyed the village.

The army is an agentive NP: an intentional, typically animate initiator of action or process. *The cannon* clearly denotes an instrument: inanimate, unintentional, noninstigatory cause. But the *earthquake* stands midway between *the army* and *the cannon* in a number of ways: It is not like *the army*, for the causality is unintentional. But like *the army*, and unlike *the cannon*, the causal force is in some way self-initiatory. Thus, *the army, the cannon,* and *the earthquake,* are characterized in varying degree by the qualities of intentionality and self-initiatory quality. The overlapping relations among these roles, and between them and noncausal roles such as location, further demonstrate the nonunitary nature of NP semantic relations in sentences, at least when this is construed in any simple fashion.

The overlap of different roles has become evident in other modern analyses. Jackendoff (1972), for example, analyzes possession as involving a type of location on various grounds. The NP *John,* in *John knows the answer,* has also been analyzed (Jackendoff, 1972) as involving a locative relation, as has *Harry* in *John is similar to Harry,* a location among a kind of abstract quality space. The last example points out a growing problem: the lack of easy intuitive classification of major categories. Classifications typically become less clear, and proliferate (e.g., countercausative for *his efforts* in *despite his efforts*) as one investigates a wider range of sentences. Classifications in modern studies of child language development have begun to show a similar diversity (e.g., one can look at the range of classifications in Bloom et al., 1975; Brown, 1973; Wells, 1974; and others).

Evidently, though the case has not been made in detail here, there are many meaningful dimensions that can be applied in varying degree among different general relations—causality, location, movement, intentionality, sensory and/or emotional experiencer, abstract and/or concrete space, benefited or hurt party—with varying degrees of subdivision (location, e.g., has been split into source [place to which], goal [place from which], and location [place at which] in modern analyses). But the way in which these meaningful relations are distributed among NP roles is neither one to one, distinct and clear, nor intuitively simple to assign. It is probably the case that rather than there being a small set of uniquely general and distinct relations, there is a large set of relations varying on a continuum in generality, importance, and clarity, represented in various degree and distribution among NP sentential roles. The application of this point to the study of children's grammar cannot be completely drawn out here. But it seems plausible, given the apparent facts about adult semantics, that children would not necessarily tend to seek uniform, clear definitions of semantic roles for NPs, but instead might formulate semantic assignments of varying clarity, generality, and overlap. Adult investigators apparently do so (again, cf. Bloom et al., 1975; Brown, 1973; Braine, 1976; Wells, 1976).

C. Constituent Structure

Simple relations among sentence structure and general semantic relations are evidently not easily found in English sentence structure, particularly in the central realm of verb, adjective, and NP relations. Persistent regularities are to be found, however, in constituent structure analyzed without regard to the semantic relation of phrases. Phrase structure rules such as:

$$S \rightarrow NP + VP$$
$$VP \rightarrow V + NP \text{ (e.g., } \textit{hit the dog, had an idea, used a hammer)}$$
$$VP \rightarrow V + PP \text{ (} \textit{looked at the dog, belongs to John, seems to me)}$$
$$VP \rightarrow V + NP + PP \textit{(blamed John for the problem, blamed the problem}$$

on John, gave a dog to his mother, bought a house from Tom)

$$VP \rightarrow V \text{ (} \textit{died, left, ran, ate)}$$
$$NP \rightarrow Det + N \text{ (} \textit{the dog, your house, this idea)}$$
$$NP \rightarrow Det + Adj + N \text{ (} \textit{the big dog, your nice house, this dumb idea)}$$
$$NP \rightarrow N \text{ (} \textit{ideas, sand, water, Sam, Joaquin)}$$

express general patterns of combinatorial possibilities of classes of items, not direct readouts of general or even specific semantic relations. We need to specify, however, how constituent structure arises from, in fact summarizes, generalizations about the combinatorial properties of individual lexical items.

The essential beginning point lies in the analysis of individual morphemes into form classes on the basis of their combinatorial behavior. These units include nouns, verbs, adjectives, prepositions, articles, and bound morphemes such as past tense *ed,* plural *s,* and so on. Such morpheme classes are defined better by combinatorial properties rather than any straightforward semantic analysis. Statistically, for example, nouns *are* more likely to denote concrete objects (persons, places, things), verbs to denote actions, and adjectives to denote attributes or states. It seems to be true in particular that no concrete object is encoded by another part of speech than the noun. These major categories may even exist in human languages because of the existence in the mind of major conceptual categories such as things, actions, and states. But in human languages, conceptual categories no longer serve to define the syntactic categories. Nouns include, besides words like *rock, Fauntleroy,* and *Idaho,* terms like *idea, action, state, relation, attribute,* and *orbit.* Verbs include nonactional state verbs such as *know, believe,* and *feel* (as in *he felt sad*). Adjectives include actional terms such as *active, reckless,* and *obnoxious,* as well as terms that can be ambiguous (compare *he is charming* to *he is being charming*—the second shows that *charming* can definitely denote an active process). Often very nearly the same concept is expressed in different combinations of form classes: *he was brave* = NP + BE + Adj, *he had courage* = NP + V + NP; *he {understood, knew}* the difficulty = NP + V + NP, *he was aware of the difficulty* = NP + be + Adj + PP.

What defines the major form classes is not their semantic definition. What members of a form class share that motivates our classifying them together is overlap of distributional privileges: they combine with other terms in similar ways. Nouns, for example, may appear directly after terms like *this* and *that* in sentence-terminal position, which adjectives and verb forms may not: *I like the {idea, dog, person},* but not **I like the {big, pushed, is}.* Verbs, unlike adjectives, can be directly inflected for tense or aspect (*push, pushed, pushes, pushing, but not pushy, *pushied, *pushies, *pushying*). Adjectives must appear after a form of *be* in order to be marked for tense or aspect: *{is, are, were, was} obnoxious, was being obnoxious.*

Constituent analysis begins with form class analysis and goes further: it attempts to describe those generalizations about sentence structure which can be captured by linear ordering of morphemes and groupings of these linear orderings. The particular intuitions it captures are these: (1) there are general possibilities for ordering units in sentences; (2) the individual units of the sentence, themselves members of general classes, form natural hierarchical groups (phrases); and (3) these hierarchical groupings of units are similar in their combinatorial possibilities to those found in other sentences.

The technique of producing this analysis is known as *immediate constituent analysis.* We can begin, for illustration, with the morpheme string *a + man + push + ed + the + girl* (assuming the analysis into morphemes), corresponding to the form class sequence Art(icle) + N(oun) + Verb + Past + Art(icle) + N(oun). At this level, a number of the units seem to group together more closely than others: *a* with *man, push* with *ed,* and *the* with *girl.* These intuitions can be represented by the following diagram, with abstract symbols assigned to the higher-order groupings:

Intuitively, however, *a man* is the same kind of higher unit as *the girl.* This intuition is borne out by their ability to appear in many similar environments across a wide range of sentences: {*the girl, a man*} *surprised us; we saw* {*a man, the girl*}, and so on. That is, what we have called X and Y are apparently units of the same type as defined by their general combinatorial properties. We shall call this unit a noun phrase (abbreviated NP). Thus, just as *man* and *girl* are classified as units of the same kind because of their commonality of combinatorial properties, *a man* and *the girl* are similarly classified as similar higher units because of their commonality of potential for combination with other units.

Push + ed, itself intuitively a unit, differs from these other units in its combinatorial possibilities: One cannot say **pushed surprised us,* or place *pushed* in other NP environments. Thus *push + ed* forms another kind of unit, here called V. These analyses have given the following partial analysis:

```
        NP            V            NP
       / \          / \          / \
     Art + N     Verb + Past   Art + N
      |   |        |     |      |   |
      A + man +  push  +  ed  + the + girl
```

It is a common intuition that the phrase *pushed a girl* also forms a unit, usually called a verb phrase, or VP. There are no other VPs in this sentence. But we find other V + NP units in other sentences that seem to combine with other units in the same way as does *pushed the girl:* thus, we may say *a man* {*pushed the girl, devised a solution, saw a house, ate a duck*} and so on. All these units, by virtue of sharing combinatorial properties in common with *pushed the girl* may be analyzed as groupings of the same type, and thus can all be called VPs.

The final constituent analysis of this sentence is that *a man* and *pushed the girl* form the highest grammatical unit, the sentence:

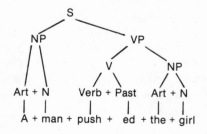

A formalization of these possibilities of combinations of classes of individual units may be found in phrase-structure rules (Chomsky, 1957). These are simply a listing of constituent analytic groupings found generally in sentences. The analyses made so far correspond to the following general possibilities:

$$S \rightarrow NP + VP \qquad VP \rightarrow V + NP \qquad V \rightarrow Verb + Past$$
$$NP \rightarrow Art + N$$

The above rules represent only a small set of the distributional possibilities found in English simple sentences, of course. Phrase-structure rules such as those noted earlier,

VP → V (as in *the man died*)
VP → V + PP (as in *the man though about the problem*)
VP → V + NP + PP (*gave a house to the girl,*
   blamed John for the problem)
NP → Art + Adj + N
NP → Art + N
NP → N

list other patterns of combination of units.

To say that a word is a verb or noun, then, is to say that it acts like other terms in how it combines with morphemes. To say that a particular combination of form classes is a noun phrase is to say that it acts like other similar groupings of similar form classes in how it combines with other groups of form classes. Constituent structure is a summary of the commonalities in patterns of distributions of individual words.

D. Transfer of Privileges

How can such a system lead to productivity, though? It appears as though these summaries say, in effect, that if a term can appear in the environment *the +* _____ ## (*I see the dog*), it is a noun. Being classified as a noun, it can appear in the environment *the +* _____ ##. If we need to hear a term in its grammatical environment to classify it, and its classification simply allows us to place it properly in its grammatical environment, how can a speaker go beyond what he hears?

The answer is that constituent rules are a shorthand for classifying the *related* privileges of terms; knowing a specific use of a term is often enough to allow its generalization to other environments than the one in which it was heard. The most powerful illustration of this kind of productivity can be made with the use of nonsense terms used in grammatical environments that make clear the distributional privileges open to the terms. The term *bik* by itself carries no cues as to its use. But if we hear it in the environment *These biks are bothering John,* we can immediately predict its possible use in a large number of other grammatical environments. Because of its appearance as a plural after the determining *these*, we know that *bik* can appear after any of the other terms called determiners, which like *these* appear before nouns in noun phrases: *this bik, that bik, those biks, a bik, the bik, a few biks*, and so on. We can also predict its use in the singular, *bik*. It can appear as well after a member of the distributional class called adjectives: *this little bik, the first bik*, and so on.

Or if the term appeared in the utterance *John biks*, the use signals that it is one of those terms which can appear after a NP, with an ending *s*, and constitute a complete sentence. As a result, we can also predict its appearance after other NPs, as in *Harry biks, the dog biks, this idea biks*, and in an even wider range of environments shared by terms with similar privileges, such as *John is bikking, Does John bik, John didn't bik, For John to bik is sad*, and so on. Not positively but possibly, *bik* might be a member of the class of terms that allows NPs afterwards as well, leading to the prediction of sentences such as *John bikked Mary, Mary was bikked by John*, and *The bikking of Mary by John was sad*.

Our tendency is to say that *bik* is a verb, as signaled by its appearance in one verb context, *John _____ + s*, and thus can appear in the syntactic contexts above. In a sense, this is backwards. It is because *bik* can enter into these environments that we call it a verb. What we should say is that one of these distributional privileges can imply the others. Viewed this way, it is not the case that children early on learn what verbs are, and then learn distributional privileges of verbs as they grow older. Rather, they associate with each other the related distributional privileges of individual terms such as appearing in the environments NP _____ + s, Did NP _____, NP *didn't* _____, NP _____ + *ed*, and learn the generality of the associations among these patterns. With time, they learn to correlate new distributional privileges with these old ones.

Grammatical possibilities comprise only part of the prediction of the use of a term, of course. If *bik* means "to contemplate a visual shape," its appearance in the context *Harry biks often* will not generalize to the grammatically possible context *this idea biks often*, because ideas do not contemplate shapes. But it is important to note once more that semantic analysis of a term does not uniquely predict its grammatical use. For example, *think* may denote thinking processes, but although we can say *The process of thinking fascinates Harry*, we cannot say *The think fascinates Harry*, because *think* appears in verb, not noun, environments.

Thus, one end product of the process of language development is the knowledge of how distributional privileges of terms are related to one another and the ability to infer or guess at new privileges for a term from hearing one. The use of constituent groupings such as NP in rules refers to the fact that many regularities in the language refer to regularities in the use of orderings of such form classes. The simple sentence rule S → NP + VP refers to the fact that every simple English sentence (i.e., every simple active declarative) begins with a grouping of terms centering around a noun (i.e., a NP).

E. Lexical Specificity

The beginning of this massive system of transfer of privileges lies in the storage of correlated individual lexical patterns. It is the fact that these related privileges each apply to a number of individual terms that allows extrapolation of related privileges to a new term that appears in one of the relevant distributional environments. The stored information must include both grammatical and semantic information; terms that encode progressive meaning with the ending *ing*, for example, can usually encode past with the ending *ed* (e.g., *considering-considered*). Toward the end of this review I shall make more specific analyses of the ways in which such possible storage and analysis systems may be conceptualized.

The adult speaker must furthermore continue to remember for many terms large amounts of partly idiosyncratic detailed grammatical and semantic-structural information. This is because the implicational relations among distributional privileges are highly variable in their reliability. Some distributional relations are perfectly reliable. For example, any term that can appear in the environment NP + *is* + *very* + _____ (*The dog is very big, happy,* and so on) can also appear in the environment determiner + _____ + N (*the big dog, this happy cat,* and so on). But sometimes distributional privileges only correlate imperfectly. Consider the privileges of terms that we call verbs. Some are highly general to most or all verbs, such as being able to appear in the environment ##NP _____ + *s...#* to denote a present or persistent state of affairs (*John likes Mary, That plumber sings*). But others are not. Some verbs must take NP objects in most circumstances (**He blamed, He blamed the girl*). Others may or may not (*He ate ducks, he ate*), while still others *can* not (**He died her*). *Die* may appear with a prepositional phrase directly after it, as in *He died from cancer; blame* cannot (**He blamed for the accident*).

The level of required memorization may be even more specific than this. *Think,* for example, can take prepositional phrase complements after it, as in *think about the problem.* But only a few prepositions are allowable, such as *about.* One cannot say **he thought under the problem* or **he thought by the problem.*[3] A speaker must also memorize much about particular allowable

---

[3]These prepositional phrase verb complements should not be confused with more general locative or manner adverbial prepositional phrases such as *under the tree* or *by the tree.* Use of these may make it seem as though verbs like *think* can take a wide range of prepositional phrase complements (e.g., *John thought under the tree*). The actual use of one of these after the verb phrase makes clear the restricted range of allowable prepositions: *He thought about the problem under the tree,* but not **he thought {by, under} the problem under the tree.*

prepositions and particles that does not follow from their more general meanings. Nothing about the usual denotation of *over* explains why one can say *He thought over the problem* but not *under*.

In fact, if we imagine a speaker beginning with the meaning he intends and choosing structures according to his lexical items of choice, it becomes apparent how general phrase-structural rules may only form summations of the generalizations implicit in a speaker's knowledge rather than strongly governing what he actually does in particular instances. Think of a speaker wishing to communicate a meaning we can roughly think of as (*X* COGITATE *Y*). Should the speaker choose the verb *consider* to encode the relation, the pattern governed by the verb is NP + V + NP (e.g., *John considered the problem*). If he chooses *think*, he may choose the pattern NP *think about* NP. This happens to correspond to the pattern NP + *think* + P + NP, but only one preposition will do. Or he may choose *think NP over (John thought the problem over)*, which = NP + *think* + NP + Particle; but again, just one particle is acceptable. Thus, major aspects of the selection of other lexical items and the ordering of NPs are governed by the individual verb, not by general phrase structure rules. So even as the formation of general distributional privileges and knowledge of their relations allows great productivity to speakers, it remains the case that a considerable amount of lexically specific information must continue to be stored and used. Nor do we know how much general vs. specific knowledge actually figures in particular processes of speech production and ocmprehension.

F. Children's Learning of Simple Sentence Structure Reconsidered

As described earlier, children's initial acquisitions display a wide variety of structures. Some children apparently attempt more general formulations of the relation between semantic relations and sentential structures, while others begin with more specific structural-meaning configurations, including single-word patterns such as *want* + *X*, or small categorical patterns such as INGESTION + INGESTED, apparently building such specific combinations into adult grammars. As should be clear, all of these tendencies are instantiated to some degree in adult grammatical structures. Very general semantic-structural correspondences are not so useful as they may have seemed though playing some role. Nor are they as prevalent in children's language as has been thought, though playing some role in varying degree for different children. At the same time, learning individual or small groups of lexical distributional-meaning configurations, which can seem like a difficult way into adult structure, nevertheless comprises in many ways a natural one. For as already summarized, the distributional regularities and transfers of privileges that characterize the grammatical productivity of adult language must begin with the storage of individual lexical information and arise from abstractions of common distributional-meaning privileges in numbers of items. And memorization of much individual lexical meaning-structural information remains necessary even to the adult. Specific lexical storages form a beginning for the acquisition of the general patterns of individual terms and their groupings that comprises adult constituent structure.

What is available of these descriptions makes it clear, however, that these initial acquisitions form only a beginning in many ways. The adult system is characterized by a great network of transfers of grammatical privileges involving constituent groupings, obligatory and optional grammatical combinatorial privileges of classes of terms, morphological regularities, and overall sentence patternings, privileges that apply to form class members not defined on semantic grounds. It is often difficult to evaluate the evidence, but children's early speech offers little indication of such formal generality. What are referred to in early speech as nouns, verbs, and adjectives, as well as other terms, have often barely begun to participate in the extensive network of privileges of adult grammar. Morphology is largely absent, as is the use of terms such as determiners and the verb *to be*, which figure importantly in defining word classes and constituent groupings. Accompanying knowledge of general sentence patterns is likewise slow to develop. Even as their sentences increase beyond two or a few words in length, children continue to leave out important obligatory constituents such as the initial noun phrase of declarative sentences or the verb itself (Brown, 1973; Bloom et al., 1975), showing a lack of awareness of the obligatory major constituent patterns of the English sentence. Early studies also suggest possible semantic subclass limitations on what eventually grow to be major grammatically defined form classes. Early verbs are largely terms denoting actions, though a few are not. Nouns remain denotational of concrete referents for a long time (lexicons of Adam, Eve, and Sarah, in unpublished grammars by R. Brown), and it might be more accurate to refer to these terms in early descriptions as object terms. In fact, initial subject nouns for most verbs are animate NPs, with a few exceptions for a few verbs (Bowerman, 1973; Bloom, 1970), and patients are usually inanimates in many children's beginning speech. When constituents such as possessive modifiers or other determiners begin to appear, thus justifying the use of the constituent analytic grouping NP rather than simple noun, they generally appear with end-of-sentence noun phrases, usually inanimates.

Ontogenetically, such beginnings, somewhat removed from the adult system of knowledge, may be advantageous in simplifying the child's analytic task. The particular case of nouns and noun phrases, for example, suggests how sometimes children may use grammatical definitions that are incorrect from the adult point of view in such a way as to attain easier encoding of the combinatorial privileges of other terms. The symbol NP in particular has been used in this chapter (and will continue to be) in the definition of the semantic-structural environments of many individual terms. For example, one privilege of most terms that we call verbs is that the relation denoted by them may be expressed as being in the past in the environment ##NP _____ + *ed*...(in which ## represents a sentence boundary). But NP itself represents in adult grammar a complex summation of the groupings and ordering privileges of individual terms. Using such abstract symbols as a means of defining the distributional properties of other terms that in the end will be summated over individual terms to define their class has a certain explanatory circularity, and is difficult to imagine in the child's initial representations. The child may initially, however, encode terms using representations such as object-phrase _____ + *ed*. Object phrase is an analytic notion less difficult to imagine the child formulating for the description of other terms.

In the end, nouns are not limited to concrete referents, as pointed out earlier. What may happen, however, is that distributional privileges of occurrence such as occurring after determiners and before verbs become associated with the originally semantically defined category of words denoting objects. With time, nonconcrete nouns such as *idea* or *game* come to be encoded on the basis of their distributional similarity with concrete nouns, and NP takes on its purely linguistic character. Providing this kind of mixture of distributional and semantic analysis for the ontogeny of the noun class may thus ease, though it does not solve, a number of analytic problems for the child.

In all these cases, then, we presently have little detailed account of the manner in which later attainment of the adult categorizations and structural groupings occurs, and the possibilities are often both myriad and plausible. What the child eventually achieves is a remarkable system of grammatical privileges and use of the relations among them instantiated in classes of individual terms. The beginnings in his speech are appropriate but far from the knowledge he will later attain.

G. Grammatical Relations and Children's Early Speech

I have not yet, however, considered one of the important issues in the description of early speech. This is the problem of whether children use purely grammatical structural relations such as subject and object in making their initial grammatical analyses. The question is what these relations are, what their use in early speech would signify, and what the evidence is that the child in some way employs them.

The general reason for interest in their possible early use is that their definition is held to be purely linguistic, abstract, and not tied in a simple way to nonlinguistic entities such as general semantic categorizations of agent or patient or to surface distributional structure. Thus, positive evidence that children employ these relations in their first linguistic formulations would support a hypothesis that children have them innately available as means for categorizing linguistic data.

It is not clear, however, that their definition is so abstruse. The first definitional facet is distributional. In simple English active declarative sentences, there is always at least one sentence-initial NP argument, as symbolized by the rule S → NP + VP. This initial NP is the subject of the sentence. A verb may also take a postverbal NP, called the object. An inspection of a range of sentences makes it clear that subject and object are indeed unassociated with any single major semantic category:

1. John kicked the table.
2. John liked the table.
3. The table pleased John.
4. John died.

In statement 1, the subject is john, who is an agent. *John* is also the subject of statements 2 and 4 but is a feeler of positive effect (experiencer) in 2 and someone who undergoes a change of state in 4. The grammatical object of statement 1 is a patient, undergoing the action of kicking. But in 2 the object is a source of affect (stimulus), and undergoes no action, while in 3 *John,* the grammatical object is an Experiencer. In fact in statements 2 and 3, the semantic roles of the sentence subjects are exactly reversed across the two sentences, as they are for the objects.

The use of subject and object in simple sentences amounts to the following pair of statements:

1. English verbs and adjectives take at least one noun phrase argument, placed initially in declarative sentences. They may take a postverbal NP as well.

2. The semantic interpretation of the NP roles must be derived from the speaker's knowledge of the structural-semantic characteristics of each predicate. For *kick,* the preverbal NP is the kicker, and the postverbal NP the thing kicked. For *like* the preverbal NP is the experiencer of a positive affect, and the postverbal NP the stimulus for the affect. And so on.

I have simplified the case slightly by not referring to the superordinate classification predicate, but in simple sentences, subject-verb-object analysis amounts to no more than this kind of combination of distributional and semantic analyses. As Bowerman (1973) has pointed out, grammatical relations such as subject and object take their abstract definition in adult grammar from their abstract organizing role in relating the grammatical and semantic characteristics of classes of sentences. The justification for the notion of underlying grammatical subject in English in particular arises most convincingly from the operation of the passive-active relationship between sentences such as *John likes Mary* and *Mary is liked by John*. No other operation in English involves the exclusive mention of deep-structure subject in its grammatical description. Even here, underlying grammatical subject may be given the interpretation of that semantic role played by the initial NP in the active sentence of an active-passive pair. Because the notion of active sentence vs. passive counterpart can be defined by distributional characteristics, this description makes grammatical subject and object a summary reference to a more complex combination of distributional-semantic analyses rather than an abstract unitary category.

In children's early sentences (and those of months and years afterwards), there is no evidence of anything like the complex knowledge of relations among sentence types that forms the essential justification for the use of subject-object relations in adult grammars. Children's early utterances could justify no more than the relatively simple combination of semantic and distributional knowledge described above for simple active sentences. Although such knowledge would be a major achievement, it would not be one that strongly requires the recruitment of abstract purely linguistic analytic categories.[4]

Nor does the available evidence even support the hypothesis that children initially have knowledge of grammatical relations as these are defined for simple sentences. If children had an expectation that predicate structures could contain the analysis verb + object, for example, we might expect a sudden acquisition of a broad range of verb-object combinations of widely varying semantic intent. Instead, as Braine (1976) and Bowerman (1976) discuss, the child's acquisition is often characterized by piecemeal acquisition of individual or small groups of word formulas such as *want + X* or *INGESTION + X*, with many potential verb-object combinations left unexpressed. Or if children automatically analyzed the underlying grammatical structure of sentences in terms of an obligatory subject-predicate analysis (McNeill, 1970), English-speaking children ought to be especially sensitive to the obligatory use of subject NPs in English declaratives. The frequent omission of sentence subjects, however, continues long after the period when sentences are only two and three words at most, with no consistent underlying principle able to be found to distinguish those cases in which omission occurs from those in which it does not (Brown, 1973).

---

[4]McNeill (1970) in fact describes the use of grammatical relations in children's early speech as being instantiated through, and isomorphic with, semantic-distributional analyses centering around the privileges of co-occurrence terms have with nouns. Given children's early concrete definition of what we symbolize as nouns, this amounts to defining terms by means of noting their order with respect to object words, an operationalization also far removed from the use of complex and abstract purely linguistic categories.

In short, the problems with which children appear to be dealing in their early acquisition could not motivate attributing to them knowledge of the complex distributional-meaning relations that characterize the definition of grammatical relations in adult speech. Nor does the actual course of acquisition support the hypothesis that they are making the general distributional analyses combined with specific semantic analyses that the early operationalization of grammatical relations would amount to. In neither a strong nor weak sense does the research of the past years support the hypothesis that children come to the acquisition task with innate knowledge of purely grammatical categories.

III. THE ACQUISITION OF MORPHOLOGICAL STRUCTURE

As we have seen, it is difficult to discover when children know and make some use of a generalization inherent in the linguistic forms they hear and use. In the case of constituent structure and simple sentence structure, the discovery is made more difficult by the demonstration that the presence in a child's speech of a number of *possible* generalized forms does not show that he has noticed or made use of these generalizations. One possible means of discovering what kinds of generalizations are psychologically relevant for the child was uncovered: seeing what constructions emerge simultaneously in the child's speech.

In the end, what is being searched for is evidence of the child's knowledge to make productive use of patterns inherent in the language (i.e., to construct novel forms according to these patterns). The case of morphological development (i.e., children's acquisition of bound morphemes such as the past *ed*, plural *s*, and possessive *s*) has offered the most powerful demonstrations to date in the field of language acquistion that children do so.

The original means of making this demonstration did not lie in naturalistic observations of children's speech but rather in an ingenious and classic experimental procedure (Berko, 1958). In a typical Berko test for verb morphology, for example, the subject is told, "Today John biks. Yesterday he _____," and a pause is left for the subject to fill in the answer (i.e., "Yesterday he bikked.").

What the experiment illustrates is the ability to generate a novel but appropriate form according to a rule. Without such a procedure, it is possible that speakers of English might have memorized each regular past-present verb pair *(pushed-push)*, just as they must memorize individual irregular past verb forms *(broke-break)*. But because forms such as *bikked* could not have been heard, they could not have been memorized; their production thus gives positive evidence of the speaker's understanding of the generality of the construction.

Berko carried out her study with children and showed that preschoolers could perform the task. Naturalistic observations (Ervin, 1964) soon gave a demonstration just as powerful, however, that children command the generalization. Children showed this, not through making up nonsense forms of their own, but through producing incorrect but clearly rule-guided sentences like *I breaked it* and *I thoughted we were going to have some.* A form like *breaked* can also not have been memorized, because the appropriate form is *broke.* The use of *breaked* illustrates that the child has inferred from the way in which *break* acts like other verb forms that it might also share with them the privilege of expressing the past in certain syntactic contexts by the addition of *ed.*

The child's acquisition of past tense verb forms does not begin, however, with the use of overgeneralized forms. His early usage shows two chief characteristics: low use of past forms and specific memorization of individual forms. The most careful analyses of the course of acquisition have been carried out by Cazden (1968) and Brown (1973). The fact that the past forms are initially memorized is evidenced by the absence of overgeneralized forms in the first period of the child's usage. He produces *broke* and *kicked,* but not *breaked.* Irregular past tense forms are in fact more common in the child's linguistic environment than regular ones (Slobin, 1971), for such forms *(ran, saw, thought, got),* though a small minority of English past verb forms, are very common in monosyllabic common verbs used around the child.

At the same time, the child at first does not usually use past forms when the nonlinguistic context indicates he should. Speaking of someone who has just fallen, he might say "he fall." Gradually, the percentage of instances rises in which he should use the past form and does. Around the time the child supplies the regular past tense marker *ed* in about half of its contexts of obligatory use, overregularized forms such as *breaked, broked, goed,* and *runned* begin to appear.

The late flowering of overgeneralized forms and the early uniformly correct use of irregular ones demonstrates that the child begins with specific, term-by-term memorizations of indidual past tense forms. Only when he has stored sufficient numbers of specific instances of past tense verb forms instantiating the rule does the general pattern emerge in his use. Thus it is clear that a child need not use a general analysis immediately for us to find that he eventually attains it, a methodological fact relevant to the studies of early sentence structure, in which general analyses failed to be instantiated in the child's initial acquisition. The study of morphological development happens to benefit from the possibility for overregularization in the case of irregular forms, a possibility not so easily discerned in the case of simple sentence constituent structure.

Earlier reports indicated that when the generalized past tense rule appears, irregular forms are completely driven out of the child's grammar (McNeill, 1966). The child for a while no longer says *broke* and *went,* but *breaked* and *goed.* Such reports, however, arose from less complete samples. What we now know is that the child during this time will alternate between possible forms. In spontaneous speech records of one child observed for an hour a week by S. Kuczaj and me, for example, the forms *breaked, broke,* and *broked* all appeared within one sample, as did forms such as *thought* and *thoughted* in another sample. Cazden (1968) reports similar alternations between *goed* and *went.* Kuczaj (1978), using a judgment task, has furthermore found that 3-, 4-, and 5-year-olds often find related forms such as *fell* and *falled,* or *broke* and *broked,* to be equally acceptable expressions.

The child thus does not necessarily lose irregular, memorized forms upon the learning of a general pattern. His acquisition lacks the characteristic of requiring absolute consistency in his expression of a form-meaning relationship. His acquisition fails to be "all or none" in another way, too. Even after the acquisition of generalizable knowledge, he does not reliably always use the past form when required. Over time, the proportion of instances in which the past form should be used and is, rises gradually, reaching asymptote at correct obligatory use only after months or years.

As Brown notes (1973), the absence of a sudden switch from nonuse to use has the feel of a gradual learning curve rather than the sudden acquisition and complete use of a rule. In the case of the past tense, however, it might be confusing to the child that sometimes the past form is regular and sometimes not, and occasionally is even the same as the present form *(hit-hit).* This cannot be the explanation, however. For gradual acquisition rather than a sudden shift to asymptotic use occurs even when the rule usage is regular. The verb ending *ing,* for example, marking a complex semantic of present ongoing activity, is almost completely regular. Any verb the meaning of which is compatible with the semantics of the ending may take the progressive. Nevertheless, the acquisition of the progressive *ing* also fails to show sudden complete use, as is so for a number of other morphemes studied by Cazden and Brown.

What does the course of acquisition, plus a consideration of how children must acquire this knowledge, tell us about their analytic abilities? A great deal. The child does not generalize possible morphological relations immediately. Instead, a number of related forms must be learned. The kinds of resemblances among forms he must be able to notice are three in nature: phonological, semantic, and distributional. The child must notice the relevance in the first place of comparing what we already know to be related forms; he must notice the relevance of comparing *dog* to *dogs, kick* to *kicked,* and so on, to draw from the initially individual storages, the generalizations about the relations between the forms. Phonological analysis has an obvious role. Morphological regularities apply to phonologically similar forms, and in particular the variation in meaning they are governed by is correlated to a phonological sequence, such as *ed* for the expression of the past on verb terms. In fact, such endings are often modulated in form according to phonological characteristics of the stem. The past tense morpheme is pronounced /t/ when following voiceless consonants, as in *kicked* and *hissed*; /d/ when following voiced consonants or vowels *(sagged, sewed)* or /əd/ after dental consonants *(fitted)*. But phonological similarity alone could not be responsible for extension to novel cases, since past-present pairs are no more phonologically related than the unrelated pairs *tick-stick* or *sick-stick*. The terms are clearly related partly on the basis of shared meaning. *Kick* and *kicked* differ in just the expression of the past meaning, as do *push* and *pushed*; otherwise they are similar. The importance of meaning is even clearer in the relation of irregular pairs such as *think-thought* and *sink-sank*, not to mention *go-went*. We know the child must eventually relate these to one another, despite their being phonologically no more related than the unrelated pair *sink-sought*. We know this because eventually they only use *thought*, for example, in the environments appropriate for expression of the past meaning of *think*. Without having induced some discreet relation between pairs like *think* and *thought,* the child would simply continue to produce the rule-derivable form *thinked* as the past of *think*.

Finally, the child must use distributional analyses for deciding the possible domain of the terms. There is nothing inherent in the meaning of many verbs that finally decides the applicability of the past tensing rule. For example, children produce overgeneralized forms such as *thoughted, seed,* and *knowed*. It cannot be that children only form the generalization that terms denoting actions or changes of state may take the *ed* ending, for *thoughted, seed,* and *knowed* do not denote actions or changes of state. In fact, these overgeneralizations produced in naturalistic speech are in many ways superior to the Berko task in demonstrating the lack of semantic limitations on children's generalized understanding of the past tense morpheme. In the Berko test, the novel form is an apparently meaningless nonsense form such as *bik*. It might be, however, that the child or adult assigns a meaningful classification to the term in hearing it in a context like *Today John biks,* assuming *bik* is an action. When they produce *Yesterday John bikked,* they might be using a semantically based generalization that action terms can take *-ed* in the past. The naturalistic use of overgeneralized nonaction terms demonstrates that children can base their overregularized usage on other grounds. (Their overgeneralizations also include any actional and change-of-state verbs such as *breaked* and *runned,* so all semantic categories are covered.)

In fact, not only do their overregularizations cross semantic categories, they scrupulously observe distributional ones. As we have seen, overregularized past tense forms occur on verbs denoting what is called a state rather than an action or change of state, verbs such as *know* and *see* and *think*. Suppose children had formed the generalization that relational terms denoting states could express the past meaning of the term by the addition of *ed*? Because many adjectives denote states, we would expect to see deviant uses such as *he happied*. Conversely, in fact, children might overgeneralize past forms appropriate to state adjectives to state verbs, resulting in sentences like *he was know*. Neither of these grammatical-class crossing operations occurs with frequency enough to have been reported in the literature, nor have I seen either kind of error in naturalistic transcripts available to me. Thus children are capable of modulating their application of morphological rules according to the distributional as well as semantic characteristics of the related terms.

This leaves open the question of what distributional resemblance between regular and irregular forms the child employs in extending the past tense usage to the irregular forms. The questions cannot be answered at this time, and the possibilities are myriad. One such possibility is the analysis that terms that take a form of *do* in negatives (*doesn't kick, don't push*) often take the past tense marker. This distributional characteristic would apply to all terms that might take the past tense marker, whatever their semantic character. Or children might use a number of distributional + meaning criteria, rather than just one, to choose the terms to which the privilege of past tensing with -*ed* might be extended. Present analyses do not address this question.

A last methodological problem for the analyst of children's language lies in the need to distinguish the determinants of the child's formulation of a general pattern from determinants of his acquisition of individual terms whose behavior happens to instantiate the general pattern without his being aware of this. This problem can be illustrated by considering actual findings concerning the possible effects of semantic analyses on the acquisition of past tense forms. As pointed out above, we know that in the end the child generalizes the past tense rule along a distributional basis, because he produces state verb overgeneralizations such as *knowed* and *thoughted* and eschews the use of forms such as *happied* and *niced*. Antinucci and Miller (1976) have reported, however, that children's first use of past tense forms tends to be confined to change of state verbs such as *broke,* in which the results of the change were present at the time of reference. Similarly, Tanouye, Lifter, and Bloom (1977) have reported that children reach 90% criterion on the use of correct past tense forms more quickly for some semantic classes of verbs than others.

Among many possibilities, what may be happening in such cases is that the child is better able to analyze the past meaning for certain kinds of relations, and so learn the *individual* past tense forms of those more easily. The child may be better able, for example, to analyze the meaning of the past for an action verb such as *kick* than for a mental verb such as *like.* This kind of semantic effect must be distinguished sharply from the case of the semantic category forming a basis for *generalization* of the rule to novel uses with other terms. How could we show a semantic basis for generalization? Essentially, the only strong evidence at present for generalization in naturalistic data consists of novel, incorrect, but reasonable forms such as *runned.* Thus, an investigator would have to show that a child who had regular past tense forms in all semantic categories of verbs (e.g., action, change of state, state) for a while generalized the regular ending incorrectly only to a specific semantic category of irregular verbs. Such a child might produce *breaked* and other overregularized change-of-state past tense forms while continuing to utter only correct, memorized irregular past state forms like *thought, knew,* and *saw.* To date, this kind of evidence for a semantically restricted pattern of generalizations has not been produced. In fact, Maratsos, Kuczaj, Fox, and Chalkley (1979) report that the production of overregularized forms such as *seed, sawed, heard,* and *knowed* can occur soon after production of actional forms such as *breaked* and *falled,* and production of irregular past forms such as *saw, heard,* and *knew,.* The available evidence thus indicates not only that children must and do use distributional criteria in the process of formulating the form classes to which morphological processes apply, but also that they may do so with relatively little error or delay.

A. Acquisition of Case-Gender Systems

The course of acquisition of morphological structures is more complex in many languages than in English, which contains comparatively few morphological rules. One of the more interesting tributes to human irrationality is to be found in those languages in which word endings on various grammatical classes are codetermined by grammatical-semantic cases such as nominative, instrumental, dative, accusative, or genitive, and arbitrary, nonsystematically based noun gender classes. For example, the English speaker needs only to learn the word *the* to denote definite reference in the grammatical class of prenominal determiners. The German child must learn the terms *der, die, das, den, der, deren,* and others, and learn to distribute them according to the case, number, and arbitrary gender class of the noun. In the singular nominative alone, for example, "the" appears as *der, die,* and *das,* depending on the individual noun. One says, *Hier ist der Löffel* ("here is the spoon"), but *Hier ist die Gabel* ("here is the fork") and *Hier is das Messer* ("here is the knife"). Nor are assignments always clear. *Der* is the determiner for the masculine singular nominative case and the feminine singular dative case. *Die* corresponds to the feminine nominative and accusative singular and the plural nominative and accusative for all nouns. Pronouns are similarly arbitrary: English "it" is variously *es, er, sie, ihn,* and so on depending on the gender of the noun denoting the intended referent. Russian has an even more complex system of case-gender codetermined endings for adjectives, prepositions, and so on.

Gender assignments of nouns are completely arbitrary, without any semantic or grammatical basis, as witnessed by the differential assignments of the words for 'knife,' 'spoon,' and 'fork' above. According to Slobin (1971, from Gvozdev, 1949), observance of the arbitrary gender distinctions causes considerable difficulty to children learning Russian, far more so than the observance of the semantic-grammatically based case categories: "In Russian, for example, the child uses a single adjective inflection for each case and number combination, but does not make gender distinctions [e.g., one singular nominative for all genders, one plural nominative, etc.] [p. 207]." Slobin also reports that case errors are infrequent, as opposed to gender errors. Such evidence forms part of the data mustered by Slobin in proposing an operating principle (cf. later discussion): The use of grammatical markers should make semantic sense.

Actually, the previous discussion of the use of tense markers in English children's acquisition introduces somewhat contrary data. For if the differences between many verbs and adjectives are distributional and not semantic, as seems the case, then tense marking is partly determined by nonsemantic grounds. MacWhinney (1978) cites a more important exception, however. Observations of German children learning determiners indicate an absence of errors in *gender* markings, and sometimes reported error in *case* markings. That is, the chldren were never observed making an error such as saying *das Gabel* instead of *die Gabel* (neuter nominative instead of feminine nominative), but at various times, sometimes rather late, might make an error such as saying *den Löffel* for *der Löffel* (masculine accusative instead of masculine nominative).[5] Furthermore, McWhinney, using a Berko-type task, produces evidence that German-speaking children sometimes as young as 3 years of age can be shown a nonsense object, and depending on the pronoun used to refer to it (accusative neuter *das,* masculine *ihn,* or feminine *sie*), select the appropriate prenoun determiner in the nominative (*das, der,* and *die* respectively).

What differentiates the child acquiring German from the child acquiring Russian, assuming these respective reports are accurate, remains mysterious at present. The difference must somehow lie in the different manner of use of gender-case endings in the two languages. What is clear from the findings in

---

[5]English-speaking (and Dutch-speaking) children also make case errors in pronominal use, saying *Me wants it* and *Why me can't go?* Case errors are not so surprising, in fact. Case is not always as clearly associated with underlying semantic class as Slobin's discussion implies. For example, in English, we say *I want him to go,* using *him* in the objective even though it is the subject of the verb *go.*

English and German, however, is that children can be impressively exact in their observance of both general and word-bound semantic distributional patterns as they acquire the generalizations inherent in the morphological systems of their languages. What is impressive, in fact, is that they acquire these systems eventually at all.

IV. TRANSFORMATIONAL RELATIONS

Constituent analysis, outlined earlier, describes the regularities of relations among morphemes that can be captured by linear ordering and hierarchical grouping of elements.[6] Transformational relations, conversely, refer to relations among structures that require other kinds of description. The variety of transformational relations makes it impossible to give a uniform characterization of them, but a few examples can give an idea of them.

Transformational relations can often be stated as a kind of statement that if there is a sentence structure or substructure of a certain form, then there is also a related sentence structure that differs from the first in a specifiable formal manner. One such well-known example is the active-passive relation between sentences such as *John will like Mary* and *Mary will be liked by John*. The basic correspondence here can be stated very roughly in this form: If there is an active sentence of the form $NP_1 + V + NP_2$, there is a corresponding sentence of identical meaning of the form NP_2 + Auxiliary + BE + V + Past Participle + *by* + NP_1. Or consider the case of yes-no questions and declaratives, exemplified in pairs like *John is going away—Is John going away?; John will leave* and *Will John leave?* The regularity is roughly this: If there is a declarative sentence with a form of *have, be,* or a modal verb (such as *can, will, should*) after the subject NP, there is a corresponding interrogative sentence requesting information about whether the described state of affairs obtains, in which what would be the postsubject *have, be,* or modal of the declarative is placed *before* the subject in the question.

As a last class of examples, consider the relation among full and truncated sentence pairs *I'll go to the store if you will go to the store—I'll go to the store if you will,* or *Yes, he has taken it away— Yes he has.* This correspondence is roughly: Under certain (hard to state) conditions, if there is a sentence of the form NP + {modal, *have*} + rest of sentence, there is a synonymous sentence of the form NP + {modal, *have*}.

The above correspondences and many others can be captured in formal descriptions by a variety of devices. Transformational grammatical descrip-

---

[6]Morphology properly belongs as part of consituent analysis, because it refers to the distribution of productive systems of bound morphemes on stems.

tions have typically taken a single underlying arrangement of elements to be common to the related types, and derived one form from the arrangement by a variety of operations including permutation of elements (passives), movement of elements (interrogatives), deletion of elements (truncated sentences above), and addition of elements (passive). Interrogatives are, for example, typically given an activelike underlying form (e.g., *John will go*) and derived by movement of the auxiliary verb to the front (*John will go → Will John go?*). Truncated forms are derived from fuller forms by deletion (*Yes he has taken it → Yes he has*). Passives are generally given an underlying activelike form, followed by the permutation of the pre- and postverbal NPs and the addition of *be* before the verb and a past participle after the verb, and an addition of *by* before the NP that was originally in subject position.

Such a description of speakers' actual representations of sentential relations would set or suggest strong constraints on the way in which children analyze, store, and relate linguistic sequences. But in fact the psychologically real mechanisms by means of which speakers capture relations among constituent structures are much in dispute (e.g., Fodor, Bever, & Garrett, 1974), and even linguists do not agree on the best descriptive means available for capturing them (e.g., cf. Bresnan, 1978). Recent years have seen a flourishing of descriptions in which relations among surface structures are captured by other means for many constructions, including the passive (Bresnan, 1978), and it turns out that in most cases a variety of formal and psychological descriptions are possible.

If this is so, what can be described about the course of acquisition of transformational relations? There is no doubt that predilections about the eventual representation of adult competence may shape one's view of how children analyze the linguistic sequences they hear, how they store these analyses, and how they further draw out the relations among their stored analyses.

By and large, I think the evidence contradicts one possible description: Children's innate tendency is to form uniformly ordered underlying representations of grammatical structures, such that transformationally related structures are analyzed by the child's immediately comparing them to relevant underlying representations. The course of acquisition instead seems to show that children may for a long time store related constructions in a closer-to-surface, more specific form without generative knowledge of the relations among sentence types, and not relate these eventually by the use of uniform underlying syntactic structures (cf. Maratsos, 1978, for further discussion). The problem is difficult, however, and in the following discussion I will attempt to concentrate on those problems and occurrences in children's acquisition of tranformational relations which illustrate aspects of development in a way that gives insight into the course of acquisition regardless of our descriptive predilections.

A. The Roles of Semantics and Distributional Analysis

Once again it is important to have a sense of the varying ways in which meaningful analysis and distributional analysis can contribute to the analysis of transformational relations. Some of this will inevitably arise in the discussions of acquisition, but a general sketch is also useful.

The role of distributional analyses is clear. Transformational relations almost by definition include descriptions which refer to grammatical classes of items and particular lexical items, rather than referring only to meaning categories. For example, the passive relation is often said to involve an agent, an action, and a patient. The agent-action-patient order of active sentences corresponds to a Patient + BE + [Action + ed] + *by* + Agent order in passives.

Passives, however, are not defined or constrained by such a semantically based syntactic formula, at least for the adult speaker. Many passives consist of nonactional sequences such as *John was liked by Mary,* corresponding to the nonactional active sentence *Mary liked John.* Nor are all actional sequences amenable to passivization. Consider the two semantically close sequences *People were being nice to John* and *People were treating John well.* Despite the semantic closeness of the sequences, only the second may passivize: *John was being treated well by people.* Attempts to passivize the first or sentences related to it turn up anomalies like **John was been being niced to by people.* The crucial variable here, of course, is that only verbs may appear in passives, not adjectives.[7]

The role of semantic analyses, however, is also clear. Though not sufficient, a requisite for making the appropriate semantic-syntactic analysis of possible pairs such as *The old men liked John* and *John was liked by the old men* is to notice that the active sentence subject (*the old men*) bears the same semantic relation to the other sentence constituents as does the *by* phrase NP of the passive. Presumably this correlation of NP roles must take place for a number of individual verb-noun phrase active and passive sets before the generalization can become productive. Furthermore, it is difficult to see how a purely distributional analysis of the relation of passives to the appropriate corresponding actives could be made. In particular, *by*, which marks the underlying grammatical subject in the passive, is syntactically just a preposition. Many other prepositions can appear in the same grammatical environment without marking the underlying grammatical subject, for example, *John was beaten {near, under, because of, despite} the old men.* A semantic analysis of particular passives is thus necessary to begin forming the correct semantic and syntactic generalizations about passive-active relations.

---

[7]The problem is not the presence of a preposition following *nice.* Passives can also be formed with V + Preposition sentences, such as *John was being talked about by people.*

Without elaboration, the same general argument applies to the usefulness of semantic analyses in the formulation of the syntactic relations between such morphologically similar sets of sentences such as *he got pushed, he got to push,* or *he pushed, he was pushing,* and *he was pushed.* The essential argument is straightforward: when the multiplicity of ways is considered in which the child *could* interpret the constituent relations between and among morphologically similar syntactic structures, and what structures he could try to relate to one another (or fail to), it becomes clear how necessary is the use of semantic analyses in determining which syntactic analyses are appropriate.

As will become clear in the following pages, of course, the child does not always make just the right structural and semantic determinations, or quickly capture the generalizations about structural relations implicit in the sentences he hears and uses. On the whole, we have little information about the child's acquisition of transformational relations, and in most cases the information fails to be detailed enough to allow final or even intermediate conclusions. But enough information is available to allow us to see something of how patterns of acquisition recur or differ according to the structural and informational characteristics of the child's analytic task, patterns that both resemble and differ from those already discussed. Though not a typical transformational system in some ways, the best studied of the child's transformational acquisitions has been his acquisition of the auxiliary verb system of English, with its associated grammar of declaratives, interrogations, and negations. I shall accordingly begin with a description of what is known of this acquisition, adding some information from unpublished sources; later discussion will involve results from the study of the development of causative verbs, conjunction, and infinitival constructions considered in a less detailed fashion.

B. Acquisition of the English Auxiliary System

The English auxiliary verbs form a key part of the English expression of the grammatical relations between interrogatives, negations, and declaratives, as well as having important interactions with the morphology of main verbs. The auxiliaries themselves include the modal auxiliaries (e.g., *can, should, will, might, could,* and others), the perfective *have,* the progressive BE, and possibly the copula verb BE, which displays mixed auxiliary and main verb characteristics (examples include *he is nice, John is in there, that is a dog*).

The set is grammatically and semantically heterogeneous. What semantic category could explain the grouping together of *will, must,* perfective *have,* and *is* as a class, while excluding the nonauxiliary verbs *gonna* (going to) or *hafta* (have to)? Even the members of the auxiliary class have considerable distributional dissimilarities. For example, modals like *will* take no inflection on the main verbs that accompany it (*he will go, *he will going*) while perfective *have* co-occurs with the past participle ending on following verbs (*he has been happy, he has seen her, he has pushed her*). Finally, the auxiliary class is a small class of verbs, unlike the class of main verbs, which is also characterized by a fair amount of semantic and distributional heterogeneity.

What makes us call the auxiliary verbs a class is their sharing of *some* distributional-semantic privileges of occurrence. All members of the class, when appearing after the subject NP, can take the negative particle *n't* (*he isn't going, can't go, didn't go, hasn't left, didn't come*). Correlated with this privilege of occurrence is the presubject occurrence in interrogatives of the same terms that can take *n't: Is(n't) he coming, did(n't) he come, can('t) he see it, have(n't) they left?* All members of the class can comprise the endpoints for truncated sentences: *he is happy—yes, he is; he can come—yes, he can; he has left—yes, he has; he died—yes, he did.*[8]

The auxiliaries also help to modulate the expression of *wh-* questions, questions such as *Where will we go?* and *Who is he talking to?* These questions are related to their declarative counterparts by two differences of structure. The more difficult of these to see is the relation of the *wh-* term to a declarative structure. Essentially, *wh-* terms like *who, what, where, when, why, how* are used to ask for information about specific sentence constituents. To say, "Where did Sandra go?" is to presuppose Sandra went somewhere and to ask for information about the locational goal. Asking, "What does Hilary think?" is to presuppose Hilary thought something and to ask for information about its nature.

Grammatically, their description involves their presence at the beginning of a sentence and the absence of a constituent in normal declarative position which would carry the same grammatical function. For example, the verb *put* requires specification of a location. One cannot say *she put it*, one must say *she put it away, she put it in the house,* and so on. The locative phrase follows *put* in declaratives. But there is a *wh-* question *Where did she put it?* in which the verb *put* is used without a locative expression after it as usual, but *Where* at the beginning seems to fulfill the required role.

Similarly, the preposition *to* requires a noun phrase object. One cannot say **Mary Anne was talking to,* even though one can say *Mary Anne was talking to someone,* which semantically is no more specific. There is a *wh-* question, however, *Who was Mary Anne talking to?,* in which *to* apparently lacks an

---

[8]The last example points up a characteristic of one of the deviant members of the class, auxiliary *do*. Unlike the other auxiliaries, *do* cannot appear in full declarative, affirmative sentences, except to express emphasis, as in *he did sing*. If the active declarative form of the sentence includes only a tensed main verb (*pushed, died*), an auxiliary *do* appears in the corresponding negatives, questions, and truncation to carry tense, leaving the main verb in uninflected form: *Did he push?—He didn't push, Yes he, did (push).*

object. *Who* at the beginning, however, clearly refers to this object, and fills the required grammatical role.

These distributional and semantic facts, along with others, have led to what is probably the best justified transformational grammatical description, in which the *wh-* term appears originally in declarativelike position, and is moved to the front of the sentence by a transformational operation:

She will put it where → Where she will put it
Mary Ann was talking to who(m) → Who(m) Mary Anne was talking to

These are not quite right, of course. What is required, assuming an activelike underlying order, is the operation of a second transformation, moving the auxiliary verb from position after the subject to position after the *wh-* term and in front of the subject:

Where she will put it → Where will she put it

Linguists have generally combined this rule of auxiliary-verb movement in *wh-* questions with that for auxiliary verb movement in yes–no questions, because both involve placement of the auxiliary in front of the subject in questions. Interestingly, there are a few *wh-*like terms which do not motivate this auxiliary verb placement, including *how come* (*how come you won't look at this?*) which in semantic function and form greatly resemble *wh-* terms like *why* or *how*. The set of *wh-* terms is itself a small set of terms and clearly does not include all the terms that might appear in it on semantic grounds.

The auxiliary verb system thus interacts with a complex set of grammatical constructions to form the English system of negatives, declaratives, yes–no, and *wh-* questions. How does its acquisition proceed?

A typical description as given in Dale (1972) marks out a number of periods and important developments. In a first stage, auxiliary verbs are absent. Yes–no questions are formed by rising intonation (*he coming?*). Negatives largely consist of a sentence-initial negative form such as *no* or *not*, with negated elements appearing afterwards: *no fall! no dog,* and so on. *Wh-* questions, rather than representing free replacement of constituents by initial *wh-* terms, consist of a few constrained formulas, such as *Where NP go?* to ask for the location of NP, *What dat?,* or *What making?*. Other kinds of locative questions are absent, and the semantic and distributional range is quite constrained.

In a second period, negatives appear sentence internally, in a number of forms: *he no singing, I not a duck, he can't sing, you don't have it,* and so on. Klima and Bellugi (1966) note that the forms *can't* and *don't* are unanalyzed negatives, for the corresponding positive forms of *can* and *do* are completely absent from children's speech at this point, in either declarative affirmatives or in interrogatives, as are other auxiliary verbs. Negative forms from earlier periods also continue to occur. *Wh-* terms expanded their usage a little, but not very much.

In a third period, a number of auxiliary verbs start to appear in a range of negatives, affirmatives, and yes–no questions. *Wh-* terms begin to appear with greater semantic-syntactic variability of use, but still appear without auxiliary verbs, in questions like *What you see?* and *Why he come?.*

A period of up to months later, *wh-* questions with auxiliaries finally appear. The auxiliary verb, which had been properly placed in presubject position in yes–no questions, now initially appears in *wh-* questions in declarativelike positions. The child says *Where we should put that?* rather than *Where should we put that?* In fact, even as positive auxiliaries finally appear in appropriate presubject position in *wh-* questions (*Where should we put that?*), negative *wh-* questions continue to display misplacements (*Why he won't go?*) (Brown, Cazden, & Bellugi, 1969). The greater complexity of *wh-* questions either in analysis or in production causes difficulties for the placement of the auxiliary for periods of months to years (Labov & Labov, 1976).

C. Lexical Specificity and Alternation in Auxiliary Verb Acquisition

The emergent picture contains elements of initial specificity of analysis, especially in the use of *wh-* terms and the beginning analyses of *can't* and *don't.* Variability and instability also are found in the alternation of negative systems in the second period. But Bellugi (1967) also describes the spread of auxiliary verbs into affirmative sentences, yes–no questions, and negatives during the third period as indicating a sudden flowering of general formulations of the auxiliary system, a flowering possibly arising from a careful gathering of data beforehand about the general related privileges of the auxiliary class. Her analysis is supported by a number of careful considerations of co-occurring developments in the use of the verb *be* and the modal verbs, particularly *will.* The pattern of development of auxiliary verbs in *wh-* questions also provides evidence for sudden shifts and flowerings of tranformational analyses in the child's development. In a number of cases, however, it turns out that a finer detailed analysis shows greater specificity, instability, and slower generalizations about classes of items than suggested in this summary.

For example the frequency of auxiliary verbs in the yes–no questions of Adam, a subject observed 2 hours every 2 weeks by Bellugi, Brown, and colleagues is shown in Table 11.1. Only the frequency of properly placed auxiliaries is reported (thus, *Mommy, they can talk?* is not tabulated, while *Does it rolls?* is).

TABLE 11.1
Adam's Auxiliary Verbs in Yes-No Position

| | | | Is | | Are | | | | |
| | | | Copula | Progressive | Copula | Progressive | | | |
Sample	Can	Will	Copula	Progressive	Copula	Progressive	Do	Does	Did
20–22	0	0	1	0	0	0	0	3	0
23, 24	1	0	0	0	0	0	0	0	0
25	23	0	0	0	0	0	0	0	0
26	41	3	1	0	0	0	0	0	0
27	13	3	3	1	1	0	1	11	0
28	18	0	15	0	0	1	13	17	9
29	20	6	9	4	4	2	9	6	9

A first impressive characteristic of the table is that it includes just seven verbs. This small set in fact makes up over 95% of Adam's yes–no auxiliaries during this period; the smallness of the yes–no auxiliary set is similar in the case of a child, Abe, observed by S. Kuczaj and me for an hour a week.

There do appear to be some relatively quick simultaneous acquisitions of related subcategories: The three forms of *do*, for example, appear within a 2-week period; *will* appears close after *can*. Even so, the auxiliaries appear to leak into yes–no question position somewhat gradually in a word-by-word fashion over a period of 8 weeks, rather than suddenly entering together.

Even within each auxiliary, in fact, a detailed analysis often indicates apparent initial lexical-semantic specificity. In Table 11.1, the auxiliary *can* seems to flourish suddenly in sample 25. All 23 of these *can*-questions, however, have *I* as subject and are requests: *Can I open it?, Can I have it?* Adam did occasionally attempt *can* questions with a subject other than *I* in samples 20–25, five times with the subjects *you, they, she,* and *we*. All of these questions, unlike the *can I* questions, contain uninverted *can*. Examples include *Mommy, they can talk?* and *She can get some more bus?* The number of properly formed *can* questions with a subject other than *I* rises from 1 in sample 26, to 10 out of 20 *can*- questions in sample 29.

Similarly, of the 11 initial appearances of *does* in sample 27, 9 are with the main verb *go* (*Does it go?*) scattered throughout the sample. The restriction is largely gone by the next sample. Adam had difficulties with choosing *do* to go with plural subjects and *does* with singular subjects, producing sentences such as *Does monkeys climb on it?*. The problem was confined largely, however, to nonpronominal subjects. In samples 27–33, *do* was correctly assigned to the plural pronouns *we* and *they* 15 times out of 16, whereas *does* was incorrectly used with nonpronominal subjects 9 times out of 12.

This pattern of initial specific lexical determination, while not universal in the data, is common. It gives the feeling that Adam was breaking into the particular auxiliary combinations holding one or two elements limited to small lexical sets and expanding the set of co-occurrence possibilities, even when wider possibilities had already been instantiated in the analysis of other auxiliaries.[9]

The various related positions of auxiliary verbs thus do not become instantiated all at once in acquisition. Furthermore, the acquisition of auxiliaries in both yes–no questions and *wh-* questions shows the familiar properties of alternation between realization and nonrealization of the pattern. Individual auxiliary verbs do not appear all at once where required, but increase in usage, as was true of past tense markings (Brown, 1973; Kuczaj & Maratsos, in preparation). The developmental sequence of omission of *wh-* question auxiliary verbs (*Where we put that?*), misplacement (*Where we should put that?*), and correct placement (*Where should we put that?*) shows similar alternation patterns. The overall developmental pattern follows roughly the sequence omission–misplacement–correct placement. But children generally make no clear developmental demarcation among the three; the same child may for months or years display all three patterns in varying degree during the same chronological sample. Omission does not stop when misplacement begins, nor does either omission or misplacement end when correct placement begins. In a fascinating and complex quantitative analysis of thousands of *wh-* questions spoken by one child, Labov and Labov (1976) furthermore found that each particular *wh-* term had its own developmental curve for the gradual replacement of omissions and misplacements by correct ones. *Why* questions continued to suffer a much higher proportion of misplacements than *where* or *what* questions for months, which in turn lagged behind *how* questions. The result persisted even when the differences among *wh-* terms in the proportion of negative vs. affirmative questions and the choice of auxiliary verbs were corrected for mathematically.

I have thrown together here a number of results that may have quite different meanings, depending on the particular operations and word class. Omission and misplacement have both been used to illustrate alternation, but the underlying mechanisms for each and determination of each may be quite different. The way in which *wh-* terms affect the placement of auxiliaries, which seems to have lexical specificity, does not necessarily operate in the same way in which individual auxiliary verbs come to attain correct placement in yes–no questions. The general point, however, is that whatever the causes, sudden rule-like shifts are the exception. Gradual growth of systems, specific lexical determinations, and oscillations among forms persist here as well as in morphological developments.

---

[9]It is important to note, however, that this analysis takes into account only uses of the auxiliaries in yes–no questions. A fuller analysis of auxiliary verb use in related constructions such as declaratives is necessary for completely certain interpretation of much of the data.

There is a sense, however, in which the auxiliary verb system may be different. Morphological marker systems, as shown earlier, readily accept members as undergoing transfers of privilege. Irregular main verbs take on the regular past tense marker; irregular nouns take on regular plurals. That is, individual terms that have some major category privileges readily take on other related privileges.

The auxiliary verb system may be acquired in a less sweeping fashion than it could be. But perhaps once the system is being acquired, or has been acquired, the child thereafter takes ready advantage of the relations among distributional privileges it exemplifies and extends them easily to new terms. One way of testing this is to look for possible overgeneralizations. The semi-auxiliary verbs *hafta* and *gonna* provide two such possible cases. *Hafta*, like modal verbs, takes an uninflected main verb after in many uses (*we hafta go, I hafta go*). Its semantics are clearly modal-like, and in fact overlap with those of the modal *must*. Nevertheless, despite its being acquired after much of the auxiliary system, no overgeneralizations of the form *Hafta we go?* or *We haftan't go* are known to me by record or report. Similarly, *gonna* is mostly used by children without the verb *to be (e.g., I gonna go)* at the time they are acquiring the declarative and interrogative uses of *will*, which it thus greatly resembles in semantic and distributional privileges in declaratives. Nevertheless, no overgeneralizations such as *Gonna we go?* or *I gonnan't go* have been reported or found. It is not that children never cross grammatical class boundaries. The copula verb *be* was mentioned before as having both auxiliary verb and main verb privileges. Instances in which it takes on main verb privileges, such as *Did it be there?* and *Because he be's my friend,* appear sporadically in transcripts of Adam and Abe.

This suggests that children transfer auxiliary verb privileges in a very conservative fashion, probably because of the very small size of the class and its highly heterogeneous semantic and syntactic nature. In fact, further evidence (Kuczaj & Maratsos, in preparation) suggests that even true auxiliaries, acquired later, do not acquire related privileges quickly. Abe rather suddenly acquired the auxiliary verb *could* in declarative sentences, using it in ways overlapping distributionally and semantically with the modal *can,* and using it 38 times in 4 hours of speech collected over 4 weeks. At this time he had been using many auxiliary verbs in declaratives and yes–no questions for months, yet he did not transfer the use of *could* to yes–no questions for 3 months, when it suddenly appeared there in high frequency. Similarly the privilege $X + n't$ signals with absolute reliability many auxiliary verb privileges. Yet experimental and naturalistic evidence from a few subjects indicates that children may first acquire *have + n't* in declaratives with no generalization to affirmative uses in declarative or yes–no questions for some time afterwards (Kuczaj & Maratsos, in preparation).

These findings do not imply anything about the formal description of how the child relates interrogatives and declaratives for auxiliary verbs. They do imply something about the degree to which transfers of privilege are actively extended and correlated. We can expect that in the end we can show that the course of acquisition includes some ability to appreciate the generalities of the auxiliary system. For example, we could give sufficiently advanced subjects such sentences as *John glixn't leave now* and show their ability to infer the use of questions such as *Glix John go to the store?* But however they are encoded—if they are encoded at all for some time—the relations among auxiliary verb privileges are apparently not actively extended even when the system has been extant for a long period.

D. Overgeneralizations in the Negation and *Wh-* Term System

What kinds of factors account for the low generality of auxiliary verb privileges? Above it was suggested that the responsible factor is the low number of auxiliaries combined with the heterogeneous semantic and grammatical nature of the class. That the low number of terms by itself is not sufficient to account for lack of generalization is indicated by other developments in the system (and in other linguistic developments). For example, when children's negatives begin to include sentence-internal negatives (*He not going, You can't come*), the early period negative morpheme *no* also appears in internal position for awhile: *He no blast off*, and *That no blue, that circle*. Naturally there is no parental model for this internal use of *no*, though there are many parental models for initial *no* (*No, you can't sit on the jello*). The use of *no* in this position thus seems to represent a real overgeneralization, one probably based on the earlier resemblance of *no* and *not* positions in the child's speech, and the semantic and phonological resemblances between *no* and various of the other negative terms (*not, can't, don't*). The latter correspondence might be strengthened by the fact that sentence-initial *no* in parental speech always appears co-occurring with another negative term (*No, you can't do that*). The point is, the other negatives, assuming that this is the important generalization set, also form a category small in number. But the semantic and distributional similarities of the members of the category are high at this time. Similarly, Kuczaj (1977) has found an overgeneralization of auxiliary verb placement privilege as modulated by the *wh-*like morphemes *how come* and *how long (until)*. These take declarative-like auxiliary verb placement in questions (*How come you can do that?*). Kuczaj found experimental evidence from an imitation task that children for some time may prefer the *wh-*like order, imitating sentences like *How come a bee will eat all the honey?* as *How come will a bee eat all the honey? How come* in particular is very close to *why* in meaning and placement, and *how long* to *when;* both are used to ask for specification of constituents. Thus, even though the *wh-* system of terms is small (and may be associated with different proportions of auxiliary verb misplacements), semantic and distributional functions are still consistent enough to cause overgeneralization of privileges to other terms. The case is similar for the very occasional use of *be* like a main verb, cited above; although main verbs do not acquire auxiliary privileges, auxiliary verbs occasionally acquire main verb privileges.[10]

E. Overregularization and Misanalysis

The overgeneralizations discussed above are the more familiar kind: A term that shares with other terms some privileges of occurrence or grammatical governance takes on still other related privileges. Another kind of overgeneralization to be found in the evidence discussed above can plausibly be interpreted as arising from *misanalysis* of surrounding grammatical environment. For example, a common error in many children's speech is redundant tensing, as found in sentences such as *Did I missed it?, Does it rolls?,* and *I didn't heard it* (Cazden, 1968; Hurford, 1975; Kuczaj, 1976). The problem is not that *missed* and *rolls* are not appropriate terms to express past tense or present generic present tense, or that *heard* is an inappropriate past. Rather, it is that the child has apparently failed to analyze in acquisition or remember in production a sufficiently large portion of the relevant string. In *Did I missed it?,* for example, there is a failure to analyze or remember that the marking of tense and number on the main verb is suspended when the environment includes ##Do-form + NP + _____ ... ##. The same process is at work in overgeneralizations such as *I don't want some soup* used instead of *I don't want any soup* (Brown & Hanlon, 1970). *Some* may certainly appear as a determiner, but is not appropriate because of the use after the negative auxiliary. Similarly for the overuse of negatives in sentences like *I'm not scared of nothing* reported in some children: *No* is an appropriate negative determiner but cannot be used after a negative auxiliary in the same clause.[11]

Though it is not so clear, some kind of misanalysis of grammatical environment is probably also responsible for the use of misplaced auxiliaries in sentences like *What we should do?* and *Why we can't go?* Auxiliaries have a natural co-occurrence with the main verb. For example, in *John will kiss*

---

[10]I also note from Abe's transcripts the following sequence, showing generalization of main verb privileges to a negative auxiliary: *Her's a nice dog; Sometimes her barks; and Sometimes her don'ts.*

[11]Not all children display this overgeneralization. Two children observed by S. Kuczaj, M. Hopmann, and me over a period of months to years at the appropriate developmental points did not produce these multiple negated forms.

Mary, it is not *John* or *Mary* that are in the future, but the reference of *kiss.* Tense and aspect are thus naturally grouped next to a verb or copula. Separation from the verb, as in questions, probably offers more difficulties on analytic grounds. In yes–no questions, the auxiliary at least appears sentence initially, which probably helps the child solidify his analysis of the separation of main verb and auxiliary, as well as helps him notice the difference from the more frequent declarative sentence order. The distortion of *wh-* question placement, relative to declaratives, is also extreme, and in this case the auxiliary is not in a perceptually conspicuous position to aid in the analysis and placement. As Brown and Hanlon (1970) have noted, embedded *wh-* clauses such as *Tell me (where he should put it)* also take a declarative-like placement of the auxiliary verb, a fact that may further bias the child toward the more usual declarative-like placement. This leaves one problem, that of why negative auxiliary terms appear in misplaced position (*Why he won't come?*) well after positive auxiliaries appear in correct position. Labov and Labov (1976) have pointed out, however, that nearly all sensible negative auxiliary *wh-* questions that take verb inversion are *why* questions. It turns out that for whatever reasons, auxiliary verb inversion in *why* questions is generally the latest to occur. In the case of the subject they studied, this consideration was apparently sufficient to account for the late correct placement of negative auxiliaries.[12]

F. Other Transformational Systems

The develolpment of the auxiliary system has thus illustrated some familiar themes: specific beginnings, alternations of forms of expression, over-regularization by extension of related privileges to inappropriate terms. New

---

[12]Another account of misplacements of auxiliaries lies in an account that assumes (or supports) the reality of transformational operations such as *wh-* preposing, verb inversion, and neg-placement (movement of the negative particle from initial sentence position to post-auxiliary verb position). In this account, the initial difficulty with *wh-* questions is that they involve two transformational operations, *wh-* preposing and auxiliary verb inversion. The child may only be able to do one, and so leaves out auxiliary verb inversion, producing *What we should do?* and so on. Similarly, when the child can perform two operations, three, as required when negation is added, are still too many, and so auxiliary verb inversion is once again foregone.

The account is not impossible, but has a number of difficulties. First, why is *wh-* auxiliary verb *omission* still common when yes-no questions are flourishing? It would be expected that at this time, auxiliary verbs would appear in *wh-* questions as well, in uninverted position. The problem looks like one of children having initial trouble analyzing the presence of the auxiliaries in *wh-* questions at all. Second, why is it always auxiliary verb inversion which fails? No sentences are reported such as *Should we do what?* in which *wh-* preposing fails. In fact, failures of *wh-* preposing are generally unseen, leading to a suspicion of the psychological reality of the transformation, which might be expected to slip occasionally.

themes have also been described: in particular, overgeneralizations corresponding to misanalysis of wider environments (e.g., *Did he missed it?*) and failures of expectable overgeneralization and even of reasonably rapid generalization of privileges to possibly related terms in the case of auxiliary verbs.

The auxiliary system, however, comprises a highly limited transformational system in one sense. The major operations may all be said to apply to small, essentially closed sets of lexical items, such as the *wh-* terms, which are essentially a small, specially functioning set of noun phrases, and the auxiliary verbs, a small and somewhat peculiar set of verbs; operations with negative morphemes and determiners may also be included.

Other transformational types of relations are less limited. The passive, for example, includes in its description the permutated relation of preverbal and postverbal NPs (*John likes Mary—Mary is liked by John*), as well as the addition of morphology to the main verb. The set of terms and groupings of terms that are thus related (NPs, verb forms) is unbounded. Other such operations that apply to large grammatical categories are some of the omission or deletion operations of transformational analysis. For example, subjectless infinitival complements like *to go* in *I want to go* are often analyzed as involving the deletion or omission of an underlying subject identical in reference to a matrix clause NP. Thus, *Harry wants to go* may be analyzed as being related to the possible but nonoccurring **Harry wants Harry to go.*

There are a few naturalistic studies of the development of the major relevant systems, such as conjunction (DeVilliers, Trager-Flusberg, & Hakuta, 1976) and sentence embedding (Limber, 1973), as well as experimental studies of constructions such as the passive, and various infinitival constructions. Though developments found in these studies are relevant to some general issues to be discussed later, a thorough review of the constructions and obtained results lies beyond the scope of this review. Bowerman (1974), however, has reported a detailed analysis of the acquisition of a passive-like nonconstruction of English, one which points up both the child's sensitivities to possible permutation relations and the limitations that may obtain on the child's applications of this understanding.

For a limited number of verbs of English, the same verb appears with both causative and noncausative meaning, with a corresponding structural change. For example, consider the relation between *The door opened* and *John opened the door.* The first sentence describes a change of state of the door. The second sentence describes *John* as having brought about this change of state. The semantic-structural relations are similar in all of the following: *The ice melted, Mamie melted the ice; The box warmed up, Dana warmed up the box; The vase broke, Marion broke the vase.* The correspondence is of this form: if there is a form NP$_i$ + V or NP$_i$ + BE + Adj, and V or Adj has a noncausative meaning, there is a sequence of the form $NP_j + V + NP_i$ in which NP_j denotes a causer of the event or process undergone by NP_i.

The relation is not at all dependable. One does not say, corresponding to *The engine died,* that **Linda died the engine.* Nor does one say, as the causative of *The button stayed here,* that **Amy stayed the button here.* Instead, there are other verbs (*kill, keep*) that contain causation as part of their meaning, but have no intransitive verb structure counterpart, as do *melt* and *open.* As a result, the causative construction is not truly productive for English.

Bowerman (1974), however, found examples of errors such as *I'm gonna stay that in there* scattered throughout the acquisition literature. She was able to make a more detailed record of Christy, one of her daughters, and found that Christy made such errors occasionally for years. For a period of a few months, in fact, the child used only the verbs *stay* and *come* as causatives rather than using the appropriate verbs *bring, leave,* and *keep* (e.g., she used *Mommy can you stay this open* instead of *Can you keep this open,* or *Come her* instead of *Bring her*). The normal verbs then began to appear once more, oscillating in use with the overextended created causatives, and gradually banishing them. Occasional errors such as *I just gonna fall this on her,* however, continued to appear for years.

Again learning of correct specific instances occurred first. Overgeneralized causatives appeared relatively late, after the child had used a variety of verbs and adjectives which instantiated the relation appropriately. Overgeneralizations also occurred only after the use of matrix verbs that directly expressed the meaning of causation, such as *make* in *make it stay there.*

As Bowerman notes, the children seem to have analyzed a transformation-like regularity governing the relation between a general meaning (causation) and a structural relation (transitive–intransitive) and generalized it to novel verbs and adjectives. The acquisition pattern brings up an important point, however: to what degree did the analysis of the semantic-structural correspondence actually give rise to a general rule? In principle, the causative construction could apply to a very large number of verbs and adjectives. Yet Christy applied it to just two consistently, for a few months. Errors did occur with many other verbs, but only very occasionally. It is as though she systematically reanalyzed those two verbs as though they were members of the causative structural set, whereas in the case of others she just occasionally noticed the resemblance to true causatives. The question is not whether the semantic-structural correspondence was noticed; it is a question of the form in which it was represented and used. Later we shall see a possible choice among representational systems of potential rules that makes this a relevant question.

V. GENERAL FACTORS AND DETERMINANTS OF GRAMMATICAL ACQUISITION

In the previous review of the development of various constructions, some general characteristics of children's development have been uncovered. Now I should like to treat briefly some general problems, these including possible roles of long-term storage of grammatical analyses, general determinants of the sequence of acquisition, including the analytic predispositions of the child, and what is known of the role of the child's surrounding speech in shaping the child's acquisitions. In all these cases, the data already discussed will help elucidate more general considerations.

A. The Role(s) of Long-Term Storage of Analyses

The major problem of accounting for grammatical development remains that of accounting for how the child can draw out information from the specific utterances he is exposed to about the general transfers of grammatical privilege that individual terms may enter into. The dimensions along which the problem may be analyzed are presently all too diverse, but a consideration of the task and the extant empirical data suggest a number of possible directions.

In all possible conceptualizations of the problem, however, it is clear that the child must use analyses from long-term storage. First, for example, the child must analyze related grammatical privileges as they obtain within individual lexical terms. In the formation of the past tense rule, for example, a number of verbs must apparently be analyzed individually into the form ##NP + $X+ed$ ... ## before the generalization forms. This analysis may take place at the time of hearing or at a later time, but in either case, comparison with stored related analyses is required. For it is difficult to see how the child could segment a word like *kicked* into *kick+ed,* with the information that *-ed* denotes the past occurrence of the relation denoted by kicking, without comparison to some other form of *kick* such as *kick* or *kicking,* presumably called up from long-term storage either at the time of hearing or after or possibly after *kicked* has been stored as an unanalyzed unit. Similarly, a more difficult relation such as that of the passive–active presumably arises from the comparison of meaning-distribution formulas within individual verbs, such as the comparison of the formula [NP_1 + ... BE + *like+ed* + *by* + NP_2 = (NP_1 denotes the one liked and NP_2 the one who likes)] to the formula for the converse distribution of NP roles for the other grammatical representations of *like.*

Beyond this, in order to form the generalization, the child must presumably note that the same privileges are related to each other within a variety of terms, as well as noting the consistency with which the privileges are related. It is doubtful, for example, that the child would form the past tensing rule or the passive–active relationship from hearing the rule apply to just one verb out of many. As has been seen in the case of the auxiliary system in particular, generalizations of transfers of privilege to possible new members may be slow or nonexistent when the members of the class are semantically and structurally heterogeneous, and their privileges are also partly instantiated in other terms (such as some main verbs).

The ways in which long-term storage of individual lexical privileges may be used, however, are also quite diverse. I shall very briefly outline just two types of model. The first possibility, which I shall call the explicit rule model, is that the network of related grammatical privileges is stated separately from the individual lexical analyses from which they presumably arise. This is the kind of model implied in abstract linguistic descriptions, in which phrase structure rules and rules such as tensing or passivization are stated as separate abstract generalizations. Various terms are then marked as participating in these rules or not.

The manner in which such a description would arise presumably involves a complex and long sifting process in long-term memory, in which the occurrence of related privileges of occurrence over a variety of terms is gradually abstracted. The final product might be a network of analysis of privileges of occurrence of terms, with statements of relations between these.

In a second model, which I shall call the implicit statement model, various structural-meaning analyses are left stored individually with the terms that centrally instantiate them. Thus, various verbs would all have information stored about their privileges of occurrence in various tense and structural environments, but there would be no separate statement of these privileges. Whereas in the explicit rule model, for example, a general rule would be separately stated that all verbs must have an initial NP in declarative sentences, in the implicit rule model, it would simply be the case that all verbs were individually marked as requiring an initial NP. Generalizations or novel productions would arise not from application of a general abstract rule, but by inspection of the analyses of related terms. To illustrate, suppose the child wished to express a relation of breaking in the past, and knows that *break* may express the particular relation. If he does not know the use of the term *broke,* or its use is not secure, he might look around (speaking far too anthropomorphically) and see that a number of terms that already share some common grammatical privileges with *break* also have the privilege ##NP + $X+ed$...# = 'relation of X in the past.' This tensing privilege is transferred to *break*, resulting in *breaked.* The sequence is basically the same for a regular verb used in a syntactic-semantic environment for the first time, or for a Berko-type nonsense word task, in which the transfer of privileges is the point of the task.

It is difficult to see which of these models is to be preferred, or if either (or still others) may not apply to various degrees at different times. The second of them has certain advantages: (1) it avoids the reification of grammatical rules; and (2) it may intuitively provide a better account of many overgeneralizations that are only occasional rather than frequent. It has been a tendency, I think, in the literature to point to occasional and frequent overgeneralizations alike and refer to either as evidence for the operation of a highly general rule. But if children have formed such highly general rules that can be applied to general classes of related items, various overgeneralizations might often be expected to be more frequent when they occur at all. For example, why should Christy have applied the causative overgeneralization so systematically to just two verbs and sporadically in the case of others? It seems to me that those two verbs were actually misanalyzed as members of the lexical class of terms that take the causative relations, whereas errors with other verbs and adjectives resulted from the occasional noticing of the resemblance of those verbs to the individually stored items to which the construction applied. If both correct and incorrect causative constructions were produced by a general rule, it is difficult to see why Christy would have produced such errors so infrequently for most terms. (3) The implicit statement account makes a continuum of rules: those generalizations that apply more consistently to terms with related privileges go more easily and feel better, but there is no sharp cutoff between rule and nonrule. This may have advantages in dealing with constructions that feel semigeneralizable—such as the English causative construction—or form class extensions like *he penciled the box*. There is often difficulty in the classification of such constructions as exemplifying a rule or not. Under this description, no clear decision is necessary.

In either kind of analysis, the fact that general knowledge depends on specific storages makes evident another possibility, one of a two-tier system of productive competence (cf. Bresnan, 1978, for related linguistic discussion). In an earlier discussion it was seen how speakers had to remember much individual information about particular constructions, such as whether a given verb required an NP object or not. Even in the case in which the construction under use falls under a general rule, it is possible that speakers may use individually stored information rather than referring to the general rule. For example, in formulating a sentence about kicking, rather than making use of the general knowledge that all the terms we call verbs require an initial NP subject in declaratives, the speaker may have it individually stored for *kick* that it does and make no reference to the general rule. Or consider the possible difference between the speaker when he produces *John kicked Mary,* versus the same speaker when he produces *John glitzed Mary,* using *glitzed* for the first time after hearing *John glitzes Mary.*

In the latter case, he must make productive use of the relation between present and past tense uses of verbs. But in using *kicked*, he could be employing an already made lexically specific analysis that the form *kicked* may express the relation of kicking in the past in the environment ##NP . . . ##. In fact, both children and adults generally do better in Berko-type nonsense tasks on real forms than nonsense ones. This is so especially when the rule is one that applies to a smaller class of terms, such as the plural of terms ending in sibilants (e.g., *niss-nissess*). If the real forms are always produced by general rule-like inferences and operations, this difficulty with nonsense forms is difficult to interpret. What the linguist describes in his rules is a summation of the regularities of the related grammatical privileges of individual terms. Often what we and the child do may be generated more directly from these individually stored analyses.

In the brief space here, it is obviously impossible to sort out all the possible formulations of how the child makes and sorts out immediate and long-term analyses of related constructions. Furthermore, clearly some constructions are more amenable to one kind of long-term representation than are others (cf. Maratsos & Chalkley, in press, for further discussion). In any case, considerations in any detail make evident the complexity of the task and the powerful analytic equipment required for it. The child must draw out from specific instances of constructions the generalizations, semigeneralizations, obligatory and optional uses, and partially arbitrary lexical subcategorizations that characterize the productive system of an adult language. At present we are a long distance from being able to outline this process in any convincing fashion, and general outlines of the relevant possibilities are all that is available.

B. Factors Affecting the Relative Ease of Acquisition of Constructions

The field of language acquisition received its greatest impetus from attempts to see how the child constructed the complex rules of his language. In particular, one primary motivation lay in the attempt to evaluate the psychological reality of transformational descriptions of the adult grammar (Brown & Hanlon, 1970). Possibly, for example, the child would learn constructions in an order related to their complexity of derivation in adult linguistic descriptions. Or his acquisition might show him building up the components and operations of the adult system such that the chronological sequence outlines the synchronic organization of adult competence.

Relatedly, evidence from the relative ease and difficulty of acquiring different constructions might also comprise means of determining the more natural or preferred means of analysis for the child (Slobin, 1973). Finally, in the case of some investigators, interest has lain not in the child's acquisition of purely linguistic formulations, but in the sequence in which various cognitively based relations are expressed, whether for reasons of linguistic or cognitive development (Bloom et al., 1975).

In none of these cases should we expect naturalistic data to provide definitive answers in a simple fashion. Clearly sequences might be determined by one of a number of factors, or a mixture of them. Instances of what should be more complex constructions may deceptively appear earlier than simpler ones because in fact the child did not properly appreciate the proper complex analysis. Nor is it easy, as we have seen, to tell from a set of related uses whether the child has drawn out the fullest level of generalization they might instantiate. Investigators have nevertheless been ingenious in seeking from both detailed analyses and diverse data the possible general determinants of acquisitional sequences.

C. Frequency of Use

A nonintrinsic but possibly determinative characteristic of the differential learning of grammatical constructions lies in their being heard with differential frequency; does greater exposure to a construction by itself guarantee earlier learning?

In some cases differential frequency clearly is determinative. Brown (1973) notes that in samples of parental utterances to young children, he found no full passives at all. The late acquisition of the passive construction (Horgan, 1978; Bever, 1970) accordingly comes as no surprise. It is more surprising that children correctly comprehend some passives as early as they do, usually around 4 and 5 years of age for middle-class children.

Even when constructions are heard reasonably often, relative frequency may also play a role. Brown and Hanlon (1970), for example, were unable to disentangle frequency of occurrence and complexity of linguistic description in their study of children's acquisition of a number of auxiliary system operations. A more recent study, however, indicates that differential frequency of exposure alone is not determinative. In a sense, acquisition data offer this generalization in a direct manner. Observers have noticed the difficulty children have in stably acquiring common terms such as *a* and *the*, or the various noun and verb inflections, compared to the relative ease of acquiring various nouns, verbs, and adjectives. Brown (1973) (also de Villiers & de Villiers, 1973) has further investigated the relation of frequency of occurrence to sequence of acquisition within a group of 14 morpheme sets, abstractly characterized for study. These sets included inflections such as the plural (*dog-dogs*), the possessive (*Harry-Harry's*), past tense *-ed*, progressive *-ing*, third person singular present *-s* (*kick-kicks*), and a variety of other forms—the copula *be* and the progressive *be* in contractible and uncontractible positions, the articles *a* and *the*, the prepositions *in* and *on*, the irregular past tense verbs, and irregular third person singular present verbs (*have-has, do-does*).

This very disjunct set of forms, including both words and morphemes, has one useful analytic characteristic in common. It is possible to judge with some—though not complete—confidence when a member of the class *should* be used, given the linguistic and nonlinguistic context. For example, if a child says *I kick it,* referring to a past event, one can infer he should have said *I kicked it.* Similarly, a child who says *I found nickel* who was not looking for a particular one can be inferred to have meant what we would say as *I found a nickel.* With other forms, usage is so optional that one cannot make such analyses. For example, prenominal adjectives are almost never required; one can only note when they actually do occur.

There are naturally some difficulties, many of which Brown carefully pointed out. For example, if a child says *Look at dog,* pointing to a particular one, he might be scored as having been obligated to say *Look at the dog;* but perhaps *Look at that dog* would have been acceptable. Furthermore, the classifications are indeed abstract ones. The plural inflection, for example, is really three sounds, depending on the end of the stem: *-s* for terms ending in unvoiced consonants like *boat, -z* for terms ending in voiced consonants, and *-iz* for terms ending in sibilants (*nose-noses*). The contractible copula *be* is a summary for a group of forms which may appear in similar grammatical environments: *is, are, am, was, were, be, 'm, 're, 's,* and corresponding negatives (*isn't, aren't, wasn't, weren't*).

If the analytic criteria are accepted, however, they may be used to define a level of stable acquisition of each morpheme set in the following manner: If a child uses a morpheme 90% of the time when it is obligatory in three consecutive 2-hour speech samples, it may be classified as stably acquired.[13] When this was done for the three children Adam, Eve, and Sarah, a very stable profile of the order of emergence of the 14 morpheme sets was found, an average correlation of 0.85 between each child. de Villiers and de Villiers (1973) corroborated this result in a cross-sectional study.

Brown found that the parents also had a relatively stable profile of frequency of use of the various morphemes. But the frequency with which parents used the morphemes correlated with the children's acquisition order only 0.26, a statistically unreliable correlation in this small set. Thus, parental

---

[13]This criterion itself bears an indirect resemblance to productive knowledge of the rule. Cazden (1968) for example noted that past tense overregularizations like *breaked* occur around the point when children use the past tense 50% of the time when it is obligatory. Ninety percent may thus be a conservative criterion. In other cases, children could conceivably reach a 90% criterion by memorization of individual instances without having a productive rule, though this is unlikely. Thus 90% is a figure selected partly for convenience, not a cutoff point selected on a necessarily principled basis.

frequency proved to have little to do with the order of acquisition for these frequently heard forms.

The result does not eliminate frequency of exposure completely as a determinant, but it points up the importance of other influences. Investigators have interested themselves chiefly in the contribution of various kinds of complexity of the linguistic forms to the child's difficulties, chiefly semantic or formal complexities.

By semantic complexity, a number of things may be understood, though all of them hinge on the child's analyzing the correspondence of the use of the form to its nonlinguistic cognitive substrate.

The basic point has been made by Slobin (1973) and MacNamara (1972): A child cannot learn the form to express something properly that he cannot conceptualize. (In fact, if he uses a form to express an incorrect meaning, we will often say he does not really command the form.) Combined with this, harder conceptualizations will lead to greater difficulty in the child's analysis of their representation in linguistic forms. Cromer (1968) thus noted that the auxiliary perfective verb *have* (e.g., *I have seen it*) emerges much later in acquisition than do auxiliary verbs that are formally no more complex. Its late acquisition, coming after children hear it used around them for years, probably stems from its subtle meaning. The difference between *I have seen it* and *I saw it* is indeed difficult to analyze. The general sense of the perfective seems to lie in a meaning of "past with present relevance."

Even when the conceptual command requisite for the use of a term is available to the child, the complexity of its instantiation in particular forms may make them difficult to acquire. For example, the progressive BE (*he was going*) is marked according to four semantic dimensions: the state-process distinction, also marked by the ending *-ing;* plural-singular (*is* vs. *are*), determined by the preceding NP; past-present (*is* vs. *was*); and person (*am* vs. *is*). Its stable acquisition follows the stable acquisition of other morphemes that express fewer of these basic semantic categories, such as *-ing,* plural *-s* on nouns, or past tense marking on verbs (Brown, 1973).

More relevant to this review is the point that the formal complexity of the expression of a given meaning also affects its acquisitional order. Brown and Hanlon (1970), for example, noted the late appearance of tag questions, questions like *isn't it?* attached to sentences to ask for confirmation (e.g., *It's cold in here, isn't it?*). English-speaking children have been observed to use early simple expressions such as *huh?* that seem to express much of the same meaning. But the complex grammar of tags, which involves initial placement of auxiliaries in a contrary negative value, pronominalization of the subject, and omission of the rest of the sentence, eludes them for years. Brown and Hanlon show that children master tags only after they master forms such as pronominalization, predicate omission, negation, and initial auxiliary verb placement in questions.

Examples also abound in the wider literature in which purely formal difficulties clearly cause difficulties. Slobin cites the Egyptian plural, a mass of mostly irregular rules with different rules for duals and number after 10, which still gives difficulty to Egyptian-speaking children into adolescence (Slobin, 1973). Finnish yes–no questions, unmarked by intonation as are their English counterparts, and marked only by complex grammatical and morphological operations, emerge late in acquisition (Bowerman, 1973).

Slobin has provided perhaps the most ambitious and extensive attempt to summarize generalizations about relative acquisition ease and difficulty for various constructions (Slobin, 1973). As he points out, language is processed by the child under the constraints of short-term memory, as an auditory stream. Characteristics of the difficulty of making such analyses, as well as the difficulty of long-term analyses, will lead naturally to consequences for children's learning. Past tensing, for example, is intuitively and distributionally associated with the verb of a sentence. When we say *John kicked Mary,* what is necessarily in the past is the act of kicking, not John or Mary. In the question form, the tense marker is separated by the subject NP from the verb: *Did John kick Mary?* Such discontinuities may be expected to cause the question form to be relatively more difficult to analyze, and it does enter children's speech later (Klima & Bellugi, 1966). Slobin has stated these generalizations about greater and lesser difficulty of learning as operating principles, principles that every child is assumed to bring to bear on the problem of language acquisition, which shape his preferred analyses. The corresponding operating principle to the problem of discontinuous elements is:

Operating principle D: Avoid interruption or rearrangement of linguistic units.

Other operating principles Slobin proposes also follow reasonably from the likely constraints on short-term and long-term analysis of generalizations, such as:

Operating principle E: Underlying semantic relations should be marked overtly and clearly.

Operating principle G: The use of grammatical markers should make semantic sense.

Referring to children's well-known tendencies to form overgeneralizations, Slobin formulates:

Operating principle F: Avoid exceptions.

With each of these he lists a number of suggested universals about the course of children's acquisition with supporting evidence. For example, under operating principle E, Slobin (1973) notes universal E4: "When a child first controls a full form of a linguistic entity which can undergo contraction or deletion, contractions or deletions of such entities tend to be absent [p. 203]." In support he cites Bellugi's finding of "the clear enunciation of 'I will'—even in imitations of sentences containing 'I'll'—at a developmental stage at which special attention is paid to the auxiliary system." Similarly, cross-cultural linguistic data from a number of languages is used in support of each of the other operating principles.

There is a difference in purpose between analyses such as Brown's and those made by Slobin. Brown (Brown & Hanlon, 1970; Brown, 1973) is essentially testing the validity of grammatical descriptions. The reasoning is that if one construction may be described as involving a rule x in its description, and another may be described as involving rules x and y, and the child analyzes the constructions in this fashion, then the second construction will appear later. Truncates, for example, may be analyzed as involving deletions of the post-auxiliary portion of a sentence. In the exchange *Will you go to the store?—Yes I will, Yes I will* can be analyzed as arising from the deletion of the VP *go to the store* under complex discourse conditions; the truncate, involving an extra rule, will arise later. On the other hand, Slobin is discussing generalizations about the necessary analysis of constructions, regardless of the particular formal description. Truncates such as *Yes, I will* might also be formulated by another formal rule: If assenting to a proposition, copy the proposition through the first auxiliary, changing the person of the subject if necessary. Or the deletion analysis might be correct.[14] But in either case, the child in figuring out the rule must analyze the grammatical and semantic relation of the truncate to the full sentence, which involves, among other things, analyzing the content of the portion of the full sentence not represented in the truncate. Similarly, interrogatives such as *Who did you talk to?* may be analyzed with an operation preposing *Who* from a position after *to*, or not so analyzed. But in either case, the child must capture the relation between the sentence-initial *Who* and the co-occurrent *to*. Thus the analysis automatically involves a discontinuity, which the transformational operation provides one form of describing. If the *wh-* question is found to arise later than corresponding declaratives in which NPs appear directly after *to* (*I was talking to John*), it may be either that the formulation of the transformation provides the difficulty, or that discovering the relation despite the discontinuity causes the problem. In most such cases, the empirical consequences of the two explanations are indistinguishable. Generally, it

---

[14]Personally, I think the copying formulation is correct. Consider the case in which someone asks a long complex question, such as, "Will you agree to try to get Harriet to come to the party tonight so that she . . . [and so on]?" It is highly doubtful for reasons of memory that the reply, "Yes, I will," comes from an exact storage of the antecedent question, with deletion of all but the subject and auxiliary.

seems to me, the extra complexity entailed by the preliminary analysis necessary to formulate the linguistic description is enough to explain the relative time of acquisition. Furthermore, such descriptions that emphasize the analysis are not as susceptible to instability as a result of changes in particular linguistic descriptions. [For example, Brown (1973) uses as his source for grammatical descriptions a work by Jacobs and Rosenbaum (1968), in which a number of operations are described by featural transformations; some of these operations are described by phrase structural constituent analyses in other transformational grammars.]

Investigators such as Brown and Slobin, in different ways, are thus attempting characterization of the analytic nature of the child. It seems to me that Slobin is doing this more directly and broadly. How good is this formulation?

Both conceptual and empirical considerations suggest that many of the operating principles currently do not give an accurate general picture. Although Slobin initially describes the operating principles as arising from factors such as limitations in short-term memory or long-term storage capacity, they are eventually presented as active preferences and strategies of the child. Slobin (1973) writes, for example, "from these operating principles, a number of more specific strategies can be derived, finally resulting in language-specific strategies for the acquisition of aspects of a given native language [p. 198]."

It seems more useful, however, to think of many outcomes arising naturally from the characteristics of the working of the equipment, rather than being active preferences about how to analyze languages. For example, as outlined above, it is natural to expect that discontinuous distributional regularities would be more generally difficult to analyze than continuous ones, given the difficulties of memory and analysis. No *active* preference is required such as is implied by operating principle D (Slobin, 1973): "Avoid interruption or rearrangement of linguistic units [p. 199]." It is not a question of avoiding discontinuities; it is a question of figuring them out at all.

At the same time, it seems to me that despite Slobin's interesting supporting examples, the operating principles that actually correspond to active preferences are presently not generally well-founded. Many of them seem to be characterizations of the child's own hypothesized productive preferences and characterizations of what he can more easily acquire. One of these, which seems presently weakest as a statement of the child's own analytic productive tendencies, is operating principle E: Underlying semantic relations should be marked overtly and clearly. For example, Bellugi's 1967 paper, which contains the *will-'ll* evidence cited by Slobin, also contains data that forms a strong exception: When children begin to control the full form of the copula BE (e.g., *he is happy*), they continue to use and extend the domain of the contracted form (*he's happy*). No apparent tendency arises to use only the full form and suspend the use of the contracted forms. Other individual developments also contradict the general formulation. An inspection of transcripts from Brown's three subjects, Adam, Eve, and Sarah, as well as Abe, shows that even when relative pronouns begin to appear (*I see one that goes*) they are usually left out when not obligatory (*Here's the onion we picked*). Also, in a number of cases children do not seem to have as much difficulty learning a form that may be analyzed as having underlying material deleted, as a fuller form. For example, de Villiers, Trager-Flusberg, and Hakuta (1976) studied the acquisition of sentential conjunction (*Harry sang and Mary sang*), NP conjunction (*Harry and Mary sang*), and VP conjunction (*Harry sang a song and danced*). Both analytically and derivationally, sentential conjunctions may be taken as the source for the others, by means of deletion: *Harry and Mary sang* can be analyzed as related to *Harry sang and Mary sang*. Similarly for VP conjunctions (*Harry sang a song and Harry danced* → *Harry sang a song and danced*). In any case, they give a fuller representation of underlying material. DeVilliers and co-workers find, however, that all three conjunction types were acquired at once in Brown's three subjects; of the three types, in fact, sentential conjunction was initially used in much lower proportion than it later was. Similarly, various observers have noticed that although subjectless infinitives may be viewed as taking their analysis from full sentential infinitives (*Harry wants to go* is thus related to an underlying *Harry wants Harry to go*), subjectless infinitives appear before full sentential infinitives (*I want Harry to go*) in children's speech.

Perhaps more important, the picture of acquisition discussed earlier of various forms shows that children continue to omit them often even after some acquisition. They leave out obligatory sentence constituents such as subjects for months to years after beginning to express them. All of the 14 morpheme sets discussed by Brown (1973) appeared more and more often over a long period in their obligatory environments, rather than suddenly appearing wherever required. Even after overgeneralizations of the past tense appear, for example, it is still often omitted. Similarly for the auxiliary verb in declaratives and questions. The picture does not suggest a child who is determined to mark underlying relations in a clear and overt fashion.[15]

In fact, earlier Slobin discusses a general principle of acquisition, one appropriate for both cognitive and linguistic acquisition, and one that

---

[15]Slobin's original principle may be limited to just those cases when the child clearly intended to express the meaning—thus the confinement to instances when the child marked with a full form rather than with a contracted or zero form. In the case of omission of obligatory forms, it may be that the child sometimes did not intend to express the meaning at all. The point that omissions take place for a long time, however, still suggests the child's general willingness not to mark relations that he can mark.

receives some empirical support (e.g., Kuczaj & Maratsos, in preparation; also see Slobin's discussion): New forms first express old functions, and new functions are first expressed by old forms. The expression of new fuunctions with old forms seems contradictory to giving a clear marking to underlying semantic relations. It seems reasonable that the child would seek out new forms to express new functions if he were more concerned with clear marking, though this may be an incorrect inference.

Recent data also shed light on another of the operating principles: Avoid exceptions. At the time Slobin wrote, it seemed, for example, that newly formed regular rule systems drove out old formulations; he described overregularized forms such as *breaked* or *broked*, for example, as driving out correct irregular ones such as *broke*. At least in the case of English, we now know this not to be so. Irregular and overregular forms continue to coexist for long periods of time. Relatedly, children have been discussed earlier as showing no tendency to make their grammatical descriptions completely uniform; for example, misplacement of auxiliary verbs in *wh-* questions alternates with correct placement for long periods (e.g., Labov & Labov, 1976).

In fact, a review of what is presently known indicates that while the child does make many overgeneralizations, there are many he could be expected to make that he does not, a problem for any theory of acquisition. For example, as full sentential infinitives entered children's speech, we might expect a reanalysis of subjectless ones as exceptions, essentially their treatment in many transformational descriptions; the result would thus be many utterances such as *I want I to go* or *He tried (for) me to come*. Such utterances are rare or, in the case of verbs that normally take only VP complements (such as *try*), nonexistent. Another example is children's learning of full and reduced post-nominal modifiers such as *The dog that is in the yard—The dog in the yard* and *The boy who is singing a song—The boy singing a song*. In all these cases, the full form could be related to the shorter form by an operation of deleting (relative pronoun + BE). Yet, for whatever the reason, children's acquisition fails to yield up forms such as *The book big,* an overgeneralization from *The book that is big*. Before we saw how possible overgeneralizations failed to occur in the auxiliary verb system because of the small and heterogeneous nature of the set. In cases such as these, the reasons are not clear; we can only say that the child either fails to notice the possible generalizations, or that somehow he does so in a manner that nevertheless fails to lead to frequent error. Our study of such problems is clearly just beginning.

Finally, I should like to consider operating principle G: The use of grammatical markers should make semantic sense. Slobin based this generalization on findings that children often became confused by arbitrary noun gender systems, while rarely crossing form class and case boundaries in their use of grammatical markers.

As discussed earlier, however, both empirical and conceptual considerations weaken the force with which this principle applies. Whatever the reasons, children learning German seem to make few errors that cross gender boundaries, whereas case errors are known there and in English (and Dutch) also, as discussed earlier. More important, form class boundaries such as verb vs. adjective are not defined by semantic categories. As discussed earlier, verbs and adjectives may share overlapping semantic characteristics. It is their distributional differences in interacting with the surrounding grammatical environment that defines them. In this way, in fact, they are similar to gender boundaries. (The distributional differences between verbs and adjectives are usually clearer than those among different noun categories, and there are some statistically though not categorically definitive semantic differences between verbs and adjectives.) Children's observance of form class boundaries in the use of grammatical markers thus shows an ability to formulate in a natural way analyses that rest on a partly nonsemantic basis.

In the end, the picture of the child that emerges, I think, is of a less actively organizing and clearly expressive organism, though still one to whom formidable analytic talents must be accorded. At the same time, the evidence indicates an organism better able to free himself from purely semantic bases in the formulation of linguistic categories and operations than we might have thought. He is thus an apt student for the learning of the human languages that surround him, which like most naturally evolved human systems are partly systematic and clear in formulation, but also in various degree unclear, unsystematic, filled with various exceptions, and based on sometimes arbitrary internal definitional grounds.

D. Parental Speech and the Learning of Language

Investigators of linguistic acquisition have sought to understand the process better not just through analyzing the child's own constructions, but also through analysis of the kind of speech children receive as data. Chomsky (1959) in particular posited that children received a very degenerate and difficult linguistic environment, an environment, like the speech of adults to each other, full of false starts, misleading pauses, and other errors, thus increasing the difficulty of the acquisition task. He did, however, assume that the child might receive examples of sentences judged as grammatical or not (1965) and might have judgments and corrections of his own utterances made by the speech community.

Chomsky both overestimated and underestimated the helpfulness of the speech surrounding the child. The overestimation lay in the notion that children might receive correction of their own grammatically incorrect sentences, with pointed exemplification of correct counterparts. Brown and Hanlon (1970) investigated this hypothesis, studying whether signs of approval such as "That's right" or "Uh-huh" were more likely to follow grammatically correct utterances, with signs of disproval such as "No, that's wrong" for ungrammatical utterances. Their findings were straightforward. Parents did give signs of approval and disapproval, but not on the basis of grammaticality. Ungrammatical utterances were as likely to receive approval as grammatical ones, and grammatical utterances were as likely to be disapproved. For what the parents chiefly commented on was the *accuracy* of the child's utterance. A child who said, "Walt Disney comes on Tuesday nights" was corrected because he named the wrong evening. A child who said "Her curl my hair" heard "Uh-huh" because her mother was curling the child's hair.

Nor were grammatical utterances more efficient in communication. Brown and Hanlon judged whether an adult response showed comprehension or not by the presence or absence of signs such as sensible conversational continuation or by signs of miscomprehension such as "What?" They found that utterances such as *Where we should put that?* communicated as effectively as more grammatical counterparts.

Among other things, these findings indicate that children come to approximate adult speech structure without overt pressure. This fact makes it difficult to understand why children apparently give up reasonable overgeneralizations and misanalyses with, to our knowledge, no application of disapproval or strong communication pressure. Perhaps the most curious aspect is why children give up generalizations because of arbitrary lexical subcategorizations. Why stop producing *breaked,* for example?

There is a related, perhaps more serious, problem, in fact, in children's learning arbitrary lexical subcategorizations about essentially regular terms. For example, *cheerful, sad,* and *happy* are semantically similar. One can say *To VP made him* {*happy, sad, cheerful*} (e.g., *To go made him cheerful*); one can also say *He was* {*cheerful, sad, happy*} *about VPing (going).* But only *happy* and *sad* appear in the environment NP + BE + _____ + *to* + VP (e.g., *He was happy to go*); *cheerful* does not (**He was cheerful to go*). Why do such uses of *cheerful* sound bad? They follow from the general patterns of the language, and numbers of similar adjectives appear in all the related environments. If the point of learning linguistic generalizations is to be able to extend terms to new uses in productive generalized ways, and to understand and produce sequences never heard before, it is difficult to see how children and adults continue to produce some novel (acceptable) utterances but give up others or refrain from others.

One possibility is this: When a number of semantic-structural sequences are possible for the instantiation of a meaning with a particular lexical item, if only one or two occur but occur with some frequency, these gain relatively high familiarity. Nonoccurring possible forms gain none, and the contrast between these levels of familiarity leads to an eventual relinquishment and disapproval of the unused form. For example, *to VP made X cheerful* or *X was cheerful about VPing* occur with some frequency in declarative uses about someone being made cheerful by a prospect; *X was cheerful to go* does not occur. The relative familiarity of the other forms for the same meaning is thus high. An explicit prediction of this hypothesis is that speakers will not have such sharp intuitions about the possible related syntactic-semantic forms for lexical terms that are rarely used at all, because none of the possibilities will gain particular strength over the other. This is certainly true of nonsense terms, which tend to sound all right in any related environment (e.g., *to go made him glix, he was glix about going, he was glix to go.*) Once again, however, it is clear that our knowledge is at a very primitive point.

Parental speech thus seems to be no direct help in channeling the child's choice of forms. It does, however, exemplify a number of characteristics that may make linguistic analysis simpler for the child. Parents (and other children, according to Schatz and Gelman, 1973) do not talk to younger children as they do to older children or each other. Their speech to younger children is shorter, more repetitive, less complex, more grammatical, more tied to the immediate speech context, and contains pauses in important structural boundaries to a greater degree (Broen, 1964; Brown & Hanlon, 1970; Phillips, 1973; Shatz & Gelman, 1973).

Investigators have found specific patterns in parental speech that may aid the child's analysis of particular constructions. Brown and co-workers (1969) report the parental use of devices such as *prompts,* in which the parent tries a form closer to the declarative order in asking *wh-* questions: *You saw what?* may follow upon the lack of answer from the child to *What did you see?* Such exchanges might aid the child in forming structural correspondences between related forms. Parents also sometimes make use of what has been called *expansions* (though many parents use these very little, Nelson, 1973), in which a parent, probably trying to make sure that he or she understands the child's sentence, repeats it in a fuller form:

Child: Mommy lunch.
Adult: That's right, Mommy is having lunch.

The efficacy of such devices in aiding acquisition is presently not generally known, though in one case the efficacy of a practice in speeding acquisition does seem supported by the evidence. Newport, Gleitman, and Gleitman (1977) found that children came to use modal auxiliary verbs such as *can* and *will* faster if their parents more frequently used these in sentence-initial positions in requests such as *Can you come here?* Findings such as these point out that in fact parents may make the acquisition task harder for children sometimes by oversimplifying the input. The use of modals in requests was generally competitive with use of a simpler imperative form (*come here*).

At present, then, the child is known to receive a linguistic input that does not guide his grammar directly by reinforcement or communication pressure but may be suited to help his acquisition in various ways. Generally, however, more specific aspects of how surrounding speech may aid his acquisition of specific constructions are not presently well understood or formulated. Nor do such possible devices obviate the problem of how the child eventually comes to relate constructions in a generalized manner, though in particular cases (e.g., prompts), characteristics of the input may aid in the analysis of specific examples.

VI. LATER ACQUIRED KNOWLEDGE

In the present review I have concentrated largely on knowledge of the development of forms arising in the preschool years. It remains to note that in a number of important cases, grammatical knowledge seems to arise relatively late, or at an unknown time. The passive, for example, comprises one of the analytically central constructions of English (Chomsky, 1957) in terms of its role in defining underlying relations across differing surface structures. Middle-class children seem to be able to comprehend passives containing action verbs (e.g., *John was hit by Mary*) by 4 or 5 years of age (Bever, 1970; Maratsos & Abramovitch, 1975). Other evidence suggests (Horgan, 1978) that the ability to produce simple actional passives in a stable and flexible manner may nevertheless be a much later acquisition. Furthermore, we have little information on children's comprehension of nonactional passives such as *John was liked by Mary,* and as noted before, it is the application of the passive–active relation across a variety of semantic types that gives it its syntactically autonomous character. In fact, experimental work with a questioning task by D. Fox, M. Chalkley, and me (Maratsos, Kuczaj, Fox, & Chalkley, 1979) indicates that children's comprehension of nonactional passives may be a much later development, indicating the lateness of children's analysis of the general, purely structural relations among active and passive sentences. Similarly, children do not seem to appreciate abstract, lexically subcategorized differences in underlying relations as controlled by different adjectives until a mental age of about 6½ (cf. Chomsky, 1969; Cromer, 1970); given sentences such as *The girl is easy to see* and *The girl is eager to see,* they tend to interpret the subject as the subject of the infinitive for both cases, even though in the *easy to see* case, the girl is the seen, not the seer. In other cases we simply have no information. A central characteristic of *wh-* questions and other constructions, for examples, lies in their unbounded nature (Ross, 1967). A *wh-* term at the beginning of a sentence may substitute for a constituent whose declarative sentence location can be in principle infinitely embedded. Not only can we ask *Who(m) was John talking to?,* but also *Whom does Mary say John was talking to?,* or even *Whom does Mary say John was trying to convince Sam that Harriet thought Hilary was talking to?* Children's spontaneous utterances, not surprisingly, offer no evidence that concerns their ability to generalize such constructions into embedded clauses, and experimental evidence is completely lacking.

It is thus true, as many have noted, that by 4 or 5 years of age a child has come to command much of the structure of his native tongue, and speaks with great fluency. But it is also true that acquisition of many central structural characteristics that help define the abstract scope of adult language are acquired either late or at a period we do not know of at present.

VII. CONCLUSIONS

The chief emphasis in this review has been on two related themes: (1) the gradual growth of children's productive use of language from specific to general analyses and the continuing tension among these both in acquisition and in adult languages; and (2) the complex interweaving of semantic and distributional analyses that the child must make in learning to speak his native language. We have seen both undergeneralization and overgeneralization in the child's analysis, not surprising given his circumstances of acquisition, and both semantic and distributional influences upon his acquisition, appropriate for the acquisition of a human language. At the same time, the evidence shows the degree to which the child is willing to observe both distributional and semantic contingencies in analyzing a language, rather than strongly favoring purely semantic bases.

Aside from particular questions, however, one central one has yet to be discussed: To what degree does the child's manner of acquiring language show him to be equipped with innate knowledge of purely linguistic ideas that he applies actively to the course of acquiring language? Despite the paucity of conclusive envidence, it seems to me that the positing of well-formed, innate, actively used, specifically linguistic ideas is presently difficult to justify. In this chapter, we have discussed how early speech offers little evidence for the use of purely linguistic formulations such as abstract underlying grammatical relations. Furthermore, despite the impressive complexity of the child's acquisition and the conceptual difficulty of imagining how he performs the task as well as he does, I think we could expect to see faster generalizations and more overgeneralizations if the child were actively analyzing the data according to general possibilities offered by well-developed innate schemas. For example, *wh*- questions appear to remain limited formulas or to remain limited to use with a small set of co-occurrent verbs and prepositions for a very long period. The operation is a common one thoughout the world's languages and is of a basic transformational type. A child with highly developed grammatical ideas, if he commands a few structural pairs such as *What you making?* and *I making NP* or *Where NP go?—NP go there,* should be able to abstract the co-occurrence relations between *wh*- terms and their declarative sentence counterpart constituents with great swiftness. Instead, the development is a slow and gradual one even after the acquisition of particular formulas (Klima & Bellugi, 1966). In other cases, we have seen how generalizations arise only slowly from a related set of instances or constructions the child commands.

This leaves open other questions, of course, such as whether the generalizations and rule schemes that emerge eventually in acquisition require our positing of innate structure-forming schemas or analytic devices specific to language. The problem is both an empirical and conceptual one: What are the characteristics of the analyses we end up devising to account for the evidence we gather? At present both the evidence and the conceptualizations—particularly the latter—are in such primitive states that there is little to be said. The distributional and semantic analysis the child makes are complex and, at present, defy our ability to describe them in any convincing way that does not entail the use of reifications such as linguistic symbols. Nevertheless, no development or analysis has yet been described in detail that defies a description in terms of combined distributional and semantic analyses of the concurrent linguistic and situation evidence available to the child. Neither distributional nor semantic analysis seems intrinsically to comprise an ability that would be confined to language in its employment, though clearly their instantiation in linguistic acquisition is more complex than we know it to be anywhere else in human cognitive functioning. This may, however, be only a result of our ignorance of other aspects of human cognitive functioning.

It should be evident, then, how much we know and yet do not know. The basic problem is that the child does not hear rules. He hears only utterances and terms used in nonlinguistic contexts in such ways that generalizations are instantiated throughout a range of utterances, each of which he hears only one at a time. We presently have some illustrative knowledge of the kinds of analyses and misanalyses the child may make, and the beginnings of methodologies for investigating these further. But our knowledge is still scant regarding the course of particular acquisitions, what specific analyses are stored, how specific analyses stored over a number of occasions are related to one another, and how the results of these final analyses are represented. Much is yet required for us to be able to make convincing delineations of how children come to learn the curious mixture of productive generality and detailed specificity that comprises a human language.

ACKNOWLEDGMENTS

This paper was written partially with the support of NIH Grant 1 R01 HD MH 09112-9. I would like to thank Dana Fox, Mary Anne Chalkley, Amy Lederberg, and Marion Perlmutter for comments during the writing of the paper. Special thanks are due to Roger Brown for permission to analyze data from the longitudinal study of three subjects followed by him and associates.

REFERENCES

Antinucci, F., & Miller, R. How children tak about what happened. *Journal of Child Language,* 1976, *3,* 167–190.

Bellugi, U. *The acquisition of negation.* Unpublished doctoral dissertation, Graduate School of Education, Harvard University, 1967.

Berko, J. The child's learning of English morphology. *Word,* 1958, *14,* 150–177.

Bever, T. G. The cognitive basis for linguistic structures. In J. R. Hayes (Ed.), *Cognition and the development of language.* New York: Wiley, 1970.

Bloom, L. *Language development: Form and function in emerging grammars.* Cambridge, Mass.: MIT Press, 1970.

Bloom, L., Miller, P., & Hood, L. Variation and reduction as aspects of competence in language. In A. Pick (Ed.), *The Minnesota Symposium on Child Psychology* (Vol. 9). Minneapolis: University of Minnesota Press, 1975.

Bowerman, M. *Early syntactic development: A cross-linguistic study with special reference to Finnish.* Cambridge, Mass.: Cambridge University Press, 1973.

Bowerman, M. Learning the structure of causative verbs: A study in the relationship of cognitive, semantic and syntactic development. *Papers and Reports on Child Language Development,* Committee on Linguistics, Stanford University, 1974, No. 8, 142–178.

Bowerman, M. Commentary on Bloom, Lightbown, and Hood. In *Structure and variation in child language. Monographs of the Society for Research in Child Development,* 1975, (Serial No. 169).

Bowerman, M. Semantic factors in the acquisition of rules for word use and sentence construction. In D. Morehead & A. Morehead (Eds.), *Language deficiency in children: Selected readings.* Baltimore: University Park Press, 1976.

Braine, M. D. S. The ontogeny of English phrase structure: The first phrase. *Language,* 1963, *39,* 1–13.

Braine, M. D. S. Children's first word combinations. *Monographs of the Society for Research in Child Development,* 1976, Serial No. 164.

Bresnan, J. A. A realistic transformational grammar. In M. Halle, J. Bresnan, & G. A. Miller (Eds.), *Linguistic theory and psychological reality.* Cambridge, Mass.: MIT Press, 1978.

Broen, P. The verbal environment of the language-learning child. American Speech and Hearing Association Monographs, 1964, (No. 17).

Brown, R. Derivational complexity and order of acquisition in child speech. In R. Brown, *Psycholinguistics.* New York: Free Press, 1970.

Brown, R. *A first language: The early stages.* Cambridge, Mass.: Harvard University Press, 1973.

Brown, R., Cazden, C., & Bellugi, U. The child's grammar from I to III. In J. P. Hill (Ed.), *Minnesota Symposium on Child Psychology* (Vol. 2). Minneapolis: University of Minnesota Press, 1969.

Brown, R., & Hanlon, C. Derivational complexity and order of acquisition. In J. R. Hayes (Ed.), *Cognition and the development of language.* New York: Wiley, 1970.

Cazden, C. The acquisition of noun and verb inflections. *Child Development,* 1968, *39,* 433–438.

Chomsky, N. *Syntactic structures.* The Hague: Mouton, 1957.

Chomsky, N. Review of Skinner's *Verbal behavior. Language,* 1959, *3,* 26–58.

Chomsky, N. *Aspects of the theory of syntax.* Cambridge, Mass.: MIT Press, 1965.

Chomsky, C. *The acquisition of syntax in children from 5 to 10.* Cambridge, Mass.: MIT Press, 1969.

Clark, R. Performing without competence. *Journal of Child Language,* 1974, *1,* 1–10.

Cromer, R. F. *The development of temporal reference during the acquisition of language.* Unpublished doctoral dissertation, Harvard University, 1968.

Cromer, R. F. Children are nice to understand: Surface structure clues for the recovery of a deep structure. *British Journal of Psychology,* 1970, *61,* 397–408.

Dale, P. S. *Language development: Structure and function.* New York: Dryden Press, 1972.

de Villiers, J. G., & de Villiers, P. A. A cross-sectional study of the acquisition of grammatical morphemes in child speech. *Journal of Psycholinguistic Research,* 1973, *2,* 267–278.

de Villiers, J., Trager-Flusberg, H., & Hakuta, K. *The roots of coordination in child speech.* Paper presented at the first annual Boston University conference on language development, Boston, October 1976.

Ervin, S. Imitation and structural change in children's language. In E. H. Lenneberg(Ed.), *New directions in the study of language.* Cambridge, Mass.: MIT Press, 1964.

Fillmore, C. J. Types of lexical information. In D. Steinberg & L. A. Jakobovitz (Eds.), *Semantics.* Cambridge: Cambridge University Press, 1971.

Fodor, J., Bever, T., & Garrett, M. *The psychology of language.* New York: McGraw-Hill, 1974.

Gvozdev, A. N. *Usvoyeniye rebenkom zvukovoy storony russkogo yazyka.* Moscow: Akad. Pedag. Nauk RSFSR, 1949.

Horgan, D. The development of the full passive. *Journal of Child Language,* 1978, *5,* 65–80.

Hurford, J. R. A child and the English question formation rule. *Journal of Child Language,* 1975, *2,* 299–301.

Jackendoff, R. S. *Semantic interpretation in generative grammar.* Cambridge, Mass.: MIT Press, 1972.

Jackendoff, R. S. Toward an explanatory semantic representation. *Linguistic Inquiry,* 1976, 89–150.

Jacobs, R. A., & Rosenbaum, P. S. *English transformation grammar.* Waltham, Mass.: Blaisdell Publ., 1968.

Katz, J. J., & Postal, P. *An integrated theory of linguistic descriptions.* Cambridge, Mass.: MIT Press, 1964.

Klima, E. S., & Bellugi, U. Syntactic regularities in the speech of children. In J. Lyons & R. J. Wales (Eds.), *Psycholinguistics papers.* Edinburgh: Edinburgh University Press, 1966.

Kuczaj, S. A., II. Arguments against Hurford's "Aux Copying Rule." *Journal of Child Language,* 1976, *3,* 423–427.

Kuczaj, S. A., II. Overgeneralization of a sentential placement rule. Manuscript submitted, 1977.

Kuczaj, S. A., II. Children's judgments of grammatical and ungrammatical irregular past tense verbs. *Child Development,* 1978, *49,* 119–128.

Kuczaj, S. A., II, & Maratsos, M. P. *The later acquisition of the English auxiliary system.* Manuscript in preparation, 1977.

Labov, W., & Labov, T. *Quantitative analysis of wh-preposing in language acquisition.* Paper presented at the International Congress of Linguistics, Glasgow, Scotland, July 1976. To appear in the proceedings of the conference.

Limber, J. The genesis of complex sentences. In T. E. Moore (Ed.), *Cognition and the acquisition of language,* New York: Academic Press, 1973.

Lyons, J. *Introduction to theoretical linguistics.* London: Cambridge University Press, 1968.

MacNamara, J. Cognitive basis of language learning in infants. *Psychological Review,* 1972, *79,* 1–13.

MacWhinney, B. Processing a first language: The acquisition of morphophonology. *Monographs of the Society for Research in Child Development,* 1978.

Maratsos, M. P., & Chalkley, M. A. The internal language of children's syntax. In K. Nelson (Ed.), *Children's language* (Vol. III). In press.

Maratsos, M. P. New models in language and language acquisition. In M. Halle, J. Bresnan, & G. A. Miller (Eds.), *Linguistic theory and psychological reality.* Cambridge, Mass.: MIT Press, 1978.

Maratsos, M. P., & Abramovitch, R. Children's understanding of full, truncated, and anomalous passives. *Journal of Verbal Learning and Verbal Behavior,* 1975, *14,* 145–157.

Maratsos, M. P., Kuczaj, S. A., II, Fox, D. E. C., & Chalkley, M. A. Some empirical studies in the acquisition of tranformational relations: Passives, negatives, and the past tense. In W. A. Collins (Ed.), *The Minnesota Symposium in Child Psychology* (Vol. 12). Hillsdale, N.J.: Lawrence Erlbaum Associates, 1979.

McNeill, D. Developmental psycholinguistics. In F. Smith & G. Miller (Eds.), *The genesis of language.* Cambridge, Mass.: MIT Press, 1966.

McNeill, D. *The acquisition of language: The study of developmental psycholinguistics.* New York: Harper & Row, 1970.

Nelson, K. Structure and strategy in learning to talk. Monographs of the Society for Research in Child Development, 1973, (Serial No. 149).

Newport, E., Gleitman, H., & Gleitman, L. Mother, I'd rather do it myself: Some effects ond non-effects of motherese. In C. Ferguson & C. Snow (Eds.), *Talking to children.* London: Cambridge University Press, 1977.

Phillips, J. R. Syntax and vocabulary of mothers' speech to young children: Age and sex comparisons. *Child Development,* 1973, *44,* 182–185.

Ross, J. R. *Constraints on variables in syntax.* Unpublished doctoral dissertation, MIT, 1967.

Schlesinger, I. M. Production of utterances and language acquisition. In D. I. Slobin (Ed.), *The ontogenesis of grammar.* New York: Academic Press, 1971.

Schlesinger, I. M. Relational concepts underlying language. In R. L. Schiefelbusch & L. L. Lloyd (Eds.), *Language perspectives: Acquisition, retardation, and intervention.* Baltimore: University Park Press, 1974.

Schatz, M., & Gelman, R. The development of communication skills: Modifications in the speech of young children as a function of listener. *Monographs of the Society for Research in Child Development,* 1973, *38* (Serial No. 152).

Sinclair, H. Sensorimotor action patterns as a condition for the acquisition of syntax. In R. Huxley & E. Ingram (Eds.), *Language acquisition: Models and methods.* New York: Academic Press, 1971.

Slobin, D. I. On the learning of morphological rules: A reply to Palermo and Eberhardt. In D. I. Slobin (Ed.), *The ontogenesis of gramar.* New York: Academic Press, 1971.

Slobin, D. I. Cognitive prerequisites for the development of grammar. In C. A. Ferguson & D. I. Slobin (Eds.), *Studies of child language development.* New York: Holt, Rinehart & Winston, 1973.

Tanouye, E., Lifter, K., & Bloom, L. *Semantic organization of grammatical morphemes.* Paper presented at the biennial meeting of the Society for Research in Child Development, New Orleans, March 1977.

Wells, G. Learning to code experience through language. *Journal of Child Language,* 1974, *1,* 243–269.

VI PARALINGUISTIC ASPECTS OF COMMUNICATION

12 Face-to-Face Interaction

Starkey Duncan, Jr.
University of Chicago

Language is acquired and used in the context of face-to-face interaction. The child acquires language only after a relatively extensive experience of interaction with others, some of this interaction involving language and some not. A child who has experienced particularly pathological interaction with significant others may not use language at all or at least not use it in any normal sense. It seems reasonable to expect that a child reared without direct contact with humans but exposed to language in terms of well-formed utterances emanating from audio speakers would not acquire language. (May this speculation never receive empirical test.) Once language is acquired, its use in everyday life commonly occurs in the context of face-to-face interaction, not only that specialized type of interaction called conversation, but also a variety of other types of interaction.

To say that language is deeply embedded in face-to-face interaction is to imply that actions traditionally considered to be "language" (as studied by linguists) frequently co-occur with other actions not traditionally considered to be language. These nonlanguage ("nonverbal") actions are observable in the speech, body motion, spatial arrangement, and other aspects of individuals who may be said to be in face-to-face interaction with each other.

Despite such considerations as these, it is a historical fact that the study of language has focused on the productions of the individual speaker and has conscientiously avoided analysis of co-occurring "nonverbal" actions.

Complementing this language-in-isolation approach is the more recent development of an extensive "nonverbal communication" literature that pays scarce attention to language.

The traditional separation of research on language from that on other aspects of face-to-face interaction is not maintained today as strictly as it has been. On the one hand, there is, for example, extensive discussion of "sociolinguistics," "speech acts," and "pragmatics" in the linguistic literature. On the other, elements of intonation and syntax are treated in some "nonverbal communication" studies. And in some studies of interaction, such as the "structural" studies discussed later, some aspects of interaction are approached from an essentially linguistic point of view.

Thus, both the study of language and the study of other aspects of face-to-face interaction may be seen as inching toward a more comprehensive view of the phenomenon and thus toward increasing mutuality of concern. Nevertheless, it seems clear that both broad fields will need to undergo some significant transformations of both conceptual framework and method before a more integrated investigation of face-to-face interaction is feasible.

Within the context of the discussion to this point, the purpose of this chapter is to undertake a review of several major approaches to research on face-to-face interaction, focusing primarily on methodological issues. Included will be certain ethnomethodological studies, the "external-variable" approach, human ethology, and "structural" studies. In each case, issues of data generation, construction of variables, and subsequent analysis will be considered, along with some discussion of the broader aims of the approach. The guiding question will be: Given the distinctive characteristics of face-to-face interaction, what research procedures seem most appropriate for producing evidence in support of claimed discoveries in the area?

In the course of the discussion a definite point of view will be expressed, though not, it is hoped, in a dogmatic manner. One cannot be so foolish as to claim solutions to the research issues raised. Rather, the issues raised and the positions taken are intended as part of the ongoing process of developing a research area.

To facilitate exposition, a couple of terminological practices will be adopted for this discussion. Although the comments below are intended to be potentially applicable to all face-to-face interaction, the discussion will be generally framed in terms of two-person interactions. The two interactants will be termed the "participant" and the "partner," the participant being the one on whom the discussion is focusing at a given moment, and the partner being the co-interactant. Thus, it might be said that the participant engages in a certain action at some moment in an interaction, and the partner responds to that action.

I. ETHNOMETHODOLOGY

Ethnomethodology seems a natural place to start this review because in their study of face-to-face interaction, ethnomethodologists have made more extensive use of language materials than any other research group to be covered.

It should be made clear at the outset that much of the work of ethnomethodologists has been difficult for me to follow. My sense of mystification in attempting to read these materials has been frequent and substantial. I make no claims either of expertise or of strong subjective certainty in my interpretations. Encountering the writings, especially the early ones, of ethnomethodologists was for me something like hearing an episode of Gangbusters broadcast in Chinese: There was considerable commotion and furor, but the story line was decidedly difficult to grasp. To ethnomethodologists, it may be apparent that I have yet to achieve an accurate decoding.

It is partially consoling to observe that this sense of mystification has not been unique to me. Weick (1969), in reviewing Garfinkel's (1967) *Studies in Ethnomethodology,* states in his first paragraph that "to comprehend even a portion of this book requires enormous effort [p. 357]." He wonders whether or not his belief that the book is "an extremely important and significant contribution to understanding human behavior [p. 357]" may not be attributable to a cognitive-dissonance effect.

There can be little doubt that ethnomethodologists, at least in an early phase of their work, saw their approach as "a radical departure from the traditional sociological thinking" (Zimmerman & Wieder, 1970, p. 295). Zimmerman and Wieder castigate Denzin (1970) for mistakenly supposing that both ethnomethodologists and symbolic interactionists shared such common concerns as "the question of how it is that social order is possible [p. 4]." Similarly mistaken in their view is Denzin's interpretation that ethnomethodologists look to "the rules, norms, definitions and meanings that members of any moral order daily take for granted" (Denzin, 1970, p. 16). Zimmerman and Wieder question any approach that assumes that "stable social action is the product of the actor's orientation to and compliance with shared, stable (if only within a particular interaction) norms or meanings [p. 268]."

If Denzin's statements fail to achieve an accurate characterization of the ethnomethodological position, what alternative do Zimmerman and Wieder propose? Their alternative may perhaps be approached through consideration of a now-famous experiment reported separately by Garfinkel (1967) and McHugh (1968). In Garfinkel's account, undergraduate subjects were told that research was being done on advice giving as an alternative to psychotherapy. Subjects were asked to describe some significant personal problem, and then to ask a "counselor" (actually an experimental confederate) questions relevant to the resolution of that problem. The one stipulation was that these questions must be framed in such a way as to permit a "yes" or "no" answer. "The subject was promised that the 'counselor' would attempt to answer to the best of his ability" (Garfinkel, 1967, p. 79). These yes/no answers were, in fact, predetermined by a table of random numbers. Garfinkel indicates that no subject perceived during the course of the experiment the true nature of the answers. Rather, subjects not only appeared to view the answers, and thus the advice, as "reasonable," but also discerned a "pattern" in the answers, often after receiving the first answer.

What is one to do with results as these (and others that Garfinkel discusses)? Zimmerman and Wieder assert that the ethnomethodological approach involves, among other things, suspending the "assumption that social conduct is rule governed, or based in and mounted from shared meanings or systems of symbols shared in common [p. 288]." Individuals do not so much act in accordance with rules, as satisfy themselves that their and others' actions are in fact rule governed. We resort to rules as a way of somehow perceiving social action as orderly. Rules provide the "*sense and appearance* of order [p. 292]." Thus, ethnomethodologists are not concerned with the description of rules that render social action orderly, but rather in the accounts that individuals construct for themselves so as to achieve the perception of orderliness in social action.

What is "radical" about this proposed research program? It does not seem radical to assert that individuals tend to perceive patterns in virtually every sort of physical and social event. Nor does it seem radical to assert that the rules applying to conduct in social situations are human creations. This notion is commonplace in social science. Bateson (1951), for example, wrote that "*man lives by those propositions whose validity is a function of his belief in them* [p. 212, italics in original]." Slightly later, Bateson (1971, but actually written in about 1955) wrote, "Of all the elements and vicissitudes of formation and re-formation of relationships, perhaps the most interesting is that process whereby people establish common rules for the creation and understanding of messages [p. 22]." If one proposes to investigate the process under which rules are created, then this is simply a legitimate issue for social anthropologists, investigators of cognitive processes, and the like.

The research program articulated by Zimmerman and Wieder appears to acquire a radical aspect at the point at which it is suggested that the notion of social order is in essence a fiction, a likely story, created by the individual striving to function somehow in a social world in which order does not otherwise exist. From this perspective, the random yes/no responses by experimental confederate in the Garfinkel-McHugh experiment is not an exceptional and highly artificial experimental manipulation, but rather a greatly simplified but accurate analogue of society itself. In his perception of social order when confronted in fact by chaos, the individual is simply making it up as he goes along. To entertain this possibility seriously is indeed to "suspend the assumption that social conduct is rule governed" (Zimmerman & Wieder, 1970, p. 288).

And it is true, as Zimmerman and Wieder indicate, that this issue must be dealt with on the level of assumptions that the investigator must either accept or reject in framing his research questions and in charting his design — that is, in deciding how to invest his research efforts. Some investigators will be willing to make the assumption that social conduct is in some sense rule governed; others will not. It turns out that other ethnomethodologists are indeed willing to make that assumption.

Schegloff and Sacks (1973) approach the notion of social order in a way entirely straightforward and familiar to other social scientists. They write, "our analysis has sought to explicate the ways in which the materials [of conversations] are produced by members in orderly ways that exhibit their orderliness, have their orderliness appreciated and used, and have that appreciation displayed and treated as the basis for subsequent action [p. 290]." Their study was designed to find the "institutionalized solution[s] [p. 298]" used by conversationalists in dealing with various problems of coordination that arise in conversations. In describing the results of their analyses, Schegloff and Sacks consistently stress the collaborative nature of the solutions to these problems (i.e., solutions achieved through the joint, coordinated action of the participants). Schegloff and Sacks describe, among other things, a series of hypothesized conversational elements and rules for using these elements. In considering phenomena associated with the exchange of speaking turns, Sacks, Schegloff, and Jefferson (1974) emphasize that "it is misconceived to treat turns as units characterized by a division of labor in which the speaker determines the unit and its boundaries, with other parties having as their task the recognition of them [pp. 726-727]." They detail the manner in which "the turn as a unit is interactively determined [p. 727]." [It may be noted in passing that they are not necessarily unique in this suggestion. See, for example, Duncan (1972, 1973, 1974, 1975).]

Similarly, Moerman (1972) states that his purpose is to "(a) document the detailed orderliness of actual conversational interaction; (b) show that participants orient to this orderliness; (c) explicate the knowledge — together with the rules for situated use of this knowledge — that members actively use in accomplishing this orderliness [p. 171]." And Cicourel (1972) asserts that, among other things, "our model of the actor must (1) specify how general rules or norms are invoked to justify or evaluate a course of action [p. 249]." He extensively considers "basic rules" that "activate short- and long-term stored information (socially distributed knowledge) that enables the actor to articulate general normative rules with immediate interaction scenes [p. 257]." ·

Sacks, Schegloff, and Jefferson (1974) raise their sights from the problem of social order within specific types of situated interaction within a particular culture or subculture, to the broader problem of potentially universal constraints on the organization of turn taking in conversations. They frame their research question as, "What might be extracted as ordered phenomena from our conversational materials which would not turn out to require reference to one or another aspect of situatedness, identities, particularities of content or context [p. 699]?"

In a number of important ways ethnomethodologists such as Jefferson, Moerman, Sacks, and Schegloff appear to share broad communalities of both method and working presupposition with other investigators of the organization of face-to-face interaction. For example, research tends to focus on naturally occurring conversations; there is a central concern with orderly sequences of action involving more than one participant in an interaction; and the proposed elements of order are viewed as institutional-ized solutions to problems involving the coordination of action among the participants. It is within the context of this recognition of broader communalities that the following more detailed discussion of research methods is developed.

A. The Methods of Ethnomethodologists

1. Type of Data Considered

Familiar to many social scientists is Garfinkel's technique of highlight-ing social phenomena of interest by having students or experimenters deliberately violate various social norms or expectations. The counseling experiment mentioned previously is of course an example. Other examples would be (1) efforts to abandon all "common knowledge" in a situation by making extremely literal interpretations of each utterance of one's partner in interaction; (2) engaging a partner in a game of ticktacktoe, only to erase the partner's mark, placing it in another square; and (3) having students act in their homes as if they were boarders.

This sort of "Candid Camera" procedure, productive of intriguing anecdotes and illustrations but of only marginally consequential social-science data, should not be permitted to obscure the fact that more systematic methods of data generation and analysis characterize a broad range of studies in ethnomethodology. Furthermore, these more systematic methods are generally applied to recordings of naturally occurring interactions of a variety of types, rather than to interactions disrupted by bizarre and artificial interventions. A strong empirical emphasis is manifest in, for example, the Schegloff and Sacks and Sacks, Schegloff, and Jefferson articles cited above, as well as in most of the contributions to the Sudnow (1972) and Turner (1974) volumes.

Among these more systematic studies in ethnomethodology, analysis is typically focused on the speech stream, especially those elements tradition-ally considered to be part of language. But some intonation and paralin-guistic (Trager, 1958) phenomena are also considered and represented in various ways in published excerpts from transcripts.

This is not to say that actions not occurring in the speech stream are denied relevance to the phenomena being considered. For example, Schegloff and Sacks (1973) acknowledge the possible relevance of "non-verbal behavior [p. 323n]" to the accomplishment of conversational closings. They simply indicate that "we have not studied these phenomena yet, and we do not have the empirical materials that would allow assertions that, and how, they work [p. 323n]."

2. Presentation of Evidence

Through detailed scrutiny of, and reflection on, their data, ethnomethod-ologists have developed a number of hypotheses regarding elements of order in face-to-face interaction. In my opinion, these hypotheses carry considerable interest and potential productivity for further research in the area. I would raise a question, however, regarding the typical approach to presenting evidence in support of these hypotheses.

It seems fair to say that a common approach of ethnomethodologists to presenting this evidence is simply to provide examples from transcriptions that are in line with the hypotheses. One or two examples of a given phenomenon are usually considered sufficient, although more may be provided. Consider the case of a greeting between A and B, such as A: "hello"; B: "hello." Schegloff and Sacks observe that "it would be redund-ant to cite multiple instances of such exchanges, or minor variants of them (though some variants would require separate treatment) [p. 291n]." Certainly, it would be difficult to quarrel with this judgment.

Undoubtedly, the multitude of anecdotes and examples provided in certain ethnomethodological articles significantly clarifies the communica-tion of the authors' ideas. But I can only question the feasibility of building a social science of face-to-face interaction using these devices as evidence. It seems clear that the type of information required to evaluate most hypotheses is not contained in examples or anecdotes.

A case in point would be the report by Sacks, Schegloff, and Jefferson (1974) that "examination of WHERE such 'next-turn starts' occur in

current turns shows them to occur at 'possible completion points' [p. 721]."
This statement is immediately followed by a sentence further specifying the
notion of "possible completion points," followed by a series of relevant
examples from transcripts.

To avoid excessive concentration on the particulars of a single instance,
the statement of Sacks and co-workers may be generalized to the following
form: "event A ('next-turn-starts') tends strongly to occur at location X
('possible completion points'), at least within a given corpus of transcribed
material." But this statement can be evaluated only on the basis of knowing
the proportion of all A's occurring at location X, together with the rate of
occurrence of location X within the corpus. To generate these proportions,
it is necessary merely to obtain from the corpus the frequency of occurrence of: (1) event A at location X; (2) event A not at location X; (3)
location X without event A; and (4) neither event A nor location X.
Clearly, none of this information can be derived from a set of examples. It
does not seem inappropriate to expect investigators to provide each other
with this sort of information in substantiation of their claimed findings.

Sacks et al. provide an interesting alternative to exclusive dependence
on examples or anecdotes for substantiating hypotheses. They are concerned with the systematics of the organization of turn taking in conversations, rather than with the specific details of that organization (p. 696).
Their purpose is to consider the general organizational implication of
"turn-allocation techniques" without becoming involved in the specific
actions by which the next turn is allocated. In proposing these general
systematics they rely for empirical support primarily on a set of "grossly
apparent facts [p. 700]" that may presumably be observed in any conversation. On the basis of these "facts" Sacks and associates propose an
interesting and insightful organization. The components and rules of this
organization deserve careful consideration by other investigators of face-to-
face interaction.

I see two general problems with this empirical strategy: one apparently
avoidable, and one not.

The avoidable problem is this. By asserting specific details for their
organization, Sacks et al. fail to maintain the high level of generality
claimed for the organization. Thus, it seems reasonable to write generally
of a "transition-relevance place [p. 703ff.]" at which "transfer of speakership [p. 703]" may properly occur. But, as mentioned above, in a later
section Sacks et al. proceed to assert that "examination of WHERE such
'next-turn-starts' occur in current turns shows them to occur at 'possible
completion points.' These turn out to be 'possible completion points' of
sentences, clauses, phrases, and one-word constructions, and multiples
thereof [p. 721]." This finding is further elaborated in immediately subsequent paragraphs. To identify specific characteristics of transition-

relevance places in this way is to become involved in a level of empirical detail for which their paper was apparently not designed, and in any event for which their empirical base — the "grossly apparent facts" — is not sufficient.

There is a second type of problem concerning the "facts" that I believe is inherent when they are the sole data source. In the first place, there seems to be no principled way of resolving differences of opinion concerning these "facts." This situation sets the stage for the discussion to degenerate into mere haggling over conflicting examples or anecdotes. I for one find the "facts" of Sacks et al. to be quite reasonable on the whole, at least for the Anglo-American conversations with which I am most familiar. But not every "fact" seems to me equally reasonable.

Let one such "fact" be an example. Fact 12 reads: "Turn-allocation techniques are obviously used. A current speaker may select a next speaker (as when he addresses a question to another party); or parties may self-select in starting to talk [p. 701]." From Fact 12, Rules 1a and 1b are developed as follows:

(1) For any turn, at the initial transition-relevance place of an initial turn-constructional unit: (a) If the turn-so-far is so constructed as to involve the use of a 'current speaker selects next' technique, then the party so selected has the right and is obliged to take next turn to speak; no others have such rights or obligations, and transfer occurs at that place. (b) If the turn-so-far is so constructed as not to involve the use of a 'current speaker selects next' technique, then self-selection for next speakership may, but need not, be instituted; first starter acquires rights to a turn, and transfer occurs at that place [p. 704].

Until reading Rule 1a, I did not appreciate the strong sense in which the word "select" is used in Fact 12. Rule 1a clearly indicates that Sacks et al. view next-speaker selection as a black-or-white process. Either the current speaker selects the next speaker (and this selection would appear to brook no alternative selection within the group), or auditors self-select with current speakers playing no part in the process. Under this interpretation, Fact 12 becomes less "grossly apparent," more salient as an empirical issue. I view such a rule format as unnecessarily and improbably simple, rigid, and absolutist. It flies in the face of the sense of mutual adjustment among participants that one often obtains from interaction materials. Certainly, it does not evidence the interactive character of conversational events described subsequently: "It is misconceived to treat turns as units characterized by a division of labor in which the speaker determines the unit and its boundaries, with other parties having as their task the recognition of them [pp. 726–727]."

A striking thing about most of the results on two-person conversations studied so far is the relative prevalence of "rules" involving optional action: participants appear to retain the choice of acting or not acting at various "transition-relevance" places. The same results suggest that speakers may indeed influence the probability of auditors' subsequent actions; but speakers do not in any sense control those auditor actions. In studying groups larger than two persons (where speaker selection becomes an issue), I would not be surprised to find some system in which there were mechanisms for both "current speaker selects next" and "self-selection," neither of these operating on an absolute basis. If such were the case, the simplest systematics would be somewhat more complicated than that proposed by Sacks et al.

But notice the direction this discussion has taken. In response to a set of postulated "facts," I have thrown up another set of possible "fa⁀ s," equally postulated. Who is to say which set is "better," or that both sets are implausible, or that any alternative set is preferable to the first two? When facts are postulated, there is a strong temptation to drift into an exchange of mere opinions, prejudices, intuitions, and anecdotes.

In contrast, imagine that studies had been conducted of turn allocation in groups of three or more participants. Sacks et al. suggest a potentially universal application for their rule system. As mentioned above, they are concerned with systematic properties "which would not turn out to require reference to one or another aspect of situatedness, identities, particularities of content or context [p. 699]." In view of these rather strong claims, if results from studies of specific groups fail to agree with the "grossly apparent facts" supporting a more universal rule system, at what point do such results begin to impinge on the proposed universal system? Would a contrary set of results from a single well-executed study be sufficient to shatter the relevant elements of the system, or would that set carry insufficient weight? If one study would be insufficient, would ten be enough? Would evidence need to be gathered from more than one culture?

Perhaps these various criticisms actually stem from my basic discomfort with the proposal of a potentially universal system for turn taking when the amount and breadth of actual, detailed studies of that phenomenon are so limited. It does not seem to me that postulating a set of "facts" is an adequate device for filling that empirical vacuum.

In any event, the criticisms voiced above are methodological. Developing appropriate methodology for studying face-to-face interaction is the central concern in this chapter. I doubt that the field of inquiry can be extensively advanced on the basis of a proliferating series of papers postulating "facts." But it should be stressed that these methodological criticisms of some ethnomethodological empirical strategies do not imply a similar criticism of the integrative effort of Sacks et al. They have demonstrated the range and breadth of conversational phenomena that can be accommodated and ordered on the basis of their elegant rule set. But until more hard, empirical descriptive studies are done, their "simplest systematics" will have to await phenomena to systematize.

B. Summary: Ethnomethodology

Ethnomethodology constitutes a major line of inquiry into the conduct of face-to-face interaction. Apart from certain exceptions, it appears that the working assumptions of most ethnomethodologists are widely shared with other investigators of face-to-face interaction. Regardless of the methodological criticisms voiced above, a number of ethnomethodological studies have produced insights and discoveries of great interest. It is to be hoped that communication will continue to expand between ethnomethodologists and other investigators of face-to-face interaction.

II. EXTERNAL-VARIABLE STUDIES

I confess to having perpetrated the infelicitous label "external-variable study." This act seems to have done little damage — the term is infrequently used, especially by investigators doing that sort of research. For all its infelicity, the term will be retained here for lack of a better one, and in any event it seems necessary to draw distinctions between various broad strategies of research on face-to-face interaction. In this case the purpose was to distinguish (1) "structural" studies designed in a roughly linguistic manner to discover elements of organization in face-to-face interaction, from (2) external-variable studies "seeking relationships between the [nonverbal] behaviors and other variables, such as personality characteristics, situation, and observers' judgments" (Duncan, 1969, p. 119). (Structural studies will be discussed in another section.) Later in that paper I also included other nonverbal behaviors as possible external variables. To this earlier characterization I would now add a crucially important attribute: a failure to consider the location of observed actions in the stream of interaction. This issue and others will be considered shortly.

When one hears a reference made to research on nonverbal communication, it is likely that the speaker has external-variable studies in mind. Constituting what must be more than 95% of the publications in the area, external-variable studies have provided the major vehicle for research on face-to-face interaction. Much of what we presently know about gaze, unfilled pauses, and the like, comes from external-variable studies.

Investigators using the external-variable paradigm have been ingenious, enterprising, and often prolific. For the most part, these workers have been psychologists — primarily, social psychologists. And the great expansion of published work on "nonverbal communication" was made possible by the early acceptance of external-variable studies by major social-psychological journals (such as *Journal of Personality and Social Psychology*, the *Journal of Experimental Social Psychology*, and *Sociometry*) when "nonverbal communication" as an area of inquiry was not included in the existing definitions of any established academic subdiscipline. For these reasons and others, investigators in the area of face-to-face interaction owe much to the external-variable literature.

In the discussion to follow, external-variable studies will be broadly characterized. Discussion will focus on serious problems in frequently used techniques. Perhaps few such studies will possess all of the characteristics described, but most will possess several. When a research literature is very large, no constructive purpose seems to be served by singling out a few studies for special criticism. For this reason, there will be a minimum of citations. It is not difficult, however, to recognize an external-variable study. Although the definition of the external-variable paradigm has changed somewhat since the 1969 review, the classification of actual studies as using that paradigm has not. And more recent studies of this sort may be identified either in terms of their characteristics or by forward searches in the Science Citation Index, based on studies described as external-variable in the review.

A. Actions

We may begin by considering the major strength of external-variable studies, one that they possess in common with virtually all studies of "nonverbal communication." Fiske (1974) has pointed out that the use as data of concrete "nonverbal behaviors," such as gaze direction, smiling, gesturing, and the like, holds a distinct advantage over certain types of measurement prevalent in social, personality, and clinical psychology. He refers to self-descriptions and ratings by peers or observers that are couched in broad trait- or emotion-oriented terms such as anxiety, dominance, and affiliativeness.

The "nonverbal" measures directed observers' attention to more specific classes of action, defined primarily in on-off terms requiring no summarizing of judgments over time. That is, observers need only indicate, for example, when a gesture begins and when it ends. More importantly, the recording of "nonverbal behaviors" required no complex inferences as to unobservable internal states of the interactants. Observers could simply note that an interactant was smiling; there was no need when recording observations to speculate on the possible implications of that smiling with respect to the purposes or internal states of the interactant. As Kendon

(1975) has noted, ratings involving such inferences fall into the paradoxical position of presupposing in the data-generation stage, the very information that the study was designed to obtain.

Thus, the concrete nature of observations of "nonverbal behavior" makes such observations an excellent source of data for social scientists of all sorts, including investigators using the external-variable paradigm. (Linguists using field data might have told us all along about the value of using specific, narrowly focused observations. It is unfortunate, though, that such linguists typically eliminate suspected "nonverbal" (nonlinguistic) behaviors from their analyses.)

The term "action" will henceforth be used to denote the kind of data generated by the sort of concrete observations briefly described above. "Action" will include observations of both "language" and "nonverbal" events, as this distinction is traditionally defined. And, because this discussion is concerned with face-to-face interaction, the actions to be considered will be those that are observed in actual face-to-face interactions or in situations in which individuals are co-present (Kendon, 1975).

B. External-Variable Experiments

External-variable studies typically place heavy emphasis on hypothesis testing through controlled experiments, even at the earliest stages of research on a given phenomenon. It would seem that this tendency can be understood only in terms of prevailing research practices in psychology, more specifically social psychology. Certainly, anthropologists do not share this emphasis. And much of the experimental work in psycholinguistics is based on hypotheses concerning the organization of language that were generated by linguists and others through an essentially exploratory-research paradigm. Some of the undesirable consequences of the premature and uncritical introduction of controlled experiments in this area will be considered shortly.

1. Variables

Part of any controlled experiment is a specification of the independent and dependent variables. It is perhaps because of an excessive concern with specifying such variables in external-variable studies that they have a strong tendency to include only one or two actions, such as gaze direction, distance between interactants, or smiling. (In specific studies these actions may be defined as independent or dependent variables.) Such studies are usually designed to test relationships between certain actions and some other, higher-level variable, such as sex differences or affiliation. This emphasis has led, in my opinion, to two undesirable consequences: (1) a wider range of actions is not considered in the study; and (2) relationships among the actions themselves are not carefully investigated.

An alternative research strategy is implied in the preceding criticisms. Face-to-face interaction may be viewed as a complex phenomenon, potentially drawing on the full range of observable actions in speech, body motion, and the like. One may ask how these many actions combine to produce the message or messages that are one product of face-to-face interaction. Of course, this sort of question focuses on the relationships among the actions themselves, rather than on the relationships between actions and other variables. And it is clear that such a strategy requires simultaneous consideration of a variety of actions. As Kendon (1975) observes, "it quickly becomes apparent that the full range of behaviors observable in interaction must be comprehended. An integrated approach to behavior becomes necessary, and we cannot be content with dealing with behavioral variables one at a time [p. 5]."

C. Experimental Control

Another essential element in the controlled experiment is, of course, the control of relevant variables. When the research area is at an early stage of development, there is an obvious difficulty in specifying a set of relevant variables to control. But there is another difficulty that will remain, regardless of the amount of research knowledge of face-to-face interaction. It is a common practice in external-variable studies to include confederates who are instructed to "control" various aspects of their actions when interacting with subjects. This type of attempted experimental control takes several distinguishable forms. In one form, confederates are requested to hold certain actions constant. A typical example would be the practice of having confederates maintain a steady gaze at the subject throughout the interaction. An obvious question would be whether or not such constancy of actions is found in naturally occurring interactions of the sort being studied. It is possible that when confederates hold one or more actions constant, the investigator may be making unnecessary sacrifices in terms of naturalness of the interaction, with consequent undesirable effects on the actions of the subject.

Two other forms of attempted control of confederates' actions may be considered together. In one of these forms, confederates are requested to maintain some general feeling tone, such as "warm and friendly," in the interaction. In another form, the instructions are somewhat more specific. An example of the latter would be the instruction to smile once at the subject and to look toward the subject 30% of the time. These approaches to attempted control raise several issues. First, is the requested pattern natural for the type of interaction under study?

Second, can the confederate actually achieve the desired constancy in his or her actions? These are, of course, empirical questions. Despite reports in the literature of training sessions and of requiring confederates to show that they can adequately perform the requested actions, there are virtually no reports of observations of confederates in the actual experimental situation, and thus no means of verifying that they did in fact achieve the desired constancy in the designated actions.

Third, what about all the other actions of the confederate, for which no "control" is requested? What evidence does the experimenter have that all other aspects of speech and body motion are irrelevant to the dependent variables?

Finally, it will be suggested later in this chapter that the organization of interaction includes appropriate sequences of actions involving both participants (in a two-person interaction). To the extent to which this is so, then certain actions by the confederate may be appropriate in response to the subject's actions. Effective control of the confederate's actions would in this case require control of the subject's actions — a paradoxical situation.

It would seem that all of this tangled web of complexity might easily be avoided simply by resorting to the careful study of interactions that are as natural as research ethics allow. It is, presumably, natural interactions that one is seeking to understand. Why not start with them?

The preceding comments have been directed at the notion of controlling the actions of confederates. In contrast, it seems reasonable to expect that control of various situational factors can be achieved with a minimum of difficulty. For example, the investigator may be interested only in female-female interactions, or in interactions in nursery schools, or in bargaining, and so forth. Only interactions having the desired characteristics will be observed. And perhaps the investigator will create the desired interactions by bringing, for example, females together to interact. Further, various features of the room, seating arrangement, and the like may be either controlled or used as independent variables without abandoning relative "naturalness" of the situation. An example here would be Becker's (1973) placing of books at various positions on tables in a library reading room, in order to observe subsequent seating patterns. None of this seems to carry the intractable difficulties resulting from confederates' attempting to control specific actions.

D. Action Sequences

There remains a difficulty shared by many external-variable studies, as well as by a number of studies of face-to-face interaction using other paradigms. I refer to the practice of gathering data on actions in face-to-face interaction simply by counting and/or timing these actions for one or both participants in an observed interaction. I shall argue that this practice is unacceptably wasteful of information available in the interaction, and that in fact the effect of this practice is to discard precisely that information that would permit meaningful interpretation of results. At this point in the discussion, the argument will be advanced on primarily an intuitive basis. Later, the position will be elaborated in terms of research results.

It seems reasonable to assert that a basic property of face-to-face interaction is that it occurs in terms of sequences of action over time, these sequences potentially involving all participants in the interaction. Interaction cannot be regarded simply as an unsynchronized display of a collection of (well-formed) signals by two individuals (in a two-person interaction). There are, rather, sequences of action and response involving both participants.

Once an interaction is begun, the taking of an action at some point is probably related in some way to other actions that preceded it. That is, to the extent that face-to-face interaction possesses some form of culturally based organization, that organization must reasonably include the specification of appropriate sequences of action.

For example, if an individual approaches me with a greeting and an offer to shake hands, there is a definite expectation that I will respond by shaking hands. My refusing to do so carries strong implications with respect to that incipient interaction. This microinteraction can be fully understood only in terms of organized sequences of action.

Other sequences of action may carry much greater optionality of response. For example, in the next section there will be a brief description of research on taking speaking turns in two-person conversations between adults. The results suggest that, in the conversations studied, the auditor retains considerable choice with respect to the points at which he speaks up to take the speaking turn. Nevertheless, there are strong regularities describable in terms of action sequences, regarding both the points at which the auditor attempts to take the turn (with respect to preceding speaker actions) and the effects of each attempt on the ensuing course of the interaction (depending on the location of that attempt).

It is simply not enough to know how many times or for how long during a stretch of interaction a given action occurs, regardless of the sophisticated treatment that is subsequently given to that information. It is necessary to know as well the location in the stream of interaction of each occurrence of that action. A smile inappropriately placed may be perceived as mocking; the same smile occurring at another point in the interaction may be perceived as sympathetic.

Similarly, one is not likely to be satisfied with knowing how many times an auditor attempted to take the speaking turn, when there is no sequential information regarding, for example, how many of these attempts were gross interruptions, and how many resulted in smooth, appropriate exchanges of the turn.

Nor is it sufficient to gather data on both participants, while ignoring sequences. For example, knowing that both participants smiled frequently tells us nothing about the incidence of mutual smiling. To the extent that there was mutual smiling, there is no information on the extent to which each participant initiated such sequences. And once again, we do not know the location of each smile with respect to other interactional events, such as paralinguistic and intonational phenomena, syntactical units, gestures, and postural shifts. Obviously, the incidence of smiling may be related to events other than smiling.

Because of considerations such as these, it is recommended that all investigation of face-to-face interaction take into account information on action sequences, and that the technique of using simple counts and timings of actions be abandoned.

Despite the relative absence of action-sequence analysis in studies of various types of face-to-face interaction, there are a number of investigators and research groups for which such analysis plays a prominent role. Examples of such work would be Altmann (1965), Brazelton, Koslowski, and Main (1974), Chapple (1970), Duncan and Fiske (1977), Jaffe and Feldstein (1970), Kaye (1976), Kendon (1967, 1976), Lewis and Lee-Painter (1974), McQuown (1971), Meltzer, Morris, and Hayes (1971), Sacks, Schegloff, and Jefferson (1974), Schegloff and Sacks (1973), and Stern (1974).

1. Action-Sequence Variables

The references cited immediately above suggest that action sequences may be studied in a number of different ways; one approach is to formulate variables in terms of sequences. Another distinct approach to analyzing action-sequence data is described in the next chapter.

There appear to be at least four essential elements in the description of an action-sequence variable: (1) the participants involved; (2) the aspects of actions relevant to the variable; (3) the type of linkage obtaining between the actions; and (4) the identification of actions as either dependent or independent. These four elements need to be considered briefly.

a. Participants. In studies of face-to-face interaction, action-sequence variables will typically include the actions of both participants (in a two-person interaction). At least in the data-generation stage of research, as well as for certain analyses, it is important to distinguish Participant A's action responses to Participant B's antecedent actions, and vice versa.

b. Aspects of Actions.   Observed actions will typically have such aspects as onset, offset, and duration; movements may have apexes and/or shifts in direction. It is important for investigators to indicate, for example, whether it is the beginning, ending, or simply the occurrence of a participant's act that is related to other actions or aspects of actions in the sequence.

c. Linkages Between Actions.   It is imperative to describe carefully the manner in which a subsequent action in an action sequence is related, or "linked," to a preceding action. This relationship may be described in terms of some time interval, or in terms of interactional events of some sort, or in terms of some combination of these two factors.

d. Independent and Dependent Actions.   It seems useful to label each action in an action-sequence variable as either independent or dependent. Independent actions would be those that either must or must not occur in order for the variable to be observed. Dependent actions are those that may or may not occur in each instance of the variable.

This abstract discussion may be made more specific by some examples:

1. *Rate of auditor attempts to take the speaking turn, given the activation of X turn cues by the speaker, when the gesticulation signal is not concurrently activated.* This action-sequence variable is drawn from studies of turn taking in two-person conversations between adults (Duncan 1972, 1974). A full statement of this variable would require detailed specification (1) of its essential terms — "turn cue," "gesticulation signal," "attempt to take the speaking turn," "speaker," "auditor," and "activation" — and (b) of the nature of the linkages. This specification is not, however, directly relevant to this example. The turn cues and gesticulation signal are independent actions, in that the turn cues must occur, and the gesticulation signal must not, in order for the variable to be observed. The auditor attempt to take the turn is a dependent action because it either may or may not occur. (This is because the variable is concerned with rate of occurrence of attempts.) Thus, the variable involves three actions; but because two of these actions are simultaneously considered (turn cues and gesticulation signal), the sequence has only two parts. Aspects of actions are as follows: (1) activation of turn cues — varied according to the definition of each cue, but primarily offset; (2) activation of gesticulation signal — duration; and (3) attempt to take the speaking turn — onset. The variable involves event-based linkages both between turn cues and gesticulation signal and between these and the turn attempt. (Data on the operation of this variable in some observed conversations may be found in Duncan, 1972.)

2. An example of a variable involving a three-part action sequence may be produced by slightly altering and expanding example 1: *Rate of*

speaker's yielding the speaking turn, given (1) that speaker's activation of at least one turn cue, when the gesticulation signal is not concurrently activated, and (2) the auditor's attempt to take the turn. In this case, the independent variable is itself a two-part action sequence involving both speaker cue signal activation and auditor turn attempt. The dependent variable is, of course, the prior speaker's yielding the turn. That yielding involves, essentially, the offset of an action, or more precisely, the non-onset of continued talking. Once again, the variable deals exclusively with event-based linkages. (Data on the operation of this variable may be found in Duncan, 1972, 1974.)

3. *Rate of participant's averting gaze from the partner within the first 6 seconds of the partner's smiling, when that smiling is not during the participant's prior smiling.* This presently uninvestigated variable involves two different actions: gaze aversion and smiling. The three-part action sequence includes a sequence of two independent actions: (1) the partner's smiling, and (2) the participant's not smiling before the partner's smile. There is one dependent action: (3) the participant's averting gaze or not doing so. The aspect involved in action 1 is duration; of actions 2 and 3, onset. The linkage between 2 and 1 is an event-based one; between 1 and 3, a temporal one.

It may be seen that the description of these variables carries considerably more information than the more commonly encountered variables, such as "number of smiles per 5-minute stretch of interaction," or "average duration of smiling." In addition, a very large number of reasonable variables can be generated with respect to the same set of observations. For example, in variable 3 above, exploratory analyses may show that some time period other than 6 seconds may prove to be more effective for certain research purposes. Similarly, the effects of various combinations of turn cues may be examined in variables 1 and 2.

The notion of action-sequence variables appears to arise naturally when the focus of research shifts from issues regarding the individual display of signals to issues regarding the process or organization of the interaction itself. It seems reasonable to expect that variables reflecting action sequences in face-to-face interaction may be an effective tool for exploring not only the organization of various types of interaction, but also individual differences in conduct within that organization.

2. CRESCAT: A Computer Program for Analyzing Action Sequences

In order to facilitate research on action sequences, a computer program is being developed by Duncan and Kenneth Kaye (also at the University of Chicago). The most important aspect of CRESCAT (not an acronym) is its on-line capability of finding complex patterns in sequences of data. Currently implemented on the IBM 370, the system is intended to be a user-oriented, "friendly" system of considerable generality. There are no limitations either on the complexity of the specified pattern or on the extent of the data file to be processed, other than those imposed by the installation.

In addition to its pattern-matching capability, CRESCAT is designed to be extremely flexible in the type and format of data that it accepts. The data may include information on the absolute or relative time events. The system will have extensive provisions for editing, copying, moving, merging, sorting, updating, creating, and deleting files. Files, tables, and graphs may be displayed in a variety of formats.

Quantitative information gathered in the course of a pattern search may be analyzed statistically by CRESCAT packaged functions or by user-written routines; alternatively, such information may be written out in a form acceptable as input to other statistical programs (e.g., SPSS) (Nie, Hull, Jenkins, Steinbrenner, & Bent, 1975).

Investigators wishing to obtain more information on the CRESCAT system may contact either Duncan or Kaye.

E. Facial Actions

Among the many actions observed in face-to-face interaction, facial expressions seem to hold a particular interest for both investigators and the public at large. In addition, facial expressions constitute a set of actions extensively investigated through the external-variable paradigm, although rarely for the purpose of studying the conduct of face-to-face interaction. Because of the first two considerations, and in spite of the third, some special — but brief — discussion of these actions seems appropriate in this section.

Undoubtedly the most active current investigation of facial expressions is being carried out by Ekman and his colleagues. In studying the face, they have chosen to limit their focus, "considering only one type of information which can be obtained from the face (information about emotion), from only one type of organism (human adults), considering only one type of evidence (empirical research) (Ekman, Friesen, & Ellsworth, 1972, p. 2)." Members of the research group have extensively reviewed the research relevant to their research aims (Ekman, 1974), developed an ingenious method of describing some facial expressions based on matching photographs rather than verbal descriptions (Ekman & Friesen, 1975; Ekman et al., 1972; Ekman, Friesen, & Tomkins, 1971), and carried out a vigorous program of cross-cultural research (Ekman, 1971; Ekman & Friesen, 1971, 1975; Ekman et al., 1972; Ekman, Sorenson, & Friesen, 1969).

Because Ekman and his colleagues have not been concerned directly with the conduct of face-to-face interaction, their methodology need not be a concern in this discussion. It may be noted, however, that they have carefully considered methodological issues and procedures have been carefully chosen, often with considerable ingenuity.

The only substantial point to be made in this discussion of research on facial actions is one also indicated by Ekman: research in this area need not be confined to external-variable studies of expression of emotion. Ekman et al. (1972) point out that "the face is not simply a display system for emotion. There are facial gestures (winks, sticking out the tongue, etc.) and instrumental actions (yawning) of the face which are not specific to any one or two emotions [p. 125]." They further suggest that "*display rules* are learned, usually early in life, for each facial behavior which specify what management technique should be applied by whom in what circumstances [p. 23, italics in original]."

In addition, facial actions may be viewed as a subset of the many actions contributing to various aspects of the organization of face-to-face interaction — in the "structural" sense described in a later section. Kendon (1976) has published a study of the role of facial actions in "regulating" the ongoing process of a "kissing round" in a courting couple. Investigations in my laboratory are currently underway on the occurrence of smiling by speaker and auditor in conversations, as related to other events in the organization of that particular type of face-to-face interaction.

It seems reasonable to suggest that facial actions may be used to comment on the status (Silverstein, 1976) or truth value, as well as other aspects, of some verbal statement or action, quite apart from emotional states.

Thus, to the extent to which the hypothesis of basic emotions continues to be supported, the work of Ekman and others may be seen as crucial contributions to that hypothesis. But it seems desirable for research on facial actions to assume a more diversified aspect, so that they may be more closely related to the process of face-to-face interaction.

F. Summary: External-Variable Studies

External-variable studies have provided a primary vehicle for the investigation of face-to-face interaction. Despite the significant strengths of such studies, two basic criticisms were made:

1. The frequent practice of attempting to control the actions of confederates seems an undesirable and avoidable research tactic.
2. Prevalent in external-variable studies is the practice of simply counting or timing observed actions, as opposed to gathering information

on the location of each action in the stream of interaction. This practice seems excessively wasteful of information and thus of potential descriptive power. The abandonment of this practice in external-variable studies is advocated. The external-variable paradigm may be replaced by one in which each variable reflects the occurrence or nonoccurrence of some specified sequence of actions.

III. HUMAN ETHOLOGY

In having its conceptual and methodological roots in a subdiscipline of biology, human ethology contrasts with the other, social-science based approaches to face-to-face interaction considered in this review. However, as a broad generalization it seems fair to say that human ethology differs from social-science based approaches more in its general conceptual framework (including a primary interest in behaviors adapted for signal function through evolution) than in specific elements of methodology. This methodological convergence is noted by Blurton Jones (1972a): "I think that the differences in the methods employed by ethologists and by psychologists are going to get smaller and smaller. There is already very little difference between the way Gewirtz and Gewirtz (1969), Ainsworth and Bell (1970, 1972) or Rheingold and Eckerman (1970) investigate mother–child relationships and the way any of the contributors to this book would do it [p. 28]." In any event, consistent with the purposes of this review, methodological issues will receive primary consideration in this discussion despite the fact that McGrew (1972) sees ethology rationale and methods as "inextricably related [p. xi]."

In order to limit the discussion, as well as to maintain consistency within this chapter, the focus will be on those human ethologists whose research has been directed primarily by an effort to understand face-to-face interaction in some specific situation in its own right. This approach may be distinguished in its relative emphasis from research primarily concerned with the issue of universal aspects of signaling. The latter concern has been succinctly expressed by Eibl-Eibesfeldt (1970): "Is there a signalling code— a language without words — common to all men [p. 297]?" Thus, in this discussion the terms "ethologists," "human ethologist," and the like should be understood as referring to a subset of the larger group.

A. General Characteristics

Among the human ethologists to be considered, there is a clear-cut preference for work with infants and children. Adults appear to be included in studies to the extent that children and infants naturally interact with them. Once again, the overriding consideration in choosing this research strategy does not seem to be a concern with communication universals. Rather, one gains the impression that these ethologists have chosen — not unwisely — to apply ethological procedures to those human subjects for whom language either does not exist or apparently plays a less prominent role than it does for adults. Ethologists seem less likely to focus on the phenomena of conversation than, say, ethnomethodologists. As Blurton Jones (1972b) observes, children have been used "as a handy brand of human subject that behaves rather than talking about behaving [p. 271]."

As might be expected, ethologists place primary methodological emphasis on careful observation of behavior in natural settings. Their studies are designed, among other things, to identify basic, repetitive elements or units of that observed behavior. (The notion of units will be further considered later in this discussion.) Blurton Jones (1972a) has suggested several aspects of the ethological approach on which there seems to be general agreement among its practitioners:

> (1) emphasis on the use of a large variety of simple observable features of behaviour as the raw data; (2) emphasis on description and a hypothesis-generating, natural history phase as the starting point of a study; (3) a distrust of major categories of behaviour whose meaning and reality have not been made clear; (4) belief in the usefulness of an evolutionary framework for determining which kinds of questions need to be asked about behaviour [pp. 4–5].

As stated in (2) above, human ethologists take a "traditionally unfashionable (non-hypothesis-testing) approach" (Blurton Jones & Leach, 1972, p. 218). Blurton Jones points out that there is another way in which this inductive bent "turns the usual [research] processes upside down. It has for long been customary to start with a concept such as 'aggression' or 'attachment' and then look for a 'good' measure of it" (p. 19). Blurton Jones states the opposite position strongly:

> This inversion implies that there are no 'psychologically meaningful variables' other than those derived from the data (these can nonetheless be very high level concepts, or complex models). This would appear to me to be an unassailable position if one's goal is a scientific study of behaviour but there are workers who prefer to determine what is meaningful either from pre-existing theory, or from introspection or intuition [p. 19].

Although contrasting with the external-variable approach, Blurton Jones' position is fully consistent with that of both the ethnomethodological studies and the so-called structural studies (considered in Section IV).

B. Categories

In line with their inductive research strategy, human ethologists place great emphasis on the careful formulation of elements of behavior to be used as basic in further observation and research. Grant (1969) begins an article by stating, "The increase in the understanding of the social behaviour of many species that has come about by the use of the ethological method has depended to a large extent on the accurate isolation and description of the characteristic behaviour patterns used by a species, i.e., on the development of a check list [p. 525]."

Behavior elements are sometimes called "units" (Brannigan & Humphries, 1972; Leach, 1972), "categories" or "behaviour categories" (Blurton Jones, 1972c; Richards & Bernal, 1972; Smith & Connolly, 1972), "motor patterns" or "behaviour patterns" (P. L. McGrew, 1970; W. C. McGrew, 1972) or all of the above (Grant, 1969). The term "categories" will be used in this discussion.

For ethologists, developing an accurate and effective set of categories is the natural starting point of research in an area. Thus, a list of such categories is often the primary result reported in a paper; this is true of many of the studies cited above. Certainly, the careful exploratory work that has been done by ethologists in category development has the potential for great usefulness to other investigators of face-to-face interaction.

The actual formulation of categories by ethologists may perhaps best be described as a highly disciplined, intuitive process, turning ultimately on the investigator's skill at observing and analyzing. Blurton Jones (1972a) suggests that "in practice an ethologist probably looks for observables which (a) are repeated in the same form, (b) look as if they affect other individuals and (c) look as if they are responses to other individuals [p. 11]." Regardless of the manner in which categories are developed, ethologists agree that the usefulness of a given category depends on the ease with which it can be observed reliably and its validity in subsequent studies.

It appears that, with few exceptions, ethological categories represent the same type of low-level observation as that described for "actions" in the preceding section. Thus, the two terms seem essentially equivalent. The general congruence is noted by Blurton Jones (1972a): "Ethological studies of children closely resemble studies proposed for kinesics (e.g., Birdwhistell, 1963) and proxemics (e.g., Hall, 1959, 1963) in their emphasis on direct observation and on recording clearly defined features of behaviour [p. 20]."

C. Analysis of Categories

Once an acceptable set of categories has been devised for studying the subjects and interactions of interest, the focus of ethological investigation moves to issues concerning the process of face-to-face interaction and the internal states of participants in interaction. Among the articles reviewed for this chapter, it seems fair to say that human ethologists are now in the process of moving into this second stage of research.

1. Characterizing Internal States

Characterizing the internal states of participants in interactions has been an integral part of ethological tradition. I would concur that such characterization is a necessary element in the adequate description of interaction. Even accepting the inductive approach that ends rather than begins with internal states, attempting to describe these is a particularly tricky endeavor. Perhaps each investigator has his own favorite list of fatal errors that have been made in this regard.

Ethologists have a variety of general terms for which they have provided special, ethologically relevant meanings, such as "causation," "intention," and "motivation." There is also a set of terms referring to more specific internal states, such as "aggression," "dominance," "appeasement," and the like. A proper consideration of issues relating to characterizing internal states would extend this discussion beyond its assigned limits and so must be deferred. It may be noted in passing, however, that Taylor (1966) and other philosophers of human action have questioned the appropriateness of concepts like "causation" when applied to voluntary human action. In order to provide a conceptual framework for human face-to-face interaction, it would seem that the distinction between voluntary and involuntary action will have to be considered carefully by both ethologists and other investigators. And it is perhaps in a dialogue between ethologists and investigators from other disciplines that some of the difficulties of characterizing internal states may be resolved in part. Further consideration of some of these issues may be found in the discussion section of Blurton Jones (1972b). The present discussion will maintain its focus on methodological issues.

2. Sequences of Action

In broadly recognizing the importance of sequences of action (as represented by sequences of categories), human ethologists differ from investigators using simple counts and timings. For example, Blurton Jones (1972a, 1972b) and Smith and Connolly (1972) advocate the analysis of sequences in studying both internal states and interaction.

But in practice, sequence analysis is infrequently employed by ethologists, apparently for two technical reasons (both discussed by ethologists).

First, observation of face-to-face interaction has been mainly done "live," that is, unaided by movie film or videotape. Clearly, there is a severe limit to the amount of information — particularly on rapid sequences of action — that can be recorded under such conditions. Second, there is the issue of how to analyze sequential data, once they are recorded. Blurton Jones (1972a) indicates that "several contemporary workers on social behaviour of children are aiming to analyse sequences of behaviour . . . but so far none have overcome fully the practical problems of getting programs written for computers that have big enough memories to analyse fairly long sequences of behaviour [p. 15]."

Despite the difficulties involved, human ethologists have succeeded in carrying out some studies of action sequences on the two broad issues mentioned above: internal states of the individual, and the process of face-to-face interaction. In studying subjects' internal states, analysis centers on sequences of categories displayed by individual subjects. That is, the sequences are observed within individuals. In studying interaction, sequences are analyzed involving both participants in an interaction. [This dichotomized approach may seem an obvious one, but it may be pointed out that in Duncan and Fiske (1977) hypotheses of internal states are based on analysis of sequences of interaction.]

Blurton Jones and Leach (1972) resort to the description of "logical sequences," that is, relationships in the data that were not recorded as sequences but that may be reasonably expected to be such. They apply this interpretation to their finding of a relationship between the "arms up" category for children, and "mother touching": mother touching presumably follows on child's arms up. Grant (1969) carried out an analysis of sequences of facial categories for single participants (not between participants in an interaction). Leach (1972) investigated sequences of actions between mother and child, but for the purposes of analysis she combined her more detailed observations into very large categories.

It appears, then, that only further development of observation and analysis techniques is required before more intensive and detailed work on sequences proceeds.

D. Summary: Human Ethology

Human ethology is a research area being carefully constructed on the basis of naturalistic observation and inductive development of concepts. Human ethologists have generally recognized the importance of analyzing sequences of actions, but there have been few studies actually using such analysis. It will be seen that many elements of the human-ethology approach are consistent with the structural studies described in the next section.

IV. STRUCTURAL STUDIES

More familiar to linguists and psycholinguists is the approach of studies designed to discover and to document the organization of face-to-face interaction in a manner roughly analogous to the way linguists hypothesize a grammar for a given language. To simplify exposition, studies of the organization of face-to-face interaction will be termed "structural studies," after Duncan (1969).

Structural studies aim at the description in formal terms of certain regularities in face-to-face interaction, although not necessarily in exactly the same way as current modes of linguistic description. It is clear, at least to me, that a description of the organization of face-to-face interaction will not center on the individual interactant but rather must include sequences of actions (as described above) involving both participants. Nor does it seem useful to become concerned exclusively with some subset of the actions observable in face-to-face interaction, such as language or "nonverbal behavior," or perhaps a few selected actions, such as gaze direction and the like. A description of the organization of face-to-face interaction would ideally encompass all actions relevant to that organization, and all relevant actions cannot be identified unless a wide range of actions are systematically and concurrently analyzed.

A. Mathematical Models of Temporal Events

Before proceeding with the discussion of structural studies, it is important to note that they do not constitute the only approach to the organization of interaction. An alternative approach entails fitting mathematical models to observations of face-to-face interaction. These observations typically include not only various types of interaction events, but also some measure of the duration of events and the time separating different events or recurrences of the same event. The organization of the interaction is represented by the model that best fits the data. This approach is considered in Chapter 13 and, therefore, receives no further attention here.

B. Studies of Sequential Structure

A second approach to studying interaction structure is closer to traditional linguistic method. Data are generated through detailed transcriptions of face-to-face interactions. A wide range of actions is observed, and the beginnings and endings of these actions are carefully located with respect to each other. Strong regularities in action sequences are sought through systematic inspection (and sometimes statistical analysis) of the transcribed material. If the search is successful, the regularities in question are described in terms of hypothesized signals, rules, units, and the like.

It has been a characteristic of these studies to date that, while sequences of actions are the essence of the analysis, considerations of time per se are not included in the hypothesized structural elements. (Time may, however, be used in the task of transcribing the interaction, in order to locate interaction events.) The omission of time for the hypothesized interaction structure is not a principled aspect of these studies, but rather it reflects a general practice of current investigators. The practice may, and perhaps should, change as research continues.

C. Early Studies

The present line of structural studies may be traced back to the early and mid-1950s. Birdwhistell (1952) was beginning his studies of "kinesics" or body motion from an essentially linguistic perspective. Hall (1959) was investigating the cultural structuring of the use of space, to which he applied the term "proxemics." At about the same time, a remarkable interdisciplinary study was being undertaken aimed at the development of "the foundation of a general theory of the structure of human communicative behavior" (McQuown, 1971, p. 5). This research project, initiated by Frieda Fromm-Reichmann, involved the collaborative efforts of Gregory Bateson, Ray L. Birdwhistell, Henry W. Brosin, Charles F. Hockett, and Norman A. McQuown, among others. Although the study was never published, it is now publicly available, as indicated in the reference. Principles of structural research, as discussed in the text and as embodied in the work itself, provide an essential theoretical and methodological foundation for present-day studies. Some of these principles were briefly mentioned above. Subsequently, Scheflen (1961, 1963, 1966, 1973) scrutinized interactions (mainly psychotherapy) from a structural point of view.

Examples of more recent work on the structure of face-to-face interaction from this second perspective would be those of Sacks, Schegloff and their colleagues described above, Kendon (1976), Duncan (1974), and Yngve (1970). A number of other investigators have contributed to a volume edited by Kendon, Harris, and Key (1975). This volume provides a contemporary and unusually comprehensive view of the considerable diversity of structural studies, as well as the wide range of traditional academic disciplines from which investigators of interaction structure have been drawn. A monograph by Duncan and Fiske (1977) describes one program of structural research and considers elements of a proposed conceptual framework for this research area.

D. Structural Methodology

Discussion of other approaches has anticipated my views on the main aspects of structural methodology. These aspects need only be summarized here as follows:

1. The categories used for observation should involve low-level description that does not require raters to make inferences with respect to unobservable entities, such as intentions or emotional states.
2. A wide variety of actions should be considered, as opposed to focusing on only one or two.
3. Data analysis must include consideration of the sequences of actions observed. (To generate accurate information on sequences, as well as on a wide variety of actions, it would seem that sound-film or videotape records of the interaction are required.)
4. Data and appropriate statistical information should be reported relevant to the investigator's claimed findings.
5. Considering the present stage of development of this area of investigation, it seems desirable for studies to have a strong exploratory, discovery-oriented approach.

Of the structural studies published to date, I would view the most common methodological weaknesses to be (1) a tendency to limit observation to only a few actions and (2) a failure to report empirical support for claimed findings. However, it seems likely that these weaknesses will be corrected as research of this sort continues to develop.

V. ELEMENTS OF A PROPOSED CONCEPTUAL FRAMEWORK

Having focused predominantly on methodological issues, I would like to conclude this chapter with a brief discussion of the conceptual framework proposed by Duncan and Fiske (1977) for research on face-to-face interaction. Only central elements of the framework will be sketched here.

The framework was developed in the course of considering both the results of the studies of speaking turns and related phenomena and the comments of other investigators. In many cases, speaking-turn phenomena will be used as examples, although familiarity with that research will not be assumed.

The primary organizing concepts are *convention* and *interaction strategy*. That is, convention and interaction strategy are suggested as two major sources of observed regularity in face-to-face interaction.

A. Convention

"Convention" refers to the structure of rules, meaningful elements and other phenomena within which the interaction takes place. The use of the term here closely follows the philosophical treatment by Lewis (1969). Convention is, apparently, what most investigators mean when they refer to the structured or rule-governed aspect of interaction; it seems directly related to Schegloff and Sacks's (1973) notion of the "orderliness" of conversations; and it is roughly analogous to the linguist's notion of grammar and to the notions of custom and practice in social science.

Given the notion of convention as a primary phenomenon in social science, what would be the elements of an adequate description of convention? Clearly, this issue has received and will continue to receive extensive consideration by social scientists. In their discussion of studies of phenomena related to speaking turns, Duncan and Fiske concluded that the following elements would have to be included, at least for those phenomena.

1. *Postulated states.* It was necessary to postulate the states of "speaker" and "auditor" for the participants in conversations in order describe actions related to the exchange of speaking turns and the like. These postulated states are necessary as well in order to square our research descriptions with our everyday intuitions.

2. *Signals.* A variety of signals was hypothesized, often together with subelements of the signals, termed "cues."

3. *Hypothesized states.* In addition to the postulated states were states hypothesized in order to describe what the signals are used for. That is, signals must bear information with respect to something, and in this case they were hypothesized to bear information with respect to internal states of the participant displaying them. For example, one signal was hypothesized to indicate some degree of willingness by the speaker to relinquish the turn. It should be stressed that these unobservable internal states were hypothesized on the basis of observed regularities in the interaction; at no point were raters required to include consideration of these states in their ratings.

4. *Moves.* The term "moves" was used to describe convention-related actions that were not signals. For example, a ship about to get underway may signal that fact by sounding one long blast on its whistle; the actual getting underway is a move. Although it is appropriate in this case for the

signal to accompany the move, either may occur without the other. The ship may signal that it is getting underway, yet fail to do so; or it may get underway without signaling. Moves may or may not have signals associated with them. A move in a chess game would be a move in the sense used here; apart from the signal "check," there are no signals that accompany chess moves.

5. *Situational requirements.* It would seem that an adequate description of a given convention must include a specification of those elements of the social situation that must or must not be present in order for the convention to be appropriately used. The situational requirements of the proposed turn conventions were not investigated systematically, and this was judged by Duncan and Fiske to be a significant omission in the description of turn-related phenomena to date.

6. *Sanctions.* Any social convention can be violated. At least theoretically, each such violation evokes negative consequences for the violator from those who adhere to the convention and who witness or hear about the violation. Presumably such negative consequences may range from severe legal or group sanctions to faintly negative impressions formed after repeated violation. In any event, it seems important to know the consequences attendant on violation of a convention.

For convenience the six elements above have been termed the "substance" of conventions. The organization of conventions is described in terms of rules:

7. *Rules.* Rules are statements specifying the relationship between any two or more elements of convention substance. A distinction may be made between signal-definition rules and interaction rules. Signal-definition rules may be said to describe the relationship between a given signal and either a convention-related state or some other signal. Interaction rules may be said to describe permissible sequences of action within the convention, given the display of certain signals and in some cases certain preceding moves by one or both participants.

B. Interaction Strategy

It does not seem reasonable to consider convention as the only major source of observed regularity in face-to-face interaction. Although it has not been subject to a great deal of empirical investigation, interaction strategy appears to provide a second major source of regularity. Interaction strategy may be generally characterized as some sort of variation in the use of convention(s). Three broad types of variation derive logically from the formulation of convention described above (although this derivation may not in every case be obvious because of the extreme brevity of the description):

1. *Exercise of permissible options.* Many conventions will provide a variety of options for those using it. For example, a chess player may in most circumstances move any one of several pieces. An auditor may or may not choose to take the speaking turn upon the activation of the turn signal by the speaker. Each such exercise of a legitimate option is an element of interaction strategy.

2. *Violation of convention rules.* A convention can always be violated, regardless of whether or not it provides for options. Thus, the fact of presence or absence of violation is an inescapable aspect of the enactment of a convention, describable in terms of interaction strategy.

3. *Formulation of situation.* In order for a participant to choose an appropriate convention in terms of its situational requirements, he must develop some formulation of the social situation in which he intends to take action. This formulating process might involve some social classification of the participant himself, the partner(s), other parties to the interaction, the social setting in which it occurs, the time of day, the season of the year, and other such factors. Most commentators on this process agree that it is not a fixed, automatic one, but rather an active construction by the participant, subject to various constraints. Once again, this is a process subject to certain options and to the possibility of violation. For this reason, formulation of the situation must be considered another element of interaction strategy. Although formulating the situation is a process internal to the participant, that formulation — more accurately, the participant's ostensive formulation — is evidenced, at least to some extent, by each convention in which he engages.

From the point of view of this conceptual framework, what one sees in a (two-person) face-to-face interaction is the interplay of two interaction strategies. Each participant must assess the social situation, choose conventions, cooperate in (ratify) conventions chosen by the partner or refuse to do so, adhere to or violate these conventions in some degree, and exercise options for which the conventions provide. All of these activities are aspects of interaction strategy. But interaction strategy cannot be described prior to an adequate formulation of the conventions involved in the interaction. Once these conventions are understood through careful analysis of interactions, the investigator can begin to describe each participant's strategy in terms of its various elements.

It may be noted that none of this involves the imputation of specific intentions to the participant. Prior to investigation, one may accept as plausible the general assumptions that each participant is acting intentionally, possesses internal states, has various sorts of information, and the like. None of this need be specified in detail, however. It is possible to describe both conventions and strategies strictly in terms of regularities in observed actions. Once a participant's interaction strategy has been described to some extent, it is possible to attempt to infer certain specific intentions from that strategy. But this stage of investigation is well beyond the present state of the art in this research area, and so it seems of little value to speculate on proper procedure for such inferences. Given the conceptual framework sketched here, the immediate task is to proceed with the careful description of interaction structure.

ACKNOWLEDGMENTS

Preparation of this manuscript has been supported in part by NSF grant SOC74-24084 awarded to S. D. Duncan, Jr., and D. W. Fiske. My thanks to Michael Silverstein for helpful comments on portions of this paper.

REFERENCES

Ainsworth, M. D. S., & Bell, S. M. Attachment, exploration and separation: Illustrated by the behaviour of one-year-olds in a strange situation. *Child Development*, 1970, *41*, 49–67.

Ainsworth, M. S. D., & Bell, S. M. Infant crying and maternal responsiveness: Reinforcement reassessed. *Child Development*, 1972, *43*, 1171–1190.

Altmann, S. A. Sociobiology of rhesus monkeys. II: Stochastics of social communication. *Journal of Theoretical Biology*, 1965, *8*, 490–522.

Bateson, G. Conventions of communication: Where validity depends upon belief. In J. Ruesch & G. Bateson, *Communication: The social matrix of psychiatry*. New York: Norton, 1951.

Bateson, G. Communication. In N. A. McQuown (Ed.), *The natural history of an interview*. Microfilm Collection of Manuscripts on Cultural Anthropology, Fifteenth Series. Chicago: The University of Chicago, Joseph Regenstein Library Department of Photoduplication, 1971.

Becker, F. D. Study of spatial markers. *Journal of Personality and Social Psychology*, 1973, *26*, 439–445.

Birdwhistell, R. L. *Introduction to kinesics*. Louisville: University of Louisville Press, 1952.

Birdwhistell, R. L. The kinesic level in the investigation of the emotions. In P. Knapp (Ed.), *Expression of the emotions in man*. New York: International Universities Press, Inc., 1963.

Blurton Jones, N. Characteristics of ethological studies of human behaviour. In N. Blurton Jones (Ed.), *Ethological studies of child behaviour*. London: Cambridge University Press, 1972. (a)

Blurton Jones, N. Non-verbal communication in children. In R. A. Hinde (Ed.), *Non-verbal communication*. London: Cambridge University Press, 1972. (b)

Blurton Jones, N. Categories of child–child interaction. In N. Blurton Jones (Ed.), *Ethological studies of child behaviour*. London: Cambridge University Press, 1972. (c)

Blurton Jones, N., & Leach, G. M. Behaviour of children and their mothers at separation and greeting. In N. Blurton Jones (Ed.), *Ethological studies of child behaviour*. London: Cambridge University Press, 1972.

Brannigan, C. R., & Humphries, D. A. Human non-verbal behaviour, a means of communication. In N. Blurton Jones (Ed.), *Ethological studies of child behaviour.* London: Cambridge University Press, 1972.

Brazelton, T. B., Koslowski, B., & Main, M. The origins of reciprocity: The early mother–infant interaction. In M. Lewis & L. A. Rosenblum (Eds.), *The effect of the infant on its caregiver.* New York: Wiley, 1974.

Chapple, E. D. *Culture and biological man.* New York: Holt, Rinehart & Winston, 1970.

Cicourel, A. V. Basic and normative rules in the negotiation of status and role. In D. Sudnow (Ed.), *Studies in social interaction.* New York: Free Press, 1972.

Denzin, N. K. Symbolic interactionism and ethnomethodology. In J. D. Douglas (Ed.), *Understanding everyday life.* Chicago: Aldine, 1970.

Duncan, S. D., Jr. Nonverbal communication. *Psychological Bulletin,* 1969, *72,* 118–137.

Duncan, S. D., Jr. Some signals and rules for taking speaking turns in conversations. *Journal of Personality and Social Psychology,* 1972, *23,* 283–292.

Duncan, S. D., Jr. Toward a grammar for dyadic conversations. *Semiotica,* 1973, *9,* 29–46.

Duncan, S. D., Jr. On the structure of speaker–auditor interaction during speaking turns. *Language in Society,* 1974, *2,* 161–180.

Duncan, S. D., Jr. Interaction units during speaking turns in dyadic, face-to-face interaction. In A. Kendon, R. Harris, & M. R. Key (Eds.), *The organization of behavior in face-to-face interaction.* The Hague: Mouton, 1975.

Duncan, S. D., Jr., & Fiske, D. W. *Face-to-face interaction: Research, methods and theory.* Hillsdale, N.J.: Lawrence Erlbaum Associates, 1977.

Eibl-Eibesfeldt, I. *Ethology: The biology of behavior.* New York: Holt, Rinehart & Winston, 1970.

Ekman, P. Universals and cultural differences in the facial expressions of emotion. In J. Cole (Ed.), *The Nebraska Symposium on Motivation* (Vol. 19). Lincoln: University of Nebraska Press, 1971.

Ekman, P. *Darwin and facial expression: A century of research in review.* New York: Academic Press, 1974.

Ekman, P., & Friesen, W. V. Constants across cultures in the face and emotion. *Journal of Personality and Social Psychology,* 1971, *17,* 124–129.

Ekman, P., & Friesen, W. V. *Unmasking the human face.* Englewood Cliffs, N.J.: Prentice-Hall, 1975.

Ekman, P., Friesen, W. V., & Ellsworth, P. *Emotion in the human face.* New York: Pergamon, 1972.

Ekman, P., Friesen, W. V., & Tomkins, S. S. Facial affect scoring technique: A first validity study. *Semiotica,* 1971, *3,* 37–58.

Ekman, P., Sorenson, E. R., & Friesen, W. V. Pan-cultural elements in facial displays of emotion. *Science,* 1969, *164,* 86–88.

Fiske, D. W. The limits for the conventional science of personality. *Journal of Personality,* 1974, *42,* 1–11.

Garfinkel, H. *Studies in ethnomethodology.* Englewood Cliffs, N.J.: Prentice-Hall, 1967.

Gewirtz, H. B., & Gewirtz, J. L. Caretaking settings, background events and behaviour differences in four Israeli child-rearing environments: Some preliminary trends. In B. M. Foss (Ed.), *Determinants of infant behaviour* (Vol. 4). London: Methuen, 1969.

Grant, E. C. Human facial expression. *Man,* 1969, *4,* 525–536.

Hall, E. T. *The silent language.* Garden City, N.Y.: Doubleday, 1959.

Hall, E. T. A system for the notation of proxemic behavior. *American Anthropologist,* 1963, *65,* 1003–1026.

Jaffe, J., & Feldstein, S. *Rhythms of dialogue*. New York: Academic, 1970.

Kaye, K. Infants' effects upon their mothers' teaching strategies. In J. C. Glidewell (Ed.), *The social context of learning and development*. New York: Gardner Press, 1976.

Kendon, A. Some functions of gaze-direction in social interaction. *Acta Psychologica*, 1967, *26*, 22–63.

Kendon, A. Introduction. In A. Kendon, R. M. Harris, & M. R. Key (Eds.), *The organization of behavior in face-to-face interaction*. The Hague: Mouton, 1975.

Kendon, A. Some functions of the face in a kissing round. *Semiotica*, 1976, *15*, 299–334.

Kendon, A., Harris, R. M., & Key, M. R. (Eds.) *The organization of behavior in face-to-face interaction*. The Hague: Mouton, 1975.

Leach, G. M. A comparison of the social behaviour of some normal and problem children. In N. Blurton Jones (Ed.), *Ethological studies of child behaviour*. London: Cambridge University Press, 1972.

Lewis, D. K. *Convention*. Cambridge, Mass.: Harvard University Press, 1969.

Lewis, M., & Lee-Painter, S. An interactional approach to the mother–infant dyad. In M. Lewis & L. A. Rosenblum (Eds.), *The effect of the infant on its caregiver*. New York: Wiley, 1974.

McGrew, P. L. Social and spatial density effects on spacing behaviour in preschool children. *Journal of Child Psychology and Psychiatry*, 1970, *11*, 197–206.

McGrew, W. C. *An ethological study of children's behavior*. New York: Academic, 1972.

McHugh, P. *Defining the situation: The organization of meaning in social interaction*. Indianapolis and New York: Bobbs-Merrill, 1968.

McQuown, N. A. (Ed.) *The natural history of an interview*. Microfilm Collection of Manuscripts on Cultural Anthropology, Fifteenth Series. Chicago: The University of Chicago Joseph Regenstein Library Department of Photoduplication, 1971.

Meltzer, L., Morris, W. N., & Hayes, D. P. Interruption outcomes and vocal amplitude: Explorations in social psychophysics. *Journal of Personality and Social Psychology*, 1971, *18*, 392–402.

Moerman, M. Analysis of Lue conversation: Providing accounts, finding breaches, and taking sides. In D. Sudnow (Ed.), *Studies in social interaction*. New York: Free Press, 1972.

Nie, N. H., Hull, C. H., Jenkins, J. G., Steinbrenner, K., & Bent, D. H. *SPSS: Statistical package for the social sciences* (2nd ed.). New York: McGraw-Hill, 1975.

Rheingold, H. L., & Eckerman, C. O. The infant separates himself from his mother. *Science*, 1970, *168*, 78–83.

Richards, M. P. M., & Bernal, J. F. An observational study of mother–infant interaction. In N. Blurton Jones (Ed.), *Ethological studies of child behaviour*. London: Cambridge University Press, 1972.

Sacks, H., Schegloff, E. A., & Jefferson, G. A simplest systematics for the organization of turn-taking for conversation. *Language*, 1974, *50*, 696–735.

Schegloff, E. A., & Sacks, H. Opening up closings. *Semiotica*, 1973, *8*, 289–327.

Scheflen, A. E. *A psychotherapy of schizophrenia: A study of direct analysis*. Springfield, Ill.: Thomas, 1961.

Scheflen, A. E. Communication and regulation in psychotherapy. *Psychiatry*, 1963, *26*, 126–136.

Scheflen, A. E. Natural history method in psychotherapy: Communicational research. In L. A. Gottschalk & A. H. Auerbach (Eds.), *Methods of research in psychotherapy*. New York: Appleton-Century-Crofts, 1966.

Scheflen, A. E. *Communicational structure: Analysis of a psychotherapy transaction*. Bloomington: University of Indiana Press, 1973.

Silverstein, M. Shifters, linguistic categories, and cultural description. In K. A. Basso & H. A. Selby (Eds.), *Meaning in anthropology*. Albuquerque: University of New Mexico Press, 1976.

Smith, P. K., & Connolly, K. Patterns of play and social interaction in pre-school children. In N. Blurton Jones (Ed.), *Ethological studies of child behaviour*. London: Cambridge University Press, 1972.

Stern, D. N. Mother and infant at play: The dyadic interaction involving facial, vocal, and gaze behaviors. In M. Lewis & L. A. Rosenblum (Eds.), *The effect of the infant on its caregiver*. New York: Wiley, 1974.

Sudnow, D. (Ed.) *Studies in social interaction*. New York: Free Press, 1972.

Taylor, R. *Action and purpose*. Englewood Cliffs, N.J.: Prentice-Hall, 1966.

Trager, G. L. Paralanguage: A first approximation. *Studies in Linguistics*, 1958, *13*, 1–12.

Turner, R. (Ed.) *Ethnomethodology*. Harmondsworth, England: Penguin, 1974.

Weick, K. Review of H. Garfinkel, *Studies in ethnomethodology*. *Contemporary Psychology*, 1969, *14*, 357–360.

Yngve, V. H. On getting a word in edgewise. *Papers from the sixth regional meeting Chicago Linguistic Society*. Chicago: Chicago Linguistic Society, 1970, 567–577.

Zimmerman, D. H., & Wieder, D. L. Ethnomethodology and the problem of order. In J. D. Douglas (Ed.), *Understanding everyday life*. Chicago: Aldine, 1970.

13 Conversational Rhythms

Joseph Jaffe
Samuel W. Anderson
Columbia University College of
Physicians and Surgeons and New York State
Psychiatric Institute

Daniel N. Stern
Cornell University Medical Center
and New York Hospital

How rhythmic can speech be? Galileo is said to have employed his own singing voice as a chronometer to discover the law of falling bodies (Drake, 1975). Such stability in vocal behavior suggests mechanisms for the control of speech timing at various levels, from the pulsating production of syllables to the time patterns that are shared and mutually understood by two persons engaged in conversation.

The fact that vocal behavior can be rhythmic enough once to have served as a physicist's chronometer should not be taken to indicate that any statistical variation in speech timing is due to error. We must immediately draw a basic distinction between casual and formal (ritual) speech. In the latter, epitomized by well-rehearsed verse, song, cheering, and oratory, the context is emotional and conventional. Rhythmic regularity here indeed approaches that of clocklike mechanisms. However, most of human verbal communication occurs in the more relaxed mode of casual speech, which includes everything from tentative, hesitant verbal formulations of unrehearsed ideas to the dithyrambic utterances of enthusiastic children. In the casual mode, departures from rhythmicity are often deliberate and expressive, and though they are greater than would be expected from considerations of timing error alone, rhythmic patterning is by no means absent. In casual speech, rhythmicity is a much more subtle phenomenon, involving a mathematically tractable stochastic element, as we shall subsequently demonstrate. Suffice it now to say that *excessive rhythmicity in casual social dialogue is boring and/or pathological:* Temporal predictability cements human relations up to a point, beyond that it can backfire.

Nevertheless, it is the optimal expression of rhythmicity that makes human relations predictable. We believe that much of what is meant by the terms "personality" and "cultural pattern" involves stability of behavioral rates. Such stable time constancies help us to recognize others, and more subtle constancies appear to be an important aspect of an individual's identity, an aspect that is sometimes disrupted in disease (Howes & Geschwind, 1964), and is present in all of us (Anderson, 1977; Buchsbaum, 1972; Stern, Beebe, Jaffe, & Bennett, 1977; see Figs. 13.1 through 13.4).

No communicative activity is more ubiquitous, more central, nor more neglected than is conversation. As philosophers increasingly acknowledge the essentially dialogic nature of all linguistic inquiry (de Laguna, 1927; Searle, 1970), we identify an analogous problem: the rhythmic coupling (entrainment) of human communicators, each of whom brings his or her idiosyncratic rhythmic propensities into the interaction.

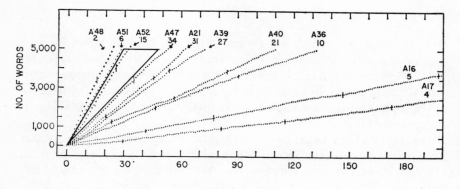

TIME IN MINUTES

FIG. 13.1.   Rate of emission of words for several aphasic patients. The ordinate specifies the cumulative number of words spoken after successive minutes of interview. A *straight line* represents a constant rate of speech. *Vertical markers* indicate the termination of one interview and the onset of another at a later date. The *triangular area* at the left indicates the range of rates in 12 normal subjects. (From Howes & Geschwind, 1964.)

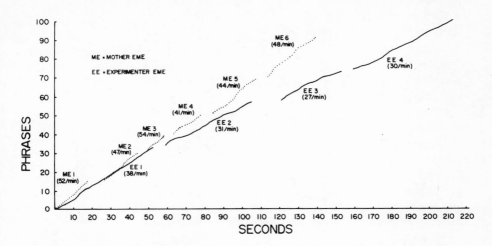

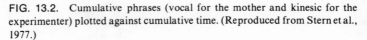

FIG. 13.2.   Cumulative phrases (vocal for the mother and kinesic for the experimenter) plotted against cumulative time. (Reproduced from Stern et al., 1977.)

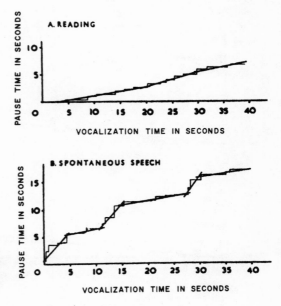

FIG. 13.3.   Cumulative pause and vocalization times from an actual talker while (A) reading and (B) speaking spontaneously. (Reproduced from Henderson et al., 1966.)

395

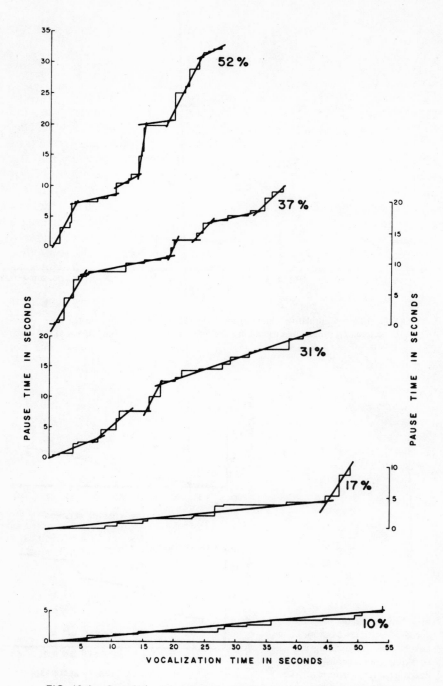

FIG. 13.4. Cumulative pause and vocalization times for the five simulated talkers at the indicated overall percentage pause times. Refer the 10%, 31%, and 52% graphs to the left-hand ordinate, the 17% and 37% to the right. (From Jaffe, Breskin, & Gerstman, 1972.)

I. HISTORICAL BACKGROUND

Early in this century, a Russian mathematician invented a new branch of probability theory. As a popular application of his ideas, he chose the convenient text of a classical drama, Pushkin's *Eugene Onegin* (Markov, 1913). We now know that he could have picked any one of a large number of nonlinguistic phenomena that could have served his purpose as well. His choice was possibly inadvertent, but was certainly felicitous, because it established Markov as an early progenitor of mathematical linguistics.[1]

Historically, Markov models have proved to be useful in communication engineering and cryptography, disciplines in which the basic problems are primarily those of linguistic performance rather than competence. Wedded to information theory, they figured prominently at the birth of quantitative psycholinguistics (Osgood & Sebeok, 1954). However, after it had been shown by Chomsky (1957, 1959) that finite state models had been injudiciously applied to issues of linguistic competence by engineers (Shannon & Weaver, 1949) and by behaviorists (Skinner, 1957), there followed a wholesale rejection of Markov models as a valid approach in both linguistics and psychology. To be sure, Chomsky's argument was not universally accepted, even at the time. For example, according to Pierce (1961):

> If we arbitrarily impose some bound on the length of a sentence, even if we limit the length to 1,000 or 1 million words, then Chomsky's grammar *does* correspond to a finite state machine. The imposition of such a limit on sentence length seems very reasonable in a practical way [p. 115].

---

[1]While Markovian theory has by now been elaborated considerably in various mathematical directions, the unadorned term "Markov model" will refer, throughout this chapter, only to Markov's original concept: "a stochastic process which moves through a finite number of states, and for which the probability of entering a certain state depends only on the last state occupied (Kemeny & Snell, 1960). More complex stochastic processes are mentioned only briefly late in the chapter, where *projected* and *semi*-Markov chains are explicitly introduced for the purpose of solving particular theoretical problems. But for the most part, applications will be made of the general two-state Markov model defined by matrix M:

$$M = \begin{array}{cc} & \begin{array}{cc} 1 & 2 \end{array} \\ \begin{array}{c} 1 \\ 2 \end{array} & \left[\begin{array}{cc} p_1 & 1 - p_1 \\ 1 - p_2 & p_2 \end{array} \right] \end{array}$$

The entries in M are *transition probabilities* between last states occupied (rows) and states entered (columns). Given that a process is in state 1, the probability of remaining there or of going to state 2 are p_1 and $1 - p_1$, respectively. If the process is in state 2, the probabilities of remaining there or going to state 1 are p_2 and $1 - p_2$. The *state diagram* for M is shown in Fig. 13.8, where it is applied as a model for stress alternation.

Chomsky deserves credit for being the first to realize that a finite state grammar, even one that generates just the thousand-word sentences, is hopelessly more inelegant and tedious than are several reasonable transformational alternatives. But, rather than launch anew into this old debate, we consider it much more important to point out that claims for non-Markovian properties of natural language have actually been supported by mathematical demonstration in the literature only for the syntactic component of grammar (Chomsky & Miller, 1963; Peters & Ritchie, 1971), leaving open the question with respect to the phonological component.

In fact, both traditional and generative theories relegate to systems of phonological rules the least computationally demanding task of the entire grammar—the selection of sound patterns to match sentence codes, the sentences usually being regarded as already preformed with respect to all properties apart from sound structure. Chomsky and Halle (1968) limit the phonological component of their grammar to a set of "local" transformations, each rule being strictly specified as to the context within which it applies. The set of phonological rules operates independently within each "phonological phrase," which is viewed as an immediate constituent of the syntactic surface structure. Unfortunately, the theory of phonological phrases is not yet completely worked out, even with respect to its fundamental axioms, and Chomsky has expressed varying degrees of enthusiasm for the task of showing either the necessity or desirability of incorporating the general use of recursive transformational cycles in phonology.

In an early formulation, Chomsky and Miller (1963) recognized that any phonological system that meets conditions of linearity and invariance is equivalent to a very simple finite automaton (p. 310ff). These two conditions (which establish, essentially, that surface strings are directly recoverable from phonetic transcriptions symbol by symbol from left to right) are known not to be met for natural languages. But it does not follow, as some have hinted, that the phonological component cannot, therefore, be Markovian. The question of whether phonology has non-Markovian properties actually depends upon one other crucial question: Does there exist a finite uper limit on the amount of contiguous contextual information that need ever be scanned to determine the sound pattern of any phone in any phonological phrase?

If the answer to this question is "no," then a formal argument applies here, as it does in syntax, which proves there can be no finite-state model for the phonological component. In our opinion, it is manifestly clear by intuition and by the examples (if not always the rules) given by phonologists, that the answer to this question must be affirmative. Proposed coarticulatory constraints across very short contexts, usually within syllables, exhaust nearly all of the known effects (see Anderson, 1975, for a review of temporal constraints). Other constraints are held to operate within words, and those interword output dependencies that do show up in studies of anticipations, perseverations, and spoonerisms are not reported across ranges of more than a few words; it is doubtful whether a spoonerism whose parts are separated by, say, 20 words, would even be recognized as a single transposition error, so strong is the intuition against such an interpretation (Fromkin, 1973).

Although Chomsky and Halle (1968) employ transformational rules in the phonological component, they follow Bierwisch in supplying a special set of "readjustment rules" to limit their range of application to finite domains (p. 372); to propose rules of this kind is to accept a finite limit.

This chapter is not the place for a full elaboration of the formal details, but it is easy to sketch out a demonstration that a finite limit on contiguous, adequate context guarantees the possibility of a Markovian phonology. First, observe that the existence of the limit implies that there is a *maximum local domain* (Δ), such that a scan of Δ surface units (including both preceding and following symbols as well as the symbol to be rewritten) will always supply at least enough information to determine completely the entire feature matrix for any phone, including segmental and coarticulatory features and stress value. Thus, the phonological component can be viewed as a Markov chain that needs no more states than the number of possible surface substrings of length Δ. And, of course, that number will be finite if Δ is finite.

Finite Δ can be regarded as an extended linearity condition, as a left-to-right scan of the surface string, Δ symbols at a time, will generate a *real-time* left-to-right phonetic string. It is important to notice that context specifications that include *following* symbols in surface structure do not violate the Markovian requirement of left-to-right processing in real time, because the entire surface string is regarded as preformed and therefore totally complete prior to the execution of the phonological rules.

Chomsky and Halle (1968) reject the mechanics of this kind of approach, because it requires treating many of their ordered phonological rules as though they were executed simultaneously rather than sequentially. It is also rejected by these authors because it is believed to require the "endless" repetition of contextual environments [p. 349]. However, we can see from the foregoing that the number of times any symbol is repeated in derivational contexts is not endless, but is equal to Δ. For example, if the maximum local domain of the phonological component were three preceding and two following units (plus the symbol itself), $\Delta = 6$, and the derivation

$$/ABCDEFGHI/ \rightarrow [ABCDEFGHI]$$

proceeds stepwise as follows, picking up the Eth symbol:

(BCDEFG)	(CDEFGH)	(DEFGHI)
$\downarrow$	$\downarrow$	$\downarrow$
[ABCDE...]	[ABCDEF...]	[ABCDEFG...]

and so on. Parentheses indicate the successive positions occupied by the moving contextual window as it generates [E], then [F], then [G]. In condensed form, this sequence can be expressed:

/A(B(C(D E F G)H)I) . . ./
    ↓ ↓ ↓
[A B C D E F G . . .]

where the surface string, enclosed by / ... /, is composed of independent surface formative symbols, or "phonemes," and the phonetic terminal string, enclosed by [...], is a fully coarticulated and suprasegmentally organized phonetic sequence. (Details, such as distinguishing terminal contexts, are omitted.)

The value of Δ for English is not definitively established; however, Liberman (1970) proposes that the limit on coarticulatory constraints is the maximum number of formatives that can occur in one "syllabic bundle" (p. 313). As it has been suggested that the most complex syllable in the language is the word "strength," Liberman's view can be taken to mean that the value of Δ for English is not more than eleven. This follows from the fact that the syllable /strIηθ/ has just six formatives, so it has both preceding and following maximal contexts of five each. As suggested above, if word-level phonology is taken into consideration, a rather larger estimate is indicated.

But, although we have shown that Markovian rules are powerful enough, under a reasonable assumption, to assign sound patterns to the output of a transformational grammar, there remains one further difficulty. It is this: The probabilities of the phonetic strings are in part determined by the probabilities of their corresponding surface strings. And, because it is not known how a transformational grammar might assign probabilities to its surface strings, the stochastic status of the model's final output cannot be determined theoretically. Nevertheless, the practical successes achieved by Markovian modeling of speech codes ranging from letter frequencies, as in cryptanalysis, to syllabic structures (see below), make it quite evident that the entire grammar does constitute a steady-state process of some kind, because it manifestly yields a stationary distribution for its phonetic repertoire.

The success of these models does not mean, of course, that any particular sentence is stochastically determined. But it does challenge any linguistic theory, if it be a theory with consequences for speech performance, to account for the gross speech statistics that are well fitted by Markov models.

Historically, it was not long after Markov's original (1913) paper that French, Carter, and Koenig (1930) collected data demonstrating short sequential constraints in actual consonant–vowel sequences of spoken English, sampled from telephone conversations. As discussed by Gerstman,[2]

---

[2]Personal communication from Prof. Louis J. Gerstman, C.U.N.Y.

TABLE 13.1
Syllable Types in Telephone Conversations

Syllable Type	Observed	Expected
CVC	33.5%	35.7%
CV	21.8	20.4
VC	20.3	18.6
V	9.7	10.6
CVCC	7.8	7.0
VCC	2.8	3.6
CCVC	2.8	2.3
CCV	0.8	1.3
CCVCC	0.5	0.5
	100.0%	100.0%

these early scientists at Bell Laboratories observed the syllable structures shown in Table 13.1.

Expected values are what would be obtained from a model that supposes that how a syllable begins is independent of how it ends; that fit is good. The result is especially clear in Table 13.2, where the data have been summed separately for syllable beginnings and endings. Cross multiplication of appropriate entries in Table 13.2 yields the predictions in Table 13.1. As should be evident from the foregoing discussion, although there are coarticulatory dependencies that extend across the syllable, they do not show up here, where allophonic covariation of vowels and consonants is not taken into account. The model asserts simply that degrees of initial and final consonant clustering occur independently.

Later in the chapter we shall show that only minor alterations are necessary to extend this orthographic model to the real-time analysis of syllabic rhythms, based on the actual durations of coarticulated phonetic segments. Gerstman's analysis shows that an abstract two-state system, based on the recurrence of spontaneously *spoken* consonants and vowels, confirms Markov's result despite large differences in language and literary style. It is but a step to move on to the real-time pattern of this simplified system, apart

TABLE 13.2
Consonant Clustering Probabilities

Initial Probabilities		Terminal Probabilities	
No consonant	0.328	No consonant	0.323
One consonant	0.631	One consonant	0.566
Two consonants	0.041	Two consonants	0.111
	1.000		1.000

from any need to determine the identities of individual letters, phones, or words. The problem can be tackled directly by means of discrete time sampling of simple phonetic features.

Chronologically, the earliest widespread application of Markovian two-state systems in real time occurred at the level of conversational analysis (see, for example, Chapple & Lindemann, 1942; Matarazzo et al., 1958; Jaffe et al., 1967). Much of this work is summarized in Jaffe and Feldstein (1970) and in Matarazzo and Wiens (1972). In the following section, we shall propose a scheme for comparing all of these results, ranging from syllable to dialogue, in a manner that permits the development of an integrated approach, comprising all levels. It would perhaps be premature to designate this scheme a theory of communication, but it is cast in as paradigmatic a form as we now feel the data, including our own work, will allow.

II.   A SYSTEMS APPROACH TO CONVERSATIONAL RHYTHMS

A nested hierarchy of finite-state systems is a simple device to organize a bewildering range of observed communication rhythms encompassing phenomena from neurophysiology to sociolinguistics. Because each level of the hierarchy is composed of but two states, the additional elegance of a unified statistical analysis is introduced, and the degree of rhythmic control at each level can be compared with control at other levels in quantitative terms. First, consider the hierarchy, as shown in Fig. 13.5.

Beginning at the bottom of Fig. 13.5, we have the *stress rhythm* (level 4), defined by the alternation of stressed vowels and intervening unstressed segments (transyllabics). A schematic state diagram for a Markov model at this level is given in Fig. 13.8. A run of alternations between these two states constitutes a phonological phrase, bounded by pauses. The stress rhythm is embedded within the *phrase rhythm* (level 3). Thus, the phrase-pause alternation is generated by a higher two-state system. Together, levels 3 and 4 represent, within the system, the common-sense notion of a monologue.

Because conversation is at least an alternation of monologues, it is tempting to construct yet a higher two-state system in which the monologue alternation is itself embedded. Depending upon the minimal definition of monologue, level 2 of the hierarchy comes close to the "turn-taking" phenomenon of Duncan (see Chapter 12). A purist would wish to equate turn taking with alternation of speaker–listener (sender–receiver) roles. But these simplistic dichotomies, however appropriate to one-way communication channels such as "walkie-talkies," are miserably inappropriate in face-to-face conversation where each participant is simultaneously and continuously a sender and receiver of messages. Though, intuitively, a listener may often

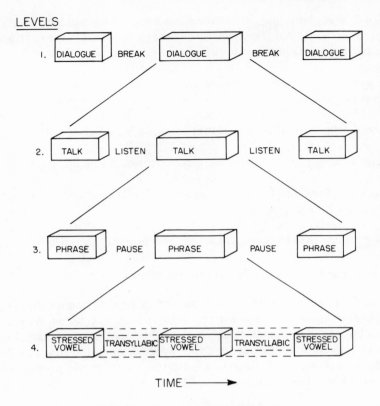

FIG. 13.5.   Conversation-level hierarchy.

respond briefly without interrupting the "turn" of the speaker, Yngve's "back-channel" behavior (1970), our completely automated analysis must adopt an arbitrary criterion that, for better or for worse, is designated as "holding the floor." Thus, a speaker gains the "floor" whenever he vocalizes unilaterally, no matter how briefly, and one-third of these unilateral vocalizations are indeed brief interjections by the listener (of duration < 1 sec) during juncture pauses of the speaker (see Fig. 13.10). By our definition, the "floor" has briefly changed hands, a so-called "speaker switch." By Duncan's definition, the speaker has not lost his "turn," but there is no conflict as long as everyone is clear about operational definitions. Thus, changes of the "floor" are equated with talk-listen alternations, and we have yet another two-state system in which the phrase rhythm of monologue is embedded. Levels 2, 3, and 4, then, constitute a dialogue, with the interpersonal decision component entering directly at level 2.

Analogously, a dialogue is bounded by breaks in the transaction at the highest level, which measures the joint decision by two persons as to when they shall engage in conversation and when not; level 1 added in with 2, 3, and 4 completes the system. Thus, the formula for a communicative relationship embodies the following rewrite rules:

Level 1. Conversational Relationship → (Dialogue + Break)*
Level 2. Dialogue → (Talk + Listen)*
Level 3. Talk → (Phrase + Pause)*
Level 4. Phrase → (Stressed Vowel + Transyllabic Segment)*

or more concisely, the formula for a conversational relationship is:

(Dialogue(Speaking(Phrase(Stressed Vowel + Transyllabic Segment) *Pause)*Listening)*Break)*

where * means that the cycle within the parentheses can repeat.[3]

A. Tempo and Rhythmicity Within the Hierarchy

That each level constitutes a two-state system permits comparison of rate (tempo) and degree of rhythmicity in common statistical terms. Assume the two states are digitized as "one" or "two" by discrete time sampling at intervals that must be shorter than the expected minimum time the system spends in any state.[4] Following digitization, a rhythmic period is then represented as a run of ones followed by a run of twos.

Let M_1 = mean duration in state 1
M_2 = mean duration in state 2
M = mean duration of a period, composed of a run of ones followed by a run of twos.
σ = standard deviation of such a period
r = subsegment correlation (i.e., correlation between durations of 1 runs and 2 runs within periods)

M defines the overall mean tempo, or rate, at a given level. Gibbon (1977) suggests that the ratio σ/M, or *coefficient of variation* (CV), be taken as an index of timing efficiency. Assuming a simple inverse relationship between variation and efficiency, Gibbon's suggestion leads to the following expression for *percent timing efficiency* (PTE):

---

[3]Although this scheme departs from previous formulations in several details, it takes the present form to emphasize the patterns of rhythmic alternation that usually occur.

[4]Hayes et al. (1970) urge caution regarding the effect of analogue to digital conversion tenchiques upon the phenomenon observed. See also Box and Jenkins (1970, p. 486).

$$PTE = 100/(CV + 1) \tag{1}$$

We consider PTE also to be an indicator for *degree of rhythmicity*. M and σ are easily calculated from the corresponding moments for the subsegments (Anderson, 1975):

$$M = M_1 + M_2 \tag{2}$$

and

$$\sigma = \sqrt{\sigma_1^2 + 2r\sigma_1\sigma_2 + \sigma_2^2} \tag{3}$$

These equations make no assumptions about the form of duration distributions, apart from the obvious requirement that they possess finite means and standard deviations.

Observations at levels 1 and 2 are satisfactorily made, especially from audio or video recordings, by an observer armed with a stopwatch, or, better, an interaction chronograph. As the time domain of level 3 approaches the lower limit of human reaction time (about 100 msec), accurate measures of phrase and pause durations are best made automatically by computer, and the use of computer-sensing is as necessary at level 4 as it is to use a microscope for the observation of protozoans (hence the term "microstructure" for speech time domains that extend below 100 msec).

In our laboratory, we employ computer processing for levels 2 through 4. We begin by measuring the stream of speech in real time as a sequence of vocalic and intervocalic segments; we shall refer to this primary measure below as the *vocalic sequence*. Primary analogue/digital sampling is performed every 400 microseconds after low-pass filtering of the speech signal at 2 kH. Vocalic segment onset is defined as a digitized signal amplitude increment of at least 6 dB above background, provided it is maintained for 20 msec or more; similarly, the end point for a vocalic segment is defined as an amplitude drop of at least 6 dB from an instantaneous maximum, provided that the drop is maintained for 20 msec or more. (For technical details, see Anderson & Jaffe, 1972.) Once the vocalic sequence of a speech sample is determined, the vowels (vocalics) and the gaps (intervocalics) between them are each subcategorized to establish their phonological status.

Vowels are regarded as stressed if they are at least 60 msec long, and unstressed if they are between 20 and 60 msec in duration (Anderson, 1975). Intervocalics are classified as pauses if they are 200 msec or longer, and as consonantal gaps if less than 200 msec. It is on the basis of this stratification of the vocalic sequence that we arrive at a chronographic model at level 4 for a stress-timed language such as English. The stress group is identified at this level as a periodic sequence that begins with the onset of a stressed vowel, continues across the following sequence of gaps and unstressed vowels (transyllabic segment), and ends with the next stressed vowel onset. Of course, no pauses can occur within a stress group, and every phrase must contain at least one stressed vowel.

The vocalic sequence remains useful, as it permits the collection of statistics on syllable rate, a most sensitive measure of word rate [see (4)].

Speech rate (words per minute) as a function of syllable rate is equal to

$$SR = K \left(\frac{\text{syllables}}{\text{phrase}} \right) \times \left(\frac{\text{phrases}}{\text{second}} \right) \tag{4}$$

where K is equal to (words/syllable) × 60. Converting to SR as a function of mean durations and combining measures from the vocalic sequence with those at level 3, we have

$$SR = K \left(\frac{M_1 + M_{iv}}{M_v + M_{iv}} \right) / (M_1 + M_2) \tag{5}$$

where M_1 = mean phrase length, M_2 = mean pause length, M_v = mean vowel length, and M_{iv} = mean intervocalic duration. The sum of M_v and M_{iv} yields the mean syllable period duration.

At level 4, the analogue of the syllable period is the *stress period,* which is approximately 1½ times as long, and is accompanied, therefore, by a stress rate that is usually less than the syllable rate in English speech. Now, Eq. (4) is replaced by Eq. (6):

$$SR = K' \left(\frac{\text{stresses}}{\text{phrase}} \right) \times \left(\frac{\text{phrases}}{\text{second}} \right) \tag{6}$$

and K by K' = (words/stress) × 60. If we further assume, as is often the case, that both phrase-initial and phrase-final vowels are stressed, we have, analogous to Eq. (5), the expression:

$$SR = K' \left(\frac{M_1 + M_{ts}}{M_a + M_{ts}} \right) / (M_1 + M_2) \tag{7}$$

where M_a = mean length of stressed vowel and M_{ts} = mean transyllabic duration (i.e., M_a corresponds to "M_1" and M_{ts} to "M_2" at level 4).

Previous research has utilized the syllable period, divided either by phonation time (excluding pauses), yielding *articulation rate,* or total speaking time (including pauses), as we do above, yielding speech rate. The common-sense notion of speech rhythm might seem to exclude pauses from consideration, although it is as yet unknown whether pause parameters are in fact independent of intraphrasal events. The "best" definition of a rhythm depends upon the empirical question to be asked: Are we concerned with the physical rhythmicity of speech as it is actually performed, with the perception of rhythmicity by a listener, or, perhaps, with the cues, both performed and perceived, that are utilized to synchronize speech between participants in conversation? There is no a priori reason to believe that any one unit will be implicated as a pacemaker for all of these disparate types of event. We consider it a virtue of the systems hierarchy that it permits a comprehensive description of speech timing without prejudgment of these issues. Our intended preconception is simply this: that any speech rhythm, whether monologic or dyadic, will almost surely involve the designated units found at one or more levels in Fig. 13.5.

Of course, rate, or tempo, is easily expressed directly in terms of system units at any level of the system; tempos obviously progress faster as one moves from top to bottom in the hierarchy. Intervals between dialogue onsets (level 1) vary widely, from minutes to decades.[5] At level 2, a person typically takes the floor (stops listening and starts talking) about three times per minute in casual conversation. Phrases usually recur at the much faster rate of 30 per minute; the pace of stressed vowels within phrases averages 180 per minute, with vowels occurring in the vocalic sequence about 1½ times as often as that. At higher levels, the tempo is relatively more sensitive to social situation; at lower levels the tempos appear to reflect psychological state. The tempos of syllable rhythms may vary in different regional dialects of English and are expected to differ markedly from our New York City norms (Anderson & Jaffe, 1976) when measured in other languages. However, we find that microstructural rhythmic stability for each individual, sampled under standard conditions, is such that it can be treated as a physiological index comparable to body temperature or heartrate. PTE [Eq. (1)], in particular, has shown that stress-period rhythmicity is reduced by various psychoactive drugs (Jaffe & Anderson, 1975). The normal range of the stress period PTE is narrowly focused at 67 to 71%, in contrast with PTE at level 3, which ranges from about 40 to 60%.

On the basis of a sample of 26 5-minute monologues performed by normal native speakers of English (15 males and 11 females, selected from data collected by Breskin, 1970), the mean durations of segments in Table 13.3

---

[5]Hayes and Cobb (1979) have identified a 90–100-minute periodicity in the onsets of dialogues under "free running" conditions, a period which matches the rapid eye movement (REM) cycle associated with dreaming in sleep. They hypothesize that the dialogue period may be the waking counterpart of the REM cycle. The explanation of this interesting concordance is not yet clear but may involve the interpersonal entrainment of endogenous biological rhythms.

TABLE 13.3
Mean Frequency and Duration (msec) of Speech Units at Levels 3 and 4,
Sampled from Monologues

	Segment	Mean Frequency	Mean Duration
Level 3	Phrase (time between pause off-set and the next pause onset)	178	893
	Pause (intervocalic ≥ 200 msec)	178	783
Level 4	Stressed Vowel (≥ 60 msec)	527	199
	Transyllabic (any nonpause separating stressed vowels)	401	121
	Alternating Stress Period	95	346
Vocalic Sequence	Vocalic (≥ 20 msec)	678	164
	Intervocalic (≥ 20 msec)	678	279

were computed. Results of this study indicate that stress (or accent) periods occur at an average rate of just under three per second during phrases and confirm familiar phonetics laboratory results that have found mean vowel durations in the vicinity of 160 msec, pause and phrase duration means of just under 1 second (Anderson & Jaffe, 1976). Looking at intercorrelations between individual mean segment durations across subjects, we obtained the correlations and significance values (t-tests) as shown in Table 13.4.

In Figs. 13.6 and 13.7, each subject's phrase and pause means are plotted, respectively, against his own standard deviations As shown in Eq. (1), constancy of timing efficiency (scalar timing) implies that a plot of σ against μ will yield a straight line. As is clear by comparison of Figs. 13.6 and 13.7, phrases more closely approximate constant timing efficiency than do pauses, at least in monologue. Stern and Gibbon (1978) report scalar timing from phrase onset to phrase onset in the playfully rhythmic speech uttered by mothers to their babies (see below), which can possibly be regarded as a dialogue situation. At any rate, it remains to be determined whether there is timing constancy across pauses when dialogue takes place between two adults.

Finally, a factor analysis was performed on the frequency and length means for all of the segment types in Table 13.3, on the total of 33 normals in the

TABLE 13.4
Correlations Between Speech Units at Levels 3 and 4

Correlated Variables (means)	Pearson R	Confidence Level
Pause frequency and pause length	–0.3907	0.05
Pause frequency and phrase length	–0.7287	0.0001
Vowel length and transyllabic length	–0.6878	0.0001
Stressed vowel length and transyllabic length	–0.7520	0.0001
Stress period length and transyllabic length	+0.3772	0.05

FIG. 13.6. Mean duration for phrases plotted against their standard deviations. Data from 33 5-minute spontaneous monologues. (From Anderson & Jaffe, 1976.)

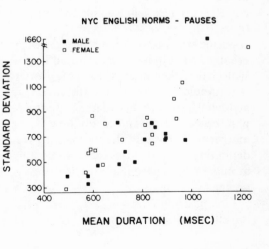

FIG. 13.7. Mean duration for pauses plotted against their standard deviations. Data from 33 5-minute spontaneous monologues. (From Anderson & Jaffe, 1976.)

409

study. As we had found earlier with the subsample, the principal factor extracted (employing varimax rotation as per BMD Program BMD08M; see Dixon, 1970) was loaded positively on syllable and accent rates, negatively on pause length. We shall call this the *speech rate* factor, Factor I.

Orthogonal to the speech rate factor are factors loaded principally on phrase rate, Factor II, and vowel length, Factor III. The speech rate factor accounted for 52% of the variance, the phrase rate factor 24%. These results indicate that normal speakers may be differentiated primarily in terms of the amount of spontaneous speech produced in 5 minutes, that pause length is inversely related to rate, and that although vowel length was found to have an inverse relationship with speech rate as Eqs. (5) and (6) predict, most of the variation between subjects on vowel length has little to do with rate of speaking, at least in comparison with the much stronger influences of pauses and phrases.

The factor analysis was repeated on the same list of segment types, but only on those instances contained within passages of speech exhibiting rhythmic stress alternation, where at least one unstressed vowel occurs between stressed vowels. Again, speech rate emerged as the most important factor (Factor I), and the other factors told essentially the same story. Factor II again loaded most heavily on phrase rate, in spite of the fact that rhythmic stress alternation occurred during only about 20% of the total speech sample. Nevertheless, Factor I and Factor II once again accounted for about one-half and one-quarter of the variance, respectively (44% and 25%). Reasoning from either result, then, it is concluded that the subjects are distinguishable in terms of the degree to which they spoke hesitantly or freely, independently of the question of rhythmic stress alternation, as well as on the total number of syllables produced, which also was uninfluenced by stress alternation. In Fig. 13.6, we see that there was a tendency for females to produce somewhat shorter mean phrase lengths than the males (Mann-Whitney U Test: $p < .002$); pause lengths, on the other hand, did not differentiate by sex ($p > .10$).

As the study also found that females produced a slightly larger number of syllables per phrase, it is ventured that if females spend less time speaking than males, they utter words at a greater rate when they do speak.

It should be noted that the factor analysis yielded almost nothing to distinguish subjects by differences in stress rhythm. Looking at total speech, it was the least important identifiable factor that was loaded on period length and virtually nothing else, accounting for only 5% of the variance. In speech exhibiting rhythmic stress alternation, this factor disappeared altogether, just as might be expected if alternating stress periodicity were a true performance universal in English.

Our finding of a primary factor identified as speech rate parallels the results of two other factor studies (Breskin, 1970; Matarazzo et al., 1958). It should be noted that these three analyses were performed on speech that involved very diverse conditions—monologue, delayed auditory feedback, and dialogue. It is not very surprising, then, that the analyses agree on little more than the identity of this primary factor. In both the other studies, the second factor is identified with pause length, whereas in monologue data, mean pause is most closely associated with the primary factor.

Because we employed our technique of virtually continuous sampling in this study, it was possible to locate the most efficient domain of timing control in the system within the region of 350 to 400 msec. It is recommended that any proposed time-series theoretic model of speech timing should sample more often than that. And, clearly, if one wishes to investigate more detailed microstructural hypotheses, such as Lenneberg's notion of a fundamental unit of 167 msec (1967, p. 114), or any function whatever of unstressed vowels or stop consonants, then sampling intervals at least as short as 10 msec are required. One final advantage of retaining sampling sensitivity in the microsecond range: it permits the identification of phonetic transitions between selected features whenever they occur and permits measurement of phase-shift in periodicities between successive occurrences of such transitions. We shall return to the importance of detecting phase-shift at the end of the chapter.

It is hard to overemphasize the importance of standard conditions in sampling stationary distributions required by simple two-state models, and, indeed, departures from stationarity are useful as an indicator of significant differences. For example, at level 2 there is evidence that longer speaking times go with longer listening times [i.e., mean talk durations are positively correlated between talkers (Matarazzo & Wiens, 1972)]. Because this effect was found in an interview situation, the attempt has been made to explain it as a tendency for questions to elicit answers of matching length. Henderson (1974) describes systematic covariation of phrase and pause lengths to produce a "cognitive stride" at level 3; Butterworth (1975) reports having confirmed it. Barik (1968) and Brähler and Zenz (1975) also have described more complex temporal patterning at levels 2 and 3.

At level three, Jaffe and Feldstein (1970) found evidence that two independent mechanisms appear to underlie phrases and pauses, as they shift systematically in different ways: Phrase length is characteristic of the individual speaker and is relatively insensitive to changes in conversational partner; in contrast, pause length is highly sensitive to social context. Talkers tend to match their average pauses, especially when rapport is good. This effect is apparently maximized when both conversational partners are field dependent (Marcus et al., 1970). Matching has also been found to increase with suggestion (Feldstein & Welkowitz, 1978), with neural maturation (Welkowitz et al., 1976), and under the influence of certain psychopharmacological agents (Natale et al., 1979).

At level 4, where timing efficiency (PTE) reaches a maximum for each individual (between 67% and 71%, compared with about 50% for units at higher levels), there is also evidence for interaction between subsegment durations. Once again, the interaction appears to be an effect of changing conditions between samples, but this is not yet clearly understood.[6] The next two sections will take up two different types of parametric interaction. We shall see that, although both phenomena are beyond the mathematical power of two-state Markov models, they can both be satisfactorily treated as Markovian *projections*.

III. TEMPORAL COMPENSATION

When a single speaker changes his parameters of rhythmic behavior at levels 3 and 4, the mean period (M) remains more stable than its components, M_1 and M_2. The effect has been seen for stress period (Anderson, 1975), for visual fixation data (Stern, 1974), and has been observed across subjects in phrase rhythm by Breskin,[7] although not within subjects by Podwall (1976). Whenever the effect occurs, it operates to maintain the characteristic degree of rhythmicity of the period in question, pointing directly to the conclusion that under different stationary conditions, within subjects or across subjects, timing is governed by a biological constraint.

The effect at level 4 is consistent with the process known in phonetics as "temporal compensation" (see Anderson, 1975), in which stressed vowels and following unstressed segments continuously change their durations in opposite direction, as if changes in one compensate for changes in the other. The phonetic hypothesis holds that the outstandingly high regularity of the stress period is accomplished by instantaneous and continuous compensatory timing control. However, we have observed numerous cases in which stress timing efficiency remains high, but the subsegment r [Eq. (3)] is not significantly less than zero (Anderson & Jaffe, 1976).

Nevertheless, it is not hard to show that even the original form of the hypothesis can be satisfied by a Markovian mechanism, whatever further modification may be necessary at such time as the phenomenon is understood. Consider first the simple two-state model for level 4 (Fig. 13.8). It is clear, by definition, that runs of 1's, extended by p_1, vary independently of

---

[6]The effect appears most often as a negative correlation between the mean durations of the two units at level 4, measured between different speech samples.

[7]Personal communication.

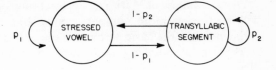

FIG. 13.8.   Schematic state diagram for stress rhythm.

runs of 2's, extended by p_2. However, as is shown by Anderson and Jaffe (1971), a Markov model can be mapped upon observable events by a *projection* that assigns more than one state to a single observable event, and because the states of such a model can encode more information than the set of observable events exhibits, the mathematical power of projected Markov models is greater than that of simple ones. The model shown in Fig. 13.9 employs a projection to generate a negative r, as predicted by the temporal compensation hypothesis. Both 1 runs and 2 runs are projected in this model, the former onto p_1 or p_3, the latter onto p_2 or p_4.

Since primary stressed vowels are longer than secondary ones as a rule, $p_1 > p_3$ by definition. For the model to exhibit compensation it is then merely necessary that $p_2 < p_4$; it will then generate sequences of stress alternations in which only primary transyllabics will follow primary stresses and secondary transyllabics will follow just the secondary stresses. It should be noticed that the projected model just defined is *obligated* to exhibit temporal compensation, a requirement fully as strict as is the *impossibility* for compensation to emerge as a stable property of the two-state model.

However, because the phenomenon itself may be episodic, we shall propose a compromise solution: There are perhaps two rhythmic modes in casual speech (e.g., fluent and hesitant). The two modes, defining two distinct degrees of rhythmicity (PTE), might be called "rhythmic speech" and "arhythmic speech." In this way we arrive at a unifying hypothesis: the four-state projected model of Fig. 13.9 is generally operative during rhythmic speech, but at times the nervous system shifts parameters so that $p_1 = p_3$ and $p_2 = p_4$. At such times, of course, there is no mathematical evidence to distinguish this degenerate case from the regular output of the two-state model.

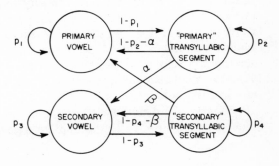

FIG. 13.9.   Schematic state diagram for stress rhythm exhibiting temporal compensation.

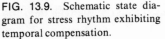

Our second use of Markovian projections is somewhat more ambitious and will lead to a more complex result. But in this exercise on temporal compensation, the basic pattern for the next problem is sketched, even to the mechanism of matching parameters under appropriate conditions.

IV.   CONVERSATIONAL COUPLING

Interoganismic matching of communicative behavior is one of the basic phenomena of biology and social science. In human conversation, a wealth of such phenomena are described (examples are catalogued in Webb, 1972), some rhythmic and some not. There is confusion when all are lumped under the general rubric of "synchrony," which has purely rhythmic connotations. For example, Feldstein (1972) avoids this error by referring to pause "congruence," which is a geometrical metaphor to describe matching of pause durations that are not concurrent.

Information theory is a teleological framework for understanding behavioral matching; that is, a communication channel assumes cognitive equivalence of sender and receiver. But the way this equivalence comes about remains to be specified. The stochastic learning models of the behaviorists and the unfolding transformational grammars of the nativists represent alternative proposals for the actual mechanism by means of which the cognitive prerequisites for a viable communication channel arise. They each represent attempts to account for the cognitive similarity of organisms, yet their relative applicability to mechanisms of competence and performance has been insufficiently emphasized. We suggest that they may be reconcilable if the highly discrepant time scales of linguistic conception (competence) and execution (performance) are kept in mind.

When the term "synchrony" is used in its strict rhythmic sense, as opposed to its looser use as "matching of formal characteristics," another body of mathematical models becomes relevant, namely, coupling of harmonic oscillators. The appeal of these models is that they account for both *intra*organismic (endogenous) rhythmicity and *inter*organismic (exogenous) entrainment thereof, yielding long-range periodicities of the dyadic system. It has been argued that finite-state Markov models of the participating organisms cannot in principle reproduce these long-range dyadic phenomena since entrainment to inherently aperiodic rhythms cannot occur (Cobb, 1973). We shall also question this argument so as to leave the issue open to empirical resolution.

Phenomena of dyadic synchrony and conversational rhythm require a model of the two-person temporal pattern (level 2) that couples the separate monologue rhythms described earlier (levels 3 and 4). The notion of a Markovian generator of such a monologue rhythm suggests a natural way to accomplish the coupling. The key is the observation (Heller, 1967) that a Markov process is simply a probabilistic finite-state automaton (PFA) with constant input. This is now explained. A PFA is a quadruple (I_j, S_k, S_{k+1}, O_l) with an internal state set (S_k). It is sensitive to a set of inputs (I_j), any one of which imposes a probability distribution upon its next state and on its set (S_{k+1}) of outputs (O_l). In a constant environment its input will be constant. It then operates to produce a subset of its possible behaviors, and this spontaneous sequence of state changes and outputs can be thought of as its intrinsic endogenous rhythm. Mathematically, it is then precisely a finite-state Markov chain.

Thus, a Markov model of monologue rhythm (levels 3 and 4) can be thought of as a PFA "running free" in a silent environment, as might be produced by an absent or nonresponsive conversational partner. This leads directly to the notion of two coupled PFAs such that the output of each is input to the other (Jaffe, 1970; Jaffe & Norman, 1964; Jaffe et al., 1967; Rapoport & Chammah, 1968). Their joint behavior should generate a set of dyadic states and outputs that we recognize as the temporal pattern of conversation. They must operate according to similar principles, but they need not be symmetrical either in their state sets or the parameters thereof. It suffices that each PFA possess a complete set of instructions as to how to respond to any joint behavior that might arise from the interaction.

An appealing feature of the model is its equal applicability to nonverbal communication. The rhythm of visual fixation during conversational interaction is well modeled by linked PFAs in both adult (Natale, 1976) and mother–infant play (Jaffe, Stern, & Peery, 1973).

A new set of problems arises when the rhythm of level 2 (Fig. 13.5) is tackled. The phenomena to be accounted for are the distributions shown in Fig. 13.10 variously designated as "talkspurts" (Norwine & Murphy, 1938), "time between speaker switches," "floor holding" (Jaffe & Feldstein, 1970), or "turn taking" (Duncan, Ch. 12, this volume). To date, we have attempted this task only in terms of the Markovian model of level 2. The active speaker is here claimed to be operating as a coupled PFA who runs free stochastically as long as his coupled partner remains completely silent. The latter, however, has an independent probability of vocalizing at any instant, the value of which is a function of the *joint output* at the previous instant. If Fig. 13.10 is conceived as a distribution of waiting times in a set of states between speaker switches, this distribution clearly cannot be generated by a four-state Markov model: A speaks alone; B speaks alone; both silent; both speak.

Nor can it be so generated even when a two step history (a 16-state model) is used for the prediction (Fig. 13.11). The shape of the distribution is obviously

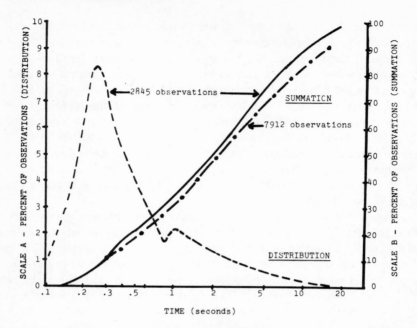

FIG. 13.10. Frequency distribution of the length of time between speaker switches (*dashed line*) and its summation (*solid line*); redrawn from a pioneering study conducted many years ago at the Bell Telephone Laboratories by Norwine and Murphy (1938), who tabulated the durations of holding the floor. They defined the event as "speech by one party, including his pauses, which is preceded and followed, with or without intervening pauses, by speech from the other party." On the basis of 2845 such events, they concluded: "Since most telephonic speech syllables are shorter than 0.3 second the modal value of 0.25 second makes it clear that monosyllabic replies are by far the most numerous." It may be seen that these, in conjunction with terse replies or questions under 1-second duration, constitute about one-third of the events. More extensive data from our own laboratory on face-to-face conversations confirm this (7912 observations, shown as summation only, in a dot–dash line). The telephonic data from Bell Labs suggest that speakers who can't see their listeners should expect to hear a brief vocal interjection every 14 seconds on the average. In the face-to-face situation in our laboratory, the rate drops to one every 18 seconds, because silent gestures probably substitute for some of the vocal ones.

underestimated for brief events and overestimated for longer ones. That these errors in fit of the model offset each other probably accounts for the fact that the means of the distribution were indeed well predicted (Jaffe et al., 1967).

The subsequent history of the stochastic modeling of conversational rhythm as coupled PFAs is largely unpublished but plays out the strategy outlined above: deducing the implicit finite state set of which the observed rhythm is a projection. The most obvious maneuver was to partition the two

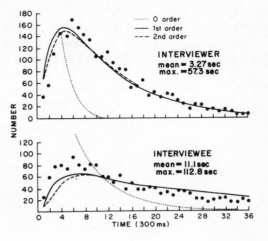

FIG. 13.11.   Data points represent average of 37 20-minute interviews, whereas the continuous curves are the respective Markovian predictions, computed for each interview separately and then averaged. (From unpublished research by J. Jaffe & J. Schwartz, 1967.)

symmetrical behavioral states, joint silence and simultaneous speech, depending upon the speaker who was holding the floor. The rationale: a speaker who has paused and resumed without interruption has obviously not lost his turn and the mean duration of such pauses need not necessarily match the analogous events for the other speaker, as would be required by a four-state model. And, though less frequent, there is also an obvious distinction between the interruptor and interruptee when simultaneous speech occurs (Feldstein et al., 1974a, 1974b; Meltzer et al., 1971). The resultant model is a six-state system of coupled PFAs (Anderson & Jaffe, 1971; Jaffe, 1970; Jaffe & Feldstein, 1970) that assigns separate parameters to speaker and listener. One of its advantages from the present point of view is that it explains the "phrase rhythm matching" phenomenon of level 2 (Fig. 13.5).

Equation (8) gives the matrix, P, that characterizes the six-state model.

$$P = \begin{bmatrix} (1 - a_1)(1 - b_1) & a_1(1 - b_1) & a_1 b_1 & 0 & (1 - a_1)b_1 & 0 \\ (1 - a_2)(1 - b_2) & a_2(1 - b_2) & a_2 b_2 & 0 & (1 - a_2)b_2 & 0 \\ (1 - a_3)(1 - b_3) & a_3(1 - b_3) & a_3 b_3 & 0 & (1 - a_3)b_3 & 0 \\ 0 & a_4(1 - b_4) & 0 & (1 - a_4)(1 - b_4) & (1 - a_4)b_4 & a_4 b_4 \\ 0 & a_5(1 - b_5) & 0 & (1 - a_5)(1 - b_5) & (1 - a_5)b_5 & a_5 b_5 \\ 0 & a_6(1 - b_6) & 0 & (1 - a_6)(1 - b_6) & (1 - a_6)b_6 & a_6 b_6 \end{bmatrix} \quad (8)$$

We have chosen not to elaborate this coupling equation in all of the tedious rigor required to show how the PFAs of the two speakers become entrained, with the output of each serving as the input to the other. Each entry in P constitutes a transition probability composed by the independent contributions from speakers A and B. It is assumed, for simplicity's sake, that the six states of A and the corresponding six states of B are entered pairwise by the two speakers such that they both track the veridical status of their conversation. Thus, the six states of P correspond to the partners' joint perception of the following events, which are held to be necessary and sufficient for the conversation to acquire its temporal organization:

State	Conversational Event
1.	Speaker A pauses, holding the floor.
2.	Speaker A speaks, taking (or retaining) the floor.
3.	Speaker B interrupts A, who retains the floor.
4.	Speaker B pauses, holding the floor.
5.	Speaker B speaks, taking (or retaining) the floor.
6.	Speaker A interrupts B, who retains the floor.

Speakers A and B make *independent* decisions to vocalize at time $t + 1$, with probabilities a_i and b_i, respectively. But each decision is contingent upon the *joint outcome* of the previous independent decision at time t, denoted by the state i, which is 1 through 6. Pause matching is accomplished by mutual adjustment of parameters a_1, a_4, b_1 and b_4.

A similar argument shows phrase matching to be dependent upon the parameters of states 2 and 5. Matching of phrase periods would thus involve the mutual adjustment of eight parameters, which can occur in many ways.

This very powerful psychological effect has been designated "congruence," a geometric metaphor that denotes a type of isochrony that is displayed in alternation. That is, the phrase rhythm of speaker A when he has the floor is "synchronized" with that of speaker B when *he* has the floor so that the phrase rhythm is smooth and unbroken, *even while possession of the floor alternates.* We have no better metaphor but that interacting speakers have mutually elected an invisible parliamentarian to direct traffic at level 2 (Fig. 13.5) but have also designated him the conductor of phrase rhythms at level 3 (Jaffe, 1977, 1978).

The major control of phrase rhythm resides in mutual adjustment of four parameters, two from each of the coupled PFAs, that regulate the duration of both speaker's pauses. One parameter is the probability that the speaker who has paused will resume; the other is the probability that the listener will remain silent. An analogous pair of parameters regulate the duration of the other participant's pauses. And because the vocalized component of the phrase rhythm is relatively insensitive to that of the other participant, the burden of phrase rhythm matching is carried by some complex adjustment of these four parameters that mutually approximate the pause components of the alternating phrase rhythms.

Yet even this projected six-state model underestimates brief "turns" and overestimates long ones, a defect in the model that can be rectified only by the rather inelegant hypothesis of three additional states per speaker whose only role is to account for this peak of interjections $<$ 1 sec in duration. This tends to confirm the intuitions of Yngve and Duncan that these brief "back channel" responses are functionally distinct from more extended utterances. Similar notions have been advanced by Dittman and Llewellyn (1969), who designate such events as "listener responses" and emphasize their synchronization with nonverbal gestures. A comparison of the frequency plots and distribution functions of Norwine and Murphy's (1938) data from telephone conversations with our own from face-to-face conversations (Fig. 13.10) suggests that there is indeed considerable overlap in time and much equivalence of communicative function between gestural and vocal modes with respect to these *interjections*. Although we have yet to identify their timing characteristics at level 4, we expect to find that they constitute the great majority of monosyllabic phrases containing just one stressed vowel.

It is not unreasonable to further speculate that it is the timing of interjections that serves as an important cue by which conversational partners entrain each other's parameters into the mutually coupled interactions modeled by Eq. (8).

An analogous line of reasoning is followed in the work of Stern (1974) and Beebe and Stern (1977) on preverbal mother-infant interaction. Results on eye contact and gaze behavior in adults have already focused on the time domains of levels 2 and 3, as it was found that listeners' eyes tend to focus on speakers' faces (Kendon & Cook, 1969), while speakers' eyes tend to wander during phrases, but return to listeners' faces during pauses. Hand gestures have been found at levels 2, 3 and 4; Kimura (1973), for example, finds that speaking is accompanied by occasional listener-directed right-hand movements that tend to synchronize with the main accents of a phrase. This gestural rhythm disappears during listening, but head nodding is likely to occur during the speaker's pauses (Matarazzo & Wiens, 1972). The binary, on-off characteristics of these nonverbal behaviors can obviously be handled as two-state systems in the same fashion as are verbal behaviors. But as for a comprehensive mathematical model for their interactions, there is as yet almost no progress outside of one or two laboratories, and if the vocal interactions are a guideline, the development of such a mathematical model will be tedious. We feel there is much more to be gained by taking a look at those simpler interactive systems that appear to be just the ones by which a time sense for communicative rhythms appears to be acquired by us all in the first place.

V. SOME DEVELOPMENTAL ISSUES

The most obvious difference between an adult–adult versus an adult–infant communicative system is that the latter is asymmetrical. The caregiver can do so many things in all the communicative channels, whereas the infant has few channels available and even in those his ability to send and receive is probably slower and certainly less well articulated. Nonetheless we need two participants to conceptualize a dialogic system.

It is useful to consider two different kinds of symmetry in the mother–infant dialogic system. Performance symmetry implies that the two participants are essentially equally proficient at performing the behaviors that constitute their half of the dialogue, and equally proficient at perceiving and discriminating the behaviors of the other. Symmetry of modality assumes that the two partners are receiving and sending in the same communicative channel, the same modality, such as vocalization–audition. In the course of development, it is more common than not, that dialogic exchanges between mother and infant are asymmetrical in one sense or the other, or even both.

One of the first developmental questions to arise is whether the infant can learn the rules and conventions of dialogic exchange in any sensory modality and motor behavior and then generalize this knowledge to other modalities and behaviors as they emerge or mature. If this is a potentially fruitful question, then we must look for the early existence of dialogic exchanges in any and all communicative modes and channels, and, particularly, we must look for exchange systems where the greatest degree of performance symmetry between mother and infant is possible, because these would be more likely to best generate the rules and conventions that define a dialogue. Clearly, vocal–auditory communication between mother and infant is a poor candidate.

The very first such candidate may be the dialogic system proposed by Kaye (1977). During feeding in the first month of life, a dialogic exchange system is described in which bursts of infant sucking alternate with bursts of mother jiggling the bottle to stimulate the infant to suck. Thus, the exchange goes: infant suck; pause; mother jiggle; pause; infant suck, etc. The pauses, which assure the alternating pattern, are a necessary part of the sequence because the mother will not start to jiggle until after the infant has stopped sucking, and, contrary to intuition, the infant will not resume sucking during the stimulation of jiggling but only after its cessation. One of the interesting features of this "dialogic system" is that while each member is acting and reacting to the other in different motor channels and through different sensory routes it is a symmetrical dialogue with regard to performance equality because each partner has roughly equal proficiency and control over the performance of the behavior that constitutes their half of the interaction.

There are other dialogic systems in early infancy. The mother–infant gazing interaction is one and has been referred to above (Jaffe et al., 1973; Stern, 1974). This system is perhaps the most unique in the early development of the infant because by the age of 3–4 months, it constitutes a dialogic system that has symmetry of both performance and modality. Due to the vagaries of developmental timetables the infant has, by the fourth month of life, essentially the same degree of control over his visual–motor system as does an adult (White et al., 1964). His motor abilities to look or gaze—to fixate, pursue an object, accommodate, avert gaze, etc.—are little different from those of his caregiver. Similarly, his abilities to see are correspondingly mature.

This gazing dialogic system is, however, quite different from the mature vocal exchanges that are the main subject of this chapter. It is not an alternating system. There is no requirement to be "silent" in order to receive information. In fact, the reverse is true, looking is necessary for seeing. (We shall return to this difference shortly.) The gazing system can operate such that if one member is looking, the other member will not be, or vice versa, or if one member looks the other will too, depending on a variety of contextual variables. In any event, the dyadic system is rule governed to the extent that what happens next is a function of the dyadic state currently prevailing. Common observation reveals that by 4 months of age the infant and mother can engage in several different exchange patterns within this system, some of which become interactive games (e.g., visual chase and dodge, early forms of peekaboo).

We have so far provided two examples of early dyadic interactive systems. There are probably many more waiting to be described and defined. We thus return to the two major developmental questions. From engaging in these interactive systems: (1) does the infant begin to learn the rules and conventions that govern dialogic exchange; and (2) if he does, is this knowledge generalizable to other channels of communication as they become functional? If the answer to these questions is positive, then we may best conceive of the foundations for vocal dialogic exchange as having been in part or even largely built up through accumulated experiences in other modalities and behaviors. To better understand the origins of vocal dialogue we would then have to intensify our exploration of both early rule-governed interactive systems and the lines of development of different interactive functions as they pass through different forms of expression.

There is one other piece of evidence that bears on this question. In a detailed examination of what a mother actually says and does while playing with her 3½-month-old infant, Stern et al. (1977) examined both vocal and nonvocal acts. Each maternal vocalization and its subsequent pause were examined and timed. Similarly, each separate maternal nonvocal act[8] and each motionless state between them were examined separately when performed by a mother for her infant and were timed irrespective of whether or not she also was vocalizing.

---

[8]A nonvocal act is any detectable movement of the body or its parts, including changes of posture.

The most interesting finding was that the mean durations of vocalizations and of acts performed *apart from vocalizing* were similar; likewise, so were the durations of pauses and states in between. Furthermore, maternal behaviors in these two channels were matched in another respect: they both showed the same striking amount of repetition (about 30% of the utterances were repeats, as was an equal percentage of the acts). Also, mean run *length* of repeats in each channel are similar.

One way to state this finding is to say that, with respect to repetition, the mother uses her body (usually her head and face) in almost exactly the same way that she uses her voice. When the baby's behaviors are also observed and timed, it is found that the mother's behaviors, regardless of which channel she uses, appear to be contingent upon the behaviors of the infant, and vice versa. Within this two-channel system it is ascertained that the temporal pattern of dialogic interaction prevails.

Much of the time, however, the mother employs the two channels in synchrony—often accompanying vocalization with acts, such as an exaggerated facial display with head posturing. Because these acts typically do not occur when she talks with adults, we have called them "infant-elicited variations" in maternal social behavior (Stern, 1977). The fact that facial display and head movement occur simultaneously with vocalization is, in itself, not surprising. It merely confirms the Condon and Ogston (1967) finding of "self-synchrony" between the vocal and kinesic behavior of mothers talking to babies as well as between pairs of adults. But, between adults, the acts are often subtle; not so with the mother addressing baby. When the mother emits a vocalization directed to her baby, she also produces simultaneous kinesic behavior of high stimulus value. The mother–baby data, certainly no less than the adult data, show that in naturally occurring interactions, we virtually never see a purely vocal interchange, even though it may be analyzed as such. Ultimately, of course, the adult acquires the ability to analyze communications himself as though the entire message were contained in the vocal channel. But we cannot easily know to what extent and at what point in development is the mother's vocal message differentiated by the infant from the entire behavioral "package" of which it is a part. This knowledge is made especially difficult because a mother will frequently establish a fairly (but not strictly) regular tempo of synchronized vocal and nonvocal behaviors for an infant. The choice of channel is less systematic than is the timing of whatever behaviors are going on: She may produce a run of vocalizations, then delete vocalizing for a behavior or two, performing silent facial displays instead, or adding a touch or tickle; all the while the tempo is not disrupted by switching modalities. In this regard, the modality of stimulation may prove to be a less crucial feature of human behavior for capturing and maintaining the interest of an infant than the temporal patterning of that stimulation. The central point is that the division we generally make between verbal and nonverbal signals may prove to be a misleading division if made too sharply when trying to understand how the infant begins to participate in the world of human communication.

When we consider the vocal environment of the prelinguistic child without concern for ongoing nonvocal behavior, we do find that it is a very interesting environment.

Although a decade ago it was assumed that the child induced the rules governing his language from the "meager and degenerate" input, often grammatically incorrect, provided by the colloquial speech of adults (Chomsky, 1965), it is now known that the caregiver's vocal input to the child represents a special communicative style that may especially facilitate this induction (Snow, 1972). And, as Slobin (1975) has noted, this style, "motherese," is not especially "meager and degenerate," but may in fact be superior to adult speech in that it is "tuned to the language processing strategies" and capabilities of the child.

These considerations refer to the speech environment provided for the child of 18 months and older, who is in fact beginning to learn to speak. The mother, however, begins to talk or vocalize in her style to the infant from the day of birth. The question thus arises as to what various developmental functions maternal speech serves during the first 18 months of life—long before speech acquisition proper is ready to begin. In addressing this question we shall leave aside the clearly important function of providing the infant with the array of speech sounds and prosodic patterns of the culture in which he will grow up. What other, more general functions might it serve?

One of the more obvious yet intriguing features of maternal vocalization to infants in the first half year of life is its stricter rhythmicity than that found among adults. On the basis of what we know about the infant's perceptual and cognitive tendencies, an ideally designed stimulus presented serially in time should have a fairly regular tempo but with perceptible variability. If the tempo were absolutely regular and fixed, there would be no deviations for the infant to notice so as to maintain his cognitive engagement. He would habituate rapidly. If, on the other hand, the deviations around the established or expected tempo were too large or irregular for the infant to "encompass," then he would presumably be incapable of perceiving them as deviations. They would appear unrelated to the referent, and, once again, the infant's cognitive engagement could not be maintained. Our current notion of the infant's attentional and cognitive process thus requires that a temporal stimulus best suited to maintain interest would have a generally regular tempo (to allow for the formation of expectancy), but with a limited, or at least lawful, variability (to engage and maintain his evaluative processes). When the tempo or timing of maternal utterances to 3½-month-old infants is examined, we find that mothers establish, for short periods, fairly regular tempos. What is more interesting is that these tempos show a variability around the expected beat, such that the standard deviation of the interval from the onset of one vocalization to the next is directly proportioned to the duration of that interval. Another way to characterize these data is to say that the coefficient of variation (σ/μ) is constant, conforming to a scalar process (Stern & Gibbon, 1979). One possible implication of these findings is that the mother vocalizes to her infant in a way that both enhances the infant's ability to form expectancies of the temporal intervals used in human communication and allows him to evaluate lawful and potentially meaningful deviations in the flow. Accordingly, one of the most important early functions of maternal speech may have little to do with speech per se but rather functions as an ideally suited serial stimulus to "teach" the infant the temporal patterning of *all* human communicative behaviors.

Another developmental issue to be raised concerns the fact that the dialogic vocalizing pattern between mothers and infants is generally not one of alternation but rather one of co-action. During the period between 3 to 4 months of age when infant vocalizations become more frequent, the mother and infant are more likely to vocalize in unison than not. Furthermore, the likelihood of their vocalizing at the same time is contributed to by both partners, because each of them is more likely to begin vocalizing *while* the other is still vocalizing rather than after the other has stopped, and each is more likely to terminate vocalizing when the other has terminated (Stern, Jaffe, Beebe, & Bennett, 1975). The study revealed that during this early period the mother (and perhaps, the infant) do indeed fashion alternating vocal exchanges, however, the pattern of vocalizing in unison was more common and appeared to occur particularly when the mother and infant were involved in more animated interactions.

These findings raise two final developmental issues. The first is that so much of early vocal behavior and dyadic vocal patterning is clearly in the service of emotional expression and interpersonal emotional exchange. In spite of this fact, we have as yet no way to conceptualize the transformation of early vocalization as a largely affective phenomenon into later vocal and verbal behaviors serving largely cognitive functions.

The second issue raised by the phenomenon of co-action and the similarity of early vocal exchanges to gazing and other nonvocal exchanges is that infants may first have to learn the "back-channeling" interjective functions of vocal behavior (see Chapter 12). This suggestion is hardly far-fetched when it is considered that the first developmental issue to be negotiated is the establishment of the signals for initiating, maintaining, terminating, and avoiding a focused interaction. It is only within that already established communication framework that the child can begin to focus his attention on the acquisition of symbolic understanding.

By now, we hope to have accumulated sufficient evidence to convince the most skeptical linguistic formalist that speech behavior not only has a temporal structure that can be described independently of conventional symbolic content, but that the structure can actually serve the function of communicating certain vital interpersonal messages in the absence of content, that this structure need not even be expressed verbally in order to serve its function, and that it may be acquired completely by the child prior to the earliest stirrings of syntax.

The chapter opened with an attempt to show that the theory of Markov models does have an important place, if albeit a circumscribed one, in the description and explanation of natural language structure. We believe that the special appropriateness that Markov models enjoy for problems of phonology is not fortuitous but is a strong indication that phonological rhythms belong to a class of biological periodicities that lie at the center of a general theory of behavioral timing in organisms. We shall close with a simplified sketch of such a theory.

VI. MARKOVIAN BIOLOGICAL CLOCKS

It has been claimed (e.g., by Cobb, 1973) that stochastic models, including Markov models, are fundamentally incapable of accounting for periodic phenomena of any kind, let alone biological rhythms. This is easily shown not to be so; take, for example, the matrix M_1:

$$
M_1 = \begin{array}{c} 1 \\ 2 \end{array} \begin{array}{|cc|} 1 & 2 \\ \hline 0.1 & 0.9 \\ 0.9 & 0.1 \\ \hline \end{array}
$$

M_1 has the steady-state vector ($p_1 = 0.5$, $p_2 = 0.5$), and its autocorrelation series is: 1, −.80, .64, −.51, .41, −.33, .26, −.21, .17, −.13, .11, −.08, .07, −.05, .04, −.03, .03, −.02, .02, −.01, 0, ... The alternation of signs and the regular attenuation of absolute values of the terms in this series demonstrate that M_1 is a damped periodic process (Cobb, 1973, p. 14).

It is simple, in this minimal case, to extract the pure periodic component of M_1 by inspection. It is M_1':

$$
M_1' = \begin{array}{c} 1 \\ 2 \end{array} \begin{array}{|cc|} 1 & 2 \\ \hline 0 & 1 \\ 1 & 0 \\ \hline \end{array}
$$

M'_1 is an oscillatory Markov chain that also possesses the stationary vector [.5, .5]. It is true that the periodic component does not yield exponential distributions of mean lengths of runs of twos or ones, but the original damped matrix M_1 does. And the fact that M_1 is both autoregressive and Markovian is shown by direct inspection of this obvious example.

Most biological clocks, however, exhibit the opposite property: They run with great regularity for rather long periods of time, being unperturbed by most stimuli and showing an extremely low threshold for disruption only by certain rare stimuli, *Zeitgebers*. Matrix M_2 is an example of a Markov model that exhibits this property (see Pavlidis, 1973):

$$M_2 = \begin{array}{c} \\ 1 \\ 2 \\ 3 \end{array} \begin{array}{ccc} 1 & 2 & 3 \\ \hline 0.9 & 0.1 & 0 \\ 0 & 0 & 1.0 \\ 0 & 1.0 & 0 \end{array}$$

The *Zeitgeber* is held to set the process in state one, otherwise it approaches the stochastic oscillatory submatrix composed of the states two and three, as the steady-state vector of the process is [0, .5, .5]. We can go on to build the rules for the *Zeitgeber* into the system: in matrix M'_2 we see that the system can be disrupted only when in state 3, and if we define the probability of the *Zeitgeber* as W, then we have a general statement for the conditions on the stationary vector. It becomes [$10kW, k, k$].

$$M'_2 = \begin{array}{c} \\ 1 \\ 2 \\ 3 \end{array} \begin{array}{ccc} 1 & 2 & 3 \\ \hline 0.9 & 0.1 & 0 \\ 0 & 0 & 1.0 \\ W & 1-W & 0 \end{array}$$

Clearly, if W is sufficiently small, this matrix will deliver an empirical oscillatory autocorrelation series of +1, −1, +1, −1, . . . for rather long periods of time whenever the system has left state one and settled down to its "free running" periodicity.

So far, we have demonstrated that Markov models can exhibit two essential properties of biological clocks: (1) isochronous periodicity; and (2) vulnerability to disruption only when in certain states, and, even at such times, only by events of certain types (*Zeitgebers*). We now show how Markovian theory can be extended to account for the third essential property: entrainability by phase shift. By way of example, we shall build this property into M'_2, to yield matrix M''_2:

$$
M_2'' = \begin{array}{c} \\ 1 \\ 2 \\ 3 \end{array}
\begin{array}{ccc}
1 & 2 & 3 \\
\hline
0.9 & 0.1 & 0 \\
0 & 0 & 1.0 \\
\omega_t & 1.0 & 0 \\
\hline
\end{array}
$$

where $\omega_t = f(t) \, dt, \ t < S$.

Unlike M_2, which shares with our earlier examples the classical Markovian assumption of an equal intertransition time (S) between all states, M_2'' permits transitions between state 3 and state 1 at any time $t < S$. Processes that permit transitions after a variable interval are called semi-Markovian (Gibbon, 1971). With the exception of this transition, it is understood, as usual, that transition probabilities hold just in case $t = S$; otherwise, they are undefined. Thus, exits from state 3 are of two types: If there is not a clock-controlled transition to state 2 at time S, then there will have been a transition to state 1 at some time $t < S$, resulting in a phase-shift. Note that after the shift, the new phase setting persists indefinitely until another phase-shift occurs, again by a transition from state 3 to 1. Of course, phase-shifts in most biological clocks are not so precise and instantaneous, and more than one semi-Markovian transition will be required to account for the local as well as the long-term effect of a *Zeitgeber,* all to be described with a bit more mathematical rigor.

But, before we leave this example, one last point. If the behavior generated by M_2'' is sampled every S seconds in a manner that is insensitive to phase-shift, the resultant data will be fitted approximately by a simple, classical model such as M_2. Of course, the parameter estimates will be indirectly influenced by the undetected shift probabilities, as

$$
W \doteq \int_0^T f(t) \, dt \qquad (T < S)
$$

Thus, to pick up a point introduced earlier, it is necessary to employ phase-sensitive sampling of signals generated by M_2'' to permit the extraction of its periodic submatrix (which, as can be seen by inspection, is equivalent to M_1). In this way we show how it is possible to succeed in identifying a Markovian clock by distinguishing it from the semi-Markovian process that resets it.

Finally, we present an example of a periodic process that is Markovian but is not solvable as an autoregressive system, because every term in its autocorrelation series is zero:

$$
M_3 = \begin{array}{c} \\ 1 \\ 2 \\ 3 \end{array}
\begin{array}{ccc}
1 & 2 & 3 \\
\hline
0 & 1.0 & 0 \\
0.5 & 0 & 0.5 \\
0 & 1.0 & 0 \\
\hline
\end{array}
$$

It is easy to see, however, that this process exhibits perfect periodicity between consecutive occurrences of the symbol "2," which always occurs on alternate transitions, while there is random selection between "1" and "3" on other occasions. M_3 constitutes an existence proof that periodicities between events of a certain type can be *embedded* among the terms of an otherwise random series and can be extracted only by specific observation of just the periodic events.

Indeed, most known biological clocks are believed to be discontinuously periodic as is M_3. It is, therefore, not surprising that interlocking periodicities also exist, while retaining some degree of independence, between the levels of our Markovian scheme for the analysis of the temporal properties of speech— not surprising, that is, if we accept the proposition that conversational rhythms are a biological phenomenon.

REFERENCES

Anderson, S. W. Ballistic control of rhythmic articulatory movements in natural speech. In D. Aaronson & R. W. Rieber (Eds.), *Developmental psycholinguistics and communication disorders.* Annals of the New York Academy of Sciences, vol. 263. N.Y.: New York Academy of Sciences, 1975.

Anderson, S. W. Language-related asymmetries of eye-movement and evoked potentials. In S. Harnad, R. W. Doty, L. Goldstein, J. Jaynes, & G. Krauthamer (Eds.), *Lateralization in the nervous system.* New York: Academic Press, 1977.

Anderson, S. W., & Jaffe, J. Projections between memory codes and some speech events not derivable from stimulus–response theory. *Mathematical Biosciences, 1971, 12,* 303–320.

Anderson, S. W., & Jaffe, J. *The definition, detection and timing of vocalic syllables in speech signals.* Sci. Rept. no. 12, Department of Communication Sciences. N.Y.: New York State Psychiatric Inst., 1972.

Anderson, S. W., & Jaffe, J. *Speech timing characteristics of normal native speakers of English in New York City.* Scientific Rept. No. 16, Dept. of Communication Sciences. New York: New York State Psychiatric Inst., 1976.

Barik, H. C. On defining juncture pauses: A note on Boomer's "Hesitation and grammatical encoding." *Lang. and Speech,* 1968, *11*(pt. 3), 156–159.

Beebe, B., & Stern, D. N. Engagement–disengagement and early object experiences. In N. Freedman & S. Grand (Eds.), *Communicative structure and psychic structure.* New York: Plenum, 1977.

Box, G. E. P., & Jenkins, G. M. *Time series analysis: Forecasting and control.* San Francisco: Holden-Day, 1970.

Brähler, E., & Zenz, H. Artifacts in the registration and interpretation of speech-process variables. *Language and Speech,* 1975, *18*(pt. 2), 166–179.

Breskin, S. *Individual differences in speech fluency under delayed auditory feedback.* Unpublished doctoral dissertation, City University of New York, 1970.

Buchsbaum, M. Individual differences in eye-movement patterns. *Percept. Mot. Skills,* 1972, *35,* 895–901.

Butterworth, B. Hesitation and semantic planning in speech. *Jour. Psycholing. Res.,* 1975, *4,* 75–87.

Chapple, E. D., & Lindemann, E. Clinical implications of measurements of interaction rates in psychiatric interviews. *Applied Anthrop.*, 1942, *1*, 1-11.

Chomsky, N. *Aspects of the theory of syntax.* Cambridge, Mass.: MIT Press, 1965.

Chomsky, N. Review of Skinner 1957. *Language, 1959, 35,* 26-58.

Chomsky, N. *Syntactic structures.* The Hague: Mouton, 1957.

Chomsky, N., & Halle, M. *The sound pattern of English.* New York: Harper & Row, 1968.

Chomsky, N., & Miller, G. A. Introduction to the formal analysis of natural languages. In R. D. Luce, R. R., Bush, & E. Galanter, (Eds.), *Handbook of mathematical psychology* (Vol. 2). New York: Wiley, 1963.

Cobb, L. *Time series analysis of the periodicities of casual conversations.* Unpublished doctoral dissertation, Cornell University, 1973.

Condon, W. S., & Ogston , W. D. A segmentation of behavior. *J. Psychiat.*, 1967, *5*, 221-235.

Dittman, A. T., & Llewellyn, L. G. Body movement and speech rhythm in social conversation. *Journal of Personality and Social Psychology,* 1969, *11,* 98-106.

Dixon, W. J. (Ed.) *BMD Biomedical computer programs.* Berkeley: Univ. of Calif. Press, 1970.

Drake, S. The role of music in Galileo's experiments. *Scientific American,* 1975, *232*(6), 98-104.

Feldstein, S. Temporal patterns of dialogue: Basic research and reconsiderations. In A. W. Siegman & B. Pope (Eds.), *Studies in dyadic communication.* New York: Pergamon, 1972.

Feldstein, S., Alberti, L., BenDebba, M., & Welkowitz, J. *Personality and simultaneous speech.* Paper presented at the annual meeting of the American Psychological Association New Orleans, August 1974. (a)

Feldstein, S., BenDebba, M., & Alberti, L. *Distributional characteristics of simultaneous speech in conversation.* Paper presented at the Acoustical Society of America, New York, April 1974. (b)

Feldstein, S., & Welkowitz, J. A chronography of conversation: In defense of an objective approach. In A. W. Siegman & S. Feldstein (Eds.), *Nonverbal behavior and communication.* Hillsdale, N.J.: Lawrence Erlbaum Associates, 1978.

French, N. R., Carter, C. W., & Koenig, W. The words and sounds of telephone conversation. *Bell System Tech. J.,* 1930, *9,* 290-324.

Gibbon, J. Scalar expectancy theory and Weber's Law in animal timing. *Psychol. Review,* 1977, *84,* 279-325.

Gibbon, J. Scalar timing and semi-Markov Chains in Free-Operant Avoidance. *J. Math. Psychol.,* 1971, *8,* 109-138.

Hayes, D., Meltzer, L., & Wolf, G. Substantive conclusions are dependent upon techniques of measurement. *Behavioral Science,* 1970, *15,* 265-269.

Hayes, D. P., & Cobb, L. Ultradian biorhythms in social interaction. In A. W. Siegman & S. Feldstein (Eds.), *Of speech and time: Temporal speech rhythms in interpersonal contexts.* Hillsdale, N.J.: Lawrence Erlbaum Associates, 1979.

Heller, A. Probabilistic automata and stochastic transformations. *Math. Systems Theory,* 1967, *1,* 197-208.

Henderson, A. I. Time patterns in spontaneous speech: Cognitive stride or random walk? A reply to Jaffe et al. *Language and Speech,* 1974, *17,* 119-125.

Henderson, A., Goldman-Eisler, F., & Skarbek, A. Sequential temporal patterns in spontaneous speech. *Language and Speech,* 1966, *9,* 207.

Howes, D., & Geschwind, N. Quantitative studies of aphasic language. In D. McK. Rioch & E. A. Weinstein (Eds.), *Disorders of communication.* Association for Research in Nervous and Mental Disease. (Vol. XLII.) Baltimore, Maryland: Williams & Wilkins, 1964.

Jaffe, J. Linked probabilistic finite automata: A model for the temporal interaction of speakers. *Mathematical Biosciences,* 1970, *7,* 191-204.

Jaffe, J. Parliamentary procedure and the brain. In A. W. Siegman & S. Feldstein (Eds.), *Nonverbal behavior and communication.* Hillsdale, N.J.: Lawrence Erlbaum Associates, 1978.

Jaffe, J. Biological significance of Markovian communication rhythms. In S. Rosenberg (Ed.), *Sentence production: Developments in research and theory.* Hillsdale, N.J.: Lawrence Erlbaum Associates, 1977.

Jaffe, J., & Anderson, S. W. *One of the most neglected physiological signals in psychopathology.* Demonstration presented at the annual meeting of the Society of Biological Psychiatry, New York City, May 1975.

Jaffe, J., Breskin, S., & Gerstman, L. J. Random generation of apparent speech rhythms. *Language and Speech,* 1972, *15,* 68–71.

Jaffe, J., & Feldstein, S. *Rhythms of dialogue.* New York: Academic Press, 1970.

Jaffe, J. Feldstein, S., & Cassotta. L. Markovian models of dialogic time patterns. *Nature,* 1967, *216,* 93–94.

Jaffe, J., & Norman, D. *A simulation of the time patterns of dialogue.* Scientific Report No. CS-4. Center for Cognitive Studies, Harvard University, 1964.

Jaffe, J., Stern, D. N., & Peery, J. C. "Conversational" coupling of gaze behavior in prelinguistic human development. *J. Psycholinguistic Res.,* 1973, *2,* 321–330.

Kaye, K. Toward the origin of dialogue. In H. R. Schaffer (Ed.), *Studies in mother–infant interaction.* London: Academic Press, 1977.

Kemeny, J. C., & Snell, J. L. *Finite Markov chains.* Princeton, N.J.: Van Nostrand, 1960.

Kendon, A., & Cook, M. The consistency of gaze patterns in social interaction. *Brit. Jour. Psychol.,* 1969, *60*(4), 481–494.

Kimura, D. Manual activity during speaking I. Right-Handers. *Neuropsychologia,* 1973, *11,* 45–50.

de Laguna, G. A. *Speech: Its function and development.* New Haven, Conn.: Yale Univ. Press, 1927.

Lenneberg, E. H. *Biological foundations of language.* New York: Wiley, 1967.

Liberman, A. M. The grammars of speech and language. *Cognitive Psychology,* 1970, *1,* 301–323.

Marcus, E. S., Feldstein, S., Welkowitz, J., & Jaffe, J. *Psychological differentiation and the congruence of conversational time patterns.* Stony Brook, N.Y.: School of Social Welfare, State University of New York, 1970.

Markov, A. A. Essai d'une recherche sur le texte du roman "Eugene Onegin." *Bull. Acad. Imper. Sci.,* St. Petersburg, 1913, *7.*

Matarazzo, J. D., Saslow, G., & Hare, A. P. Factor analysis of interview interaction behavior. *J. Consult. Psychol.,* 1958, *22,* 419–429.

Matarazzo, J. D., & Wiens, A. N. *The interview.* New York: Aldine-Atherton, 1972.

Meltzer, L., Morris, W. N., & Hayes, D. P. Interruption outcomes & vocal amplitude: Explorations in social psychophysics. *Pers. Soc. Psychol.,* 1971, *18,* 392–402.

Natale, M. A Markovian model of adult gaze behavior. *Jour. Psycholoing. Res.,* 1976, *5,* 53–63.

Natale, M., Dahlberg, C. C., & Jaffe, J. The effect of LSD and dextroamphetamine on therapist–patient matching of speech "rhythms." *Jour. of Communication Disorders,* 1979, *12,* 45–52.

Norwine, A. C., & Murphy, O. J. Characteristic time intervals in telephone conversation. *Bell System Technical Journal,* 1938, *17,* 281–291.

Osgood, C., & Sebeok, T. (Eds.) Psycholinguistics. *J. Abn. Soc. Psychol.,* 1954, Supplement.

Pavlidis, T. *Biological oscillators: Their mathematical analysis.* New York: Academic Press, 1973.

Peters, P. S., & Ritchie, R. W. On restricting the base component of transformational grammars. *Info. & Control,* 1971, *18,* 483–501.

Pierce, J. R. *Symbols, signals & noise.* New York: Harper, 1961.

Podwall, F. N. *How do speakers parse time?* Unpublished doctoral dissertation, City Univ. of New York, 1976.

Rapoport, A., & Chammah, A. *Prisoner's dilemma.* Ann Arbor: Univ. of Michigan Press, 1965.

Searle, J. *Speech acts.* Cambridge: Cambridge Univ. Press, 1970.

Shannon, G. L., & Weaver, W. *The mathematical theory of communication.* Urbana, Ill.: Univ. Illinois Press, 1949.

Skinner, B. F. *Verbal behavior.* New York: Appleton, 1957.

Slobin, D. On the nature of talk to children. In E. Lenneberg & E. Lenneberg (Eds.), *Foundations of language development* (Vol. I). New York: Academic Press, 1975.

Snow, C. Mother's speech to children learning language. *Child Dev.,* 1972, *43,* 549–565.

Stern, D. N. Mother and infant at play. In M. Lewis & L. Rosenblum (Eds.), *The origins of behavior* (Vol. I). New York: Wiley, 1974.

Stern, D. N. *The first relationship: Infant and mother.* Cambridge, Mass.: Harvard Univ. Press, 1977.

Stern, D. N., Beebe, B., Jaffe, J., & Bennett, S. L. The infant's world during social interaction: A study of caregiver behaviors with special reference to repetition and timing. In H. R. Schaffer (Eds.), *Studies in mother–infant interaction.* London: Academic Press, 1977.

Stern, D. N., & Gibbon, J. Temporal expectancy during mother–infant play. In E. Thoman (Ed.), *Origins of the infant's social responsiveness.* Hillsdale, N.J.: Lawrence Erlbaum Associates, 1979.

Stern, D. N., Jaffe, J., Beebe, B., & Bennett, S. L. Vocalizing in unison and alternation: Two modes of communication within the mother–infant dyad. In D. Aaronson & R. W. Rieber (Eds.), *Developmental psycholinguistics and communication disorders. Ann. N.Y. Ac. Sci.,* 1975, *263,* 89–100.

Webb, J. T. Interview synchrony: An investigation of two speech rate measures. In A. W. Siegman & B. Pope (Eds.), *Studies in dyadic communication.* Elmsford, N.Y.: Pergamon Press, 1972.

Welkowitz, J., Cariffe, G., & Feldstein, S. Conversational congruence as a criterion of socialization in children. *Child Dev.,* 1976, *47,* 269–272.

White, B. L., Castle, P., & Held, R. Observations on the development of visually directed reaching. *Child Dev.,* 1964, *35,* 349–364.

Yngve, V. H. On getting a word in edgewise. *Papers from the sixth regional meeting Chicago Linguistic Society.* Chicago: Chicago Linguistic Society, 1970.

VII APPLICATIONS OF PSYCHOLINGUISTICS

14

The Naming Act and Its Disruption in Aphasia

Davis Howes
*Boston Verterans Administration Hospital
and Boston University School of Medicine*

> *The words of language name objects—sentences are combinations of such names. In this picture of language we find the roots of the idea: every word has a meaning. This meaning is coordinated to the word. It is the object for which the word stands.*
> —Ludwig Wittgenstein (*Philosophical Investigations,* Section 1, 1953)

> Socrates. *And is not naming a part of speaking? For in giving names men speak. And if speaking is a sort of action and has a relation to acts, is not naming also a sort of action?*
> —Plato (*Cratylus,* ca. 400 B.C.)

An unwary reader might suppose that these two passages, written more than two millennia apart, have accidentally been assigned to the wrong authors. For the first, taken from the final work of one of the progenitors of modern logical positivism, verges on the doctrine of philosophical idealism we generally associate with Plato; and the second, with its empirical (even behavioristic) cast, suggests the kind of analysis of natural language typified by the later Wittgenstein. Both quotations, to be sure, are out of context. Yet it is fair to say that Wittgenstein, while attempting to demonstrate the inadequacy of the conception of language I have quoted, never in fact strayed far from it; and that Plato, however far beyond empiricism his theory of universals may have taken him, got there by pursuing the act of naming to its logical conclusion.

Taken together, as if written by a single individual, these passages serve to demonstrate three points:

1. The act of naming is fundamental not only to our understanding of natural language, but to our understanding of how we know things as well.

2. Naming is immensely complex in its ramifications. The simplicity of the model stated by Wittgenstein is intentionally deceptive; for how can a meaning be the object for which a word stands? What is the meaning of the word anyway? And in what way do names combine to form sentences?

3. 2000 years have added little to our knowledge of the subject of naming.

This last point enables me to state the modest aims of this chapter without apology. I shall make no attempt to provide an integrated theory of the naming process, nor shall I endeavor to survey the efforts of others to attain that goal. In the spirit of Plato's question (and of Wittgenstein's treatise), I shall confine myself to an examination of naming as an act of natural language, but from one special point of view: to indicate what the breakdown of the naming function observed in patients with aphasia can tell us about the normal process by which words, objects, and meanings are linked.

The advantages of approaching the subject of naming from this perspective are several. Foremost, perhaps, is the fact that we are dealing with people who, a few weeks or months earlier, had performed the naming function much as the rest of us do. We are thus studying the same physiological process that provides the starting point for the inquiries of Plato, Wittgenstein, and others pursuing the nature of human understanding. True, we cannot exclude the possibility that in performing the task of naming the patient may utilize structures in his brain that formerly were not put to that use. But at least we are dealing with a subject who has known what it is like to perform the naming function in the natural way. This we cannot say of the study of naming or signing in animals (even the clever chimpanzee) or of its development in children.

Of course, it might be argued by the same token that it is even more advantageous to investigate naming in the normal adult. But experimental work on naming is limited by the extraordinary flexibility and facility of the process itself. Apart from a few basic types of measurement, experimenters interested in the problem have been obliged to introduce other factors such as memory or judgment in order to study the naming function. The results of such investigations, while often of considerable interest, tell us more about the ancillary processes than about the naming function itself.

One can also turn to the armchair experiment, examining the implications of the utterances we might be expected to produce in special situations in much the way that Plato, Wittgenstein, and other philosophers have done. This indeed appears to be the favored method of current psycholinguistics. The slow and uncertain pace of discovery by this approach, however, is evidenced by our comparison between Plato and Wittgenstein. By its nature, the armchair procedure can tell us nothing that we do not already know—a feature that has been canonized in recent years by Chomsky and his circle under the name of "competence." The natural scientist is justfiably skeptical of this approach. It is too easy to pick and choose examples that seem to favor our preconceived notions of what we think we know about language. To cite Wittgenstein (1953) again: "One cannot guess how a word functions. One has to look at its use and learn from that. But the difficulty is to set aside the prejudice that stands in the way of doing this. This is no simple-minded prejudice [Section 340]." An important advantage of viewing the naming function from the perspective of aphasia is that nature does not necessarily share our prejudices.

There are, finally, two elementary facts about aphasia that make it a particularly valuable mirror to normal language. These are often left unstated by aphasiologists, who take them for granted; yet they are by no means evident from normal observation, and their significance can easily be overlooked in the maze of controversy that surrounds other aspects of aphasia. The first is that aphasias are produced by focal lesions in the brain: lesions responsible for aphasias invariably encroach upon a specific territory representing perhaps 10% of the cerebral cortex. The second is that different lesions within this territory give rise to qualitative as well as quantitative differences in the pattern of aphasic disorders. It is these two facts that mark language as part of the biological inheritance of the species, not an invention like tools or agriculture, and that differentiate language functionally and structurally from other cognitive processes and modes of communication that in normal experience seem to be inseparable from it. They show, too, that the smooth surface of natural language is not the result of some unitary symbolic process, but of the interplay between functionally and anatomically distinct central processing systems.

Beyond these two elementary facts the literature on aphasia seems to the outsider a maelstrom of conflicting assertions and counterassertions by equally qualified experts. Perhaps it is this chaotic appearance of the aphasiological literature that has deterred psychologists concerned with language and cognitive processes from making proper use of this important source of information. (Though this was not always so; William James, for example, was fully conversant with the subject.) Actually, all is not as confusing as it seems. Most of the controversy concerns two broad issues: the classification of different clinical pictures into functional types; and the localization of particular syndromes within the territory reserved for language. If these two issues are set aside, there is to be found a large body of factual information on aphasic disorders about which there is relatively little difference of opinion. Because the aim of this chapter is to formulate the disorders of naming observed in aphasia for readers who do not have extensive experience with clinical material, I shall avoid the issues of localization and classification as far as possible. This naturally limits the scope of the presentation from the viewpoint of the aphasiologist; but I hope it will have compensating advantages for the reader trained in other disciplines who would like to become acquainted with the field.

I. PRELIMINARY REMARKS ON NAMING

A subject at once so complex and so elemental as the act of using names does not lend itself to definition. Characterization by example is a more useful method of clarifying terminology. The following remarks are intended to introduce some of the more important aspects of naming that arise in the consideration of aphasic disorders.

A. Confrontation Naming

1. The prototype for all naming acts is naming a concrete object. All considerations of the subject, so far as I know, start from that vantage point. Following neurological usage, I shall refer to naming in such situations as *naming to confrontation.* For example, suppose you show me a banana and ask me "What do you call this?" or "What is this?" If I respond with the word "banana;" that is confrontation naming.

Both the object and its name are commonly designated by the same word. Hence it is helpful to distinguish these two usages by a typographical convention. Italics will be used here to denote the object or stimulus, capital letters to denote the name. Thus in the above example I name the object *banana* by speaking the word BANANA.

2. The term "confrontation naming" applies only when the expected response is a single word or word compound. For instance, if my reply had been "It's a yellow fruit that's white inside, good to eat, and imported from Central America," it would not be naming to confrontation even though the reply designates the object satisfactorily. Replies of this kind are called *naming by description.*

3. Confrontation naming is not limited to the universe of concrete objects or to nouns. A picture or line drawing of the object can in almost all cases be substituted without detectable effect on naming. Similarly, a wave, a smile, or a wink can be presented in lieu of an object. Whether the naming responses in such instances are construed to be nouns or verbs is a moot point in English, but responses inflected as verbs can be elicited by modifying the question to, say, "What did I do?" Adjectives and adverbs can also be elicited by analogous modifications. Hence the use of nouns is not essential.

Tactile or auditory stimulation may be used as well as visual. In these cases the names elicited are either names of objects (e.g., PENCIL by touch or

MOTORCYCLE by sound) or of types of sensory experience (ROUGH or SMOOTH to touch, COUGH or WHISTLE to sound).

Although a thorough examination of confrontation naming in patients should include items covering these extensions, it should be noted that most clinical testing of aphasics is confined to visually presented objects or pictorial representations of them.

4. From the above it is evident that the essential requirement for studying confrontation naming is control over a stimulus configuration to which there corresponds a unique word (or small set of synonymous words) in the vocabulary of normal speakers. In other words, confrontation naming is tested in patients by presenting to them stimulus configurations that are practically certain to produce the expected response in a normal speaker. Hence we can assume that, but for the presence of cerebral disease, the patient would have named each item correctly with probability approaching 1.

5. The variety of stimulus configurations that typically evoke any given name is of course enormous (consider, e.g., ASHTRAY). This convergence upon a single name may occur because each of the stimulus configurations arouse the same "concept," which stands in one-to-one correspondence with the name. For example, the various stimulus configurations presented by different *ashtrays*, each viewed from different perspectives, may be processed so that they all converge on the same perceptual or conceptual event, which in turn corresponds to the name ASHTRAY.

This assumption, though widely held, rests more on convenience and plausibility than on hard evidence. It is also possible, for example, that each stimulus configuration excites only one of a numerous set of independent 'concepts,' each of which corresponds to the same name. In this case there is no single central event common to all these configurations other than the name itself. For example, suppose the stimulus configurations associated with one particular *ashtray* arouse one "concept" that is independent of the "concept" aroused by the configurations associated with a different *ashtray*, though both elicit the same word ASHTRAY in the naming situation. In the latter case the convergence of stimulus configurations on a common name takes place at two levels: (1) between stimulus configurations and "concept," and (2) between "concepts" and the common name.

This distinction, despite its abstruse appearance, will prove useful in discussing some of the implications of naming in aphasia. As the term "concept" is generally associated in psychological theory with the assumption of a one-to-one correspondence with a name, I shall substitute the more neutral term "cognition" for the intermediary event when that assumption is not invoked. Thus, in stating the proposition that a given *ashtray* arouses a cognition that in turn evokes the name ASHTRAY, no assumption is implied whether that cognition is different from, or the same as, the cognition aroused by any other *ashtray*.

It may be noted in passing that the phenomenon of homonymy (e.g., the smoker's PIPE contrasted with the plumber's PIPE) presents no special problem in this connection but is readily interpreted under either assumption.

6. It follows from the above that a failure of confrontation naming will result if either (1) the stimulus configuration fails to arouse an appropriate cognition or (2) the cognition when aroused does not elicit the associated name. The former represents a failure of recognition (*agnosia*) rather than of the naming process itself. In most cases this distinction is clinically obvious: any evidence that the patient has recognized the presented object (whether by actual use, by gesture, or by verbal description of function) is sufficient to establish the absence of agnosia. There are in the literature, however, some cases of naming disorder reported as aphasia where internal evidence indicates that agnosia was present (e.g., Freund, 1889).

7. The power of a stimulus configuration to evoke a name is therefore the product of its power to arouse an appropriate cognition and the power of that cognition to evoke the name. Both of these may be graded quantities. There is evidence from experimental work with normal subjects that familiar objects have roughly equivalent power to arouse appropriate cognitions in the naming task (Wingfield, 1966; Oldfield, 1966). On this assumption, performance on a confrontation naming task measures the power of the cognition to evoke its associated name in patients free of agnosia. If, however, the stimuli are atypical examples of objects (e.g., an unusual model of a *telephone*), or if the test is expanded to include items other than concrete objects, this assumption obviously is not justified.

8. The naming process itself, from cognition to the actual speech act, necessarily involves two phases: (1) the *selection process* by which the appropriate name is determined from the set of possible words; and (2) the *production process* by which the selected word is uttered. Obviously these are not simple one-stage processes. The distinction is important, however, because the type of information processed in the two phases is fundamentally different. The first is essentially semantic, the second articulatory. Consequently, failures of the production process are readily distinguished from failures of the selection process. If a patient shown a *watch* says something like WORSH, where the target word WATCH is recoverable by purely phonemic/phonetic transformations, the failure is evidently one of production; if he says TELEGRAPH, on the other hand, the failure is of the selection process (assuming recognition has been demonstrated independently). Of course failures may also occur in ways that do not clearly distinguish between these two phases (as by saying nothing, or I CAN'T, or LATCH).

9. The inverse of confrontation naming is the task of presenting a name to the subject for recognition of its meaning. The criteria used to assess recognition in this situation are much the same as in the direct naming task: pointing to the named object; demonstrating how to use it either by gesture or

by description; responding YES/NO to a pairing of the name with an appropriate/inappropriate object; etc. Tasks of this kind are usually called tests of verbal comprehension in the literature on aphasia, but that term is also used to designate other procedures for evaluating the capacity to understand spoken language where the constraints of confrontation naming do not apply. To avoid ambiguity I shall therefore use the term *inverse naming* to designate a comprehension task that fulfills the general requirements of confrontation naming.

10. One of the most ubiquitous assumptions about language, albeit one that is seldom explicit, is that naming and inverse naming are equivalent; that is, the process of passing from name to cognition is simply the process of passing from cognition to name executed in reverse order. The progression of ideas in the opening passage from Wittgenstein offers a good example: from the assertions first that words name objects and second that every word has its meaning we are led to the proposition that this meaning is coordinated or associated (*zugeordnet* is the original German) with the word. The directionality of the relationship between word and meaning is by implication of no consequence; and indeed, throughout the *Philosophical Investigations* Wittgenstein introduces examples of language acts in one direction or the other as if they were interchangeable. The assumption is no less pervasive in current psycholinguistic theory: semantic issues are analyzed almost exclusively in the context of inverse naming (understanding the meaning of a word or sentence), yet the semantic concepts so derived are employed without reservation in theoretical models of how sentences are generated. A further indication is the symmetry with which the terms "encoding" and "decoding" are applied to natural language, so that one man's "encoding" is another's "decoding," depending on whether he writes from the viewpoint of a listener or speaker.

This assumption that naming is a reversible process presupposes the existence of "concepts" corresponding to words as discussed in Section 5 above. It is implicitly assumed that there is a fairly direct connection or bond between the word and its corresponding "concept" or meaning by which either one can evoke the other. If on the other hand we suppose that there is convergence from a large number of cognitions to a single name, as envisaged in Section 5, then the naming process is convergent in one direction and divergent in the other and therefore cannot be strictly reversible.

We have then a hierarchy of assumptions about the relationship of naming to inverse naming: (a) they are equivalent processes in the sense of reversibility, as commonly assumed; (b) they are not reversible, but there exists a set of concepts in essentially one-to-one correspondence with names; (c) there is an extensive convergence between cognitions and names, so that neither reversibility nor concepts are assumed. To these may be added the minimum assumption (d) that naming and inverse naming are performed by independent systems or structures. Normal language function offers little evidence to indicate how far down in this sequence it is necessary to go; hence the prevalence of the strongest assumption in discussions of language based on the armchair method.

B. Related Verbal Tasks

Confrontation naming invites comparison with several other verbal procedures that call for single-word responses. The assumption that such tasks utilize the same production process then can be invoked. The following are of particular interest in relation to naming in aphasia.

1. Repetition of Single Words

In principle, repetition can be performed either with or without cognition. In the former case inverse naming is used to arouse an appropriate cognition and then direct naming to produce the expected response; in the latter (called *echoic* repetition) the response is mapped directly on the acoustic representation of the stimulus configuration without intervention of a cognition. If a patient consistently fails on inverse naming of words that he repeats correctly, the repetition is ordinarily assumed to be echoic. The converse, however, does not imply that repetition is not echoic, because inverse naming could be performed in parallel with echoic repetition. Other criteria are invoked to indicate that repetition is cognitive rather than echoic (e.g., if repetition is substantially better for common words than for rare words or nonsense syllables).

2. Reading Aloud

The distinction between performance with and without cognition applies here as well. This task is less useful than repetition because of the prevalence of alexias (failures of inverse naming for written material) in association with aphasia. Preservation of reading aloud in the face of other deficits, however, is sometimes useful in demonstrating that the production process is intact.

3. Word Association

The subject is presented a word with the instruction to say the first word that comes to mind other than the word presented to him. The task requires inverse naming of the stimulus word, and the production process appears to be the same as in confrontation naming. The selection process, however, is open to several interpretations. The advantage of this test is that the relative frequencies of different responses to certain stimulus words are known from studies of large groups of normals (Kent & Rosanoff, 1910; Postman & Keppel, 1970). Although the distribution of associative frequencies in individual subjects has never been studied quantitatively, the associations given by normal subjects generally conform to the expected frequencies based on the tabled values (Cramer, 1968). Hence departures from the normal are fairly easy to detect.

4. Naming to Category

Here the patient is asked to give all the names belonging to a specified category, such as animals, clothing, makes of car, etc. The task requires inverse naming of the generic word and repeated use of the naming process. As in the case of word association, the process by which the initial generic cognition gives rise to specific names is a matter of speculation. In normal subjects it is known that the rate at which new names are introduced decays approximately as an exponential function of time, and that there is a tendency for names to occur in relatively short bursts or clusters (Bousfield & Sedgewick, 1944; Indow & Togano, 1970). The constants of the function vary considerably between individuals and categories, however, and satisfactory data defining this range of variation for normal subjects are lacking. Consequently, failures of category naming are demonstrable only when they are relatively severe. (A variant of this task frequently used in testing patients is to ask for all words beginning with a specified letter. The task is ill suited for work with aphasic patients because failures are confounded by secondary effects of disorders affecting the processing of letters in alexia and dysarthria, as well as by the educational level of the patient.)

II. NAMING DISORDERS IN APHASIA

Disorders of confrontation naming appear in practically all cases of aphasia, the deficit varying quantitatively from total abolition to nearly normal performance with only occasional errors. Because our interest here is primarily in the character of the naming disorder in relation to the pattern of aphasia, the severity of the deficit is of secondary interest. In what follows I shall briefly describe the typical forms of naming errors in several varieties of aphasia. I shall then review in greater detail some of the systematic factors that affect naming performance in aphasia and the way in which specific classes of words are sometimes affected. It should be mentioned that naming is disturbed in other pathological conditions that are not considered here; Geschwind (1967) has discussed some of these.

A. Naming in Different Forms of Aphasia

Aphasia is a consequence of any disease affecting the region of the brain reserved for speech and language. The most common causes are cerebral vascular disease (including hemorrhage, thrombosis, embolism, etc.), tumors, abscesses, and head injury. The characteristic pattern of the aphasia is, by and large, independent of the disease process. The progression of symptoms, on the other hand, depends on the nature of the disease and not on the type of aphasia. Thus, in cases of tumor the onset of the aphasia is generally insidious and the progression is one of steadily increasing severity, whereas in vascular cases the onset is usually sudden ("stroke") followed by a progression of steady improvement to a stable state. In discussing the clinical pictures of aphasia, observations from the acute stage (the terminal phase of progressive disease or the initial phase of vascular disease) are generally excluded from consideration because the patient's condition is unstable and the focal effects of the disease are obscured by more widespread consequences.

In the following survey I describe the characteristic failures of confrontation naming in several well-known clinical patterns of aphasia. In selecting these patterns as prototypes I do not wish to imply that they constitute a typology by which aphasias can be classified according to the functional nature of the disorder. They are introduced rather as prototypes, well documented in the literature and familiar to anyone with extensive experience with aphasia, that are of particular interest for the study of naming. I hope thereby to escape some of the controversial issues that surround the questions of classification and localization of aphasias. These prototypes are not to be taken as descriptions of individual cases but as indicative of the observations one would expect to find in different cases corresponding roughly to the same prototype.

In describing the disorders of naming in these prototypes I have imagined a test of confrontation naming consisting of about 50 familiar objects (or line drawings thereof) presented successively and in random order. In this section the items are considered as if they were equivalent; later we shall consider the possibility that some items are more prone to elicit errors than are others.

1. Broca's Aphasia (Motor Aphasia, Verbal Aphasia)

The patient's spontaneous speech is effortful and sparse, but his comprehension of speech is by contrast relatively unimpaired. Typically the phonemes are not clearly enunciated (*dysarthria*), although in context they are usually recognizable. The dysarthria is not uniform: the same phoneme may be mispronounced in different ways at different times, and simple phrases (e.g., I DON'T KNOW), expletives, or well-known sequences of words (e.g., counting from 1 to 20, or reciting the Lord's Prayer) are frequently uttered faultlessly and without effort. There are also frequent phonemic errors (substitutions, deletions, additions, and displacements), though these are usually rare enough that the intended words can be detected without difficulty. In most cases (but by no means all), conversational speech is to some degree telegraphic in style because of a paucity of connective words (*agrammatism*). The patient also has difficulty getting out specific content words that he wants (*word finding difficulty*).

Practically all oral commands are performed without hesitation, and the patient appears to follow conversational speech addressed to him with only occasional difficulty. Reading comprehension is often equally effective, but in many cases it is considerably worse than comprehension of oral speech (*alexia*). The majority of cases corresponding to this prototype are paralyzed on the right side (*hemiparesis*), with the arm usually more affected than the leg. Writing is typically no better than speech, but the great majority of cases can be tested only with the nonpreferred hand because of the associated paralysis of the right side. When the hemiparesis is slight or absent, writing with the preferred hand usually is no better than speech; but there are numerous reports of cases in which writing is almost normal or at least markedly better preserved than speech.

Confrontation naming in this type of patient is generally consistent with his spontaneous speech. The performance is effortful, dysarthric, and slow. The frequency and pattern of errors depends somewhat on the severity of the case. Let us imagine two patients: A, who can sustain conversational speech at a rate of 50–60 words per minute (roughly a third to a half his premorbid rate); and B, whose rate is less than 20 words per minute and who has difficulty sustaining any continuous discourse. If the set of 50 common objects is presented for naming to each of those patients, we can expect to find that patient A will attempt all items and will give dysarthric approximations to the correct phoneme sequence for 75–90% of them. In the other instances, the phoneme pattern of the target word will be evident and will include deletions, insertions, and translations as well as phoneme substitutions. When the error constitutes an English word it will be related to the target word in sound but not in meaning (e.g., CLAY for *key*). Latencies will be two or three times normal, and there will be a number of instances of false starts (word fragments) in which the initial phonemes of the target word appear. The principal differences for the more severe case, B, will be that the patient will fail to produce any response on a number of items (say 25–50%), and phonemic errors will increase both in frequency and degree; some of the responses will be so badly mangled that their relationships to the target words cannot be recognized (*neologism*).

Repetition of single words in such patients is comparable to naming, usually slightly better. The pattern of errors and of dysarthria is similar. In word association the proportion of common to rare associations is essentially normal for a patient of the severity of A, if obvious phonemic errors are discounted; the latencies are increased by roughly the same factor as in naming. In a severe case such as B, however, the patient may fail to give any response to 25–35% of the stimulus words. Although he continues to give nearly a normal proportion of high-frequency associations, the response is likely to be perseverative or irrelevant when the latency is extremely long (say, greater than 10 seconds). Naming to category is generally done quite well by a patient of moderate severity.

2. Wernicke's Aphasia (Sensory Aphasia, Jargon Aphasia)

In the prototypical case the patient speaks rapidly, clearly, and without effort, but produces a jumbled sequence of words (*jargon*) that makes no sense to the listener (e.g., MORE ABOUT IT THERE ISN'T VERY MUCH WITH IT WHEN I WAS WORKING WITH ME NOTHING ABOUT MY TIME I WAS DOING MY WORK). The rate may be faster than normal (*logorrhea*), sometimes by as much as 50%; but this is not always the case. Comprehension of spoken language is severely impaired: only a few oral commands are regularly obeyed (e.g., "close your eyes" or "stand up"), although the patient is evidently attentive and cooperative. There is at best only a loose thematic relationship between what is said to him and what he says or does. Questions calling for specific information are quite useless, though the patient will usually respond with jargon utterances that indicate that he understands that a verbal answer is called for (Boller & Green, 1972). Most of his spontaneous speech consists of standard English words, some of which recur with excessive frequency (TIME and WORK in the patient quoted above), and the syntax is preserved as far as the sequence of connective and substantive words is concerned. There are, however, occasional phonemic errors. These often stand out quite prominently because of their clear articulation, although they make up only 1–2% of his output. Apart from the verbal sphere, the patient is well oriented toward his social environment, takes care of himself, finds his way about, and obeys simple visual signals such as beckoning him to come or holding up one's hand to him to stop.

In very severe cases of this type confrontation naming, inverse naming, repetition, association, and category naming are all abolished. It is difficult in such cases to determine whether the patient understands what is expected of him, especially with the more complex tasks like word association or category naming. Usually, however, it is possible to tell that he is attempting the correct task by his facial expression, verbal gestures, and the appropriate length of his utterances. In less severe cases, moreover, it is evident that the patient knows what he is supposed to do. He may correctly name 5–10% of a series of simple objects (e.g., *cup, door*), and others may be embedded in longish jargon utterances (e.g., to presentation of a *chair:* AND THEN ON THE CHAIR I

HAVE MADE MY WAY ON A STOOL, STOOL IN FRONT OF THIS . . .), sometimes without showing any indication that he recognizes he has produced the correct word. Less common in such a patient is naming by functional definition (to a *cigarette,* IT'S A THING THAT YOU PUFF OUT A SMOKE WITH). Phonemic transformations of the target word are exceptional, although they may be present in the irrelevant part of the jargon utterances. The jargon may contain words related in meaning to the stimulus word (e.g., to the picture of an *octopus* the word PICKEREL in a 30-word response), but unless this occurs frequently it is impossible to know whether such occurrences are coincidental or not. Unlike the patient with severe Broca's aphasia, the patient with Wernicke's aphasia almost never responds with silence or a simple confession of failure (e.g., I CAN'T or IT WON'T COME OUT); indeed, the shortest responses usually are the correct ones, and even these are seldom uttered as single words (e.g., IT'S A CUP or IT'S PART OF A CUP instead of just CUP).

Inverse naming appears to be of the same order of magnitude as naming in such patients, although clinical testing procedures do not provide a clear basis for quantitative comparisons. The word association test is often feasible, the patient giving enough very common associations (perhaps 5%) to demonstrate that he is endeavoring to perform the task. Another 10–20% of his responses may be associations of low frequency (1–20 per thousand in standard tables of normal responses.). The remaining responses will consist of words not in the tables (but often vaguely related in meaning to the stimulus word), wholly irrelevant words, and jargon utterances. Category naming is not often tested with such patients; my personal experience suggests that it is practically abolished, even in the patient who carries out the naming and association tasks.

Repetition of words in these less severe patients is successful for about the same proportion of items as naming, but the pattern of errors is quite distinct. Practically all errors are of the phonemic type. Usually the target word is evident in the response (e.g., FULLOFF for "foot"), but in perhaps 20–30% of the responses the errors are so severe that no relationship can be detected (e.g., PINNED for "bay"). The envelope of the target word, however, is almost always preserved at least approximately: long jargon utterances, which abound in the naming or association tasks, are exceptional in the same patient's attempts at repetition.

3. Conduction Aphasia (Central Aphasia of Goldstein)

The patient speaks at a normal rate, without apparent effort or dysarthria, but the flow of speech is interrupted by frequent phonemic errors. Comprehension of oral commands and of conversational speech is good. The phonemic errors in his spontaneous speech may affect only a small proportion of the words uttered (2–5%), and many of the errors are simple enough that the target word is understandable in context (e.g., POPPER for *paper*), but in perhaps half the distortion is so great that the meaning of the passage is lost. The words affected are commonly content words (nouns, verbs, adjectives), but connectives are not immune. Frequently the patient makes several attempts to say the word, showing that he recognizes the error, but the sequence does not progress regularly toward the target word. The words affected by errors at one time are pronounced correctly and with ease on another occasion (very long words, however, may be marred by errors in every instance). In some cases the patient's speech may seem to be loosely constructed or vague and circumlocutory, apart from the phomemic disorder. Reading aloud is more severely disturbed by phonemic errors than is spontaneous speech, even in those exceptional cases where comprehension of written language is fairly good. Writing is still more severely affected.

Confrontation naming is grossly disturbed by phonemic errors. The proportion of errors increases as a function of the length of the name, but even monosyllabic names are frequently affected by phonemic errors (perhaps 20–30% of items). Only a small percentage of three- and four-syllable names are produced correctly. Despite his difficulty, the patient is able to produce a response that resembles the target word closely enough to demonstrate that his selection is correct in practically every instance. Repeated attempts are commonly required. It is generally believed that the sequence of successive attempts progresses in the direction of the target word, but the progression is certainly far from regular, and on occasion the sequence may first converge and then diverge from the target. It is worthy of note that in practically all cases that have been tested extensively a small proportion of the responses (perhaps 5%) have consisted of words related to the target semantically but not phonemically (e.g., WATCH to presentation of an *alarm clock*).

Repetition of single words exhibits essentially the same pattern of disorder. Following an early suggestion by Wernicke (1874), repetition has been singled out on theoretical grounds as the functional disturbance characteristic of this type of aphasia (Kleist, 1962; Geschwind, 1965). This emphasis would suggest that the severity of the disturbance is greater for repetition than for confrontation naming. A survey of cases published in the literature, however, reveals that where data on both repetition and naming are reported in sufficient detail there is no evidence that one is more severely impaired than the other (Green & Howes, 1977). Recently Lecours and Lhermitte (1969) have developed an elegant and comprehensive method for the analysis of phonemic errors. Their method, if applied to the responses generated by repetition and naming of the same items, opens up the prospect of a definitive answer to this question.

Word association in these patients indicates little change in the selection of associations from the normal tables, if one limits consideration to those items for which the target words can be detected. In this task, however, unlike naming and repetition, the target word is frequently uncertain. This leaves open the possibility that in those instances the patient has selected associations that are beyond the scope of the standard tables of normal associations. Naming to category also is difficult to evaluate precisely, for successive attempts to pronounce a single name often cannot be distinguished from phonemically disturbed attempts to produce different names.

4. Nominal Aphasia (Amnestic Aphasia, Anomic Aphasia, Paraphasia)

The patient's conversational speech might be taken for normal except that occasionally the flow is broken while he searches for a particular word he needs to convey his thought (*word-finding pauses*). These difficulties usually occur when the patient tries to explain some relatively complicated thought, and they affect content words rather than connectives. Both phonemic errors and word substitutions are common in such episodes. The hiatus may so distract the patient that he loses his train of thought, and he often talks about the problem while the search goes on. In addition to these obvious failures of word finding, the patient's speech typically contains slight errors that are often missed unless his speech is recorded and transcribed. Among these will be both phonemic errors (e.g., DUFF for "tough") and word substitutions (e.g., WE GO ONCE A YEAR. WE SPENT ("met") A LOT OF NICE PEOPLE THERE). The proportion of words affected by errors is much less than in conduction/central aphasia (perhaps 1% or even less), but much greater than one would find in normal conversational speech. The character of the errors, moreover, rarely resembles the kind of error that has been documented for normal speech (cf. Fromkin, 1973). The patient readily follows oral commands, and his understanding of conversational speech is generally good. Nevertheless, his comprehension of conversational speech is noticeably fragile. A three-party conversation, for example, may be extremely difficult for him to follow even if he seems to understand everything when conversing one on one. Reading and writing are usually more severely impaired, although there are exceptions.

The most striking feature of this type of aphasia in the patient's difficulty with confrontation naming. He may in fact name 70–80% of common objects presented to him correctly, yet even so the failures are far out of proportion to his spontaneous speech and comprehension. Even very common items (*cup, chair*) may be missed. Of those named correctly, moreover, half may be named only after a long latency and evident effort of concentration. Unnecessary additions (*augmentation*) occur in other instances (e.g., SCREW-NAIL to presentation of a *screw*). Errors are usually of several types. Most numerous, usually, are simple errors in which the patient says nothing or utters simple carrier phrases (e.g., LET'S SEE . . . , or IT'S A . . .), until finally, after 10–20 sec, he gives up. This he will usually signify verbally by saying something like I CAN'T or I KNOW WHAT IT IS BUT I CAN'T SAY IT. Another common type of error is for the patient to describe the object, usually by indicating its function, without giving its name. Irrelevant conversation, however, such as one encounters in Wernicke's aphasia, is rare. The most striking type of failure is the word substitution. This is usually produced with the same intonation as a correct name and is almost always related in meaning to the target word. The relationship is sometimes quite close and seemingly natural (e.g., SPOON to a *fork*), but more often is not predictable (e.g., TROUGH to *cup*). These substitutions are often quite picturesque, and the patient may be as struck by their oddity as is the examiner. They are produced, however, as though they were correct names, for after producing one the patient seldom continues to try to produce the correct name, unless specifically asked to do so. Although these semantic errors are characteristic of patients with nominal aphasia, their frequency is often exaggerated. Rarely do they constitute more than 25% of all naming failures. Indeed, phonemic errors, which are sometimes ignored in discussions of this type of aphasia, are often more common than word substitutions.

The patient's difficulty with confrontation naming is particularly striking by contrast with his performance on both repetition and inverse naming. Both of these are performed flawlessly and without effort for the same words used in the test of naming. A few very difficult words ("hippopotamus") may give difficulty on repetition. Inverse naming is equally faultless when the test is limited to names of common objects. With more difficult tasks, however, the patient's comprehension is usually found to be fragile.

Word association in patients with nominal aphasia presents an interesting comparison with confrontation naming. The patient gives almost as many high-frequency associations (table frequencies greater than 200 per thousand) as a normal subject. Perhaps 25–35% of his responses are of this kind. But he gives a much larger proportion of responses that are very rare in the tables (frequencies of 0–1). These responses are vaguely, but clearly, related in meaning to the stimulus word (e.g., THICK to "deep," LARGE to "soft," VALLEY to "river"). Looked at individually, each of these responses might be found among the associations given by a normal subject; but the proportion of unusual associations is two or three times the normal proportion. Failures to give any association ("blocks"), on the other hand, are not appreciably more common than among normals (perhaps 2–4%). Latencies for most of the responses are within the normal range, but there is a greater proportion of long latency responses (10 seconds or more) than in the normal subject. One regular feature of the associations given by these patients has no counterpart in normal subjects. This is the recurrence of specific words as associations to different stimulus words. These are not given perseveratively (i.e., to successive stimulus words), and they generally appear only to stimulus words for which some relevance can be seen. For instance, one patient gave the association WINDOW to the stimulus words "house" (frequency 23/1,000), "chair" (frequency 3/1,000), "bath" (frequency 0/1,000), "stove" (frequency 0/1,000), and "street" (frequency 0/1,000); each recurrence of this response was separated by at least eight other associations. The recurrent words depend on the individual patient, but practically all patients of this type show at least one, and sometimes two or three.

Naming to category is also severely disturbed in the patient with nominal aphasia. A patient who gives no more than 15% errors on confrontation naming may be able to produce only 15–25 animal names in 10 min, compared to 60–90 for a normal subject of comparable experience. The patient himself is usually perplexed by the difficulty of the task. He may try various devices, such as imagining himself to be in a zoo or a barnyard, but the names do not come forth.

5. Other Aphasic Syndromes

Several patterns of aphasia that are of much rarer incidence than the preceding ones are of interest here because of their effects on naming and related tasks. In *word deafness* the patient has great difficulty understanding what is said to him, although there is no hearing loss sufficient to explain the receptive disorder. Thus he may be able to hear the faint tick of a watch held 4 in. from his ear, yet be unable to respond to oral commands or questions. This is one of the few aphasic syndromes in which confrontation naming may be wholly unimpaired. Traces of the kind of errors found in nominal aphasia, however, are sometimes observed. Repetition and inverse naming are, of course, severely disturbed.

In *echoic aphasia* (isolation syndrome) the patient has practically no spontaneous speech or comprehension and yet repeats long sentences spoken to him. A few simple linguistic transformations (such as "you" to ME) sometimes appear in appropriate places. The repetition clearly is performed without comprehension, and generally is compulsive in that the patient is unable to inhibit it upon request. In these patients confrontation naming and inverse naming are wholly abolished. It may in fact be difficult to get the patient to repeat single words in the format of a test, although he repeats much longer passages when not asked to do so.

In cases of *section of the corpus callosum* (cf. Sperry, Gazzaniga, & Bogen, 1969) the patient gives essentially normal responses to all stimuli presented to his dominant (usually left) hemisphere, but fails when they are directed to the opposite hemisphere. Of particular interest is the behavior of these patients when objects are presented for naming to the right hemisphere (e.g., in the left visual field or left hand). A few of them may be correctly named (the proportion is still a matter of controversy). But in most instances the patient will confabulate, rather than simply say I DON'T KNOW. In this respect their performance compares with that of the patient with Wernicke's aphasia, although the character of the confabulation is of course entirely different.

6. Summary Table

In order to permit more direct comparisons between the different patterns of naming disorder I have put into tabular form as much of the above information as possible. Table 14.1 shows the relative preponderance of nine types of naming error in each of the four main aphasic prototypes (two grades of severity are distinguished for Broca's aphasia). Each type of error is rated on a scale of 0 to 4. In assigning the ratings I have attempted to reflect actual protocols, but the scale values are not intended to represent uniform intervals of relative frequency. A rating of 0 is assigned to errors that practically never occur in clean cases of the given prototype, and a rating of 1 to those that are very rare but that undeniably occur in some cases. A rating of 2 signifies a type of error that is not common, but neither is it so rare as to surprise when it does appear. Ratings of 3 and 4 indicate the more common types of error, with the 4 given to those that tend to predominate. Thus types of error rated less than 2 are extremely rare, whereas those rated greater than 2 are the common ones.

The types of error listed in the upper half of the table (B through E) consist of responses that are appropriate as to length (i.e., one-word responses) whereas those in the lower portion (F through I) represent responses that

TABLE 14.1
Estimated Prevalence of Different Types of Naming Error
in Four Aphasic Prototypes

	Broca's				
Type of Error	Mild	Severe	Conduction	Wernicke's	Nominal
A. No Response	1	4	1	1	4
B. Dysarthric Response	4	4	1	0	0
C. Phonemic Errors	2	3	4	1	2
D. Neologism	1	2	3	1	1
E. Word Substitution	1	1	1	2	3
F. Augmentation	1	1	2	2	2
G. Embedded Naming	0	0	1	2	2
H. Naming by Description	1	1	1	3	4
I. Extended Jargon	0	0	0	4	1

Key: 0 = Practically never   3 = Fairly common
     1 = Very rare   4 = Predominant
     2 = Occasionally

involve excess verbiage. A few remarks and qualifications may help to clarify the abbreviated designations in the table. Type A (No Response) is not limited to total silence, but includes instances where the patient's remarks are parenthetical (e.g., I CAN'T, or IT JUST WON'T COME). Types B (Dysarthric Response) and C (Phonemic Errors) are used only when the target word is apparent to the examiner. If distortions of either type (or both) are so severe that the patient's production does not appear related to the target word, the response is classified under Type D (Neologism). Type E (Word Substitution) refers to substitutions that are not phonemically similar to the target word; phonemic errors that accidentally form a word (e.g., CLAY for *key*) are classified under C. Type F (Augmentation) does not include the use of carrier phrases (e.g., IT'S A . . .), but is restricted to the addition of unnecessary substantive words or short phrases, whether or not the response includes the target word (e.g., FISHTAIL for *fish*). Type G (Embedded Naming) refers to instances where the patient actually produces the target word as part of a longer sequence but does not seem to recognize that he has produced it. Type H (Naming by Description) refers to the use of a description of the item or of its function as a substitute for its name; if the patient parenthetically describes the item while searching for the name, the response would not be so classified. Type I (Extended Jargon) is reserved for lengthy responses that do not make good sense to the examiner; such strings may include nonsense words or be composed wholly of perfectly ordinary English words in meaningless order.

Examined column by column, this table recapitulates the main patterns of aphasic naming disorder described above. For Broca's and conduction cases the errors lie mainly in the upper part of the table, whereas the errors for Wernicke's aphasia are concentrated in the lower portion. One point brought out clearly by the table is the greater variety of errors encountered in nominal aphasia. Descriptions of this type of aphasia are apt to stress the occurrence of word substitutions to the exclusion of other types of errors. Examination of protocols of naming tests, however, does not sustain that picture. As the table shows, I have rated six of the nine types of error as common enough not to be surprising in these cases.

Looking at the table row by row, we see that most types of error are absent (or nearly so) either in the two prototypes affecting production (Broca's and conduction) or in Wernicke's aphasia. The greatest amount of overlap is for phonemic errors, which appear in the naming responses of three of the four prototypes with at least some degree of regularity. It would be interesting to know whether the distribution of phoneme substitutions and displacements are the same or different in these three types of aphasia. This is a question that cannot be answered by ordinary tabulation of data, but which the computer analysis of phonemic errors devised by Lecours and Lhermitte (1969) should be able to settle definitively.

B. Systematic Factors Affecting Confrontation Naming

In surveying the naming disorders in different aphasic syndromes I have been concerned with the characteristic types of errors without considering the type of item that is most likely to produce errors. Some stimulus configurations are of course much more prone to produce errors than others. One might expect this factor to interact strongly with the type of disorder. On this point, however, the results to date have been disappointing, although the possibility that more precise experimental investigations may reveal some unexpected relationships is certainly not to be discounted. I shall therefore describe these effects on naming performance generally, making reference to specific aphasic prototypes only as necessary.

Two quantitative factors that have pronounced effects on the aphasic's ability to name are the frequency with which the name is used in the language and the length of the word itself. The pioneering studies on the effect of word frequency are those of Rochford and Williams (1962–1965). Having noted that a set of objects they were using in naming tests with aphasics could be arranged in order of difficulty, they found that a large proportion of the most difficult items were those with very low-frequency names. But except at the extreme end of the scale, Rochford and Williams found only a weak association between item difficulty and word frequency. They were equally impressed by the observation that names learned early in childhood, but not necessarily common in adult speech, were often among the items named with ease by their patients.

The studies of the Oxford group on naming in normal subjects (Oldfield & Wingfield, 1965; Oldfield, 1966) led to a thorough study of the word frequency effect in aphasic naming (Newcombe, Oldfield, & Wingfield, 1965; Newcombe, Oldfield, Ratcliff, & Wingfield, 1971). They corroborated the main findings of Rochford and Williams, but attributed the absence of a pronounced relationship except at the very low frequencies to the small proportion of errors with words of frequencies greater than 20 per million. Using latency of the naming response in place of the proportion of errors, they were able to demonstrate a linear relationship to the logarithm of word frequency over the entire experimental range. This function parallels the results they obtained with control subjects, the aphasic latencies averaging about twice the control values. The correlation between latency and log word frequency, moreover, was of the same order of magnitude for aphasics as for controls, and indeed not far below the estimated reliability of word-frequency measurements for normals (Howes, 1954). These results led the authors to conclude that the naming performance of aphasics differs only in degree from normals.

The evidence assembled by this group is impressive. It can be wondered, however, if their method has not limited their findings. In common with a recent trend in neuropsychological research, they have treated their aphasics as a single group for comparison with control and other brain-damaged groups. It is at least conceivable that some of their aphasics do not conform to the normal functional relationship betwen latency and frequency, but that this evidence is washed out by pooling their data with those from other patients. In my own experience with the Oldfield-Wingfield set of items, I have observed that in certain patients, specifically those with relatively severe nominal or mild Wernicke's aphasias, the word-frequency effect seems to be very weak indeed. It would take a much larger set of items to test this impression adequately, but it accords well with the views expressed by Rochford and Williams. In general, when a quantative relationship known to hold for normal subjects is investigated in an aphasic patient we can expect one of three types of result: (1) performance that is within normal limits; (2) performance that is significantly worse than normal, but in which the functional relationships are preserved with shifted constants (the outcome reported by Newcombe et al.); and (3) performance in which the normal functional relationships are themselves disturbed. This last type of result, which is of particular importance for understanding the mechanisms of language, is inevitably obscured when the data are pooled with those from other patients whose results conform to 1 or 2.

The effect of word length on naming performance has received little attention in the literature, despite its evident impact in clinical examination of patients. Indeed, some of the effect of frequency in the previously cited studies may be attributable to length, because the two variables are so highly correlated in natural language that it requires considerable effort to disentangle them. A recent study by Goodglass, Kaplan, Weintraub, and Ackerman (1976), although directed primarily at another issue, provides the best data on the subject. They presented a set of 48 pictures for naming to a group of 48 aphasics, with Broca's, Wernicke's, conduction and nominal aphasias represented in roughly equal proportions. The pictures had been preselected to represent names of one, two, three, and four/five syllables, 12 of each length, with word frequency carefully matched between lengths. A picture was considered to be correctly named if the target word was clearly recognizable; errors of articulation and phonemic substitutions were thus ignored unless they were so extreme as to obscure the target word. (This turns out to be an important point.)

The results showed clear evidence of a word length effect on naming failures ($p < .001$). On the average, twice as many failures (36% vs. 18%) occurred with the four/five syllable names as with monosyllabic ones, despite careful balancing for frequency. Of greater interest is the question whether the effect of word length depends on the type of aphasia. Goodglass and co-workers report a significant interaction ($p < .01$) between length and type of aphasia. This may, however, represent an artifact of the use of analysis of variance on discrete incidence data. A χ^2 test on the total number of naming failures partitioned by length and type of aphasia, which makes minimal assumptions, does not reach significance ($\chi^2(9) = 14.37, p > .10$). The χ^2 test, however, confirms the powerful effect of length ($\chi^2(3) = 55.64, p < .001$).

Irrespective of the statistical question, the differences between the four types of aphasia in their data are certainly much smaller than most clinically experienced observers would expect. This may reflect the fact that the main purpose of their study required a selection of patients that minimize differences between groups in the proportion of naming failures. Their analysis of variance, for example, showed no significant difference between patient groups in this respect, although certainly an unselected or "random" sample of Wernicke's patients would yield many more naming failures than a "random" sample of nominal aphasics. Even when one takes this selective bias into account, however, these data constitute impressive evidence that the effect of word length on naming is far more uniform in different aphasic syndromes than clinical experience suggests. The importance of their procedure of ignoring phonetic and phonemic errors must be stressed in this connection. In clinical examination, the innumerable phonemic and dysarthric errors are so striking in the attempts of patients with conduction or Broca's aphasia to name polysyllabic words that a uniform word-length effect could easily be missed without the use of a scoring criterion such as the one adopted by Goodglass and associates.

One other systematic effect on naming performance is cueing, either by saying to the patient the first sound or syllable of the target word (*phonemic cueing*) or by providing him with a definition, synonym, or familiar context in which the target word occurs (*semantic cueing*). The success of this procedure with many patients has long been noted, and Weigl (1961; Weigl & Bierwisch, 1973) in particular has emphasized its significance both for understanding the nature of naming disorders and for treatment of the patient. Certainly it is true that some patients who unaided can name only a small proportion of objects to confrontation are able to produce practically all of those names after only minimal phonemic cueing. The question is whether the success of cueing, particularly of the two different modes of providing cues, depends on the type of aphasia. Intuitively, it is tempting to speculate that phonemic cueing should be particularly useful in Broca's and conduction aphasia (where problems with speech production predominate), whereas semantic cueing should be more useful in Wernicke's and nominal aphasia. In my experience there is little substance to this idea. In the first place, semantic cueing seems to be relatively ineffective in all cases, except in the form of automatic sequences (e.g., "red, white, and _____"), which can be interpreted as essentially phonemic rather than semantic. Second, cueing seems to have little success with relatively severe patients of any type. Finally, phonemic cueing can facilitate naming in all four syndromes. It is perhaps of some conceptual interest that phonemic cueing can have considerable success in patients with nominal aphasia, or even with mild cases of the Wernicke's type. Although the main problem in these cases may relate to semantic or cognitive processing, partial information about the physical structure of the word can help to overcome their difficulties.

A related question raised by neurologists in the nineteenth century, particularly Thomas and Roux (1895), is whether the aphasic possesses some "mental image" of the word he cannot produce in a confrontation naming task. This was tested by asking the patient to select the first syllable of a word from a series spoken to him, or by some similar procedure. Exaggerated claims and counterclaims were the main result at that time. New life has been infused into this question by the study of Goodglass and co-workers (1976) cited previously. Whenever one of their patients failed to name an object they asked him first to point to its initial letter on a printed alphabet card and then to indicate the number of syllables in it by pointing to one of five alternative outlines on a specially prepared card. The patients with conduction aphasia were decidedly superior at both tasks, succeeding on 34% of their naming failures. The Broca's patients were not far behind (20%). By contrast, the nominal aphasics were correct with only 5% of the initial letters and 10% of the syllable lengths (chance performance), with the Wernicke's only slightly better. Thus it does appear that patients with the production types of aphasia possess some partial information about the physical structure of the name they cannot produce, whereas this type of information is not available to nominal or Wernicke's patients.

The success of phonemic cueing in the different syndromes thus appears to result from different mechanisms. In nominal and Wernicke's aphasia the patient gains information he is lacking; in Broca's and conduction aphasia cueing gives the patient an acoustic model to imitate, thus helping him to overcome his difficulty in producing the word.

C. Specific Naming Difficulties

A question of great theoretical interest is whether a single processing system underlies all naming acts or whether some types of names utilize different structures from others. If the former, the analogy with the modern digital computer in processing various forms of input would be striking. It is already implicit from the foregoing review that for most simple objects, or representations of objects, the naming difficulties of aphasics are to all appearances uniform, once a few systematic factors like the frequency and length of the name are taken into account. But there are some exceptions to this rule. In this section, the naming of aphasics is examined for certain specific classes of cognitions that exhibit, or might be expected to exhibit, special deficits or facilitation.

1. Proper Names

Probably the most salient distinction among names in normal language is between proper and common names, a distinction recognized by the use of capitalization in English. Proper names for persons, places, etc., are so uniquely bound to their referents that it is reasonable to suppose that they do not require a conceptual stage of processing, in the sense used here. They also frequently employ phonemic combinations that are rare among common names and that even contravene the combinatory rules of the language. On either of these grounds we might expect aphasics of one prototype or another to exhibit a markedly more severe impairment with proper nouns than with common nouns. In the early literature on aphasia there were occasional reports of such cases, but these were chiefly based on the patient's own complaints and were in the context of a more general naming deficit. There are of course many more occasions when a patient feels the inability to use a proper name of extremely low frequency than common nouns of comparable frequency, for which he may readily find a substitute expression. To my knowledge there is no documented case showing a selective impairment of the use of proper names, a fact that is the more remarkable because the distinction is so obvious to the patient as well as the clinician.

2. Technical Nomenclature

Specialized fields, particularly the sciences, employ a host of special names that seem to function much like proper names in the narrow range of cognitions to which they are associated and in their utilization of phonemic combinations foreign to the rules of the language. Although patients with such specialized skills abound in the contemporary world, there has been little exploration of the effect of aphasia on technical vocabulary. I once examined an aphasic patient who had been a professional computer programmer, with the hope of making use of his skills while he was in our hospital. In the course of this effort he was able to use quite a lot of technical terminology in a reasonable manner, and his facility with the console was quickly restored; but when it came to useful programming, the project was a total loss.

3. Parts of Speech Other Than Nouns

Once again, there has been no systematic study of this question. But there is a great deal of clinical experience with trying to elicit verbs and adjectives either from specially designed pictures or from events as they occur in the testing situation. The experience of all observers I know is the same: verbs and adjectives are produced to confrontation neither better nor worse than nouns, given that the appropriate cognition is clear and that the words are of comparable length and frequency.

4. Stimulus Modality

In 1889 C. S. Freund described eight cases of what he termed "optic aphasia," which he interpreted as a disconnection between the visual centers of the occipital lobe and the language areas more anterior in the left hemisphere. This led to a sizable literature of case reports of optic aphasia accepting the same interpretation. But at least five of Freund's cases had clear visual agnosias by his own description, and in the others he did not carefully examine whether naming to tactile or auditory presentation was equally disturbed. His followers were for the most part equally uncritical. The interest in optic aphasia gradually subsided as investigators began to carry out parallel tests with both tactile and visual presentation and repeatedly found parallel naming deficits. My own review of this literature yielded not a single case in which there was satisfactory evidence for optic aphasia. In recent years the concept has been revived by Spreen, Benton, and Van Allen (1966) to account for a carefully tested case in which naming was superior for tactile over visual presentation of objects on seven separate testing occasions. Only on the first of these tests, however, does the difference they report approach statistical significance ($p < .05$). The difference between the total number of items named to visual and tactile presentation on all seven tests, as tabulated from their data, is not significant ($\chi^2(1) = 2.50$, $p > .10$). A procedural difference may explain the consistency of the slight superiority of tactile naming: The objects were presented one at a time for tactile naming but in sets of 10 for visual naming. All the evidence to date, then, is consistent with the assertion that the naming deficits in aphasia are independent of the sensory modality through which the cognition is received.

This equivalence does not of course apply to cases involving section of the corpus callosum, discussed previously. These are not properly regarded as aphasias, because stimulus events routed to the left hemisphere via any sense modality are promptly named.

5. Numerals and Letters

Naming of numerals and two- or even three- and four-digit numbers is in some cases much better preserved than the naming of objects, though as a rule there is no demonstrable discrepancy. In cases of conduction aphasia the superiority of number naming can be particularly striking and has been documented repeatedly. The interpretation of this observation is much debated. The most common hypothesis is that the effect is somehow related to the fact that there are only 10 digits compared to about 40 English phonemes. But this can hardly be sustained in view of the absence of the phenomenon in most cases. The naming of letters, on the other hand, is often disturbed with what appears to be disproportionate severity. The question arises whether the production of letter names or number names should be regarded as naming in any functional sense, since it is unclear that any cognition is necessary to the process. Indeed, the fact that these are among the most striking anomalies picked up by tests of naming serves to underscore the generality of the rule that naming is independent of the nature of the cognition to be named.

6. Names of Colors and Body Parts

The two indisputable exceptions to the preceding statement are to be found in the naming of colors and body parts in cases of nominal aphasia. In this syndrome it is almost the rule rather than the exception to find one or the other (or both) of these specific classes of stimuli disproportionately disturbed. The discrepancy may be extremely dramatic: one highly intelligent patient I examined, who performed better than 95% on tests of object naming, could do no better than chance when naming colors shown to him, and completed the sentence "the sky is . . . ?" with the response RED. The specific difficulty for naming of body parts is seldom this dramatic; but neither are statistical tests necessary in most cases to prove its existence. Certain body parts are particularly prone to errors of naming: chin and cheek, the neck and the calf, for example; and the joints (elbow, wrist, knee, and ankle) are typically substituted one for the other. It is significant that in naming colors and body parts the patient's errors almost invariably are incorrect names belonging to the same class.

These specific naming deficits are not found in Broca's aphasia and rarely, if ever, in conduction aphasia. Whether they occur in Wernicke's aphasia is a moot point because of the generalized difficulty of naming in those cases. Severely impaired color naming is also a common accompaniment of alexia without agraphia, even when no nominal aphasia is evident (Benson and Geschwind, 1969).

One clue to the interpretation of these strange specific disorders may be that they usually, if not always, apply also to inverse naming (single-word comprehension test). This is so even though they appear in the context of nominal aphasia, where inverse naming is only lightly affected if at all. In this respect they appear to be more akin to the finger recognition (and naming) problems of Gerstmann's syndrome, or to the specific loss of capacity for recognizing (and naming) faces (*prosopagnosia*) (Brown, 1972). They remain, in any case, a challenge to the otherwise general rule that naming disorders apply generally to all stimuli irrespective of the nature of the cognition to be named.

D. Localization of Aphasic Naming Disorders.

Each of the main aphasic patterns discussed here is associated with its own characteristic site of lesion. This is not to deny that the question of localization is fraught with controversy. But if we restrict ourselves to cases corresponding closely to the prototypes, acknowledge that data on localization are intrinsically of limited precision, and admit to the existence of occasional cases that do not correspond to the characteristic clinico-pathological relationships, it is possible to state some general principles that few aphasiologists would contest. In the present context, it should be noted, the evidence of localization is of interest primarily for its bearing on the question whether the different patterns of naming defect should be considered to result from damage to distinct physiological systems. For this limited purpose, as contrasted with attempts to construct a model of language function on anatomical considerations, it is not essential that the data be of high precision.

To simplify the subject I ignore here the complicated issues that arise from occasional cases of aphasia from right-hemisphere lesions. These constitute less than 5% of cases of aphasia and therefore do not affect the overall picture.

The localization of Broca's aphasia has probably been the subject of more argument than that of any other aphasic syndrome. At least in part this is accounted for by the legacy of Broca himself in fixing upon the posterior part of the third frontal convolution (Broca's area) as the seat of articulate speech. From the time of Pierre Marie's famous attack on this assumption (Marie, 1906), carefully documented by Moutier (1908), it has been abundantly clear that this restricted area is not involved in all cases of Broca'a aphasia, perhaps not even in a majority of them (cf. Mohr, Pessin, Finkelstein, Funkenstein, Duncan, & Davis, 1978). If the limits of Broca's area are extended to include the adjoining frontal operculum and anterior portion of the insula, however, this enlarged zone is affected in practically all cases corresponding to the prototype of Broca's aphasia as described above.

The zone to which Wernicke originally assigned the type of aphasia that bears his name (the posterior third of the first temporal convolution) has fared somewhat better. But again one must be wary of attempting to define this zone too narrowly. The lesions that have been reported in most of the cases fully corresponding to the prototype are quite large and extend well beyond the first temporal convolution.

There is general agreement that the classical pattern of conduction or central aphasia is associated with lesions in the vicinity of the tip of the Sylvian fissure (supramarginal convolution). In a recent survey of the literature on this subject, Green and Howes (1977) found 25 cases with autopsy, in all of which the damage extended within a centimeter or two of the parieto-temporal junction. The principal question at issue concerning the pathology in these cases is not the site of the damage, but whether the symptoms result from destruction of cortical tissue, as Goldstein (1912) contended, or from a functional disconnection of Wernicke's from Broca's area caused by the interruption of long fiber pathways, as originally conceived by Wernicke and supported in recent years by Geschwind (1965). This question cannot be resolved on pathological evidence, because in the cases that have come to autopsy both cortex and white matter have been affected. In any case, those who hold to the disconnection view are not in serious disagreement about the characteristic site of the lesions in these cases (e.g., Benson et al., 1973). It is perhaps significant that no cases of this syndrome have yet been reported with lesions limited to the anterior portion of the superior longitudinal (arcuate) fasciculus connecting Wernicke's area with the Broca zone.

Nominal aphasia is characteristically associated with lesions of the angular gyrus or posterior-inferior temporal lobe (second and third temporal convolutions). Perhaps because of the wide extent of this region (only part of which is usually affected in any given case), it is commonly held that this pattern of aphasia has less localizing value than other classical types (cf. Geschwind, 1967). However, in a review of over 180 case reports of this form of aphasia published in the journal literature I have found that all but 5 of the 44 cases with autopsy are associated with lesions in the region described.

These clinico-pathological relationships are indicated on the lateral projection of the left hemisphere in Fig. 14.1. Such a two-dimensional projection of course cannot adequately represent cortical regions below the external surface of the hemisphere that are associated with aphasia, such as the anterior portion of the insula. The shaded areas, moreover, are intended to indicate the zones only for cases corresponding closely to the four major prototypes that have been described. These comprise only a small proportion of the aphasias that occur. Given this restriction, it is a fair estimate that in at least 80%, perhaps in 90%, of cases corresponding to each prototype, the lesions affect the appropriate zone. This accuracy, although too crude perhaps to support a theoretical structure, is more than sufficient to establish the weaker point that the naming deficits associated with each prototype represent the malfunction of separate neural structures.

The geometrical distribution of the zones indicated in Fig. 14.1 suggest some functional relationships. It is easy to see that the four zones divide naturally into two groups along the anterior/posterior dimension, with Broca's aphasia associated with the anterior zone and the other three prototypes associated with the posterior region. Because the output of patients with Broca's aphasia is characteristically slow, effortful, and dysarthric, whereas the output in each of the other prototypes is characteristically copious and effortless, the latter are frequently called *fluent* and the former *nonfluent* aphasias. This distinction is quite satisfactory when one limits consideration to the major prototypes considered here. But the rule does not hold generally; many cases in which output is limited to simple stereotyped utterances have lesions limited to the posterior zones, and it is not uncommon for patients with anterior lesions to exhibit little dysarthria. The most general rules are of exclusion: if the patient's output is copious and effortless, the anterior zone is rarely implicated; if his output is markedly dysarthric and effortful, the lesion is rarely confined to the posterior region.

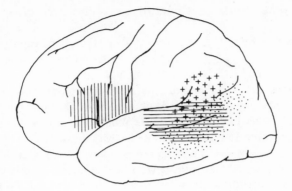

FIG. 14.1. Lateral aspect of the left hemisphere showing the regions generally affected in four aphasic syndromes: Broca's aphasia (vertical stripes), Wernicke's aphasia (horizontal stripes), conduction aphasia (crosses), and nominal aphasia (stipling).

Because the middle cerebral artery serves both the anterior and posterior regions, however, both the anterior and posterior regions are affected in a large proportion of cases.

It is surprising to find that the two aphasic prototypes that mainly affect the production of speech, Broca's and conduction aphasia, are associated with opposite poles of the total speech territory. Failure to distinguish these two clinical types obviously hinders any attempt to localize aphasias. For this reason, the classification of aphasias into "predominantly expressive" and "predominantly receptive" types, introduced by the influential work of Weisenburg and McBride (1935), inevitably leads to an underestimation of the evidence for localization. The fact that Broca's aphasia and conduction aphasia, seemingly so closely related in function, should be associated with lesions at opposite ends of the speech territory is of considerable theoretical interest. It suggests a sharp functional distinction between articulatory control and processing at the phonemic level. Further, the close proximity of the zone for conduction aphasia to those for Wernicke's and nominal aphasia, where speech production is not affected, suggests that there may be a functional requirement that the structures concerned with the phonemic representation of a word be in intimate contact with those involved in the selection process.

III. CONCLUDING REMARKS

In this survey we have focused on the simplest of naming acts: speaking the name of a familiar object presented alone and in plain view. It is so primitive an act that Wittgenstein does not even consider it among his word games, and the patient without aphasia is puzzled, sometimes even indignant, if he is examined for it.

Yet even with a highly educated normal speaker, confrontation naming is not the automatic symbolic process it is taken to be. The expressions "thingumabob" and "whachamacallit" would not exist otherwise. Oldfield's smooth average curves showing the speed of naming objects in relation to the frequency of their names mask a basic variability that is easily overlooked, but which all of us have experienced. What goes on in those occasional failures of confrontation naming in the healthy individual? That they occur more often for rare names than for common ones is true. But this evades the basic issue: Why should an object we have named promptly and without effort hundreds or thousands of times suddenly fail to call up its name for seconds or minutes? The workings of this process are tightly closed off from conscious view. When it fails, we can only sit helplessly and hope for lightning to strike.

The disintegration of confrontation naming in aphasia reveals at least some of the complexity of this process. In my preliminary remarks I pointed out that elementary informational considerations require that two phases of the naming act be distinguished—a selection process and a production process. The disorders of confrontation naming we have reviewed clearly respect this division, with the Broca's and conduction cases on the production side and the Wernicke's and nominal cases on the selection side. But the patterns of naming error in these cases suggest that each of these two phases is of considerably greater complexity than we might have anticipated from observation of normal speech.

A. The Production Phase

Let us consider the production phase first. That the production aspect of naming should be affected by lesions in two separate regions, situated at opposite poles of the speech territory, could hardly be predicted from a consideration of normal naming as an informational process. Yet this finding is perhaps best understood in that light. Let us assume that the systems damaged in conduction aphasia are primarily involved in the coding (and/or transmission) of the phonemic representation of a name after its selection has been accomplished, and that the systems impaired in Broca's aphasia are primarily concerned with the control and execution of commands to the many neuromuscular elements involved in the actual production of the name. Because neither is directly concerned with the selection phase, damage to them should not affect inverse naming (which utilizes different input-output systems) but should of course extend to the production of words in other single-word tasks like repetition, reading aloud, and association. These are indeed salient findings in the two syndromes.

The large distance separating the regions affected in the two production types of aphasia is puzzling at first. But if we accept the need for two separate systems, one for phonemic coding and one for control and execution of the muscular act of speech, these peculiar spatial arrangements can be understood in relation to informational requirements. The control/execution system must have direct access to many pathways in the motor tracts descending from the cortical motor centers of the ascending frontal convolution. At the other end, the process of determining the phonemic code of a name from a purely cognitive input imposes an enormous informational load. By comparison, transmission of the phonemically coded representation of a name (with only 40 or so alternatives to be considered at a time) requires little channel capacity. Consequently, if it is impossible for the systems engaged in all three of these informational transitions to be contiguous, it is most advantageous to introduce a physical separation between the systems performing phonemic coding and motor control.

Some model of this general type seems justified by the facts. But the complexity of the observations summarized in Table 14.1 must not be forgotten. The occurrence of some phonemic naming errors in Wernicke's and nominal aphasia presents no theoretical problem, but what of the phonemic errors in Broca's aphasia? Can they be dismissed as merely extreme articulatory variations that pass beyond phoneme boundaries? And what of the numerous naming failures of the "no response" type both in Broca's and (to a lesser extent) in conduction aphasia? Do these simply represent total failure of the production systems, or could they be failures of the selection process? These questions can be answered clearly only with the aid of more powerful methods of measurement than those that have been customary in this area, such as the method for analyzing phonemic errors developed by Lecours and Lhermitte (1969). Improved measurements, however, will be of little use unless they are addressed to explicit theoretical conceptions.

B. The Selection Phase

The selection phase of the naming process is affected in the other two of our four prototypes, Wernicke's aphasia and nominal aphasia. This interpretation is evident in the case of nominal aphasia, for the word-substitution type of error is pathognomonic of a selection disorder, and the preservation of both repetition and inverse naming in these patients establishes that neither the production nor reception of speech is impaired. With Wernicke's aphasia it is equally evident that the production phase of processing is not disturbed, but the disorder is obviously much more complex, with both repetition and inverse naming severely impaired. Wernicke (1874) supposed that the failure to comprehend spoken language in these patients resulted from disordered "word images," presumably implying that the patient cannot recover the correct sequence of phonemes from the acoustic input in which the word is embedded. Luria (1947/1970) and Luria and Hutton (1977) continue to maintain this position. The evidence is now overwhelming, however, that Wernicke's aphasia represents a true central-processing disorder with little or no significant impairment of phonemic processing. This has long been recognized by many astute observers (cf. Brain's, 1961, choice of the term "central aphasia" for this syndrome), because practically all of these patients respond reliably to a few simple commands (e.g., "stand up" or "close your eyes"). It is hard to see how a defective "auditory analyzer" could pass these particular phoneme sequences and reject others. Recently more systematic studies have established that even when these patients cannot answer a question, they reliably discriminate between real questions and similar nonsense utterances or the same questions asked in foreign languages (Boller & Green, 1972). Further, they can discriminate pairs of phonemes that are either the same or different (Blumstein, Baker, & Goodglass, 1977; Naeser, 1974). The disorder of comprehension thus appears to arise from a more central phase of the process.

Wernicke's aphasia, though the most fascinating of all aphasic syndromes, is nevertheless so severe that it gives us little information about the selection phase of the naming process. For this purpose the cases of nominal aphasia are of greatest interest. We have noted the occurrence of particularly severe naming problems for body parts and colors in these patients. Aside from these special classes of words, the striking feature of their naming disorder is the apparent randomness of their failures and successes. A patient who one day fails to name an *ashtray* saying YOU PUT YOUR CIGARETTE OUT IN IT, may on a later test name the same *ashtray* promptly but fail on a *cigarette,* and then call the examiner's attention to the fact that the last time he had done the reverse. This variability suggests that the disorder does not affect the patient's vocabulary, in the sense of the permanent store of information used in the selection process, but represents a lowered efficiency of the systems by which that store is searched ("retrieval"), an interpretation also suggested by analysis of the vocabulary in samples of continuous discourse (Howes, 1964).

The word-substitution errors given by these patients are intriguing. They almost always bear a semantic relationship to the target word, but they are not easy to categorize for statistical purposes. The word associations of normal subjects, for example, are far more coherent. It is tempting to think of these substitutions as representing "semantic fields" that offer a clue to the semantic structure of the vocabulary. If so, the structure must be much more diffuse and idiosyncratic than has been assumed.

On one point of theoretical interest the evidence from nominal aphasia is definite. This is the asymmetry of the deficits in naming and inverse naming. The significance of this fact seems to have escaped attention, perhaps because the observation itself is so ordinary in clinical experience. One of the most ubiquitous assumptions in the literature on language and semantics is that naming and inverse naming are equivalent processes executed in reverse directions, as I noted in my preliminary remarks on naming. Closely related is the hypothesis, frequently evoked in the psychological literature, that a specific stimulus elicits its name by first arousing a generic "meaning" or "concept" appropriate to that name. If words and their corresponding concepts are so closely bound, it is difficult to understand why the direct passage from cognition to word should be so much more difficult than the reverse passage from word to cognition. The conception of naming as a convergent process, with many different cognitions independently capable of arousing the same name, offers a simple explanation of the asymmetry. Finding the name for a stimulus, then, depends on the probability that the retrieval system can succeed for the specific cognition presented to the patient. Inverse naming, on the other hand, requires only that the retrieval system succeed for *any one* of the cognitions associated with the word. If many cognitions are associated with the same word, and they are not equally available at any given time, inverse naming will have a much greater probability of success than direct naming.

In this chapter I have limited the subject of naming in aphasia to confrontation naming and to four specific aphasic syndromes. Each of these restrictions carries with it a loss of generality. But narrowing down the topic has compensating advantages. Within such a limited focus it is possible to formulate propositions that in principle can be tested directly and quantitatively on individual patients. Admittedly, the data now available do not permit a rigorous analysis; the treatment of the subject here is necessarily based on clinical impression aided by scattered protocols and research findings for groups of patients. Yet these observations at least hold out the promise that a fairly rigorous theoretical treatment of confrontation naming in specific aphasic syndromes is possible. In the long run, such a theory, though limited to a narrow domain, is perhaps more likely to give us a better understanding of so complex a process as human naming than are more speculative theories addressed to a broad domain.

REFERENCES

Benson, D. F., & Geschwind, N. The alexias. In P. J. Vinken & G. W. Bruyn, *Handbook of clinical neurology* (Vol. 4). Amsterdam: North Holland, 1969.

Benson, D. F., Sheremata, W. A., Bouchard, P., Segarra, J. M., Price, D., & Geschwind, N. Conduction aphasia. *Arch. Neurol.*, 1973, *28*, 339–346.

Blumstein, S., Baker, E., & Goodglass, H. Phonological factors in auditory comprehension in aphasia. *Neuropsychologia*, 1977, *15*, 19–30.

Boller, F., & Green, E. Comprehension in severe aphasics. *Cortex*, 1972, *8*, 382–394.

Bousfield, W. A., & Sedgewick, C. H. W. An analysis of sequences of restricted associative responses. *J. Gen. Psychol.,* 1944, *30,* 149–165.

Brain, W. R. *Speech disorders.* London: Butterworths, 1961.

Brown, J. W. *Aphasia, apraxia, and agnosia.* Springfield, Ill.: C. C. Thomas, 1972.

Cramer, P. *Word association.* New York: Academic Press, 1968.

Freund, C. S. Ueber optische Aphasie und Seelenblindheit. *Arch. Psychiat. Nervenkr.,* 1889, *20,* 276–297; 371–416.

Fromkin, V. (Ed.), *Speech errors as linguistic evidence.* Netherlands: Janus Lingarum, 1973.

Geschwind, N. Disconnexion syndromes in animal and man. *Brain,* 1965, *88,* 237–294; 585–644.

Geschwind, N. The varieties of naming errors. *Cortex,* 1967, *3,* 97–112.

Goldstein, K. Die zentrale aphasie. *Neurol. Zentralbl.,* 1912, *12,* 739–751.

Goodglass, H., Kaplan, E., Weintraub, S., & Ackerman, N. The "tip-of-the-tongue" phenomenon in aphasia. *Cortex,* 1976, *12,* 145–153.

Green, E., & Howes, D. H. The nature of conduction aphasia: A study of anatomic and clinical features and of underlying mechanisms. In H. Whitaker & H. Whitaker (Eds.), *Studies in neurolinguistics* (Vol. 3). New York: Academic Press, 1977.

Howes, D. H. On the interpretation of word frequency as a variable affecting speed of recognition. *J. Exp. Psychol.* 1954, *48,* 106–112.

Howes, D. Application of the word-frequency concept to aphasia. In A. V. S. de Reuck & M. O'Connor (Eds.), *Disorders of language* (Ciba Foundation Symposium). London: Churchill, 1964.

Indow, T., & Togano, K. On retrieving sequence from long-term memory. *Psychol. Rev.,* 1970, *77,* 317–331.

Kent, G. H., & Rosanoff, A. J. A study of association in insanity. *Amer. J. Insanity,* 1910, *67,* 37–96.

Kleist, K. *Sensory aphasia and amusia.* Oxford: Pergamon Press, 1962.

Lecours, A. R., & Lhermitte, F. Phonemic paraphasias: Linguistic structures and tentative hypotheses. *Cortex,* 1969, *5,* 193–228.

Luria, A. R. *Traumatic aphasia: Its syndromes, psychology and treatment* (rev. and transl.). The Hague: Mouton, 1970. (Originally published, 1947.)

Luria, A. R., & Hutton, J. T. A modern assessment of the basic forms of aphasia. *Brain and Language,* 1977, *4,* 129–151.

Marie, P. Revision de la question de l'aphasie. La 3ᵉ circonvolution frontale gauche ne joue aucun role special dans la fonction du langage. *Sem. Med.,* 1906, *21,* 241–247.

Mohr, J., Pessin, M. S., Finkelstein, S., Funkenstein, H. H., Duncan, G. W., & Davis, K. R. Broca aphasia: Pathologic and clinical aspects. *Neurology,* (Minneap.), 1978, *28,* 311–324.

Moutier, F. *L'aphasie de Broca.* Paris: Steinheil, 1908.

Naeser, M. A. *The relationship between phoneme discrimination, picture-perception and language comprehension in aphasia.* Paper presented at the meeting of the Academy of Aphasia, Warrenton, Va., October 1974.

Newcombe, F., Oldfield, R. C., & Wingfield, A. Object-naming by dysphasic patients. *Nature* (*Lond.*), 1965, *207,* 1217–1218.

Newcombe, F., Oldfield, R. C., Ratcliff, G. G., & Wingfield, A. Recognition and naming of object drawings by men with focal brain wounds. *J. Neurol. Neurosurg. Psychiat.,* 1971, *34,* 329–340.

Oldfield, R. C. Things, words and the brain. *Quart. J. Exp. Psychol.,* 1966, *18,* 340–353.

Oldfield, R. C., & Wingfield, A. Response latencies in naming objects. *Quart. J. Exp. Psychol.,* 1965, *17,* 273–281.

Postman, L., & Keppel, G. *Norms of word association.* New York: Academic Press, 1970.

Rochford, G., & Williams, M. Studies in the development and breakdown of the use of names. *J. Neurol. Neurosurg. Psychiat.* 1962, *25*, 222-227; 228-233. 1963, *26*, 377-381. 1965, *28*, 407-413.

Sperry, R. W., Gazzaniga, M. S., & Bogen, J. E. Interhemispheric relationships: The neocortical commissures; syndromes of hemisphere disconnection. In P. J. Vinken & G. W. Bruyn (Eds.), *Handbook of clinical neurology* (Vol. 4). Amsterdam: North-Holland, 1969.

Spreen, O., Benton, A. L., & Van Allen, M. W. Dissociation of visual and tactile naming in amnesic aphasia. *Neurology* (Minneap.), 1966, *16*, 807-814.

Thomas, A., & Roux, J. C. Du defaut d'evocation spontanee des images auditive verbales chez les aphasiques moteurs. *Soc. Biol.*, 1895, *2*, 733-735.

Weigl, E. The phenomenon of temporary deblocking in aphasia. *Z. f. phon. Spr. u. Komm.* 1961, *14*, 337-364.

Weigl, E., & Bierwisch, M. Neuropsychology and linguistics: Topics of common research. In H. Goodglass & S. Blumstein (Eds.), *Psycholinguistics and aphasia*. Baltimore: Johns Hopkins Press, 1973.

Weisenburg, T., & McBride, K. E. *Aphasia: A clinical and psychological study.* New York: The Commonwealth Fund, 1935.

Wernicke, C. *Der aphasische Symptomenkomplex.* Breslau: Cohn & Weigart, 1874.

Wingfield, A. *The identification and naming of objects.* Unpublished doctoral dissertation, Oxford University.

Wittgenstein, L. [*Philosophical investigations*] (G. E. M. Anscombe, trans.) New York: Macmillan, 1953.

15 Language in Psychotherapy

Donald P. Spence
Rutgers Medical School—CMDNJ

Where traditional linguistics concerned itself with the study of *la langue* and its underlying principles, the new schools of psycholinguistics are moving gradually toward the study of *la parole* and a focus on natural language. Continuously engaged in one form of natural language study is the psychotherapist. Decoding, parsing and otherwise responding to spontaneous utterances is his stock in trade, and in the service of understanding everything possible about the patient, the therapist becomes an expert on one person's language — his patient's. Some of the forms of this language are not intelligible; others convey several sets of meanings; and yet others are more implicit than explicit. The therapist, in order to capture all possible meanings, learns to listen on different levels and develops an almost poetic sensitivity to form and content, to metaphor and simile. This sensitivity can be carefully taught (see Sharpe, 1950, for some good examples; Sharpe was formerly a student of literature); more often, it is learned in passing, as an outgrowth of the therapist's experience.

Guiding his approach to language is the principle of multiple function, one of the key assumptions of dynamic psychotherapy (Waelder, 1936). This principle states that any piece of behavior fills many roles simultaneously; indeed, it cannot emerge as behavior, goes the theory, unless it serves both conscious and unconscious needs. This principle alerts the therapist to the unconscious meaning in an apparently innocent remark and sensitizes him to the importance of ambiguity and double meaning in everyday speech. It trains him to ask himself, at frequent intervals, questions such as the following: Why is the patient using that word? Why is he omitting that detail? Why is he phrasing it that way? Not only is he sensitized to obvious language mistakes, such as slips of the tongue; he is also quick to notice peculiar choice of word, unnecessary repetition, and other detailed aspects of the patient's speech. In the sections to follow, I shall discuss some of the more common ways in which clinical listening makes use of well-known linguistic phenomena.

I. SURFACE STRUCTURE AND DEEP STRUCTURE IN CLINICAL LISTENING

Evidence has been accumulating for some time (see Bransford & Franks, 1971, and a recent review by Jenkins, 1974) that suggests that we tend to focus on the meaning, or deep structure, of an utterance and ignore, or pay only casual attention to, its surface structure.

Item. Bransford and Franks (1971) gave subjects a list of complex sentences to learn of form (1):

(1) The old car pulled the trailer up the hill

They were next given a second set of simpler forms (e.g., 2):

(2) The car climbed the hill

The second set had different surface structure but partially overlapping deep structure. Subjects were asked whether each form of the second set was either new — had never been seen before — or old. In fact, none of the second set had previously been presented, yet certainty was uniformly high that they had been presented before. Subjects were apparently attending to the deep structure and ignoring small differences in surface structure.

Item. If I make the statement:

(3) Are you wearing your watch?

and you respond

(4) Yes, it's about 3:15

I consider the dialogue to be unexceptional and essentially complete, despite the fact that you ignored my literal question; i.e., you disregarded the surface structure of (3). But if you had focused on the surface structure and replied:

(5) No

I would have felt misunderstood, frustrated or both. We are sensitized to listen to the deep structure components of an utterance and ignore everything else — within limits. The limits, however, raise some interesting questions.

Studies by Sachs (1967) on memory for form and content make a similar point. Subjects were asked about the form (surface structure) and meaning (deep structure) of a target sentence embedded in a larger paragraph. After a very short delay (80 to 160 syllables of interpolated material), recognition of surface structure dropped significantly whereas recognition of deep structure persisted. For example, if the original target sentence was:

(6) There he met an archeologist, Howard Carter, who urged him to join in the search for the tomb of King Tut

and the matching sentence, for testing recognition, was:

(7) There he met an archeologist, Howard Carter, and urged him to join in the search for the tomb of King Tut

a high proportion of the subjecs recognized the change in meaning even though it was carried by the single word "and" in place of "who." On the other hand, if the matching sentence was:

(8) There he met an archeologist, Howard Carter, who urged that he join in the search for the tomb of King Tut

only one subject out of eight recognized the difference between (8) and (6). The remaining subjects called (8) the same as (6), even though they had been instructed to respond to *any* change whatsoever. These findings make it clear, once again, that people are sensitized to the underlying meaning and disregard changes in form when the meaning remains invariant.

Lakoff (1972) has documented how the surface structure can vary to express certain social norms, as in the difference between:

(9) You may have some cake

and

(10) You must have some cake

But whether we choose to attend to these distinctions is a matter of social context and situational demand, and in many settings, these and other differences are simply ignored.

The opposite situation seems to be the case in psychotherapy — particularly in analytically based therapies. If the patient made the following statement:

(11) I can't stomach any more fights with my boss

we would listen on two levels. On the one hand, we would hear the core proposition:

(12) I am tired of fighting

but, in addition, we would notice the use of the word "stomach" and form the tentative hypothesis that arguments make his stomach hurt. In this instance, we have cancelled the usual rule and switched our attention from deep structure to surface structure.

Listening to both kinds of structure is one aspect of what Freud has called listening between the lines, or listening with evenly hovering attention. The well-known slip of the tongue is the most familiar example. If the patient makes the following statement:

(13) When I went to the doctor last week he (sic) felt feverish

we would switch our attention from listening to his intended meaning to the substitution of the word "he" for "I," and suspect that the patient was denying certain feelings about himself and attributing them to the doctor. Slips of this kind are obvious perturbations of the surface structure and produce, in almost all listeners, an immediate shift in attention. But slips are only the most obvious example. Wherever possible, the therapist trains himself constantly to focus on surface structure and ask such questions as "Why is he using this word?" "Where have I heard that word before?" and the like. Consider the following example:

(14) I'm scared to death of needles

Most people, if asked to summarize this sentence, would say something about the person being afraid of needles (presumably injections) and would consider (15) a reasonable translation:

(15) I have an extreme dislike of injections

But the therapist listening to (14) might pay particular attention to the word "death" and assume that it had a significance above and beyond what was required by the familiar expression "scared to death." This assumption stems directly from the psychoanalytic concept of multiple function, described above, which states, in effect, that a given piece of behavior can have many causes and can fill many roles.

Some supporting evidence for the proposition that the word "death" may, in fact, be quite significant, comes from a recent study of women at risk for cervical cancer (Spence, 1977). Patients were interviewed just after a cone biopsy was taken but before the results of the biopsy became known; thus, neither the patient nor the interviewing physician were aware of the actual diagnosis. Nevertheless, the word "death" appeared significantly more often ($p < .01$) in the sample of women who were later diagnosed positive. Of particular linguistic interest is the fact that a high proportion of usages are metaphoric (e.g., "froze to death," "scared to death," "tickled to death," etc.); moreover, when only the metaphors are considered, the cancer patients still use the word at a significantly higher rate than the controls.

Suppose we focus on one such sentence, uttered by one of the cancer patients:

(16) The first year we were married we almost froze to death

Regarded as a speech act, it has the clear intention of conveying to the interviewer a sense of extreme discomfort, and we might interpret the phrase "froze to death" as an attempt to be humorous, to elicit his sympathy, or as the literal truth. In context, the last seems unlikely; people do not freeze to death any more unless they are explorers, sailors, or otherwise exposed to extreme conditions, and this was not the case with the patient in question. But we have reason to think that the marker word "death" is not entirely accidental, because of the fact that it occurs significantly more often among our cancer patients, and for two additional reasons. From an exploratory pool of 181 words, "death" is the only one that discriminates between cancer patients and controls with a level of significance greater than 1 in 100; and when an independent sample of judges was asked to give word associations to the stimulus word "cancer," the response "death" was by far the most popular response.

One way to approach the problem of surface vs. deep structure is to look at the phenomenon of language transparency. Polanyi (1958) captures it nicely in the following anecdote:

My correspondence arrives at my breakfast table in various languages, but my son understands only English. Having just finished reading a letter I may wish to pass it on to him, but must check myself and look again to see in what language it was written. I am vividly aware of the meaning conveyed by the letter, yet know nothing whatever of its words. I have attended to them closely but only for what they mean and not for what they are as objects. If my understanding of the text were halting, or its expressions or its spelling were faulty, its words would arrest my attention. They would become slightly opaque and prevent my thought from passing through them unhindered to the things they signify [p. 47].

Under what conditions does transparency disappear? With faulty execution, as Polanyi points out; also with unfamiliarity. The better we know a language, the more transparent it seems; conversely, in learning a new language, we come face to face with its unreasonable opaqueness, we struggle with every word and we are much more conscious of form (word order, verb endings, etc.) than we are of content. Transparency also disappears when meaning is ambiguous. Given the well-known ambiguous sentence:

(17) The shooting of the hunters is terrible

with no context to guide us, we have no choice but to come back to the individual words and perhaps to the paralinguistic cues attached to them in an effort to decode the meaning. And finally, transparency disappears when we hear an unusual word; in a sentence like:

(18) He gave a rather *recondite* impression

our reading of the speaker's meaning is incomplete and we are suddenly confronted with the surface structure of the sentence and with the word "recondite" in particular; once we ask him to explain, the language becomes transparent again and we resume listening to meaning (deep structure).

These examples make it clear that transparency is easily clouded — but they tend to be the exceptions. Because we are overtrained to listen for meaning, we tend to ignore minor changes in the surface structure that might — if we were listening closely — make the transparency disappear. Usually, however, the transparency remains unblemished, and we continue to focus on meaning. As a result, the surface structure becomes a perfect vehicle for carrying ancillary meanings, a kind of sideband that is loosely coupled to the deep structure of the sentence but that rarely comes into focal awareness. There is a large middle ground where transparency is momentarily clouded, but so briefly that the interruption never comes to our attention. Slips of the tongue provide a good example; sometimes they are noted, but only for an instant; more often they are ignored, sensed as a momentary interference in the speech process (similar to a cough or sneeze). Slightly deviant verbalizations — less extreme than (18) above — are another example of this middle ground; they may briefly force us to switch attention to the surface structure, but frequently they go unnoticed.

Now we are in a position to return to:

(16) The first year we were married we almost froze to death

This sentence is a good example of those cases that contain additional information in the surface structure but that are not sufficiently deviant to attract attention. Additional training is needed (and may be explicitly provided to hopeful psychotherapists) that can sensitize the listener to variations in the surface structure and give him the option of moving back and forth from surface to depth.

To what extent does the listener register surface information when he is not aware of surface structure changes? This is one of the key problems for future research. If we assume a symmetry between language production and language comprehension, we could argue that the same structures that code additional meanings into the surface structure of a phrase could also decode these meanings at the other end. One set of structures (called conversational implicatures) is described in Section III of this chapter; they deal primarily with continuity and discontinuity of the deep structures of a conversation and the extent to which the meaning of one speaker is continued by the second. A second set of structures may operate on the surface structure, enabling the speaker to disguise certain information in metaphor or other figure of speech, and/or enable him to deploy telltale marker words (such as "death") that escape notice when randomly sprinkled through a conversation; a similar structure may be available (spontaneously or through training) for accumulating these marker words, amplifying their significance, and returning this new meaning to the center of awareness. The study of natural language should help us to isolate spontaneous examples of such coding and decoding operations, enabling us to understand the nature of the underlying structures.

A. Form Is More Revealing Than Content

Generally speaking, this rule suggests that the therapist can understand more by paying particular attention to the *way* in which things are said and listening to the specific words used in an utterance, than by listening to *what* is being intended. In practice, the rule implies that the therapist must continually try to resist the transparency of each utterance. For example, he might note the continuous use of the passive voice (see Schafer, 1968) and use this formal property of the patient's language as a key to his defensive style. As such a patient begins to improve, one might expect that changes in his language would begin to reflect this improvement and that his constructions would actually become more active.

I have noted the overuse of certain words as markers of underlying pathology; when the marker occurs as a metaphor, we have a clear instance of where form is clinically more important than content. In the sentence "I was tickled to death . . . " the intended meaning is clearly at odds with the specific word "death," and unless the clinician is listening very carefully, he will be likely to miss it. We might hypothesize that form is particularly significant when it is clearly at odds with content; this kind of juxtaposition would provide a perfect hiding place, as it were, for all kinds of conflictual meanings because the listener is almost certain to disregard form and choose content instead. When disguise is further increased by the use of metaphor, the chances of evading awareness are significantly increased; and when the frequency of such utterances falls below a certain lower limit, the human listener can no longer detect the marker, and some kind of computer search is necessary. But the computer may be only a temporary tool; once the judge has been sensitized to a certain pattern, he may be able to pick it up on his own. This possibility has clear implications for the use of computer analysis in the training of clinicians, for once we isolate certain principles, we can sensitize the clinician in very specific ways and probably increase his general effectiveness.

B. Position Is More Important Than Content

This rule can best be illustrated by the following detail from a psychoanalysis (Gray, 1973):

> A young woman given occasionally to impulsive decisions or arrangements, after about six months of analysis achieved a deepening degree of involvement in the analytic process. Part way through an hour, she began to speak of her success in overcoming shyness at work. She said this was allowing her, during the past several days, to persuade her boss that the company could in fact pay her way to a neighboring state for a week during the coming month for research purposes which would be valuable for the company. She remarked upon the pleasure the experience and the travel would provide for her.
>
> I silently observed, among other things, that within the ideas she had just expressed was the thought of her being at some distance from the analytic setting and from the analyst. It can be surmised from the material that the patient was also referring to memories of currently contemplated behavior — to an impulse which, if it persisted, might in fact carry the patient briefly away from the analysis in the near future [p. 479].

The patient refers to an event that occurred outside the analytic hour — her attempt to persuade her boss to let her take a trip. The significance lies in its relation to other events within the hour. As it happened, the key remark followed closely on an expression of disappointment over the location of the analyst's office — the patient was implying that it was hard to reach. The analyst concluded that the allusion to the chance to travel could be seen as a disguised expression of disappointment; crudely translated, the sequence might read: Because it is is so hard to come to the office, and, in particular, so hard to express my feelings, I would rather take a trip.

This conclusion could not have been reached had the analyst listened only to the content of the patient's remarks; that is, to the reference to an outside event. Its significance lies in its position in the stream of speech. Once we look at position, and such related issues as continuity, contrast, closeness, distance, etc., we start to focus on the utterance as a speech act, in a specific context.

Another example of this principle comes from some further data on the patients at risk for cervical cancer (Spence, 1977). We know from clinical experience that one way to avoid awareness of a certain theme is to break it into two parts and separate the parts in time. This defense — a particular form of the mechanism of isolation — could be studied in our corpus of cancer interviews by looking at the relation between the position of the marker word "death" and its presumed referent — the word "cancer." Denial through isolation might take the form of separating these two words over the course of the interview. We measured the *minimal* distance separating the two words (to get around the fact that each word is frequently used more than once during the hour). These patients had also been rated for concern over the possibility of cancer by two judges who looked through the interviews and assigned a rating from 1 (unconcerned) to 7 (highly anxious). When we looked at the minimum distance between "death" and "cancer," we found that it was significantly longer for the patients who were unconcerned about the possibility of cancer. Once again, position of an utterance is clinically significant. Unconcerned patients who were at pains to deny the risk of cancer "allowed" more time to elapse between the use of the word "death" and the word "cancer." How the spacing is accomplished is still to be discovered, but the data underline the importance of position and support the clinical rule of thumb to the effect that the position of an utterance in the hour is just as important as its content.

The rule on position and the rule on form are obviously interrelated. Position cannot be studied unless an utterance is isolated as a speech act — as a specific piece of behavior — and this kind of isolation can occur only when we shift focus from the thing being said to the way in which it is expressed. The striking part of the data on the word "death" is the fact that its appearance is doubly concealed — first, by being placed in a metaphor, and second, by being separated in time from the word "cancer." Occurrence of specific words is not only nonrandom within a sentence, but it seems to be nonrandom between sentences. Which rule takes precedence? Is it more important to allocate markers over time (i.e., between sentences) and then let them emerge as necessary, or does the speaker exert some control over the position within sentences as well?

To say that the positioning of markers is under the speaker's control, however this is defined, is to imply that we may have innate structures for allocating the distribution of significant words over time; more specifically, that we can control frequency and density of significant words. Given these kinds of performance structures, it seems natural to assume that we have the latent capacity to *detect* changes in frequency and density, even at fairly low levels. Given the proper kind of training, it should be possible to make therapists highly sensitive to these parameters, assuming a symmetry between speech production and speech understanding.

II.   EPISODIC AND SEMANTIC MEMORY

The process of dynamic psychotherapy consists in large part in finding past answers to present questions. To the extent that it invokes the past, it calls on memory; and Tulving's recent distinction between episodic and semantic memory (Tulving, 1972) has particular significance for the practice and theory of therapy.

Episodic memory, as defined by Tulving, refers to personal experiences and their temporal relations. The memory of my trip to the state fair last Saturday is a typical example. The events in this memory were experienced in a real time sequence, and this time dimension is used to organize the events in my long-term store, coded along with the content of each event. When an event loses its distinctive time-marking, it is lost from the episode because there is usually no other marker that links it to other events in the episode. Episodic memories tend to be self-contained and not related to other memories; as a result, they are more difficult to access from other locations in long-term store. If someone asks me, for example, what happened *after* we got off the Ferris wheel at the state fair, I must rehearse all events in sequence in order to arrive at a reasonable answer.

Semantic memory, by contrast, is the kind of information tapped by an intelligence test. We know that Madrid is the capital of Spain without ever having been there. Semantic memory is abstractly organized, with many links between items; each item, as a result, is open to access from a number of different locations. Semantic memory tends to be primarily abstract and does not have an experiential component; thus I remember the multiplication table without the memory of when or where I learned it.

Tulving points out that forgetting is more likely to occur in episodic memory because individual items tend to be nested in rather shallow networks and typically are accessed only in connection with that particular event. By contrast, an item in semantic memory is embedded in a tight network of concepts and tends to be multiply marked and multiply accessed. Forgetting of episodic events frequently (says Tulving) comes about as the result of losing the time code; because the time thread is often the only connection that links all the items, its loss is critical.

From one point of view, the problem of therapy can be seen as the problem of how to translate episodic memory, which is highly personal and subject to forgetting, into semantic memory, which is more abstract and permanent. Memories accessed during therapy tend to be primarily episodic, because what is significant to the patient tends to cluster around certain current events. Some of these events are clearly remembered at all times, whereas others are sometimes remembered and sometimes forgotten. And there are various styles of forgetting. The therapist is familiar with many kinds of smaller distortions in episodic memory, produced by a variety of defense mechanisms, all used in the service of minimizing anxiety. The time frame may be preserved, but certain unpleasant elements may be dropped out and the sequence somewhat collapsed. Because the missing items are not linked to other conceptual frameworks, their loss easily goes unnoticed. If the distortion becomes particularly severe, we may see an episodic memory that is completely untrue. This form of memory, called a screen memory (see Freud, 1899), is subjectively impossible to distinguish from a true episodic memory. It includes a dating in the patient's past and may be linked to other real events; however, it has never happened. A typical screen memory may be invented as a substitute for a real, but painful episodic event; when the real memory is restored, the screen drops away.

One of the important aspects of episodic memory is its relation to a particular time frame. Frequently the key event can be recalled *only* under conditions similar to those that existed at the time of storage. This restriction — called the principle of encoding specificity (see Tulving & Thomson, 1970) — is of key importance in psychotherapy and tends to be supported by clinical experience. The analyst encourages the patient to reexperience early life events as vividly as possible *in order to* bring about further recall. Free association is the key to complete access, and the concept has a crucial relation to episodic memory. By encouraging the patient to say what comes to mind, telling everything and withholding nothing, remembering with no attempt to organize or add regularity, the therapist is encouraging him to experience events in an episodic mode. Truly free association permits a certain amount of reliving; as new memories are accessed, they are then seen from a more contemporary point of view, given a new organization, and put into semantic memory. In this way, the patient gains access to parts of his forgotten past.

A. Semantic Resistance

Although psychotherapy can be seen as the translation from episodic to semantic memory, the timing is all-important, and too hasty translation can interfere with the process. Premature interpretation, which often fails, can be interpreted as taking a piece of episodic memory and forcing it into a semantic net. For example, the therapist might listen to an account of the patient's childhood that was heavily preoccupied by eating and label it "oral fixation" without hearing the full range of events that provided the context for this scene. The patient, as a result, may subsequently experience the incident as an example of eating behavior and be even less able to make contact with other events which served other needs. Just because they have no consistent thematic core, episodic events are especially prone to a thematic organization that serves some elements and ignores others. Because bad interpretations often have this effect, Glover (1931), in a well-known paper, pointed to the danger of inexact interpretation and how it may augment the resistance. Episodic memories are particularly vulnerable to retrospective emphasis or falsification, and one of the tasks of therapy is to encourage the patient to suspend judgment and deliberately not search for themes, in order that a more complete (i.e., episodic) recall can take place. Premature interpretation, by establishing a dominant theme, may prematurely transfer the memories from episodic to semantic mode and prevent further exploration.

Something similar seems to happen when a therapy is conducted in the patient's second language (see Greenson, 1950). The terms used to designate early childhood events and situations, if they come from the patient's second language, belong to his semantic store; they were not learned during childhood but much later in life. As a result, they are thematically organized, not linked with early behaviors, and cannot be used to access other memories that are not currently in awareness. The second language tends to emphasize rationality and organization, and the denotative sense of a word tends to be emphasized over its connotative sense. (Translations of poetry are notoriously poor, and a user of a second language has particular difficulty with metaphor.) Semantic nets, in effect, are being used to capture episodic experiences, which may explain why therapy in a second language often takes on a stilted and intellectual flavor — the difference between mediocre autobiography and Proust. Greenson (1950) has described how shifting to the patient's "mother tongue" appeared to facilitate her analysis.

B. Conclusions

What can the lore of psychotherapy contribute to Tulving's rather significant distinction? First, some episodic memories should be regarded with suspicion; they may well be screen memories that have an episodic flavor but no real-time referent. Second, the time code is only one of many organizing principles in episodic memory; an underlying theme may serve as well, and a time sequence is sometimes distorted in order to make room for a thematic organization. For example, a patient may remember events in the wrong time sequence because they are linked by some other attribute; he might collapse the memories of two separate trips to the Swiss Alps into a recollection of one vacation. The time code, as Tulving has noted, is particularly vulnerable to distortion; one reason for this may be that, with one or two exceptions, it does not leave its trace on the events in question. Only occasionally (as in watching sunsets or time-lapse movies) do we have the experience of watching time "pass" as it were; once events are removed from a time frame, it is relatively easy to rearrange their sequence with no one the wiser. The studies by Bartlett on remembering (1932), recently updated by Paul (1960), give many examples of time distortion in recall.

Third, the choice of memory model is partly defensive. By that I mean that a memory is sometimes left in an episodic mode, because to reorganize it and place it in a more semantic (i.e., permanent) context may force the person to draw interpretations he would rather not face. For example, a patient may remember that when he was growing up, his father never went to work before one o'clock in the afternoon and usually returned around three o'clock, 2 hours later. He may also remember, around the same period of his life, seeing NRA (National Recovery Act) signs on a store window when he went to buy groceries when his mother was sick. Integration of these two episodic memories make it clear that the patient is describing a time period during the Depression; therefore his father was probably *looking for work* in the afternoon, not *going to work* for a short time; therefore — to put the events into a semantic frame — the father was unemployed. So long as the two memories remained episodic, they would tend to remain isolated and the concept of unemployed could never be attached to his father, with all of its disturbing implications. Because many of the translations from the episodic to the semantic mode confront the patient with unpleasant discoveries, the work is often halting and encounters continuous resistance. To hold a memory in an episodic mode may serve a strong defensive need.

III.   CONVERSATIONAL IMPLICATURES

The distinction between what is said in a conversation as opposed to what is meant, implied, or suggested has long been observed but never fully formalized. Grice (1967) has developed the concept of conversational *implicature* (or rule), which attempts to formulate the commonly observed gap between the literal meaning of an utterance and its meaning as a speech act, which is embedded in an ongoing conversation. These distinctions overlap in part with the earlier distinctions drawn between deep structure and surface structure but focus in particular on the need for cooperation in the dialogue and on the sharing of goals that makes a conversation possible.

Grice approaches the problem by proposing a cooperative principle, tacitly assumed by both parties, which underlies the goals of a conversation. He then proceeds to show how the intentional violation of the principle makes possible such effects as irony, sarcasm, humor, etc. I will list four main parts of this principle, with examples, to show what happens when they are violated, and then I will give some examples of how Grice's argument can be extended to the peculiar dialogue of psychotherapy.

Grice sets out four categories of the cooperation principle — quantity, quality, relation, and manner — modeled after the four categories of Kant. I will discuss each of these in turn.

1. *Quantity.* Applied to a conversation, this rule stipulates that one's contribution should be as informative as is required for the purposes of the exchange and (a corollary) should not be more informative than is required. The following exchange violates this rule:

A: Do you have your watch on you?
B: Yes.

The quantity of *B*'s response is insufficient and does not meet the level set by *A*. The following exchange is also a violation.

A: Do you remember "Deep Purple"?
B: Oh, very well. I first heard it in the late 1930s when Susie and I. . . .

2. *Quality.* Try to make your contributions true; do not say what you believe to be false; and do not say something for which you lack adequate evidence.

A: What is the date today?
B: February 31.

B's false answer forces a sarcastic interpretation on the exchange.

3. *Relation.* Be relevant.

A: I heard that your partner Horace just sold out without telling you.
B: Horace is a fine friend.

We assume that *B* is being relevant and, therefore, is adding to the information being exchanged — hence, he must be telling us something new — ergo, he is being ironical, or saying the opposite from what appears. This works because we assume Rule 2 — that is, that *B* is telling the truth. But we know that Horace is not a fine friend; therefore the only way B can be sincere is by being ironical.

A: How is Sue?
B: She is the cream in my coffee.

Sue is clearly not cream; *B* is, we presume, being both relevant and saying the truth (Rule 2); therefore we take what is relevant and presume that he is applying the properties of cream (smooth, sweet, etc.) to Sue. The same rule applies to any use of metaphor or simile; note that it takes place automatically except with certain types of very literal-minded patients and fails completely with young children.

A: Mrs. X (who happens to be in the room) is an old bag.
B: It's nice weather we're having.

B is intentionally violating the rule of relevance in order to draw *A*'s attention to his gaffe, force him to change the subject, and protect Mrs. X.

4. *Manner.* Avoid obscurity and ambiguity; be brief and orderly.

In general, Grice sees a conversation as a special case of a cooperative effort in which: (1) the participants have some common immediate aim; (2) each party identifies himself with the transitory conversational interest of the other; and (3) the transaction will continue in appropriate style until both parties agree that it should terminate. Violation of the four principles may take place in the following ways:

1. One party may, without calling attention to the fact, violate a maxim either to expand his range of meaning or to introduce some additional information. These violations can (but need not) lead to misunderstandings.

2. One party may opt out from the cooperative principle (e.g., "Sorry, my lips are sealed").

3. One party may be faced by a clash of rules; for example, he may be unable to fulfill the first maxim of quantity without violating the second maxim of quality. In such cases, the conversation may continue, somewhat impoverished, degenerate into small talk, or stop altogether.

4. One party may blatantly fail to fulfill a maxim; for example, he might simply lie.

Here are some examples in which one or more principles are superficially violated, with the goal of reaching a new level of meaning.

A: How is *C* getting on in his new job at the bank?
B: Oh, quite well — he likes his colleagues and he hasn't been to prison yet.

B seems to be violating the rule of quantity because his answer includes much more information that would seem to be required (a simple "fine" or "badly" might have sufficed). He also seems to be violating Rule 3 — his answer seems irrelevant. Yet if we assume that he is upholding the cooperative principle, then we assume: (1) that the additional information is needed to satisfy our question's minimum requirements; and (2) that his answer is indeed relevant, even though it doesn't seem that way. Therefore, he is telling us something about *C* — namely, that he is potentially dishonest.

A: Smith doesn't seem to have a girlfriend these days.
B: He has been paying a lot of visits to New York lately.[1]

B seems to violate the rule of relevance. Because we assume that *B* is following the cooperative principle, we conclude that going to New York has something to do with the matter of girlfriends — namely, that Smith has a girl in New York. Notice that we cannot draw this conclusion if we assume that *B* is not following the cooperative principle and has not heard our question, is distracted, or perhaps is brain-damaged.

A. Applications to Psychotherapy

Grice is speaking about normal conversational exchanges, and yet much of what he describes can be applied to the therapeutic situation. We depend heavily on the rule of relevance — it forms the basis for our belief in the

---

[1]The bulk of the examples in this section are taken from Grice (1967).

importance of contiguity and our assumption that two ideas closely associated in time are associated in meaning. We apply the rule to slips of the tongue — that is, we assume that an apparently unrelated word is not a mistake but merely continues the thought in another form. And we put our faith in the cooperative principle, as explained later.

In psychotherapy, we always assume the rule of quality — that the patient is telling the truth, either factually, in terms of content, or formally, in the sense that he is telling us *everything* that comes to mind and where possible in the order in which it occurs to him. When we have evidence that either relevance or quality is violated, we usually make some intervention — we might interpret (or comment on) a slip, and we would certainly point up an apparent lie.

The rule of quantity is treated somewhat differently; more exactly, it is *expected* by both, but more often observed by the patient. The patient will frequently ask why a question is not being answered, acting on the belief that in normal conversation, an answer would be expected, and we are clearly violating that rule. On the other hand, we apply it to the patient; that is, his response to an interpretation is treated as if it were maximally informative, and if it is not — if, for example, he falls silent or becomes vague or cryptic — we usually will query him.

The cooperative principle becomes an important part of the therapeutic contract. That is to say, we agree to participate in a conversation in the interests of treatment; given this contract, we feel compelled to honor the related rules of relevance, quality, manner, and (to some degree) quantity.

I referred earlier to an incident described by Paul Gray; let me go back now to that event, consider each of the possible responses discussed by Gray, and analyze them with the help of one or more of Grice's rules. The patient, you recall, was considering the possibility of leaving the analysis for a week on company business, and Gray considers three possible responses:

1. *Point out to the patient that this move would interrupt the analysis.* An answer of this kind can be described as a simple application of the rule of relevance, and *because* of that, a mistake. The patient says she might leave, and the analyst replies in kind. From the standpoint of therapy, this remark can be criticized on the grounds that it attempts to control behavior without getting at the underlying reasons; consequently, similar problems might be expected to emerge in the future, and the patient would be none the wiser. From the standpoint of Grice's cooperative principles, we can add a further dimension. By applying the rule of relevance in so straightforward a manner, the therapist is treating the patient's statement as if it were an ordinary remark; by extension, he runs the danger of turning the therapy into an ordinary conversation. An answer such as this, because

it turns on the rule of relevance, would encourage the patient to use it in turn and to listen to the conversational aspects of what the therapist was saying or of his preceding remarks (e.g., the manifest content) and not to their deeper meanings. More generally, overuse of the rule of relevance would tend to emphasize the rational and everyday aspects of the therapeutic dialogue and would prevent the patient from exploring his less accessible thoughts and feelings.

2. *Suggest that it would be important to analyze such an impulse before carrying it out.* Here the therapist is violating the rule of manner; the patient has voiced a thought, following the rule of free association, and the therapist has responded with what looks like a prohibition. In other words, he seems to be taking a stand on the issue, rather than listening in the traditional, nonjudgmental manner he is supposed to follow. The implied prohibition may have the effect of discouraging further free associations, and the patient may try to slant her remarks in a way that will please the therapist and avoid further prohibitions. To respect the rule of manner, the therapist would either say nothing or make some comment on the underlying dynamic aspects of the patient's thought — which brings us to the final possibility.

3. *The therapist could point to the sequence of events in the hour and show how the thought of being many miles away on a job assignment followed immediately after the patient had voiced her disappointment over the location of the analyst's office, a location that made it difficult to reach.* In this instance, the therapist is drawing attention to the connection within the hour between the statement of disappointment and the thought about the trip. In so doing, he infers a casual link from the contiguous juxtaposition of two seemingly unrelated statements. He is, first, obeying the rule of manner, responding to a set of free associations in a complementary way (i.e., by drawing attention to their underlying theme). Second, he is obeying the rule of relevance, but in modified form — he is responding to one of the latent themes of the material.

Now we are in a position to add two more rules to Grice's basic four, in order to provide for the special features of the therapeutic "conversation." The first rule is what is usually known as the basic rule — free association. At the beginning of therapy (and particularly, psychoanalysis) the patient is instructed to say whatever comes to mind with no attempt to select or eliminate material. To do so is to follow the basic rule. The therapist, in turn, is expected to indicate where the rule is not followed and to point up underlying connections, missing links, and in other ways direct the patient to continuities in the underlying stream of associations. The therapist may also associate to the patient's remarks but does not always verbalize these thoughts. Thus the basic rule is one of the key assumptions underlying the therapeutic dialogue, and failure to follow it is usually interpreted.

The second rule might be called the rule of depth. Where possible — and this becomes an issue of timing and technique—the therapist should respond to the deeper layers of a statement. This rule can be seen as an extension of the rule of relevance, on the grounds that any remark has many meanings, and a reply can be relevant for one meaning but not for another. The rule of depth instructs the therapist to make his reply relevant to the most latent meaning that he feels still lies within the patient's understanding.

For example, suppose the patient reported a dream in which she took an overnight train, got off, and watched the train disappear into the distance. The therapist might make the interpretation, "When do you plan to terminate treatment?" Superficially unrelated, his answer responds to the latent content of the dream because he is interpreting the train trip as a representation of the therapy and getting off as representing termination. He has observed both the rules of depth and relevance.

Consider some further examples (*A* is always the patient):

A: I forgot to come last week.
B: You are more disturbed about the therapy than you realized.

The therapist, following the rule of depth, is responding to one meaning of forgetting — namely, that the patient did not want to come. He seems to be violating the rule of relevance, but only in order to sensitize the patient to one of the latent meanings of forgetting. By violating the rule, he is adding a new dimension to the interchange; he is also following the rule of free association to the extent that the patient's statement triggered an association about not wanting to come, and the therapist proceeded to voice that association.

A: I don't follow what you are saying.
B: You may not want to see the connection between the two points I just raised.

Again, the therapist seems to be violating the rule of relevance; his apparent violation sensitizes the patient to another level of meaning and encourages him to examine the causes of his failure to understand, rather than focus on the simple fact that it happened. Notice that the therapist is also ignoring another implication (i.e., that he should repeat what he just said in simpler language).

Where the earlier examples showed that breaking the relevance rule permitted the expression of irony or sarcasm, the last examples, taken from a therapeutic context, suggest that ignoring relevance frequently lays the ground for an interpretation. The extent to which rules are broken, therefore, can be used as a way of gauging the depth of the therapy; the less often broken, the more the two parties are responding to the manifest content of the material. But there is a danger; violation of relevance, because it sometimes leads to sarcasm or ridicule, can often disrupt the course of therapy. The therapist must be on the lookout for these and other more personal interpretations and must be ready to respond appropriately. As a rough generalization, we might say that the therapist obeys the rule of relevance when he wants to offer support and violates the rule when he wants to extend the patient's awareness and move a bit below the manifest content. In these cases, he will probably obey the rule of depth. Problems of countertransference or just plain bad therapy come about when the therapist ignores both the rules of relevance and depth and obeys the rule of free association — that is, he voices a private thought that has nothing to do, on any level, with the patient's statement. These problems also appear when the therapist violates the rule of quality and says something that is either untrue or misleading.

Because of its special nature, the therapeutic conversation depends much more heavily on the violation of rules than on the observance of rules to convey the special meaning being considered. Each time a rule is broken, the patient (or therapist) is warned that some other meaning, in addition to the conventional deep structure, is being brought into play. The addition may take into account specific aspects of the surface structure, as in our previous example:

A: I can't stomach any more fights with my boss.
B: I wonder if your ulcer is bothering you again.

or it may encourage the patient to consider his language in a new way, as in the following exchange inspired by Schafer (1976):

A: My unconscious made me forget my keys.
B: I'm not sure I would implicate your unconscious; I think you did the forgetting, but for reasons which are not altogether clear.

As a result of these and other interchanges of a similar kind, the patient learns to listen to himself in a new way. He gains a greater awareness of ambiguity and learns, along with the therapist, to switch from deep structure to surface structure when the need emerges [patients in therapy, because of their greater exposure to the details of surface structure, might be able to remember both form and content in Sachs' (1967) procedure].

But there is an even more important conclusion to be drawn. The process of therapy depends partly on the linguistic data — the spoken content — but, in addition, it relies heavily on what is not said — the expectations that are violated when the therapist ignores what is superficially relevant. The trigger for an interpretation, for example, is often what is not said; the cue for a response may lie in the latent content of a remark that has only a sketchy relationship to the words spoken. A therapy protocol, because it so constantly violates the rule of relevance, seems to be a collection of non sequiturs. For this reason, the complete transcription of a therapy hour may be disappointingly sketchy because it does not contain some of the most important data — the unvoiced expectations of the patient and the suppressed associations of the therapist. A complete recording of a case may be less valuable than clinicians had supposed 5 years ago (see Luborsky and Spence, 1971, for arguments in favor of recording that capture the flavor of the period). The next section will take up these issues in more detail.

IV. THE IMPORTANCE OF WHAT IS NOT SAID

In the three earlier sections of this chapter, we discussed the process of therapy from three somewhat overlapping points of view. Each of these has touched on a part of the therapeutic process, and yet a therapist might come away feeling that what concerns him most of the time has not concerned us. It is time to raise the question directly — to what extent can the therapeutic process be captured by language and studied by linguists? To what extent, on the other hand, does the central focus of the hour run through our fingers?

Consider the following exchange:

Patient: It feels cold in here.
Therapist: That's your imagination.
Patient: (Silence)

The effect of the patient's announcement can be only partly inferred from the text. We gather that the room is not cold; we are less clear as to why the therapist was somewhat abrupt (or even scolding); and we are even less clear as to why the patient lapsed into silence, although we might assume (with increasing uncertainty) that he felt rejected. Note that these conjectures constitute the essence of therapy, and yet there is nothing in the transcript that can clearly support such interpretations. We can all agree on what was said, but the impact on the listener is much harder to determine.

We are talking about the consequences of specific speech acts. To put the matter in more formal language, following the innovative work of

Austin (1962), we are concerned with the distinction between the locution-ary act — what was said — and the perlocutionary act — what we bring about by saying something. Words such as persuade, deceive, encourage, irritate, amuse, inspire, embarrass, and bore have a heavy perlocutionary loading, in contrast to a more neutral set such as report, ask, express, thank, and promise. The effect of the statement — its perlocutionary aspect, if you will — may or may not be intentional, depending on the skill of the therapist, his way with words, the predictability of the patient, and a number of other variables. But we would all agree that the therapeutic process is intimately tied to the perlocutionary dimension of what was said because ultimately, the therapist wants to make some impact on the patient.

We now see the beginning of a paradox. The *impact* of the therapist's remarks is frequently unmarked in the transcript. The therapeutic effect of an interpretation, which is a special and carefully planned variation of its perlocutionary dimension, cannot be read from the text, or even from an audiovideo recording of the session. And the paradox is deepened by the fact that the more intense the relationship — the "deeper" the therapy, if you will — the greater the number of perlocutionary acts, the larger their significance, and the less revealing the surface, or locutionary, dimension of the transcription.

At this point, we might consider a section from a therapy hour that, fortunately for the point under discussion, is annotated by the therapist. These annotations (Goldman, 1976, p. 107) capture the impact of the therapist's remarks on the patient as conceived by the therapist — that is, they capture one of the many possible perlocutionary meanings of a statement. They also capture the impact of the patient's remarks upon the therapist, and here the comments are probably much more complete. Here is the excerpt (*C* stands for client; *T* for therapist):

Actual Dialogue	*Translation*
C: You don't happen to have a cup of coffee do you?	(I feel needy. Make me feel better.)
T: I don't . . . umm.	(I can't.)
C: That's all right.	(I'm disappointed but I can accept it.)
T: There's a meeting, an oral going on in that room over there, for a graduate student, or I would be glad to do it . . . or I would be glad to get you some.	(I wish I could make you feel better.)
C: It's not vital to . . . (pause) what a day!	(That scares me. Let's change the subject.)
T: Did you just come up today? (Pt. is from out of town.)	(O.K.)

(continued)

Actual Dialogue	Translation
C: Yeah, I got up and . . . I can't remember this dream. I keep trying to remember these dreams. This morning John woke me up so I told him, I don't know why I said it, but I said that I dreamed that he had a sister that committed suicide, and that's all I can remember.	(Here's where I am. I'm worried about living, and about knowing myself and trusting myself, or my boyfriend.)
T: Umm, humm	(O.K.)
C: I remember saying that, but I don't remember dreaming it at all.	(Especially the trusting part.)
T: Oh-h-h.	(Are you?)
C: It's frustrating me.	(I'm frustrated and scared.)
T: You mean you're really trying to remember?	(Because you want to help yourself and don't feel you can?)
C: Yeah, I really am. I used to be able to think to myself, now, I want to remember what I'd dream or something like that, and then I would sort of be conscious of it . . . in a way, or something, (pause), but I can't. . . .	(Yes.)
T: You mentioned that last time . . . about wanting to and not being able to	(You feel that this is an important problem for yourself.)
C: Yeah, it's strange to me. (Sigh) Boy. . . .	(Yes.)
T: Here is an ash tray.	(I will help you look at it.)
C: Thank you. How often do you have to do these tapes?	(I'm not sure if I can stand to look at it.)
T: Well. . . .	(Aren't you?)
C: About fifty hours or something?	(Do you need help, too)
T: No, — uh, I just thought I would tape a few and see what they sounded like and choose one, or several. I really don't know exactly how many they want, so if I tape you it will probably help out.	(Sure, but I don't feel desperate about it.)

Several conclusions can be drawn from this interchange. First, we have a much clearer picture of the perlocutionary effect of the patient's statements on the therapist than we have of the effect of the therapist's remarks on the patient, despite the fact that the latter is more central to the success of the therapy. Second, we can distinguish (along with Austin, 1962, p. 117) between the object of a perlocutionary act (largely intended, as "I am warning you that this is the last time") and its sequel, which includes the reaction of the listener, which is largely unintended. For example, the listener, in response to the warning just quoted, might burst into laughter, a discomforting and (probably) unanticipated sequel. Or consider the therapist's statement quoted above: "Here is an ashtray." Its intent (we gather from the therapist's notes) was to put the patient at ease; its sequel (or at least a visible part of same) is the patient's unexpected question: "Thank you. How often do you have to do these tapes?" The difference between intention and sequel is what makes therapy so hard to teach. Contributing to this difficulty is the fact that, as Austin (p. 118) points out, perlocutionary acts often achieve their response in a nonconventional manner, a paradox caused, in part, by the simple fact that people usually do not like to be told what to do and, to prove that point, may react to an instruction (such as a warning, a promise, or whatever) by explicitly behaving in some quite different fashion.

For this and many other reasons, we may produce an effect in therapy without knowing why, or we may intend one effect and instead produce another. Glover (1931) has devoted a paper to this subject; it discusses the unintended effects of what he terms inexact interpretations, which, in Austin's language, would constitute one of the nonconventional sequels of a perlocutionary act. Glover makes the point that such interpretations, because they bring about an intellectual understanding, can often increase the patient's resistance and make his treatment more difficult; they probably have other unintended effects as well.

Third, we see right away that attention must be paid to the problem of how to mark the perlocutionary content of the therapy protocol. Until that is done, we have no way of approximating the gist of the interaction, and a glance at the transcript shows that the comments in the right column do not fully supply this need. And because we have no standard notation — because we must always make inferences from the raw text, no matter how faithful the recording, because the important information is never spoken — we are left with many possible interpretations of any one exchange. It now becomes clear why audio or video fidelity is not the answer: The information is not contained in what is spoken, but in its impact on the listener, and only a portion of this impact is conveyed by the response. In an ironical manner, the much maligned process notes of the early therapists may —because they contain some of their inner responses and some sense of the context within which the therapy hour is being experienced — contain more crucial information than highly sophisticated recordings, despite the current trend to substitute the latter for the former. The recordings may be more sophisticated, but they are also, at certain levels, more impoverished.

How could perlocutionary acts be marked so as to bring out the full significance of what is intended and the effects of this act on the listener? Some of the distinctions made earlier in this chapter may help us here. First, we can learn a lot from abrupt changes in the continuity of theme — as, for example, in the exchange already quoted:

T: Here is an ashtray.
C: Thank you. How often do you have to do these tapes?

This shift in topic gives us the clue that getting the ashtray is having an unintended effect that can be read several ways. On the one hand, it may have reassured the patient and allowed her to open a new and somewhat threatening topic—the need for the tape recorder. But the larger context suggests a contrary reading — to wit, that the patient is not fully reassured and is seeking further ways to avoid looking at the dream. Whatever the "true" effect, the change in continuity alerts us to the probability that something important is taking place that is not contained in the transcript. Generalizing from this example, we might argue that when a conversational implicature is violated, we may conclude that the statement preceding the violation contained a rather significant perlocutionary loading — in other words, something in the statement unexpectedly derailed the conversation. The break in continuity is the outer marker, so to speak, of an unintended consequence; the content of this consequence, by contrast, is usually unmarked, and its decoding depends largely on such other clues as the position of the utterance and its precise surface structure. These (and other clues) can be combined to approximate the impact on the listener, but because a certain amount of inference is necessary, they can hardly be called markers in the usual fashion. These clues are often used, in fact, by the therapist to fashion his next remark. When the approximation is a good one, we can speak of empathy; when it is bad, we can speak of inexact interpretations.

The importance of the perlocutionary component brings up a warning. To pay too close attention to the language of therapy may cause one to miss the forest for the trees. The precise wording of a carefully thought out interpretation may be irrelevant to its effect, precisely because its effect depends heavily on its unintended perlocutionary meanings. It may also follow that the "inexact" interpretation may have unexpectedly good side effects because of its place in the context of the hour (i.e., its timing), its tonal quality, its rhythm, or any of a number of paralinguistic qualities (see Chapter 12 for a fuller description of these features). Perlocutionary sequels can stem from all of these dimensions, and once we understand that the *consequence* of a statement is all-important, we begin to minimize the importance of mere words.

To argue in this fashion is not to say that a linguistic analysis of a therapy protocol is futile — not at all. It only means that we must be careful to look closely at the consequences of a speech act and find ways of marking them and linking them to the raw text of the utterance. Careful study of these links may show that more consequences can be predicted than Austin assumed, that even this level of meanings has a certain lawfulness about it, and those that cannot be predicted can often be reasonably approximated. Once we have a system for transforming the surface structure of an utterance into a inclusive subset of likely consequences, we will be a good bit closer to developing a linguistic model of the therapeutic process.

REFERENCES

Austin, J. L. *How to do things with words.* New York: Oxford University Press, 1962.

Bartlett, F. C. *Remembering.* Cambridge: Cambridge University Press, 1932.

Bransford, J. D. & Franks, J. J. The abstraction of linguistic ideas. *Cognitive Psychology,* 1971, *2,* 331–350.

Freud, S. [*Screen memories* (Vol. III)] (James Strachey, trans.). London: Hogarth Press, 1962. (Originally published, 1899.)

Glover, E. The therapeutic effect of inexact interpretation. *International Journal of Psychoanalysis,* 1931, *12,* 397–411.

Goldman, J. *Becoming a psychotherapist.* Springfield, Ill.: C. C Thomas, 1976.

Gray, P. Psychoanalytic techinique and the ego's capacity for viewing intrapsychic activity. *Journal of the American Psychoanalytic Association,* 1973, *21,* 474–494.

Greenson, R. R. The mother tongue and the mother. *International Journal of Psychoanalysis,* 1950, *31,* 18–23.

Grice, H. P. *Logic and conversation.* Unpublished manuscript, William James Lectures at Harvard, 1967.

Jenkins, J. J. Remember that old theory of memory? Well, forget it! *American Psychologist,* 1974, *29,* 785–795.

Lakoff, R. Language in context. *Language,* 1972, *48,* 907–927.

Luborsky, L., & Spence, D. P. Quantitative research in psychoanalytic therapy. In A. E. Bergin & S. L. Garfield (Eds.), *Handbook of psychotherapy and behavior change.* New York: Wiley, 1971.

Paul, I. H. Studies in remembering: The reproduction of connected and extended verbal material. *Psychological Issues.* 1960, *1*(2), 1–152.

Polanyi, M. *Personal knowledge.* New York: Harper Torchbooks, 1958.

Sachs, J. Recognition memory for syntactic and semantic aspects of connected discourse. *Perception and Psychophysics,* 1967, *2,* 437–442.

Schafer, R. On the theoretical and technical conceptualization of activity and passivity. *Psychoanalytic Quarterly,* 1968, *37,* 173–198.

Schafer, R. *A new language for psychoanalysis.* New Haven: Yale University Press, 1976.

Sharpe, E. F. Psycho-physical problems revealed in language: An examination of metaphor. In E. F. Sharpe, *Collected papers on psychoanalysis.* London: Hogarth Press, 1950.

Spence, D. P. Lexical derivatives in patients' speech: Some new data on displacement and defense. In B. Freedman & S. Grand (Eds.), *Communicative structures and psychic structures.* New York: Plenum, 1977.

Tulving, E. Episodic and semantic memory. In E. Tulving & W. Donaldson (Eds.), *Organization of memory.* New York: Academic Press, 1972.

Tulving, E., & Thomson, D. M. Associative encoding and retrieval: Weak and strong cues. *Journal of Experimental Psychology,* 1970, *86,* 255–262.

Waelder, R. The principle of multiple function. *Psychoanalytic Quarterly,* 1936, *5,* 45–62.

16 Educational Psycholinguistics: Defining the Domain

Aaron S. Carton
SUNY, Stony Brook

Lawrence V. Castiglione
Queens College, CUNY

In this chapter we propose an initial mapping of the domain of educational psycholinguistics by deriving its problems from the nature of education. The surface manifestations of an educational psycholinguistics will, of course, occur in such areas as foreign language learning, the acquisition of reading skill, concerns for individual language variation, and the development of rhetorical skills. But a systematic discipline must be founded on questions for research and a coordinated set of problems with an underlying theme. The mere application of existing findings to specific instructional tasks will not suffice. Worse than merely failing to define a discipline, such mechanical procedures also lead to a lack of circumspection and confusion in educational practice.

If educational psycholinguistics is a definable domain, it is one that has emerged or is emerging. To our knowledge, no formal, self-conscious attempt [such as Osgood and Sebeok's (1965) attempt for psycholinguistics in general] has been made to define educational psycholinguistics. Nor can educational psycholinguistics as yet specify self-conscious conferences, journals (journals on "applied linguistics" notwithstanding), or organizations given over entirely to the issues that comprise its purview. There are, on the other hand, a number of scholars who would, doubtlessly, be glad to call themselves educational psycholinguists. If the domain is to be defined as a coherent discipline and not the mere intersection and overlap between education and psycholinguistics, it must be mapped from the problems of education as well as from observations of its activities and the structure of interrelations among those activities; it must be mapped from the contributions of scholars who work as educational psycholinguists.

I.   SOME DIMENSIONS OF EDUCATION

Educational practice (call it an art or technology as you wish) is essentially concerned with devising or selecting strategies, procedures, or methods to be used in any given set of educational circumstances. What is to be taught — that is, subject matter or curriculum — and who the learner is are, of course, ultimate determinants of appropriate methods. But the prevailing values in which an educational system functions determines, in turn, the selection of that subject matter and the categories of learners who will receive instruction. Because the ends of education are so often intrinsically contained in its means, values turn out to be an important determinant in the selection of methods as well.

A wide range of strategies, procedures, approaches, or "methods" is available to education. They extend from the explicit inculcation of "facts" or the conduct of highly disciplined drill to relatively unstructured "discovery procedures," "open classrooms," and various forms of self-initiated, self-directed learning. Traditionally, for example, English spelling has been taught by requiring students to recite from memory the letters that comprised the words that appeared in the arbitrarily ordered lists of "spellers." Other approaches grouped words by "families" of spelling patterns and involved students in "word study" or in the analysis of the morphological and etymological composition of words. In the most "open" currently used procedures, children are encouraged to write using whatever spelling seems to them to communicate the words they wish to use while it is anticipated — or fondly hoped — that eventually their spelling will converge upon the accepted norms. (See C. Chomsky, 1975.)

Elsewhere we have characterized a dimension along which educational methods and strategies can be arrayed as ranging from *instructive* to *educative* (Carton & Castiglione, 1976). Roughly, instructive educational strategies correspond to those often associated with "traditional" education and are based on the initiatives of teachers who seek to "build into" their students certain knowledge or skills. Eductive strategies might be associated with "progressive" educational philosophies and might be characterized (as the derivation of the term is intended to suggest) as seeking to "lead forth" from the student the development of knowledge and skills. This dimension should be thought of as a continuum rather than as a dichotomy. Attempts to classify the various educational procedures that have ever been used or proposed would result in arraying each procedure at some intermediate point on this continuum.

The continuum can be further exemplified by the extensive range of methods for teaching reading. An extremely instructive approach would consist of informing pupils of the phonetic values of written characters and then requiring them to intone a text. The teacher might provide a model or even intone the text in unison with the pupil before the pupil intones it independently. (The reading of Hebrew is sometimes taught in this way for religious purposes without any reference to the meaning of the text.) Highly systematized "programmed instruction" methods for teaching reading may also be classified as instructive. At the eductive extreme, children may be placed in rooms with books and expected to explore the texts. Profusely illustrated books and the availability of familiar, frequently recited stories enhance the possibility that they may be able to decipher the texts. In this approach, reading acquisition may be allowed to proceed "naturally" as it seems to in the case of some of a limited number of children who come to school with reading skill or who learn to read in preschool or kindergarten. The "experience chart" method may, perhaps, be placed somewhere in the middle of the continuum as it involves the pupil in dictating a text to the teacher who transcribes it and returns it to the pupil as a reading assignment.

The applicability of the dimension can also be observed in respect to the teaching of formal grammar. The instructive approach requires students to memorize the definitions of parts of speech and treats diagramming and the parsing of sentences as algorithms that are to be followed mechanically. A more eductive approach asks pupils to underline in "Sentence B" the word that corresponds to the underlined word in "Sentence A." Later, in this method, pupils learn that they have been underlining "nouns" and "verbs," and they are encouraged to make explicit the defining characteristics of the parts of speech that they had hitherto perceived only intuitively. Similar procedures may be used for identifying subjects and predicates and eventually for the complete parsing of sentences.

The selection of what should be taught and, to a considerable degree, the selection of the procedure to teach it are very largely a consequence of the image a culture will harbor as to what its educated individuals ought to know and how they ought to behave. Social, political, economic, and cultural values, sometimes explicitly articulated and justified and sometimes operating as unanalyzed presuppositions, are central determinants of the knowledge a society has to offer its young, of the selection of knowledge it chooses to transmit, and of its preferred educational approaches. Thus, for example, up until a few generations ago, Latin and Greek were considered marks of the "educated man." In the seventeenth century, such an assertion, perhaps without much examination or critical justification, was reason enough for studying Latin and Greek, whereas in the late nineteenth and early twentieth centuries the study of Latin required justification in utilitarian terms (e.g., "doctors need it") or for the purpose of other educational objectives (e.g., "it helps to build vocabulary"). Now, in the twentieth century black activists in the United States often seek to include Swahili in the education of Blacks as an assertion of national identity, ethnic minorities ask for bilingual programs, and Irish nationalists in Ireland urge the use of Gaelic.

Social values may also determine how education is to be conducted. A preference for eductive methods may logically be associated with an image of an educated person who can continue to learn by himself, make independent discoveries, and perhaps conduct research, whereas instructive methods may be associated with cultures seeking to develop individuals who conform with desired patterns or established traditions and which may prize expertise over creativity.

Standard research paradigms can offer little in the way of *prescribing* what values a society ought to harbor. It was not a research finding that prompted the change in the status of classical languages from the *sine qua non* of education to their place as merely interesting subjects for those who might be interested in them. Changes in social conditions and attendant changes in values lead to metamorphoses of school curricula that sometimes occurred with justification and sometimes occurred as though they were merely minor inadvertent alterations. But research can *describe* relations and associations between values and preferences in the selection of subject matter and of educational approaches. Research can also evaluate the "success" of educational procedures by testing the association of any approach or procedure with the values that students eventually acquire. The problem of evaluating values, nevertheless, remains a baffling one. Because education is itself a process of value assertion, the implication for educational research and for an educational psycholinguistics is that it must confront value considerations much sooner than "pure" research is likely to.

Educational psycholinguistics will be concerned with the acquisition of certain aspects of language and with language use. One of the research tasks of the field is the characterization of various aspects of language, as subject matter or curricula, in a manner that is relevant to the way in which they are likely to be learned. A relevant dimension along which subject matter or the curriculum might be arrayed can be characterized as ranging from *opaque* to *transparent*. By transparent subject matter we mean material that we can learn as the relationships among its elements become apparent to us; we perceive the logic of its structure. Transparent subject matter is axiomatic; or, at least, it "stands to reason." It is intended to be "understood." Opaque subject matter seems arbitrary to us. It provides us with no structure, logic, or internal mnemonics by which parts can be derived or inferred from other parts without previous exposure. Opaque subject matter must somehow be "fixed in memory": it will not help to think about it.

Of course, opacity and transparency may exist in varying degrees in any given subject matter. Or the educator may find possibilities for manipulating the amount of transparency that will be exhibited by any element he seeks to teach. Emphasis may be placed either on transparent or opaque elements. For example, a word meaning may be communicated as though it were a completely opaque or arbitrary element. If the meanings of its component morphemes are provided and its structure is opened for extraction by the student, however, some amount of transparency, or "motivated" character, may be imparted with its meaning. If the pupil has available the possibility of deriving the meanings of the component morphemes from other, already known, words, even more transparency is provided. A discipline such as mathematics can be taught with emphasis on "understanding" (or transparency) and can involve the student in derivations and in the reformulation of proofs the curriculum requires him to learn. Some teachers of mathematics, on the other hand, may require the memorization of formulas to suffice.

The possibility that eventually one must regress to at least a few completely "basic" and arbitrary elements is open to question. Still, it is easily shown, when anticipation, guessing, and inference are encouraged, that the more one knows in a given domain, the more transparent new elements become (cf. Carton, 1966, 1971). Variations in sequencing transparency and opacity are also possible. Formulas may be memorized and left to be "understood" later, or a formula can be learned by a "discovery" procedure from the outset. A poem may be memorized in childhood to be pondered upon for its meaning and to be understood when the intellect matures or exposure to the poem can be saved until the child is prepared to understand it. Wertheimer's classic work *Productive Thinking* (1945) provides many excellent analyses of what we have called transparency in the subject matter of mathematics and science (as well as in games and in social affairs). From his theoretical point of view, Wertheimer is rather hostile to allowing opacity — or what he calls "ugly proofs" — to occur in educational materials. Yet, standard linguistics almost invariably regards language to be arbitrary, at least from a philosophical point of view. Consequently the educational psycholinguist may of necessity be more tolerant of opaque subject matter than some educators in other domains.

It is to be noted that in the preceding discussion and examples, we have considered mainly the transformation of subject matter from opaque to transparent and vice versa. We have left open for continuing debate between nativists and empiricists — between cognitivists and behaviorists — the question of whether elements of knowledge are *intrinsically* opaque or transparent. On the other hand, we can see that one class of methods of education can consist of manipulations in the nature of subject matter. Further, the selection of subject matter is, as we noted, largely a matter of social values. So might the selection of method be. Or the selection of method might be based upon considerations of educational efficiency, itself a utilitarian value. All in all, the relations among values, subject matter, and educational methods are obviously intimate and complex.

Finally, the selection of educational procedures is related to the nature of the learner. Different from value considerations, reasonable prescriptions for educational practice can follow relatively logically and easily from the research analysis of the principles that relate methods of learning to learners and to subject matter. Yet one should be wary of crudely pragmatic tests of "what works," because these fail to consider the relations among methods, the learner, and subject matter. Such tests yield results that are not general — that are not likely to be germane to changed circumstances and varieties of learners — and that may mislead the practitioner. Though much educational research is concerned with such tests, they defeat optimistic expectations of practicality. Because current general psycholinguistics is so vigorously concerned with relating analyses of language to the methods of learning and the use of language that humans exhibit, there are foreshadowings of an emerging educational psycholinguistics that will be more analytic and productive than some other branches of educational research have been heretofore.

A simple practical example follows from experiments in teaching autistic children to speak and studies of language acquisition of normal children. Experiments with autistic children suggest that such children need palpable reinforcers to learn and that the methods of behavior modification have shown themselves to be promising with such a population. In contrast, "normal" children do not seem to need such methods to acquire language. There are intimations of innate mechanisms that facilitate learning — be they a "language acquisition device," "natural curiosity," "a predisposition to imitate," responsiveness to relatively subtle types of reinforcers, etc. There are, therefore, those who would advise against using methods that work on abnormal populations with normal ones lest the "natural" mechanisms that facilitate learning be disrupted by artificial educational manipulations. In another domain, the decision to teach reading in English before or after reading in Spanish to children in bilingual programs may be expected to be best made when it takes into consideration the experience each child has had with each language; when it takes into account the different cognitive processes involved in coping with the relatively systematic phoneme-grapheme correspondences of Spanish as opposed to the relatively complex system of underlying morphemic structures and varying phoneme-grapheme patterns of English; and when instruction can be adjusted to the intellectual capacities and cognitive styles of each child.

The learner, or the "mind" of the learner, may be characterized by means of a relevant dimension we have conceived as ranging from *autonomous* to *docile*. Autonomy here implies that learning occurs as a result of processes attributable to the learner, which originate from within and which are directed by the learner. By docility we mean responsiveness. E. C. Tolman (1932) characterized living organisms as *docile,* implying (as the etymology of the word does) that they are "teachable," "malleable" to the contingencies of the environment, and capable of changes in behavior that bespeak environmental influences. In the sense proposed here, the usual connotations of "tractability" and "submissiveness" may be permitted to contribute to our formulation of the conception.

Ironically, Tolman regarded docility to be a necessary condition for purposive behavior. But Tolman's purposiveness derives its goals, at least in part, from environmental conditions. His system posits docility as the means by which the organism can acquire information, such as cognitive maps about its environment, and thereby make its molar behavior appropriate. Our conception of docility need not be regarded as being at variance with Tolman's.

However, our conception of autonomy should not be regarded as being synonymous with behavioristic — environmentally determined — conceptions of purposiveness, such as Tolman's. With the term autonomy we mean to subsume and accommodate certain nativistic posits that are said to characterize the organism and are not be discovered in environmental conditions. Such posits typically assume the form of underlying structures that account for behavioral sequences and include notions such as implicit behavioral programs or inherent linguistic competence that seek to account for rule-governed behavior and syntax. Behaviorism typically eschews such posits.

The posit of a language acquisition device (LAD) by some psycholinguists suggests a view of the child as an autonomous learner of language. The assumption that parents act as reinforcers of the imitative behavior or communicative behavior of the infant implies a view of the infant as a docile learner. Studies of parent–child observation — conducted generally in an observational rather than experimental mode — suggest that a multiplicity of processes play a role in language acquisition (see Chapter 11, by Maratsos, this volume).

The autonomy-docility dimension is applicable in a number of ways in educational thought. Educational philosophies can be characterized by the extent to which they assume pupils to be generally docile or autonomous. There are, there were, or there can be, educational theorists who assume that pupils are basically autonomous but need to be molded into docility before education can occur. Or there may be those who feel that effective learning depends on autonomy and will seek practices that will rouse pupils from a presumably natural docile condition. The dimension can be applied to distinguish individual students from each other, noting that some exhibit initiative or curiousity while others are submissive or indifferent. It can be applied as characterizing temporary sets of pupils and developmental stages. It can be seen as applicable to minute perceptual phenomena, such as the recognition of letters, for which the terms *inquiry* and *suggestion* were recently proposed (Navon, 1975, cited by Broadbent, 1977). This dimension may also apply to problem-solving activity and to the motives and inducements that account for persistence. The ends of the dimension have been perceived as an antinomy reflecting basic oppositions in a view of man and other organisms (e.g., Allport, 1937; Skinner, 1971), or as complementary processes whose alternation account for what we learn (Navon, 1975).

Consideration of the empirical validity of the assumptions we may make about these educational dimensions — of transparency/opacity, and of autonomy/docility — leads us to note that opacity or transparency of *subject matter* must be evaluated by *learners,* and the determination of autonomy or docility in *learners* depends on presenting them with *subject matter.* The logic and scientific paradigms that we can bring to bear on the problem dictate this interrelatedness. Typically, we proceed in research either by reducing variability in subject matter in order to study individuals or by allowing the responses of individuals to characterize the subject matter. The yield of such experimental strategies is a set of statements of relations among variables applicable to circumscribed classes of subject matter with circumscribed types of students. Anticipations for simple, broad, or grand generalizations are defeated by the complexity and specificity of empirical findings. The unraveling of what comprises opaque or transparent subject matter and of what determines autonomy and docility in students proceeds laboriously. As we now turn to the specific of an educational psycholinguistics, other methodological complexities will emerge.

II.   FOREIGN LANGUAGE EDUCATION

The matrix of dimensions we have attempted to sketch prepares us with reference points for analyzing how specific tasks of language education have been approached and for defining the research problems that comprise — or may comprise — an educational psycholinguistics.

Although we might seek the origin of a psycholinguistics for foreign language learning in antiquity, a good historical point of departure for our purposes seems to be the early contacts of modern linguistic science with foreign language instruction. We find that as early as the 1940s Leonard Bloomfield (1942b) was responsible for establishing an important contact between linguistics and foreign language education in the form of programs he devised for "exotic" languages for soldiers in the United States Army. A cursory review of the issues in foreign language education since the development of those programs will illustrate how the dimensions of education may be dealt with.

Because Bloomfield was a linguist, one might properly anticipate that his efforts to contribute to foreign language education would lie in attempting to clarify the nature of language, which he characterized as being arbitrary (see Bloomfield, 1933). Admittedly he sought linguistic structures. But his justification for searching seems to have been merely a scientist's faith that the phenomena of nature were systematic, structured, and orderly. Bloomfield did not reason — as Chomsky (1971) did later — that linguistic structures were derived from the structures of the human mind and were, therefore, in certain aspects transparently compelling to it. Bloomfield's linguistic structures were to be formulated by the rigorous application of a systematic method of analysis.

A close analysis of Bloomfield's statements about pedagogy and his psychological assumptions (cf. Carton, 1976) reveals an almost doctrinaire consistency with the atomistic behaviorist psychology of his period. Indeed, consistencies can be discerned between Bloomfield's view of language and Clark Hull's (1943) view of behavior in general.

An applied linguistics (rather than a psycholinguistics) of foreign language instruction seems to have followed close upon the heels of Bloomfield's formulation of the "Army method." The central issue for linguists who sought to try their hand at teaching foreign languages seems to have been the idea that the grammatical structure of the target language should determine the sequencing of the curriculum and the nature of the drills for pupils. (The idea at that time, when French grammar might be tortured on the Procrustean bed of Latin grammar, was more radical than it might seem now.) So "pattern practice" replaced conjugations, and dialogue memorization replaced analyses of texts. The structural linguists held that "Speech is primary," and so reading was delayed for the sake of phonology and "near-native pronunciation." *Meaning* was not an explicit issue in the syllabi, and vocabulary building was incidental to the acquisition of grammatical structures.

Titles such as "Speaking Russian (Arabic, Tagalog, etc.) Before You Know It," appeared in this period, and they suggest the important intuition into the psychology of learning that linguists had then acquired. Fluent grammatical, or patterned, speech — today we speak of "rule-governed behavior" — was not to be acquired from studying explicit rules. The mediation by language was, ironically, found to be of as little use for learning how to talk as it was for acquiring any other kind of motor behavior, such as walking, running, or playing the violin. Modeling and practice seemed to be the relevant pedagogical procedures for acquiring such skills, and after the invention of the "Army method" for foreign language instruction, drill became the method of choice.

When psychologists turned their attention to what Bloomfield and applied structural linguists were doing, they perceived them to have reconciled an antinomy between doctrines. The pattern practice that supplanted the grammar-translation method represented a behavior-oriented, behavioristic approach. Wilga Rivers (1964) wrote of "mimicry-memorization," and John Carroll (1963) called it the "mim-mem" approach. It was regarded by many, if not most, to be vastly superior to the "cognitive code" approach, which relied on the awkward intervention of overtly formulated rules that a speaker would need to evoke each time some linguistic elements were to be ordered into an acceptably formed utterance. For psychologists, the argument hinged upon the role of the Hullian construct of *habit strength*. The theoretical fare of the 1940s, 1950s, and early 1960s provided "habits" (and little else) as a construct by which preconscious, prompt, fluent, and predictable (or patterned) behavior could be accounted for. In this view, the mind of the student acquiring a language was clearly regarded to be on what we would call the docile side.

In last analysis, the dialogue about foreign language learning between linguists and psychologists from about 1940 to about 1965 — which occurred, of course, amidst the cross-talk of the advocates for a myriad of other more or less traditional and less theoretically minded language-education procedures — cannot be said to have constituted a true psycholinguistics. It would seem rather, that a tentative partnership developed. Psychologists never questioned the analyses linguists adduced for the writing of curricula. When, for example, contrastive analyses appeared (Rivers, 1964), psychologists could readily assume that such analyses could be aptly used to reduce retroactive interference effects between languages. In general, linguists were to characterize the nature of language, and psychologists would specify how it was to be learned. Such a partnership, however, kept the disciplines separate.

The psychology of learning that was brought to bear on the problem of foreign language acquisition was a laboratory-based science that proceeded by testing hypotheses drawn from behavior theory. In effect, it was engaged in testing whether certain manipulations *could* produce learning. It did not observe learning *in situ* and could not produce an account of all the ways learning might actually occur. Learning theory provided the *rationalization* for what pedagogues had long been doing; conducting drills and using a bit of reward and punishment to keep the drills under control. And teachers had been doing that — drilling Latin declensions and conjugations in European gymnasia and American schools — long before the dawn of modern scientific linguistics or formal psychology. The audio tape, the language laboratory, and the programmed instruction format added improved mechanization, but little else, to a mechanistic concept of learning.

In the meantime, the program of twentieth-century linguistics — the formulation of analyses of languages that were *true to each language analyzed* — became the source of the real issue. As linguistically motivated curricula developed (e.g., *The Audiolingual Materials* [A/LM] of the Modern Language Materials Development Center, 1961) for each language, various types of pattern practice appeared such as substitution drills, expansion drills, and transformation drills. These drills implied a new model of language processing. Each of the types of drills eventually listed in the linguistically sophisticated "methods" texts for foreign language teachers of the late 1960s and early 1970s might be subsumed under a heading of *syntactic* drills (Kadler, 1970). Gone were the paradigmatic drills — the declensions and conjugations — that concerned themselves with each form class in isolation and that examined the morphology of only those constituent structures adjacent to stems or bound to them.

Superficially, the approach that emerged resembled the later Chomskian generative approach. Syntactically oriented transformational grammar theory also markedly departs from paradigmatic linguistic analysis and suggests the organization of speech in longer units. [Only in the highly artificial and educationally irrelevant situation of "word-association tests" do adults — not even children — produce paradigmatic responses. See Ervin (Tripp), 1961]. Yet behaviorist-motivated drills remained superimposed on a kind of linguistic analysis that was later felt to be inimical to behaviorism. In 1965, Chomsky told the Northeast Conference on the Teaching of Foreign Languages (Chomsky, 1966; Allen & Van Buren, 1971) that he was "frankly, rather skeptical about the significance, for the teaching of languages, of such insights and understanding as have been attained in linguistics and psychology."

Chomsky's skepticism was, of course, completely consistent with his general position. He was in agreement with one of the structuralist views that had hitherto dominated applied linguistics: a conscious knowledge of formal statements of grammar is not a necessary condition for the acquisition of fluent language skills. But Chomsky did not believe, as some structuralists did, that knowledge of such a grammar would hinder language acquisition. Nor did he have in mind the same kind of grammar the structuralists were concerned with.

The formal grammar Chomsky thought would be of *no* help in language acquisition was the transformational-generative grammar of deep structures, which he was then developing. Ironically, structuralist grammars, which were largely concerned with surface structures, were, in Chomsky's estimation, possibly useful as "practical" or "teaching" grammars if they met a number of other conditions. Further, the mere organization of syntagmatic drills — the development of a transformational text — did not satisfy the conditions necessary to develop generativity. Under the generative rubric, segments derive their implications from syntax, and no amount of patterned stringing together of elements on a surface structure could be the equivalent of generating a sentence from its deep structure. Most importantly, the fluency or "nonconsciousness" (if we may be allowed such a term) that both the structuralists and the generativists perceived as the most desired characteristic of language mastery, could not, for Chomsky, be a matter of habit strengths. For Chomsky, such fluent, orderly linguistic behavior was spontaneous, and not merely responsive to environmental conditions. The source of grammatical performance was linguistic competence, which was to be defined as the presence of abstract representations of linguistic structures in the mind. The source of competence, in turn, was largely the *native* human predilection or predetermination to derive grammar from minimal exposure to language or to linguistic data of even a very debased sort.

If one notes that Chomsky's conception of linguistic inquiry is the ascertaining of the abstract linguistic structures that comprise the competence of any individual who speaks a language, we may perceive that the linguist is engaged in attempting to get to "know" (in a formal sense) what the speaker already "knows" (in an intuitive sense). Such a speaker knows more than the linguist does, just as nature may be said to know more than the science that seeks to describe it. Linguists cannot tell speakers how to speak any more than natural scientists can tell nature how to be. It will be recalled, however, that behavioristic psychology emerged from an *experimental* scientific paradigm that equates knowledge with successful implementation. The generativist paradigm placed greater emphasis on observational research methods. That paradigm later infiltrated some segments of psychology. It does not associate science with technology as closely as the experimental paradigm does. Nor is the generativist paradigm easily assimilated into a simple conception of an educational psycholinguistics.

A staunchly nativistic position such as Chomsky's produces problems for "educationists" (i.e., the community of teachers, educational philosophers, educational researchers, administrators, etc.), because it invades the domain of the teacher and the work of the school. It returns a substantial amount of that territory to pupils. It threatens even the most "eductive" of educational philosophies. If the theory does not develop a definition of boundaries between areas in which autonomous learning may occur and where instruction is necessary, the educationist is deprived of expectations that his interventions may be effective. The mandate to teachers to "form the mind" of the child is revoked. And the educational system may even be bereft of indications as to *what* it should teach or, at least, what it should "expose" to the pupil.

In addition to Chomsky's skepticism, two other issues — bilingualism as a psycholinguistic phenomenon and the question about the optimal age for initiating foreign language instruction — seem also to point to constraints upon what were considered possibilities and ranges of action for those who would teach second languages.

The formulation of a taxonomy of bilingualisms that distinguished between "compound bilinguals" who depend upon the mediation of their native language, and "coordinate bilinguals" who can function in one or another language independently from any other language (Ervin & Osgood, 1954) was dependent upon a behaviorist approach that used the construct of "mediation" in its learning theory. Eventually, the distinctions became attributable to "contexts of acquisition" (Lambert, Havelka, & Crosby, 1958). The logic of the analysis and the data to support it ominously suggest that the kinds of formal instruction usually conducted in schools are much less likely to produce fluent and effective functioning in a second language than are settings in which the student is somehow set free upon his own recognizance. When the psycholinguistic research of investigators such as Lambert is considered for its applicability to instructional settings, that applicability seems to assume the form of recommendations for introducing procedures that may simulate or approximate conditions that occur when individuals acquire second languages in nonschool settings. Examples of these recommendations include efforts to manipulate attitudes and motivations to resemble or approximate those of learners in "natural" settings, to select individuals with such attitudes for instruction (Gardner, Ginsberg, & Smythe, 1976), or to propose exchange programs and the like (Cziko & Lambert, 1976).

A movement in the United States, Britain, and Canada to initiate foreign language instruction in the early grades (Foreign Language in the Elementary School, or FLES), found much of its justification in the biological (and, by implication, nativistic) theorization about speech and brain mechanisms of Wilder Penfield (Penfield & Roberts, 1959). In the United States, individual attempts and experiments to begin French, Spanish, or even German in the third grade or as early as kindergarten could be observed to collapse even while enthusiasm for the movement was spreading. It rapidly became obvious that whatever neurological magic there was which accounted for the success with which Swiss children acquired their bilingualism, it was not easily evoked by the instructional methods and curricula that were available for instruction in the elementary school classroom. In Britain (Burstall, 1975), where a 10-year systematic study of FLES was initiated in 1963, the age for starting foreign language study was not found to be crucial to the amount or kind of achievement of pupils. The circumstances of instruction, motivational factors of both children and teachers, and sex of the child were, however, among the variables that accounted for achievement. In Canada, social and political factors — which, in turn, are related to motivational variables — seem to be related to the success of the St. Lambert experiment and other programs. In addition to formal instruction in a language, the Canadian experiments included opportunity for functional use by conducting instruction in the target language for varying amounts of time (Stern, 1976).

The Canadian experience serves notice to the educational psycholinguist that the educationist may not choose his level of discourse as freely as does the academic researcher. He must be prepared in his problem solving to consider social, political, economic, and psychological variables simultaneously. Further, he must distinguish between learning in schools and learning elsewhere. Reports of the British experience implied to commentators that: "the data of the . . . study suggest that the primary factor in the attainment of proficiency in French (and presumably, any foreign language) is the amount of instructional time provided" (Carroll, 1975, cited by H. H. Stern, 1976). On the other hand, a recent study by Oyama (1976) of Italian immigrants who had spent varying amounts of time in the United States persuasively demonstrates that it is the age of initial contact with the nonnative language, and not the duration of contact, that is the crucial factor in the effective acquisition of a nonnative phonological system. This finding is confined to phonology and is in agreement with earlier claims and beliefs (see Stern, 1963). The question of whether the acquisition of vocabulary, morphology and syntax can be shown to follow similar patterns in nonschool settings remains wide open to further research. Oyama's results, nevertheless, clearly imply once more that the set of factors that are to be found in operation when foreign language acquisition is studied in individuals who have been exposed to "natural" conditions is quite different from the set of factors that account for learning that occurs in the context of school instruction. The differences between these sets of factors are again suggested by the occurrence of bilingualism as a worldwide phenomenon among the poorest people, in remote places, involving many pairs of languages, pidgins, and creoles; and by the fact that immigrant children seem to benefit from their youth in acquiring a second language, whereas children learning second languages in schools seem to be handicapped by their youth.

We have suggested elsewhere that an important distinction is to be made between education, as it occurs in school settings, and learning, which may be said to occur in the "world" (Carton & Castiglione, 1976). The school, it seems, seeks to be like a garden or a farm where growth is cultivated to maximize the achievement of specific objectives and to minimize waste. Learning in noneducational settings — in the "real world" — can be likened to life in the wilds. Errors and waste are frequent *in natura*. Animals in the wilds frequently fail to reach maturity and seeds frequently fail to germinate. Similarly, much passes the learner unnoticed and unlearned.

In gardens we may use methods and materials for cultivation and fertilization that do not occur in nature and disregard methods and materials that are natural. In schools we may induce learning with procedures and curricula that are not a part of daily living and omit the use of many methods of learning and presentations of knowledge that are part of the "world." Gardeners select crops for their value as schools select subject matter and objectives. Values are not to be discerned in the wilds, and learning *in natura* may not be determined by the desires of educators; only the survival value of what is available in the environment determines the knowledge of those who are without formal education.

The case of native language acquisition illustrates this point. The cardinal observation of developmental psycholinguistics has been that children throughout the world learn (or can learn) their first language without any instruction beyond mere exposure. But of the thousands of different words that may pass an infant's ears at any one time, only a few may be acquired in that time. Although there is no orderly sequencing in the presentation of grammatical principles that are acquired, the infant seems to acquire language in an orderly pattern of his own. Yet "errors" (overregularizations) are an intrinsic part of the process. Psycholinguistic research exploring whether foreign language acquisition in "the wild" follows similar patterns may prove valuable, indeed.

Observations such as this may be found among the arguments adduced to support a nativistic theory of language acquisition. We do not adduce them for that reason. Indeed, the one conclusion of which the continuing debate among theoretical positions persuades us is that such facts can be construed in a variety of ways. The research paradigm of developmental psycholinguistics is important because it suggests a strategy relevant to studying learning *in natura*. This strategy emerged with the anecdotal reports that appeared early in this century on the development of certain monolingual and bilingual children (e.g., Stern & Stern, 1907). Such a strategy involves an emphasis upon observation and the extraction of principles from relations that are suggested by the data, as opposed to an experimental strategy, which relies upon prior assumptions about relationships and upon the researcher's interventions in the learning process.

There are, of course, strengths and weaknesses to every method of inquiry, but it is important to make note of the possibility that different methods may yield different findings. An "experimental manipulative" method cannot be easily applied to studying the developmental psycholinguistics of normal children whose language acquisition might be imperiled by some misguided intervention. Advocates of the behaviorist viewpoint have at times been reduced to post hoc extrapolations of the operation of behaviorist principles, which they attributed to environmental factors (e.g., mothers "naturally reinforce the speech of babies") — see Bellugi & Brown, 1964, and Carton's review, 1965). For example, the successful behavior modification of autistic children only suggests what *can* work under exceptional circumstances. It is not very persuasive that its underlying principle is the only operative one in normal circumstances, or that it is the only principle that exists. The educational psycholinguist might be forewarned, therefore, that the analysis of languages, the sequences of presentations, and the drills that can work in school situations may not be the only ways in which learning can take place. However, evidence gathered from observations or even from "test-developmental methods" that determine what individuals can do at various stages of their growth does not easily yield up principles to account for the learning which occurs (cf. Carton, 1976). Nonexperimental research seems to tend to foster theoretical constructions that can be criticized for their lack of parsimony. However, Piaget's "clinical" method (Flavell, 1963; Piaget, 1929), used to study developmental phenomena, has, despite the theoretical debates it aroused, incontrovertably illustrated how revealing observational and exploratory strategies can be.

It seems obvious that harnessing the learning processes that occur outside schools would constitute a worthwhile challenge for educational psycholinguistics. Some attempts, intentional or otherwise, to utilize natural learning processes in the foreign language field have included "total immersion" programs, exchange programs, or "bilingual education" programs, that involve conducting all school instruction in one or another language for large parts of the day or lengthy parts of the school year. Such approaches involve efforts at simulating or approximating natural conditions but are, of course, usually rather uneconomical for schools as we know them, or practicable only when suited to special ethnic configurations of local populations. Further, there is reason to believe that the most effective solution does not lie in the mere replication of natural conditions. (The concept of schools would have been abandoned early in human history, were this the case.) In one study of an overseas program Carton and Carroll (1960) found that the better students were prepared with formal instruction in a foreign language (Russian) before going abroad, the more their language skills benefited from their experience abroad.

In another instance, Carton (1966, 1971) sought to analyze language as a system by which we generate cues from which messages are reconstructed. He also sought to analyze the "inferencing," or guessing and reconstructive propensities, of the students. He concluded that comprehension and the acquisition of new lexical and linguistic structures could be facilitated by alerting students to various types of cues, freeing them to use certain "inferencing" skills that many students appear intuitively prepared to use, and by helping them to develop additional inquiry procedures. Many questions remain, however, about the "inferencing" abilities of students at various stages of cognitive development and the interactions between cues and the guesses made about them. Of course, "inferencing" cannot be proposed as a complete instructional method; it can only supplement other approaches. Yet attempts to encourage inferencing in the context of a method that is more "instructive" (and hence inimical to it) may be unwise [cf. Mueller's (1970) review of Carton (1966)]. Finally, inferencing is relevant to the acquisition of productive skills only to the extent that receptive linguistic competence may eventually facilitate productive linguistic skills.

III. A PSYCHOLINGUISTICS OF READING

The name of Leonard Bloomfield figures prominently as the initiator of a "linguistics of reading" (Bloomfield, 1942a; Bloomfield & Barnhart, 1961). Subsequently many other linguists have offered contributions. The various linguistic approaches to reading appear to be counterparts of analyses of the nature of writing that "reading specialists" had previously suggested. Linguists had found themselves embroiled in the conventional disputes (albeit with sophisticated linguistic insights) between wholistic and analytic views of written materials that had preoccupied reading educators for decades (cf. Carton, 1969, 1976; Chall, 1967; Wardhaugh, 1968, 1971). With the emergence of the concept of deep structures and the suggestion of the possibility that writing might constitute an alternative to speech as a possible surface structure, it became possible for some researchers to escape the Bloomfieldian notion of the primacy of speech and the assumption that writing necessarily involved a recoding into speech signals. A view of reading as a process of reconstruction of cues into meaningful messages emerged. The psycholinguistic models of speech perception that have developed in the 1960s and early 1970s (for a review, see Cairns & Cairns, 1976) emerged as applicable to the reading process — and, perhaps, to Carton's "inferencing" view of foreign language comprehension. The proponents of a "psycholinguistics of reading" (Carton, 1976; Goodman, 1965, 1968a, 1968b, 1969, 1970; Kolers, 1968a, 1968b, 1970, 1972; Smith, 1971; and others) produced considerable evidence that reading was largely an autonomous process — or a process that depended, at least, upon alternations between suggestion from the text and inquiries by the reader, coupled with integrations or reconstructions at higher cognitive levels. The implications for pedagogy to date seem more likely to assume the form of injunctions against interfering with the autonomous processes than suggestions for instructive actions to be applied to children. For example, the psycholinguistic analysis of reading reveals that errors are often generated by the character of the text and are also often indicative of effective reconstructions of messages and intelligent comprehension (Goodman, 1968a, 1968b, 1969).

Closer consideration of what educationists have long considered "methods" of reading instruction seems to suggest, however, that a very large portion of educational strategies proposed for the teaching of reading — be they instructive or eductive — have been concerned with inducing students to attempt to read and to maintain reading behavior and inquiry procedures. Some of the blandishments, uses of grades, rewards, and threats of punishment that are prescribed are quite removed from the reading process itself. Their value and possible deleterious effects upon pupils have been the topic of much discussion. Other methods of instruction are concerned with setting up inquiry procedures by asking students to extract information from texts. Another very large portion of "reading instruction" consists of developing for presentation to students analyses of the nature of writing. Consideration of the psycholinguistic analysis of the intimate relation between the nature of writing and the processes a reader can bring to bear upon the text seems to some degree to suggest that, at best, reading instruction can hope only to stimulate the pupil's inquiry processes: As we learn more about the reading process, narrowly explicit techniques of reading instruction seem to become farfetched. Reading is a *receptive* process, and there are no drills or overt behaviors that can induce it or produce it. Indeed, even the autonomous drills that developmental psycholinguists have noted in native language acquisition (Weir, 1962) are not relevant to the comprehension process; only autonomous inquiry processes are. Thus, a psycholinguistics of reading will undoubtedly find itself concerned essentially with determining which inquiry and reception processes are most appropriate for various aspects of written language (or visual communication in general) and with developing techniques for analyzing and diagnosing which procedures a given student of reading may employ at any instant. The educational procedures of the psycholinguistically sophisticated teacher of reading may consist largely of the manipulation of texts and reading tasks in order to elicit inquiry procedures more advanced than those the student has available or, when necessary, to induce him to use procedures more appropriate to his task. The data and the theorization to be derived to date from a psycholinguistics of reading strongly suggest eductive strategies. Many children already arrive in school with reading skills acquired, most likely in interaction with natural environments composed of the adults around them. Text has only recently become a normal part of the experience of children, and only in some parts of the world. Printing dates back to about 1450, whereas language is about as old as humankind.

IV. RHETORIC

A significant branch of education is, of course, concerned with rhetoric or "language arts." And much has been written relating human development, and in particular language development, to school curricula in the language arts (e.g., Britton, 1970; Cazdan, 1972; for a more linguistic analysis, see also Halliday, McIntosh, & Strevens, 1964).

Many curricular and instructional practices concerned with speaking, writing, and communication skills in general reflect the sophistication afforded by linguistics and psycholinguistics. Yet educational psycholinguistics is markedly more amorphous in respect to rhetoric than it is in respect to foreign language learning or reading. The reason, we believe, lies with a problem of values, a problem that does not exist once a decision to teach reading or a foreign language is made, but which attracts attention in the very act of choosing to teach rhetoric. Modern linguistics finds its origins as a descriptive science passionately eschewing any prescriptivism, and psycholinguistics has embraced the attitude of its parent in this regard. Schools, on the other hand, are almost by definition places where prescriptions are made. They have always been concerned with teaching the standard languages and the prestige dialects of their societies. So schools have often found the objective descriptivism and detached liberalism of linguistics difficult to comprehend, and linguists have hesitated before participating in the standard educational activity of teaching prescriptive grammar.

The difference in view between linguists and educators has not prevented linguists from eventually becoming involved in preparing curricula about language. There are many curricular units that use advanced linguistic analyses and that are intended to help students analyze their own language and develop a modicum of metalinguistic awareness. One of these even rather ingeniously capitalizes on the linguistic intuitions that all speakers of a given language have in order to develop a formal analysis of parts of speech and English morphology (Roberts, 1959). Essentially, such curricula constitute nothing less than an introduction to the science of linguistics adjusted to the grade levels of elementary schools. But such linguistic studies make no pretenses at teaching pupils how to talk. Although educators may have addressed themselves directly to this problem, linguists produced only an extensive literature concerned with what should be taught.

The discussion about education in rhetoric may be said to be more sociolinguistic than psycholinguistic, and indeed it may well be that many of the prominent figures in the discussion (Shuy, 1970; Stewart, 1969, 1970) count themselves to be sociolinguists or even sociologists (Bernstein, 1970). Disputes revolve upon the acceptability of dialects associated with racial groups (e.g., black English vernacular) and with poverty stricken and deprived groups low on the status scales of their societies (e.g., Burling, 1973). Much is made of the regularity and complexity and even poetic character of the language of these groups. Some opponents of the view that dialects should be taught merely "take for granted" the need to acquire the standard language (Bereiter & Engelmann, 1966; Engelmann, 1970). Others thoughtfully question whether lower-class speech is suited for communicating the concepts involved in technical, scientific, and aesthetic discussions (Bernstein, 1970). Although much interesting work has been done and remains to be done describing nonstandard varieties of English — or any other language — and the social phonemena that surround them, for education the debate reduces itself to a matter of social and political values, about which, as we have noted above, research has little to say. The choices available include attempting: (1) to persuade the ascendant members of the society to become more tolerant of the speech of the disenfranchised; or (2) to make available to the disenfranchised opportunities to acquire the ascendant speech patterns; or (3) to continue the hierarchical structure that linguistic differences perpetuate. In the last analysis the discussion is really about which form of social justice or injustice the disputants prefer (or believe more practical) and which the society, with its educational system, will choose (see Williams, 1970).

There is room, however, for an educational psycholinguistics of rhetoric to conduct research in three areas. The first would be a psycholinguistics in which the psychological component would be concerned with personality considerations such as self-image and identity and interpersonal perception. It is in this domain that the factual validity of certain assertions about the social justice of one or another language policy for education can be tested. For example, one proposition that is in need of validation is whether a minority child who is encouraged to speak his own dialect (or even his own nonprestige language) will in fact develop a better self-image and realistic self-esteem and will function more effectively in respect to all of life's challenges.

The second area would concern itself with that evasive issue of the relation between language and thought. Recurrently, the assertion appears that some modes of expression are specifically suited to certain modes of thought, and vice versa, both in respect to different language systems (e.g.,

Whorf, 1956) and in respect to class dialects (e.g., Bernstein, 1958). Suggestive evidence is frequently alluded to, but, for us at least, convincing evidence either to support the assertion or to lay the issue to rest has not as yet been developed. Until it is, we cannot be certain about the consequences of policies that might be selected on the basis of social values or unsubstantiated *beliefs* that the consequences of a chosen policy will be in accord with the values that motivated its selection.

Finally, an educational psycholinguistics of rhetoric needs to concern itself with precisely what constitutes effective communication and with procedures for developing such skills. At the time of writing, linguistics — operating indistinguishably from psycholinguistics — has begun to make notable progress in pragmatics and semantics. With the exception of some exciting work on the relation of language structure to comprehension and memory, the purely psychological concomitant of the phenomena under consideration have hardly begun to be explored (cf. Bransford, Barclay, & Franks, 1972). Such exploration may well have important implications for education.

V. CONCLUSION

Indeed, many issues of educational psycholinguistics remain unexplored. What we have attempted in this chapter is to provide a rough map of the domain of educational psycholinguistics. Our examination of the domain has been extensive, but very cursory. We hope, however, that the salient and significant features of the domain have been correctly identified and not distorted by anything more than the omission of many details. We believe that by taking the problems of education as our point of departure we have been able to suggest a field that may be productive of some theoretical notions important to both educational psycholinguistics itself and to its parent, psycholinguistics. It seems reasonable to expect that educational psycholinguistics will develop special methodologies and, at the same time, characteristic formulations of problems, combining reason with experience in a very distinctive way.

REFERENCES

Allen, J. P. B., & Van Buren, P. *Chomsky: Selected readings.* New York: Oxford University Press, 1971.

Allport, G. W. *Personality: A psychological interpretation.* New York: Holt, 1937.

Bellugi, U., & Brown, R. W. (Eds.). *The acquisition of language.* Monograph of the Society for Research in Child Development, 1964, *29*(1), (Serial No. 51).

Bereiter, C., & Engelmann, S. *Teaching disadvantaged children in the pre-school.* Englewood Cliffs, N.J.: Prentice-Hall, 1966.

Bernstein, B. Some sociological determinants of perception: An inquiry into sub-cultural differences. *British Journal of Sociology,* June 9, 1958, 154–174.

Bernstein, B. A sociolinguistic approach to socialization with some reference educability. In F. Williams (Ed.), *Language and poverty.* Chicago: Markham Publishing, 1970.

Bloomfield, L. *Language.* New York: Holt, 1933.

Bloomfield, L. Linguistics and reading. *Elementary English Review,* 1942, *19,* 125–130; 183–186. (a)

Bloomfield, L. *Outline guide for the study of foreign languages.* Baltimore: Linguistic Society of America, 1942. (b)

Bloomfield, L., & Barnhart, C. L. *Let's read.* Detroit: Wayne State University Press, 1961.

Bransford, J. D., Barclay, J. R., & Franks, J. J. Sentence memory: A constructive versus interpretive approach. *Cognitive Psychology,* 1972, *3,* 193–209.

Britton, J. *Language and learning.* Harmondsworth, England: Penguin, 1970.

Broadbent, D. E. The hidden preattentive process. *American Psychologist,* 1977, *32*(2), 109–118.

Burling, R. *English in black and white.* New York: Holt, Rinehart & Winston, 1973.

Burstall, C. French in the primary school: The British experiment. *Canadian Modern Language Review,* 1975, *31*(5), 338–402.

Cairns, H. S., & Cairns, C. E. *Psycholinguistics: A cognitive view of language.* New York: Holt, Rinehart & Winston, 1976.

Carroll, J. B. Research on the teaching of foreign languages. In N. L. Gage (Ed.), *Handbook of research on teaching.* Chicago: Rand McNally, 1963.

Carroll, J. B. *French in eight countries.* New York: International Education Association, 1975. (Cited by Stern, H. H., *Canadian Modern Language Review,* 1975, *32*(3).

Carton, A. S. Theory of baby-talk — Review of *The acquisition of language* (U. Bellugi & R. Brown, Eds.). *Contemporary Psychology,* 1965, *10*(11).

Carton, A. S. (with the assistance of N. Magaud). *The "method of inference" in foreign language study.* Office of Research and Evaluation, City University of New York, 1966. (Available from the author or ERIC)

Carton, A. S. Linguistics and reading instruction. In J. Allen (Ed.), *Reading and realism.* Newark, Del.: International Reading Association, 1969 (pp. 571–581, figure 1).

Carton, A. S. Inferencing: A process in using and learning foreign languages. In P. Pimsleur & T. A. Quinn (Eds.), *Papers on the psychology of second language learning.* Cambridge, England: Cambridge University Press, 1971.

Carton, A. S. *Orientation to reading.* Rowley, Mass.: Newbury, 1976.

Carton, A. S., & Carroll, J. B. *The 1959 summer Russian language learning program: Report to the inter-university committee on travel grants.* Cambridge, Mass.: Laboratory for Research in Instruction, Harvard University, 1960. (Mimeo)

Carton, A. S., & Castiglione, L. V. Psycholinguistics and education: Directions and divergences. *Journal of Psycholinguistic Research,* 1976, *5*(3), 233–244.

Cazdan, C. B. *Child language and education.* New York: Holt, Rinehart & Winston, 1972.

Chall, J. *Learning to read: The great debate.* New York: McGraw-Hill, 1967.

Chomsky, C. Invented spellings in the open classroom. *Word,* 1975, *27*(1-2-3), 499–518. (Special issue)

Chomsky, N. Linguistic theory. In R. G. Mead (Ed.), *Language teaching: Broader contexts.* Northeast Conference Reports, 1966.

Chomsky, N. Implications for language teaching. In J. P. B. Allen & P. Van Buren (Eds.), *Chomsky: Selected readings.* London: Oxford University Press, 1971.

Cziko, G., & Lambert, W. E. A French–English school exchange program: Feasibility and effects on attitudes and motivation. *The Canadian Modern Language Review*, 1976, *32*(3), 236–242.

Engelmann, S. How to construct effective language programs for the poverty child. In F. Williams (Ed.), *Language and poverty*. Chicago: Markham, 1970.

Ervin (Tripp), S. Changes with age in the verbal determinants of word-association. *American Psychologist*, 1961, *74*(3), 361–372.

Ervin (Tripp), S., & Osgood, C. E. Second language learning and bilingualism. In C. E. Osgood & T. A. Sebeok (Eds.), *Psycholinguistics*. Special supplement to *Journal of Abnormal and Social Psychology*, 1954, *49*, 139–146.

Flavell, J. *The developmental psychology of Jean Piaget*. Toronto: Van Nostrand, 1963.

Gardner, R. C., Ginsberg, R. E., & Smythe, P. C. Attitude and motivation in second-language learning: Course related changes. *Canadian Modern Language Review*, 1976, *32*(3), 243–266.

Goodman, K. S. Dialect barriers to reading comprehension. *Elementary English*, December 1965, pp. 853–860.

Goodman, K. S. *A study of children's behavior while reading orally*. Final Report to the United States Department of Health, Education and Welfare, March 1968. (Mimeo/ERIC) (a)

Goodman, K. (Ed.). *The psycholinguistic nature of the reading process*. Detroit: Wayne State University Press, 1968. (Mimeo/ERIC) (b)

Goodman, K. S. *A study of oral reading miscues that result in grammatical retransformations*. Final Report to the United States Department of Health, Education and Welfare, June 1969. (Mimeo/ERIC)

Goodman, K. S. Reading: A psycholinguistic guessing game. In H. Singer & R. B. Ruddell (Eds.), *Theoretical models and processes of reading*. Newark, Del.: International Reading Association, 1970.

Halliday, M. A. K., McIntosh, A., Strevens, P. *The linguistic sciences and language teaching*. Bloomington, Ind.: Indiana University Press, 1964.

Hull, C. C. *Principles of behavior*. New York: Appleton-Century-Crofts, 1943.

Kadler, E. H. *Linguistics and teaching foreign languages*. New York: Van Nostrand Reinhold, 1970.

Kolers, P. A. The recognition of geometrically transformed text. *Perception and Psychophysics*, 1968, *3*, 57–64. (a)

Kolers, P. A. Reading temporally and spatially transformed text. In K. S. Goodman (Ed.), *The psycholinguistic nature of the reading process*. Detroit: Wayne State University Press, 1968. (b)

Kolers, P. A. Three stages in reading. In H. Levin & J. P. Williams (Eds.), *Basic studies on reading*. New York: Basic Books, 1970.

Kolers, P. A. Experiments in reading. *Scientific American*, 1972 *227*(1), 84–91.

Lambert, W. E., Havelka, J., & Crosby, C. The influence of language-acquisition contexts on bilingualism. *Journal of Abnormal and Social Psychology*, 1958, *56*, 239–244.

Modern Language Materials Development Center. *Teachers' Manual*. New York: Harcourt Brace and World, 1961.

Mueller, T. (Review of *The method of inference in foreign language study* by A. S. Carton). *The Modern Language Journal*, 1970, *54*(5), 378–379.

Navon, D. *Global precedence in visual recognition*. Unpublished doctoral dissertation, University of California, San Diego, 1975. (Cited by Broadbent, 1977.)

Osgood, C. E., & Sebeok, T. A. (Eds.). *Psycholinguistics: A survey of theory and research problems*. *Journal of Abnormal and Social Psychology* (Supplement) *49*, 1954. Reissued: Indiana University Press, Bloomington and London, 1965.

Oyama, S. A sensitive period for the acquisition of a nonnative phonological system. *Journal of Psycholinguistic Research,* 1976, *5*(3), 261–284.

Penfield, W., & Roberts, L. *Speech and brain mechanisms.* Princeton, N.J.: Princeton University Press, 1959.

Piaget, J. *The child's conception of the world.* New York: Harcourt, Brace, 1929.

Rivers, W. *The psychologist and the foreign language teacher.* University of Chicago Press, 1964.

Roberts, P. *Patterns of English.* New York: Harcourt, Brace, 1959.

Shuy, R. W. The sociolinguistics of urban language problems. In F. Williams (Ed.), *Language and poverty.* Chicago: Markham Publishers, 1970.

Skinner, B. F. *Beyond freedom and dignity.* New York: Knopf, 1971.

Smith, F. *Understanding reading.* New York: Holt, Rinehart & Winston, 1971.

Stern, C., & Stern, W. *Die Kindersprache. Eine Psychologische Und Sprachtheoretische Untersuchung.* Leipzig: Barth, 1907.

Stern, H. H. *Foreign languages in primary education.* Report on an International Meeting of Experts, April 9–14, 1962. UNESCO Institute for Education, Hamburg, 1963.

Stern, H. H. Optimal age; myth or reality. *Canadian Modern Language Review,* 1976, *32*(3), 283–294.

Stewart, W. A. On the use of Negro dialect in the teaching of reading. In J. C. Baratz & R. W. Shuy (Eds.), *Teaching black children to read.* Washington, D.C.: Center for Applied Linguistics, 1969.

Stewart, W. A. Toward a history of American Negro dialect. In F. Williams (Ed.), *Language and poverty.* Chicago: Markham Publishers, 1970.

Tolman, E. C. *Purposive behavior in man and animals.* New York: Appleton-Century, 1932. (Reprinted University of California Press, 1949)

Wardhaugh, R. *Is the linguistic approach an improvement in reading instruction?* Paper presented at the 13th Annual Convention of the International Reading Association, May 1968.

Wardhaugh, R. Theories of language acquisition in relation to beginning reading instruction. *Reading Research Quarterly,* 1971, *VII*(1), 168–194.

Weir, R. H. *Language in the crib.* Gravenhage: Mouton, 1962.

Wertheimer, M. *Productive thinking.* New York: Harper and Bros., 1945.

Whorf, B. L. *Language, thought and reality* (John B. Carroll, Ed.). Cambridge, Mass.: M.I.T. Press, 1956.

Williams, F. (Ed.). *Language and poverty.* Chicago: Markham Publishers, 1970.

Author Index

Subject Index

A

AB fusion, 242
Absolute neutralization, *see* Neutralization
Abstract:
  and concrete sentences, 68, 95
  representation, *see* Representation,
    abstract
Abstractness, 148–153
Acceptability:
  vs. grammaticality, 233–234
Acquisition of behavior, 118, 124–127
Action, 368–369
  joint, 269–271, 277, 282
  sequence variables, 373, 375
  sequences, 371–373, 381–384
Affective polarity and linguistic marking,
  211
Allophone, 136, 145
American sign language, 55
Animal communication, 112–113
Aphasia, 18, 37, 436, 443–467
  category naming in, 443, 446–451
  cerebral localization, 460–463
  clinical forms, 444–453, 459
  confrontation naming, 444–460, 463–467
    cueing effects, 456f.
    special word classes, 457–460
    types of error, 445–453, 466
    word frequency effect, 454f.
    word length effect, 455f.
  inverse naming, 445–451, 460, 465–467
  optic, 459
  repetition disorders, 442, 445–451
  word association, 442f., 445–451, 466
Applications, 17–20
  educational, 19–20
  neurological, 18
  psychotherapy, 18–19
Applied psycholinguistics at the Royal
  Society, 40
Associationists, 34
Attention, 271–272, 274
Auditory feedback:
  role in acquisition and performance,
    201–202
Augmented transition networks (ATNs), 233
Autonomy as a characteristic of learners,
  502–504
  in conducting drills, 514
  in learning to read, 513–514

B

Behavior theory, 111–124
Behavior therapy, 112, 116
Bilingual education, 512
  in English for Spanish-speaking children,
    502
Bilingualism, 509–510
  cognate, 509
  contexts of acquisition, 509
  coordinate, 509

Biological clock, 425–427
  autoregressive system, 427
  equal intertransition time, 427
  Markovian, 425
  phase shift, 427
  semi-Markovian process, 427
  unequal transition times, 427
  zeitgebars, 426
Body and mind, 28
"Book-reading," 274, 276
Breakdowns (structure), 249–250
Buffer stores, 66–67, 72–74, 87

C

Caracteristique universelle, 31
Cartesian linguistics, 28–29
Center-embedding, 235
Chimpanzee language, 54–56
Chomsky and Halle, 133, 147
Chukchansi, 151, 157
Chunking, 235–236
Classical conditioninng, 113–116, 117,
  120–124
  conditional response, 113–116
  conditional stimulus, 113–116, 120, 123
  interoceptive, 116
  unconditional response, 113–166
  unconditional stimulus, 113–116, 123
Cloze procedure, 119, 126
Co-articulatory constraints, 399–401
  consonant–vowel sequences, 400–401
  maximum local domain, 399
Coding:
  accumulations, 72–74
  patterns, 98–102
  procedure, 88–93
  representation 88, 90–91, 93–95
  time, 68–74
Cognition:
  processes, 6, 9–13
  role in naming act, 439–444, 467
Communication, 11, 14–17
  comparative study of, 53
  mother–child, 266–283
Competence:
  grammar, 232–236, 238–239
  linguistic, 230
  -performance distinction, 10–11, 84–85
Comprehension, 91–103
  sentence, 229, 231
Compressed speech, 69–70, 73
Concepts:
  role in naming act, 439, 441, 467
Concrete representation, *see* Representation,
  concrete
Congruity:
  law of, 35
Constituent structure, 297–309
  distributional analysis and, 300–305
  semantic relations and, 297–300
  transfer of privileges and, 303–305